ACCA

Strategic Professional

Advanced Performance Management (APM)

Practice & Revision Kit

For exams in September 2023, December 2023, March 2024 and June 2024

BPP

First edition 2007

Seventeenth edition 2023

ISBN 9781 0355 0126 7

(Previous ISBN 9781 5097 4413 8)

e-ISBN 9781 0355 0079 6

Cataloguing-in-Publication Data

A catalogue record for this book is available from the British Library

Published by

BPP Learning Media Ltd

BPP House, Aldine Place

London W12 8AA

www.learningmedia.bpp.com

Printed in the United Kingdom

Your learning materials, published by BPP Learning Media Ltd, are printed on paper obtained from traceable, sustainable sources.

We are grateful to the Association of Chartered Certified Accountants for permission to reproduce past examination questions. The suggested solutions in the practice answer bank have been prepared by BPP Learning Media Ltd, unless otherwise stated.

A note about copyright

Contents

Question index

The headings in this checklist/index indicate the main topics of questions, but questions often cover several different topics. Past exam questions are designated with the date of the exam in which they featured, although some have been amended to reflect subsequent changes to the syllabus or in the format of the exam. Prior to September 2018, Advanced Performance Management (APM) was known as P5 Advanced Performance Management.

Since September 2015 there have been four exam sittings per year, but ACCA generally only publish two exams' worth of questions per year. These releases are compiled from questions selected from the preceding sessions. These compilation exams are denoted as 'Mar/Jun' and 'Sept/Dec' in the index below.

Topic index

Listed below are the key APM syllabus topics and the numbers of the questions in this Kit covering those topics. We have also included a reference to the relevant Chapter of the BPP APM Workbook, the companion to the BPP APM Practice and Revision Kit, in case you wish to revise the information on the topic you have covered.

If you need to concentrate your practice and revision on certain topics or if you want to attempt all available questions that refer to a particular subject, you will find this index useful.

Syllabus topic	Question numbers	Workbook chapter
A1 Introduction to strategic management accounting	1, 15, 42, 50, ME1 Q1, ME3 Q1	1, 2, 3
A2 Performance hierarchy	10, 16, 41, 44, 46, 51, 52	2
A3 Performance management and control of the organisation	2, 3, 4, 5, ME1 Q2	3
A4 Changes in business structure and management accounting	4, 11, 26, 43, 48	4
A5 Environmental, social and governance factors	6, 7, 9, 29, 37, 47	4
B1 Performance management information systems	10, 11, 13, 38, 41, 44, 48 ME3 Q1	5
B2 Sources of management information	10, 12, 35, 41	5
B3 Recording and processing systems and technologies	14, 48	5
B4 Data analytics	10, 14, 25, 44, 48	5
B5 Management reports	40, 42, 43, 44, 47, 48, 50, 52, ME1 Q1	1, 5
C1 Strategic performance measures in private sector	15, 30, 34, 40, 41, 43, 44, 45, 46, 52, ME1 Q3, ME2 Q3	6, 7
C2 Divisional performance and transfer pricing issues	16, 17, ME3 Q1, ME3 Q2	7
C3 Strategic performance measures in not-for-profit organisations	19, 20, 21, 22	8
C4 Non-financial performance indicators	28, 31, 38, 45, 46, 49, 50, ME2 Q2	9
C5 The role of quality in management information and performance measurement systems	8, 23, 25, 26, 30, 35, 46, 47, 49, ME2 Q2	10

Syllabus topic	Question numbers	Workbook chapter
C6 Performance measurement and strategic Human Resource Management issues	7,18, 25, 26, 30, 32, 40, 6, 51, ME1 Q1	11
C7 Other behaviour aspects of performance measurement	22, 25, 27, 49	11
D1 Alternative views of performance measurement and management	28, 31, 33, 34, 36, 45, 49	12
D2 Strategic performance issues in complex business structures	7, 10, 36, 37, 49, ME3 Q3	13

ME refers to mock exams at the end of the Practice & Revision Kit.

The exam

Computer-based exams

Strategic Professional exams are all computer-based exams (CBE).

Approach to examining the syllabus

When answering APM questions, some of the key qualities that you will need to be able to demonstrate include:

(a) **The application of strategic planning and control models in performance management.** The models stress the need to take a holistic view of the factors that affect a business and to consider them when giving strategic advice on performance. Good candidates often distinguish themselves by being able to synthesise disparate detailed points into an overall, strategic approach for an organisation.

(b) **Factors external to the business, and the impact of risk and uncertainty on organisational performance.** Candidates need to move beyond the internal factors associated with traditional management accounting to consider the information needs of the strategic level of management as well as the operational and tactical levels.

(c) **The information that management require and the systems that are needed for its delivery.** Candidates are expected to be aware of the effect of information technologies on performance management decision making rather than the detail of these technologies. Candidates will not be required to have detailed technical knowledge of hardware and software, but they should be conversant with the broad hardware and software trends and issues, and how these interact with the provision of performance information throughout the organisation. In particular, candidates need to recognise the impact that technology (and developments in technology) can have on performance management and decision making in an organisation.

4 and 5: **The fourth capability** is the **application** of the techniques and assumed knowledge to specific scenarios. You shouldn't simply discuss theories and models in general terms; you need to apply them specifically to the scenario identified in the question, in order to evaluate an organisation's performance and identify potential ways to improve organisational performance. **The fifth capability**, which builds directly on the fourth, is being able to take performance measurement information and turn it into **advice which is commercially valuable for strategic decision makers.**

Summarising the advice ACCA's examining team gives for APM:

Candidates should do the following:

- Understand the objectives of the exam as explained in the syllabus and prepare the detailed topics in the Study Guide.
- Be very comfortable with the areas tested in *Performance Management* (at Applied Skills level) which constitute brought forward knowledge for APM.
- Ensure that their preparation for the exam has been based on a programme of study set for the required syllabus and exam structure.
- Use an ACCA-approved study materials for APM. They are structured around the syllabus and ACCA's examining team reviews them so that they give an effective coverage of what is examinable.
- Practise questions under exam conditions in order to improve speed and presentation skills, ensuring these test discursive, computational and analytic abilities.
- Study all the technical articles relevant to APM that are published on ACCA's website.
- Be able to clearly communicate understanding and application of knowledge in the context of a business scenario.

The questions tend to be wide-ranging, as the examining team wants to link topics and mix ideas up. So you are better knowing something about every part of the syllabus than a lot of detail about a few areas only.

Format of the exam

The Advanced Performance Management syllabus is assessed by a **3 hour 15 minute exam**. The pass mark is **50%**. All questions in the exam are **compulsory**.

The format of the exam is:

		Number of marks
Section A:	One 50-mark case study question. **Ten professional skills marks are available.** This was introduced in September 2022 and is explained later in this section.	50 (40 for technical content, 10 for professional skills)
Section B:	Two questions worth 25 marks each **Ten professional skills marks are available (5 marks in each section B question).** This was introduced in September 2022 and is explained later in this section.	50 (40 for technical content, 10 for professional skills)
		Total: 100

Section A will contain **one case study question** worth **50 marks in total**, but comprising three or four requirements relating to the same scenario information. The detail of the requirements will be **embedded in the scenario**. The 'requirements' at the end of the scenario then ask you to respond as you have been instructed in the scenario. Therefore, you need to refer back to the detailed requirements in the scenario in order to answer each part of the question.

The case study scenario will be based on an organisation in a particular business context, and will include the organisation's mission and strategic objectives. Candidates will be expected to assess the methods by which the organisation is controlling, managing and measuring performance in order to achieve its objectives. This assessment could include an evaluation of the organisation's performance report, its information systems, new strategies or projects, and its performance management and measurement systems. Candidates could be expected to undertake calculations, draw comparisons against relevant information where appropriate, and be prepared to offer recommendations as needed.

Candidates should expect to see Section A of the exam focus on a **range of issues from across syllabus sections A, B and C**, although the issues will vary depending on the business context of the organisation in the scenario.

Section B will comprise a further two 25-mark questions. Again, the detail of the requirements **will be embedded in the scenario** (this has been introduced from the September 2022 sitting). The 'requirements' at the end of the scenario then ask you to respond as you have been instructed in the scenario. Therefore, you need to refer back to the detailed requirements in the scenario in order to answer each part of the question.

These questions are more likely to assess a range of discrete subject areas from the main syllabus section headings. However, they will still require evaluation and synthesis of information contained within a scenario, and the application of this information to the question requirements.

Although one subject area is likely to be emphasised in each Section B question, candidates should not assume that questions will be solely about content from that area.

One of the Section B questions will come mainly from **syllabus section D**. The other question can come from **any other syllabus section**.

The **pass mark** for the APM exam is 50%.

Remote invigilated exams

In certain geographical areas it may be possible for you to take your exam remotely. This option, which is subject to strict conditions, can offer increased flexibility and convenience under certain circumstances. Further guidance, including the detailed requirements and conditions for taking the exam by this method, is contained on ACCA's website at https://www.accaglobal.com/an/en/student/exam-entry-and-administration/about-our-exams/remote-exams/remote-session-exams.html.

Analysis of past exams

The table below provides details of when each element of the syllabus has been examined in the ten most recent sittings, and whether it was examined as part of a Section A or Section B question. We have also included a reference to the relevant Chapter of the BPP APM Workbook, the companion to the BPP APM Practice and Revision Kit, in case you need to revise the information on the topic covered.

Since September 2015, ACCA have generally been issuing two sample exams each year, one after the December exam session, the other after the June sitting. These exams will be compiled from questions selected from the two preceding sessions, eg in December 2017 the sample questions were compiled from the September 2017 and December 2017 exams.

Note that in exams prior to September 2018 there were three questions in Section B so that four questions in total are referenced for those exams.

Workbook chapter		Sept/Dec 2022	Mar/June 2022	Sep/Dec 2021	Mar/June 2021	Sep/Dec 2020	Mar/ June 2020	Sep/Dec 2019	Mar/June 2019	Dec 2018	Sep 2018
	STRATEGIC PLANNING AND CONTROL										
1	Strategic management accounting		A							A, B	
2	Performance hierarchy				A	A		A	A		A

Workbook chapter		Sept/Dec 2022	Mar/June 2022	Sep/Dec 2021	Mar/June 2021	Sep/Dec 2020	Mar/ June 2020	Sep/Dec 2019	Mar/June 2019	Dec 2018	Sep 2018
3	Performance management and control	A			A				B		
4	Organisational change, environmental & ethics			B		B		A			B
	PERFORMANCE MEASUREMENT SYSTEMS AND DESIGN										
5	Performance management systems and design		A	A	A	B	A*	A		A	B
	STRATEGIC PERFORMANCE MEASUREMENT										
6	Strategic performance measures in the private sector			A	B*		A*	A			
7	Divisional performance and transfer pricing issues	B	A, B				B				
8	Not-for-profit organisations					A					
9	Non-financial performance indicators				B	A					A
10	The role of quality in performance management	A		B			B		A	B	
11	Performance management and strategic HR issues	B		A, B							A
	PERFORMANCE EVALUATION										
12	Alternative views of performance measurement and management	B			B		B	B	B	B	A
13	Strategic performance issues in complex business structures		B			B					

* Contained an area that is no longer in the APM syllabus; for this reason, this question has not been included in this Practice and Revision Kit.

IMPORTANT!

The table above gives a broad idea of how frequently major topics in the syllabus are examined. It should not be used to question spot and predict, for example, that a certain topic will not be examined because it has been examined in the last two sittings. The examining team's report indicate that they are well aware that some students try to question spot. The examining team avoid predictable patterns and may, for example, examine the same topic two sittings in a row. Equally, just because a topic has not been examined for a long time, this does not necessarily mean it will be examined in the next exam

Syllabus and Study Guide

The complete APM syllabus and study guide can be found by visiting the exam resource finder on the ACCA website.

Helping you with your revision

BPP Learning Media – ACCA Approved Content Provider

As an ACCA **Approved Content Provider**, BPP Learning Media gives you the **opportunity** to use revision materials reviewed by the ACCA examining team. By incorporating the ACCA examining team's comments and suggestions regarding the depth and breadth of syllabus coverage, the BPP Learning Media Practice & Revision Kit provides excellent, **ACCA-approved** support for your revision.

These materials are reviewed by the ACCA examining team. The objective of the review is to ensure that the material properly covers the syllabus and study guide outcomes, used by the examining team in setting the exams, in the appropriate breadth and depth. The review does not ensure that every eventuality, combination or application of examinable topics is addressed by the ACCA Approved Content. Nor does the review comprise a detailed technical check of the content as the Approved Content Provider has its own quality assurance processes in place in this respect.

BPP Learning Media do everything possible to ensure the material is accurate and up to date when sending to print. In the event that any errors are found after the print date, they are uploaded to the following website: www.bpp.com/learningmedia/Errata.

The structure of this Practice & Revision Kit

The 25-mark questions in the exam typically focus on one main syllabus area. The 25-mark questions in this Kit have been grouped according to the section of the syllabus (Parts A-D) to which they mainly relate.

The 50-mark questions in the exam cover a number of different syllabus areas, so the 50-mark questions in this Kit are found in a single bank of questions.

There are also four mock exams which provide you the opportunity to refine your knowledge and skills as part of your final exam preparations.

Question practice

This is the most important thing to do if you want to get through. Many of the most up-to-date exam questions are in this Kit. Practice doing them under timed conditions, then go through the answers and go back to the Workbook for any topic you are really having trouble with. Come back to a question a week later and try it again – you will be surprised at how much better you are getting. Be very ruthless with yourself at this stage – you have to do the question in the time, without looking at the answer. This will really sharpen your wits and make the exam experience less worrying. Just keep doing this and you will get better at doing questions and you will really find out what you know and what you don't know.

Selecting questions

To help you plan your revision, we have provided a full topic index which maps the questions to topics in the syllabus (see page viii).

Making the most of question practice

At BPP Learning Media we realise that you need more than just questions and model answers to get the most from your question practice.

- Our Top tips, included for all questions, provide essential advice on tackling questions, presenting answers and the key points that answers need to include.
- We include marking guides to show you what the examining team rewards.
- We include comments from the examining team to show you where students struggled or performed well in the actual exam.

Attempting mock exams

There are four mock exams, including the ACCA Specimen Exam, which provide practice at coping with the pressures of the exam day. We strongly recommend that you attempt them under exam conditions. All the mock exams reflect the question styles and syllabus coverage of the exam.

Topics to revise

ACCA's Study Guide for APM highlights that 'candidates should expect to see Section A of the exam focus on a range of issues from across syllabus sections A, B and C'. The Study Guide also notes that 'one of the Section B questions will come mainly from syllabus section D' while 'the other Section B question can come from any other syllabus section'.

Taken together though, these points mean that the questions in your exam could cover any area of the syllabus. Moreover, because **all the questions in the APM exam are compulsory**, it is essential to learn the **entire syllabus** to maximise your chances of passing. There are no shortcuts – trying to spot topics to be examined is dangerous and will significantly reduce the likelihood of success. As this is an advanced ('Strategic Professional') level exam, it also assumes knowledge of topics covered in Performance Management at Applied Skills level.

That said, the **main capabilities** in the syllabus (which is shown on ACCA's website) take you through what the examining team expects you to be able to do when you have completed your studies:

- Use strategic planning and control models to plan and monitor organisational performance.
- Identify and evaluate the design features of effective performance management information and monitoring systems and recognise the impact of developments in technology on performance measurement and management systems.
- Apply appropriate strategic performance measurement techniques in evaluating and improving organisational performance.
- Advise clients and senior management on strategic business performance evaluation.

These four areas are the syllabus areas covered in sections A-D (the technical part) of the syllabus for Advanced Performance Management.

However, whilst it is important that you work through your way through the Workbook and cover all the different syllabus areas, it is also important to try and think how the areas might relate to each other, and how they could be used to help managers in an organisation control and improve the performance of that organisation. Remember, this exam is about performance **management**, as well as performance **measurement**; and you should treat both of these aspects (measurement and management) with equal importance as you are studying for your APM exam.

Remember to come out of the detail once you have finished a chapter and practised some questions. Take some time to reflect on how the chapter has covered the syllabus and how it feeds back into the capabilities which you will need to display in order to pass the APM exam.

Gaining the easy marks

Your technical knowledge (including knowledge brought forward from Performance Management) should enable you to score a small number of relatively easy marks. There are likely to be a small number of marks available in certain requirements for definitions or explanations that don't have to be related to the scenario. However, don't assume that you can ignore all the scenarios and still pass! The level of marks available in APM for knowledge alone (without application) is around 20-30% and so is nowhere near enough to pass the exam.

Professional marks are available in Section A and Section B questions, and some of these should be easy to obtain. For example, there are likely to be marks available for presenting your answer in section A in the format, style and tone, requested (eg a report).

Essential skill areas

We think there are three areas you should develop in order to achieve exam success in Advanced Performance Management (APM):

(a) **Knowledge application:** Technical knowledge does not in itself count for a high number of marks, but without a good broad knowledge of the syllabus you will find it difficult to score marks for applying your technical knowledge to the scenario, and there are many marks available in the exam for doing this.

(b) **APM Professional skills:** These are worth 20% of the marks in the APM exam (from September 2022 onwards) and are explained in detail in this section.

(c) **Exam success skills:** These are general skills required in the application of good exam technique and apply to any exam.

At the revision and final exam preparation phases these **should be developed together as part of a comprehensive study plan of focused question practice.**

These skills are shown in the diagram below.

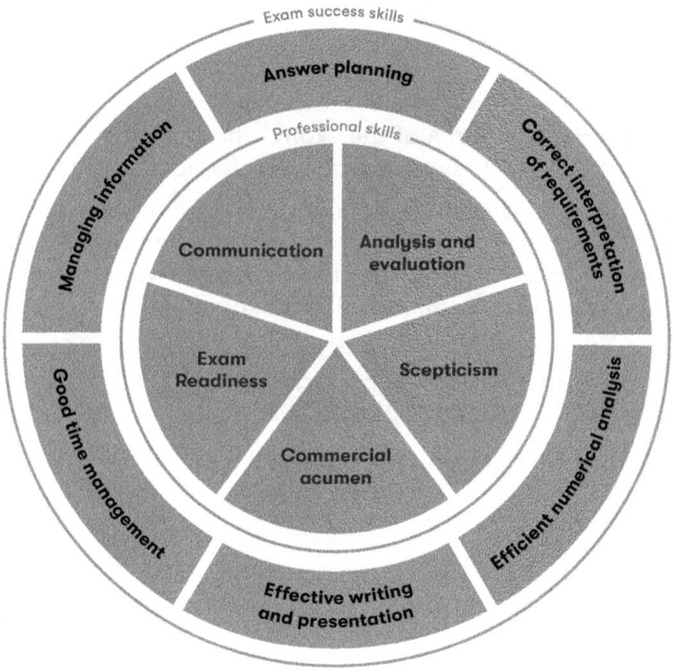

APM professional skills

From the September 2022 exam onwards, 20 marks will be available for demonstrating the 'professional skills' that would be expected from a proficient senior financial professional.

There are four professional skills – these skills are important and are worth 20 marks in the exam. A brief summary of each skill is given below.

ACCA professional skill: Definition	Three aspects of each professional skill
Communication To express yourself clearly and convincingly through an appropriate medium, while being sensitive to the needs of the intended audience.	Inform target audience using clear format Persuade with logical argument Appropriate use of technology

ACCA professional skill: Definition	Three aspects of each professional skill
Commercial acumen To show awareness of the wider business and external factors affecting business, and use commercially sound judgement and insight to resolve issues and exploit opportunities.	Practical considerations Recognise constraints Awareness of alternative opportunities to those suggested
Analysis and evaluation To appraise information objectively and to draw logical conclusions, recognising the impact on relevant stakeholders.	Consider the meaning of data Assess impact on stakeholders Apply analysis to the company in the question
Scepticism To probe, question and challenge information and views presented to you, to fully understand business issues and to establish facts objectively, based on ethical and professional values.	Question the validity of approaches Challenge opinions Identify new information needed

All of the professional skills will be examined in Section A of the exam, which is a single 50-mark case study, with 10 of the 50 marks being allocated to demonstrating professional skills.

Section B will consist of two compulsory scenario-based 25-mark questions. Each section B question will allocate 5 marks to professional skills, so 10 marks in total will be available for professional skills marks in Section B. Each question will contain a **minimum of two professional skills from Analysis and Evaluation, Scepticism and Commercial Acumen.**

The professional skills marks should not be thought of as being separate from the technical requirements; these marks are earned by providing comprehensive and relevant responses to the technical requirements. Each professional skill is outlined in the following sections.

These are covered in more detail in the APM Workbook.

Exam success skills

Passing the APM exam requires more than applying syllabus knowledge and demonstrating the specific APM skills; it also requires the development of excellent exam technique through question practice.

We consider the following six skills, or exam techniques, to be vital for exam success.

Try to consider your performance in all six Exam success skills during your revision stage question practice, and reflect on your particular strengths, and your weaker areas, which you can then work on.

Exam success skill 1

Managing information

Questions in the exam will present you with a lot of information.

The CBE functionality demonstrated below can help you to manage this information on the screen.

In the computer-based exam (CBE) the **highlighter tool** provided in the toolbar at the top of the screen offers a range of colours:

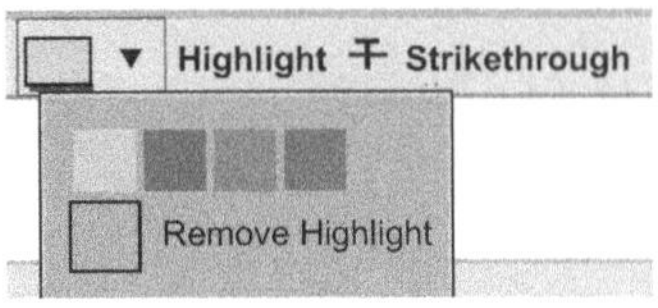

This allows you to choose **different colours to answer different aspects to a question**. For example, if a question asked you to discuss the pros and cons of an issue then you could choose a different colour for highlighting pros and cons within the relevant section of a question.

The **strikethrough function** allows you to delete areas of a question that you have dealt with – this can be useful in managing information if you are dealing with numerical questions because it can allow you to ensure that all numerical areas have been accounted for in your answer (although this is of limited use in the APM exam).

The CBE also allows you to **resize windows** by clicking on the bottom right-hand corner of the window as highlighted in the following section:

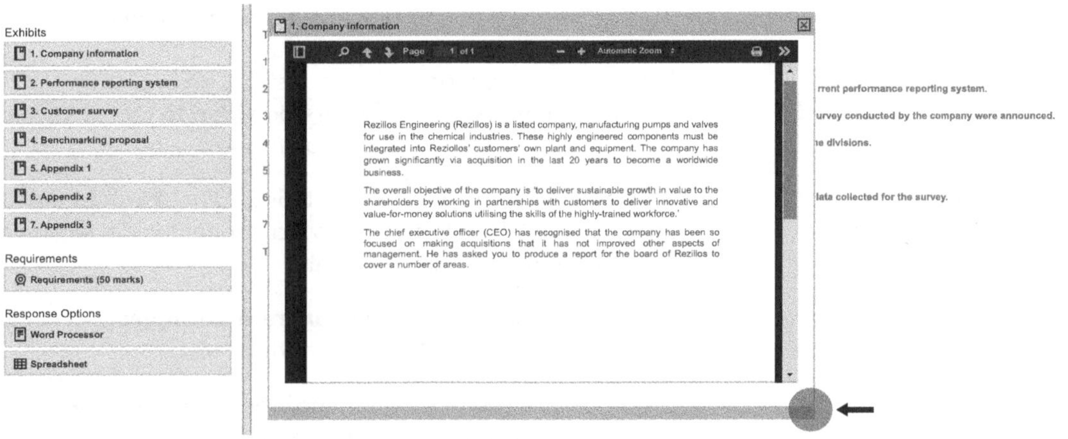

This functionality allows you to **display a number of windows at the same time**, so this could allow you review:

- The question requirements and the exhibit relating to that requirement, at the same time; or
- The window containing your answer (whether a word processing or spreadsheet document) and the exhibit relating to that requirement, at the same time.

Exam success skill 2

Correct interpretation of the requirements

The active verb used often dictates the approach that written answers should take (eg 'explain', 'discuss', 'evaluate'). It is important you identify and use the verb to define your approach. The **correct interpretation of the requirements** skill means correctly producing only what is being asked for by a requirement. Anything not required will not earn marks.

Advice on developing this skill

This skill can be developed by analysing question requirements and applying this process:

Step 1 Read the requirements slowly and carefully

Read the requirement a couple of times slowly and carefully, and **highlight the active verbs**. Use the active verbs to define what you plan to do. Make sure you identify any sub-requirements within a requirement, this is **often signalled by the use of the word 'and'** within a requirement. In APM, remember that the requirement will be embedded in the question scenario.

Important active verbs for APM include the following:

Verb	Meaning
Advise	This requires you to provide someone with useful information, or **to tell them what you think they should** do based on a consideration of the issues presented in a scenario.
Analyse	This requires you **break an issue into separate parts** and discuss, examine, or interpret each part.

Verb	Meaning
	This may require you to **give reasons for** the current situation or what has happened.
Assess	This requires you to **judge the importance** or estimate the nature, quality or significance of an issue.
Discuss	This will require you to consider and debate/argue about the **pros and cons** of an issue.
Evaluate	This will require you to present a **'balanced' discussion** of an issue looking at both the positive and negative issues. Where numbers feature in a question, an evaluation will require you to use the numbers provided to create a value from which **a judgement** can be made.
Explain	This involves making an idea clear and could require you to, for example, show logically how a concept is developed or to **give the reason for** an event.
Illustrate	This will require you to **give concrete examples**, normally drawn from the question's scenario.
Recommend	If you are asked to **'recommend'** then you are expected to **use details presented in the scenario** to create a logical and **justified** course of action.

Step 2 Read the requirements slowly and carefully

Read the requirements a couple of times slowly and carefully and **highlight the active verbs**. Use the active verbs to define what you plan to do. Make sure you identify any sub-requirements within a requirement; this is **often signalled by the use of the word 'and'** within a requirement.

In APM, remember that the requirement will be embedded in the question scenario. For example, in the scenario, the CEO may ask you analyse or evaluate something, and then the requirement will ask you to respond to the CEO's instruction.

Step 3 Read the requirement again

Read the requirement again to remind yourself of the exact wording before starting your written answer. This will capture any misinterpretation of the requirements or any missed requirements entirely. This should become a habit in your approach and, with repeated practice, you will find the focus, relevance and depth of your answer plan will improve.

Exam success skill 3

Answer planning: Priorities, structure and logic

This skill requires the planning of the key aspects of an answer which accurately and completely responds to the requirement.

Advice on developing this skill

In a computer-based **exam** you can use the copy and paste functions to **copy the question requirements to the beginning of your answer**. This will allow you to ensure that your answer plan addresses all parts of the question requirements.

You can also **copy the question requirements to the main body of your answer**. This will allow you to create sub-headings for your answer, again ensuring that your answer addresses all parts of the question requirements.

Copying and pasting simply involves highlighting the relevant information and either right clicking to access the copy and paste functions, or alternatively using Ctrl C to copy and Ctrl V to paste.

Exam success skill 4

Efficient numerical analysis

It is important to use the spreadsheet provided to produce clear and efficient numerical analysis.

It is **not a sensible idea** to perform calculations on a calculator and then manually transfer them to the spreadsheet because this will **not show the marker where the numbers have come from.**

Using a spreadsheet allows you to **show the marker how numerical values have been calculated,** because the basis for a calculation is displayed if the marker clicks onto a cell.

Clear labelling should also help to show the marker what the numbers are intended to mean.

For example, in the following spreadsheet the marker can see that the highlighted calculation in cell K9 is calculated as I9/G2 because this is what is recorded in the spreadsheet cell (as shown in the first row), and can also see from the headings in cells C9 and K4 that this is meant to be a measure of the appraisal costs as a percentage of sales.

K9 fx =I9/G2

	A	B	C	D	E	F	G	H	I	J	K	L	M
1		Cost of quality report											
2					Sales		4500						
3													
4		**Cost of conformance**					$000s		$000s		% sales		
5			**Prevention costs**										
6					Maintenance		8		8		0.18%		
7													
8					Quality audit		2						
9			**Appraisal costs**		QC supervisor		35		37		**0.82%**		
10												1.00%	

WORKINGS

If the workings are visible in the cell and reflect straightforward calculations, as is the case here, then there is **less need to show detailed workings.**

However, a **workings section** will sometimes be a useful feature of a spreadsheet answer if more detailed calculations are involved. This reduces the likelihood of errors being made (if calculations are complex).

Keep your workings as clear and simple as possible and ensure they are cross-referenced to the main part of your answer. Where it helps, provide brief narrative explanations to help the marker understand the steps in the calculation. This means that if a mistake is made you should not lose any subsequent marks for follow-on calculations.

Spreadsheet short-cuts

You can also use useful spreadsheet short-cuts to improve the efficiency of numerical analysis. For APM useful short-cuts include the ability to calculate totals and averages and also to calculate NPV, IRR and MIRR.

Further details are given in the following table:

Function	Guidance and examples
Sum	=SUM(A1:A10) adds all the numbers in spreadsheet cells A1 to A10.
Average	=AVERAGE(A1:A10) averages the numbers in spreadsheet cells A1 to A10.
NPV	Net present value is based on future cash flows, assuming that the first cash flow is in one year's time. For example, if the future cash flows from a project arise over five years and need to be discounted at 10% then the formula could be as follows: =NPV(0.1, B10:F10)

Function	Guidance and examples
	This would give the present value of cash flows from time period 1-5; the cash outflow in time 0 would then need to be deducted to calculate the net present value.
IRR	Internal rate of return is based on future cash flows, looking at cash outflows and inflows in each year of a project, from time 0 onwards. For example, to identify the internal rate of return of the future cash flows from a project arising over five years then the formula could be as follows: =IRR(A10:F10)
MIRR	Modified internal rate of return is based on future cash flows (looking at cash outflows and inflows) in each year of a project, from time 0 onwards. The formula is =MIRR (values, finance rate, reinvestment rate). The finance rate and reinvestment rate will normally be the same. For example, to identify the MIRR of the future cash flows from a project arising over five years (involving time periods 0-5), where the cost of capital to be applied to cash outflows (the finance rate) and cash inflows (reinvestment rate) is 10%, then the formula could be as follows: =MIRR (A10:F10, 0.1, 0.1)

Where numerical calculations require commentary then this can be provided in a word processing document with a **reference to calculations provided within the spreadsheet**.

Exam success skill 5

Effective writing and presentation

Written answers should be presented so that the marker can clearly see the points you are making, presented in the format specified in the question. The skill is to provide efficient written answers with sufficient breadth of points that answer the question, in the right depth, in the time available.

Advice on developing this skill

Step 1 *Use headings*

Using the headings and sub-headings from your answer plan will give your answer structure, order and logic. This will ensure your answer links back to the requirement and is clearly signposted, making it easier for the marker to understand the different points you are making. Underlining your headings will also help the marker.

Step 2 *Write your answer in short, but full, sentences*

Use short, concise sentences with the aim that every sentence should say something different and generate marks. Write in full sentences, ensuring your style is professional.

Exam success skill 6

Good time management

This skill means planning your time across all the requirements so that all tasks have been attempted at the end of the 3 hours 15 minutes available and actively checking on time during your exam. This is so that you can flex your approach and prioritise requirements which, in your judgment, will generate the maximum marks in the available time remaining.

Planning time

In APM it is crucial to spend time on planning before starting to write your answer. This allows time for a candidate to immerse themselves in the question scenario. Approximately 20% of your time should be allocated to planning, to ensure that you are able to assimilate the key features of the scenario before starting to write.

For a 50-mark question, planning time should be 50 marks × 1.95 × 0.2 = 20 minutes.

For a 25-mark question, planning time would be 25 marks × 1.95 × 0.2 = 10 minutes per question.

Writing time

For time management purposes, candidates should allocate time based on the technical marks available. Professional skills marks should not be thought of as separate requirements as they are earned by providing comprehensive and relevant responses to the technical requirements.

Writing time can be calculated by multiplying the technical mark allocation for each requirement by 1.95 minutes [as the 20% of time spent planning is exactly offset by the extra 20% of marks available for professional skills marks].

So, time planning for a 25-mark question with, for example, a 12 mark part (a) and a 8 mark part (b) (and 5 professional skills marks) should be as follows:

Total time: 25 marks × 1.95 minutes per mark = 49 minutes

Planning time: 49 minutes × 0.2 = 10 minutes

Writing time: part (a) = 12 × 1.95 minutes per mark = 23 minutes

Writing time: part (b) = 8 × 1.95 minutes per mark = 16 minutes

At the beginning of a question, work out the amount of time you should be spending on each requirement and note the finishing time next to each requirement on your exam.

Keep an eye on the clock

Aim to attempt all requirements, but be ready to be ruthless and move on if your answer is not going as planned. The challenge for many is sticking to planned timings. Be aware this is difficult to achieve in the early stages of your studies and be ready to let this skill develop over time.

If you find yourself running short on time and know that a full answer is not possible in the time you have, consider recreating your plan in overview form and then add key terms and details as time allows. Remember, some marks may be available, for example, simply stating a conclusion which you don't have time to justify in full.

Question practice

Question practice is a core part of learning new topic areas. When you practise questions, you should focus on improving the Exam success skills – personal to your needs – by obtaining feedback or through a process of self-assessment.

This exam is a computer-based exam, so practising as many exam-style questions as possible in the ACCA CBE practice platform will be key to passing this exam. You should attempt questions under **timed conditions** and ensure you produce full answers to the discussion parts as well as doing the calculations. Also ensure that you attempt all mock exams under exam conditions.

ACCA have launched a free on-demand resource designed to mirror the live exam experience, helping you to become more familiar with the exam format. You can access the platform via the Study Support Resources section of the ACCA website navigating to the CBE question practice section and logging in with your myACCA credentials.

Questions

STRATEGIC PLANNING AND CONTROL

Questions 1 to 9 mainly cover strategic planning and control, the subject of Part A of the syllabus for Advanced Performance Management (APM).

1 Stokeness (June 2013, amended) (49 mins)

Respond to the CEO's request for work on the following areas:

(a) The external business environment and performance measures **(15 marks)**

(b) The risk appetite of the venture capitalists and performance measurement **(5 marks)**

Professional marks will be awarded for the demonstration of skill in analysis and evaluation, and commercial acumen in your answer. **(5 marks)**

(Total = 25 marks)

Exhibit 1: Company information and mission

Stokeness Engineering's (Stokeness) mission is to provide world-leading, reduced-emission, fuel efficient power products for the motor industry in order to optimise shareholder returns.

Stokeness has existed for only five years and is owned by its management and venture capitalists (VCs). The management were all engineers who had been working on the basic research associated with new fuel technologies and saw the opportunity to commercialise their expertise. Stokeness is highly regarded in the industry for its advanced, efficient fuel cell designs. As a result, the VCs were eager to invest in Stokeness and have assisted by placing experienced managers into the business to aid the original engineering team.

Exhibit 2: New product development

Stokeness is developing hydrogen fuel cells for use in powering large motor vehicles such as buses and trucks. They will replace standard petrol/diesel engines. The fuel cells have a clear advantage over these older technologies in having lower carbon dioxide (a greenhouse gas) emissions. The governments of many developed countries are keen to see cuts in such emissions and are supportive of a variety of possible technological solutions to this issue (such as fuel cells, electrical batteries and compressed natural gas).

Exhibit 3: External business environment

It takes five to ten years to develop a viable product for sale in this motor market. There are a number of companies developing fuel cells but Stokeness is believed to have a two-year lead over them and to be only three years away from commercial launch.

Alternate power technologies, like the hydrogen fuel cells, would be fitted by the major international vehicle manufacturers into their vehicles for sale to their customers. The vehicle manufacturers will need to form a close partnership with any engine producer in order to make their technologies compatible, and this has already begun to happen, with two of the major manufacturers signing deals with other engine makers recently.

A major problem that needs to be overcome with any of these new technologies is that there must be an infrastructure accessible to the end users for refuelling their vehicles (as the petrol station chains do for petrol engine vehicles at present).

Governments have indicated their desire to support the development of such technologies to address environmental issues and to try to establish new, high-value industries in their jurisdiction. They may do this through tax breaks and investment to support the development of the refuelling infrastructure.

Production of Stokeness's fuel cells uses a special membrane that requires rare and expensive elements. Also, it has partnered with two other engineering firms to subcontract the production of certain components in the fuel cell. Stokeness has had to share much of its fuel cell design with these firms in order to overcome certain engineering difficulties.

Also, there are a number of start-up companies developing the other technologies mentioned above, as well as large, existing diesel and petrol engine manufacturers who are constantly reducing the emissions from their existing engines.

The VCs have stressed the need to analyse competition and competitive advantage in order to understand how to make the business profitable in the long term.

The chief executive officer (CEO) of Stokeness wants to understand the external business environment and its effect on performance management. She has requested an assessment, using Porter's five forces model, of the impact of the external business environment on the performance management of Stokeness and a justified recommendation of one new performance measure for each of the five force areas.

She is also interested in the risk appetite of the venture capitalists and how this might impact on performance measurement at Stokeness, and has also asked for an assessment of this.

2 CRC (Mar/Jun 2019, amended) (49 mins)

It is now 1 September 20X5.

Respond to the CEO and the board's requests for work on the following areas:

(a) Moving from its current budgeting system to ABB **(10 marks)**

(b) Completing the analyst's work and explaining the variance for July 20X5 **(10 marks)**

Professional marks will be awarded for the demonstration of skill in analysis and evaluation, scepticism and commercial acumen in your answer. **(5 marks)**

(Total = 25 marks)

Exhibit 1: Cortinas Retail Clothing (CRC): Company information

CRC started as a clothing retailer 20 years ago with one store. The business expanded steadily and had 10 stores after 18 years of trading. Since then, the rate of expansion has increased rapidly with an average of four stores opening per year.

CRC is planning to open its first large out of town store soon and is also considering the acquisition of a food retailing business. Both of these will be supplied with items using CRC's existing central warehouse.

Exhibit 2: Introduction of RFID system

At the beginning of the 20X5 accounting year, to cope with this rapid growth, CRC acquired a RFID (radio frequency identification device) system at its single central warehouse. This was to help manage inventory more effectively and speed up the processes for receiving items from suppliers and despatching them to stores. Items are still moved manually by staff in the CRC warehouse where there is little automation compared to competitors. There has been some resistance from staff to the RFID system, which they find difficult to use. CRC is currently trying to reduce the number of suppliers it has to help increase efficiency in the warehouse.

Exhibit 3: Budgeting system

The budget setting process has remained unchanged since CRC was formed. All managers prepare draft budgets using spreadsheets and submit them to the CRC board for approval. Managers use the previous year results as a starting point when drafting the budgets and increase the variable costs in line with any anticipated growth in volumes. For example, when preparing the budget for the year ending 30 June 20X6, the manager of the central warehouse used the actual costs of running the warehouse from the previous year and increased them all by the same percentage. This was to reflect an anticipated increase in volumes in 20X6 over 20X5. Managers are appraised on their performance against the approved budgets.

CRC has needed all its financial resources to fund its expansion and so it has only old and basic IT systems, which are not enterprise resource planning systems, unified databases or networked systems.

It has been suggested to the CRC board that the current system of budgeting is no longer suitable and that the business should move to activity-based budgeting (ABB).

The CEO has asked you to evaluate whether CRC should move from its current budgeting system to ABB.

Exhibit 4: Central warehouse activity in July 20X5

The board has never seen an activity-based budget before and is unsure how it could be used to explain variances between actual and budgeted performance in the central warehouse. As an example, they would like to see how an activity-based budget for the year ending 30 June 20X6 could be used to explain variances from the actual results for the month of July 20X5.

The two key activities which drive costs in the central warehouse are receipts of items into the goods inwards section and despatches of items from the goods outwards section. A receipt into good inwards involves accepting a delivery of items from a supplier, tagging those items and putting them away in the warehouse. Receipts from suppliers contain variable numbers of individual items. Despatches of items from goods outwards are to CRC's own retail stores. Cost driver rates for these two activities will be used to set monthly cost budgets for the warehouse.

The board asked an analyst to prepare an activity-based budget for the central warehouse for the year ending 30 June 20X6. The analyst has collected relevant information on the costs for the year needed to prepare the activity-based budget and has begun the work (Appendix 1).

The total annual cost relating to goods inwards needs to be determined. This should be used to calculate the budgeted cost of each receipt into goods inwards, in order to explain the variance between the budgeted cost and the actual cost of receipts of goods inwards for the month of July 20X5. The analyst has already correctly included the costs of the warehouse manager's salary and the lease of the RFID system into the incomplete activity-based budget in Appendix 1.

The board has asked you to complete the analyst's work in Appendix 1 as required by the board and explain the variance between the budgeted cost and the actual cost for each receipt into goods inwards for July 20X5.

Exhibit 5: Appendix 1

Analyst's incomplete activity-based budget for the central warehouse for YE 30 June 20X6.

	Total	*Goods inwards*	*Goods outwards*	*Other*
	$	$	$	$
Warehouse manager's salary (1)	55,000	–	–	55,000
Lease of RFID system (2)	75,000	45,000	30,000	–
RFID tagging (3)				
Warehouse staff wages (4)				
Heating and lighting (5)				

Sub-total cost of activities driven by the receipt of goods inwards

To enable you to complete your calculations, you are told that in July 20X5 there were 650 receipts into goods inwards. These receipts contained 100,000 items, which is the same as the budgeted number of items for the month. The actual total cost of activities driven by receipts into goods inwards for the month was $18,000.

Analyst's notes

Relevant information on costs in the central warehouse for the year ending 30 June 20X6

Notes.

1 The cost of the warehouse manager's salary relates to all sections of the warehouse and cannot be apportioned directly to goods inwards or goods outwards.

2 The cost for the RFID system is invoiced by a lease company. 60% of this cost is allocated to goods inwards and the remainder relates to goods outwards.

3 The cost of RFID tagging is the wages cost for specially trained staff, known as taggers. Their only job is to attach RFID tags to items when they are received, before the items are put away in the warehouse. All items received are RFID tagged and the costs of tagging are allocated entirely to the cost of goods inwards. Three taggers will be required, each paid an annual salary of $24,000. The cost of each individual RFID tag is negligible.

4 There are expected to be 14 full-time warehouse staff throughout the year to 30 June 20X6 each paid an annual salary of $22,500; 50% of the warehouse staff work in goods inwards and 50% in goods outwards.

5 The cost of heating and lighting relates to all sections of the warehouse and cannot be apportioned directly to goods inwards or goods outwards. The actual heating and lighting cost for last year was $10,000, and the warehouse manager has proposed a budget of $10,500 for the coming year. The general cost of inflation though is expected to be zero.

6 The annual number of receipts into goods inwards expected is 9,000, containing a total of 1,200,000 items. These are expected to occur evenly over the year.

3 Framiltone (Sep/Dec 2016, amended) (49 mins)

Respond to the CEO's request for work on the budgeting system.

Note. There are 12 marks available for the first part of the work required on this area and there are 8 marks available for second part of the work required on this area. **(20 marks)**

Professional marks will be awarded for the demonstration of skill in analysis and evaluation, scepticism and commercial acumen in your answer. **(5 marks)**

(Total = 25 marks)

Exhibit 1: Company information

Framiltone is a food manufacturer based in Ceeland whose objective is to maximise shareholder wealth. Framiltone has two divisions: Dairy Division and Luxury Division. Framiltone began manufacturing dairy foods 20 years ago and Dairy Division, representing 60% of total revenue, is still the larger of Framiltone's two divisions.

Exhibit 2: Dairy division and Luxury division

Dairy division

This division manufactures cheeses and milk-based desserts. The market in Ceeland for these products is saturated, with little opportunity for growth. Dairy Division has, however, agreed profitable fixed price agreements to supply all the major supermarket chains in Ceeland for the next three years. The division has also agreed long-term fixed volume and price contracts with suppliers of milk, which is by far the most significant raw material used by the division.

In contrast to Luxury Division, Dairy Division does not operate its own fleet of delivery vehicles, but instead subcontracts this to a third-party distribution company. The terms of the contract provide that the distribution company can pass on some increases in fuel costs to Framiltone. These increases are capped at 0.5% annually and are agreed prior to the finalisation of each year's budget.

Production volumes have shown less than 0.5% growth over the last five years. Dairy Division managers have invested in a modern production plant and its production is known to be the most efficient and consistent in the industry.

Luxury division

The Luxury division was set up two years ago to provide an opportunity for growth which is absent from the dairy foods sector. Luxury Division produces high quality foods using unusual, rare and expensive ingredients, many of which are imported from neighbouring Veeland. The product range changes frequently according to consumer tastes and the availability and price of ingredients. All Luxury Division's products are distributed using its own fleet of delivery vehicles.

Since the company began, Framiltone has used a traditional incremental budgeting process. Annual budgets for each division are set by the company's head office after some consultation with divisional managers, who currently have little experience of setting their own budgets. Performance of each division, and of divisional managers, is appraised against these budgets. For many years, Framiltone managed to achieve the budgets set, but last year managers at Luxury Division complained that they were unable to achieve their budget due to factors beyond their control. A wet growing season in Veeland had reduced the harvest of key ingredients in Luxury's products, significantly increasing their cost. As a result, revenue and gross margins fell sharply and the division failed to achieve its operating profit target for the year.

Exhibit 3: Budgeting system

Framiltone has just appointed a new CEO at the end of Q1 of the current year. They have called you as a Performance Management Expert to ask for your advice.

'In my last job in the retail fashion industry, we used rolling budgets, where the annual budget was updated to reflect the results of every quarter's trading. That gives a more realistic target, providing a better basis on which to appraise divisional performance. Do you think we should use a similar system for all divisions at Framiltone?' they asked.

You have obtained the current year budget for Luxury Division and the division's Q1 actual trading results (Appendix 1) and notes outlining expectations of divisional key costs and revenues for the rest of the year (Appendix 2).

The new CEO has two requests:

- Using the data in the appendices, you are asked to recalculate the current year budget to the end of the current year and to briefly comment on the overall impact of this on the expected operating profit for the year.
- To evaluate whether a move from traditional incremental budgeting to a system of rolling budgets would be appropriate for Dairy and Luxury Divisions.

Exhibit 4: Appendix 1

Luxury Division current year budget

	Q1	*Q2*	*Q3*	*Q4*	***Total***	*Q1 actual*
	C$'000	C$'000	C$'000	C$'000	**C$'000**	C$'000
Revenue	10,000	12,000	11,000	7,000	**40,000**	10,400
Cost of sales	(6,100)	(7,120)	(6,460)	(4,720)	**(24,400)**	(6,240)
Gross profit	3,900	4,880	4,540	2,280	**15,600**	4,160
Distribution costs	(600)	(720)	(660)	(420)	**(2,400)**	(624)
Administration costs	(2,300)	(2,300)	(2,300)	(2,300)	**(9,200)**	(2,300)
Operating profit	1,000	1,860	1,580	(440)	**4,000**	1,236

Exhibit 5: Appendix 2

Expected key costs and revenues for remainder of the current year

(1) Sales volumes are expected to be 2% higher each quarter than forecast in the current budget.

(2) Average selling price per unit is expected to increase by 1.5% from the beginning of Q3.

(3) The exchange rate between the Ceeland Dollar (C$) and the Veeland Dollar (V$) is predicted to change at the beginning of Q2 to C$1.00 buys V$1.50. For several years up to the end of Q1, C$1.00 has been equivalent to V$1.40 and this exchange rate has been used when producing the current year budget. Food produced in the Luxury Division is despatched immediately upon production and Framiltone holds minimal inventory. The cost of ingredients imported from Veeland represents 50% of the division's cost of sales and suppliers invoice goods in V$.

(4) The rate of tax levied by the Ceeland Government on the cost of fuel which Luxury uses to power its fleet of delivery vehicles is due to increase from 60%, which it has been for many years, to 63% at the beginning of Q3. 70% of the division's distribution costs are represented by the cost of fuel for delivery vehicles.

(5) Administration costs are not expected to change.

4 Godel (June 2014, amended) (49 mins)

Respond to the CEO's requests for work on the following areas:

(a) Analysing variances into planning and operational elements **(6 marks)**

(b) Evaluating the current budgeting system and the beyond budgeting proposal **(14 marks)**

Professional marks will be awarded for the demonstration of skill in analysis and evaluation, scepticism and commercial acumen in your answer. **(5 marks)**

(Total = 25 marks)

Exhibit 1: Company background and strategy

Godel Goodies (Godel) manufactures a variety of own-label sweets for the two largest supermarket chains in Seeland. The business makes several different flavours of the same basic product. The strategy of the business has been to be a cost leader in order to win the supermarkets' business. The sales of Godel vary up and down from quarter to quarter depending on the state of the general economy and competitive forces. Most of the sweet manufacturers have been in business for decades and so the business is mature with little scope to be innovative in new product development. The supermarkets prefer to sign suppliers to long-term contracts and so it is difficult for new entrants to gain a foothold in this market. The management style at Godel is very much command-and-control which fits with the strategy and type of business. Indeed, most employees have been at Godel for many years and have expressed their liking for the straightforward nature of their work.

Exhibit 2: Variance analysis

The chief executive officer (CEO) of Godel has asked your firm of accountants to advise them as their finance director (FD) will be absent for several months due to a recently diagnosed illness. As the CEO is preparing for the next board meeting, they have obtained the operating statement and detailed variance analysis from one of the junior accountants (Appendix 1).

The CEO is happy with the operating statement but wants to understand the meaning of the detailed operational and planning variances, given in Appendix 1, for the board meeting. They also need to know what action should be taken as a result of these specific variances.

Exhibit 3: Budgeting process

The FD had been looking at the budgeting process before they fell ill. The CEO has decided that you should help them by answering some questions on budgeting at Godel.

Currently, the budget at Godel is set at the start of the year and performance is measured against this. The company uses standard costs for each product and attributes overheads using absorption costing based on machine hours. No variations are allowed to the standard costs during the year. The standard costs and all budget assumptions are discussed with the relevant operational manager before being set. However, these managers grumble that the budget process is very time-consuming and that the results are ultimately of limited value from their perspective. Some of them also complain that they must frequently explain that the variances are not their fault.

The CEO wants to know your views on whether the current way of budgeting is appropriate and whether the managers' complaints are justified. They are satisfied that there is no dysfunctional behaviour at Godel which may lead to budget slack or excessive spending and that all managers are working in the best interests of the company.

In the last few months, the FD had been reading business articles and books and had mentioned that there were a number of organisations which were trying to go 'beyond budgeting'.

The CEO is concerned that they do not understand what budgeting does for the business and this is why they want you to explain what are the benefits and problems of budgeting at Godel before considering replacing it with a 'beyond budgeting' approach. They want a recommendation on whether or not to adopt beyond budgeting.

Exhibit 4: Appendix 1

Note. You may assume that all figures in this Appendix are correct.

Operating statement for Godel

Period: May 20X4

	$	$	
Budgeted profit		214,200	
Budget fixed production costs		264,180	
Budgeted contribution		478,380	
Sales variances			
Volume	20,100		Adverse
Price	8,960		Adverse
		29,060	Adverse
		449,320	

Actual sales minus standard cost of sales

	Favourable	Adverse		
	$	$	$	$
Variable cost variance				
Material price		4,200		
usage	3,500			
rate	1,100			
efficiency	24,480			
idle time		5,600		

	Favourable	Adverse			
	$	$	$	$	
Variable overhead expenditure		1,080			
efficiency	3,060				
	32,140	10,880			
				21,260	Favourable
				470,580	
Actual contribution				470,580	
Budgeted fixed production overhead			271,728		
Expenditure variance			18,696		Adverse
Actual fixed production overhead				290,424	
Actual profit				180,156	

	$	
Detailed variances		
Total variable cost variances		
Planning	20,680	Favourable
Operational	580	Favourable
Sales price variances		
Planning	15,600	Adverse
Operational	6,640	Favourable

5 Perkin (Sep/Dec 2015, amended) (49 mins)

Respond to the institutional shareholder's requests for work on the following areas:

(a) Perkin's current budgeting system **(14 marks)**

(b) Evaluation of Perkin's poor performance **(6 marks)**

Professional marks will be awarded for the demonstration of skill in analysis and evaluation, and commercial acumen in your answer. **(5 marks)**

(Total = 25 marks)

Exhibit 1: Company background and objectives

Perkin manufactures electronic components for export worldwide, from factories in Ceeland, for use in smartphones and handheld gaming devices. These two markets are supplied with similar components by two divisions, Phones Division (P) and Gaming Division (G). Each division has its own selling, purchasing, IT and research and development (R&D) functions, but separate IT systems. Some manufacturing facilities, however, are shared between the two divisions.

Perkin's corporate objective is to maximise shareholder wealth through innovation and continuous technological improvement in its products. The manufacturers of smartphones and gaming devices, who use Perkin's components, update their products frequently and constantly compete with each other to launch models which are technically superior.

Exhibit 2: Budgeting process

Perkin has a well-established incremental budgeting process. Divisional managers forecast sales volumes and costs months in advance of the budget year. These divisional budgets are then scrutinised by the main board, and revised significantly by them in line with targets they have set for the business. The finalised budgets are often approved after the start of the accounting year. Under pressure to deliver consistent returns to institutional shareholders, the board does not tolerate failure by either division to achieve the planned net profit for the year once the budget is approved. Last year's results were poor compared to the annual budget. Divisional managers, who are appraised on the financial performance of their own division, have complained about the length of time that the budgeting process takes and that the performance of their divisions could have been better but was constrained by the budgets which were set for them.

In P Division, managers had failed to anticipate the high popularity of a new smartphone model incorporating a large screen designed for playing games, and had not made the necessary technical modifications to the division's own components. This was due to the high costs of doing so, which had not been budgeted for. Based on the original sales forecast, P Division had already committed to manufacturing large quantities of the existing version of the component and so had to heavily discount these in order to achieve the planned sales volumes.

A critical material in the manufacture of Perkin's products is silver, which is a commodity which changes materially in price according to worldwide supply and demand. During the year supplies of silver were reduced significantly for a short period of time and G Division paid high prices to ensure continued supply. Managers of G Division were unaware that P Division held large inventories of silver which they had purchased when the price was much lower.

Initially, G Division accurately forecasted demand for its components based on the previous years' sales volumes plus the historic annual growth rate of 5%. However, overall sales volumes were much lower than budgeted. This was due to a fire at the factory of their main customer, which was then closed for part of the year. Reacting to this news, managers at G Division took action to reduce costs, including closing one of the three R&D facilities in the division.

However, when the customer's factory reopened, G Division was unwilling to recruit extra staff to cope with increased demand; nor would P Division reallocate shared manufacturing facilities to them, in case demand increased for its own products later in the year. As a result, Perkin lost the prestigious preferred supplier status from its main customer who was unhappy with G Division's failure to effectively respond to the additional demand. The customer had been forced to purchase a more expensive, though technically superior, component from an alternative manufacturer.

The institutional shareholders' representative, recently appointed to the board, has asked you as a performance management expert for your advice. 'We need to know whether Perkin's budgeting process is appropriate for the business, and how this contributed to last year's poor performance.'

The shareholder representative acknowledged that external factors had contributed to Perkin's poor performance and suggested it would be helpful if Perkin's performance reports distinguished between variances resulting from its own operational performance and those due to changes in circumstances that could not have been anticipated when the budgets were produced.

The shareholder representative has two requests:

- First, an evaluation of the weaknesses in Perkin's current budgeting system and whether it is suitable for the environment in which Perkin operates.
- Second, an evaluation of the extent to which Perkin's poor performance for the last year can be attributed to external factors.

6 Jolt (Sept 2018, amended) (49 mins)

Respond to the board of Jolt's request for work on the BPR proposal.

Note. There are 12 marks available for the first part of the work required on this area and there are 8 marks available for second part of the work required on this area. **(20 marks)**

Professional marks will be awarded for the demonstration of skill in analysis and evaluation, scepticism and commercial acumen in your answer. **(5 marks)**

(Total = 25 marks)

Exhibit 1: Company information

Jolt manufactures high quality swimwear and cycling clothing in its only factory, which employs 1,000 manufacturing staff and 200 support staff. Its products are used by both amateur and professional sports players in its home country. Jolt is known for its high ethical standards towards its workers, suppliers and the environment, and has voluntarily published a corporate sustainability report for many years.

Jolt is organised into traditional functional departments such as procurement, finance and sales, most of which have their own unreliable spreadsheet-based systems for planning and reporting. As a result, Jolt often fails to produce accurate, timely and consistent data to monitor its own performance, which contributes to failures in achieving the performance targets set by its retail customers.

Jolt's market is seasonal and competitive. Retailers, who are Jolt's customers, for both swimwear and cycling clothing have two key demands: they want lower prices to pass on to consumers and they also require suppliers to meet performance targets relating to lead times and quality.

To help them comply with the retailers' demands, Jolt's competitors have closed down all of their own manufacturing facilities and outsourced all production to overseas suppliers, who have much larger factories and lower costs. To mitigate the cost of shipping goods over long distances, Jolt's competitors have invested in sophisticated software to consolidate orders so that each shipping container is completely full before despatch from their suppliers. Purchase invoice processing is also automated by the integration of information systems into the suppliers' bespoke systems.

Exhibit 2: BPR proposal

In order to reduce costs, it has been proposed to outsource the manufacture of swimwear, which is 50% of Jolt's total output, to a supplier 17,000 km away. A comparison of the cost of manufacturing and the cost of outsourcing swimwear is given in Appendix 1.

The change to outsourced supply for swimwear will mean that staff from Jolt's functional departments will reorganise into multi-disciplinary teams, each serving major customer accounts. Each team will perform all aspects of account management from taking sales orders and procurement through to arranging shipping and after sales service. Team members dealing with customers will work in Jolt's home country, while those managing quality and supplier audits will work close to the manufacturing site. Teams will be given greater autonomy to set selling prices to reflect market conditions. Many support staff will work in unfamiliar roles or be offered new jobs overseas after the reorganisation.

A consultant has advised Jolt's board of directors that the outsourcing and reorganisation proposal has characteristics of re-engineered processes and could be described as business process re-engineering (BPR). They advised that, as well as evaluating how BPR will improve its business performance in meeting its customers' demands and requirements, Jolt should take into account any ethical aspects of the proposed changes.

In response to the consultant's advice, the board have asked you to help them. The work the board requires in in two parts:

- First, the board would like an evaluation of how the BPR proposal could improve Jolt's performance in relation to its retail customers' two key demands, and
- Second, an assessment of the potential impact of Jolt's high ethical standards on the BPR proposal and consequently on business performance.

Exhibit 3: Appendix 1

Comparison of the average cost of manufacturing and outsourcing swimwear production

	Manufacturing	*Outsourcing*
Average cost per unit	$	$[1]
Material cost	1.85	–
Labour cost	2.20	–
Factory overhead	0.95	–
Purchase cost from supplier[2]	–	3.50
Total	5.00	3.50

Notes.

1 Purchase cost of outsourced products is translated into $ from the supplier's home currency.

2 In addition to the purchase cost from the supplier, Joly must pay for shipping costs at the rate of $5,000 for each large, standard sized shipping container, regardless of the number of units in it. Each contains holds 10,000 units when fully loaded.

3 Due to changes in international trade tariffs expected in the near future, swimwear imports in to Jolt's home country will be subject to 10% import duty on the cost of imports excluding shipping cost.

7 Pattack (Sept/Dec 2021) (49 mins)

The following **exhibits** provide information relevant to the question:

(1) Company information – the background, overall aim and structure of the company: Pattack

(2) Current delivery process – information related to how Pattack currently manages its delivery service

(3) BPR proposal – details of a business process re-engineering (BPR) proposal and new bonus scheme for delivery drivers put forward by a management consultant

(4) Appendix 1 – flowcharts of both the current and proposed processes

Required

Respond to the CEO's request for work on the proposed new system.

Note. There are 13 marks available for the first part of the work required on this area and there are 7 marks available for second part of the work required on this area. **(20 marks)**

Professional marks will be awarded for the demonstration of skill in analysis and evaluation, scepticism and commercial acumen in your answer. **(5 marks)**

(Total = 25 marks)

Exhibit 1: Company information

Pattack is a company in Geeland which specialises in the delivery of parcels. Pattack collects parcels from online retailers and delivers them to the end user. Pattack's overall aim is: 'to maximise shareholder value through having a strategic focus on costs, by being the best delivery company in Geeland, and by having an engaged and committed workforce.'

Despite enjoying several years of growth, Pattack's performance has suffered recently as there have been new entrants into the marketplace.

Pattack's current functions are run along departmental lines:

- Collections – the collection drivers who collect parcels from retailers
- Internal operations – the computer operators who enter the orders
- Delivery administration – the administrators who schedule the deliveries
- Deliveries – the delivery drivers who deliver the parcels to the end user

Exhibit 2: Current delivery process

Currently, Pattack collects parcels from the retailer and brings those parcels back to its premises. Collection drivers are employed for this purpose.

When on Pattack's premises, the parcels are then logged on Pattack's computer system. All details of the delivery are recorded at this time. These details are: the name of the retailer, the name of the end user to whom the parcel has to be delivered and the expected delivery date and time. On-time delivery is a key metric in the parcel delivery industry.

Pattack's drivers' delivery schedules are prepared for them by delivery administration after the computer operators have entered the order details. These schedules are presented to the drivers in paper form and the schedules are organised based on the time each order is due to be delivered.

The drivers return their completed delivery schedules after the day's deliveries. Computer operators should record the date and time of the actual delivery at this point. However, the operators are often too busy logging the delivery details of outgoing parcels for the next day to undertake this task and, additionally, the delivery drivers do not always record the actual time when the delivery was made. A lack of accuracy of recorded delivery data has been the cause of complaints from the retailers Pattack delivers for.

The manager of the deliveries department does not have a vehicle tracking system and assumes that the delivery drivers are following the schedule they have been given in the morning.

Exhibit 3: BPR proposal

The chief executive officer (CEO) of Pattack recently met with a management consultant who advised him that the entire current operation should be re-engineered. The management consultant suggested that Pattack invests in a barcoding system which would electronically barcode all parcels with all details of the delivery. This coding could be undertaken by the retailers, which would ensure this data was entered as soon as the order is allocated to Pattack. This data would be electronically communicated to Pattack, enabling deliveries to end users to be arranged at this time.

Drivers collecting parcels from the retailers would be the same drivers who deliver the parcels to the end user. These drivers would know the delivery schedule in advance of collecting the parcels. End user receipt would be acknowledged by issuing each driver with a digital handheld device which would require a signature from the end user and which would also automatically note the delivery time when the parcel was signed for. Additionally, each vehicle would be fitted with a vehicle tracking device which would ensure its exact location could be checked at any time.

Appendix 1 provides a flowchart of the old process and the re-engineered process.

The management consultant also suggested that Pattack's bonus system should relate to the new process and indicated that they felt the drivers should be awarded a bonus when overall retailer satisfaction exceeded 85%.

The CEO has requested two pieces of work:

- First, an evaluation of how the BPR proposal could improve Pattack's performance in relation to its overall aim
- Second, an evaluation of the bonus scheme for delivery drivers identified by the management consultant

Exhibit 4: Appendix 1

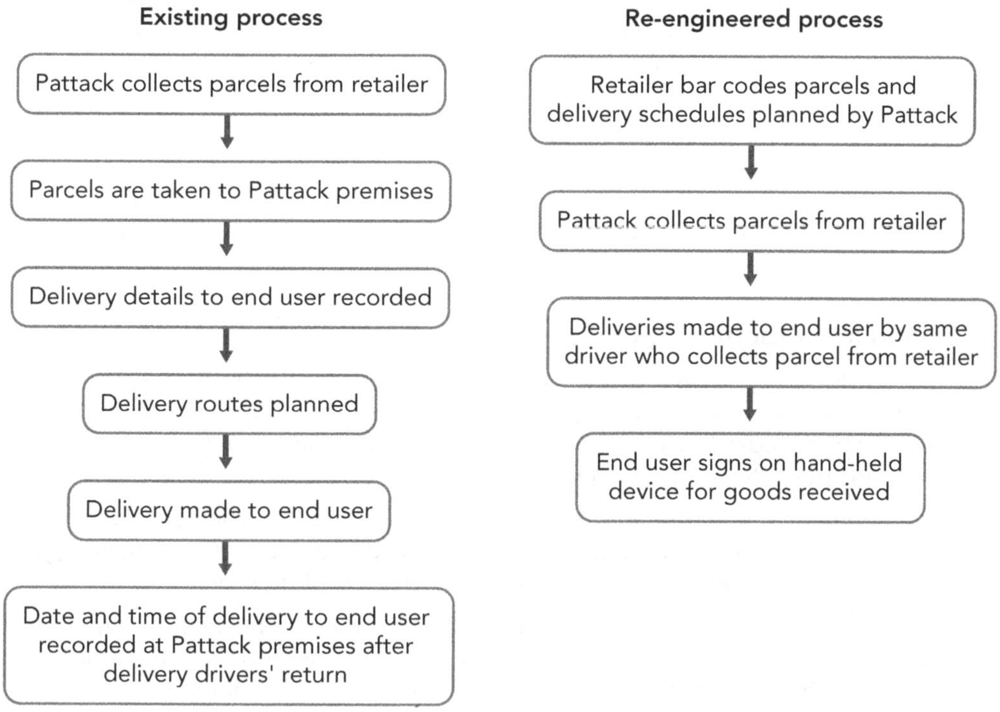

8 Sgoltaire (Sept/ Dec 2021) **(49 mins)**

The following **exhibits** provide information relevant to the question:

(1) Company information – the background, main objective and product range of the company: Sgoltaire

(2) Kayland manufacturing plant – details of a proposal to build a new manufacturing plant overseas in Kayland, to produce Chemical K

(3) Environmental impact of Chemical K – information relation to the impact that the production of Chemical K will have on the environment

(4) Environmental management accounting – details of work required on how environmental management accounting (EMA) may be used to improve business performance

(5) Appendix 1 – the present value (PV) of the costs to decommission and clean up the site used for manufacturing Chemical K

This information should be used to answer the question **requirements** within your chosen **response option** provided.

Required

It is now 1 September 20X5.

Respond to the board's request for work on the following areas:

(a) Ethical issues **(8 marks)**

(b) EMA **(12 marks)**

Professional marks will be awarded for the demonstration of skill in analysis and evaluation, scepticism and commercial acumen in your answer. **(5 marks)**

(Total = 25 marks)

Exhibit 1: Company information

Sgoltaire is a large company listed on the Jayland stock exchange. Its main objective is to maximise the long-term wealth of its shareholders. The largest shareholder is a pension fund which only invests in companies which behave ethically towards their stakeholders and the environment. All companies listed in Jayland must produce an annual corporate sustainability report (CSR).

Sgoltaire manufactures a diverse range of chemicals, ranging from those for use in industrial processes to household detergents and cleaning products. Sgoltaire is a well-known and trusted brand in Jayland. Many of its household products command premium prices because they use ingredients and manufacturing processes which cause less harm to the environment than those of competitors.

Exhibit 2: Kayland manufacturing plant

As part of a wider strategy, Sgoltaire plans to produce a new product, Chemical K, which will require the building of a new manufacturing plant. The company has always manufactured in Jayland, but in order to increase business performance, the board is considering whether to build the new plant overseas at a site identified in Kayland.

Due to high unemployment in Kayland, labour costs are lower there. Environmental regulations are also much less strict than in Jayland. Kayland is a hot, dry country where there is often insufficient water available to meet the needs of the population and their livestock.

Sgoltaire's largest shareholder, the pension fund, is aware that the company lacks experience in operating outside Jayland. Because of this, the shareholder is concerned that the board may pay insufficient attention to the impact of ethical issues on both strategy formulation and business performance, when taking the decision whether to manufacture in Kayland.

Exhibit 3: Environmental impact of Chemical K

The manufacture of Chemical K would consume large volumes of water taken from a nearby river. To comply with the limited environmental regulations in Kayland, some of this water would be used to dilute a toxic waste product, Waste Product A (WPA), which arises from the manufacturing process. The diluted WPA would then be discharged back into the nearby river. The discharge of WPA into rivers is not permitted in Sgoltaire's home country of Jayland because there is some scientific evidence that contact with WPA may cause serious long-term health problems to people, which may not become apparent for many years.

Production of Chemical K would cease after ten years, and the plant must be decommissioned. The site would remain contaminated with harmful chemicals for many years after decommissioning, unless a separate cleaning operation is undertaken.

The board have requested your advice on how ethical issues may affect the decision to manufacture in Kayland.

Exhibit 4: Environmental management accounting

It has been suggested that Sgoltaire uses environmental management accounting (EMA) to improve business performance. EMA is the identification, collection and analysis of information related to the physical and financial impact of an organisation's activities on the environment. The board wants advice on how EMA will help the following four areas:

(1) Calculating costs

(2) Investment appraisal

(3) Setting performance measures and targets

(4) Product pricing

In relation to investment appraisal, the board calculated that the net present value (NPV) of the proposal to manufacture Chemical K in Kayland is $240m, compared to $200m if the manufacturing was done in Jayland. It has since been identified that the costs of decommissioning the plant and cleaning the site were not included in these calculations, so the board has now begun the work of estimating the present values of the costs to decommission and clean the two possible sites (Appendix 1).

The board have asked for your advice on how EMA will help Sgoltaire in the four areas identified.

Exhibit 5: Appendix 1

Present value of the costs of decommissioning the plant and cleaning the site

Cost	*Jayland*	*Kayland*
	$m	$m
Decommissioning the plant[1]	20	30
Cleaning the site[2]	60	–
Total	80	30

(1) The board has estimated that because of logistical difficulties due to Kayland being 8,000 km from Jayland, decommissioning costs, which do not include the costs of cleaning the site, would be 50% higher than in Jayland.

(2) The board has not yet estimated the costs of cleaning the site in Kayland, though because of the same logistical difficulties which apply to decommissioning costs, costs of cleaning the site in Kayland will also be higher than in Jayland.

9 Alflonnso (Sept/Dec 2016, amended) (49 mins)

Respond to the CEO's request for work on the following areas:

(a) Calculating the total waste treatment costs and R&D costs of the three new products **(3 marks)**

(b) Calculating and commenting on the profit per litre of the new products **(9 marks)**

(c) Advice on EMA **(8 marks)**

Professional marks will be awarded for the demonstration of skill in analysis and evaluation, and commercial acumen in your answer. **(5 marks)**

(Total = 25 marks)

Exhibit 1: Company information

Alflonnso is a large producer of industrial chemicals, with divisions in 25 countries. The Agrochemicals Division produces a chemical pesticide, known internally as 'ALF', to control pests in a crop which is of worldwide significance, economically and for food production. Pesticides such as ALF only remain effective for a limited time, after which pests become resistant to them and a replacement product needs to be found. A scientific study has shown that the current variant, ALF6, is becoming ineffective in controlling pests, and in some places it has accumulated in the soil to levels which may significantly reduce crop yields in the future if it is continued to be used. The Agrochemicals Division is evaluating three new products to find one replacement for ALF6.

Exhibit 2: Potential new products

ALF7

ALF7 is produced by a small chemical modification to the existing product and requires little research and development (R&D) resources to develop it. As it is closely related to the current variant, it is only expected to remain effective, and in use, for three years. It is unclear whether ALF7 will accumulate in the soil in the same way as ALF6 does.

Red

Red is a new type of pesticide which will incur large amounts of R&D expenditure to develop a commercial version. In addition, the Agrochemicals Division will have to fund a long-term scientific study into the effect of Red on the environment at a cost of $4m for each of the 15 years that the product will be in use, and for five years afterwards.

Production of Red generates large amounts of toxic by-products which must be treated in the division's waste treatment facility. The production plant used to produce Red must also be decommissioned for cleaning, at an estimated cost of $45m, at the end of the life of the product.

Green

Green is a form of a naturally occurring chemical, thought to be safe and not to accumulate in the environment. It is expected to remain in use for eight years. Production of Green requires relatively large amounts of energy. Significant R&D expenditure is also needed to produce an effective version, as Green remains active in the environment for only a short time. Because of this, Green is unsuitable for use in climates where crop production is already difficult.

Exhibit 3: Global Food Production Organisation

The Global Food Production Organisation (GFPO) is a non-governmental organisation which funds new ways to increase global crop production, especially in regions where food for human consumption is already scarce. The GFPO has agreed to make a significant contribution to the R&D costs of producing a replacement for ALF6, but will be unwilling to contribute to the R&D costs for Green because it cannot be used in every region. Similarly, a number of governments, in countries where Alflonnso has licences to operate its other chemical businesses, have warned the company of the potential public disapproval should the Agrochemical Division choose to replace ALF6 with a product unsuitable for use in areas where food production is scarce.

Exhibit 4: New CEO

The newly appointed chief financial officer (CFO) for the Agrochemicals Division has asked you, as a performance management consultant, for your advice.

One of our analysts in the Agrochemicals Division has produced a single period statement of profit or loss (Appendix 1) to show the profitability of the three new products we are considering as replacements for ALF6.

I think the analyst's calculations are too simplistic,' they continued. 'The costs of the waste treatment are apportioned based on the expected revenue of the new products. This is consistent with Alflonnso's traditional group accounting policy, but I don't think this gives an accurate costing for the new products. Also, I watched a presentation recently about the use of life cycle costing and also how environmental management accounting (EMA) can help reduce costs in the categories of conventional, contingent and reputation costs, and as a result improve performance.

The new CEO has requested for your help in three areas:

- Calculating the total waste treatment costs and R&D costs of the three new products, using activity-based costing, and excluding the value of the grant from the GFPO.
- Using this analysis, your answers from part (a), calculate the average net profit per litre of each of the three alternative new products over their expected life cycles and comment on the results.
- Advice on how EMA may help improve the performance of the Agrochemicals Division.

Exhibit 5: Appendix 1

	ALF7	*Red*	*Green*
Revenue per litre ($)	8.00	13.00	11.00
Quantity sold and produced (million litres)	100	85	75

Single period statement of profit or loss for the replacement products for ALF6 (Note 1)

	$m	$m	$m
Revenue	800	1,105	825
Direct material, labour and energy	(524)	(724)	(565)
Factory overheads	(80)	(122)	(74)
Environmental study	–	(4)	–
Waste treatment of toxic by-products (Note 2)	(54)	(63)	(71)
Net profit (Note 3)	142	192	115
Average profit per litre ($)	1.42	2.26	1.53

Notes.

1 All figures exclude the contribution from the GFPO towards the R&D costs of the new product.

2 Waste treatment is an overhead cost incurred in the division's waste treatment facility. Currently, costs of waste treatment are apportioned to products according to expected revenue. The total annual cost of the waste treatment facility, which processes a total of 55 million litres of waste each year, is $300m. Any waste treatment capacity not used by any of the three new products can be used to treat waste created during the manufacture of other products in the division. One litre of waste by-product is produced for every 12.5 litres of ALF7 produced, for every 2.5 litres of Red produced, and for every 100 litres of Green.

3 R&D costs are incurred in the division's R&D facility. In accordance with the group's accounting policy, R&D expenditure is not currently apportioned to individual products. The annual cost of the R&D facility is $60m and has a total of 30,400 R&D hours available, of which 800 hours would be required to develop ALF7, 8,500 hours to develop Red, and 4,000 hours to develop Green.

PERFORMANCE MEASUREMENT SYSTEMS AND DEVELOPMENTS IN TECHNOLOGY

Questions 10 to 14 cover performance measurement systems and developments in technology, the subject of Part B of the syllabus for APM.

10 Luvij (Mar/Jun 2018, amended) (49 mins)

Respond to the board's request for work on the following areas:

(a) External information **(12 marks)**

(b) The measurement and management of the performance of the joint venture **(8 marks)**

Professional marks will be awarded for the demonstration of skill in analysis and evaluation, and commercial acumen in your answer. **(5 marks)**

(Total = 25 marks)

Exhibit 1: Company background

Luvij manufactures high quality, luxury women's footwear. It sells its products on its own website and also to small independent retailers.

Exhibit 2: Data collection and performance analysis

In order to monitor performance and aid decision making, Luvij collects sales data on all of its footwear ranges and feedback on its designs from customers and retailers. In addition, to ensure that prices remain competitive, Luvij has a team of staff to monitor the prices of similar products on competitors' websites and to identify design trends in the market, which change frequently, and from season to season. Generating new footwear designs consistent with changing market trends is a critical success factor for Luvij. The large volume of data collected is entered into a complex spreadsheet by one data entry clerk.

Luvij operates a functional structure with different departments for sales, production, purchasing and design. The spreadsheet is sent by email to the senior manager of each of these departments at the end of each quarter. The senior manager for the sales, production and buying departments are expected to generate the relevant sales, production and purchasing forecasts by analysing information contained in the spreadsheet. The senior manager of the design department uses the information to generate new footwear designs consistent with market trends.

Exhibit 3: Potential joint venture

Luvij has a strategic objective to become the market leader in the sale of high quality, children's footwear to small independent footwear retailers. It has already invested heavily in market research and developing innovative designs. To reduce the risks of not achieving this strategic objective, for example, by having insufficient capacity to produce a larger range of footwear styles, the board is considering entering into a joint venture with Shirville.

Shirville is a large manufacturer of exclusively children's footwear. Its advanced manufacturing machinery and production techniques mean that it can produce the high volumes required to supply supermarkets and chain stores* found on the main streets of most towns and cities. Shirville's objective for the joint venture is to utilise spare production capacity it has in a factory which it holds on a lease which expires in three years.

Exhibit 4: Director's concerns

One recently appointed board member at Luvij has commented:

> I believe that the external information on market trends and competitors' prices compiled in the quarterly spreadsheet is of limited usefulness as I have heard complaints from managers that they have difficulty understanding the large volume of data given to them, and that they often

receive this too late. The company I worked for in my previous job used a unified corporate database to share information in real time across all parts of the business. A similar unified corporate database may be useful for Luvij.

I am also concerned about the potential problems of measuring and managing the performance of the joint venture with Shirville. The fact that the two businesses have different objectives is just one example of why these problems may occur, though there will also be other reasons.

*Chain stores are large retailers with multiple stores based in different locations.

As a result of these concerns the board have asked for your assistance with two areas:

- An explanation of the factors which might limit the usefulness of the external information currently used by Luvij, and how the use of a unified corporate database could help to overcome these limitations
- Advice on the potential problems with the measurement and management of the performance of the joint venture with Shirville

11 Clonyard (Sep/Dec 2020, amended) (49 mins)

It is now 1 September 20X5.

Respond to the CEO of Elrig's request for work on the following areas:

(a) Alignment between Elrig and Clonyard **(10 marks)**

(b) The introduction of an ERPS **(10 marks)**

Professional marks will be awarded for the demonstration of skill in analysis and evaluation, scepticism and commercial acumen in your answer. **(5 marks)**

(Total = 25 marks)

Exhibit 1: Company information

Clonyard is a private company which sells shoes to adults and children. Clonyard has several retail shops. The mission of Clonyard is 'to satisfy customers by providing footwear of excellent quality for the modern world.' Clonyard has built its reputation on providing footwear to those who have specialist needs in footwear, such as minor medical issues, and Clonyard's staff excel at spending time with customers to determine customers' correct requirements. Clonyard has achieved modest growth over the past five years.

Twelve months ago, Clonyard was the subject of a successful but hostile take-over bid by Elrig, a listed company. Elrig's mission is 'to return value consistently to our shareholders by growing our market share and by offering unrivalled value for money for our customers.'

Elrig's primary motivation for the takeover was to enhance its market share by acquiring a niche operator. In addition, Elrig's directors also believe that there is likely to be consolidation in the industry in the near future and the purchase of Clonyard by Elrig is a reaction to that belief. Having acquired Clonyard, Elrig is keen to retain the Clonyard brand and is also keen to ensure that all aspects of Clonyard's business operations are integrated into those of Elrig.

Exhibit 2: Business alignment

Elrig has taken a decision at board level that a similar range of inventory is maintained throughout all Elrig and Clonyard shops. Managers of Clonyard's individual shops are unhappy with this as this is contrary to the individual specialisms which shop managers were encouraged to develop previously. As a result, several managers have left the business.

In order to help with the integration of Clonyard into Elrig's business, Elrig has ensured that each Clonyard shop will have at least one of Elrig's employees working there. Clonyard's staff have complained that the Elrig members of staff are more focused on ensuring a sale is made than spending the required time with customers. Clonyard staff have also expressed concern about the lack of technical product knowledge of Elrig's staff.

Elrig has retained most of Clonyard's directors. These directors have found it challenging to adjust to Elrig's focus on pursuing market share and recently said, 'It's as though they don't measure anything else. Every report we get is about market share and the message is always that we need more of it, as quickly as possible.'

The chief executive officer (CEO) of Elrig was recently told by a management consultant that Elrig should consider using the McKinsey 7S model to help with the integration of Clonyard into Elrig's operation. The management consultant indicated that they felt that Elrig should only focus on the soft elements in this model for now.

The CEO would like you to evaluate whether Elrig is properly aligned with Clonyard using **only** the skills, staff and style components of the soft elements.

Exhibit 3: Introduction of an ERPS

Introduction of an ERPS Elrig and Clonyard are currently utilising different computer systems. It is therefore difficult for staff at all levels of Elrig's operations to obtain access to Clonyard's performance data. The board of Elrig has complained that any information it receives on Clonyard's operations or performance is too late to enable the board to make decisions. The director of operations for the group, for example, has indicated that they do not see any reports on inventory levels at each Clonyard shop until at least three months into the financial year. They have also indicated that Clonyard shops appear to wait too long for goods to be delivered to them from their suppliers.

The group sales director indicated that the data he receives on Clonyard's monthly financial performance is at least three weeks late. This offers no opportunity to introduce discounted products at an appropriate time, which is a very common sales approach for Elrig.

Elrig's employees in general have expressed concern that Clonyard's computerised information systems are outdated and that Clonyard's employees do not use the computer system as much as they should. For example, it was reported that it is common practice for a Clonyard employee to place an order for inventory over the telephone and not enter the order onto the computer system until after the order has been delivered.

The board of Elrig has decided that it needs real time access to Elrig's overall business operations, including Clonyard, and is considering the purchase of an enterprise resource planning system (ERPS). Further, a director of Elrig has indicated: 'the use of a shared up-to-date information system such as an ERPS will ensure that the Clonyard operation is completely integrated within the Elrig one. The Clonyard employees will also be delighted with the brand-new system.'

The CEO wants you to evaluate the introduction of an ERPS into Elrig's overall business, including Clonyard.

12 Quark Healthcare (Dec 2013, amended) (49 mins)

Respond to the CFO's request for work on the following areas:

(a) The impact of the RFID system on performance management at Quark **(13 marks)**

(b) The RFID information system and lean systems **(7 marks)**

Professional marks will be awarded for the demonstration of skill in analysis and evaluation, scepticism and commercial acumen in your answer. **(5 marks)**

(Total = 25 marks)

Exhibit 1: Organisational background

Quark Healthcare (Quark) runs a number of large hospitals which provide general medical care for the people of Veeland. Veeland is an advanced economy and healthcare is considered to be a high skill, high technology and high-status industry. It is compulsory for the people of Veeland to purchase health insurance and then the insurance companies reimburse the healthcare providers for services delivered. The insurance companies audit the healthcare providers and grade them for value for money. As there are a number of hospital chains (such as Quark), the insurers will encourage their insured customers to use those which are most efficient. The ultimate sanction for a healthcare provider is for an insurance company to remove them from the list of acceptable providers.

Quark has large amounts of capital tied up in expensive medical equipment and a drug inventory. The existing systems for accounting for these items are traditional ones aimed at avoiding theft and obsolescence. Quark has an inventory system which requires regular (weekly) physical checks of the drugs in inventory in order to update it. It is important that the right drugs must be in easily accessible stores (located throughout the hospital) in order to act quickly in case of a medical emergency. Also, the accounting staff at Quark maintain a non-current asset register (NCAR) which logs the location of all major assets including medical equipment. The problem with the NCAR is that it is often out of date as doctors will take equipment in time of emergency and not properly log its new location. This often leads to equipment lying unused in one area of the hospital while being searched for in another area, to the detriment of patient care.

Exhibit 2: Radio-frequency identification devices (RFID)

Quark has recently instituted a tagging project where radio-frequency identification devices (RFID) will be attached to the most valuable pieces of equipment used in treatment and also to batches of high-value drugs. The hospitals are fitted with wifi networks which can pick up the RFID signal so that the RFID tags will be detectable throughout a hospital. The tags will identify the object which they are attached to by a unique identification number and will give its location. The identifier number will link to the inventory system which will identify the product, the quantity initially delivered in that batch and the date of delivery. The RFID information will be accessible through the computer terminals throughout the hospitals.

The chief financial officer (CFO) of Quark has asked you to advise him on the impact of this new system on performance management at Quark. They have suggested that you look at the costs and benefits which will be associated with producing the information from the RFID system, the impact of the nature of the information supplied, the changes to performance management reporting and how the new information could be used for improved control at the hospital. They are keen to be seen to be at the forefront of accounting and management developments and have been reading about cost control techniques.

Exhibit 3: Lean systems

Recently, the CFO has heard about 'lean' systems, so wants to know how the RFID system and its impact on the hospital fit with this concept. The CFO has asked you to evaluate whether the overall management of the hospital can be considered to be 'leaner' as a result of the RFID information system.

13 Nelson, Jody & Nigel (Mar/Jun 2017, amended) (49 mins)

Respond to the board's request for work on the following areas:

(a) The existing warehouse information system **(8 marks)**

(b) The three proposals suggested by the management consultant **(5 marks)**

(c) The performance metrics in Appendix 1 **(7 marks)**

Professional marks will be awarded for the demonstration of skill in analysis and evaluation, and commercial acumen in your answer. **(5 marks)**

(Total = 25 marks)

Exhibit 1: Organisational background

Nelson, Jody and Nigel (NJN) operates a warehouse and distribution centre, storing and distributing 5,000 product lines on behalf of its client, an overseas sports equipment manufacturer.

Exhibit 2: Warehouse information system

NJN receives goods in shipping containers, which should include a packing list of the items they contain. Sometimes, packing lists are lost in transit and the manufacturer is asked for duplicates. Packing lists are manually input into NJN's warehouse information system (WIS) in batches, usually within 48 hours of the goods being received. Goods are first unpacked into a sorting area, and later moved to wherever there is available warehouse space once the packing list has been input. The WIS records the location within the warehouse where each item is located. The client's customers, who are retail stores, place orders by email, and do not currently have access to real-time inventory levels in NJN's warehouse.

Each morning picking lists are printed in the warehouse office. These lists show the quantities of items to be picked and the items' 12-digit product codes. Staff use these codes to retrieve items from the warehouse locations for despatch to retailers. In 8% of picking lists, at least one item is not in the location or does not have the quantity specified by the WIS. As a result, the item is not despatched, or the wrong item is picked. A small team investigates these discrepancies, using special reports which the warehouse manager extracts from the WIS. The team manually reconciles quantities of missing items in the warehouse to the sports equipment manufacturer's own records of the items which should be in inventory. If missing items cannot be found, the customer is informed via an email that they are unavailable.

Exhibit 3: Recent issues

The sports equipment manufacturer has a service level agreement with NJN, covering the accuracy of picking and the proportion of customers' orders successfully fulfilled. NJN's performance on these has deteriorated, especially when there is increased seasonal demand for certain products. At these times staff are under increased pressure to pick items quickly, and so picking accuracy deteriorates and absenteeism increases. There have also been accidents where goods have not been safely placed or safely picked from warehouse locations at busy times. These accidents have resulted in minor injuries to some employees.

The sports equipment manufacturer has threatened to end NJN's contract if performance does not improve. In response, NJN has recruited more staff to investigate discrepancies between items physically in warehouse locations, and those shown on the WIS at busy periods. It has also begun a series of cyclical inventory counts where every product line is counted every month to correct the quantities and locations shown on the WIS. NJN has rented an additional nearby warehouse in which to sort incoming items before they are put away.

The board is concerned about these issues and has asked for an assessment of whether NJN's existing warehouse information system (WIS) is effective in reducing waste and adding value in NJN's workflow.

Exhibit 4: Lean principles

NJN has hired a management consultant who is an expert in 'lean' principles and the application of these to management information systems. They believe that the WIS is wasteful, not adding value to the business or to its customers, and have suggested that NJN would benefit from the application of lean principles to this system.

They have suggested three proposals – that NJN:

- Reorganise the warehouse by storing high volume items close to the despatch area,
- Shut down the additional warehouse; and
- Discontinue the cyclical inventory counts.

The board of NJN has asked you to advise whether the three proposals suggested by the management consultant will help to eliminate the different types of waste identified under lean principles.

To help with the adoption of lean principles in the warehouse reorganisation, the management consultant recommends NJN apply the '5Ss'* of lean principles, and they have suggested performance metrics which can be used to evaluate NJN's progress towards adopting these (Appendix 1).

The board has asked you to evaluate whether the application of each of the 5Ss following the warehouse reorganisation at NJN is adequately measured by the performance metrics in Appendix 1.

*: Structurise, Systemise, Sanitise, Standardise, Self-discipline

Exhibit 5: Appendix 1

Performance measures for 5Ss relating to warehouse reorganisation

(1) Warehouse manager's daily assessment of the tidiness of the warehouse on a scale of 1–10.

(2) The proportion of inventory not stored in order of its alphabetical description with products with names beginning with 'A' nearest the despatch area and 'Z' furthest away.

(3) The number of accidents caused by goods being incorrectly stored or picked.

14 Amal (June 2012, amended) (49 mins)

Respond to the CEO's request for work on the following areas:

(a) Analysis of the three airlines' performance **(12 marks)**

(b) Data analysis **(8 marks)**

Professional marks will be awarded for the demonstration of skill in analysis and evaluation, and commercial acumen in your answer. **(5 marks)**

(Total = 25 marks)

Exhibit 1: Company background and objectives

Amal Airline (Amal) is the national airline of Jayland. The airline's objective is to be the best premium global airline.

Exhibit 2: Recent events

Amal provides long- and short-haul services all over the world and is based at its hub at Jaycity airport. Amal has been hit by a worldwide reduction in air travel due to poor economic conditions. The most recent financial results show a loss and this has caused the board to reconsider its position and take action to address the changed environment.

Amal has cut its dividend in order to conserve cash and it is trying to rebuild profitability by reducing costs by 14%. The airline is capital intensive as it needs to maintain a large fleet of modern aircraft. The two major costs for the airline are staff and fuel. In trying to renegotiate working conditions and pay, the management have angered the unionised workforce. There has already been some strike action by the unions representing the aircraft crew and ground staff and more is threatened.

Additionally, the board is pushing forward a large project to improve the design of the company website in order to increase the number of passengers who check in online and so would not require as much assistance at the airport. The new design is also aiming to increase the number of passengers who book their tickets through the company's website rather than other resellers' websites or at booking agents.

The board has also been considering taking advantage of new technology in aircraft engines by making a large investment ($450m) in new low-noise, fuel-efficient aircraft in an effort to reduce the environmental complaints surrounding air travel and also cut costs.

Exhibit 3: Performance analysis

The chief executive officer (CEO) has provided the data for Amal and two of its main competitors (shown in Appendix 1). Kayland Air is a government-owned and run airline in the neighbouring country of Kayland. It has a similar mix of business to Amal and targets a similar market. Cheapo Air is currently one of the most successful of the new privately owned airlines that have gained significant market share over the last 15 years by offering a cheap but basic short-haul service to customers in and around Jayland. Cheapo Air subcontracts many of its activities in order to remain flexible.

The CEO has requested an analysis, using the data provided, of the three airlines using appropriate performance indicators and a commentary on the results of this analysis.

Exhibit 4: Big Data Analysis

The CEO believes that Amal could be making more use of Big Data Analysis. They recently returned from a conference about 'Big Data Analysis in the Airline Industry' where one of the speakers talked about the benefits of Big Data Analysis in relation to four key areas:

- Identifying trends in passenger demand and using this to set prices
- Understanding and influencing the customer's selection process (in particular reducing the number of potential customers who start booking a flight online but do not go on to complete the transaction)
- Boosting revenue from in-flight sales by optimising the on-board store for individual flights
- Understanding customer sentiment and improving customer satisfaction

Amal currently offers the same selection of in-flight products on all its flights.

The CEO has asked you to explain how using big data analysis in these four areas could help Amal improve its performance.

Exhibit 5: Appendix 1

Data provided by the CEO:

Data for the most recent calendar year

	Amal	*Kayland Air*	*Cheapo Air*
Passengers ('000)	23,649	38,272	35,624
Passenger kilometres (millions)	79,618	82,554	40,973
Revenue ($m)	5,430	7,350	2,170
Costs			
Fuel ($m)	1,480	1,823	535
Staff ($m)	1,560	2,998	238
Staff numbers	32,501	56,065	5,372
Operating profit ($m)	630	54	127
Number of aircraft	182	361	143
Average aircraft size (seats)	195	163	125
Seat kilometres (millions)	100,654	105,974	46,934

Note. A seat kilometre is generated for every one kilometre flown by an **available** seat on the company's aircraft.

STRATEGIC PERFORMANCE MEASUREMENT

Questions 15 to 27 cover strategic performance measurement, the subject of Part C of the syllabus for APM.

15 Chicory (Sept/Dec 2017, amended) (49 mins)

Assume it is now December 20X7.

Required

Respond to the board's request for work on the following areas:

(a) The relative financial performance of Chicory using:

(i) ROCE **(5 marks)**

(ii) EBITDA **(8 marks)**

(b) Problems of using the benchmarking exercise **(7 marks)**

Professional marks will be awarded for the demonstration of skill in analysis and evaluation, scepticism and commercial acumen in your answer. **(5 marks)**

(Total = 25 marks)

Exhibit 1: Company background

Chicory operates a chain of depots in Deeland, supplying and fitting tyres and other vehicle parts to lorries, buses and agricultural vehicles. Chicory's objective is to maximise shareholder wealth. Due to a slowdown in the Deeland economy, Chicory's recent performance has been weak. An unsuccessful acquisition has also caused cash flow problems and a write-off of goodwill of $24.7m in the year to 30 June 20X7.

Exhibit 2: Benchmarking exercise

The board has commissioned a benchmarking exercise to help improve Chicory's performance. This exercise will involve comparison of a range of financial and other operational performance indicators against Fennel, a similar business in Veeland. Fennel has agreed to share some recently available performance data with Chicory as they operate in different countries. The reason Fennel was chosen as a benchmark is that as well as supplying and fitting tyres and parts to heavy vehicles, a large part of Fennel's business involves supplying electricity to charging points to recharge electric cars. Fennel installs and operates the charging points in public places, and users pay Fennel for the electricity they use. The board of Chicory intends to follow a similar business model as the use of electric cars is increasing in Deeland.

The Veeland economy is growing strongly. Electric car use there has increased rapidly in the last two years, encouraged by tax incentives for businesses, like Fennel, to install and operate charging points. The Veeland government has also underwritten loans taken out by businesses to finance this technology, which has enabled Fennel to borrow funds for the significant capital investment required. The cost of components used in the charging points is falling rapidly. Capitalisation of development costs related to this technology is permitted in Veeland, but not in Deeland. In 20X5, Fennel invested heavily in IT systems which significantly improved performance by increasing the availability of parts in its depots, and reducing inventories.

Chicory uses return on average capital employed (ROCE) as its main financial performance indicator, and this is to be benchmarked against Fennel. One board member suggested that, though it may have some disadvantages, EBITDA (earnings before interest, tax, depreciation and amortisation) could have advantages as a performance measure over the existing measure, and should also be included in the benchmarking exercise.

You have been given the most recently available financial data for both businesses in Appendix 1, with the data for Fennel being converted into dollars ($) from its home currency.

The board has requested your help with two issues:

- An evaluation of the relative financial performance of Chicory against Fennel using the two financial performance measures identified in the benchmarking exercise, and an evaluation of their use as performance measures in this situation.
- Advice on the problems of using the benchmarking exercise with Fennel as a way to improve Chicory's performance.

Exhibit 3: Appendix 1

Benchmark data

Extract from statement of financial position

	30 June 20X7 Chicory	*31 December 20X5 Fennel*[1]
	$m	$m
End of year		
Total assets	140.0	296.0
Current liabilities	(81.0)	(120.0)
Beginning of year (Note 1)		
Total assets	138.0	290.0
Current liabilities	(60.0)	(120.0)

Income statement

	30 June 20X7 Chicory	*31 December 20X5 Fennel*
	$m	$m
Revenue	175.1	350.0
Cost of sales	(130.1)	(299.0)
Gross profit	45.0	51.0
Administrative expenses	(11.0)	(25.0)
Write off of goodwill	(24.7)	–
Operating profit (Note 2)	9.3	26.0
Interest payable	(1.8)	(8.0)
Profit before tax	7.5	18.0
Tax	(3.0)	(1.0)
Net profit	4.5	17.0

Notes.

1 $6m of new capital was introduced into Fennel on 31 March 20X5. Normally, new net investment is spread evenly over the year.

2 Operating profit is after charging depreciation of non-current assets of $18m in Chicory, and $25m in Fennel.

16 Landual Lamps (June 2013, amended) (49 mins)

Respond to the FD's request for work on the following areas:

(a) The current system of transfer pricing at Landual **(8 marks)**

(b) The impact of changing the transfer pricing policy for housing components **(4 marks)**

(c) Evaluate the impact of the change in proposed divisional structure **(8 marks)**

Professional marks will be awarded for the demonstration of skill in analysis and evaluation, scepticism and commercial acumen in your answer. **(5 marks)**

(Total = 25 marks)

Exhibit 1: Company background and organisation structure

Landual Lamps (Landual) manufactures and delivers floor and table lamps for homes and offices in Beeland. The company sells through its website and uses commercial logistics firms to deliver its products. The markets for its products are highly competitive. The company has traditionally relied on the high quality of its designs to drive demand for its products.

The company is divided into two divisions (components and assembly), plus a head office that provides design, administrative and marketing support. The manufacturing process involves:

(1) The Components Division making the housing components and electrical components for the lamp. This is an intricate process as it depends on the specific design of the lamp and so serves as a significant source of competitive advantage for Landual.

(2) The Assembly Division assembling the various components into a finished lamp ready for shipment. This is a simple process.

The finance director (FD) of Landual is currently overloaded with work due to changes in financial accounting policies that are being considered at board level and has been unable to look at certain management accounting aspects of the business.

As a result of this, they have asked you to evaluate the current transfer pricing policy between the Components and Assembly Divisions.

Exhibit 2: Transfer pricing policy

The current transfer pricing policy at Landual is as follows:

- Market prices for electrical components are used as these are generic components for which there is a competitive external market.
- Prices for housing components based on total actual production costs to the Components Division are used as there is no external market for these components since they are specially designed for Landual's products.

Currently, the Components Division produces only for the Assembly Division in order to meet overall demand without the use of external suppliers for housing and electrical components. If the Components Division were to sell its electrical components externally, then additional costs of $269,000 would arise for transport, marketing and bad debts.

Exhibit 3: Potential changes

The FD is considering two separate changes within Landual: one to the transfer pricing policy, and a second one to the divisional structure.

First, the transfer pricing policy for housing components would change to use variable cost to the Components Division. The proposal will reduce the revenue of the Components Division (and correspondingly the cost of sales of the Assembly Division) by the fixed production costs relating to housing components: $1,302,000.

The FD wants to know the impact of the change in transfer pricing policy on the existing results of the two divisions and the company. (No change is proposed to the transfer price of the electrical components.)

She has asked for your advice on the impact of changing the transfer pricing policy for housing components, as suggested by the FD, and a comment on the results.

Second, as can be seen from the divisional performance report below, the two divisions are currently treated as profit centres. The FD is considering splitting the Components Division into two further separate divisions: an Electrical Components Division and a Housing Components Division. If the board agrees to this proposal, then the Housing Components Division will be treated as a cost centre only, charging its total production cost to the Assembly Division. The Electrical Components and Assembly Divisions will remain as profit centres.

The FD needs to understand the impact of this proposed new divisional structure on divisional performance assessment. They have asked you to evaluate the impact of the change in proposed divisional structure on the profit in the divisions as directed by the FD.

They have asked that, in order to keep the discussion on the new divisional structure simple, you use the existing transfer pricing policy to do illustrative calculations. They stated that they would reallocate head office costs to the two new components divisions in proportion to their cost of sales.

Financial and other information for Landual is provided in Appendix 1.

Exhibit 4: Appendix 1

ACTUAL DATA FOR LANDUAL FOR THE YEAR ENDED 31 MARCH 20X3

	Components Division	*Assembly Division*	*Landual*
	$'000	$'000	$'000
Sales:			
Electrical	1,557		
Housing	8,204		
Sub-total	9,761	15,794	15,794
Cost of sales:			
Electrical	804	1,557	
Housing	6,902	8,204	
Sub-total	7,706	9,761	7,706
Fixed production costs:			
Electrical	370		
Housing	1,302		
Sub-total	1,672	1,268	2,940
Allocated head office costs	461	2,046	2,507
Profit	(78)	2,719	2,641

Note. The Components Division has had problems meeting budgets recently, with an adverse variance of $575,000 in the last year. This variance arises in relation to the cost of sales for housing component production.

17 Laudan Advertising Agency (Sep/Dec 2016, amended) (49 mins)

Respond to the directors' request for work on the following areas:

(a) The KPI for the requirement to purchase 90% of design work internally **(5 marks)**

(b) The need for a formal transfer pricing policy at LAA **(8 marks)**

(c) Advice on using a market value transfer price **(7 marks)**

Professional marks will be awarded for the demonstration of skill in analysis and evaluation, scepticism and commercial acumen in your answer. **(5 marks)**

(Total = 25 marks)

Exhibit 1: Company background, and objectives

Laudan Advertising Agency (LAA) is based in Geeland and has three autonomous subsidiaries: A, B and C. All three subsidiaries are profit centres and LAA seeks to maximise the long-term wealth of its shareholders. A is based in Geeland, while both B and C are located in other parts of the world. LAA is a highly respected advertising agency, which in the last five years has created advertising campaigns for 25 of the world's top 100 most recognised brands.

LAA's four key objectives published on its website are to:

- Delight our clients by the quality of our work
- Provide excellent value for money to our clients
- Give our clients access to specialist and local knowledge
- Ensure our clients return to us time after time

There are three main functions within LAA:

(1) Campaign management, which involves researching and understanding clients' requirements and budgets and designing a suitable advertising campaign for them

(2) Creative design, which is where the visual appearance of the advert and graphics are created

(3) Media buying, which negotiates prices with, and buys advertising time and space from, magazine and newspaper publishers, internet search engines and TV companies

Each subsidiary has its own department for campaign management and for media buying. Only A, however, has a creative design department.

The directors at LAA believe that without visually appealing design, any advertising campaign is unlikely to be successful and meet the expectations of the client. They identified the importance of being able to produce high quality creative design as a critical success factor for the business. Two years ago, they decided to concentrate all of LAA's creative design at a 'centre of design excellence' within A. The intention was to improve the quality of creative design within the business by giving staff access to the latest design technology, and by attracting the most talented designers to work there.

Exhibit 2: Additional key performance indicator

To encourage the three subsidiaries to use the internal creative design department within A, instead of external third-party design agencies, the directors created a new additional key performance indicator (KPI) on which to appraise the performance of all subsidiaries and of subsidiary managers

- All subsidiaries, including A, must purchase at least 90% of creative design work internally from A.

Prior to the introduction of this performance indicator, 40% of creative design work in each of the three subsidiaries was purchased from external design agencies.

The directors of LAA have become concerned that the introduction of the new KPI may be causing managers to operate in ways which are not helping to meet LAA's stated objectives. They have asked for comments from subsidiary managers (Appendix 1) about whether they have met the 90% target in the most recent period and, if not, to explain why this is.

The directors have requested your help with three issues:

- An evaluation of whether setting the KPI for the requirement to purchase 90% of design work internally will help LAA to manage performance in order to achieve its stated objectives.
- An assessment of the need for a formal transfer pricing policy at LAA.
- Advice on whether LAA should use a market value transfer price as suggested by the manager of Subsidiary C

Exhibit 3: Appendix 1

Subsidiary managers' comments on achievement of KPI for 90% creative design work purchased internally.

Subsidiary A

'A purchased 86% of design work from our internal design department in the period. It would have been almost 100%, but we won a large order for a new client who operates in a specialised industry of which we have no experience. As a result, we had to use the services of a specialised external design agency, which was much more expensive than using our in-house team.'

Subsidiary B

'B purchased 62% of design work internally in the period. Though the quality of the designs is good, they were more appealing to consumers in Geeland than here in Veeland. Many of the designs were rejected by a key client, by which time the internal design department had insufficient capacity to finish the work so we had to use an external agency.

As there is no formal transfer pricing policy in place at LAA, the basis of the transfer price charged by the internal design department is also unclear to us. It appears to be based on full cost of the design work, including apportioned overheads and an allowance for bad debts and marketing expenses, plus a very substantial mark-up. We have spent a long time trying to negotiate this price with A, which is much more expensive than external designers. Also we are currently being investigated by the tax authorities here in Veeland who have indicated that the prices charged by A for design seem well in excess of market rates.'

Subsidiary C

'C purchased 91% of design work from the internal design department in the period, as well as achieving all our other performance targets. A key client of ours ran a major advertising campaign during the period. We used the internal design department for the first time for this campaign. The client was very unhappy with the extra cost that this incurred, as the number of design hours and the hourly rate was much higher than for previous campaigns. The internal design department refused to reduce the price after long negotiations and we had to give a large discount to the client before they would settle our invoice. As a result, our gross profit margin for the period was significantly reduced. It would be much fairer if the transfer price charged by A was based on the market price of the services provided.'

18 Jenson, Lewis and Webb (Mar/Jun 2017, amended) (49 mins)

Respond to the directors' request for work on the following areas:

(a) Evaluating the comments of the export division manager **(7 marks)**

(b) The bonus for the manager of the Export Division **(8 marks)**

(c) Problems in the use of economic value added (EVA™) **(5 marks)**

Professional marks will be awarded for the demonstration of skill in analysis and evaluation, scepticism and commercial acumen in your answer. **(5 marks)**

(Total = 25 marks)

Exhibit 1: Company background and objectives

Jenson, Lewis and Webb (JLW) manufactures tubes of acrylic paint for sale to artists and craft shops in Kayland and Seeland. JLW has two divisions, Domestic Division and Export Division, both based in Kayland. All costs are incurred in Kayland dollars ($KL). Domestic Division is an investment centre and sells only to customers in Kayland. Export Division is a profit centre and exports all its products to Seeland, where customers are invoiced in Seeland pounds (£SL), at prices fixed at the start of the year. The objective of JLW is to maximise shareholder wealth.

Exhibit 2: Capital expenditure

At the beginning of the year ended 31 December 20X6, the head office at JLW purchased new production machinery for Export Division for $KL2.5m, which significantly increased the production efficiency of the division. Managers at Domestic Division were considering purchasing a similar machine, but decided to delay the purchase until the beginning of the following financial year. On 30 June 20X6 the $KL weakened by 15% against the £SL, after which the exchange rate between the two currencies has remained unchanged.

Exhibit 3: Performance appraisal

The managers of the two divisions are currently appraised on the performance of their own divisions, and are awarded a large bonus if the net profit margin of their division exceeds 8% for the year. Extracts from the management accounts for the year ended 31 December 20X6 for both divisions are given in Appendix 1. On being told that they would not be receiving a bonus for the financial year, the manager of Export division has commented that they have had difficulty in understanding the bonus calculations for their division as it is not based on traceable profit, which would consider only items which relate directly to the division. They also do not believe it is appropriate that the net profit margin used to appraise their performance is the same as 'that which is used to evaluate the performance of Export division itself'. They have asked for a meeting with the directors to discuss this further.

The directors have asked you to evaluate the comments of the export division manager.

JLW's directors intend to award divisional managers' bonuses on the basis of net profit margin achieved in 20X6 as planned, but have asked you as a performance management consultant for your advice on the comments of the export division manager in advance of their meeting. They have asked you to recommend, using appropriate calculations, whether the manager of the Export Division should receive their bonus for the year.

One director has also suggested that, in future, economic value added (EVA™) may be a good way to evaluate and compare the performance of the two divisions. You are asked to briefly discuss potential problems in the use of economic value added (EVA™) as a measure of divisional performance (you are not required to perform an EVA™ calculation).

Exhibit 4: Appendix 1

EXTRACTS FROM MANAGEMENT ACCOUNTS FOR YEAR ENDED 31 DECEMBER 20X6

	Export Division	*Domestic Division*
	$KL'000	$KL'000
Revenue (Note 1)	8,000	12,000
Cost of sales	(4,800)	(7,800)
Gross profit	3,200	4,200
Depreciation	(395)	(45)
Allocated head office costs	(360)	(540)
Other overheads (Note 2)	(1,900)	(2,300)
Net profit	545	1,315

QUESTIONS

	Export Division	Domestic Division
	$KL'000	$KL'000
Net profit margin on revenue	6.8%	11.0%
Capital employed (Note 3)	6,500	8,500

Notes.

1 Revenue accrues evenly over the financial year.

2 Other overheads for Domestic Division include the creation of a bad debt provision equivalent to $KL75,000 for a wholesale customer who had financial difficulties during the year, and $KL90,000 for advertising a new range of paints launched at the end of the year.

3 JLW is financed in equal proportions by debt and equity. The cost of equity is 8% and the after-tax cost of debt is 5%.

19 Essland Police Forces (December 2013, amended) (49 mins)

Respond to the CEO's request for work on the following areas:

(a) The calculations used in the league table **(15 marks)**

(b) Application of a league table approach in policing **(5 marks)**

Professional marks will be awarded for the demonstration of skill in analysis and evaluation, scepticism and commercial acumen in your answer. **(5 marks)**

(Total = 25 marks)

Exhibit 1: Company background and objectives

You are a performance management expert brought in by the chief executive officer (CEO) of the Department of the Interior for the country of Essland. The department is a branch of the Essland Government which handles security, policing, immigration and border control. The CEO is a civil servant and reports to the Minister for the Interior. The Minister for the Interior is an elected politician selected by the Prime Minister of Essland, who leads its government.

Exhibit 2: League tables

The newly elected Minister for the Interior has instructed the CEO to implement their policy for improving the regional police forces' performance by copying the method used for schools. In a recent initiative by the School's Ministry, a league table for the hundreds of schools in Essland was created, showing the best and worst in terms of examination performance only, in order to motivate senior school managers to improve. The league table was used to create targets for assessing the schools' and their managers' performance. Additionally, parents in Essland have the right to choose which school their children attend and so often base their selection on league table performance. Therefore, the Minister has had a policy review body draw up a method of creating a league table for the police forces.

The CEO has requested your help to clarify their own thinking on this new policy for the four regional police forces in Essland (Cashire (C), Dashire (D), Eshire (E) and Fashire (F)).

The CEO needs you to assess the use of the league table using the policy review body's suggested method and has collected the data and calculation of the league table given in Appendix 1 to assist you. They also want to assess whether the table will help in meeting the Department's aim and goals for the police.

The CEO has asked you to evaluate the method of calculating and measuring the force scores for use in the league table in achieving the Department of the Interior's aims and goals.

Exhibit 3: Aim and goals

The overall aim of the Department (and its police forces) is 'to provide a value-for-money service to ensure that the community can live in safety with confidence in their physical and legal security'. The detailed goals of the Department are to:

- Tackle the underlying causes of crime and achieve long-term sustainable solutions
- Bring perpetrators to justice
- Provide protection and support for individuals and communities at risk of harm
- Respond to community needs by being accessible and engaging with their concerns

The CEO is concerned about importing the use of a league table from the schools sector, as it might not be appropriate here.

The CEO has asked you to identify and explain whether the application of a league table approach is less appropriate in the context of policing.

The CEO warned you, 'I'm not interested in the performance of the forces. I'm interested in the method of assessment, so don't waste time with your ideas on how to improve actual policing.'

Exhibit 4: Appendix 1

The appendix defines the policy review body's method for scoring each force, provides the basic data for each force and then calculates the current force score placing the forces into a league table:

Force score = Rank 1 × 0.25 + Rank 2 × 0.25 + Rank 3 × 0.25 + Rank 4 × 0.25

Where each rank is the ranking from 4 to 1 which each force gets for each of the following variables (4 is best, 1 is worst):

- Rank 1 is based on the number of crimes per 10,000 of population.
- Rank 2 is based on the solution rate for crimes reported in the year.
- Rank 3 is based on the user satisfaction score (based on a survey of the population).
- Rank 4 is based on the percentage of calls to police answered within ten seconds.

For example, a force which was top ranked in each of the ranks would get a force score of 4 (= 4 × 0.25 + 4 × 0.25 + 4 × 0.25 + 4 × 0.25).

Data by region:

For the calendar year 20X2

	C	D	E	F
Population	1,250,000	900,000	1,700,000	1,500,000
Number of crimes reported in year	62,500	47,250	83,300	63,000
Number of crimes solved in year	31,250	22,680	45,815	33,390
User satisfaction score	71%	80%	73%	68%
Percentage of calls to police answered within ten seconds	92%	93%	91%	94%
Number of police force employees	6,200	4,400	8,500	7,900
Cost of police force for year ($m)	404	298	572	510

Calculation of force score:

	C	D	E	F
Number of reported crimes per 10,000 of population	500	525	490	420
Rank 1	2	1	3	4
Solution rate for crimes reported in year	50%	48%	55%	53%
Rank 2	2	1	4	3
Rank 3 (user satisfaction)	2	4	3	1
Rank 4 (call handling)	2	3	1	4
Force score	2	2.25	2.75	3

The league table for 20X2 is:

	Force	*Score*
1	F	3.00
2	E	2.75
3	D	2.25
4	C	2.00

Note. You should assume that the calculations in Appendix 1 are accurate.

20 Beeshire Local Authority (December 2014, amended) (49 mins)

Respond to the senior management team's request for work on the following areas:

(a) Value for money **(13 marks)**

(b) Qualitative performance measures **(7 marks)**

Professional marks will be awarded for the demonstration of skill in analysis and evaluation, scepticism and commercial acumen in your answer. **(5 marks)**

(Total = 25 marks)

Exhibit 1: Waste collection in Beeshire

Beeshire Local Authority (BLA) is a local government body which provides a range of services for the area of Beeshire within the country of Seeland. Beeshire is a wealthy area within the country with many tourist attractions. One of BLA's tasks is to ensure that waste is collected from the homes and businesses in Beeshire. The goal for BLA's Waste Management Department is 'to maintain Beeshire as a safe, clean and environmentally friendly place where people and businesses want to both stay in and return to'. The need for waste collection is linked to public health concerns, the desire to keep the streets clean and attractive and the desire to increase the amount of rubbish which is recycled. BLA is funded through a single local tax and does not charge its residents or businesses separately for most of its services, including waste collection. There is no public or political appetite for outsourcing services such as waste management.

Waste collection is performed by the workforce using a fleet of vehicles. The waste is either taken to recycling plants or else to landfill sites for burying. BLA obtains revenues from all the recycled waste but this only just covers the cost of running the recycling facilities.

Against a background estimate that waste will increase by 1% p.a. in the future, the national Government has ordered local authorities, such as BLA, to promote the recycling of waste and has set a target of 40% of all waste to be recycled by 2015. In order to discourage the creation of non-recyclable waste, the Government has imposed a levy per tonne of waste buried in landfill sites and has stated that this levy will rise over the next five years in order to encourage continuing improvement in the amount of recycled waste.

Exhibit 2: Performance measures

Currently, Seeland is in a long recession and so local authority revenues have fallen as tax revenues reflect the poor state of the economy. Along with other local authorities, BLA has tried to cut costs and so has focused on financial measures of performance. In a recent, private meeting, the chief executive of BLA was heard to say: 'keep costs under control and we will worry about quality of service only when complaint levels build to an unacceptable level'. As one of the area's largest employers, cutting staff numbers has been very difficult for BLA due to the impact on the local economy and the reaction of the residents.

The current performance indicators used at BLA are drawn from the existing information systems with national figures given for comparison. Those relating to waste collection for the year ending 31 March 20X4 are shown in Appendix 1.

BLA's senior management team have requested your help in two areas:

- Explaining how the value for money provision of waste services by BLA should be assessed, by suggesting and calculating justified performance indicators using the scenario information.
- Discussing the difficulties of measuring qualitative factors of performance, suggesting appropriate solutions for BLA.

Exhibit 3: Appendix 1

BLA – Performance information for year ending 31 March 20X4

	BLA	*National total*
Total cost ($m)	250	2,850
Volume of waste		
landfilled (tonnes)	1,250,000	13,750,000
recycled (tonnes)	950,000	9,500,000
total (tonnes)	2,200,000	23,250,000
No. of staff	3,500	39,900
Staff cost ($m)	110	1,190
No. of households	2,380,952	26,190,476
No. of complaints about waste uncollected	18,250	200,750
	BLA	*National average*
Frequency of waste collections (days)	14	12

Notes.

1 Cost data and number of households comes from BLA's financial systems.

2 Waste data comes from weighing lorries at the landfill sites and recycling facilities.

3 Staff data is collected from BLA's HR system.

4 Complaints data is based on numbers of letters and phone calls to the Waste Management Department.

5 Frequency of collection data is obtained from the department's vehicle schedules.

21 Teeland Universities (Mar/Jun 2016, amended) (49 mins)

Respond to the request for work on the following areas:

(a) Value for money **(11 marks)**

(b) League tables **(9 marks)**

Professional marks will be awarded for the demonstration of skill in analysis and evaluation, scepticism and commercial acumen in your answer. **(5 marks)**

(Total = 25 marks)

Exhibit 1: Objectives

Universities in Teeland have three stated objectives:

(1) To improve the overall standard of education of citizens in Teeland

(2) To engage in high quality academic research

(3) To produce well-qualified university graduates to meet the needs of the graduate jobs market in Teeland

Exhibit 2: Government funding

Each university is funded by a fixed sum of money from the Teeland Government according to the number of students studying there. In addition, universities receive extra funds from the Government and also from other organisations, such as large businesses and charities. These funds are used to support academic research.

Following the onset of an economic recession, the Teeland Government has stated its intention to reduce spending on publicly funded services such as the universities.

Proposal to introduce league tables

One senior politician, following a recent visit to neighbouring Veeland, was controversially quoted as saying:

> The universities in Veeland offer much better value for money for the citizens there compared to our universities here in Teeland. There are 25 students for each member of academic staff in Veeland, whereas in Teeland, the average number is 16, and yet, the standard of education of citizens is much higher in Veeland. The Veeland Government sets targets for many aspects of the services delivered by all the universities in Veeland. Furthermore, league tables of the performance of individual universities are published on the internet, and university leaders are given bonuses if their university falls within the top quarter of the league table. In Veeland, the system of performance measurement of the universities is considered so important that there is a special government department of 150 staff just to measure it.

They went on to add:

> I want to see a similar system of league tables, targets and bonuses for university leaders being introduced here in Teeland. To appear near the top of the league tables, I think we should expect each university to increase the number of graduates entering graduate jobs by at least 5% each year. I would also like to see other steps taken to increase value for money, such as reducing the number of academic staff in each university and reducing the salary of newly recruited academic staff.

You have been asked to assist the Teeland Government on two areas:

- Advice on how it could assess the value for money of the universities in Teeland, using the performance data in Appendix 1
- Discussion of the proposal to implement league tables in order to improve the performance of universities in Teeland

Appendix 1 contains details and existing performance data relating to four of the best known universities in Teeland.

Northcity University is famous for its high teaching standards and outstanding academic research in all subjects. As such, it attracts the most able students from all parts of the world to study there.

Southcity University is a large university in the capital city of Teeland and offers courses in a wide range of subjects, though most of the funding it receives for academic research is for science and technology, in which it is particularly successful.

Eastcity University is a small university specialising in the teaching of arts and humanities subjects such as history and geography.

Westcity University currently offers less strict entry standards to attract students from more diverse backgrounds, who may not normally have the opportunity of a university education.

Exhibit 3: Appendix 1

Existing university performance data

	North	*South*	*East*	*West*
Number of students	17,600	30,400	5,200	11,200
Number of academic staff	1,750	2,400	485	625
Entry requirements (Note 1)	100	77	72	48
Total annual payroll cost of academic staff	\$109m	\$149m	\$20m	\$37m
Graduate jobs filled each year (Note 2)	4,180	6,555	1,154	1,750
Funds received for academic research	\$491m	\$474m	\$26m	\$14m
TSOR survey rating (Note 3)	84%	76%	73%	90%
Position in league table (Note 4)	1	11	14	21

Key to performance data

Notes.

1 Entry requirements represent students' average attainment in examinations prior to entering university. The entry requirement of the highest-ranking university is scored as 100, with the score of all other universities being in proportion to that score.

2 The number of graduates each year who go on to further study or who begin jobs normally undertaken by university graduates. In Teeland, students attend university for an average of 3.2 years.

3 The Teeland students' overall satisfaction rating (TSOR) survey is undertaken by the Teeland Government to assess students' overall satisfaction with the standard of teaching, the social and support aspects of university life and their optimism for their own future job prospects.

4 The Education Department of the Teeland Government has produced a provisional league table ranking the overall performance of each of the 45 universities in Teeland, with 1 being the highest ranking university. This has been compiled using a number of performance measures, weighted according to what the Government believes are the most important of these measures.

22 Tosemary and Rhyme Hospital (Sept/Dec 2017, amended) (49 mins)

Respond to the request for work on the following areas:

(a) Non-financial performance indicators **(5 marks)**

(b) Value for money **(10 marks)**

(c) Budget-constrained approach **(5 marks)**

Professional marks will be awarded for the demonstration of skill in analysis and evaluation, scepticism and commercial acumen in your answer. **(5 marks)**

(Total = 25 marks)

Exhibit 1: Organisational background

Tosemary and Rhyme Hospital (TRH) is a small hospital for the treatment of patients with only minor injuries. Patients arriving at TRH with more serious injuries are referred to a larger hospital nearby. Those with minor injuries are admitted into TRH and wait to be seen by a doctor. After treatment, most patients leave the hospital and need not return. If their treatment has failed, however, they are re-admitted for additional treatment.

Patients do not have to pay for treatment at TRH, which is a not-for-profit, public sector hospital. It is funded entirely by the government from taxation and a fixed level of funding is received from the government each year. It is up to TRH to allocate its funding to different areas, such as doctors' salaries, medicines and all other costs required to run a hospital.

Exhibit 2: Objectives

TRH's objectives are:

- To give prompt access to high quality medical treatment for patients
- To provide value for money for the taxpayer, as measured by the '3Es' framework of economy, efficiency and effectiveness
- To contribute to medical science by developing innovative ways to deliver treatment to patients

Exhibit 3: Concerns about performance measurement systems

It has been suggested to TRH that the hospital has inadequate performance measurement systems in place to assess whether it is achieving its objectives, and that insufficient attention is given to the importance of non-financial performance indicators and too much attention is placed on short-term financial performance; this style is sometimes described as being 'budget-constrained'.

You have been asked for your advice, and have met with some of the doctors to get their opinions.

One senior doctor has told you:

> I think TRH always delivers value for money. We've always achieved our total financial budgets. Doctors here work much longer hours than colleagues in other hospitals, often without being paid for working overtime. There is not enough government funding to recruit more doctors. At busy times, we've started referring more patients arriving at TRH to the larger hospital nearby. This has helped reduce average waiting times. Patients arriving at TRH are now seen by a doctor within 3 hours 50 minutes rather than 4 hours as was previously the case. So, we're already doing all we can. I don't know how much time we spend developing innovative ways to deliver treatment to patients though, as most of the performance data we doctors receive relates to financial targets.

Recent performance data for TRH and national average information has been provided in Appendix 1. This is indicative of the data which the doctors at TRH receive.

You have been asked to provide assistance in three areas:

- Explaining why non-financial performance indicators are particularly important to measure the performance of not-for-profit organisations such as TRH
- Justifying one performance measure for each of the components of the value for money framework used at TRH and, using the measure, evaluating whether TRH is delivering value for money
- Advising on the implications of this budget-constrained approach for managing TRH's performance

Exhibit 4: Appendix 1

Data for the year ended 31 August 20X7

	TRH	National *average* (Note 1)
Number of doctors	25	24
Total doctors' salaries including overtime	$3.75m	$4.20m
Total doctors' salaries budget including overtime	$3.75m	$3.20m
Number of patients treated	24,375	20,000
Average staff satisfaction rating (Note 2)	9%	89%
Number of patients re-admitted	1,830	300

Notes.

1 National average for other public sector minor injuries hospitals.

2 Staff satisfaction rating was obtained by conducting a survey of all 25 doctors. A survey score of 100% represents 'totally satisfied', and a score of 0% represents totally unsatisfied.

23 Pitlane (Mar/Jun 2017, amended) (49 mins)

Respond to the request for work in the Booster project.

Note. There are 6 marks available for the first part of the work required on this area and 14 marks available for the second part of the work required on this area. **(20 marks)**

Professional marks will be awarded for the demonstration of skill in analysis and evaluation, scepticism and commercial acumen in your answer. **(5 marks)**

(Total = 25 marks)

Exhibit 1: Company background

Pitlane Electronic Components (Pitlane) manufactures components for use in the electricity distribution network in Deeland. Demand from Pitlane's biggest customer, to replace identical but worn out components, has been constant for many years. Pitlane has recently renewed an exclusive long-term supply agreement with this customer, who has always agreed to buy the components for their total standard cost plus a fixed profit margin of 15%. Variances between standard and actual costs of the components are negligible. Pitlane runs several production lines in two factories located in different areas of Deeland. The factories' layout is poorly designed and the production process requires components to be transported around and between the factories.

Exhibit 2: Government incentives

The Deeland Government wants to encourage renewable electricity generation. It is offering a three-year subsidy scheme, beginning in 20X8, for consumers to have solar panels installed on the roofs of their homes. As an added incentive, businesses will be exempt from tax on profits made on the sale of solar panels and related components.

Exhibit 3: New product development (Booster project)

To take advantage of this scheme, Pitlane has built a prototype of a new electrical component, known as the 'Booster', which increases the output from domestic solar panels. The Booster will be sold to installers of solar panels and not directly to consumers. Pitlane's marketing department has estimated market data for the duration of the scheme based on a similar scheme in Veeland (Appendix 1). As a result of its products being unchanged for many years, Pitlane has little recent experience of developing new products and estimating costs and potential revenues from them. It is expected that many competitor products will be launched during the scheme, at the end of which demand is expected to fall greatly, and production of the Booster will discontinue.

Pitlane's shareholders insist that for the Booster project to go ahead, it must meet the financial performance objective of achieving a 15% net profit margin, after all costs, for the duration of the scheme.

The Booster's total fixed costs during the scheme are estimated to be $10m, including $2.8m upfront development costs to enable the Booster to communicate the amount of solar energy generated directly to consumers' smartphones via an app. The product development team at Pitlane believes this feature, and the use of highest quality packaging, will allow it to charge 10% more that the average price of its competitors. The marketing team, however, has questioned the overall value of these two features and whether customers would be prepared to pay extra for them, as most of the Deeland population do not yet own smartphones.

Pitlane has estimated the direct costs for the Booster (Appendix 2). The largest direct cost is for the four main sub-components. These are bought in bulk from six different suppliers in Deeland, though all are readily available from suppliers worldwide. The sub-components are fragile. During production of the Booster prototype, many sub-components were found to be damaged during the production process by workers incorrectly assembling them. This resulted in the completed prototype Boosters being scrapped after testing by the Quality Control Department. The manufacturing director is concerned that the incorrect assembly of sub-components by workers may mean that it may not be profitable for Pitlane to start full scale production of Boosters. To counteract these quality problems, Pitlane will employ more highly skilled workers, who are paid around 30% more than most other workers in the business which is accounted for in the cost estimate given in Appendix 2. Pitlane staff have never been encouraged to suggest any ways to improve the manufacturing process.

Pitlane's directors are concerned that the Booster project will not meet the shareholders' financial performance objective. They have asked you, as a consultant experienced in target costing and other Japanese business practices such as Kaizen costing, for your advice on two areas:

- Calculating the cost gap per unit in each of the three years of the Booster's life, taking into account all estimated costs
- Advice on the extent to which target costing would help Pitlane to achieve the financial performance objective set by the shareholders

Exhibit 4: Appendix 1

ESTIMATED MARKET DATA FOR BOOSTER

	20X8	*20X9*	*20Y0*
Total market size (units)	600,000	500,000	460,000
Average price of competitors products ($/unit)	180	170	160
Booster market share of total market	10%	15%	20%

Exhibit 5: Appendix 2

ESTIMATED UNIT DIRECT COST OF BOOSTER

	$
Sub-components	94
Assembly labour	21
Packaging	10
Distribution	2
Internal transport and handling	7
Total	134

24 Posie (Sep/Dec 2015, amended) (49 mins)

Respond to the CEO's request for work on the following areas:

(a) The Six Sigma project **(15 marks)**

(b) The impact on Posie's information requirements **(5 marks)**

Professional marks will be awarded for the demonstration of skill in analysis and evaluation, scepticism and commercial acumen in your answer. **(5 marks)**

(Total = 25 marks)

Exhibit 1: Company background and structure

Posie is a large business which manufactures furniture. It is made up of two autonomous divisions in Deeland.

The Manufacturing Division purchases raw materials from external suppliers, and performs all manufacturing and packaging operations. All sales are made through the Retail Division which has 95 retail stores in Deeland, as well as through Posie's own well-developed website. Posie has retail operations in eight other countries as well as in Deeland. These overseas businesses operate as independent subsidiaries within the Retail Division, each with their own IT and accounting functions.

The furniture is sold in boxes for customers to assemble themselves. About 10% of the products sold by Posie are purchased already packaged from other manufacturers. All deliveries are outsourced through a third-party distribution company.

Exhibit 2: Customer returns and complaints

Posie's corporate objective is to maximise shareholder wealth by producing 'attractive, functional furniture at low prices'. This is how customers generally perceive the Posie brand. The chief executive officer (CEO) of Posie is concerned about increasing levels of returns made by customers and increasing numbers of consumers complaining on online forums about products purchased from Posie.

Concerned about the impact on the Posie brand and the cost-leadership strategy, the CEO has asked you, as a performance management expert, to help Posie implement the Six Sigma technique to reduce the number of products returned and in particular to define customers' requirements and measure Posie's existing performance.

The production director has been appointed to sponsor the project and you will be supported by a small team of managers who have recently received training in Six Sigma. The board member responsible for manufacturing quality recently resigned because they thought it was unfair that the Manufacturing Division was being held responsible for the increased level of customer returns.

You have been given access to some information concerning the reasons why customers return goods to help you measure existing performance in this area (Appendix 1). This is an extract from the management reporting pack presented to the board at their monthly meetings. The returns data, however, are only compiled every six months due to the lengthy analysis required of data from Posie's overseas retail operations. It is included twice a year in the board report along with the key performance indicators (KPIs) for customer satisfaction. The last time this information was produced 93% of customers indicated they were satisfied with the quality of the manufacture of Posie's products.

You have been asked to advise the board, using the data provided in Appendix 1, how the Six Sigma project at Posie to reduce returns from customers could be implemented using DMAIC methodology.

Exhibit 3: Information requirements

The CEO has heard that Six Sigma requires 'large amounts of facts and data'. They suggested that the returns data contain insufficient detail and that as part of your project you may need to do more analysis; for example, on why customers are not satisfied with the manufacturing quality.

They also added, 'I'm not sure that our current IT systems are capable of generating the data we need to identify which responsibility centres within the Manufacturing Division are the root causes of the problem of customer returns.'

The CEO has request that you evaluate the impact on Posie's information requirements arising from the need to identify and improve on the level of customer returns.

Exhibit 4: Appendix 1

Reasons given by customers for returning goods

Category	*Reason for return of goods*	*% responses*
1	Difficult to assemble or pieces missing	48
2	Goods arrived damaged	14
3	Goods were not as described or were defective	25
4	Goods were of poor quality or no longer wanted	11
5	Arrived late	2
Total		100

25 Albacore (2013 Pilot Exam, amended) (49 mins)

Respond to the Chair's request for work on the following areas:

(a) The existing branch information **(8 marks)**

(b) The performance management style and performance appraisal system **(12 marks)**

Professional marks will be awarded for the demonstration of skill in analysis and evaluation, and commercial acumen in your answer. **(5 marks)**

(Total = 25 marks)

Exhibit 1: Company background

Albacore Chess Stores (Albacore) is a chain of 12 shops specialising in selling items associated with the game of chess: boards, pieces, clocks, software and books. Three years ago, the company was the subject of a venture capital buyout from a larger group. A new senior management team was put in place after the buyout. They have the aim of running the business in order to maximise profits.

Exhibit 2: Budgeting process

The chief financial officer (CFO), along with the other members of senior management, sets the annual budget and uses a standard costing approach with variance analysis in order to control individual shop performance. The head office handles all capital purchases and brand marketing. All inventory purchasing is done centrally and the shop opening times are set as standard across the company. As an illustration of senior management attitude, the CFO had set the budget for staff costs for 20X1 at $7 per hour for part-time staff, and this was rigorously observed in the period.

Each shop is run by a manager who reports their financial results to head office. The shop managers recruit and manage the staffing of their shop. They have some autonomy in setting prices locally and have been given authority to vary prices by up to 10% from a master list produced by the CFO. They also have a local marketing budget agreed each year by the shop's manager and the marketing director as part of the annual appraisal process.

Exhibit 3: Performance appraisal and reward systems

The shop managers have approached the Chair of Albacore to complain about the way that they are managed and their remuneration. They feel that their efforts are unrecognised by senior management. One manager commented:

> I have had a successful year in hard economic circumstances. I have run a number of promotions in the shop that have been well received by the customers. However, the budgets that are set are impossible to achieve and as a result I have not been paid any bonus although I feel that I have done everything in my power to bring in good profits.

The shop managers at Albacore are paid a basic salary of $27,000 with bonuses of up to 30% of basic salary dependent on two factors: performance above budget and the operational director's performance assessment. The budget for the next year is prepared by the CFO and presented at the shop manager's annual appraisal.

The Chair is concerned about the system of performance assessment for the shop managers and the reward systems at Albacore. They have heard of variance analysis but is unsure about what would be relevant in this situation. They have provided the following illustrative information from the previous year for one shop:

ALBACORE CHESS STORES

TUNNY BRANCH YEAR TO SEPTEMBER 20X1

		Budget	*Actual*	*Variance*
		$	$	$
Sales		266,000	237,100	–28,900
Cost of sales		106,400	94,840	11,560
Gross profit		159,600	142,260	–17,340
Marketing		12,000	11,500	500
Staff costs:	manager	27,000	27,000	0
	part-time staff	38,000	34,000	4,000
Property costs		26,600	26,600	0
Shop profit		56,000	43,160	–12,840

Notes.

1 Property costs includes heating, lighting and rental.

2 Positive variances are favourable.

The manager of this shop commented at the appraisal meeting that they felt that the assessment was unfair since their failure to make budget was due to general economic conditions. The industry as a whole saw a 12% fall in revenues during the period and the budget for the period was set to be the same as the previous period. They were not paid a bonus for the period.

The Chair has asked for two pieces of work:

- An evaluation of the suitability of the existing branch information given as a means of assessing the shop manager's performance
- An analysis of the performance management style and evaluate the performance appraisal system at Albacore (including suggestions for suitable improvements to its reward system for the shop managers)

26 Cuthbert (Mar/Jun 2016, amended) (49 mins)

Respond to the board's request for work on the following areas:

(a) The proposed use of BPR **(12 marks)**

(b) Reward systems **(8 marks)**

Professional marks will be awarded for the demonstration of skill in analysis and evaluation, scepticism and commercial acumen in your answer. **(5 marks)**

(Total = 25 marks)

Exhibit 1: Company background

Cuthbert is based in Ceeland and manufactures jackets for use in very cold environments by mountaineers and skiers. It also supplies the armed forces in several countries with variants of existing products, customised by the use of different coloured fabrics, labels and special fastenings for carrying equipment. Cuthbert incurs high costs on design and advertising in order to maintain the reputation of the brand.

Each jacket is made up of different shaped pieces of fabric called 'components'. These components are purchased by Cuthbert from an external supplier. The external supplier is responsible for ensuring the quality of the components and the number of purchased components found to be defective is negligible. The cost of the components forms 80% of the direct cost of each jacket, and the prices charged by Cuthbert's supplier for the components are the lowest in the industry.

Exhibit 2: Production process

There are three stages to the production process of each jacket, which are each located in different parts of the factory:

Stage 1 – Sewing

The fabric components are sewn together by a machinist. Any manufacturing defects occurring after sewing has begun cannot be rectified, and finished garments found to be defective are heavily discounted or, in the case of bespoke variants, destroyed.

Stage 2 – Assembly

The garments are filled with insulating material and sewn together for the final time.

Stage 3 – Finishing

Labels, fastenings and zips are sewn to the finished garments. Though the process for attaching each of these is similar, machinists prefer to work only on labels, fastenings or zips to maximise the quantity which they can sew each hour.

Jackets are produced in batches of a particular style in a range of sizes. Throughout production, the components required for each batch of jackets are accompanied by a paper batch card which records the production processes which each batch has undergone. The batch cards are input into a production spreadsheet so that the stage of completion of each batch can be monitored and the position of each batch in the factory is recorded.

There are 60 machinists working in the Sewing Department, and 40 in each of the Assembly and Finishing Departments. All the machinists are managed by 10 supervisors whose duties include updating the batch cards for work done and inputting this into a spreadsheet, as well as checking the quality of work done by machinists. The supervisors report to the factory manager, who has overall responsibility for the production process.

Machinists are paid an hourly wage and a bonus according to how many items they sew each week, which usually comprises 60% of their total weekly wages.

Supervisors receive an hourly wage and a bonus according to how many items their team sews each week. The Factory Manager receives the same monthly salary regardless of production output. All employees are awarded a 5% annual bonus if Cuthbert achieves its budgeted net profit for the year.

Exhibit 3: Recent problems and issues

Recently, a large emergency order of jackets for the Ceeland army was cancelled by the customer as it was not delivered on time due to the following quality problems and other issues in the production process:

- A supervisor had forgotten to input several batch cards and as a result batches of fabric components were lost in the factory and replacements had to be purchased.
- There were machinists available to sew buttons onto the jackets, but there was only one machinist available who had been trained to sew zips. This caused further delay to production of the batch.
- When the quality of the jackets was checked prior to despatch, many of them were found to be sewn incorrectly as the work had been rushed. By this time the agreed delivery date had already passed, and it was too late to produce a replacement batch.

This was the latest in a series of problems in production at Cuthbert, and the directors have decided to use business process re-engineering (BPR) in order to radically change the production process.

Exhibit 4: BPR and changes to the production process

The proposal being considered as an application of BPR is the adoption of 'team working' in the factory, the three main elements of which are as follows:

(1) Production lines would reorganise into teams, where all operations on a particular product type are performed in one place by a dedicated team of machinists.

(2) Each team of machinists would be responsible for the quality of the finished jacket and, for the first time, machinists would be encouraged to bring about improvements in the production process. There would no longer be the need to employ supervisors and the existing supervisors would join the teams of machinists.

(3) The number of batches in production would be automatically tracked by the use of radio frequency identification (RFID) tags attached to each jacket. This would eliminate the need for paper batch cards, which are currently input into a spreadsheet by the supervisors.

You have been asked, as a performance management consultant, to assist the board in two areas:

- Advising on how the proposed use of BPR would influence the operational performance of Cuthbert
- Evaluating the effectiveness of the current reward systems at Cuthbert, and recommending and justifying how these systems would need to change if the BPR project goes ahead

27 Beach Foods (June 2015, amended) (49 mins)

Respond to the board and the CEO's requests for work on the following areas:

(a) EVA™ **(4 marks)**

(b) ROI and RI **(7 marks)**

(c) Control and management style **(9 marks)**

Professional marks will be awarded for the demonstration of skill in analysis and evaluation, scepticism and commercial acumen in your answer. **(5 marks)**

(Total = 25 marks)

Exhibit 1: Company background and structure

Beach Foods (Beach) is a family-owned business which has grown strongly over its 100-year history. The objective of the business is to maximise the family's wealth through their shareholdings. Beach has three divisions. It manufactures a variety of foods in two of the divisions: Beach Baby Foods (Baby) and Beach Chocolate Foods (Chocolate). Each of these divisions knows its own market and sets prices accordingly. The third division (R&D) researches new products on the instructions of the other divisions and is considered to be vital to the survival and growth of Beach. The board of Beach has been considering the impact of using a divisional structure and has come to you as a performance management consultant to ask for your advice.

Exhibit 2: Divisional performance measures

There is disagreement at board level about the correct choice of divisional performance measure to be used in the two manufacturing divisions. Currently, the business uses EVA™ but two directors have been questioning its value, complaining that it is complicated to understand. These directors have been promoting the use of either residual income (RI) or return on investment (ROI) as alternatives. The board wants to use the same measure for each division. As well as qualitatively evaluating these different measures, the board needs an assessment of the impact of a change in performance measure on their perception of these divisions' performance.

The board has therefore requested two pieces of work on these areas:

- Comments on the usefulness of EVATM as a divisional performance measure for the manufacturing divisions at Beach
- Calculation and discussion of the use of ROI and RI at Baby Division, given the data in Appendix 1, and an assessment of the impact of the assumptions made when calculating these metrics on the evaluation of the performance of this division and its management

Exhibit 3: Divisional control and management style

The chief executive officer (CEO) of Beach has engaged a business analyst to perform a study of the portfolio of manufacturing businesses which make up Beach. This has been completed in Appendix 2. The CEO wants your comments (based on the categorisation given in Appendix 2) on how this work will impact on the performance management of the divisions. Specifically, the CEO has asked for your recommendations on how to control each division; that is, whether each division should be treated as a cost/profit/investment centre and also the appropriate management style to use for handling staff in each division. The CEO commented to you:

> I have heard of different approaches to the use of budget information in assessing performance: budget-constrained, profit-conscious and also a non-accounting style. I need to know how these approaches might apply to each division given your other comments.

The CEO has then requested that you provide justified recommendations for each division's control and management style.

All of this work has been partly prompted by complaints from the divisional managers. The Chocolate divisional managers complain that they had to wait for a year to get approval to upgrade their main production line. This production line upgrade has reduced wastage and boosted Chocolate's profit margin by 10 percentage points. The Baby Division has been very successful in using the ideas of the Research and Development (R&D) Division, although Baby's managers do complain about the recharging of R&D costs to their division. Head office managers are worried about Chocolate as it has seemed to be drifting recently with a lack of strategic direction. Chocolate's managers are considered to be good but possibly not sufficiently focused on what benefits Beach as a whole.

Exhibit 4: Appendix 1

Figures from Beach management accounts for year ended 31 March:

Baby Division	*20X5*
	$m
Revenue	220
Costs	
Divisional operating costs	121
R&D costs recharged	11
Allocated head office management fees	28
Profit before tax	60
Capital employed	424

Notes.

1 Baby launched a new product with a large publicity campaign during the year.

2 The notional cost of capital for Baby is estimated by the chief financial officer at 11%. Weighted average cost of capital (WACC) for Beach is 7.5%.

3 ROI for similar entities is 20%.

4 EVA™ for Baby is calculated as $35m.

Exhibit 5: Appendix 2

Star Baby: Market growth 18% Relative market share 105%	**Question mark**
Cash cow Chocolate: Market growth 3% Relative market share 120%	**Dog**

Relative market share is the market share of the division compared to that of the market leader. If an organisation is a market leader, then its market share is compared to the next largest competitor.

Note. You may assume that the calculations and this categorisation are accurate.

PERFORMANCE EVALUATION

Questions 28 to 39 cover performance evaluation, the subject of Part D of the syllabus for APM.

28 Veyatie (Sep/Dec 2019, amended) (49 mins)

It is now 1 September 20X5.

Respond to the board's requests for work on the following areas:

(a) The customer satisfaction data **(7 marks)**

(b) The balanced scorecard **(13 marks)**

Professional marks will be awarded for the demonstration of skill in analysis and evaluation, scepticism and commercial acumen in your answer. **(5 marks)**

(Total = 25 marks)

Exhibit 1: Company information

Veyatie is a fashion clothing retailer which caters for both male and female customers of all adult age groups. Veyatie has ten retail stores. The company's information systems are basic for a business of its size and focus solely on financial information.

Veyatie's strategic objectives are 'To maximise shareholder wealth by increasing the number of retail stores, making our customers completely satisfied, ensuring our stores are attractive and offering the widest range of fashion clothing in our market.'

The Veyatie board has seen little need for non-financial performance indicators (NFPIs) so far, preferring instead to focus attention on cost control and working capital management. As a result, all senior managers are appraised against targets for operating profit margin, inventory turnover and the current ratio.

Exhibit 2: Customer satisfaction

Following a period of poor financial performance, Veyatie began collecting data on one aspect of non-financial performance, customer satisfaction, as the board had been advised that this is a key driver of financial performance.

The data collection began at the start of Quarter 3 20X3 and there is now data available for two complete years (Appendix 1). Veyatie has found it difficult to interpret this qualitative data and also the trends in this data. Some board members question its usefulness and propose reverting back to reporting just the financial indicators which they are used to.

Veyatie collects this data by asking customers to rate their satisfaction with their visit to the store as they are paying for their items. The scores range from 1 (completely dissatisfied) to 5 (completely satisfied). The mean score is the performance indicator reported to the board and the senior managers. Customers are encouraged to leave a score by having their names entered into a quarterly prize draw to win tickets to major football matches, concerts and amusement parks.

The board have requested your help in assessing the difficulties in using and interpreting the customer satisfaction data at Veyatie.

Exhibit 3: Balanced scorecard

A consultant has suggested to the board that the introduction of a balanced scorecard approach may improve business performance, as Veyatie is unlikely to achieve all of its strategic objectives in the near future. The board has already heard what the benefits of the balanced scorecard are, but are sceptical about these.

The board has asked for your advice on the problems of implementing and using the balanced scorecard approach at Veyatie. One aspect of this advice should focus on the selection of suitable performance measures and the consultant has already chosen some performance measures which could be included in a balanced scorecard at Veyatie (Appendix 2). These have been provided to help you illustrate your advice on the problems of using the balanced scorecard.

Note. The board would welcome your advice on how to refine the performance measures as part of your advice on the problems of using and implementing the balanced scorecard, but does not want you to give a detailed evaluation of the advantages and disadvantages of each performance measure, or to suggest completely new measures.

Exhibit 4: Appendix 1

Customer satisfaction data

Percentage of customers giving customer satisfaction scores* between 1 and 5

			20X3				*20X4*		*20X5*
Narrative	*Score*	*Q3*	*Q4*	*Q1*	*Q2*	*Q3*	*Q4*	*Q1*	*Q2*
Completely satisfied	5	5%	5%	50%	5%	5%	0%	5%	45%
Very satisfied	4	10%	5%	0%	14%	15%	5%	20%	1%
Satisfied	3	70%	65%	0%	56%	50%	65%	45%	1%
Somewhat satisfied	2	10%	20%	0%	20%	25%	25%	25%	8%
Completely satisfied	1	5%	5%	50%	5%	5%	5%	5%	45%
Mean score		3.00	2.85	3.00	2.94	2.90	2.70	2.95	2.93

* Satisfaction scores were collected from a large number of customers when paying for their items.

Exhibit 5: Appendix 2

Perspective	Performance measure
Financial	Operating profit margin Inventory turnover Current ratio
Customer	Customer satisfaction Market share
Internal business processes	Stock out percentage[1]
Learning and innovation	Total employee training days[2]

Notes.

1 Stock out percentage is the percentage of product lines which are unavailable for sale in each store at the beginning of each trading day.

2 The human resources department already records the total number of employee training days. Employee training covers the three main areas of health and safety training, training in handling customer complaints and training staff to understand the range of products available and how to display them attractively in the store.

29 Pharmaceutical Technologies (2013 Pilot Exam, amended) (49 mins)

Respond to the board's requests for work on the following areas:

(a) The measures proposed for customer and learning & growth aspects of PT's balanced scorecard **(5 marks)**

(b) Analysis of stakeholder influence for BDR **(8 marks)**

(c) Differences in the application of the balanced scorecard approach **(7 marks)**

Professional marks will be awarded for the demonstration of skill in analysis and evaluation, scepticism and commercial acumen in your answer. **(5 marks)**

(Total = 25 marks)

Exhibit 1: Company background

Pharmaceutical Technologies Co (PT) is a developer and manufacturer of medical drugs in Beeland. It is one of the 100 largest listed companies on the national stock exchange. The company focuses on buying prospective drugs (which have shown initial promise in testing) from small bio-engineering companies. PT then leads these drugs through three regulatory stages to launch in the general medical market.

The three stages are:

(1) To confirm the safety of the drug (does it harm humans?), in small-scale trials;

(2) To test the efficacy of the product (does it help cure?), again in small-scale trials; and

(3) Finally, large-scale trials to definitively decide on the safety and efficacy of the product.

The drugs are then marketed through the company's large sales force to healthcare providers and end users (patients). The healthcare providers are paid by either health insurance companies or the national government dependent on the financial status of the patient.

Exhibit 2: Industry regulator

The Beeland Drug Regulator (BDR) oversees this testing process and makes the final judgement about whether a product can be sold in the country.

Its objectives are to protect, promote and improve public health by ensuring that:

- Medicines have an acceptable balance of benefit and risk;
- The users of these medicines understand this risk-benefit profile; and
- New beneficial product development is encouraged.

The regulator is governed by a board of trustees appointed by the Government. It is funded directly by the Government and also through fees charged to drug companies when granting licences to sell their products in Beeland.

Exhibit 3: Balanced scorecard

PT has used share price and earnings per share as its principal measures of performance to date. However, the share price has underperformed the market, and the health sector, in the last two years. The chief executive officer (CEO) has identified that these measures are too narrow and is considering implementing a balanced scorecard approach to address this problem.

A working group has drawn up a suggested balanced scorecard. It began by identifying the objectives from the board's medium-term strategy:

- Create shareholder value by bringing commercially viable drugs to market.
- Improve the efficiency of drug development.
- Increase shareholder value by innovation in the drug approval process.

The working group then considered the stakeholder perspectives:

- Shareholders want a competitive return on their investment.
- Payers/purchasers (governments, insurers and patients) want to pay a reasonable price for the drugs.
- Regulators want an efficient process for the validation of drugs.
- Doctors want safe and effective drug products.
- Patients want to be cured.

Finally, this leads to the proposed scorecard of performance measures:

- Financial – share price and earnings per share
- Customer – number of patients using PT products
- Internal business process – exceed industry standard on design and testing; time to regulatory approval of a product
- Learning and growth – training days undertaken by staff; time to market of new product; percentage of drugs bought by PT that gain final approval

The balanced scorecard now needs to be reviewed to ensure that it will address the company's objectives and the issues that it faces in its business environment.

The working group has requested the following:

- An evaluation of the performance measures proposed for customer and learning & growth aspects of PT's balanced scorecard
- A brief description of a method of analysing stakeholder influence and an analysis of the influence of four different external stakeholders on the regulator (BDR)
- Using the external stakeholder analysis, a description of how the application of the balanced scorecard approach at BDR would differ from the approach within PT

30 Victoria-Yeeland Logistics (June 2015, amended) (49 mins)

Respond to the CFO's requests for work on the following areas:

(a) Performance metrics for each customer perspective success factor and comments on using customer complaints **(11 marks)**

(b) Reward management issues **(9 marks)**

Professional marks will be awarded for the demonstration of skill in analysis and evaluation, scepticism and commercial acumen in your answer. **(5 marks)**

(Total = 25 marks)

Exhibit 1: Company background and objectives

Victoria-Yeeland Logistics (Victoria) is a logistics support business, which operates a fleet of lorries to deliver packages of goods on behalf of its customers within the country of Yeeland. Victoria collects packages from its customers' manufacturing sites or from the customers' port of importation and delivers to the final user of the goods. The lorries are run and maintained from a set of depots spread throughout Yeeland.

The overall objective of Victoria is to maximise shareholder wealth. The delivery business in Yeeland is dominated by two international companies and one other domestic business and profit margins are extremely tight. The market is saturated by these large operators and a number of smaller operators. The cost base of Victoria is dominated by staff and fuel, with fuel prices being highly volatile in the last few years.

Exhibit 2: Balanced scorecard

In order to improve performance measurement and management at Victoria, the chief financial officer (CFO) plans to use the balanced scorecard (BSC). However, they have been pulled away from this project in order to deal with an issue with refinancing the business's principal lending facility.

The CFO has already identified some suitable metrics but needs you, as their assistant, to complete their work and address any potential questions which might arise when they make their presentation on the BSC to the board. The CFO has completed the identification of metrics for three of the perspectives (Appendix 1) but has yet to complete the work on the metrics for the customer perspective. This should be done using the data given in Appendix 2.

Therefore, the CFO has requested a justified recommendation, and calculation, of a suitable performance metric for each customer perspective success factor. The CFO also wants a commentary on the problems of using customer complaints to measure whether packages are delivered safely and on time.

Exhibit 3: Reward management issues

Additionally, two issues have arisen in the reward management system at Victoria, one in relation to senior management and the other for operational managers. Currently, senior management gets a fixed salary supplemented by an annual bonus awarded by the board. Shareholders have been complaining that these bonuses are not suitable. The operational managers also get bonuses based on their performance as assessed by their management superiors. The operational managers are unhappy with the system. In order to address this, it has been suggested that they should be involved in bonus target setting as otherwise there is a sense of demotivation from such a system.

The CFO wants an evaluation of this system of rewards in light of the introduction of the BSC and best practice.

Exhibit 4: Appendix 1

Financial perspective (How do we appear to our shareholders?)

Return on capital employed

Profit margin

Revenue growth

Customer perspective (How do we appear to our customers?)

Success factors:

Ability to meet customers' transport needs

Ability to deliver packages quickly

Ability to deliver packages on time

Ability to deliver packages safely

Internal process perspective (What business processes must excel?)

Time taken to load and unload

Lorry capacity utilisation

Learning and growth perspective (How do we sustain and improve our ability to grow?)

Leadership competence (qualitative judgement)

Training days per employee

Exhibit 5: Appendix 2

The process: A customer makes a transport request for a package to be collected and delivered to a given destination. The customer is supplied with a time window in which the delivery will occur. Packages are then loaded onto lorries and delivered according to a route specified by the depot's routing manager.

Total number of customer transport requests	610,000
Total number of packages transported	548,000
Total number of lorry journeys	73,000
Total package kilometres	65,760,000
Total package minutes	131,520,000
Number of delivery complaints from customers:	
from damaged packages	8,220
from late delivery (outside agreed time window)	21,920

Notes.

1 All figures are for the last financial year.

2 A package kilometre is defined as a kilometre travelled by one package.

3 A package minute is defined as a minute spent in transit by one package.

31 Harray Keyboards (Mar/Jun 2021) (49 mins)

It is now 1 September 20X5.

Respond to the CEO of Harray's request for work in the use of the performance pyramid.

(20 marks)

Professional marks will be awarded for the demonstration of skill in analysis and evaluation, scepticism and commercial acumen in your answer. **(5 marks)**

(Total = 25 marks)

Exhibit 1: Company information

Harray Keyboards (Harray) is a family-owned business which manufactures computer keyboards. It has contracts to supply three large desktop computer manufacturers. Harray won its contracts to supply these manufacturers under severe price competition as the manufacturers themselves have seen the price of their whole desktop package fall in the past 10 years. The contracts are for five years and have at least three years each left to run. At the end of the contract, the desktop manufacturers will retender for suppliers and Harray expects to be in a strong position as the existing supplier to win more work.

The chief executive officer (CEO) and leader of the Harray family is Graham Harray. They and the board believe that the success of the business has been built on an emphasis on strategic focus. They recently declared at a board meeting, 'Cost leadership wins business in our niche market and we should not over-stretch ourselves into non-core activities – we make cheap keyboards!'

Exhibit 2: Performance pyramid

The CEO has indicated that they want to use the performance pyramid to analyse the performance indicators used at Harray. They have asked you, as the company's performance management expert, to undertake two pieces of work on this area.

First, the CEO would like you to complete the analysis provided in Appendix 1. Appendix 1 contains the work done so far by a junior accountant on the pyramid headings and their associated indicators for Harray, with additional notes and information about Harray's performance. They would then like you to evaluate only the operational performance indicators at Harray.

Second, there are a number of non-financial indicators used in the performance pyramid and the CEO would like some advice on the reliability of these indicators compared to the financial ones which are usually presented in the board reports. They would like this part of the work to focus on the methods of measuring such indicators including the information sources, and the methods of processing and checking which is normally undertaken. They have told you to use the operational indicators from the first part of the work to illustrate your advice.

Exhibit 3: Appendix 1

Harray's performance indicator information (for the year ended 30 June 20X5)

Pyramid heading	Indicator	Value
1 Vision	Cost leadership in keyboard manufacturing	
2 Financial	Profit in the financial year	$600,000
3 Market	Market share	12%
4 Customer satisfaction	Customer complaints	0.4% of keyboards
5 Flexibility	Time from order to delivery	28 (average)
6 Productivity	Operating profit margin	7.2%
7 Waste		
8 Quality		
9 Delivery		
10 Cycle time	Working capital cycle	37 days

Notes.

1. Vision does not have an indicator. There is a separate project being carried out within the finance department to deal with this.
2. The absolute profit figure is used.
3. Market share is measured by an external marketing expert.
4. Customer complaints are measured by customer returns.
5. Many orders require customisation of the production process. Customers see timely delivery as critical.
6. There are a number of other margins available for use in measuring productivity in specific areas of operations, but operating margin is used as the summary indicator of productivity.
7. There are 16 manufacturing production lines in the factory. These lines are active for nine hours a day for six days a week (52 weeks a year). A keyboard is produced from the production line every 2.2 minutes (including set-up time), while the machines are operating. Last year, the factory produced 1.05 million keyboards.
8. The number of keyboards rejected by quality inspectors in the factory was 15,750 in the year. Of these, 9,450 were able to be reworked at an average cost of $2 and the rest were scrapped. The standard cost of a keyboard is $8.
9. Harray uses an external logistics firm (Achall) to handle all deliveries. Harray calls Achall to collect an order and Achall's lorry fleet picks up orders from Harray's factory and delivers to the customer. There are service level agreements governing how long Achall has to deliver the goods to Harray's customers. Achall supplies Harray with data from its own systems on the number of packages delivered and how many were late.

   Below is the report for last year:

Deliveries made (in total in the period)	5,127
Deliveries made within agreed time after Harray's order received	4,717
Total time taken to deliver Harray's goods (ie the total, over all the orders, of the number of days each order spends in transit)	17,423

10 Working capital cycle is calculated as: inventories days (22) + trade receivables days (42) – trade payables days (27).

32 APX Accountancy (June 2011, amended) (49 mins)

Respond to the requests for work on the following areas:

(a) The existing performance management system at APX **(7 marks)**

(b) Improvements from the introduction of a building block approach **(8 marks)**

(c) The marketing manager's statement **(5 marks)**

Professional marks will be awarded for the demonstration of skill in analysis and evaluation, and commercial acumen in your answer. **(5 marks)**

(Total = 25 marks)

Exhibit 1: Company background

APX Accountancy (APX) is an accountancy partnership with 12 branches covering each of the main cities of Emland. The business is well established, having organically grown over the last 40 years to become the second largest non-international practice in Emland. The accountancy market is mature and expands and contracts along with the general economic performance of Emland.

APX offers accountancy, audit, tax and business advisory services. The current business environment in Emland is dominated by a recession and the associated insolvency work is covered within the business advisory area of APX.

Exhibit 2: Performance management

At present, the practice collects the following information for strategic performance evaluation:

	Audit	*Tax*	*Business advisory*	*Total*
Revenue ($m)				
APX	69.1	89.2	64.7	223.0
Accounting industry	557.0	573.0	462.0	1,592.0
Change in revenue on previous year				
APX	3.0%	8.0%	22.0%	10.0%
Accounting industry	2.5%	4.5%	16.0%	6.8%
Profit margin at APX	6.4%	7.8%	10.5%	8.1%
Customer service score (1 to 5, with 5 being excellent)				
APX	3.4	3.9	4.1	

The figures shown are for the most recent financial year and illustrate the metrics used by APX. Equivalent monthly figures are produced for each of the monthly partner meetings which review practice performance.

The staff are remunerated based on their grade, with non-partners obtaining a bonus of up to 10% of basic salary based on their line managers' annual review. The partners receive a fixed salary with a share of profit which depends on their contractual responsibilities within the partnership.

The managing partner of APX is dissatisfied with the existing performance management system, as they have not convinced that it is helping to achieve the long-term goal of expanding and ultimately floating the business on the national stock exchange.

Therefore, they have asked you to consider the impact of applying Fitzgerald and Moon's building block approach to performance management in the practice.

You have been requested to:

- Evaluate the existing performance management system at APX by applying the building block model.
- Explain the main improvements the introduction of a building block approach to performance management could provide, and suggest specific improvements to the existing system of performance measures at APX in light of the introduction of the building block model.

In addition, the marketing manager at APX believes that the firm as a whole doesn't pay enough attention to customer service. At the last management meeting they said that, in their opinion, the customer service score(*) was the most important figure out of the performance metrics currently used by APX, and felt it was no coincidence that the area of the business with the highest customer service score had also performed best financially.

You have been requested to briefly evaluate the marketing manager's statement about the customer service score.

* Customer service scores reflect ratings given by customers in relation to the level of service they feel they have received from APX.

33 Vunderg (March 2019, amended) (49 mins)

It is now 1 September 20X5.

Required

Respond to the requests for work on the activity-based management (ABM).

Note. There are 11 marks available for the first part of the work required on this area and 9 marks available for the second part of the work required on this area. **(20 marks)**

Professional marks will be awarded for the demonstration of skill in analysis and evaluation, scepticism and commercial acumen in your answer. **(5 marks)**

(Total = 25 marks)

Exhibit 1: Vunderg: Company information

Vunderg manufactures windows and related products. The overheads in the business are high and primarily relate to procurement, customer administration and product design. Procurement and customer administration overheads relate to all of Vunderg's product groups. Design overheads currently relate to only two product groups, glasshouses and conservatories. Vunderg's current costing system has been in use for a long time and absorbs overheads into product costs on a direct labour hours basis. The current costing system does not involve identifying the factors which drive the costs of the company's activities and allocating overheads to products based on their usage of those factors.

Exhibit 2: Current product range

Windows

For many years, Vunderg has manufactured UPVC window frames used for residential house building. Vunderg buys the glass from an external supplier, inserts it into a frame and sells the completed window units to a small number of large construction companies. These window units all have standard designs, specifications and sizes. This market is very competitive, and Vunderg must offer a complete range of windows for sale to the construction companies.

Glasshouses

Five years ago, Vunderg developed a range of small garden glasshouses, for non-commercial use, made of attractive and high quality materials. After initial quality problems due to the use of materials and manufacturing methods new to Vunderg, glasshouse production is now efficient, quality is high and the glasshouses now command premium prices.

The glasshouses are sold nationwide through 40 retailers, who vary significantly in the size of orders they place and the level of customer support and trade discounts which they receive from Vunderg. As a result, the profitability of selling to different retailers, or types of retailer, varies significantly.

Conservatories

More recently, Vunderg began manufacturing conservatories* using the same materials as its glasshouse range. These conservatories are expensive and are made to measure for individual customers' houses. There are a wide range of finishes and options available to choose from. Conservatories which match garden glasshouses have become popular with customers who can afford them. Unlike Vunderg's other products, these are sold directly to individual home owners.

*Conservatories are structures made mainly of glass, which are attached to the side of residential houses. They form an additional room in a house and are popular in cool climates.

Exhibit 3: Future product development

Vunderg is looking to move into another new market soon, as the market for making windows for houses is now saturated. This new market will be the manufacture and design of large windows to be installed in the entrance halls of large, prestigious commercial buildings. These will be bespoke items, designed and manufactured to customers' own specifications.

Exhibit 4: Recent performance

The CEO is concerned by a recent fall in overall net profit margin, despite modest revenue growth and good control of direct costs. In particular, they have said:

> The conservatories part of the business may not be as profitable as its positive contribution (Appendix 1) may suggest. For example, our procurement department spends a lot of time sourcing special materials and finishes requested by customers. Many conservatories have leaked in the rain so we have to rectify these faults and work on a new design to prevent this happening. As we have only basic information systems, it is unclear how much some of these activities are costing. Over 20% of our factory space is dedicated to manufacturing conservatories. We may be better off discontinuing these products.

The CEO has some experience of activity based costing (ABC) in a previous role and believes that activity based management (ABM) could help to improve Vunderg's strategic performance. They are keen to have some further analysis in this area before they make a decision to implement ABM. You have therefore been requested to:

- Advise the CEO how activity based management (ABM) could help improve the strategic performance of Vunderg.
- Assess the limitations of using the ABM method for Vunderg's products and customer types, and the problems with its implementation.

Exhibit 5: Appendix 1

Contribution by product type for the year ended 30 June 20X5

Product type	*No. of units sold*	*Total contribution*
		($'000)
Windows	175,000	9,800
Glasshouses	3,800	969
Conservatories	650	910

34 Bazeele (Mar/Jun 2018, amended) (49 mins)

Respond to the CEO's requests for work on the following areas:

(a) Value-based management **(10 marks)**

(b) Economic value added **(10 marks)**

Professional marks will be awarded for the demonstration of skill in analysis and evaluation, scepticism and commercial acumen in your answer. **(5 marks)**

(Total = 25 marks)

Exhibit 1: Organisational background

Bazeele hires out plant and machinery to small firms working in the construction industry. Bazeele's senior managers, including the chief executive officer (CEO), have worked in the business since it was established 30 years ago, and they own the majority of the shares. During that time, Bazeele has acquired many smaller plant hire businesses. Of these business units, those which have underperformed after acquisition have either been sold on or restructured, for example, to increase their operating margins. Bazeele has recently diversified by hiring out large items of plant to large construction firms working on major infrastructure projects. These projects can last for up to ten years. Strong growth in the general economy has increased the number of these large projects and has also led to a predicted large increase in bank interest rates.

The shareholders' objective is for Bazeele to maintain its historic return on capital employed (ROCE). Managers at business units are given the objective of maintaining net profit margins of their own business units. Similarly, managers at individual branches of business units are given the same objective according to their own areas of responsibility.

Exhibit 2: Value-based management

Following two years of poor performance, it has been suggested to the CEO that Bazeele would benefit from adopting a value-based management (VBM) approach.

The CEO requires your advice and has said:

> The shareholders are unsure what VBM is, whether it will benefit Bazeele, and what changes the business would need to make if it were to adopt it. All managers in the business are already clear what their objectives are.
>
> For example, one business unit manager recently postponed some expensive staff training on improving customer satisfaction, which I believe was the correct decision.
>
> Our recent poor performance has meant we cannot afford this sort of expenditure, especially as we have no information on what levels of customer satisfaction actually are. Personally, I dislike change, but would not object to the adoption of VBM if it was thought to be beneficial for Bazeele.
>
> I am concerned about what changes we would need to make to our performance measurement and performance management systems if we were to adopt a value-based management approach. The shareholders have heard that economic value added (EVA™) can be used to measure whether Bazeele has created or destroyed value for its shareholders, but this has not yet been calculated.

The CEO has therefore requested:

- An evaluation of whether a value-based management approach is appropriate for Bazeele
- Advice, using the information in Appendix 1, on whether Bazeele has generated economic value for its shareholders

Exhibit 3: Appendix 1 – details of recent performance

Notes from Bazeele's management accounts for the most recent year end:

Notes.

1 Net profit after tax for the year: $10m

2 Capital employed at the start of the year: $250m

3 The interest charge for the year was $15m on a variable rate loan with an interest rate of 10%. Bazeele is funded 60% by debt and 40% by equity. The cost of equity is 12%. Bazeele pays tax at a rate of 20%. The weighted average cost of capital is 9.6%.

4 The depreciation charge for non-current assets for the year was $6.0m; the economic depreciation of which was $14.0m. At the start of the period, the accumulated economic depreciation of non-current assets exceeded its accounting depreciation by $16.0m.

5 Brought forward at the start of the year was a provision of $4.8m which was made in respect of a debt owed by a customer who has since repaid it.

6 Within the current profit or loss account there is an expense for $0.6m for advertising in trade magazines. This led to several enquiries from new customers involved in large infrastructure projects, which has resulted in Bazeele signing at least two large contracts after the end of the accounting period.

35 Dibble (Mar/Jun 2016, amended) (49 mins)

Respond to the CEO's requests for work on the following areas:

(a) The use of ABC in the Timber and Steel Divisions **(8 marks)**

(b) How ABM could be used to improve business performance **(12 marks)**

Professional marks will be awarded for the demonstration of skill in analysis and evaluation, and commercial acumen in your answer. **(5 marks)**

(Total = 25 marks)

Exhibit 1: Organisational background

Dibble is formed of two autonomous divisions, Timber and Steel, and manufactures components for use in the construction industry. Dibble has always absorbed production overheads to the cost of each product on the basis of machine hours.

Timber Division

Timber Division manufactures timber frames used to support the roofs of new houses. The timber, which is purchased pre-cut to the correct length, is assembled into the finished frame by a factory worker who fastens the components together. Timber Division manufactures six standard sizes of frame which is sufficient for use in most newly built houses.

Steel Division

Steel Division manufactures steel frames and roof supports for use in small commercial buildings such as shops and restaurants. There is a large range of products, and many customers also specify bespoke designs for short production runs or one-off building projects. Steel is cut and drilled using the division's own programmable computer aided manufacturing machinery (CAM), and is bolted together or welded by hand.

Steel Division's strategy is to produce novel bespoke products at a price comparable to the simpler and more conventional products offered by its competitors. For example, many of Steel Division's customers choose to have steel covered in one of a wide variety of coloured paints and other protective coatings at the end of the production process. This is performed off-site by a subcontractor, after which the product is returned to Steel Division for despatch to the customer. Customers are charged the subcontractor's cost plus a 10% mark-up for choosing this option. The board of Steel Division has admitted that this pricing structure may be too simplistic, and that it is unsure of the overall profitability of sales of some groups of products or sectors of the market.

Recently, several customers have complained that incorrectly applied paint has flaked off the steel after only a few months' use. More seriously, a fast food restaurant has commenced litigation with Dibble after it had to close for a week while steel roof frames supplied by Steel Division were repainted. Following this, the Production Manager has proposed increasing the number of staff inspecting the quality of coating on the frames, and purchasing expensive imaging machinery to make inspection more efficient.

Exhibit 2: Activity-based costing and activity-based management

The chief executive officer (CEO) at Dibble has approached you as a performance management expert for your advice. 'At a conference recently, I watched a presentation by a CEO at a similar business to ours talking about the advantages and disadvantages of using activity-based costing (ABC) and how over several years the adoption of activity-based management (ABM) had helped them to improve both strategic and operational performance.'

'I don't want you to do any detailed calculations at this stage, but I'd like to know more about ABC and ABM, and know whether they would be useful for Dibble,' they said.

Specifically, the CEO has requested you to:

- Assess whether it may be more appropriate to use ABC in Timber and Steel Divisions than the costing basis currently used.
- Advise how ABM could be used to improve business performance at Dibble.

Exhibit 3: Extracts of the most recent management accounts for Timber and Steel Divisions

You are provided with extracts of the most recent management accounts for Timber and Steel Divisions:

Division	*Timber*	*Steel*
	$'000	$'000
Revenue	25,815	20,605
Materials	12,000	10,100
Direct labour	4,500	850
Subcontract costs	75	650
Analysis of production overheads		
Set-up time for CAM machinery	–	575
Machining time	–	2,777
Storage of goods awaiting or returned from subcontractors	120	395
Transfer of goods to and from subcontractors	50	300
Inspection and testing	35	425
Total production overheads	205	4,472
Gross profit	9,035	4,533

36 Zones (Sep/Dec 2018) (49 mins)

Respond to the CEO's requests for work on the following areas:

(a) The Lynch and Cross performance pyramid **(4 marks)**

(b) The new measures in Appendix 2 **(8 marks)**

(c) Whether the two measures defined in Appendix 3 are suitable for use in the DMAIC method. **(8 marks)**

Professional marks will be awarded for the demonstration of skill in analysis and evaluation, and commercial acumen in your answer. **(5 marks)**

(Total = 25 marks)

Exhibit 1: Zones: Company information

Zones is an overnight parcel delivery business. Since it was founded by the current CEO, it has grown rapidly due to a boom in online shopping. It now operates 1,000 delivery vehicles of various sizes. Recently, financial performance and market share have deteriorated. Zones has had no clear corporate vision, an excessive focus on financial objectives and inadequate systems to measure and manage performance of the underlying processes driving its financial performance.

Exhibit 2: Business model

Zones' collection and delivery service uses delivery vehicles to transport parcels to and from local depots and individual addresses. Vehicles may also pick up parcels from the addresses to which they deliver. Each time the vehicle calls to pick up or deliver parcels is known as a stop, and the time of day for each stop is booked in advance. At the end of each day, vehicles, along with any parcels not delivered, return to the depot. Regardless of who pays for the service, Zones regards anyone to whom it delivers, or from whom it picks up parcels, as a customer. In the long term, the requirements of both of these groups for a competitively priced, reliable and flexible service will be similar.

Exhibit 3: Performance improvement proposals

The CEO believes that reductions in customer satisfaction and flexibility, caused by a decline in operational performance, may have led to the recent deterioration in financial performance and market share. It has been suggested that Zones use the Lynch and Cross performance pyramid (Appendix 1) to reverse this deterioration, and three new measures for operational performance have been suggested in Appendix 2. The CEO has stated that Zones' corporate vision should be:

'To increase shareholder wealth by becoming the leading overnight parcel delivery business, providing quality, reliability and value for customers.'

It is also proposed to use the DMAIC (define, measure, analyse, improve and control) method to implement the Six Sigma methodology to improve the quality of delivery. Two measures have been defined in Appendix 3 which may help improve Zones' delivery performance.

To assist with these proposals, the CEO has requested you to:

- Advise on the features of the Lynch and Cross performance pyramid that can help Zones achieve its corporate vision.
- Using the performance pyramid, evaluate the extent to which the suggested new measures in Appendix 2 can be used to measure and manage operational performance at Zones.
- Advise whether the two measures defined in Appendix 3 are suitable for use in the DMAIC method to implement the Six Sigma methodology in order to improve delivery performance.

Exhibit 4: Appendix 1

Lynch and Cross performance pyramid

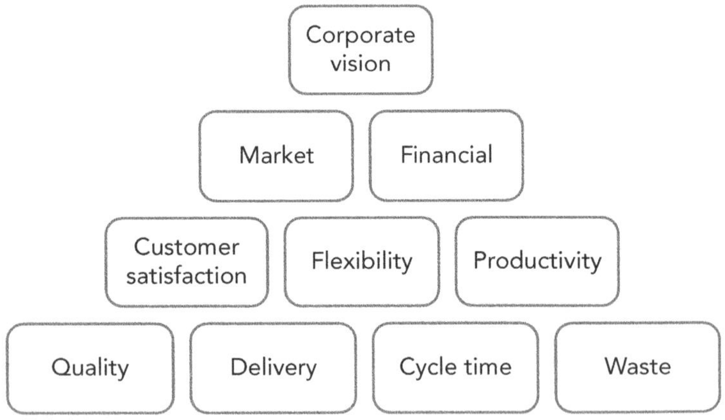

Exhibit 5: Appendix 2

Suggested new measures for operational performance

Measure	Description
Vehicle utilisation	Average utilisation of all vehicle capacity. This is measured by taking the average of vehicle load as a percentage of capacity when the vehicle leaves the depot at the beginning of each day and the vehicle load as a percentage of capacity when the vehicle returns to the depot at the end of each day. Capacity is measured either according to the internal volume or the length of the vehicle, depending on the type of vehicle being used.
Fuel consumption	Average litres of fuel per kilometre travelled for all vehicles.
On-time stops	Percentage of stops made within 30 minutes* of the booked time.

* Zones receives complaints from customers relating to deliveries not made on time. Of these, less than 0.0001% relate to deliveries made within 30 minutes of the booked time.

Exhibit 6: Appendix 3

Suggested new measures for improving quality of delivery using the DMAIC methodology

Measure	Description
On-time stops	Percentage of stops made within 10 minutes of the booked time.
Failed deliveries	Percentage of deliveries which cannot be made due to the customer being unavailable to take the delivery, or by parcels being incorrectly addressed. Currently, 5% of deliveries are failed and have to be returned to the depot.

37 Roan (Sep/Dec 2020, amended) (49 mins)

It is now 1 September 20X5. Respond to the RSU management board's request for work on the following areas:

(a) Managing and measuring performance in the RSU joint venture **(14 marks)**

(b) Performance measures for stakeholder groups **(6 marks)**

Professional marks will be awarded for the demonstration of skill in analysis and evaluation and commercial acumen in your answer. **(5 marks)**

(Total = 25 marks)

Exhibit 1: Background

Roan University (Roan) is based in Teeland, which is a developed country. The government of Teeland has stated that it will cut part of the funding for the university and has made it clear that Roan must develop new replacement income streams. Roan will remain state owned.

Saugh University (Saugh) is based in Deeland, which has a developing economy, and which is culturally different to Teeland. Saugh's funding is from the government of Deeland and this funding is secure for the foreseeable future. The government of Deeland has indicated that it wants the university to develop joint ventures and alliances with universities in developed countries.

Roan and Saugh have recently entered into a joint venture to set up a new university in Deeland. The new university is called RS University (RSU). Roan and Saugh each own 50% of the joint venture and a new purpose-built campus has been constructed. RSU will welcome students within three months.

Exhibit 2: Details of the joint venture

Roan and Saugh have established a joint management board (MB) to manage the long-term and short-term operations of RSU. The MB's membership is 50% from each university, plus at least one government representative from Deeland. The MB meets at least three times per annum and the position of chairman on the MB rotates between Roan and Saugh on a meeting-by-meeting basis. The MB have asked you, as a performance management expert, to assist them with some tasks.

Roan has stated that its aim for the joint venture RSU is 'to internationally expand our provision and lead educational developments in the global arena by enhancing our revenue streams from innovative sources.' Saugh, however, has made it clear that it will view the success of RSU by the quality of the graduates who are produced and by the contribution these graduates make to society.

Saugh is keen that Roan sends as many home-based staff from Teeland to teach at RSU in Deeland as is possible, but Roan would prefer to recruit local staff in Deeland to undertake its teaching obligations at RSU. Roan's teaching staff have voiced concerns about the extensive travel involved to teach at RSU and have also indicated that their work at Roan is likely to suffer if they teach at RSU. Specifically, they feel that they would not be able to effectively undertake their teaching duties, research activities or supervision of students at Roan. Negotiations are currently taking place between the teachers' trade union, which Roan's staff belong to, and management at Roan which could result in all Roan's teaching staff refusing to teach at RSU.

The management board would like you to discuss the problems that will be encountered when managing and measuring the performance in the RSU joint venture.

Exhibit 3: Stakeholder views

There has been some criticism of the joint venture within the local community in Teeland. A parent of one of the students studying at Roan has written, on behalf of a newly-formed public pressure group, to the local newspaper saying, 'All the attention at Roan is on this inappropriate joint venture. My son was refused any help or guidance as the staff who could assist were all overseas helping with the development of RSU. Their exam results were three weeks late as there was no one there to mark the exams. This is not acceptable. Roan should exist to educate Teeland students primarily. Everything else is secondary.' Membership of the public pressure group is growing.

Roan has undertaken an analysis of its stakeholders using Mendelow's matrix. Part of this work is supplied in Appendix 1, along with the justifications for the categorisation of the three stakeholder groups.

For each of the three stakeholder groups, the management board would like you to justify an appropriate performance measure which could be used by Roan.

Exhibit 4: Appendix 1

Stakeholder analysis

		Level of interest	
		Low	High
Power	Low	A	B
	High	C	D

Government of Teeland – The government would be keen to know of any financial problems or difficulties with the joint venture but, generally, it would belong in segment A so minimal effort should be expended.

Roan teachers' trade union – The teachers' trade union's power could be high if it has the backing to recommend to the management of Roan that Roan employees will not travel to or teach at RSU. If Roan can recruit local staff for RSU, the power and interest of the trade union will both be low as there will be little or no need for its involvement. If Roan cannot recruit local staff, then the power and interest of the trade union will both be high and it will fall into category D of being a key player.

Public pressure group in Teeland – The group has a very high level of interest in the joint venture and its power may be determined by its size. If it grows significantly, then its power may become high also. For the present, its power is likely to be low so the group will fall into category B – kept informed.

38 Forion Electronics (June 2015, amended) (49 mins)

Respond to the board of Forion's request for work on the following areas:

(a) The ERPS **(6 marks)**

(b) The usefulness of the three critical areas in the alliance agreement **(8 marks)**

(c) The relative reliability of financial and non-financial data **(6 marks)**

Professional marks will be awarded for the demonstration of skill in analysis and evaluation, scepticism and commercial acumen in your answer. **(5 marks)**

(Total = 25 marks)

Exhibit 1: Company background

Forion Electronics (Forion) manufactures a range of electronic goods. Its business has grown rapidly over the last ten years and is now complex and international. Forion manufactures over 100 different products, selling into 25 different countries. There is a supplier base of over 200 companies from which Forion sources. As the business has become more complex, the board has found it difficult to pull together all the information that it requires in order to make decisions.

Exhibit 2: Information systems

The current information systems are developed in-house and are based in the functional departments (such as purchasing, manufacturing, warehousing and delivery, selling and marketing). The organisation uses the financial system as a means of bringing together information for an overview of corporate performance.

There have been a number of examples of problems encountered with information in Forion:

- There are inefficiencies arising from ordering the wrong amount of subcomponents.
- There are often stock-outs or obsolescence of unsold goods in the warehouses, although the Marketing Department prepares good sales forecasts.
- Sometimes, there are insufficient delivery vehicles available to meet customer deadlines.

The board of Forion believes the problems arise from poor information sharing within the company. It is considering the purchase of an enterprise resource planning system (ERPS) to be the single information system for the whole organisation.

The board have requested you to discuss how the ERPS may impact on performance management issues at Forion.

Exhibit 3: Potential strategic alliance

Also, Forion is planning to launch a smartphone. However, in order to make it competitive they need to have high-visibility, durable screens. As the cost of screen development is considerable, it has been decided to form a strategic alliance with a well-known screen manufacturer to provide this key component for the new smartphone. Bon Accord Screens (BAS) has been chosen as the strategic ally, as it has a strong reputation for its quality of manufacturing and new product development. BAS has been trying to break into the smartphone market for several years.

The alliance agreement has stipulated three critical areas of performance for BAS's supply to Forion:

(1) Quality of manufacturing, measured by fault rates of screens supplied being within agreed tolerances (so that they fit Forion's phone bodies)

(2) Time of delivery, measured by the number of times a shipment is more than one day overdue

(3) The ability to provide technical upgrades to the screens as the market demands

The service level agreement will be based on these three points and there will be financial penalties built into the agreement if BAS fails to meet these.

The board of Forion have requested that you evaluate:

- The usefulness, from Forion's viewpoint, of the three critical areas in the alliance agreement for measuring the performance of BAS
- The relative reliability of financial and non-financial data from internal and external sources in the context of the alliance between Forion and BAS

39 Callisto Retail (Jun 2012 amended) (49 mins)

Respond to the Jeff and George's request for work on the following areas:

(a) Assessing performance measurement and performance management in complex business structures **(15 marks)**

(b) Evaluating the proposed report **(5 marks)**

Professional marks will be awarded for the demonstration of skill in analysis and evaluation, and commercial acumen in your answer. **(5 marks)**

(Total = 25 marks)

Exhibit 1: Company background

Callisto Retail (Callisto) is an online reseller of local craft products related to the historic culture of the country of Callistan. The business started ten years ago as a hobby of two brothers, Jeff and George. The brothers produced humorous, short video clips about Callistan which were posted on its website and became highly popular. They decided to use the website to try to sell Callistan merchandise and good initial sales made them believe that they had a viable business idea.

Callisto has gone from strength to strength and now boasts sales of $120m per annum, selling anything related to Callistan. Callisto is still very much the brothers' family business. They have gathered around themselves a number of strategic partners into what Jeff describes as a virtual company. Callisto has the core functions of video clip production, finance and supplier relationship management. The rest of the functions of the organisation (warehousing, delivery and website development) are outsourced to strategic partners.

The brothers work from their family home in the rural North of Callistan while other Callisto employees work from their homes in the surrounding villages and towns. These employees are involved in video editing, system maintenance, handling customer complaints and communication with suppliers and outsourcers regarding inventory. The employees log in to Callisto's systems via the national internet infrastructure. The outsourced functions are handled by multinational companies of good reputation which are based around the world. The brothers have always been fascinated by information technology and so they depend on email and electronic data interchange to communicate with their product suppliers and outsourcing partners.

Exhibit 2: Recent issues

Recently, there have been emails from regular customers of the Callisto website complaining about slow or non-delivery of orders that they have placed. George has commented that this represents a major threat to Callisto as the company operates on small profit margins, relying on volume to drive the business. They believe that sales growth will drive the profitability of the business due to its cost structure.

Exhibit 3: Contracts and service level agreements

Jeff handles the management of outsourcing and has been reviewing the contracts that exist between Callisto and its strategic partner for warehousing and delivery, RLR Logistics. The current contract for warehousing and delivery is due for renewal in two months and currently has the following service level agreements (SLAs):

(1) RLR agrees to receive and hold inventory from Callisto's product suppliers.

(2) RLR agrees to hold 14 days' inventory of Callisto's products.

(3) RLR agrees to despatch from its warehouse any order passed from Callisto within three working days, inventory allowing.

(4) RLR agrees to deliver to customers anywhere in Callistan within two days of despatch.

Breaches in these SLAs incur financial penalties on a sliding scale depending on the number and severity of the problems. Each party to the contract collects their own data on performance and this has led to disagreements in the past over whether service levels have been achieved, although no penalties have been triggered to date. The most common disagreement arises over inventory levels held by RLR, with RLR claiming that it cannot be expected to deliver products that are late in arriving to inventory due to the product suppliers' production and delivery issues.

Jeff requires an assessment of the difficulties of performance measurement and performance management in complex business structures such as Callisto, especially in respect of the performance of their employees and strategic partners.

Exhibit 4: Employee productivity

George has also been increasingly concerned about the length of time it is taking for customer complaints to be addressed, and the damage which delays in replying to customer complaints could have on Callisto's reputation. In this respect, they are also worried that Callisto's employees are not working as productively as they could be.

Consequently, they have designed a daily report which lists all the employees in alphabetical order, and then shows four columns of data for each employee:

(1) How long they have been logged on to Callisto's system

(2) How many videos they have edited

(3) How many complaints they have handled

(4) How many suppliers or outsourcers they have contacted

George has requested an evaluation of this proposed report.

SECTION A QUESTIONS

Questions 40 to 52 are 50-mark questions, covering a range of topic areas, as will be the case in your APM exam. In the exam, you should expect Section A questions to focus on a range of issues from across **syllabus sections A, B and C**.

40 Freuchie Retail (Sept/Dec 2021) (98 mins)

The following **exhibits** provide information relevant to the question:

(1) Company information – industry information and mission for the company: Freuchie Retail (Freuchie)

(2) Performance reporting: Quantitative – details of the chief executive officer's (CEO) request to review the current performance report starting with the quantitative elements

(3) Performance reporting: Narrative – further details about work on the narrative aspects of the current performance report, to build on the review already requested by the CEO

(4) Operational gearing and cost structures – and explanation of the work to be prepared on operational gearing and its implications for Freuchie

(5) What gets measured, gets done – instructions from the CEO for an assessment of the quote

(6) Appendix 1 – the current performance report of Freuchie

(7) Appendix 2 – additional data supplied for Freuchie

This information should be used to answer the question **requirements** within your chosen **response option(s)**.

Required

It is now 1 September 20X5.

Write a report to the chief executive officer (CEO) of Freuchie to respond to their instructions for work on the following areas:

(a) Current performance reporting: Quantitative **(16 marks)**

(b) Current performance reporting: Narrative **(10 marks)**

(c) The calculation of operational gearing and its implications **(7 marks)**

(d) The quote, 'what gets measured, gets done' **(7 marks)**

Professional marks will be awarded for the demonstration of skill in communication, analysis and evaluation, scepticism and commercial acumen in your answer. **(10 marks)**

(Total = 50 marks)

Exhibit 1: Company information

Freuchie Retail (Freuchie) is a family-owned business which sells a range of clothes from a chain of shops across Beeland. Freuchie's mission is 'to deliver returns to shareholders above the average for the retail sector by providing a superior customer experience from the appearance of the stores to the attractive range of clothes which are sold with enthusiasm'.

The board feel that performance has been poor compared to other similar retailers in the past five years. As a result, a new chief executive officer (CEO) was appointed a year ago and has spent this time conducting a fundamental review of the business. The review has identified a number of areas for improvement including those associated with performance reporting and management.

Exhibit 2: Performance reporting: Quantitative

The CEO is concerned that performance towards this mission and its subsidiary objectives are not being usefully discussed at board meetings. They believe that the fault lies in the board's performance report for annual strategic review. Therefore, they want you to do an assessment of the current performance report in two parts in light of their concern (see Appendix 1 for the most recent example). The first part of the assessment should consider the quantitative elements of the report and can include some discussion of improved indicators and also, more generally, should take into account what is best practice for reporting performance.

Exhibit 3: Performance reporting: Narrative

The second part of the performance reporting assessment should be a review and rewrite of the current narrative commentary on the report. The CEO believes the current commentary is especially weak and wants a critical assessment of it, followed by an improved example based upon what you consider to be the crucial aspects of Freuchie's performance. They have stated that the improved example commentary should consist of no more than four points in order to focus attention on the key areas. You should include figures to illustrate the points you have included using the data given where it is available, but some can be left blank to be filled in later if the underlying data is not available.

Exhibit 4: Operational gearing and cost structures

The CEO was at a business networking meeting recently where one speaker, a highly regarded management consultant, made a number of comments about fixed and variable costs, operational gearing and the importance of these to the operation of a store. The CEO did not understand the presentation, complaining that there was too much jargon. They want to understand what operational gearing is and how it relates to fixed and variable costs. Therefore, they want a calculation of operational gearing for Freuchie using current data (Appendices 1 and 2) and an assessment of the implications of the result for Freuchie's management.

Exhibit 5: What gets measured, gets done

At the same business networking meeting, another CEO mentioned that they found the quote 'What gets measured, gets done' a useful starting point for thinking about the management implications of new performance indicators. They then used another list of jargon phrases that Freuchie's CEO did not follow. As a result, the CEO wants an assessment of the problems that the quote identifies and also, how phrases such as 'tunnel vision, sub-optimisation and gaming' might link to the quote. They want illustrations from Freuchie's business.

Exhibit 6: Appendix 1

Freuchie Retail: Strategic Performance Report

Year to 30 June 20X5

	Budget	*Actual*	*Actual*	*Costs and profit as a % of revenue*	*Change on previous year*
	20X5	*20X5*	*20X4*		
	$m	$m	$m		
Revenue	641	638.1	577.7		10.50%
Cost of sales	380.5	378.9	342.1		
Gross profit	**260.5**	**259.2**	**235.6**	40.60%	10.00%
Staff costs	136.2	135.8	123.1	21.30%	10.30%
Other operating costs					
Rent and property costs	71	71	63.4		
Marketing	34	34	34	5.30%	0.00%

	Budget	Actual	Actual	Costs and profit as a % of revenue	Change on previous year
	20X5	20X5	20X4		
	$m	$m	$m		
Head office costs	11.9	11.7	11.9		
Total	**116.9**	**116.7**	**109.3**	18.30%	6.80%
Operating profit	**7.4**	**6.7**	**3.2**	1.00%	109.40%
Finance costs	4.9	4.9	4.8		
Group profit before tax	**2.5**	**1.8**	**-1.6**	0.30%	
Tax	0.5	0.4	-0.3		
Group profit after tax	**2**	**1.4**	**-1.3**	0.20%	
Other data:					
Number of employees		5,103	4,607		10.80%
Dividend per share ($)		0.51	0.51		0.00%
Inventory obsolescence/loss write-downs ($m)		13.1	12.7		3.10%
Number of stores		42	38		10.50%

Commentary:

- Overall performance is satisfactory as the business has maintained its dividend.
- Revenue is up by 10.5% on the previous period.
- Gross margin has held at about 41%.
- Inventory write-downs were in line with the increased stock held at the stores.

Exhibit 7: Appendix 2

Freuchie – additional data

Cost of sales includes:

	Budget 20X5	Actual 20X5	Actual 20X4
	$m	$m	$m
Insurance	18.2	18.2	16.2
Utilities	12	11.9	10.8
Depreciation	17	17	15.3
Total	**47.2**	**47.1**	**42.3**

Staff costs:

The employees are all paid an annual salary as a fixed sum stated in their contract, except for a bonus pool of 1% of revenue which is divided up between the sales staff who exceed their target revenue.

41 Iron Chicken (Iron Chicken (2013 Specimen exam, amended)) (98 mins)

Write a report to the CEO of Iron Chicken in response to their instructions for work on the following areas:

(a) The use of economic value added (EVA™) as the key performance metric at IC **(15 marks)**

(b) Current key performance indicators **(6 marks)**

(c) The two improvement projects **(10 marks)**

(d) The impact of the proposed new information system on the two improvement projects **(9 marks)**

Professional marks will be awarded for the demonstration of skill in communication, analysis and evaluation, scepticism and commercial acumen in your answer. **(10 marks)**

(Total = 50 marks)

Exhibit 1: Company information and mission

Iron Chicken (IC) is a multinational business which manufactures commercial building control systems. Building control systems include heating and air-conditioning systems, lighting controls, power and water monitoring and security systems (eg keypad access, alarms and CCTV). IC's manufacturing takes place at a number of factory sites where some products have a long product life and are simple and mass-produced while other products are complex and have a short product life due to changing technologies.

IC's mission statement is 'to create value for shareholders through control products which improve productivity, save energy and increase comfort and safety'.

A new chief executive officer (CEO) has been appointed to address a decline in IC's share price in the last three years. This CEO has identified that the business has grown through acquisition and as a result they stated, 'senior management have focused on making corporate deals and not making control systems'. The CEO has declared that the business must focus on optimising its value generation rather than just getting larger through acquisitions. They have developed an improvement programme for IC.

You are a performance management expert within IC, and the CEO has tasked you with aiding them on four aspects of their improvement programme:

Exhibit 2: Economic value added (EVATM)

The CEO wants your views on the use of economic value added (EVA™) as the key performance metric at IC. You have been supplied with the current EVA™ calculation (Appendix 1) but there is some doubt about whether the junior management accountant who has done this work was sufficiently trained in the method.

Therefore, the CEO requires you to evaluate its accuracy and the assumptions which form part of the calculation and advise them on your results, providing calculations as needed.

Exhibit 3: Critical success factors (CSFs) and key performance indicators (KPIs)

The CEO believes that the poor performance of the company can be addressed by ensuring that the mission statement flows down into the performance management of the business.

To that end, the following critical success factors (CSFs) and the associated key performance indicators (KPIs) have been identified.

CSF		Associated current KPI
1	Greater staff productivity	Units produced per labour hour
2	Reduction of wastage in production	Power consumed per unit produced
3	Greater innovation of products	Number of new products launched

The CEO wants you to briefly explain a weakness of the current KPI associated with each CSF and then provide a justified alternative KPI.

Exhibit 4: Improvement projects

In order to improve performance, the CEO plans to implement initiatives associated with 'lean' manufacturing.

Specifically, there are two projects which have been suggested, and the CEO needs your advice on these:

(1) Move to just-in-time (JIT) manufacturing

(2) Use Kaizen costing

The CEO has stated that they need you to explain what these improvement projects are, how they will help to meet the CSFs at IC, and also how they will impact the existing three KPIs.

Exhibit 5: New information system

The CEO is concerned about the implications of the improvement projects for IC's information systems as they feel that the systems are not currently suitable for the plan that they have. The current information systems of the company are based around the functional departments of the business such as manufacturing, marketing, finance and logistics. Each department has developed its own system, although all feed into the finance system which is the main one used for strategic decision making. In order that the department systems can all feed through to the current finance system, these current systems only handle quantitative data. The company is considering the implementation of a new information system. This new system will introduce networking technology in order to bring together all of the departmental systems into a new, single, corporate database. The CEO would like an assessment of the impact of this proposed, new information system on the improvement projects.

Exhibit 6: Appendix 1

Economic value added		*Year ended 30 June 20X5*	
		$m	Note
Operating profit		551.4	
Add back:	Non-cash expenses	15.1	
	Marketing capitalised	23.1	5
Less:	Tax	134.8	6
	Lost tax relief on interest	24.5	7
Net operating profit after tax (NOPAT)		430.3	
Capital employed			
From the statement of financial position		2,401.0	10
Marketing spend capitalised		23.1	5
Adjusted capital employed		2,424.1	

BPP

WACC = (1/2 × 16%) + (1/2 × 6.8%) = 11.4%

EVA™ = NOPAT – (WACC × capital employed) = 154

Assumptions and notes

Notes.

1 Debt/equity: 100.0%
2 Cost of equity: 16.0%
3 Tax rate: 30.0%
4 Cost of debt (pre-tax): 6.8%
5 There has been $23.1m spent on marketing each year for the last two years in order to build the brand of IC long term.
6 Tax paid in the year was $130m while the tax charged per the accounts was $134.8m.
7 Interest charged in the period was $81.6m.

   Lost tax relief on this interest was 30% × $81.6m.
8 The only research and development spending identified in the last five years was $10m expensed during this year on a new product.

   The product has not been launched yet.
9 Capital employed during the period (from the statement of financial position):

	$m
Opening	2,282.0
Change in period	119.0
Closing	2,401.0

42 FIAG (Mar/June 2021) (98 mins)

It is now 1 September 20X5.

Write a report to the chief executive officer (CEO) to respond to their instructions for work on the following areas:

(a) The performance reporting at Fiag focused on:

   (i) The question of manipulation in the board report **(12 marks)**

   (ii) Whether the report addresses the company's objectives and the report's presentation **(14 marks)**

(b) The consultant's report on the external business environment **(14 marks)**

Professional marks will be awarded for the demonstration of skill in communication, analysis and evaluation, scepticism and commercial acumen in your answer. **(10 marks)**

(Total = 50 marks)

Exhibit 1: Company information

Fiag Bicycles (Fiag) is a large national bicycle manufacturer in the well-developed country of Beeland. It was a family-owned business until three years ago when it raised new funds from a venture capitalist (VC) to develop new models of bicycle. Of the eight models in its current range, two have been significantly redesigned and one totally new model has been launched in 20X4. This new model (the Zoam) has been developed over five years and is Fiag's most radical development to date, as it is lightweight and has an electrical battery which can assist less physically fit riders to cycle up hills.

The VC invested $30m in 20X2 and insisted that Fiag produce a mission statement as a clear indication of the company's objective. The objective of Fiag is 'to give the shareholders sustainable growth in returns by developing and manufacturing the best quality bicycles and so bring the joy of cycling to a broad customer base in Beeland'.

Exhibit 2: Performance reporting

The VC has a non-executive director on the board of Fiag. They have criticised the executive directors over the most recent performance report that was presented to the board meeting in order to review the annual performance to 30 June 20X5 (Appendix 1). Firstly, they were very unhappy about what they perceived to be attempts to manipulate the picture presented in the report.

Secondly, they repeated criticism given in earlier board meetings that the report does not address the company's objectives. They then demanded that the executive directors take action on these points immediately and asked that the board meeting be reconvened once this is done.

The chief executive officer (CEO) wants you, as a performance expert in the company, to give them advice on these matters. They are committed eventually to a redesign of the performance reporting at Fiag but needs to understand the non-executive director's concerns more clearly before this begins. They are happy that there are no arithmetic errors in the presentation of the performance report but wants a critical review from you:

(1) Addressing the question of manipulation in the impression given by the report

(2) Assessing whether the current report addresses the company's objectives and briefly, any other issues in its presentation

Exhibit 3: External business environment

The CEO has recognised that the company operates in an increasingly volatile external business environment. Therefore, they have employed a consultant to perform a PEST analysis and given you the relevant extracts of their report (Appendix 2). They stated that they don't not want you to re-perform the consultant's analysis of the external environment. Instead, they want you to focus on the implications of the PEST factors identified on Fiag's business and then on providing a justified recommendation of suitable performance indicators to measure the impact of each of those factors.

Exhibit 4: Appendix 1

Performance report

Year to 30 June	*20X5*	*20X4*	*Improvement year on year*	*Industry average*
	$m	$m	%	%
Revenue	73	289	-6	
Costs of sales	131		137	
Gross profit	142	152	-7	
Administrative expenses	50	52		
Distribution expenses	28	29		
Selling and marketing expenses	51	52		
Operating profit	13	19		
Operating margin	4.8%	6.6%		11%
Exceptional costs	0	12		
Net financing costs	0	0		
Profit before tax	13	7		86%

Commentary:

- Revenue from new and redesigned bicycle models grew by 200% in 20X5.
- PBT has improved by 86%.
- Operating margin has fallen by a small 1.8%.

Notes.

1 Administrative expenses include the income from a two-year government grant of $5m pa (in 20X5 and 20X4) relating to Zoam.
2 Revenue includes revenue from the Zoam (new electrical bicycle) ($25m in 20X5, $5m in 20X4).
3 Exceptional costs are the costs of developing the new electrical bicycle.

Exhibit 5: Appendix 2

External business environment at Fiag (August 20X5): Extract of report by A Consultant

Political environment

- The government of Beeland has recently provided tax allowances to citizens who use a bicycle to commute to work.
- It has also supported cycling by building many new dedicated cycle-paths.

Economic environment

- Beeland has seen steady economic growth for the last 20 years and this wealth has spread through all parts of society.
- The introduction of significant import tariffs has surprised many businesses such as Fiag, who import raw materials or sub-components for final assembly.

Socio-cultural environment

- Having a healthy lifestyle has become an increasingly popular aspiration for the people of Beeland.
- The population of Beeland is ageing with increasing numbers of retired people.

Technological environment

- Cheap, new materials are enabling lighter bicycles to be built without compromising their strength.
- Battery technology has rapidly advanced so that it is feasible to fit lightweight electrical power units to bicycles.

43 Merkland Sportswear (June 2015, amended) (98 mins)

Write a report to the board of MS to respond to the CEO's instructions for work on the following areas:

(a) Assessment of the existing dashboard metrics; your suggested improvements to them

Note. You should ignore the impact of the Nush scandal in this part of the question. **(16 marks)**

(b) The impact of Response 1 on performance management at MS **(8 marks)**

(c) The impact of the new factory on the values and choice of metrics in the existing dashboard **(10 marks)**

(d) The implications of using the value chain for performance management **(6 marks)**

Professional marks will be awarded for the demonstration of skill in communication, analysis and evaluation, scepticism and commercial acumen in your answer. **(10 marks)**

(Total = 50 marks)

Exhibit 1: Company information, mission and business aims

Merkland Sportswear (MS) is the market leader in sportswear in Ceeland, selling a variety of sportswear products under its own well-known brand. It is primarily a product development and marketing business as it contracts out all of its manufacturing to third parties around the world and it mostly sells its products through third-party retailers. It has only one store which is located in the capital city of Ceeland. The purpose of this store is to act as a centre for its marketing activities and to be a tangible representation of the MS brand. However, the main marketing activity for MS is the recruitment and promotion of star sportsmen and women as MS brand ambassadors. MS tries to have the most well-known sports star in each of the ten most popular sports in Ceeland as an ambassador.

You are a performance management adviser to MS, brought into the company by the chief executive officer (CEO) to help the board with a number of issues.

Exhibit 2: Performance dashboard

The first area in which the board of MS requires your input is in a review of the existing performance dashboard for MS, and you have been given a copy of the dashboard (Appendix 1). The dashboard is deliberately kept focused as it is for board use and the CEO has indicated that the three performance headings of 'financial, design and brand' will be kept at this time. The board has accepted that there may need to be up to two metrics for each of 'brand' and 'design' but they want to keep the number of financial metrics at three.

The mission statement of the business is designed to be broadly appealing. It is 'to inspire Ceelanders to compete'. From a business perspective, the aims are more focused; MS aims to grow as a business and to maximise shareholder wealth. The CEO further clarified the broad strategy to achieve these aims saying, 'We want to inspire competition not just in our customers but also within the company, to seek our greatest competitive advantage. We will achieve this by creating innovative products which provide reduced risk of injury and enhanced sporting performance supported by the best marketing operation in Ceeland.'

Exhibit 3: Review of competitive position

In order to assist in providing more detailed strategies to achieve the company's aims, the board has instituted a review of the competitive position of MS by commissioning a SWOT analysis, and you have also been given a copy of this (Appendix 2).

The CEO wants to you assess the existing dashboard metrics (Appendix 1) and then use the SWOT analysis to suggest improvements to the dashboard metrics within the constraints the CEO has outlined.

Exhibit 4: Child labour scandal

You have been given details on a recent new development in the market.

Nush Sportswear, one of the major competitors of MS, has recently suffered a scandal which has been widely reported. An investigative reporter discovered that one of the suppliers who manufactured sports shoes for Nush had been using child labour. The country in which the manufacturer worked had rules prohibiting child labour, but enforcement of these rules was very weak. This story has been widely covered in the media and has led to consumer boycotts and a review by the Ceeland business regulator into Nush's sourcing policies. It has been discovered that this is common practice in the sports footwear business where manufacturing is outsourced to such countries.

Potential responses to the child labour scandal

MS's shareholders have reacted with alarm to the potential damage that this could do to MS's brand. They have asked the board to consider changing their policy of outsourcing footwear manufacture.

The board is considering two alternative responses:

(1) Review and ensure that all outsourced footwear manufacture complies with appropriate employment terms and conditions (where necessary manufacturing would move to third-party companies in countries with appropriate regulation and enforcement); or

(2) Create a manufacturing operation for MS in order to have full control of operations.

In Response 1, the review of existing third-party manufacturers is being performed by a team from the Procurement Department. They have also considered the impact of moving all footwear sourcing to more strictly regulated environments. The results of this investigation are given in Appendix 3.

The CEO has asked you to assess the qualitative and quantitative impact of this response on performance management at MS, using the data in Appendix 3.

In Response 2, the board is considering setting up a factory for the manufacture of all MS footwear, but it wants to understand the impact of this on MS's existing performance metrics.

This has prompted the CEO to give you some further tasks.

Exhibit 5: Impact of the new factory on dashboard metrics

The board also wants to know how the new factory will impact on the existing performance dashboard. The CEO wants you to use an estimate of $103m profit before interest and tax from the new factory to evaluate the impact of the new factory on the dashboard. (This estimate is before product development and marketing costs as it only represents the manufacturing operation at the factory.) Also, $36m will be required to invest in new buildings, and $11m in working capital.

The CEO wants you, using 20X5 figures as a base, to evaluate the impact of the new factory on the values and choice of metrics in the existing dashboard.

Exhibit 6: Value chain

The consultant who prepared the SWOT analysis has mentioned to the board that if it is thinking of reviewing its existing strategies, then it should consider using the value chain to secure competitive advantage.

The CEO would like an explanation of the implications of using the value chain for performance management at MS. (An outline of the value chain is given in Appendix 4.)

Exhibit 7: Appendix 1

MS performance dashboard

REPORT FOR THE YEAR TO MARCH 20X5

	20X5	*20X4*	*20X3*	*Change 20X5/20X4*
Financial				%
Revenue ($m)	273	238	209	14.7
Operating profit ($m)	71	60	54	18.3
ROCE (%)	41.7	37.5	36.0	11.2
Design				
Design awards won	2	2	1	0.0
Brand				
Awareness (%)	64	63	59	1.6

Note. Design awards are national clothing design awards which address both the look of and technology in a product. Brand awareness is the percentage of those sampled who could identify the company's logo and can name at least one of its products.

Exhibit 8: Appendix 2

SWOT (completed before the Nush scandal was reported)

S:	W:
• High market share • Excellent brand awareness • Strong revenue growth (compared to industry average of 11%) • Supply chain management	• Loss of a key brand ambassador (who was injured when tripping over the laces of their MS boots) • Weak IT expertise
O:	T:
• New products in the market for new sports (such as those being introduced at each World Championships)	• Growth of social media as main marketing channel

Exhibit 9: Appendix 3

Procurement review of new outsourced footwear manufacturers

Currently, MS buys two million pairs of shoes at an average of $21 per unit (a pair of shoes) and we assume an average selling price of $75. Cost per unit will increase by 10%. Additionally, there will be a need to perform annual audits of these suppliers which will cost $0.5m.

The change of policy will be marketed as sustaining the values of MS. The MS ethics code states 'we will play fair and source our goods responsibly'. This marketing will cost $0.8m p.a. but it is hoped that this will produce a gain in market share. However, the increase in sales cannot be estimated at this time as competitors are making similar moves. The reviewer commented, 'It would be helpful to know how many units we would need to sell in order to cover these increased costs so this can be used as a marketing target.'

Exhibit 10: Appendix 5

Value chain analysis

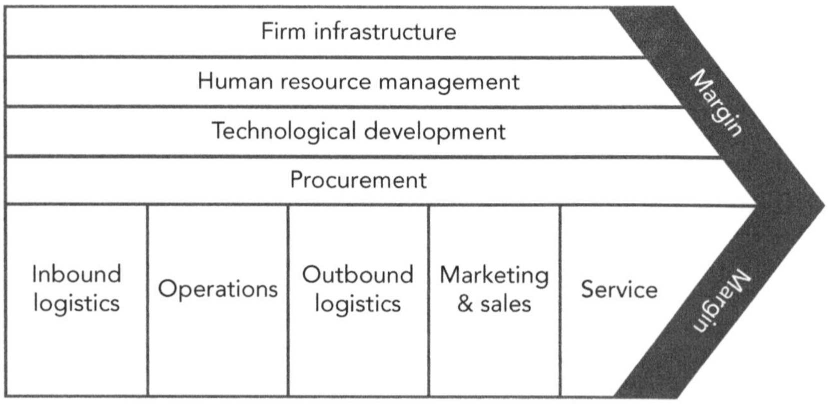

44 Flack (Mar/Jun 2016, amended) (98 mins)

Write a report to the board of Flack, in response to the CEO's instructions for work on the following areas:

(a) Evaluation of Flack's performance report **(14 marks)**

(b) Evaluation of the new performance measures (revenue and operating profit per square metre) **(9 marks)**

(c) Changing the divisional performance measure **(9 marks)**

(d) The use of data analysis **(8 marks)**

Professional marks will be awarded for the demonstration of skill in communication, analysis and evaluation, scepticism and commercial acumen in your answer. **(10 marks)**

(Total = 50 marks)

Exhibit 1: Company information and mission

Flack Supermarkets (Flack) is a multinational listed business operating in several developing countries. The business is divided into two divisions: Metro, which runs smaller stores in the densely populated centres of cities, and Hyper, which runs the large supermarkets situated on the edges of cities. Flack sells food, clothing and some other household goods.

Competition between supermarkets is intense in all of Flack's markets and so there is a constant need to review and improve their management and operations.

Flack mission is to be: 'the first choice for customers by providing the right balance of quality and service at a competitive price. We will achieve this through acting in the long-term interests of our stakeholders: earning customer loyalty, utilising all our resources and serving our shareholders' interests.'

Exhibit 2: Performance report

You are a performance management expert working for Flack, and the chief executive officer (CEO) wants your views on the company's performance report and whether it is fit for the purpose of achieving the company's mission. The CEO has provided you with a copy of the company's most recent report as an example (Appendix 1).

This report is used at Flack's board level for the annual review of the company's performance. The divisional boards have their own reports.

The CEO has mentioned to you that there has been criticism of the board of Flack in the financial press, saying that the board is 'short-termist'.

Therefore, the CEO has asked you to evaluate the performance report to see if it is fit for the purpose of achieving the company's mission. However, the CEO also wants your evaluation of the performance report to include comments in relation to the criticism that the board is short-termist.

Exhibit 3: Performance measures

The board is considering introducing two new performance measures to address the objective of 'utilising all our resources'. These are revenue per square metre, and operating profit per square metre.

The CEO wants an evaluation of these two measures, explaining: how they might address the objective, what those ratios currently are, and how they could be used to manage business performance. The CEO told you that the information in the board report (Appendix 1) will assist in this work.

There have been disagreements between Flack's divisional management about capital allocation. The divisions have had capital made available to them. Both sets of divisional managers always seem to want more capital in order to open more stores but historically have been reluctant to invest in refurbishing existing stores. The board is unsure of capital spending priorities given that the press comments about Flack included criticism of the 'run-down' look of a number of its stores.

The CEO has asked you to assess the effectiveness of the current divisional performance measure of divisional operating profit and the possibility of replacing this with residual income, in the light of these problems. The CEO has told you that you are not required to calculate the current values.

Exhibit 4: Information system

The CEO has proposed to the board that better data analysis could help to improve the businesses sales. The company already has a loyalty card programme with a data warehouse collecting information from customers' cards regarding their purchases, but currently the programme is only used to identify customers preferences so that targeted marketing messages can be sent to them. The CEO believes that greater analysis of this data could help the business improve sales.

The CEO has asked you to include in your report an explanation of data analysis, including descriptive, diagnostic and predictive data analysis, and explain how using these techniques on the data from the loyalty card programme could help to improve sales.

Exhibit 5: Appendix 1

Board's performance report

FLACK YEAR TO 31 MARCH

	Metro budget 20X6	Metro actual 20X6	Hyper budget 20X6	Hyper actual 20X6	Flack budget 20X6	Flack actual 20X6	Flack actual 20X5	Change on PY
	$'000	$'000	$'000	$'000	$'000	$'000	$'000	
Revenue								
Food	1,039,521	1,104,567	5,421,277	5,542,119	6,524,798	6,646,686	6,513,752	2.04%
Clothes	765,465	773,197	3,801,894	3,879,483	4,567,359	4,652,680	4,536,363	2.56%
Other goods	328,056	331,370	1,629,383	1,662,636	1,957,439	1,994,006	1,964,096	1.52%
Total	2,187,042	2,209,134	10,862,554	11,084,238	13,049,596	13,293,372	13,014,211	2.15%
Cost of sales	1,994,583	2,014,750	10,199,936	10,408,099	12,194,520	12,422,829	12,186,796	1.94%
Gross profit	192,459	194,404	662,617	676,139	855,076	870,543	827,415	5.21%
Other operating costs	34,993	35,346	173,801	177,348	208,794	212,694	208,227	
Operating profit	157,466	159,058	488,816	498,791	646,282	657,849	619,188	6.24%
Operating margins		7.20%		4.50%		4.59%		
Finance costs					76,993	79,760	75,482	
Group profit before tax					569,289	578,089	543,706	6.32%
Tax					142,322	144,522	135,926	
Group profit after tax					426,967	433,567	407,780	6.32%
Total shareholder return						3.1%	2.7%	
Return on capital employed	13.2%	13.3%	13.2%	13.5%	13.2%	13.4%	13.2%	

	Metro budget 20X6	Metro actual 20X6	Hyper budget 20X6	Hyper actual 20X6	Flack budget 20X6	Flack actual 20X6	Flack actual 20X5	Change on PY
	$'000	$'000	$'000	$'000	$'000	$'000	$'000	
Number of stores			533		208			
Total square metres			161,227		841,967			

45 Monza Pharma (Sept/Dec 2016 amended) (98 mins)

Write a report to the board of Monza to respond to the CEO's instructions for work on the following areas:

(a) The problems of using a balanced scorecard **(7 marks)**

(b) The performance measures currently used, and those proposed by the consulting firm **(12 marks)**

(c) The different measures of return on investment **(11 marks)**

(d) The quality costs in the Manufacturing Division and the impact of implementing TQM **(10 marks)**

Professional marks will be awarded for the demonstration of skill in communication, analysis and evaluation, scepticism and commercial acumen in your answer. **(10 marks)**

(Total = 50 marks)

Exhibit 1: Company information and objectives

Monza Pharma (Monza) is a developer and manufacturer of medical drugs, based in Beeland but selling its products all over the world. As a listed company, the overall objective of the company is to maximise the return to shareholders and it has used return on capital employed (ROCE) as its performance measure for this objective. There has often been comment at board meetings that it is good to have one easily understood measure for consideration.

The company has three divisions:

- The Drug Development Division develops new drug compounds, taking these through the regulatory systems of different countries until they are approved for sale;
- The Manufacturing Division then makes these compounds; and
- The Sales Division then sells them.

Exhibit 2: Balanced scorecard

Monza's share price has underperformed compared to the market and the health sector in the last two years. The chief executive officer (CEO) has identified that its current performance measures are too narrow and is implementing a balanced scorecard (BSC) approach to address this problem. The current performance measures are:

- ROCE
- Average cost to develop a new drug
- Revenue growth

The CEO engaged a well-known consulting firm which recommended the use of a BSC. The consultants began by agreeing with the board of Monza that the objective for the organisation's medium-term strategy was as follows:

- Create shareholder value by:
  - Innovating in drug development

- Efficiency in drug manufacturing
- Success in selling their products

The consulting firm has presented an interim report with the following proposed performance measures:

- Financial: ROCE
- Customer: Revenue growth
- Internal business process: Average cost to develop a new drug
- Learning and growth: Training days provided for employees each year

The CEO and the lead consultant have had a disagreement about the quality and cost of this work and as a result the consultants have been dismissed. The CEO has commented that the proposed measures lack insight into the business and do not appear to tackle issues at strategic, tactical and operational levels.

The CEO has decided to take this work in-house and has asked you as the performance management expert in the Finance Department to assist him by writing a report to the board to cover a number of areas.

Exhibit 3: Balanced scorecard and performance measures

Following the disagreement with the consultants, the CEO is worried that the consultants may not have been clear about the problems of using the BSC in their rush to persuade Monza to use their services.

Therefore, the CEO would like you to assess the problems of using a balanced scorecard at Monza.

The CEO also wants you to evaluate the choice of performance measures currently used by Monza, and those proposed by the consulting firm.

Exhibit 4: ROCE calculations

There has been a debate at board level about how ROCE should be calculated. The marketing director stated that they were not sure what profit figure (of which at least four were available) should be used and why, especially given the large variation in results which this gives. They also wondered what the effect would be of using equity rather than all capital to calculate a return on investment.

You have been provided with some basic data (Appendix 1) to assist you in quantifying and evaluating these possibilities.

The CEO has asked you to evaluate the effect of choosing different profit and capital measurements for different measures of return on investment, and to recommend a suitable approach for Monza.

Exhibit 5: Total quality management

In addition to these concerns about performance measurement, the board is considering introducing a total quality management approach within Monza. Quality of output is critical in such a heavily regulated industry where the products can be a matter of life and death. There has been discussion about testing this idea within the Manufacturing Division. However, first, the CEO wants to understand, the costs associated with quality issues within that division. To help you with the work required, they have supplied some detailed information in Appendix 2.

The board also requires an outline evaluation of how a total quality management (TQM) approach would fit within the Manufacturing Division.

The CEO has summarised the work you are required to do here: 'Analyse the current quality costs in the Manufacturing Division, and then briefly discuss how implementing TQM would affect the division.'

Exhibit 6: Appendix 1

Financial data for Monza for the most recent accounting period

	$m
Revenue	8,001
Costs	2,460
Gross profit	5,541
Other costs	3,248
Restructuring costs	482
Operating profit	1,811
Finance costs	266
Profit before tax	1,545
Tax	419
Profit after tax	1,126
Capital structure from the statement of financial position	
Shareholders' equity	1,161
Long-term debt	8,739

Note. Restructuring costs relate to a major project which completed during the period.

Exhibit 7: Appendix 2

Cost information for the Manufacturing Division for the most recent accounting period

(1) Batches rejected at factory valued at $17m which have a scrap value of $4m

(2) Training of factory staff which cost $8m

(3) Regulatory fines costing $5m (due to drug compounds being outside the specified range of mix of chemical ingredients)

(4) Discounts given following customer complaints due to late delivery costing $22m

(5) Factory product testing department cost $12m

(6) Cost of raw materials was $1,008m

46 Dargeboard Services (Mar/Jun 2017 amended) (98 mins)

Write a report to the board of Dargeboard Services (DS) in response to the CEO's instructions in for work on the following areas:

(a) The links between the key performance indicators (KPIs) at DS and its mission **(8 marks)**

(b) The assumptions and definitions used in the calculation of the KPIs **(12 marks)**

(c) DS's performance dashboard compared to best practice **(8 marks)**

(d) The building block model **(4 marks)**

(e) Assessment of the two reward schemes **(8 marks)**

Professional marks will be awarded for the demonstration of skill in communication, analysis and evaluation, scepticism and commercial acumen in your answer. **(10 marks)**

(Total = 50 marks)

Exhibit 1: Company information and mission

Dargeboard Services (DS), a listed company, provides facilities management (FM) services where it manages such activities as cleaning, security, catering and building services on behalf of its clients. Clients can outsource to DS a single activity or often outsource all of these aspects in a full service contract.

The mission of DS is 'to give the shareholders maintainable, profitable growth by developing the best talent to provide world-class services with maximum efficiency'.

Exhibit 2: Systems review

The board have asked the chief executive officer (CEO) to review the effectiveness of Dargeboard's systems for performance measurement and management. They have turned to you to begin this process by considering the strategic performance dashboard of DS. They have supplied the most recent example in Appendix 1.

They have tasked you with aiding them in writing a report to the board which will cover some key aspects of strategic performance reporting at DS.

The first thing the CEO wants you to do is to evaluate the links between the current key performance indicators (KPIs) at DS (as shown in Appendix 1) and its mission, and therefore how well the KPIs measure the achievement of the mission. The CEO has asked you to do this by showing how each KPI links to all or part of the mission. However, they have told you that they do not want suggestions of new indicators.

Next, the CEO has asked you to look at each of the current set of indicators in turn, and to examine the assumptions underlying the calculation of those indicators, as shown in Appendix 1. There has been a suggestion made in the press that DS is producing a biased set of results aimed to mislead the markets. This would then artificially boost the share price and so boost the value of the senior management's share holdings. As a result, the CEO wants you to assess the assumptions and definitions used in the calculation of the indicators.

Third, the CEO has asked you to evaluate the other presentational aspects of Dargeboard's strategic performance dashboard against best practice.

Exhibit 3: Reward and remuneration schemes

The idea of employee share ownership has always been at the heart of DS's remuneration schemes. Its aim is to support an entrepreneurial culture and is a key differentiator in the market for new employees. The current reward system grants shares based on the appraisal of the individual by the line manager against vague categories such as leadership and entrepreneurship. The results of this scheme have been that only about 5% of staff received their maximum possible bonus in previous years and half of them received no bonus at all. Increasingly, this has led to the staff ignoring the reward scheme and describing it as 'only for the bosses' favourite people'.

In response to this, the board have been discussing methods of analysing and improving the rewards system at DS. One non-executive director suggested using Fitzgerald and Moon's building block model. The CEO was asked to consider this as a project separate from the issues of performance measurement mentioned above.

The CEO will select suitable indicators from the dimensions but has asked you to explain to the board what is meant by results and determinants in this context, and how the dimensions link to standards and targets.

Finally, the CEO believes that there are two types of reward scheme which might suit DS, and she they have provided you with details of the schemes (Appendix 2). The CEO would like an assessment of the relative strengths and weaknesses of the two reward schemes.

Exhibit 4: Appendix 1

Dargeboard Services: Strategic performance dashboard Year to 31 December 20X6

	Cleaning	*Security*	*Catering*	*Building services*	*Full service*	*Total*	*Total 20X5*
Operating profit margin	6.5%	6.4%	6.5%	4.9%	5.9%	5.9%	5.8%
Secured revenue	76%	85%	92%	88%	93%	88%	87%
Management retention	86%	74%	87%	82%	89%	85%	87%
Order book ($m)	1,160	875	357	1,553	3,359	7,304	6,807
Organic revenue growth	7.1%	4.3%	5.0%	8.1%	7.9%	7.2%	4.6%
ROCE						17.2%	16%

KPI definitions and notes

Notes.

1 Cleaning, security, catering and building services headings are for single service contracts.

2 No commentary is provided as the CEO talks the board through the dashboard at each board meeting.

3 Secured revenue is long-term recurring revenue. This is the percentage of budgeted revenue which is already contracted. The budget is often not completed until well into the year as it is a complex process. In 20X6, the original budget showed revenue of $1,565m with the final budget signed off at the end of Q1 showing $1,460m. The secured (contracted) revenue for the period was $1,285m. The accounts show a year end revenue of $1,542m.

4 Management retention is the percentage of managers who were still employed throughout the whole year. The figure only includes those employees on full-time contracts (about 65% of all managers).

5 Order book is the total cash value of future contracted revenue. DS has contracts which run up to 10 years into the future.

6 Operating profit margin. This excludes exceptional items such as the reorganisation of the catering business which cost $55m in 20X6, where revenue was $245m.

7 Organic revenue growth is calculated by using the total revenue figure as reported in the accounts. It includes net acquisitions which brought in revenue of $48m in 20X6.

8 Return on capital employed (ROCE). Capital employed is total assets less current liabilities from the statement of financial position.

Exhibit 5: Appendix 2

The CEO is considering two schemes, one based on the current scheme and a new scheme.

Scheme 1 (based on the current scheme)

The reward system grants shares in DS based on the appraisal of the individual by the line manager against vague categories (leadership and entrepreneurship). The line managers have been informed that their bonus will in turn be partly dependent on how well they perform this appraisal. The expectation will be that as a result, 20% of staff will receive their maximum possible bonus and 20% will receive no bonus.

Scheme 2 (the new one)

Under scheme 2, employee targets are to be derived from the strategic indicators depending on the employee's area of responsibility. The senior management (with help from line management where appropriate) will cascade down the strategic indicators to the relevant operational or tactical level for that employee.

There will be five targets set by senior and line management in consultation and the employee will then get up to 50% on top of their basic salary as a bonus (10 percentage points for each of the targets achieved).

47 Thyme Engine Products (Sept/Dec 2017 amended) (98 mins)

Write a report to the CEO of Thyme to respond to their instructions for work on the following areas:

(a) The award-winning dashboard **(13 marks)**

(b) The impact of integrated reporting on the type of information prepared by the company's management accountant **(5 marks)**

(c) The target cost gap for the new engine, and the fit between target costing and the existing TQM approach **(10 marks)**

(d) The costs of quality **(12 marks)**

Professional marks will be awarded for the demonstration of skill in communication, analysis and evaluation, scepticism and commercial acumen in your answer. **(10 marks)**

(Total = 50 marks)

Exhibit 1: Company information and objectives

Thyme Engine Products (Thyme) manufactures jet aircraft engines for the commercial aircraft market. This is a worldwide business although Thyme's production and development are all based in the country of Beeland. Thyme is a listed company and its stated overall objective is to be 'a world-class jet engine manufacturer trusted by our customers to deliver excellent products'. Its promise to its shareholders is that it will maximise their returns. The strategy to achieve this is to use world-class engineering to design engines and high-quality production and customer service in order to drive profitable growth.

Thyme's share price has recently suffered as a result of the failure of a new engine design which led to large cash losses and a difficulty in obtaining new financing. There has also been a bribery scandal involving a senior manager and one of its key customers. As a result, a new chief executive officer (CEO) has been employed and they have begun a major review of systems at Thyme.

Exhibit 2: Performance reporting – dashboard

The first area which the CEO wants to examine is the information given to the board for strategic decision making in both the planning and controlling of the business. The Government of Beeland has been encouraging information sharing between businesses and has recently sponsored awards for management accounting. The winner of the engineering sector has produced a sample dashboard template (with dummy figures) for an annual review and this is given in Appendix 1. The CEO realised that the winner had a very similar overall objective and strategies to Thyme and wants to know what it is about this dashboard that helped it win the award. To this end, they have asked you to evaluate why the dashboard in Appendix 1 was award winning. The CEO does not want a new dashboard for Thyme at this stage, although they think there may be some useful, specific comments to make about the contents of the dashboard given Thyme's recent problems.

Exhibit 3: Integrated reporting

The CEO has also recently been reading about integrated reporting and in the light of this review of the dashboard, the CEO has also asked for you to include a section in your report explaining your views on how integrated reporting might have an impact on the type of information prepared by the company's management accountants.

Exhibit 4: Total quality management

As high-quality engineering products lie at the heart of Thyme's competitive advantage, there has been a total quality management (TQM) approach to the management of all resources and relationships throughout the business. Thyme currently has a project under consideration to develop a new simple jet engine which would compete in the crowded market for small corporate jets. In order to compete in this market, it is believed that a target costing approach to this new engine would be beneficial. You have been given some data about the price and cost of the new engine (Appendix 2).

The CEO wants you to calculate the target cost gap for the new engine using the data you have been given, and then they want you to comment on whether the use of target costing would fit within the existing TQM approach for this new engine.

Exhibit 5: Quality costs

The new engine project has further raised the profile of quality as a broad issue at Thyme and the CEO wants your advice on the costs associated with quality. They need to know the cost of each of the four categories of quality costs. They have gathered data in Appendix 3 for this exercise. They are happy that they have identified that prevention costs are complete, but are worried that some of the possible costs for the other three categories are missing and needs suggestions of cost areas to be examined to identify these missing items. In addition, they want advice on the relative importance to Thyme of each of the four categories. They have summarised the work they require from you as follows: 'I would like you to categorise and calculate the costs of quality, using the data I have given you. I would then like you to suggest cost areas to be examined, and to evaluate the relative importance of each category to Thyme.'

Exhibit 6: Appendix 1

Award winning performance dashboard

Report for the year to June 20X7

				Budget variance	*Growth*	*Budget*
	20X5	*20X6*	*20X7*	*20X7*	*20X6 to 20X7*	*20X8*
Financial						
Revenue ($m)	10,652	11,213	11,500	234 (F)	2.6%	11,776
Operating profit margin	16.2%	16.8%	17.2%	0.2 % points (F)	0.4 % points	17.2%
EVA™	746	774	815	48 (F)	5.3%	803
Total shareholder return	6.5%	6.8%	11.1%	4.5 % points (F)	4.3 % points	7.5%
Design						
Class leading products in:						
Fuel efficiency	3	3	3	0		3
Noise levels	2	2	3	1 (F)		3
Chemical emissions	1	2	3	1 (F)		3
Manufacturing						
% of orders right first time	92.0%	92.4%	93.7%	0.7 % points (F)		93.0%
Delivery						
Deliveries on time	88.0%	89.9%	88.2%	0.2 % points (F)		88.0%
Market share						
(As % of market leader)	33.0%	35.2%	38.1%	1.1 % points (F)		39.0%

Commentary:

- The revenue growth of the business remains strong above the average growth for the sector of 1.5%.
- EVA™ is positive and growing indicating increased shareholder wealth.
- Healthy and continuing growth in market share reflects an increased number of class-leading products and improvements in 'right on time' service to customers.
- There have been no major new business risks arising during the period while market volume growth continues as expected.

Exhibit 7: Appendix 2

New jet engine

		$'000/engine
Competitor price		2,500
Raw materials		200
Subcomponents bought in		600
Skilled labour		625
General labour		125
Production overheads		275
Planned profit margin	15%	

Notes.

1 Design and development has cost $120m and the engine is expected to sell approximately 1,200 units over its lifetime.

2 Sales and marketing costs are expected to be approximately 20% of the selling price.

3 The planned selling price is expected to match the competitor's price with the brand reputation of Thyme providing the competitive edge.

Exhibit 8: Appendix 3

Quality costs identified in current year

	$m
Repairs and replacements under customer warranties	223
Customer relationship management – complaint handling	56
Performance testing of final assembly	110
Performance testing of subcomponents from suppliers	28
Costs of re-inspection after repairs arising from final assembly testing	95
Training in quality control	11
Maintenance of inspection equipment	36

Notes.

1 The company spent $92m in the year buying higher quality raw materials to use in manufacture.

2 The company's revenue was $11,500m in the current year.

48 Chiven (Mar/Jun 2018, amended) (98 mins)

Write a report to the board of Chiven to respond to the CEO's instructions for work on the following areas:

(a) Evaluation of the existing measures and presentation in the current performance report **(15 marks)**

(b) The new performance measures you recommend **(8 marks)**

(c) The implications on performance measures and systems of simplifying the supply chain **(7 marks)**

(d) Evaluation of the use of analysis of social media discussions, and the meaning and benefits of sentiment analysis. **(10 marks)**

Professional marks will be awarded for the demonstration of skill in communication, analysis and evaluation, scepticism and commercial acumen in your answer. **(10 marks)**

(Total = 50 marks)

Exhibit 1: Company information and aim

Chiven Stores (Chiven) is a listed clothing retailer in Beeland. Its overall aim is 'to become the largest clothing retailer in Beeland and deliver exceptional value to its shareholders'. It has recently dropped down the clothing retailer rankings from fourth to fifth largest. Shareholders have expressed concern at the lack of dividend growth at a time when spending in the Beeland clothing market has been growing.

Exhibit 2: Performance reporting

There has been a recent change of chief executive officer (CEO) and the new CEO has identified that the performance reporting at Chiven is not fit for the needs of the business. They have asked you to prepare a report to the board to address the performance measurement and management issues which they see as most important. Their plan is to achieve the overall aim by 'maximising our opportunities from new technology and increasing our currently small web presence'. They want a detailed evaluation of the current performance report which is used by the board for its annual review of the business (Appendix 1). However, they want this overall task split into two separate parts in your report, with the first being an evaluation of the existing set of measures and their presentation. In relation to this, the CEO has stated that the current performance report does not need a commentary though, as they and the finance director talk through the report in detail with the board.

For the second part of the task, the CEO wants you – using the data in Appendix 1 – to recommend, and justify, three new measures which you believe address key issues for the business but are not currently on the report. The CEO also wants you to include appropriate calculations for each of the measures you recommend.

Exhibit 3: Business integration and supply chain

In an additional effort to drive improvement and gain competitive advantage for Chiven, the board has decided to use the value chain as a business integration tool. The CEO has provided a copy of the value chain diagram which was discussed at the last board meeting (Appendix 2). They believe that further improvements in Chiven's performance can be achieved through simplification of the supply chain. The CEO believes that this has implications for the performance measurement and information systems at Chiven and wants your report to address this as well. They have asked you to advise on appropriate performance measures and systems for Chiven when using the value chain approach to simplify the supply chain.

Exhibit 4: Data analysis

Finally, the CEO believes that Chiven should make use of state-of-the-art data analytics to get more feedback about what customers and potential customers really think about Chiven's products. They have heard that many businesses now analyse discussions on social media about their products and services. They have also heard that many use 'sentiment analysis' as a tool to analyse these conversations. The CEO thinks that the board should be briefed about these two developments.

The CEO needs you to include a section in your report for the board which evaluates the use of analysis of discussions on social media and explains the meaning and benefits of sentiment analysis.

Exhibit 5: Appendix 1

Chiven Stores

Annual performance report for year ended March 20X8

								20X8	20X7
Revenue ($m)			*Region*	*A*	*B*	*C*	*Total*	*Total*	*Total*
	Clothing								
		Men's		178	356	178	712		
		Women's		297	593	297	1,187		
		Children's		119	237	119	475		
			Total	594	1,186	594		2,374	2,351
	Other								
		Men's		19	39	19	77		
		Women's		32	65	32	129		
		Children's		13	26	13	52		
			Total	64	130	64		258	255
							Total	2,632	2,606

								20X8	20X7
Operating profit margin ($m)			*Region*	*A*	*B*	*C*	*Total*	*Total*	*Total*
	Clothing								
		Men's		15.5	15.7	15.2			
		Women's		16.2	16.3	15.9			
		Children's		18.1	18.3	18.0			
	Other								
		Men's		15.5	15.8	15.2			
		Women's		16.2	16.4	15.8			
		Children's		18.1	18.2	17.8			
							Overall	16.5	16.5

	20X8	*20X7*
Number of stores	542	540
EPS ($)	0.56	0.56
Dividend per share ($)	0.28	0.28
EVA™ ($m)	21	24

	20X8	20X7
Inventory turnover rate (days)	32	32
Average number of product line bought per supplier	66	64
Floor space (square meters)	850,000	828,00
Market share (%)	9.8	10.1
Number of employees	40,500	39,400
Number of suppliers	161	161
ROCE (%)	8.3	8.5
Number of accidents in stores	256	255
Average queuing time for customers (seconds)	125	128
WACC (%)	5.8	5.7
Average time between customer entry and employee greeting (seconds)	248	232
Inventory obsolescence/loss write-downs ($m)	25	25

Exhibit 6: Appendix 2

Value chain diagram

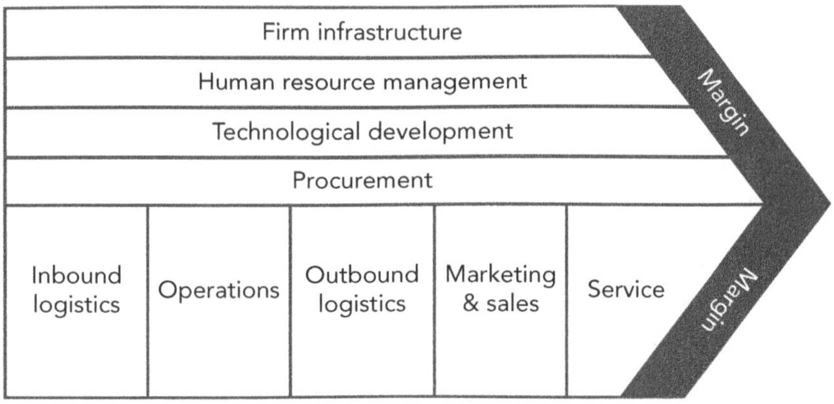

49 Fearties (Sept 2018, amended) (98 mins)

It is now 1 September 20X5.

Write a report to the CEO of Fearties in response to their instructions for work in the following areas:

(a) Key performance indicators (KPIs) and the balanced scorecard **(22 marks)**

(b) Non-financial performance indicators (NFPIs) **(8 marks)**

(c) The management style at Fearties **(10 marks)**

Professional marks will be awarded for the demonstration of skill in communication, analysis and evaluation, scepticism and commercial acumen in your answer. **(10 marks)**

(Total = 50 marks)

Exhibit 1: Company background

Fearties Security (Fearties) is a business, owned and run by the Feartie family, which provides security personnel for other businesses (eg factory guards and security staff at large public events, for example, music concerts). The business has grown along with the market for outsourcing of security personnel roles and Fearties is one of the largest of such service providers in Beeland.

The Feartie family has always managed the business to increase profits without excessive risk-taking. Most of the family are financially dependent on the business through their pay and dividends. The founder of the business was an accountant and it has become a family tradition that the chief executive officer (CEO) would always have an accounting background. As a result, the performance reporting has always focused on financial results.

Exhibit 2: Recent events

A new generation of the family has risen to power with a goal of increasing growth by expanding Fearties' operations into different countries, using its existing reputation for reliability. The newly appointed CEO has recognised that the choice of key performance indicators (KPIs) may not be suited to the current business environment, where the company is facing various issues:

- Changing government regulation with most customer-facing Fearties staff now required to hold a certificate showing they are aware of the relevant laws and health and safety procedures regarding their duties. Indeed, this factor is a reason for the growth of outsourcing to Fearties;
- Difficulty in recruitment and retention as the pay for customer-facing staff is low by Beeland's standards (even though Fearties provides full training for them); and
- Legal difficulties arising from claims of Fearties staff being too aggressive in the pursuit of their duties.

The CEO has asked you to prepare a report to the board on several performance management matters for Fearties.

Exhibit 3: KPIs and balanced scorecard

The CEO is considering the introduction of a balanced scorecard approach and wants you to perform an evaluation of whether the existing key performance indicators cover the financial perspective for the board. They have provided you with a draft copy of the most recent board report to illustrate current reporting (Appendix 1) and other financial information (Appendix 2). This draft has been prepared quickly by a junior accountant and the CEO believes that there is an error in the return on capital employed calculation which you should correct.

They then require reasoned recommendations for two indicators within each of the remaining three perspectives (customer, internal business process and innovation and learning). These indicators should address the issues facing the business.

Exhibit 4: Non-financial performance indicators

In the past, the board has resisted the introduction of customer surveys due to worries about the ability to measure performance using this method. The CEO is aware that many of the new indicators from the introduction of the balanced scorecard are likely to be non-financial. Therefore, they have asked that you evaluate for the board the problems associated with measuring and managing performance using non-financial performance indicators (NFPIs) at Fearties, using customer surveys as an illustration.

Exhibit 5: Management style

Given these changes, there may have to be changes to the management style at Fearties. Therefore, the CEO also wants your assessment of the existing management style at Fearties and provide a justified recommendation for an appropriate approach. They have been taught about Hopwood's styles of using budget information (budget-constrained, profit-conscious, non-accounting) and so wants a brief definition of these prior to your assessment and recommendation.

Exhibit 6: Appendix 1 Key performance indicators

	20X5	20X4
	$m	$m
Revenue	686	659
Operating profit	36	34
Cash flow from operating activities	64	64
Dividends paid	14	13
Return on capital employed	21.1%	20.4%

Exhibit 7: Appendix 2 – Other information:

Fearties Security

Year ended 30 June 20X5

Profit information

	20X5	20X4
	$m	$m
Revenue	686	659
Operating profit	36	34
Profit after tax	20	19
Assets and liabilities		
Non-current assets	54	51
Current assets	213	211
Current liabilities	151	148
Non-current liabilities	21	21
Net assets	95	93
Equity	95	93

Dividend history

	$m
20X5	14
20X6	13
20X4	13
20X3	13
20X2	11
20X1	10

50 Rezillos (December 2018 amended) (98 mins)

It is now 1 December 20X8.

Write a report to the board of Rezillos to respond to the CEO's instructions for work on the following areas:

(a) Evaluation of the performance reporting system used at board level **(12 marks)**

(b) Assessment of the analysts' criticisms of the customer survey results **(9 marks)**

(a) Evaluation of the usefulness of the type of benchmarking proposed **(5 marks)**

(ii) Completion of the benchmarking exercise, and commentary on it **(14 marks)**

Professional marks will be awarded for the demonstration of skill in communication, analysis and evaluation, scepticism and commercial acumen in your answer. **(10 marks)**

(Total = 50 marks)

Exhibit 1: Company information

Rezillos Engineering (Rezillos) is a listed company, manufacturing pumps and valves for use in the chemical industries. These highly engineered components must be integrated into Rezillos' customers' own plant and equipment. The company has grown significantly via acquisition in the last 20 years to become a worldwide business.

The overall objective of the company is 'to deliver sustainable growth in value to the shareholders by working in partnership with customers to deliver innovative and value-for-money solutions utilising the skills of the highly-trained workforce'.

The chief executive officer (CEO) has recognised that the company has been so focused on making acquisitions that it has not improved other aspects of management. They have asked you to produce a report for the board of Rezillos to cover a number of areas.

Performance reporting system

The CEO would like an evaluation of the performance reporting system used at the strategic board level by Rezillos. The current performance report used for the annual review at board meetings is given as an example (Appendix 1).

Exhibit 2: Customer survey

At the most recent round of meetings with stock market analysts, the board has been criticised about a customer survey whose results were announced at these meetings. The criticisms centred on the method of calculation, sampling and the disclosures in the press release. The board of Rezillos is concerned by the impact of this on their reputation in the market and needs to understand whether the criticism is justified. The press release and some further internal details about the method and the results of the customer survey are given in Appendix 2. The CEO wants you to assess the analysts' criticism of the customer survey results.

Exhibit 3: Benchmarking proposal

Rezillos has three divisions based in its three countries of operation (Beeland, Teeland and Veeland). In order to drive forward the integration of the divisions, the CEO has decided that they should be benchmarked against each other. However, they are aware that this is not the only method of benchmarking. Therefore, initially, they want you to evaluate the usefulness of the proposed type of benchmarking for the divisions.

Finally, the CEO has supplied the data in Appendix 3 and has asked you to complete the benchmarking exercise and to comment on the metrics used and the results.

Exhibit 4: Appendix 1

Rezillos

	Year to 30 September							
	Beeland	*Teeland*	*Veeland*	*Total*	*Total*	*Growth*	*Profit as a % of revenue*	
	20X8	*20X8*	*20X8*	*20X8*	*20X7*		*Company*	*Industry average*
	$m	*$m*	*$m*	*$m*	*$m*			
Revenue	738	2,030	923	3,691	3,504	5.34%		
Cost of sales	497	1,391	601	2,489	2,363			
Gross profit	241	639	322	1,202	1,141		32.6%	29.8%
Other operating costs								
Selling and distribution costs	89	208	101	398	380			
Administration costs (note 1)	74	171	83	328	321			
Total	163	379	184	726	701			
Operating profit	78	260	138	476	440	8.18%	12.9%	9.7%
Finance costs				88	88			
Group profit before tax				388	352		10.5%	
Tax				78	71			
Group profit after tax				310	281		8.4%	
Return on capital employed (ROCE)				8.64%				

Note. Administration costs contain an allocation of product development costs to each division.

Exhibit 5: Appendix 2

Press release from Rezillos: Customer survey results

Rezillos has performed an extensive survey of its customer base and is proud to announce an average customer rating of 7.0 (out of 10). This bears positive comparison with a leading competitor of Rezillos who performed a survey last year scoring an average rating of 6.0.

The survey asked for a customer rating on a scale of 0 to 10, where 10 was exceptional, 5 was good and 0 was unacceptable.

End of press release

Extract from Rezillos internal document on calculation of customer rating

The survey was carried out by the staff at head office who sampled customers from all three divisions.

Customer number	*Rating*	*Account size ($m)*	*Division*
1	10	1.5	Beeland
2	9	3.3	Beeland
3	9	2.1	Beeland
4	6	6.4	Beeland
5	6	152.0	Teeland
6	6	11.2	Beeland
7	6	10.5	Beeland
8	6	74.0	Veeland
9	5	21.0	Veeland

Notes.

1 The company has 180 customers in total.

2 The customer number is an identification number for administrative purposes.

3 Each division has its own marketing and customer support function although product development is a head office function.

Exhibit 6: Appendix 3

(All data is for 20X8 unless otherwise stated.)

The benchmarking exercise is partly complete with the metrics needing to be calculated identified by question marks.

	Beeland	*Teeland*	*Veeland*
Benchmarking metrics			
Growth of market	8.5%	3.2%	5.0%
Revenue growth	12.5%	3.2%	4.8%
Operating margin	10.6%	12.8%	15.0%
Inventory days	162	162	?
Order book growth	5.2%	5.3%	?
Number of face-to-face interactions with division's top 10 key customers	260	120	40
Percentage of revenue from new products introduced in the last three years	24.9%	29.0%	?
Reduction in incident rate	3.4%	0.0%	?
Utilisation of learning and development programme	1.20	1.26	?

Notes.

1 The industry standard method of calculating incident rate is:

Incident rate = number of incidents per year × 200,000/number of employee labour hours paid

2 The company's employees work on average 40 hours per week for 50 weeks per year.
3 Utilisation of learning and development programme is measured by the number of training days per employee.
4 Key customers are designated by the divisional management.
5 A single inventory management system has been implemented across the whole company.

The following data has been collected to assist in the completion of the benchmarking exercise:

	Veeland
Revenue from new products introduced in the last three years ($m)	163
Cost of sales ($m)	601
Inventory ($m)	267
Number of incidents (20X8)	68
Number of incidents (20X7)	74
Number of employees (20X8)	6,600
Number of employees (20X7)	6,250
Order book ($m) 20X8	932
Order book ($m) 20X7	885
Number of training days	6,450

51 Folt (March 2019, amended) (98 mins)

It is now 1 September 20X5.

Write a report to the CEO of Folt Manufacturing (Folt) to respond to the instructions for work on the following areas:

(a) Key performance indicators **(15 marks)**

(b) Target costing **(10 marks)**

(c) Quality (conformance) costs **(6 marks)**

(d) Information systems **(9 marks)**

Professional marks will be awarded for the demonstration of skill in communication, analysis and evaluation, scepticism and commercial acumen in your answer. **(10 marks)**

(Total = 50 marks)

Exhibit 1: Company information

Folt Manufacturing (Folt) is a company, which is majority owned by its management team. A number of years ago, it was bought out of a larger multinational business by the management team. The management were supported by a venture capital firm, who provided the remaining equity and now supply all the debt required by the business at market rates. The business manufactures and sells digital imaging devices for use in a variety of industrial situations. A key component in its products is the image processing software which is included. Folt has a small team of software developers who are beginning to gain a reputation for innovative solutions.

Folt has faced increasing pressure in its home market of Beeland, from manufacturers in countries with lower cost bases. As a result, it has decided to invest in developing its image processing software rather than compete on the manufacturing of the hardware (the imaging devices). It will continue to sell the imaging devices but the manufacturing will be outsourced.

Folt's overall objective is unchanged and it is 'to provide an adequate return to its capital providers while growing the business into a world-class supplier in its areas of expertise'. The chief executive officer (CEO) has identified three factors which are critical success factors (CSFs) to achieving this objective. These are:

(1) Keep capital providers satisfied;

(2) Build a world-class software development team; and

(3) Ensure that quality of the imaging devices meets market standards.

Exhibit 2: Performance measurement system

The CEO requires assistance from a performance management expert to create an appropriate performance measurement system for Folt. First, they need recommendations of suitably justified key performance indicators (KPIs) for each CSF. The CEO has indicated that there should be a maximum of two KPIs per CSF in order to avoid information overload. Then, they want an assessment of the use of this group of KPIs to measure the strategic performance of Folt.

Exhibit 3: Outsourced manufacturing: Initial plans

The company has selected a suitable manufacturer for the outsourced work. Xela Manufacturing (Xela) is based in Ceeland, which is a much lower cost environment than Beeland. Folt is preparing to enter into detailed contract negotiations with Xela.

The manufacturing will be done under licence from Folt. This means that Folt supplies the product designs but retains the intellectual rights to them and Xela manufactures to agreed standards of quality. Xela then despatches the devices back to Folt who add the software, package the product and send it to their customers. The quality standards will be set by the service level agreements (SLAs), which will be agreed in the contract.

In preparation for these negotiations, the CEO needs advice on the following three critical areas (target costing, responsibility for quality areas and sources of information) for the negotiation of the agreement.

Exhibit 4: Target costing

The CEO would like a better understanding of the cost structure of the products in order to have a firm basis for price negotiation with Xela. They have heard that target costing could be helpful. Therefore, they need to know how target costing works and how it might be used in this situation. In order to clarify the explanation, they have gathered information (Appendix 1) on one product (Product 123) which requires a redesign before being relaunched into the market. They want an example calculation of the target cost gap and an explanation of how the result of this would impact on negotiations with Xela.

Exhibit 5: Responsibility for quality areas

The maintenance of existing quality is a critical concern for Folt, since it will focus on software as the key selling point, but this will not be sufficient for market success if the hardware does not meet market standards. The CEO wants to understand, in terms of the four areas of quality costs, how responsibility for conformance costs (prevention and appraisal costs) should be treated under the proposed contract between Folt and Xela.

Exhibit 6: Sources of information

Folt has appropriate information systems in place for its existing manufacturing operation. The CEO and board are happy with their operation at present. However, Xela has indicated that its current information systems are purely financial, aiming to collect the required information for its financial reporting duties. The CEO is worried about this and wants an assessment of the impact of this on the management of quality within the contract.

Exhibit 7: Appendix 1

Information on Product 123

The company aims for a profit margin of 20% on Product 123. Target price is $175 per unit, based on sales and marketing department research.

Cost details:

(1) The remaining commercial life of the product is two years.

(2) It is estimated that 250,000 units will be sold over the remaining life of the product.

(3) Materials cost $37 per unit.

(4) Each unit will take 0.5 hours of labour at an average cost of $25 per hour.

(5) Each unit will use 1.1 hours of machine time at an average cost (including overheads) of $32 per hour.

(6) Packaging and delivery will cost $8 per unit.

(7) The design costs of the unit are expected to total $2m.

(8) Inspections cost $100,000 per annum – the redesign will not affect this.

(9) The rate of failed products, either spotted by customers or by the inspection team, is expected to remain at 2.5%.

(10) Failed products will be reworked at an average cost of $20 per unit.

(11) The software package supplied by Folt costs $40 per unit.

52 Arkaig (Sep/Dec 2019, amended) (98 mins)

It is now 1 September 20X5.

Write a report to the chief executive officer (CEO) of Arkaig to respond to their instructions for work on the following areas:

(a) The performance reporting at Arkaig **(10 marks)**

(b) The introduction of economic value added (EVA™) **(15 marks)**

(c) The information requested on the performance hierarchy **(9 marks)**

(d) The value chain analysis prepared by the consultant **(6 marks)**

Professional marks will be awarded for the demonstration of skill in communication, analysis and evaluation, scepticism and commercial acumen in your answer. **(10 marks)**

(Total = 50 marks)

Exhibit 1: Company information

Arkaig Manufacturing (Arkaig) is a world-leading, listed manufacturer of production machinery for other industries. It has customers in the mining, cement and chemicals sectors and seeks to provide them with the equipment, software and service for their products.

The aim of Arkaig is 'to maximise shareholder wealth by providing world-class, tailored automation solutions, which use technology innovatively, show improved machine downtime and reduced energy consumption for our customers.' This is supported by an entrepreneurial culture among all employees who should 'treat the business as if they owned it'.

Exhibit 2: Strategic internal performance reporting

There has been criticism of the business' current performance reporting by one of the directors at a recent board meeting. However, the chief executive officer (CEO) believes that the reporting system, which they put in place two years ago, is an excellent one.

In preparation for the next board meeting, the CEO needs an evaluation of the current report. As an example, a recent report used by the board for its strategic review is given in Appendix 1. The CEO stressed that it was the report and not the performance of the business which should be evaluated.

Exhibit 3: Economic value added

Another criticism of the performance management of Arkaig was that it lacked an over-arching measure of performance. As a result, the CEO is considering the introduction of economic value added (EVA™) to replace return on capital employed (ROCE) as a principal performance measure. The CEO wants to present this idea at the next board meeting and so needs an illustrative calculation of EVA™ along with a brief explanation of its benefits as a replacement for ROCE. The data in Appendix 2 should be used for the calculation.

Exhibit 4: Performance hierarchy

The earlier work requested focuses on the strategic level of the organisation and the CEO is keen to ensure that the other levels of the organisation (tactical and operational) do not get ignored in this discussion. However, before undertaking any specific work, they want to make a presentation at the next board meeting. Therefore, they want you to provide him with a brief description of the nature of the information required for performance measurement at these three different levels and explain how this information is influenced by the extent of planning and controlling activity at each of the levels of the performance hierarchy. They want examples which would be relevant to Arkaig to illustrate these points in order that the presentation is made more concrete for the directors. They will then prepare the slides for the presentation themselves.

Exhibit 5: Value chain

In order to analyse the operational aspects of Arkaig, the CEO has employed a consultant to produce a value chain analysis (Appendix 3). The value chain analysis has highlighted certain critical activities within Arkaig where there was concern about the performance management aspects. The CEO would like you to assess the performance management implications of the consultant's comments on the critical areas identified for Arkaig. An explanation of the value chain is not required.

Exhibit 6: APPENDIX 1

Arkaig: Strategic performance report

	Year ended 30 June 20X5					
	Mining	*Cement*	*Chemicals*	*Total*	*Previous year total*	*Industry average*
	20X5	20X5	20X5	20X5	20X4	
Orders ($m)	5,204	6,898	5,900	18,002	17,878	
Revenue ($m)	5,100	6,756	5,784	17,640	18,166	
Revenue growth (%)	0	–1.8	–6.5	–2.9		
Net profit ($m)	220	350	302	872	798	
Net profit margin (%)	4.3	5.2	5.2	4.9	4.4	4.6
ROCE (%)	16.1	17.3	17.4	16.8	15.7	15

Commentary:

(1) The company has increased its return on capital employed on the previous year and exceeded the industry benchmark.

(2) Revenue has fallen by 2.9% on the previous year but the order book has grown by 0.7%, indicating sustained sales levels going forward.

(3) The net profit margin has increased to 4.9%, again exceeding the industry benchmark of 4.6%.

(4) The company has continued to emphasise its entrepreneurial culture to its employees.

Exhibit 7: APPENDIX 2

Economic value added

The following details have been gathered for the 20X5 EVA™ calculation:

(1) The operating profit of Arkaig was $3,175m. This includes a depreciation charge of $1,780m.

(2) Amortisation charges of $95m in the year have been incurred.

(3) The corporation tax rate is 25%. Tax of $694m was paid in the year.

(4) The company has spent $90m this year and each year for the previous ten years on long–term brand building.

(5) The economic depreciation for the year is estimated to be $1,907m.

(6) This year and each year for the previous ten years, economic depreciation has included a $10m write-down of the value of brand building.

(7) Research and development expenditure of $705m was incurred in the period leading to an economic asset of $4,233m at the year end.

(8) Interest paid in the period was $213m.

(9) Capital employed during the period (from the statement of financial position):

	$m
Opening	19,404
Change in period	977
Closing	20,381

(10) Cost of capital:

Equity	12.0%
Debt (pre-tax)	3.8%

(11) Gearing: 45% debt/(equity + debt)

Exhibit 8: APPENDIX 3

Value chain analysis

Primary activities:

- Inbound logistics (receiving, handling and storing inputs) and outbound logistics (delivering the product to customers) – Warehouse and distribution operations are controlled by an old information system which feeds into operations management information.
- After-sales service – This is an important area of revenue generation for Arkaig. However, certain directors are worried about over-focusing on this activity.

Secondary activities:

- Human resource management – Arkaig aims to recruit, retain and motivate staff who can fit with its entrepreneurial culture.

Note. Other areas of the value chain, not mentioned here, do not require comment.

Answers

1 Stokeness

Workbook reference

Porter's five forces model and risk appetite are both discussed in Chapter 2 of the Workbook.

Top tips

Part (a).

Although this part of the question should offer some relatively easy marks (for analysing the impact the different forces could have on Stokeness), it is important that you realise that the requirement isn't only about the impact of the five forces. You also have to recommend a performance measure for each of the five forces.

This second element of the requirement (recommending new performance measures) requires careful thought. The performance measures need to measure the strength or impact of each of the **five forces** themselves, not primarily different aspects of Stokeness's own performance. So, for example, what would be a suitable measure to indicate the threat of new entrants?

Also, in relation to the first part of the requirement, note that you are asked about the impact of the five forces on **performance management** at Stokeness, not, for example, how the five forces could be used to assess the attractiveness of the industry.

In other words, you should be thinking about how Stokeness could use an understanding of the five forces to improve its performance or develop its strategy, rather than simply identifying that a particular force is strong or weak.

Part (b).

Even though this part of the question is only worth five marks, in effect there are still two different elements to it: the VCs' risk appetite, and key issues in performance measurement at Stokeness.

Stokeness appears to be a technology start-up company, which suggests the VCs were prepared to accept a relatively high degree of risk by investing in it. Equally, they will expect returns from the company in the future.

However, currently, Stokeness is still three years away from a commercial launch. So, for the moment, the key aspects of its performance relate to this pre-launch phase; for example, has Stokeness got sufficient cash to sustain it until it can begin to sell its products? If Stokeness runs out of money before it launches its fuel cells, then there is little chance of it generating any returns for the VCs in future.

Examining team's comments

Part (a) was generally well done, with candidates making good use of the information in the scenario to give useful performance management advice to Stokeness.

However, many candidates appeared not to read the second part of the requirement fully: this asked for a **justified** recommendation of **one new** performance measure for each of the five forces. Instead, they simply produced a list of performance measures for each area, often also including market share, meaning that they failed, in three different ways, to answer the question.

In **part (b)**, many candidates wasted time listing the different possible risk appetites, despite these not being required by the question set. Candidates are reminded that it is vital to read the requirement carefully, and to answer the question asked – not an alternative question of their own creation.

Marking guide	Marks
(a) For each of Porter's five forces:	
Up to 4 marks for performance management implications of the force, and justifying a suitable performance measure	
Total for part (a): Up to 15 marks	
Maximum	15
(b) For assessing the risk appetite of the VCs – 1 mark per valid point; up to 2 marks	
For assessing the VCs' impact on performance measurement at Stokeness – 1 mark per valid point; up to 3 marks	
Total for part (c): up to 5 marks	
Maximum	5
Professional skills	
Analysis and Evaluation	
• Use of information provided to perform a suitable/comprehensive evaluation of five performance measures for each of the five forces	
• Demonstration of reasoned and balanced judgement/assessment of the impact of the external business environment on these performance measures	
• Demonstration of ability to consider relevant factors applicable to Stokeness Co's situation	
Commercial acumen	
• Effective use of examples and/or calculations from the scenario information and other practical considerations related to the context to illustrate points being made relating to performance measures	
Maximum	5
Total	25

(a) **Threat of new entrants**

Barriers to entry – The threat of new entrants into the fuel cell market will be determined by the extent of the barriers to entry into the market. The barriers to entry appear to be high, given the technical skills and the length of time required to develop a viable product.

These barriers to entry will be strengthened further by the need to develop a relationship with the vehicle manufacturers who will be the customers for the fuel cells. Even if a potential new entrant develops a viable product, they will not be able to establish themselves in the market unless they can attract any buyers for their product.

Performance measure: Patented revenue – One of the ways in which technology firms can create a barrier to entry into their markets is by registering patents over new products or technologies. In this respect, Stokeness needs to ensure that it obtains patents for new cell designs or technology processes which could provide it with competitive advantage.

A suitable performance measure to use here would be the percentage of revenue which is generated from patented protects. This will indicate the degree to which Stokeness's patents will act as a barrier to entry.

Other performance measures:

Customer loyalty – If vehicle manufacturers (customers) are committed to using Stokeness's cells on a long-term basis, this will make it harder for new entrants to join the market.

To this end, it would be useful to measure customer loyalty by looking at the number (and value) of the long-term contracts Stokeness has to supply fuel cells to vehicle manufacturers.

Ratio of fixed cost to total cost – This gives an indication of the capital required to develop and produce fuel cell products, and therefore the level of amount of capital a potential new entrant would need to be able to enter the market. If large amounts of capital are required, this could make it harder for new entrants to join the market.

Threat of substitutes

Alternative fuel sources – The existing petrol/diesel engines remain a substitute for Stokeness's products, especially as their manufacturers are reducing the level of carbon dioxide emissions from these engines. Equally, electrical batteries and compressed natural gas products could also be substitutes for the fuel cells.

The petrol/diesel engines still have a number of strengths in the market; in particular, they are the only fuel source for which there is an infrastructure in place which enables end users to refuel their vehicles easily.

Performance measure: Output – The level of threat from substitute products could be measured by analysing the power output of different types of power supply compared to the level of emissions they produce and the cost of producing the power.

The cost of creating different engine types and the price of the fuels required to run them are likely to be very significant in determining the extent to which different types of engine are considered viable by vehicle manufacturers.

Bargaining power of suppliers

Component elements – The membrane which is used to produce the fuel cells requires rare and expensive elements. As a result, the **suppliers' bargaining power is high**. Stokeness's ability to produce the fuel cells will depend on the price and availability of the elements required for the membrane.

In particular, if the supply of these elements is controlled by a small number of suppliers they will be in a particularly strong position to dictate the price of the elements.

Subcontractors – The engineering firms to which Stokeness has subcontracted the production of certain components for the fuel cell also have a high bargaining power because of the knowledge they have gained of Stokeness's products. In this respect, it is important that there is a non-disclosure agreement in place to protect any commercially sensitive details of the products.

The size of the two engineering firms relative to Stokeness is not clear from the scenario, but it is possible that one of them may also consider some kind of forward vertical integration if they feel that Stokeness's products are going to be commercially successful.

Performance measure: Switching cost – The power of the suppliers could be measured by estimating the cost involved in switching to an alternative supplier. This cost could include any penalty fees payable to the existing suppliers, as well as the opportunity cost of lost sales arising as a result of delays incurred in switching supplier. These delays could be quite significant, given the specialist nature of Stokeness's product, which any new suppliers would have to understand, and tailor their processes to, before production could re-commence.

Other performance measures:

Proportion of cost – An alternative measure of the suppliers' bargaining power could be taken as the price of the suppliers' components in relation to the cost of the fuel cell as a whole. Such a measure can give an indication of the importance of the components to the overall fuel cell.

Number of suppliers – It could also be useful to monitor the number of suppliers, because this will indicate the level of competition in that market. If the number of potential suppliers available to Stokeness increases, this could reduce their bargaining power.

Bargaining power of customers

Large manufacturers – Stokeness's customers are manufacturers of large vehicles, such as buses and trucks. It is likely there will only be relatively few of these companies, but they will be quite large, giving them significant bargaining power. Crucially, the manufacturers have a choice of what fuel source to use (for example, fuel cells or standard petrol/diesel engines), and before they agree to use Stokeness's cells they will need to be sure that the cells are compatible with the existing technologies used in the vehicles.

Switching costs – However, once customers have committed to using a particular type of power source, the cost of switching to an alternative source is likely to be high. This may reduce the bargaining power of customers, but only once Stokeness has secured them as customers. In this respect, the fact that Stokeness has a two-year lead over the other companies developing fuel cells could be a significant advantage to it, if it can secure some significant contracts before the competitors have developed their cells.

Given the relative size of Stokeness compared to the manufacturing companies, and the potential importance of the fuel cells in the engine production process, one of the manufacturers might try to acquire Stokeness. However, this might prove to be an attractive option for the venture capitalists, depending on the price offered.

Performance measure: Discounts requested – The level of discount which customers request would provide Stokeness with an indicator of how strong the customers perceive their bargaining power to be. If the customers feel that Stokeness's fuel cells will provide them with a significant competitive advantage, then they will be less likely to press hard for a discount.

Other performance measures:

Switching costs – The costs which a manufacturer would incur to switch from one power source to another could also be used as an indicator of the strength of the bargaining power of customers. The higher these costs are, the less likely a customer will want to switch power source, thereby reducing their bargaining power. Although Stokeness is unlikely to be able to calculate this figure exactly, it should nonetheless be able to make an estimate of it.

Number of alternative suppliers – The number of alternative suppliers which customers could choose from could also affect the customers' bargaining power.

Competitive rivalry

Development advantage – As Stokeness has a two-year lead over the other companies developing fuel cells, the level of existing competition from these companies currently seems low. If Stokeness patents any key technologies it develops, this should help sustain its competitive advantage over its direct competitors.

Moreover, if Stokeness is able to secure contracts with some of the vehicle manufacturers before the other companies have developed their products, this will make it harder for the competitors to break into the market. In turn, this could help reduce the level of competitive rivalry in the industry in the future.

Performance measure: Launch date – Once Stokeness and then the competitors have launched their products, it will be possible to measure the strength of competitive rivalry by analysing market share. Until that point, however, there isn't a 'market' to analyse. Instead, the time until the commercial launch date of a viable fuel cell is a key performance measure. Although it may be difficult to obtain exact information about competitors' expected launch dates, Stokeness should try to monitor these alongside its own.

This measure highlights the importance of avoiding any overruns in the development process, and in delivering a commercially viable product as soon as possible, thereby maintaining Stokeness's competitive advantage over the other companies which are also developing fuel cells.

Other performance measures:

Partnership agreements – An alternative measure could be the number of partnership agreements signed, with vehicle manufacturers, or the projected revenues – or volumes – under such agreements.

(b) **Technology start-up** – Stokeness seems to be a technology start-up company, which suggests that it is a risky company for external investors to invest in. Equally, however, it offers the prospect for high returns if its fuel cell technologies prove successful. Therefore, it appears that the VCs are risk seeking by investing in Stokeness.

However, it appears that the VCs have tried to moderate the level of risk to some degree by placing commercially experienced managers into the business to assist the engineers who founded it. Moreover, because the VCs now have some of their own employees on the management team, this will give them a high degree of influence at Stokeness.

Medium/long-term returns – Given that Stokeness is still three years away from the commercial launch of its cells, the VCs will not begin to see any returns from their investment until the medium to long term. However, Stokeness could use net present value calculations, based on projected returns, as a performance measure in this respect.

Cash flow and cash control – In the shorter term, it is vital that Stokeness does not run out of cash while it is still developing its product (and hence not yet generating any revenue from it). Consequently, monitoring actual expenditure against budget and cash outflows will be key performance measures, to ensure that spending is kept under control.

Development targets – Stokeness needs to measure key non-financial aspects of performance as well as financial ones. Crucially, the point at which Stokeness can start selling a commercially viable product and therefore start acquiring customers will have a significant impact on its cash flow and NPV calculations. If the launch of the product falls behind schedule, this will increase the risk of the company running out of cash.

Therefore, it will be important for Stokeness to measure operational progress against key milestones: for example, completing successful test runs of the product.

Customer acquisition – Equally it will be important for Stokeness to sign contracts with customers, in order to secure revenue. Therefore, performance measures showing the number of definite customers signed up and the number of potential leads would also be useful.

2 CRC

Workbook reference

Budgeting systems are covered in Chapter 3 of the Workbook.

Top tips

Part (a) required an evaluation of whether a clothing retailer should consider the implementation of activity based budgeting (ABB). The key to scoring well was to evaluate the pros and cons of the current system before moving on to consider whether the current and future plans of the company were a good fit with ABB (which on balance they probably were).

Don't forget to score easy marks for defining your terms (such as ABB and incremental budgeting, but keep these definitions brief.

Part (b) required the completion of work by an analyst of an annual ABB budget. A sensible approach would be to use this information to create a budget for a specific month and then to measure actual performance against the budget.

Examining team's comments

Part (a)

The use of the word 'evaluate', as has been highlighted in previous Examiner's Reports for this examination means that candidates should assess the strengths and weaknesses of the arguments that arise, in relation to the scenario that is detailed, before coming to a justified conclusion as to what the company should do. Seen in that light, this should have been a question where most candidates were scoring at least ten marks. Both the budgeting methods would have been well known from Performance Management and the issues that arose from them were very clear from the scenario.

Part (b)

Candidates tended to err with regard to the heating and lighting costs in this part of the question, not realising that the proposal for an increase in cost in an environment of zero inflation should not be accepted in an activity based budget. This was a key part of demonstrating the difference between the inefficiencies that the traditional system would allow to be carried forward from year to year and the new system which required justification for the figures used.

Marking guide		Marks
(a) 1 mark per point		
Advantages and disadvantages of current system	6	
Advantages and disadvantages of ABB	6	
Maximum		10
(b) Calculations		
RFID tagging	1	
Warehouse staff wages	1	
Heating & lighting	1	
Cost per receipt	1	
Total variance	2	
Variance per receipt	2	
Commentary on the variances	3	
Maximum		10

Professional skills

Analysis and Evaluation

- Use of information provided to perform a suitable/comprehensive evaluation of variances
- Demonstration of reasoned and balanced judgement / assessment of alternative budgeting systems
- Demonstration of ability to consider relevant factors applicable to CRC's situation
- Identification of further analysis, which could be usefully carried out
- Balanced appraisal of information

Scepticism

- Effective challenge and critical assessment of alternative budgeting systems
- Demonstration of effective challenge the assumptions of warehouse heating and lighting costs

Commercial acumen

- Effective use of examples and/or calculations from the scenario information and other practical considerations related to the context to illustrate points being made relating to CRC
- Recommendations are practical and plausible in the context of CRC Co's situation

Maximum	5
Total	25

(a) **Advantages of the current budgeting system**

CRC managers use the previous year's results as a starting point when drafting their budgets, and increase the variable costs according to any anticipated growth in volumes. This is an example of incremental budgeting.

An advantage of incremental budgeting is that it is quick and easy to prepare. The budgeting system at CRC has remained unchanged for a long time and it is unlikely managers will have experience in any other method of budget setting. While CRC was growing steadily, and relatively slowly at approximately one new store every two years (approximately 18 years/10 stores), the use of incremental budgeting may have been appropriate. But as CRC is now entering new locations, such as out of town shopping centres and possibly food retailing, incremental budgeting is unlikely to be appropriate.

Incremental budgets can also be flexed according to anticipated activity levels. The manager of the central warehouse has done this, rather simplistically, by increasing costs of running the warehouse to reflect the anticipated increase in volumes in 20X6.

Disadvantages of current budgeting system

The use of incremental budgets can encourage slack. This includes incorporating extra costs into the budget to make it more achievable, or spending up to the budgeted amount to ensure that a larger budget is set next year. This may be the case particularly at CRC, as managers are appraised based on achieving their budget. The manager of the central warehouse appears to be building in slack by increasing the budget for heating and lighting when the general rate of inflation is zero. This will make it more likely that the manager will receive a positive appraisal next year, as it will be easier to achieve the budget.

Incremental budgeting does not encourage CRC to look for new and innovative ways of doing things. The level of automation in the warehouse is lower than in competitors and CRC appears to have just increased the budget for more staff to manually handle items in response to increased volumes. The introduction of the RFID system is, though, an example of the use of technology to increase efficiency in the warehouse.

Incremental budgeting is only appropriate where costs are already well controlled and operations are efficient. Otherwise, poorly controlled costs and inefficiencies are just incorporated into the next period's budget. Staff resistance to the introduction of the RFID system, and their difficulties in using it, suggest that this might not be the case.

Advantages of activity-based budgeting (ABB)

The principle of ABB is that it is activities, such as the goods inwards and goods outwards in the central warehouse, which drive costs. By understanding what drives the cost, such as the number of receipts from suppliers and the number of despatches to stores, CRC can take action to control the drivers of the costs and eliminate activities which are not value adding. ABB is particularly useful where overhead costs form a large part of total costs.

ABB can help identify critical success factors which CRC must do well, such as being able to put items away in the warehouse quickly and accurately and to retrieve them efficiently. This is more likely to be done right first time as ABB focuses on the whole of an activity.

ABB is useful, as CRC is changing the nature of its operations. It is undergoing rapid expansion by opening four new stores a year. There is also likely to be a change in the nature of its business, with the opening of its first out of town store and possible acquisition of a food retailing business. The incremental approach to budgeting may no longer be appropriate given the scale and nature of these changes. ABB may be more suitable as the business becomes more complex.

Disadvantages of activity-based budgeting (ABB)

One of the main disadvantages of ABB is the time and resources which are needed to implement it, for example, by identifying activities and their costs drivers. In the short term, overheads may not be controllable, which will reduce the benefits of implementing ABB.

CRC has used all its financial resources to fund its expansion and has only old and basic IT systems compared to its competitors. Its current systems are not enterprise resource planning systems (ERPS), unified databases or networked systems. Significant investment in CRC's IT systems will be needed to collect and process large volumes of data on cost drivers and activities which would be required to implement ABB. There may also be resistance to the change from staff, who may also require extensive training, as they will be unfamiliar with the ABB approach.

Conclusion

CRC should adopt ABB, mainly as a response to the significant changes in the business and its increasing complexity.

The out of town store and the food retailing business will both be supplied from CRC's existing central warehouse. The nature of these businesses may be different from the existing business. For example, out of town stores may require despatches that each contain a larger number of items from the goods outwards section. Food retailers may require smaller, more frequent despatches to prevent spoilage. The current approach of incremental budgeting, in the central warehouse at least, is unlikely to be appropriate. The benefits of implementing ABB do, however, need to be compared to the financial cost and disruption of doing so.

(b) **Activity-based budget for the central warehouse for YE 30 June 20X6**

	Total	*Goods inwards*	*Good outwards*	*Other*
	$	$	$	$
Warehouse manager's salary*	55,000	–	–	55,000
Lease of RFID system*	75,000	45,000	30,000	–
RFID tagging (W1)	72,000	72,000	–	–
Warehouse staff wages (W2)	315,000	157,500	157,500	–
Heating and lighting (W3)	10,000	–	–	10,000
Total	527,000	274,500	187,500	65,000

Annual number of receipts into goods inwards expected	9,000
Cost ($) per receipt into goods inwards	30.50
	(274,500/9,000)

*As already calculated by the analyst

Comments on variance analysis

The total expected cost for receipts into goods inwards for July 20X5 was $19,825 ($30.50 budgeted cost per receipt × 650 receipts). The actual cost was $18,000, giving a favourable variance of $1,825. The cause of this cannot be identified, on the basis of the information available, as the breakdown of the $18,000 actual cost would be required. It would be useful to have this information.

100,000 items were processed in July 20X5 which is the same as the budgeted amount. However, the number of receipts budgeted was 750 (9,000/12), whereas the actual number of receipts was only 650, equivalent to $27.69 ($18,000/650) per receipt. This is a favourable variance of $2.81 per receipt.

It appears that the favourable variance may be due to the receipt of larger quantities of items from suppliers in each delivery. If some of the goods inwards costs are variable with the number of items, this would result in a cost saving. This could be because of the reduction in the number of suppliers, with fewer suppliers individually supplying more items.

Workings

1 ***RFID tagging***

3 × $24,000 = $72,000

2 ***Warehouse staff wages***

Total warehouse staff wages = 14 × $22,500 = $315,000

Of which $157,500 (50% of $315,000) relate to each of goods inwards and goods outwards

3 ***Heating and lighting***

As inflation is zero the cost included in the budget should be $10,000 the warehouse manager should not be allowed to introduce unnecessary padding into the budget.

3 Framiltone

Workbook reference

Different approaches to budgeting (including rolling budgets and incremental budgets) are discussed in Chapter 3 of the BPP Workbook.

Top tips

Part (a). Although we often tell you that the majority of the marks in APM relate to analysis and evaluation, calculations are still an important part of performance management – and therefore you should still expect there to be some calculations in the exam.

Most of the marks in part (a) of this question relate to calculation, and if you worked carefully through the information provided in Appendix 2 you should be able to score a good number of these.

However, it is important not to rush the calculations, and to think about the points carefully. For example, the increase in sales volume (point 1) will affect not only revenue but also cost of sales and distribution costs.

Similarly, point 2 tells you that the selling price increases from the beginning of Q3, so it only affects Q3 and Q4 (not Q2). However, don't forget the volume increase (from point 1) when calculating the impact of the price increase.

It is very important to lay out your workings carefully to give yourself the best chance of picking up these points. The calculations themselves aren't difficult, but it is very easy to drop marks by making careless mistakes or not thinking through the implications of the points in Appendix 2 carefully. (For example, will the movement in exchange rate increase Framiltone's costs or reduce them?)

Finally, note that as well as recalculating the budget you are asked to comment briefly on the impact this has on the division's expected operating profit.

Part (b). A sensible way to approach this question will be to think about the benefits and drawbacks of both approaches to budgeting, and the situations where each is likely to be most appropriate.

You should have identified from the scenario that the two divisions are very different: the Dairy Division is well established, operating in a saturated market (with little opportunity for growth), and much of its business is governed by long-term contracts. By contrast, the Luxury Division is a new business, focusing on growth, and with rapidly changing product ranges.

These contrasts between the two divisions should have helped you to think about which approach to budgeting might be more appropriate for each. (The key point here – and a fundamental point you should have been aware of – is that an incremental approach is likely to be appropriate in stable conditions (Dairy), whereas rolling budgets are likely to be more appropriate in dynamic conditions (Luxury).)

Examining team's comments

Part (a) wasattempted well by many candidates, and the layout of the answers were generally excellent. Although some of the calculations were tricky, candidates who read the requirement carefully should have had few problems here. However, the examining team was disappointed to see how many candidates could not adjust forecasts by a set percentage, or struggled to compensate for a change in an exchange rate. Candidates must also ensure that all relevant workings are shown. In a number of cases, incorrect answers were presented without supporting calculations, and therefore potential marks for using the correct method (even if the final answer was incorrect) were lost.

Part (b) was generally well answered, and it was pleasing to see many candidates adopting a sensible structure to their answer – explaining the budget systems (incremental; rolling), discussing their advantages and disadvantages for both divisions, and then making a suitable recommendation. Identifying a clear structure for their answers in this way helps candidates ensure that all areas of the requirement are covered.

Marking guide

	Marks	
Calculations:		
Use of Q1 actual figures as starting point	1	
Revenue: Sales volume increase	1	
Sales price change from Q3 onwards	1	
Cost of sales: Sales volume increase	1	
Exchange rate percentage	1	
Application of exchange rate change	1	
Distribution costs: Sales volume increase	1	
Fuel tax percentage	1	
Application of fuel tax charge	1	
Comments on calculations (impact on operating profit) – up to 2 marks		
Total for part (a): up to 11 marks	11	
Use of incremental budgeting in the divisions – up to 5 marks		
Use of rolling budgeting in the divisions – up to 5 marks		
Total for part (b): up to 9 marks	9	
		20

Professional skills

Analysis and Evaluation

- Appropriate use of the data to support discussion and draw appropriate conclusions
- Demonstration of reasoned and balanced judgement / assessment of budgeting systems
- Demonstration of ability to consider relevant factors applicable to Framiltone Co's situation
- Balanced appraisal of information

Scepticism

- Demonstration of effective challenge the comments of the new CEO

Commercial acumen

- Effective use of examples and/or calculations from the scenario information and other practical considerations related to the context to illustrate points being made relating to budgeting systems
- Recommendations are practical and plausible in the context of Framiltone Co's situation

Maximum	5
Total	25

Recalculate the budget for Luxury Division to the end of the current year.

	Q1 (Actual)	*Q2*	*Q3*	*Q4*	*Total*
	C$'000	C$'000	C$'000	C$'000	C$'000
Revenue (W1)	10,400	12,240	11,388	7,247	41,275
Cost of sales (W2)	(6,240)	(7,020)	(6,370)	(4,654)	(24,284)
Gross profit	4,160	5,220	5,018	2,593	16,991
Distribution costs (W3)	(624)	(734)	(682)	(434)	(2,474)
Administration costs	(2,300)	(2,300)	(2,300)	(2,300)	(9,200)
Operating profit	1,236	2,186	2,036	(141)	5,317

Recalculating Luxury Division's budget for the year to reflect current conditions gives a more realistic target for the division managers. For the coming year, the effect of this is very significant and represents a much more challenging target for managers as it increases the expected total annual operating profit by 33% (5,317/4,000) over the original budget.

Workings

1 ***Revenue***

	Q1 (Actual)	*Q2*	*Q3*	*Q4*	*Total*
	C$'000	C$'000	C$'000	C$'000	C$'000
Original budget	10,400.0	12,000.0	11,000.0	7,000.0	40,400.0
2% sales volume		240.0	220.0	140.0	600.0
1.5% sales price			168.3	107.1	275.4
Total	10,400.0	12,240.0	11,388.3	7,247.1	41,275.4

2 ***Cost of sales***

	Q1 (Actual)	*Q2*	*Q3*	*Q4*	*Total*
	C$'000	C$'000	C$'000	C$'000	C$'000
Original budget	6,240.0	7,120.0	6,460.0	4,720.0	24,540.0
2% sales volume		142.4	129.2	94.4	366.0
6.67% exchange rate*		(242.2)	(219.7)	(160.6)	(622.5)
Total	6,240.0	7,020.2	6,369.5	4,653.8	24,283.5

*6.67% = 1 – (1.4/1.5), applied to 50% of cost of sales

3 ***Distribution costs***

	Q1 (Actual)	*Q2*	*Q3*	*Q4*	*Total*
	C$'000	C$'000	C$'000	C$'000	C$'000
Original budget	624.0	720.0	660.0	420.0	
Non-fuel (30% of original) × 1.02 uplift for sales		**220.3**	**202.0**	**128.5**	
Fuel pre-tax (70% of original × 1.02 uplift for sales (÷ 1.6 for old tax))		321.3	294.5	187.4	
Fuel adjusted for tax (× 1.6 in Q2, and × 1.63 for new tax in Q3 & 4)		**514.1**	**480.1**	**305.5**	
Total (non-fuel + fuel post tax)	**624.0**	**734.4**	**682.1**	**434.0**	**2,474.4**

Incremental budgeting

This is the type of budgeting which Framiltone currently uses. The starting point of incremental budgeting is usually the previous year's actual performance or budget. This is then updated for any known changes in costs, or for inflation. The budget would normally remain unchanged for the remainder of the year.

Incremental budgeting is suitable for use in organisations which are stable and not undergoing significant changes. This is the case for Dairy Division, which operates in a saturated market and has little opportunity to grow.

ANSWERS

Production volumes in Dairy Division have only increased by 0.5% over a full five years, so it is a very stable business. Dairy Division has stability of both revenues and costs. It has long-term fixed cost and volume supply agreements with its supermarket customers. It also has similar fixed contracts with its suppliers of milk, the most significant raw material ingredient used in its products.

Though the third-party distribution company is able to pass on some increases in fuel costs to Dairy Division, these are capped at only 0.5% per year. This is significantly less than the tax increases which will increase Luxury Division's fuel costs after the start of Q3. It appears that Dairy Division has relatively little exposure to rising fuel prices.

Furthermore, these increases are agreed prior to the setting of the current year budget, so there is no need to update these costs on an ongoing basis throughout the year.

As the dairy foods market is saturated and stable, there is little opportunity for the division to incur discretionary costs such as research and development of new products.

Incremental budgeting is only suitable for business where costs are already well controlled. This is because a big disadvantage of incremental budgeting is that it perpetuates inefficient activities by often simply building inflation into previous year results or budgets. It appears that Dairy Division, having been in existence for a relatively long time, does have good cost control as it has a modern production plant and is recognised as having the most efficient production processes in the industry.

Incremental budgeting may, however, build in budget slack. Managers may spend up to their budgeted amounts in one year, so that their budget is not cut the next, which may affect their appraisal and reward in the future. It is unclear whether this is occurring at Dairy Division, though for many years (while Dairy Division was the only division at Framiltone) the budgets set following consultation with divisional managers have just been achieved. This may be consistent with the stability of the division, but could also indicate that budgets were not set at a challenging enough level, even though Dairy Division had the best performance of the two divisions last year.

It is not therefore advisable that rolling budgets are introduced in Dairy Division, as the current incremental process appears satisfactory. This is especially so since divisional managers have little experience of setting their own budgets, and the time and cost of using rolling budgets would exceed the value of them to the division.

Rolling budgets

Rolling budgets are continually updated to reflect current conditions and are usually extended by budgeting for an additional period after the current period, for example, a quarter, has elapsed. That way, the budget always reflects the most up to date trading conditions and best estimates of future costs and revenues, usually for the next four quarters.

Rolling budgets are suitable for businesses which change rapidly or where it is difficult to estimate future revenues and costs.

Luxury Division was only set up two years ago, and is therefore a relatively new business. It also operates in quite a different sector of the industry to that in which Dairy Division operates and where Framiltone has most experience. There is likely to be considerable uncertainty as to future costs and revenues as Framiltone has little direct experience on which to base its forecasts.

Whereas Dairy Division operates in a saturated and stable market, Luxury Division uses rare ingredients which are subject to variations in availability and cost, for example, as a result of poor harvests. There is no indication that Luxury Division has fixed price and volume contracts with its customers or suppliers and is therefore likely to suffer from instability of supply as well as demand resulting from changes in consumer tastes.

The frequent changes in the product range are also likely to make forecasting for a year ahead difficult. The fact that a large proportion of ingredients are imported from Veeland makes costs susceptible to changes in the C$:V$ exchange rates which can quickly make an annual budget out of date, though managers may use methods such as forward contracts to reduce these movements. If managers are appraised on a budget which is out of date or unrealistic, they are likely to give up trying to achieve the budget, which will negatively affect the performance of Framiltone.

Rolling budgets will provide a more accurate basis on which to appraise managers at Luxury Division as they incorporate the best known estimates of future costs and revenues. It can be seen by the recalculation following Q1 results that Luxury Division's revised budgeted operating profit for the year has increased significantly by 42% (5,660/4,000), most of which is due to exchange rate changes. Where costs and revenues are likely to change during the period, rolling budgets give a much more realistic basis on which to appraise divisional performance and appraise and reward divisional managers. Budgets are likely to be achievable, which will motivate managers to try to achieve them.

Though the regular updating of the budget required in rolling budgeting is costly, time consuming and possibly a distraction for divisional managers, it does seem that rolling budgets are more suitable for Luxury Division than the current incremental approach particularly as, being realistic and achievable, they will increase managers' motivation to achieve the budget and so improve the performance of the business.

4 Godel

Workbook reference

Approaches to budgeting, and 'Beyond budgeting' are discussed in Chapter 3.

Top tips

Part (a). It is important that you focus specifically on the planning and operational variances here rather than discussing the variances shown in the operating statement more generally. As such, the figures you need to be looking are those shown in the 'Detailed variances' at the bottom of the operating statement.

Part (b). The requirement here is to 'evaluate' the proposal and therefore by implication the existing budgeting system. An 'evaluation' should include both the advantage and the disadvantages of the system. As the examiner's comments (below) indicate, if you are asked to evaluate something, it is important that you give a balanced argument – and don't focus only on the advantages or the disadvantages.

Note that you are also asked to give a recommendation at the end of your answer, about whether or not Godel should move to a 'beyond budgeting' method; so make sure you do this, as well as evaluating the method.

The context of the scenario is crucial here. Godel is a well-established business, operating in a mature market, and its management style – which fits with the company's strategy and the type of business – is a 'command and control' style. Does this suggest that Godel is suited to a more 'beyond budgeting' or might the old/traditional approach be more appropriate?

Examining team's comments

In **part (a)**, most candidates appeared not to know the definitions of operating and planning variances, and so those who attempted this question talked about all the other variances in the Appendix rather than answering the question.

Part (b) of this question was also inadequately attempted. Too many candidates saw only the negatives of the existing system, and few identified its positives for a traditional company like Godel in a mature market. Many candidates appeared to assume that because beyond budgeting was 'new' – and the company's existing approach was 'old'/'traditional' – then the move to beyond budgeting would automatically be beneficial for it. However, by making such an assumption, candidates failed to take account of the context of the scenario. The characteristics of the company and its environment were well-suited to the existing approach, and so a move to 'beyond budgeting' would not generate any significant benefits for the company.

Just because an approach or idea is 'new', this does not necessarily make it suitable for a company to adopt it.

Marking guide	Marks
(a) Definitions of planning and operational variances – 1 mark Advice about planning and operational elements of total variable cost variances – up to 3 marks Advice about planning and operational elements of sales price variance – up to 3 marks Total for part (a): up to 6	
	6
(b) Benefits of budgeting for Godel – 1 mark per relevant point – up to max of 5 Points could include: • Planning and co-ordination – meeting overall strategy • Responsibility • Integration • Motivation • Evaluation of performance Problems with budgeting – 1 mark per relevant point – up to max of 4 Points could include: • Time consuming and unnecessary • Lack of recognition of planning failures • Insufficient planning and operational analysis • Impedes continuous improvement Description of beyond budgeting – up to 2 marks Evaluation of appropriateness of beyond budgeting for Godel – up to 5 marks Recommendation: 1 mark	
	14
Professional skills	
Analysis and Evaluation • Use of information provided to perform a suitable/comprehensive evaluation of the implication of variances • Appropriate use of the data to support discussion and draw appropriate conclusions • Demonstration of reasoned and balanced judgement / assessment of budgeting systems • Demonstration of ability to consider relevant factors applicable to Godel Co's situation • Identification of further analysis, which could be carried out to enable an appropriate recommendation to be made.	
Scepticism • Demonstration of effective challenge the managers' complaints	
Commercial acumen • Effective use of examples and/or calculations from the scenario information and other practical considerations related to the context to illustrate points being made relating to budgeting systems • Recognition of problems and opportunities • Recommendations are practical and plausible in the context of Godel Co's situation	
Maximum	5
Total	25

(a) **Planning variances** result from the assumptions or standards used in the original budget-setting process not being accurate. For example, if the original budget assumed that sales prices would be increased by 2%, but market conditions have meant that sales prices could only be increased by 1%, the resulting sales price variance should be treated as a planning variance.

In effect, a planning variance is the difference between the original budget and the budget as it would have been revised with the benefit of hindsight.

Operational variances, in effect, are the differences between this 'revised' budget, and actual performance. Operational variances result from the decisions of operational managers, rather than issues with the original budget-setting process.

Variable cost variance

The total variable cost variance considers a number of costs together, and so it is unlikely that any gains or problems highlighted by it can be attributed to one individual. As such, the variable cost variance has little use for Godel, although highlighting the total variance could, in turn, identify the need for more detailed analysis to identify the specific causes of the variance.

The $20,680 favourable planning variance suggests that the standard costs have been set too high, and therefore most of the apparent cost improvements are due to this. Compared to the planning variance, the operational variance is very low ($580) which suggests that the operational managers have had little impact in driving down costs in the month.

Sales price variance

The sales price variance indicates the extent to which sales prices were incorrectly estimated in the budget (planning variances) and how effective the sales managers have been in negotiating higher prices with customers (operational variances).

The adverse planning variance ($15,600) suggests that the original budget was too optimistic in the initial price it set for Godel's sweets. However, the favourable operational variance ($6,640) suggests that the sales managers have been quite successful in their price negotiations with customers, although not successful enough to overcome the adverse planning variance.

The initial price-setting process should be examined, to identify why prices were budgeted too high. For example, Godel's market intelligence about the prices being set by competitors, or the commercial situation of its customers (the supermarkets) may have been faulty.

(b) Godel's competitive strategy is based on it being a cost leader, and therefore it will be very important for the company to control its costs effectively.

The budgeting system provides a mechanism for monitoring costs, and overall it seems that Godel is being successful in controlling its costs – as its total costs show a favourable variance.

Planning – More generally, budgets can be used to help communicate and co-ordinate all the management activities within Godel towards its overall strategic plan – minimising costs, and winning supermarkets' business.

Responsibility – The budget can also help to attribute responsibility for performance, and to identify which managers are responsible for which costs. For example, the favourable material usage variance indicates that fewer raw materials were required than planned, which suggests the production manager has been able to reduce waste and/or improve the efficiency of the production process.

Motivation – Although the managers do not appreciate the time taken by the budgeting process, the standard costs and assumptions being used in the budget are nonetheless discussed with them before being included in the budgets. The fact that the managers have the chance to participate in the budget process should help to motivate them to achieve the budget figures set.

In particular, it is important that managers are given the chance to identify any areas of the budget which they think are not realistic or achievable – otherwise the budget will become demotivating to the managers and their teams.

The CEO's feeling that there is no dysfunctional behaviour at Godel, and that all the managers are working in the best interests of the company, suggests that the budgeting system is not damaging motivation, even if it is not necessarily doing anything to enhance it.

Evaluation – Budgets assist performance evaluation by identifying variances which can then be analysed and investigated. This is particularly important for areas where actual performance is adverse to budget, to enable corrective action to be taken to improve future performance.

At Godel, sales are under-performing the budget both in terms of volume and price. However, more favourably, labour costs are considerably under budget – with the favourable labour 'efficiency' variance suggesting that staff are working efficiently.

Problems with Godel's budgeting system

Although the top-down nature of Godel's budgeting system fits with the organisation's strategy and management style, nonetheless there are still several problems with it.

Time-consuming – The nature of Godel's business – in a mature market, and with little scope for innovation or new product development – suggests that budget-setting should not be a complex process. However, the managers' complaints that it is very time-consuming process.

The managers may be exaggerating here, and their complaints may be more of an indication of the fact that the budgets ultimately have limited value to them (because the operational variances are relatively small), and therefore they do not want to spend much time preparing them.

Nonetheless, there appears to be a danger that Godel's current budgeting system may have become more complicated than it needs to be.

Planning variances – The bulk of the variances at Godel relate to planning variances, rather than operational variances. This reinforces the suggestion that there is little point spending lots of time on the operational aspects of the budget, but, instead, more time could be spend analysing the external factors with a view to reducing the level of planning variances.

Responsibility – The fact that the operational managers are frequently asked to explain variances which are not their fault suggests that the distinction between operational and planning variances needs to be more extensive.

Currently, the analysis between operational and planning variance is quite limited in scope. However, for example, instead of only analysing the total cost variance into operational and planning variances, some of the main cost headings in the operating statement could also be analysed in this way, so that managers are only held responsible for the operational variances.

No incentive to reduce cost – Although the CEO does not believe the managers build slack into their budgets, the use of standard costing nevertheless does not provide any incentives for them to try to reduce costs further. Given Godel's strategy as a cost leader, it would be beneficial to it if the budget system encouraged a system of continuous improvements in relation to efficiency gains and cost reductions.

However, given the mature nature of the business, Godel's senior management may feel that it is unlikely there will be a need to update budgeted costs on a regular basis and that a review of them once a year is sufficient.

Beyond budgeting

'Beyond budgeting' approaches move away from having an annual system of centrally created budgets, and replace them with a more flexible system of targets. Advocates of beyond budgeting argue that traditional budgets add little value and require too much management time, which would be better spent elsewhere. This argument may be appropriate at Godel, given the managers' grumbling about the time-consuming nature of the budgeting process and the limited value it provides them.

Under a 'beyond budgeting' approach, the purpose of performance measurement changes from monitoring variances against budget towards measuring achievement of strategic goals, adding value, or performance against suitable benchmarks.

Crucially, the 'flexible' nature of 'beyond budgeting' means that it will use forecasts produced and revised more regularly than the annual budgets currently used at Godel. However, it will also devolve control and decision-making to the line managers. Moreover, the targets set are intended to guide managers, rather than to constrain them. (This, in conjunction with devolved control and decision-making should help to improve managers' motivation.)

However, 'beyond budgeting' is not necessarily approporiate for all organisations, and the nature of Godel's business and culture may limit the potential benefits it could gain from moving beyond budgeting.

Decentralisation – Beyond budgeting enables a more decentralised way manger, and helps to create a culture of personal responsibility and self-management. However, Godel has a top-down 'command-and-control' management style, and its employees will be familiar with this, because most of them have worked for the company for many years. Therefore, moving 'beyond budgeting' will require a significant change to the culture and the management style in the business, which may prove difficult to achieve.

Moreover, the lower level managers may have little interest in preparing their own forecasts, particularly if they – like the staff – value the straightforward nature of their work. And, at a practical level, the managers are likely to need training in the process of budgeting and forecasting before they can begin doing it.

Dynamic environments – On of the advantages given for beyond budgeting is that it enables managers and staff to respond quickly to emerging events – as a result of the devolution of responsibility to them. However, this is more likely to be beneficial in dynamic markets than in a mature business and a relatively stable environment such as Godel.

Similarly, the focus at Godel appears to be on cost control (which is well-suited to traditional budgeting approaches) rather than continuous improvement (which is better supported by 'beyond budgeting'.)

In general, the nature of Godel's business and its environment, suggests that there may not be a need to revise Godel's budgets regularly, as would be the case under 'beyond budgeting.' Moreover, the additional work required in generating more regular forecasts and updates is likely to exacerbate the grumbling and complaints from the operational managers about the length of time taken up by the budgeting process.

Recommendation

As such, it does not appear appropriate for Godel to move 'beyond budgeting'. The potential benefits which could be gained from it appear limited given the nature of Godel's business; and the culture and management style at Godel does not appear to fit with the 'beyond budgeting' approach. Therefore, Godel should not move to a 'beyond budgeting' approach.

5 Perkin

Workbook reference

Budgeting and budgeting systems are discussed in Chapter 3 of the Workbook.

Top tips

Although good exam technique is important in all APM questions, it is particularly useful in this one – especially reading all three requirements and identifying how the different parts of the question fit together.

Part (a). The scenario highlights a number of problems which Perkin has experienced, so one approach to this requirement could be just to work through the scenario and identify which of these are due to weaknesses in the current budgeting system, or its lack of suitability for the environment in which Perkin operates.

However, a more structured approach for trying to identify the weaknesses might be to use 'PRIME' as a framework for your answer.

Plan – Does the budget process encourage budget holders to plan how to achieve targets which support the company's overall strategic objectives?

Responsibility – Do the budgets help to allocate responsibility, and specify which managers control which costs?

Integration – Does the budget structure help to ensure that the activities of one area support another?

Motivation – Do the budgets help to motivate managers?

Evaluation – Do the budgets allow trends in performance to be identified and investigated?

The scenario identifies a number of issues where Perkin's budgeting system does not help to achieve these 'PRIME' characteristics; and so you can then highlight these as weaknesses of the system.

However, note that you are asked to evaluate the system's suitability for Perkin's environment, as well as the weaknesses in the system. A key point to realise here is that Perkin is operating in a dynamic, fast-moving environment. Therefore, to what extent are incremental budgets, which are produced annually and enforced rigidly, likely to be suitable?

Although the requirement does not ask you to recommend an alternative budgeting system, it could be helpful to think whether the characteristics of alternative budgeting models (eg rolling budgets) would make them more appropriate than Perkin's current system. If another model seems more suitable, briefly mentioning this could help support your evaluation of the suitability (or unsuitability) of the current system.

Part (b). The scenario clearly identifies a number of external factors which have affected Perkin's performance during the year (eg rising silver prices; the fire at the customer), and these factors in themselves are outside Perkin's control.

In effect, however, this requirement is looking at the extent to which factors can fully be classified as controllable or uncontrollable. The key question in Perkin's case is: Although the initial factors were external (uncontrollable), has Perkin's internal response (controllable) also had an impact on its performance?

Marking guide	Marks
(a) Evaluation of current budgeting system	
Weaknesses in current system – 1 mark per relevant point – up to 12 marks	
Suitability of the system for Perkin's environment – 1 mark per point – up to 5 marks	
Conclusion – 1 mark	
Total for part (a): up to 14	
	14
(b) Discussion of controllable and non-controllable aspects – up to 2 marks	
Identifying external factors which contributed to Perkin's poor performance – 1 mark	
Evaluating the extent to which the external factors as opposed to internal weaknesses were responsible for Perkin's poor performance – 1 mark per relevant point; up to a maximum of 4	
Total for part (b): up to 6	
	6

Marking guide	Marks
Professional skills	
Analysis and Evaluation	
• Use of information provided to perform a suitable/comprehensive evaluation of the budgeting system	
• Demonstration of reasoned and balanced judgement	
• Demonstration of ability to consider relevant factors applicable to Perkin Co's situation	
Commercial acumen	
• Effective use of examples and/or calculations from the scenario information and other practical considerations related to the context to illustrate points being made relating to Perkin's performance	
Maximum	5
Total	25

(a) Perkin uses a traditional approach to budgeting, which has a number of weaknesses.

First of all, the budgeting system does not seem aligned with Perkin's **corporate objective** which focuses on innovation and continuous product improvement. Innovation is a key competitive advantage to both component and device manufacturers in this industry and the products which incorporate Perkin's components are subject to rapid technological change as well as changes in consumer trends. The markets in which the two divisions operate appear to be evolving, as seen by the high popularity of the smartphone model which was designed for playing games. This may mean the distinction between smartphone and gaming devices could be becoming less clear cut. Management time would probably be better spent considering these rapid changes and currently the budgeting process does not facilitate that.

In reality, the budget process at Perkin is **time consuming** and probably therefore a costly exercise. Divisional budgets go through a lengthy process of drafting and then revision by the main board before they are approved. The approval often happens after the start of the period to which they relate, at which point the budgets are already **out of date**. This also means divisional managers are trying to plan activities for the next financial year without a set of finalised targets agreed, which could impact the effectiveness of decisions made.

Another weakness is that the budgets are **only prepared annually**, which is clearly too infrequent for a business such as Perkin. The process is also rigid and inflexible as deviations from the planned targets are not tolerated. Sticking to rigid, annual budgets can lead to problems such as P Division not being able to cope with increasing popularity of a particular product and even other short-term changes in demand like those driven by seasonal factors, or one-off events such as the factory fire. Linked to this problem of budgetary constraints is that to cut costs to achieve the budgeted net profit, managers closed one of the three research and development facilities in G Division. As identified at the outset, a successful research and development function is a key source of long-term competitive advantage to Perkin.

It also appears that Perkin fails to **flex the budgets** and consequently the fixed budgets had discouraged divisional managers from deviating from the original plan. P Division did not make technical modifications to its components due to the cost of doing so, which meant they were unable to supply components for use in the new model of smartphone and had to discount the inventories of the old version. It is unclear why G Division did not take on additional staff to cope with increased demand following the reopening of their customer's factory, but it may be because managers felt constrained by the budget. This then caused long-term detriment to Perkin as it lost the preferred supplier status with its main customer.

Another problem created by annual budgeting is the **management of short-term changes in costs and prices**. A key component of Perkin's products is silver, which fluctuates in price, and though it is not clear how much effect this has on Perkin's costs, any problems in supply could disrupt production even if only a small amount of silver were required. Also Perkin exports goods worldwide and probably also purchases materials, including silver, from overseas. The business is therefore exposed to short-term movements in foreign currency exchange rates which may affect costs and selling prices.

Similarly, there also seems to be **considerable uncertainty** in sales volumes and prices which creates problems in the forecasting process for the two divisions. P Division did not anticipate the high demand for the new component which meant it had to discount products it had already manufactured in order to achieve its forecast sales volumes. G Division did correctly forecast the demand, but based on past growth in the market which may be too simplistic in a rapidly changing industry. Lack of up to date information will hinder decision making and overall performance at Perkin. Perkin would perhaps be better adopting a rolling basis for forecasting.

The two divisions share manufacturing facilities and are likely to compete for other resources during the budgeting process. The current budgeting system does not encourage resource, information or knowledge sharing, for example, expertise in forecasting silver requirements. Divisional managers are **appraised on the financial performance of their own division** and hence are likely to prioritise the interests of their own division above those of Perkin as a whole. P Division would not reallocate its manufacturing facilities to G Division, even though G Division needed this to cope with extra demand following reopening of the customer's factory. The current system is therefore not encouraging goal congruence between the divisions and Perkin as a whole and a budgeting system, if done effectively, should encourage co-ordination and co-operation.

Managers may find the budgeting process **demotivating** because it is **time consuming** for them and then the directors override the forecast which they had made. It is also unfair and demotivating to staff to appraise them on factors which are outside their control. This also identifies another weakness in Perkin's budgeting system related to control, as there does not seem to be any planning and operating variance analysis performed to assess exactly where performance is lacking, and so no appropriate management information is provided.

Planning variances result from actual events and circumstances differing from the assumptions used in the original budget. For example, the fire at its main customer meant that the annual growth of 5% anticipated in G's sales forecast was too high (because the budget had not anticipated the fire). The lost sales resulting from the fire should be treated as a planning variance. In effect, a planning variance is the difference between the original budget and the budget as it would have been revised with the benefit of hindsight. By isolating the planning variances, Perkin can get a better insight into the degree to which the original budget was inaccurate. If it becomes clear that the majority of the variances result from changes in circumstance, which couldn't have been known when the annual budget was originally set, this could reinforce the argument for moving away from the current budgeting system – for example, to rolling budgets.

Operational variances then reflect the differences between this 'revised' budget and actual performance. Operational variances result from the ongoing decisions of divisional managers, rather than issues with the original budget-setting process.

Perkin could then get a fairer reflection (through the operational variances) of how well the **divisional managers** are performing. This will also increase the effectiveness of the budgeting system as a **control mechanism** – comparing the manager's actual controllable performance against budgeted targets. Currently, the divisional managers are appraised on the financial performance of their divisions, so they are being held responsible for planning variances as well as operational variances. However, as the budgets are determined by the main board, the managers should not be held responsible for planning variances over which they have little (or no) control.

It is not even clear just how often divisional managers receive reports on performance throughout the year. Any budgeting system without regular feedback would be ineffective. It should even be noted that for the industry in which Perkin operates the use of only budgetary targets as a measure of performance is narrow and internal. It should be utilising information from external sources as well to assess performance in a more relevant and contextual way.

In conclusion, given the rapidly changing external environment and the emphasis on innovation and continuous product development, the current budgeting method does not seem appropriate for Perkin.

(b) As the shareholder representative noted, external factors have adversely affected Perkin's performance over the last year. However, the way Perkin has responded to the external events has also contributed to the problems it has faced. As such, it is important that Perkin doesn't simply use the external factors as an excuse for its poor performance, thereby failing to acknowledge the internal factors and behaviours which have also contributed to it.

The current lack of any detailed analysis into the reasons why Perkin's actual performance varies from budget means it is difficult to hold managers to account for their performance. However, as the three examples we evaluate below demonstrate, the factors that affect performance cannot be categorised entirely as controllable (internal) or as uncontrollable (external). Instead, Perkin's performance reflects a combination of both types of factors.

The **unexpectedly high popularity of the new smartphone** with the large screen was an external factor. However, P Division's inability – or unwillingness – to make the necessary technical modifications to its own components to support the new screen was an internal factor, resulting – as we noted in part (a) – from the fact that Perkin does not flex its budgets.

Similarly, the **global shortage of silver** during the year (and the corresponding increase in silver prices) was an external factor. However, the lack of communication between G Division and P Division which led to G buying silver when P already held large inventories reflected an internal weakness. If the two divisions had liaised more effectively, the impact of the short-term increase in silver prices could have been reduced (or perhaps even avoided) if Perkin was able to wait until prices fell again to top up its inventories.

Again, the **fire which affected G's main customer** was an external factor. However, G's refusal to recruit extra staff to fulfil increased demand when the customer's factory reopened, and P's refusal to allow some of its manufacturing facilities to be used to meet this demand, are both internal decisions. However, it was these responses – rather than the fire itself – which led to Perkin losing its preferred supplier status with the customer.

As we noted in part (a), the response to the silver price increase and the fire both reflect the lack of goal congruence between the divisions and Perkin as a whole. Again, though, this is an internal weakness, reflecting dysfunctional behaviour which has resulted from the way divisional performance is rigidly assessed against budget. Therefore, although external factors have contributed to G's poor performances, internal weaknesses have also played a significant part in G's poor performance.

6 Jolt

Workbook reference

Business process re-engineering is discussed in Chapter 4 of the Workbook, as are ethical issues and their impact on business performance. Information systems are discussed in Chapter 5.

Top tips

Part (a) – Although the requirement has been set within the overall context of business process re-engineering (BPR), the key issue for Jolt here is how the proposal could improve its performance specifically in relation to its retail customers' key demands:

- Lower prices
- Meeting performance targets in relation to lead times and quality

Therefore, a useful way to structure your answer would to look at each of the demands in turn, and to evaluate the impact the proposal could have on them.

Also, as you have been given cost information in Appendix 1, it is important that you use that. As Jolt is under pressure to lower prices, a key question in relation to the outsourcing plan should be: what impact will it have on Jolt's costs? BPR aims to achieve 'dramatic' improvements in performance – but will outsourcing provide any significant reductions in costs?

As with all APM questions, it is also important to think about the context of the scenario in practical terms. For example:

- What impact might outsourcing the manufacture of swimwear to a supplier 17,000 km away be expected to have on lead times?
- Similarly, will outsourcing affect Jolt's ability to control the quality of its products?

Part (b) – Although the requirement just asks you to assess the 'potential impact of Jolt's ethical standards', did you notice that the opening paragraph told you 'Jolt is known for its high ethical standards towards its workers, suppliers, and the environment'?

Having identified this, a useful way to structure your answer could be to use each of the aspects – workers; suppliers; the environment – as headings, and then assess how they could be affected by the proposals, or how the desire to behave ethically in relation to them might affect the acceptability of the proposal. For example, in relation to suppliers: will the new outsourced manufacturer have the same high standards the Jolt has? (And if it doesn't, what implications might this have for Jolt?) Or, in relation to the environment: what impact might shipping goods from a supplier 17,000 km away have on Jolt's environmental credentials?

Marking guide	Marks
Explanation of BPR – 2 marks	
Evaluate impact of proposal in relation to lower prices – 1 mark per relevant point – up to 6 marks	
Evaluate impact of the proposal in relation to meeting performance targets – 1 mark per relevant point – up to 6 marks	
Total for part (a): up to 12	
For assessing the impact of ethical standards relating to workers – 1 mark per relevant point – up to 4 marks	
For assessing the impact of ethical standards relating to suppliers – 1 mark per relevant point – up to 3 marks	
For assessing the impact of ethical standards relating to the environment – 1 mark per relevant point – up to 3 marks	
Total for part (c): up to 8	
	20
Professional marks	
Analysis and Evaluation:	
• Use of the data in Appendix 1 to determine relevant calculations to analyse the outsourcing proposal	
• Comprehensive evaluation of how the BPR proposal could improve performance of the customers' two key demands is undertaken	
Scepticism	
• Recognition that the BPR proposal will bring additional challenges to Jolt, not just potential improvements	
• Identification that information related to customer lead times is missing	
Commercial Acumen:	
• Comprehensive assessment of the possible ethical consequences of the BPR proposal	
Maximum	5
Total	25

BPR

BPR is the fundamental and radical redesign of business processes to achieve dramatic improvements in performance. For Jolt, the BPR proposal aims to meet the retailers' demands for lower prices and the requirement to meet performance targets relating to lead times and quality.

Lower prices

To be able to sell swimwear at lower prices, Jolt proposes reducing costs by outsourcing production to an overseas supplier. The current average production cost of manufacturing is $5·00 per unit. The cost of purchasing from an external supplier is $4·00, which is $3·50 purchase cost, plus $0·50 ($5,000/10,000) shipping costs. This 20% ($1·00/$5·00) saving is a significant improvement in financial performance, but not a dramatic one, and may not fit the definition of BPR.

Exchange rate movements could reduce the cost saving significantly. In the near future, expected changes to international trade tariffs will increase the unit cost to $4·35 ($4·00 + 10% of $3·50), and reduce the cost saving to just 13% ($0·65/$5·00).

Unless Jolt decides to outsource the remaining 50% of production and close its factory completely, factory overheads of $0·95c per unit may still be incurred and just be re-allocated to Jolt's other sportswear products, possibly totally eliminating the cost saving.

Combining several jobs into one is a characteristic of a re-engineered process. As such, reorganising staff into multidisciplinary teams may create overhead savings, such as by reducing the number of staff employed by the automation of purchase invoice processing. These savings will be offset by additional costs, such as investment in new information systems, retraining staff to work in unfamiliar roles, or incentivising them to work overseas.

Re-engineered processes often allow workers more autonomy to make decisions. Giving teams more autonomy to set prices may allow Jolt to set prices reflecting the customers they serve and to prevailing market conditions.

Meeting performance targets

Lead times

Current lead times for customer orders are unknown. As the proposed supplier is 17,000 km away, goods will take several weeks to be transported by sea. This may increase lead times significantly, though may be offset by faster production times in larger factories. As Jolt's sales are seasonal, retailers may pre-order in advance, reducing the importance of long lead times. To minimise shipping costs, shipping containers must be full, which may mean deliveries will be in larger quantities and which may increase the lead times.

Quality

Jolt is already known for producing high quality products. The quality of the new supplier's products needs to be ensured. Any deterioration in the quality of Jolt products would undermine its reputation and reduce long-term business performance as fewer consumers would buy them. Monitoring of quality standards is more difficult when using external suppliers, especially at long distances, than when manufacturing in Jolt's own factory. In re-engineered processes, work is performed where it makes most sense to do so. In this respect, having staff responsible for quality and supplier audits working close to the manufacturing site will help Jolt maintain performance in supplier relationship management.

Impact on workers

Jolt is known for its high ethical standards towards workers. Following the BPR, at least 500 (50% of 1,000) manufacturing workers are likely to be left without jobs. As Jolt's competitors have already closed their factories, these workers may be unable to find new jobs doing similar work, though jobs may be created in the new supplier's factory.

Staff who remain in work may become demotivated if they think that BPR will be extended to all of Jolt's products. This may reduce financial performance by reduced productivity, increased staff turnover or difficulties recruiting new staff.

Staff may also be demotivated if they are placed in unfamiliar roles or may be unwilling to learn new skills. Other staff may welcome, and be motivated by, the opportunity to perform new types of work, learn new skills or work overseas. This will probably increase their individual performance.

Suppliers

Any association with unethical practices, for example, if the new supplier were found to be using unacceptable working practices, could seriously harm Jolt's reputation for high ethical standards. This could reduce financial performance, as consumers may not buy Jolt's products, or potential investors could be discouraged from providing capital. Part of the team located close to the manufacturing site is responsible for supplier audits, which may help to reduce this risk.

Environment

Jolt should consider the environmental impact of shipping goods long distances. The environmental credentials of the new supplier are unknown. This will be amplified if Jolt decide to ship containers that are not full, increasing the carbon footprint generated per item. As Jolt voluntarily publishes a corporate sustainability report, any deterioration in its performance on environmental issues will become widely known. This could lead to reduced financial performance if consumers switch to competing products.

7 Pattack

Marking guide		Marks
Definition of BPR – 1 mark		
1 mark per relevant point: Strategic focus on costs		
Being best delivery company		
Engaged and committed workforce		
Maximisation of shareholder value		
Identifying Pattack's customer – 1 mark	1	
Bonus scheme – 1 mark per relevant point, up to 6 marks	6	
Conclusion – up to 2 marks	2	
Maximum		20

Professional skills marks

Analysis and Evaluation:

- Application of analysis to the specific situation regarding the company in the scenario
- Balanced and reasoned appraisal eg of the bonus scheme given the specific situation in the scenario

Scepticism:

- Demonstration of the ability to question problems with the bonus scheme
- Recognition that extra information is required regarding the BPR proposal

Commercial Acumen:

- Practical and plausible points that recognise the scenario information and other practical considerations

Maximum	5
Total	25

Business process re-engineering (BPR) involves rethinking how a process is undertaken at a fundamental level and is based on the radical redesign of business processes to achieve dramatic improvements. It starts by asking questions such as: 'why do we do things this way?' and 'would we do things exactly the same way if we were starting again?'

Pattack has an overall aim supported by several strategies. The main aim is to maximise shareholder value and this will be achieved through having a strategic focus on costs, by being the best delivery company in Geeland, and by having an engaged and committed workforce. It is likely that all these goals can be better achieved by the BPR proposal.

Strategic focus on costs

There are several areas in the new proposal where costs will be saved over the long term. Upon collection by Pattack drivers, the parcels will not now require to be taken to Pattack's premises to enable the delivery schedules to be planned by delivery administration. Instead, the deliveries will be planned through the electronic transfer of data from the retailers. This will save costs in two main areas. First, the drivers are not required to return to Pattack's premises which will save the costs of the drivers' time, vehicle fuel and associated vehicles costs. Second, the same drivers who collect the parcels from the distributors will deliver the parcels to the end users. This will save cost as there is no need to employ two different types of driver for two different purposes. The process has merged the collection and delivery functions and therefore there is only a requirement for one type of driver.

There will also be a cost saving as the date and time of delivery to the end user is now undertaken automatically and accurately. The current process is not accurate and has been a source of complaints from the retailers. The current process is likely to damage Pattack's relationship with the retailers and Pattack is likely to lose business in an increasingly competitive environment. Introducing a system whereby the end user has to sign for receipt of the parcel, along with the date and time of the confirmed receipt, will save Pattack the costs associated with recording the data when the drivers return to Pattack's premises. It will also save the cost of the damage to Pattack's relationship with the retailer and may help ensure future business.

The fundamental idea of a strategic focus on costs is that cost savings are considered over the long term. The barcoding technology and the hand-held devices used by the drivers would certainly represent an expense in the short term. However, it is clear that the benefits in terms of process improvement represent a permanent change to Pattack's processes. From the evidence in the scenario, it is very likely that such process improvement will result in significant cost savings in the long term.

Being best delivery company

The redesign of the process to tag the parcel at source will also help Pattack achieve its aim of being the best delivery company in Geeland as it will enable route planning to be undertaken on a more pro-active basis. Routes can now be planned as orders are communicated from retailers instead of waiting until all parcels have been brought back to Pattack's premises. This is likely to enhance retailer satisfaction with the service Pattack is offering.

Electronic vehicle tagging will enable the delivery manager to respond to any requests from the retailers concerning delivery. Pattack can thereby demonstrate that it is reacting to retailer demands for real time information regarding delivery and can show that it is putting the overall retailer experience at the centre of its process redesign.

The receipt by the end user, combined with the original bar coding of the order, would enable a digital audit of every order Pattack received to be undertaken in the event of any subsequent problem the retailer may have with the end user. This would enhance retailers' trust in Pattack and their overall satisfaction with the service Pattack is providing.

Engaged and committed workforce

Much of the work currently undertaken by the computer operators will now be addressed by the bar-coding operation. It is not clear, however, if there is a new position for these staff members within the new process. Likewise, there is no need now for both collection and delivery drivers and it has to be assumed that Pattack will require fewer drivers overall. The main purpose of the BPR proposal is to make Pattack's operations more efficient and it is clear that long-term cost reduction is part of that. It is inevitable that this will include employees as some of the tasks they perform are replaced by enhanced technology. There would clearly be an effect on staff morale if some workers were made redundant and this may lead to the workforce feeling under threat rather than committed or engaged.

There are some elements of the BPR proposal, however, which are likely to enhance employee engagement and commitment. The remaining drivers, for example, should have schedules which are better planned and more efficient than the current ones, which should enhance their trust and faith both in the organisation generally and in the redesigned processes which has been initiated specifically. The delivery manager should also feel that they have has more control over the entire process if they are able to see where delivery vehicles are at any given moment.

Maximisation of shareholder value

It is not clear from the scenario if Pattack has undertaken or will undertake a net present value calculation for the BPR proposal. This would allow Pattack to make a more objective judgement as to whether the proposal is adding to shareholder value.

However, Pattack's aim is to maximise shareholder value by undertaking the strategies outlined above. It is very unlikely that the BPR proposal will enhance strategic performance in all those areas and not contribute to the maximisation of shareholder value. Overall, therefore, it is extremely likely that the BPR proposal will help with Pattack's aim of maximising shareholder value.

Drivers' bonus

The retailers are Pattack's customers as it is the retailers who employ Pattack to deliver the parcels on their behalf. The end user is the retailer's customer, not Pattack's, so it is appropriate to measure satisfaction of the retailer.

Clarity

The measurement of satisfaction has to be clearly defined. Pattack may choose to measure this by a survey of the retailers but would need to be clear with regard to the questions asked and, in particular, the options offered in terms of potential responses. Surveys are well-known, for example, for respondents choosing middle values on a scale of one to five. There may also be a lack of shared understanding around the word satisfaction and perhaps measuring customer delight, happiness or something more tangible such as the possibility of the retailer using Pattack for its next delivery may be more meaningful.

It should also be clear as to when a bonus will be awarded and whether there is a scale to it. For example, it should be made clear to the drivers that a basic bonus will be awarded when overall customer satisfaction reaches the specific detailed figure of 85% and if the bonus will increase if this satisfaction level reaches 90% or 100%. As it currently stands, the bonus scheme does not identify these levels.

Controllability

There are some factors which are in control of the drivers in their interaction with the retailers and, in that sense, the measure can be seen as a fair one. For example, they are in control of how they personally interact with the retailers when they collect the parcels and as such are in control of how Pattack is represented in this part of the relationship. They are also in control of the physical condition of the parcels and should be able to assure the retailers that the parcels will be delivered in the same condition that they were collected.

The other area of most concern to the retailer will be whether the goods are delivered on time, and this is only partly in the drivers' control. They cannot control the conditions on the roads and there may be accidents, traffic jams, adverse weather conditions and problems with access to end user premises for certain type of vehicles, which could affect delivery. If deliveries are late, the end users are likely to complain to the retailers and, as a result, the retailers' satisfaction with Pattack could potentially be affected adversely. Such an eventuality may mean that the drivers are not awarded their bonus on the basis of factors beyond their control.

The drivers are also not in control of the entire relationship with the retailer. The retailer's view of satisfaction will be influenced by all their dealings with Pattack, which will also cover such things as the ordering process, invoicing and customer relations with Pattack's office staff. These factors may adversely affect the retailers' view of their satisfaction with Pattack and are out of the drivers' control.

It seems unfair, therefore, to award the drivers a bonus based on these significant factors which are out of their control.

Motivation

Motivation to achieve a bonus is usually related to how clear it is and how achievable it is deemed to be. As neither the potential scale of the bonus nor the monetary reward attached to it is clear, and it appears to contain several aspects which are beyond the control of the drivers, it is unlikely that they will be motivated to achieve it as it is currently presented.

There is a danger with this bonus system that the drivers focus on this measure to the exclusion of other factors. For example, the need to deliver parcels on time as part of ensuring the retailers' satisfaction may cause the drivers to break speeding laws or to take more chances than they would normally when driving.

Conclusion

As a starting point, the idea of basing drivers' bonus based on retailer satisfaction does sound appropriate, but the proposed bonus could be further clarified and should also be better defined to relate to the specific elements which are in the drivers' control. As it stands, the scheme is too general and should not be adopted.

8 Sgoltaire

Workbook reference

Ethics and environmental management accounting are covered in Chapter 4.

Top tips

An issue to note here is that guidance was contained within the scenario about how to structure the answer to both part a (in Exhibit 2 of the question) and part b (in Exhibit 4 of the question).

Part (a)

Make sure that you don't fall into the trap of discussing ethical issues without relating these to the decision to invest overseas.

A sensible approach would have been to identify each of the ethical issues detailed in the scenario and then to advise how each of these issues would affect the decision, including both the potential positive and negative impacts on the performance of the company.

A good answer required practical comments on these areas, not in overly theoretical terms.

Part (b)

Make sure that you discuss EMA methods in a way that relates to the question ie how they can be used to improve business performance.

Answers that were structured under the four headings given in the question generally scored better than unstructured answers and better answers will use the figures given in Appendix 1 of the question to create an adjusted NPV.

Marking guide		Marks
(a) 1 mark per point:		
Impact of ethics on strategy formulation – up to 5 marks	5	
Impact of ethics on business performance – up to 5 marks	5	
Marks Available	10	
		8
(b) 1 mark per point:		
Calculating costs – up to 3 marks	3	
Investment appraisal – up to 3 marks	3	
Calculations – up to 2 marks	2	
Setting measures and targets – up to 3 marks	3	
Product pricing – up to 3 marks	3	
		12

ANSWERS

Marking guide	Marks
Professional skills marks	
Analysis and Evaluation:	
• Appropriate use of the data to support discussion and draw conclusions	
• Balanced and reasoned appraisal of the impact of the overseas investment on stakeholders	
Scepticism:	
• Demonstration of the ability to question the ethicality of the proposed overseas investment	
Commercial Acumen:	
• Practical and plausible pointes that recognise the scenario information and other practical considerations especially relating to the use of EMA	
Maximum	5
Total	25

(a) **Strategy formulation**

Business ethics relates to behaviour expected by society, but not codified in law. Developing strategies which demonstrate high standards of ethical behaviour, for example, towards the environment, will help create long-term, sustainable competitive advantage. This is because stakeholders may react negatively to poor ethical behaviour.

For example, Sgoltaire's biggest shareholder only invests in ethical companies. This stakeholder has high power and interest and will strongly influence strategy formulation to ensure that this is consistent with its own principles and objectives. Ultimately, the pension fund could sell all of its shares, which may reduce Sgoltaire's performance by making it harder to raise finance. The creation of long-term, sustainable economic competitive advantage is consistent with Sgoltaire's main objective, which is to maximise the long-term wealth of its shareholders.

Apart from the business and economic consequences of the investment in Kayland, ethical issues need to be considered. Although Kayland's environmental regulations allow the discharge of diluted WPA into rivers, it would clearly be unethical to take action which could harm human health in the long term. Significantly, the discharge of WPA into rivers is not permitted in Jayland.

The use of scarce river water to dilute WPA, in order to conform to Kayland's limited environmental regulations, is also an ethical issue. Using scarce water in such a way may cause harm to the local population and their livestock.

The board has not yet estimated the costs of cleaning up the proposed site at Kayland once production ceases. This could be a deliberate strategy as the board could think this is unnecessary due to the less strict environmental regulations there. Leaving the site contaminated with harmful chemicals, after decommissioning the plant, could affect the company's reputation in the long term and is unethical.

Conversely, the board does have a duty to develop strategies which benefit internal stakeholders such as shareholders and employees. For example, incurring costs to find safe ways of disposing of WPA, which could eventually turn out to be harmless, could reduce long-term shareholder wealth. Also, while many employees may want to work for a business with ethical strategies, the financial costs of these may reduce their job security by making the business less profitable.

Business performance

Poor ethical behaviour can have a big impact on Sgoltaire's reputation, leading to customers boycotting its products and a reduction in financial performance. For the proposed project in Kayland, Sgoltaire's reputation could be damaged in the short term if it were found to be paying local workers unacceptably low wages.

A strategic decision to discharge WPA into rivers or not clean up the site could increase the interest of environmental campaigners, who may join forces with other stakeholder groups such as consumers and the government in order to increase their power. This will increase any possible damage to Sgoltaire's reputation. Managing these groups will incur cost and management time and possibly risk fines and penalties for poor environmental performance. These costs could, in the long term, exceed the costs of disposing of WPA in an environmentally safe manner. The use of water, which is a scarce resource, could also increase the interest of environmental campaigners.

Poor ethical behaviour could also reduce long-term financial performance, if people were to become ill as a result of contact with WPA; as well as the impact on reputation, there could be fines and lawsuits, the value of which is hard to quantify. Formulating an alternative strategy for the safe disposal of WPA may therefore be beneficial to long-term performance, even if there were a short-term cost to this.

Behaving ethically can have a positive effect on business performance, for example, by creating brand loyalty.

This already appears to be the case, as Sgoltaire is a well-known and trusted brand. Its household detergents and cleaning products command premium prices because they use ingredients and processes which cause less harm to the environment than those of competitors.

The publication of the annual CSR report will communicate how ethically Sgoltaire behaves towards a wide range of interested stakeholders. The stakeholders who value ethical behaviour will react positively to ethical behaviour by Sgoltaire. Customers may choose to buy its products, or investors to buy its shares because of this.

(b) Environmental management accounting (EMA) relates to the production and analysis of financial and non-financial information to help a business identify environment-related costs and manage its performance in respect of the environment.

Calculating costs

As Sgoltaire is listed in Jayland, it must produce an annual CSR report which demonstrates its performance in environmental and other social and ethical matters. The company will need to measure environment-related costs to compile this. The sophistication of the company's information systems is unclear, but traditional information systems do not capture environment-related costs, such as the costs to dispose of WPA, which may be hidden in overheads.

EMA helps to capture these hidden costs as well as contingent costs, for example, in cleaning up contaminated sites after production ceases. Of all the environment-related costs, the reputation and relationship costs which may occur, for example, if discharged WPA harms the health of large numbers of people, may be the largest cost.

By the use of techniques such as environmental activity-based costing, input/output analysis and lifecycle costing, EMA can be used to develop a clearer understanding of costs, particularly environment-related costs, meaning that budgets will be more realistic. This will make them more useful for planning purposes. Managers appraised using these budgets, which could include budgets specifically relating to environment-related costs, would be more motivated to achieve any targets set.

Sgoltaire may have to invest in more sophisticated information systems in order to capture environment-related costs which are currently hidden within overheads. The cost of this needs to be compared against the benefits of doing so.

Investment appraisal

EMA helps to ensure that all environment-related costs are included in an investment appraisal. For example, the board's calculations of NPV of the proposal to manufacture Chemical K in either Jayland or Kayland did not include estimates for the present values of decommissioning the plant or of cleaning the sites when production ceases.

If investment appraisals do not include all relevant costs such as these, business performance may decrease as Sgoltaire may start to manufacture products which will have a low, or even negative, NPV which will not generate long-term shareholder wealth.

If the project were to take place in Jayland, these costs would reduce the NPV of the project by 40% (W1), which is a large amount. The board has not estimated the present value of the costs to clean up the site in Kayland. As a result of logistical difficulties due to Kayland being 8,000km from Jayland, decommissioning costs would be 50% higher than in Jayland and so for the same reason, clean-up costs in Kayland might also cost 50% more.

On this assumption, the NPVs of both alternatives would be $120m. The board would probably choose to manufacture in Jayland, as there are lower risks by operating in the home country. If the environment-related costs of decommissioning and clean up were not taken into account, the board may have chosen to undertake the project in Kayland because the NPV of the project was $40m ($240 – $200) more than in Jayland.

Setting performance measures and targets

EMA can be used to set targets for improving performance in respect of the environment, for example, by reducing environment-related costs, fines or taxes. This is important as Sgoltaire publishes an annual CSR report, so its environmental performance is clear to a range of stakeholders, many of whom have an interest in environmental matters.

Performance targets could be financial or non-financial, for example, physical quantities. If the production of Chemical K were to commence in Kayland, a non-financial target could be the volume of water taken from the local river. This is because water is a scarce resource in Kayland and taking too much of it may have a harmful effect on the local environment, the human population, and their livestock.

Environmental performance measures could be internal or external. Targets could relate to both short-term and long-term performance. The number of cases of ill health due to contact with WPA is an external measure relating to long-term performance.

Product pricing

Using EMA to develop a clearer understanding of costs also helps Sgoltaire in setting a price for Chemical K. EMA will help Sgoltaire to understand all of the costs in the product's lifecycle and what drives them. These will include environment-related costs which are incurred before or after production begins or after it ends, such as decommissioning or clean-up costs. Sgoltaire can price the product to ensure that all of these costs are covered. This should ensure that the company can make an acceptable profit on the sale of the product over its lifecycle and can choose not to make products which are likely make losses. This will improve long-term financial performance.

Environment-related costs occurring after production ceases may be incurred in many years' time. Predicting these costs may be significantly affected by inflation, changes in the cost of capital and the possible introduction of stricter environmental regulations in the future.

By demonstrating that production of Chemical K is made in such a way as to minimise harm to the environment, Sgoltaire may be able to charge a premium price to customers to whom this is important. Though the use of Chemical K is unclear, many of its household products already command premium prices for this reason.

Working

NPV of the two proposals after including decommissioning and clean-up costs

	Jayland	*Kayland*
	$m	$m
NPV of project estimated by the board	200	240
Decommissioning cost	(20)	(30)
Cleaning cost	(60)	(90)*
NPV after decommissioning and cleaning	120	120
Decommissioning and cleaning costs as a % of the estimated NPV (80/200:120/240)	40%	50%

*Cleaning costs of Kayland estimated at 50% higher than in Jayland.

9 Alflonnso

Workbook reference

You should already be familiar with activity-based costing from your earlier studies (in Performance Management), but it is revisited, in the context of activity-based management, in Chapter 12 of the Workbook. Environmental management accounting is discussed in Chapter 4.

Top tips

Part (a). The calculations themselves should be relatively straightforward. However, note that the overheads are not allocated only to these three products. For example, the $300m of waste treatment costs relates to the total of 55 million litres, not just to the quantities of waste by-product generated by ALF7, Red and Green.

Part (b). The figures shown in Appendix 1 should have provided some context for this requirement. Appendix 1 suggests that Red is the most profitable of the three products. However, will this still be the case using ABC, and considering the products' entire life cycles?

The calculations themselves for this question are not difficult, but there are a number of elements to them, so it is important to follow a structured approach:

- Appendix 1 shows profits for a single period, and the waste treatment costs calculated in (a) (ii) are also for a single period (year). So, first you need to calculate a revised annual profit for each product.
- Next you need to multiply the revised annual profit by the product's life cycle, to find life cycle profit.
- The life cycle profit then has to be adjusted for any pre-production or post-production costs (for example, decommissioning costs).
- Finally, the total life cycle cost has to be divided by the number of litres produced over the product's life cycle to identify the average profit per litre over the life cycle.

Once you have done the calculations, don't forget you also need to comment on the results. How does the relative profitability of each of the products compare to that in Appendix 1, and what are the main reasons for any differences?

Part (c). In the scenario, the CFO talks about a presentation they watched which showed how EMA can help to reduce three categories of cost – conventional, contingent and reputation – and improve performance as a result.

As such, a sensible approach would be to use each of these categories as headings in your answer, and to consider how EMA could affect them. For example, how might EMA affect decision making, which in turn could affect the division's performance in relation to each of the categories?

The scenario highlights some potential reputation issues quite clearly – for example, about Green's unsuitability for use in climates where crop production is already difficult. The sequence of the requirements in the question should also help you here. For example, one of the main life cycle costs in your calculations in part (b) should have been decommissioning costs, which would be a good illustration of contingent costs.

Examining team's comments.

In **part (b)**, many candidates showed a fundamental lack of technical competence by failing to distinguish between costs that occurred on an annual basis and those that related to the product's overall life.

Candidates must also appreciate that if they are asked to comment on the results, then what is required is more than simply saying 'this figure is larger than that one' – which can be seen from the figures themselves. Instead, in a question like this, the commentary should consider the implications of the figures: will they change a decision? Does the use of one technique fundamentally change the cost or product, and what are the implications of this?

In **part (c),** the majority of the marks available were for applying EMA to the practices of the Agrochemicals Division. Would practice change? How? What might be involved? However, a number of candidates' answers largely only defined and/or explained EMA, without considering its potential benefits to the division. Unfortunately, answers based on theory alone can only score around 25% of the marks available, meaning they fall well short of the number of marks required to pass.

Marking guide	Marks
(a) Waste treatment costs – 2 marks	
R&D costs – 1 mark	
	3
(b) Revenue, direct costs, overheads (given in scenario) – 1 mark	
Waste treatment costs – 1 mark	
Total net profit over life cycle (before other life cycle costs) – 1 mark	
Scientific study – 1 mark	
Decommissioning cost – 1 mark	
R&D costs – 1 mark	
Total litres – 1 mark	
Average profit per litre over life cycle – 1 mark	
Comments on calculations – up to 3 marks	
Total for part (b): up to 9	
	9
(c) Description of EMA – up to 2 marks	
Impact of EMA on each cost category: conventional, contingent, reputation – up to 3 marks per category	
Total for part (c): up to 8	
	8
Professional skills	
Analysis and Evaluation	
• Use of information provided to perform a suitable/comprehensive evaluation of profit	
• Appropriate use of the data to support discussion and draw appropriate conclusions	
• Demonstration of reasoned and balanced judgement or assessment of the overall usefulness of EMA	
• Demonstration of ability to consider relevant factors applicable to Alflonnso Co's situation	
• Balanced appraisal of information	
Commercial acumen	
• Effective use of examples and/or calculations from the scenario information and other practical considerations related to the context to illustrate points being made	
Maximum	5
Total	25

(a) **Calculation of waste treatment cost**

	ALF7	*Red*	*Green*
Quantity of waste by-product (m litres)	8.0	34.0	0.75
[m litres produced/no. of m litres to make 1 litre of waste]	[100/12.5]	[85/2.5]	[75/100]
Allocated total $300m according to quantity of waste as proportion of total 55m litres:			
Annual waste treatment allocated ($m):	43.6	185.5	4.1
	[8 × 300/55]	[34 × 300/55]	[0.75 × 300/55]

R&D cost

	ALF7	*Red*	*Green*
Allocated total $60m according to required hours of research as proportion of total 30,400 hours:			
R&D treatment allocated ($m):	1.6	16.8	7.9
	[800 × 60/30,400]	[8,500 × 60/30,400]	[4,000 × 60/30,400]

(b) **Average unit cost of each product over total life cycle**

$m	*ALF7*	*Red*	*Green*
Revenue (given)	800.0	1,105.0	825.0
Direct material, labour and energy (given)	(524.0)	(724.0)	(565.0)
Factory overheads (given)	(80.0)	(122.0)	(74.0)
Waste treatment (from part (a))	(43.6)	(185.5)	(4.1)
Total annual net profit	152.4	73.5	181.9
Life cycle duration (years)	3	15	8
Total net profit over life cycle (before other life cycle costs)	457.2	1,102.5	1,455.2
Scientific study ($4m × 20 years)	–	(80.0)	–
Decommissioning cost	–	(45.0)	–
R&D cost (from part (a))	(1.6)	(16.8)	(7.9)
Total net profit over life cycle	455.6	960.7	1,447.3
No. of litres produced over the life cycle (m)	300	1,275	600
Average profit per litre over life cycle	$1.52	$0.75	$2.41

From the analyst's calculations in Appendix 1, Red has the highest profitability per litre of the three products at $2.26, but this only covers a single period. As such, it does not consider costs which occur before production commences or after it ceases. When the costs of the products over their entire life cycles are taken into account, Red has the lowest average unit profit, the highest being Green at $2.41. This change has occurred as the R&D costs, the cost of the study which will span 20 years and the decommissioning costs have now been recognised. Knowing the costs over the entire life cycle of a product will help the Agrochemicals Division to better evaluate its investment decisions, determine appropriate prices and generate an acceptable margin.

(c) **EMA**

EMA involves the production of non-financial and financial information to support internal environmental management processes. This could involve measuring the physical movements of inputs to a production process, such as materials and energy, and outputs such as waste.

The Agrochemicals Division could also record financial data on costs and savings related to the environment. It appears that, in common with most other businesses, these costs are not currently identified by Alflonnso's accounting system and they lie hidden within overheads.

Managers have no incentive to reduce these environment-related costs as they are not even aware of them, or the costs of poor environmental practices. EMA allows an organisation to identify environment-related costs and take steps to control them. Such costs are often categorised into conventional costs, contingent costs and reputation costs.

Conventional costs

These costs include the cost of energy and raw materials, and may remain hidden within overheads. The energy costs of the three new products in the analyst's income statement are simply combined with raw material and direct labour costs. This does not, for example, highlight the relatively high energy cost to produce Green. Being unaware of this cost, managers are unable to take steps to redesign the specification or production process for the product in order to reduce the cost. Techniques such as ABC can improve the visibility of environmental costs by charging these costs on the basis of the activities which drive them – which are research hours and volume of waste by-products, for R&D costs and waste treatment costs respectively – will give a more accurate costing. This will provide a better basis on which to evaluate the new products and set appropriate prices.

Contingent costs

These are costs which are incurred in the future, for example, the decommissioning costs of the plant used to manufacture Red. This cost is significant, at an estimated $45m, but occurs 15 years in the future and so the estimation is unlikely to be accurate.

Identification of these contingent costs will at least allow the Agrochemicals Division to more accurately estimate the cost of each of the three new products. Also, by identifying these costs at an early stage, this may allow managers to redesign the specification or production process for the product in order to reduce the cost and help prevent managers from focusing only on short-term performance.

Reputation costs

Reputation costs are incurred where an organisation acts in a way which may cause harm to the environment, and include sales lost as a result of loss of reputation. These costs are hard to quantify. For example, the accumulation of the existing product, ALF6, in the soil is said to have a potential effect on crop yields which may lead to future claims from users of the product or to loss of sales due to its potential harm to the environment.

Similarly, Alflonnso's failure, by producing Green, to improve crop yields in countries where food production is already scarce is likely to arouse disapproval by public and governments in the 25 countries where it operates. This again may result in lost sales or refusal by governments to grant licences for Alflonnso to operate.

Making managers aware of these reputation costs should focus their attention on the need to manage the risks of them occurring.

PERFORMANCE MEASUREMENT SYSTEMS AND DEVELOPMENTS IN TECHNOLOGY

10 Luvij

Workbook reference

The characteristics which affect the usefulness of information are discussed in Chapter 5 of the Workbook, as are unified corporate databases. Performance management issues in relation to joint ventures are discussed in Chapter 13.

Top tips

Part (a). The final paragraph in the scenario provides some useful clues for this requirement: for example, by highlighting the managers have difficulty understanding the large volume of data; and that they often receive it too late for it to be useful. They are clearly issues which reduce the value of the information to them.

A useful way to approach this requirement could be to think of the characteristics of good information, and then whether Luvij's information demonstrates those characteristics. As the requirement asks you about 'factors which might limit the usefulness' of the information, you need to focus specifically on problems, or potential problems, with the information.

However, as well as explaining the potential limitations of the current information, you are also asked to evaluate how the use of a unified corporate database could help to overcome these limitations.

We have structured our answer so that after each 'limitation' in the current information we evaluate how using a unified corporate database could help to overcome the limitation. However, you could equally look at all the potential issues with the current information first, and then evaluate how a unified database could help to overcome them.

Crucially though, to score well, it is important that you address both parts of the requirement, and assess them specifically in the context of Luvij, rather than making generic points about the characteristics of good information, or the benefits of using a unified corporate database. For example, the second paragraph highlights that design trends in the market change frequently – so it is important of receiving information quickly. The current spreadsheet is only circulated at the end of each quarter. So will that limit its usefulness, and could the unified corporate database help to ensure information is available more quickly?

Part (b). The requirement here also has two elements: advising the board about problems, first, with measuring the performance of the joint venture; and second, managing the performance of the joint venture.

Again, though, the final paragraph provides a useful clue to some of the issues here, by highlighting that the businesses have different objectives. These objectives have been explained in more detail earlier in the scenario: with Luvij wanting to expand its capacity in order to become the market leader, but Shirville simply wanting to use up spare capacity in its factory until the lease expires in three years' time.

A key question to ask yourself here is: what are the implications of these differences in objectives, and how could they create problems for the joint venture?

Similarly, the scenario tells us that Luvij aims to sell high quality children's footwear to independent footwear retailers, while Shirville produces high volumes for supermarkets and chain stores. So this should also prompt you to think about the different strategies each company is pursuing (differentiation vs cost leadership?) and therefore the aspects of performance which will be most important for them to measure and manage. If the two partners are prioritising different aspects of performance, what implications could this have for the joint venture and its chances of success?

Examining team's comments

Part (a) was generally well answered. Candidates identified the missing areas of information needed by the company and then connected these to the benefits which could achieved by using a unified corporate database.

Candidates also generally performed well in **part (b)** with many answers describing the differences between the two organisations and how this would affect the joint venture.

Marking guide

	Marks
(a) 1 mark per relevant point	
Limitations of the usefulness of the external information currently used – up to 7 marks	
Evaluation of the use of a unified corporate database to overcome those limitations – up to 7 marks	
Maximum for part (a): 12 marks	
	12
(b) 1 mark per relevant point	
Problems of performance measurement – up to 5 marks	
Problems of performance management – up to 5 marks	
Maximum for part (b): 8 marks	
	8
Professional skills	
Analysis and Evaluation	
• Use of information provided to perform a comprehensive evaluation of existing information	
• Demonstration of reasoned and balanced judgement / assessment of the potential benefits of a database	
• Demonstration of ability to consider relevant factors applicable to Luvij Co's situation	
Commercial acumen	
• Effective use of examples and/or calculations from the scenario information and other practical considerations related to the context to illustrate points being made relating to Luvij	
• Recognition of problems	
Maximum	5
Total	25

(a) **Usefulness of information**

> **Tutorial note.** This suggested solution uses the characteristics of good information as a framework for assessing the external information Luvij currently uses. However, there are a variety of ways to structure this answer, and you would receive credit for relevant points you make, even if the structure of your answer is different from the suggested solution.

Relevant

For the external information to be useful, it should be relevant to the needs of the users. The information in the quarterly spreadsheet contains sales data as well as information on market trends in designs. All of this information may not be relevant for all of the departments to which it is circulated. For example, data on design trends may not be relevant to the production department using it to plan production capacity.

A unified database, integrating data from different sources, would make data more relevant to users by giving users only information and reports which are relevant to them and sharing data from all relevant departments. Users would not waste time interpreting data which is irrelevant to them.

Timely

For external information to be useful, it must be available when needed. This is particularly so in the fashion industry where designs change quickly and where competitors may offer short-term discounts. The external information at Luvij is only sent at the end of each quarter, which is likely to be too infrequent in the fast moving industry in which Luvij operates. Additionally, as the information is prepared by one staff member, there could be delays in producing it if they were on sick leave, for example.

A unified database would ensure that data was available instantly, especially if linked to retailers' own systems' real-time sales data. This should improve the speed of decision making.

Accurate

To be useful, information must be accurate. Entering large volumes of data into a complex spreadsheet is prone to error, as well as being time-consuming. Inaccurate data may lead to poor decision making.

A unified database would process all data automatically with minimal human intervention, and would thus be less prone to inaccuracies. All departments would share identical data.

Communication

Although the spreadsheet of external information at least ensures that all departments have access to the same data, the large volume of data may be difficult to understand. Managers may be overloaded with data, much of which they do not need.

A unified database would allow users access only to information which they need. This would be in an easy to use format, perhaps with the ability to drill down to more detailed information held in the database.

Emailing data to a large number of staff may mean that confidential or commercially sensitive information, such as on design trends, is shared with staff who do not require it. A unified database would restrict access to information, using passwords, only to staff who are authorised to receive it.

Cost effective

The cost of producing the external information should not exceed the benefits of doing so. Costs of the current system include not only the costs of employing the team to compile the information but also time spent collecting, processing or interpreting data which may be inaccurate, irrelevant or out of date.

Using a unified database would incur costs of buying, maintaining and developing the system, as well as staff training. An evaluation must be made whether these costs are justified by the benefits. Some adaptation of the existing system, such as increasing the frequency of reporting the information, or sending different sets of information to different departments, may be more cost effective.

(b) **Problems of performance measurement in the joint venture**

Measuring the performance of the joint venture may require Luvij and Shirville to share confidential information, which they may be unwilling to do. Luvij's innovative designs for children's footwear and Shirville's knowledge of advanced production techniques are both likely to be commercially sensitive.

It is unclear exactly what each of the parties contributes to the joint venture. Luvij is providing innovative designs, and Shirville is providing advanced manufacturing machinery and production techniques. As each party is providing different things to the joint venture, it may be hard to measure the contribution, to profit for example, from each party.

Luvij and Shirville will have their own information systems. These may be incompatible, or it may be difficult or costly to integrate them. Each party may measure or collect information in a different way, which will mean information used to measure the performance of the joint venture is not prepared on a consistent basis.

Problems of performance management

Luvij's objective for the venture is to become the market leader in high-quality children's footwear. Shirville's objective is to utilise spare production capacity in a factory where the lease is due to expire in three years. As the parties have different objectives, it may be hard to develop performance metrics for the joint venture. The share of the chosen market may be a key performance metric for Luvij, and return on capital employed may be appropriate for Shirville. The metrics chosen may conflict, and their relative importance may be unclear. This will make it difficult for managers to manage the joint venture according to each of the venture partner's objectives.

Luvij's objectives for the joint venture are long term, whereas Shirville may choose to end the joint venture upon expiry of the factory lease in just three years. Establishing timescales for performance objectives may be difficult as each party has different time horizons for the venture.

Luvij is entering a new market and has already invested heavily in market research and product design. Shirville seems to have a much lower risk appetite, as it only wants to utilise spare capacity. Managing performance may be difficult because Luvij may wish to make decisions which involve a higher level of risk than Shirville may wish to accept.

The parties have may have different expectations of the level of quality of products arising from the joint venture. Luvij manufactures high-quality footwear and will want its range of children's footwear to be of a quality consistent with its women's footwear range. Shirville supplies supermarkets and high street stores, probably with lower quality products. Disagreement about acceptable levels of quality may damage performance of the joint venture.

11 Clonyard

Workbook reference

The 7S model is covered in Chapter 4 and ERPS is covered in Chapter 5 of the Workbook.

Top tips

Part (a)

The appendix to the question presented the 7S model and identified which parts represented soft elements. The candidate was then required to apply the stated soft elements (staff, skills, style) to the scenario to illuminate the difficulties in integrating Clonyard. A good answer required practical comments on these areas, not in overly theoretical terms; 1 mark was available per point.

Part (b)

This required an assessment of both the possible advantages and also possible disadvantages of the introduction of an ERPS using the clues provided in the scenario. A good answer would apply a basic understanding of an ERPS to the scenario provided.

Marking guide	Marks
(a) Skills – up to 3 marks	
Staff – up to 3 marks	
Style – up to 3 marks	
Conclusion – up to 2 marks	
	10
(b) Advantages of ERPS – up to 6 marks	
Disadvantages of ERPS – up to 6 marks	
	10

Marking guide	Marks
Professional marks	
Analysis and Evaluation:	
• Reasoned assessment of the three soft elements of the McKinsey 7S model in relation to the alignment of Elrig and Clonyard	
• Balanced and reasoned appraisal of the ERPS proposal	
Scepticism:	
• Recognition that the McKinsey 7S model has overlap between the elements and the company has not attempted to align them	
• Recognition that the ERPS won't integrate the two companies beyond initial operational benefits	
Commercial Acumen:	
• Recommendation on the introduction of an ERPS clearly demonstrates an understanding of the issues facing Clonyard and Elrig and is commercially sound	
Maximum	5
Total	25

(a) **Skills**

It is clear that Clonyard and Elrig train and develop their staff in different ways. Clonyard has placed an emphasis on detailed product knowledge and on ensuring that the individual's needs are met. Such training and development is very much aligned with a company that has a specialist niche. It is also clear that Elrig's focus is less on meeting individual requirements than in pursuing a sale and it is likely that Elrig's staff have been trained and developed more in terms of sales techniques than with regard to product knowledge. This means that the staff from Clonyard have a different skill set and it is clear, from their reaction to the Elrig staff working in Clonyard shops that no attempt has been made to develop the skill set of either group of employees in order to align them with each other.

Staff

It is clear, especially given the point above, that staff are treated in a different way in both organisations. It is also evident from the scenario that Clonyard staff are leaving the organisation. It is likely that staff have been given responsibility for inventory and shop management in Clonyard and that the focus in the company has been on developing the individual to enhance their range of specialist knowledge. Elrig's singular focus on market share would suggest that Elrig's staff are more likely to be trained and developed in the areas of financial performance measures and be aware of costs, margins and the financial implications of the decisions being made. Indeed, the fact that Elrig's staff are seeking to make a sale quickly suggests that they are aware of the cost of the time they spend with each customer and it is likely that there is an ideal time per sale that they will work towards.

Style

Style usually represents the corporate culture of the organisation and it is clear that the cultures are very different within Elrig and Clonyard. The issue of the takeover being hostile in the first instance is perhaps an indicator that the styles of the organisations are very different. Style is also indicative of how an organisation presents itself to the outside world and again it is clear, through the interactions with customers, which Clonyard would seek to satisfy the customer's specific requirements whereas Elrig would try to sell a product to the customer with the minimum time spent on the transaction. Such a contrast in styles would inevitably be reflected in the customer experience and it may prove to be very damaging for Clonyard if its style is aligned with that of Elrig. Customers may feel that there is no longer any reason to visit Elrig if its main differentiators of individual service, product specialism and time spent with the customer are removed.

Conclusion

It is clear that there is overlap and interconnectivity between each soft element of the 7S model. Elrig appears to have made no attempt to align these differing elements and as a result there are different styles of operation and different skill sets in the respective staff.

The 7S model has been useful in addressing this lack of alignment and provides evidence to Elrig that it must revert to the mission of Clonyard and decide if this now needs to change in the light of the takeover. If not, and as the 7S model has shown, Elrig might be best advised to allow Clonyard to operate as it was doing quite successfully beforehand and consider integration and alignment as a long term rather than a short-term goal.

(b) **Advantages**

An ERPS would help alleviate the problems detailed with regard to inventory control in that the current inventory levels would be very clear on the ERPS and any sale would register immediately, thereby showing the effect on the inventory overall. Minimum inventory levels may be set within the ERPS and an order to the supplier automatically triggered when inventory reaches that level. An ERPS will also allow details of the delivery to be tracked and the ERPS will enable staff at the appropriate level to discover how long deliveries are taking and to manage the supplier relationship accordingly.

The discounting of product lines in certain areas is clearly a key part of Elrig's strategy to enhance its market share and the sales manager is correct in that it is impossible to impose this strategy on Clonyard with such old data. An ERPS would ensure that the sales manager has access to immediate sales of each product and could compare this with both planned sales of the product and past sales of the product. The ERPS may also permit the inclusion of some external data which could inform the company of any changes in the market for particular products or distinct product lines. This would certainly enable the sales manager to take real time decisions with regard to which products might be discounted and to what level. The ERPS would be of great benefit to him in this endeavour.

The ERPS, as highlighted above, has the ability to remove the responsibility for the ordering of inventory from the employee and undertake this function based on the minimum inventory levels that have been input. This would certainly solve the problem of Clonyard employees not entering the purchase order into the computer system and would ensure that the relevant people in the organisation are fully aware of the inventory both on order and in store.

Disadvantages

However, the view of the director of Elrig appears to be that they can use the introduction of an ERPS to impose Elrig's strategy on Clonyard and this is something which should be avoided. The strategies of the two companies should be aligned initially and any shared computer system, and the information that it might generate, should be agreed thereafter.

There are other significant potential negative effects of introducing the ERPS based on the director's view. For example, it may further enhance the feeling of alienation that many Clonyard employees appear to be feeling if another system is imposed on them without discussion and agreement. Their motivation would suffer and Clonyard's ability to maintain its position in the market may be affected. This market position is, after all, the main reason for Elrig's purchase of Clonyard in the first place.

There is evidence from the scenario that Clonyard is delaying the information that it offers Elrig as even manual systems could offer more up to date data than that detailed by the operations manager and the sales manager. This sub optimal behaviour has perhaps been a reaction by Clonyard staff to the imposition of Elrig's systems. Much as the removal of any sub optimal behaviour should be encouraged, the introduction of the ERPS without discussion and agreement may enhance those feelings of Elrig imposing its operations upon Clonyard. This stresses again the dangers of introducing a computer system to integrate one company's operations into another and further highlights the need to come to a common approach with regard to the future strategic direction of Clonyard.

It is also naïve of the Elrig director to assume that Clonyard employees will be enthusiastic about the introduction of a new computer system. Aside from the potential negative aspects associated with control that are highlighted above, there is evidence from the scenario that Clonyard employees are not engaging fully with their own computer system. This may be because they have not been properly trained and the prospect of the introduction of a new and much more complex system may be very threatening for them.

Alongside the difficulties associated with the introduction of the ERPS into the Elrig/Clonyard operation, an ERPS has other well established and more generic disadvantages such as its cost, its difficulty in adapting to the specifics of some individual business operations and the time taken to implement the system.

Overall, the introduction of an ERPS would certainly help with regard to some operational aspects detailed in the scenario. The overall benefits are likely to be much wider than this with, for example, the access to real time information being very useful to Elrig/Clonyard in their current environment. However, the introduction of the ERPS should not be used as a way of integrating Clonyard within Elrig's operation. This needs to be done at a much more fundamental level where strategic direction is agreed. Using an ERPS to integrate without this agreement first is likely to lead to more problems with regard to integration than it will solve.

12 Quark Healthcare

Workbook reference

Developments in IT systems (such as the introduction of RFID tags)are discussed inChapter 5 of the Workbook. Lean systems are also discussed in Chapter 5.

Top tips

Part (a)

It is very important that you think about the impact of the RFID system specifically in the context of the areas highlighted by the CFO: (i) the costs and benefits associated with producing information from the system; (ii) the impact of the system on the nature of the information supplied; (iii) changes to performance management reporting; and (iv) how the new information could be used to improve control at the hospitals.

To this end, it would be sensible to use each of the CFO's suggestions as headings in your answer, to make sure you cover all of them.

The 'control' issues and their impact on performance should be relatively easy to identify from the scenario – for example, staff are unable to find equipment because it hasn't been replaced after being used, and as a result patient care is delayed while staff waste time trying to find the equipment.

The problems staff face in finding equipment and drugs provide a link between parts (a) and (b) of the question. One of the key principles of 'lean' systems is the removal of waste and non value adding activities. Time spent looking for equipment or drugs clearly doesn't provide any value to hospital patients. Similarly, 'lean' systems aim to promote efficiency.

So, a sensible way to approach **part (b)** will be to evaluate how far the RFID system can reduce waste and improve efficiency at the hospital.

Marking guide	Marks
(a) Costs and benefits associated with producing the information from the RFID system – 1 mark per relevant point up to a maximum of 3 marks	
Impact of the RFID system on the nature of the information supplied – 1 mark per relevant point up to a maximum of 3 marks	
Changes to performance reporting resulting from the implementation of the new system – 1 mark per relevant point up to a maximum of 3 marks	
Use of information from the new RFID system to improve control at the hospitals – 1 mark per relevant point up to a maximum of 6 marks	
Total for part (a): up to 13	13

ANSWERS

Marking guide	Marks
(b) Definition of lean systems – up to a maximum of 2	
Analysis of the impact of the RFID system on the management of the hospital – 1 mark per relevant point, up to a maximum of 7	
(Within this 7 marks, up to 2 marks are available for definition of the 5 Ss of lean)	
Total for part (b): up to 7	
	7
Professional skills	
Analysis and Evaluation	
• Use of information provided to perform a suitable/comprehensive evaluation of the RFID system	
• Demonstration of reasoned and balanced judgement	
• Demonstration of ability to consider relevant factors applicable to Quark Co's situation	
Scepticism	
• Effective challenge and critical assessment of the RFID system	
Commercial acumen	
• Effective use of examples and/or calculations from the scenario information and other practical considerations related to the context to illustrate points being made relating to Quark Co	
• Recognition of problems in implementing the new system	
Maximum	5
Total	25

(a) **Costs and benefits of the system**

Cost – There is likely to be considerable cost associated with the hardware and software needed to establish the RFID system. A significant amount of time may also be required to tag the equipment and drugs which are to be included in the system.

However, the costs should be compared to the benefits which will accrue from the system:

Efficiency savings – Hospital staff will save time because they will no longer have to search for items once those items have been tagged.

Patient care – Improvements in patient care as a result of hospital staff being able to find equipment or drugs immediately rather than having to search for them.

Impact of the nature of the information supplied

Non-financial information – Although the information being supplied about Quark's equipment and inventory is non-financial (relating to the location and quantity of equipment and drugs in Quark's hospitals), it should already be included in the hospital's information systems.

Timeliness and accuracy – However, the major impact of the new system should come from the improvements it can provide to the timeliness and accuracy of the information being recorded. The RFID tags will update information on a **real-time basis**. Moreover, because movements are **recorded automatically** the problem of the register not correctly reflecting the physical location of an asset will be overcome.

Batches of drugs – However, the quality of the information provided by the RFID tags may be less reliable for the drugs which are delivered in a single packaged batch. If a tag is applied to a batch as a whole when it is delivered to the hospital, then the information provided by the tag will no longer be reliable once the batch is opened and drugs are used from it.

Instead, there will still be a need for the hospital to physically count the quantities of these drugs actually held in inventory, rather than relying on the RFID information alone.

Performance management reporting

Weekly physical checks – Under its existing systems, Quark has to make weekly physical checks of the drugs held in inventory in order to update its records on the basis of those checks. However, the information provided by the RFID tags should mean that inventory records can be updated on a real-time basis, rather than being dependent on these weekly checks.

Access to information – The fact that the RFID information will be available on terminals throughout the hospitals should also help the speed with which staff can locate items of inventory or equipment. The ease and speed with which staff can search the information will depend on the number of terminals which are installed. It would also be useful for relevant staff to receive training on how to search for information on the terminals.

Improved control

Control over drugs – Quark's existing accounting systems aim to avoid theft and obsolescence of equipment and drugs. RFID tags should improve controls over security by providing greater transparency about the location of assets. For example, the tags will make it easy for staff to check that all the high-value drugs are stored in secure locations, thereby reducing the risk of them being stolen.

Reduced obsolescence – Additionally, the information available about the date drugs were delivered should help staff identify the order in which different batches of a drug should be used to prevent obsolescence and wastage.

Tagging equipment – We have already noted that tagging items of equipment will allow staff to find them more quickly and thereby provide faster service to patients. However, the RFID tags will also enable the hospitals' management teams to ensure that pieces of equipment are replaced and locked away in secure areas once they have been used. This again should help reduce the risk of theft, but perhaps equally importantly staff should be reminded of the importance of replacing items after they have been used, and of storing them in useful locations. This also links to the ideas of 'lean' systems which the CFO is interested in.

Practical issues – The **medical staff** are likely to be key stakeholders in the hospitals, so their attitude to the new system is likely to be very important. If they resist the system, then its implementation is unlikely to be successful, as appears to have been the case with the new method for recording drugs administered to patients.

In this respect, it will be important to consult the medical staff over the design and implementation of the RFID system. Not only does consulting them recognise their position as key stakeholders, but also it gives them the opportunity to ensure the system is designed in a way which provides them with the information they need.

(b) **Lean systems**

Removal of waste – The aim of 'lean' systems is to minimise the amount of resources (including time) which are consumed by the activities of an organisation. A key element of this comes from identifying and eliminating all non value adding activities. In this context, 'lean' also involves the systematic elimination of waste.

In relation to information systems, waste arises from difficulties in accessing and retrieving information, or from having to correct inaccurate information. This kind of 'waste' has clearly been an issue for Quark – for example, where staff have had to waste time looking for equipment or drugs which have not been not stored in the correct place. Such activity is clearly not value adding; rather it detracts from the value (care) which Quark can offer to its patients.

Improved efficiency – In contrast to this, the goal of a 'lean' operating system is to get the right things to the right place at the right time. In the context of Quark, this could mean enabling staff to know where equipment is so that it can be made available in the right place when it is needed by patients. Consequently, introducing the RFID system should help the operations management at the hospitals become leaner.

'Lean' systems can also have wider cultural implications which could be beneficial at the hospitals, in particular in relation to changing attitudes towards 'waste' and 'inefficiency'. The instances of equipment lying unused in one area of the hospital while being searched for in another area (to the detriment of patient care) would seem to be symptomatic of waste and inefficiency in the hospitals.

5 Ss – Lean principles are often characterised through 5 Ss, which could usefully be introduced at Quark:

Structurise – Identify the things which are most important and introduce order where possible. At Quark this could mean identifying the optimal locations for storing equipment, on the basis of where it is used most frequently.

Systemise – Arrange essential items in order so that they can be quickly and easily accessed. The RFID system will make it easier for staff to locate the equipment and drugs they need.

Sanitise – Keep the working environment clean. Be tidy, and avoid clutter. Although the RFID system should help staff to find drugs and equipment more easily, there is a danger that staff may think that this reduces the need for them to replace them after use, or to keep stocks of drugs tidy and in order.

Standardise – Make cleaning and checking a routine. For example, the RFID information could be used by management to check that equipment is replaced after use; and staff could even be monitored on the extent to which they keep their sections of the hospitals tidy.

Self-discipline – Sustain via motivation; for example, by reporting on performance. The system could produce exception reports highlighting pieces of equipment which had not been returned to a secure store once they were no longer being used. Corrective action can then be taken to return the equipment to an appropriate store area.

Impact of the RFID system

In some organisations, 5Ss has become a cleaning and housekeeping exercise only, and the underlying philosophy behind the concept has been lost. If this happens, then RFID's ability to make the management system leaner will be reduced. However, if the RFID information system is seen as an important part of quality management at the hospitals, then its impact should be more beneficial.

13 Nelson, Jody & Nigel

Workbook reference

Performance management information systems, and lean principles, are discussed in Chapter 5 of the Workbook.

Top tips

Part (a)

There are two aspects of the information system you need to assess here: whether it is effective in reducing waste; and whether it adds value to NJN's workflow.

A sensible approach to this requirement is to work through the scenario and identify features in the current system which relate to waste or adding value. Do these features reduce waste? Or are they actually creating waste?

For example, (in paragraph 2) we are told 'Packing lists are manually input...' and in the third paragraph we are told that in 8% of packing lists, at least one item is not available in the location or the quantity specified by the WIS, and these discrepancies have to be investigated. Do features like these suggest the system is effective in reducing waste?

Similarly, in the second paragraph of the scenario we are told the retail stores 'do not currently have access to real-time inventory levels'. As such, is the system adding any value – compared, for example, to a system in which the retail stores could see the inventory levels, and therefore didn't try to order an item which was unavailable?

The scenario provides a number of hints towards points to include in your answer, so if you use these efficiently you should be able to score well on this part of the question.

Part (b)

Before we can identify whether the three proposals will help to eliminate the different types of waste we first need to identify what these types of waste are. The sixth paragraph of the scenario suggests one: activities which do not add value to the customer; but waste can also result from over-production or holding excess inventory.

Having identified the causes of waste, we then need to ask will the proposals help to address then (or, are there problems with the proposals which will limit their effectiveness. One way to consider this might be to ask what changes NJN will have to make as a result of the proposals (and whether these will be beneficial)? For example, shutting down the additional means NJN will be able to hold less inventory (which is one of the types of waste).

Part (c)

Since the question asks whether 'each of the 5Ss' is adequately measured by the performance metrics a sensible way to structure your answer would be to use each 'S' as a sub-heading, and then to ask:

- What does that 'S' involve?
- Do any of the measures (in Appendix 1) relate to those aspects of performance?

For example, 'Sanitise' involves being tidy and avoiding clutter, so assessing the tidiness of the warehouse would help to measure this.

Note the verb is 'evaluate' so – where possible – you should try to present a balanced argument: identifying areas where 'S's are adequately measured, as well as areas where they are not.

Examining team's comments

Part (a). This was generally well done, with candidates able to identify and discuss the problems from the scenario. The better candidates then tied these problems to the operation of the information system and often made good suggestions for improvements.

Part (b). Although candidates were asked to view the reduction of waste as an application or lean principles, few structured their answers using lean ideas about waste. Nonetheless, by keeping their answers focused on the specifics of the scenario and the proposals, candidates still scored well in this requirement.

Part (c). Candidates' performance on this part of the question was mixed, as many did not appear to know the meaning of the lean principles (5Ss) given. However, candidates did offer some useful evaluation of the indicators from first principles (about reducing waste or increasing efficiency).

Marking guide	Marks
(a) Assessing whether the existing WIS is effective in reducing waste and adding value – 1 mark per relevant, valid point Total for part (a): up to 8	
	8
(b) Advising whether the three proposals will help to eliminate waste – 1 mark per relevant, valid point Total for part (b): up to 5	
	5
(c) Evaluating whether performance metrics adequately measure the 5Ss. 1 mark per relevant point, up to a maximum of 2 for each 'S' Total for part (c): up to 7	
	7

ANSWERS

Marking guide	Marks
Professional skills	
Analysis and Evaluation	
• Demonstration of reasoned and balanced judgement	
• Demonstration of ability to consider relevant factors applicable to NJN Co's situation	
• Balanced appraisal of information	
Commercial acumen	
• Effective use of examples from the scenario information and other practical considerations related to the context to illustrate points being made relating to NJN	
Maximum	5
Total	25

(a) **Manual input**

At NJN, at least some of the inputs to the WIS are manual, and that means they are prone to error. This is time consuming and costly.

The packing lists which are received in the shipping containers are input manually. If incorrectly input, the quantities of items in the locations in the WIS will also be incorrect. Incorrect information in the WIS wastes time by needing teams to investigate the discrepancies, reconcile inventory records with those held by the manufacturer, and correct the information held on the WIS.

Furthermore, customers will not receive the items they have ordered, as in 8% of picking notes, items are not in the location they should be, or are in insufficient quantities. This is a high proportion of errors. Staff will waste time looking for items stored in the wrong locations. This will cause customer dissatisfaction and mean that larger quantities of inventory will need to be held, which is a wasteful use of storage space. Fewer complete orders can be fulfilled per unit of warehouse space, than would otherwise be the case. Both of these are sources of waste.

In the longer term, this means NJN staff must undertake a series of cyclical inventory counts in order to correct the information held in the WIS. This is wasteful activity which does not add value to customers, and should be eliminated.

The provision of accurate inventory information will also be of value to the retailers who can place orders only for items which are available, rather than only finding out about unavailable items by receiving an email from NJN. This would lead to increased customer satisfaction by avoiding having stock outs of particular items by ordering alternatives.

NJN should consider the use of barcodes or radio frequency identifiers (RFIDs) on products, to ensure that accurate data is input into the WIS. Using these devices, the product numbers and quantities of goods entering and leaving the warehouse could be automatically read into the WIS, without any intervention from warehouse staff. This would reduce the time taken to manually input the data and improve its accuracy.

An effective information system may interface directly with the manufacturers' and retail customers' information systems through electronic data interchange (EDI). This would increase service levels by ensuring that all parts of the value chain had access to accurate and timely information.

Time delays

The packing list batches are not available until up to 48 hours after receipt of the goods. The information held in the WIS will therefore be out of date. Items which are required for sales orders may be unavailable for picking. The use of automated input, where possible, will increase the timeliness of the information input into the WIS. This will reduce the labour cost of correcting the system and improve the number, accuracy, and completeness of orders despatched to customers.

Currently, all picking notes are printed in the warehouse office, which may be some distance from the area where items are picked. This also implies the existence of a bottleneck in the provision of information to the staff picking the items and wastes staff time moving to and from the warehouse office to pick up the reports. An improvement would be to ensure that information is available when and where it is needed, using terminals in the warehouse, or portable devices such as tablets. This would reduce time spent collecting picking information.

Similarly, in order to investigate discrepancies, staff have to obtain special reports which the warehouse manager extracts from the WIS. Again, this is a bottleneck which could delay staff getting the correct information, and may mean that the reports are inconsistent depending on the parameters set to run them. An effective system would eliminate these problems by providing standardised reports when requested, and in an optimal location.

Complex presentation of information

Effective systems add value to information when they organise and present the information in a clear way, without excessive detail. This allows the users to easily and quickly identify the information they need. It prevents wasting time obtaining the information in the first place, and correcting errors caused by interpreting it incorrectly.

The picking sheets show the 12-digit product codes which can easily be misread, increasing the likelihood of errors. A better system would present the information in a more accessible way and prevent information overload; for example, showing product descriptions or product codes only for the items to be picked.

(b) **Eliminating waste**

There are two main types of waste at NJN which can be identified using lean principles: waste which does not add value to the customer, and waste which occurs due to variations in demand and demands on staff.

Reorganising the warehouse to place high volume items near to the despatch area will help reduce the type of waste where the movement of staff to pick goods is more than should be required. Less movement, which means less staff time and cost, will be required by staff to pick these items and bring them to where they are to be despatched. It may be, however, that large and bulky items should be placed nearer to the despatch area instead, to save on the time spent transporting them to the despatch area. This may also address the increased seasonal demand for certain types of product, as products which are popular for that specific period could be stored more closely to the despatch area.

The cost of absenteeism is a waste caused by demanding too much of staff at busy times to compensate for inefficient organisation in the warehouse and errors in the WIS. The cost of searching for items which have been put in the wrong physical location at busy times is a waste due to variation in activity levels.

Another type of waste which does not add value to the customer is holding excessive inventory, for example, the additional warehouse space which NJN has rented. By not making efficient use of the warehouse space it has, NJN is reducing its level of output, and revenue, relative to the resources available to it. In addition, the extra warehouse space means more time spent by staff moving through the warehouses trying to locate goods.

The cyclical inventory counts which the Management Consultant has suggested do not add value to the customer and are also more demanding for staff. This is a wasteful activity, correcting the errors which have occurred in the WIS. NJN should instead concentrate on ensuring that errors do not occur in the first place, which will cost less than correcting them.

(c) **Lean principles (5Ss)**

The 5Ss in the adoption of lean principles during the warehouse reorganisation are Structurise, Systemise, Sanitise, Standardise and Self-discipline.

Structurise

This involves introducing order where possible, for example, by ensuring that items in the warehouse are arranged so that they are easy to find. This would also include segregating damaged or obsolete inventory, or discarding it from the warehouse.

The management consultant has suggested the measure of the proportion of inventory not stored in order of its alphabetical description, with 'A' nearest the despatch area and 'Z' furthest away. This may measure how easy to find each product is, but would not necessarily make best use of all available space or make the picking process more efficient. It may also be subjective and prone to errors caused by the interpretation of the product description, for example, in deciding if cricket balls should be measured under 'C' or 'B'.

Systemise

This principle involves organising items so that they are easy to use. At NJN, this means being able to accurately pick the correct items in the shortest possible time. It could also cover access to other resources, such as having computer terminals close to where they are needed.

The measure relating to the storing of goods alphabetically seems to conflict with the Consultant's recommendation to place the high volume lines close to the despatch area. Whereas storing goods alphabetically may make items easy to find, it does not necessarily make them easy to use (pick). By storing the high volume items near to the despatch area, the average time taken to pick orders would be reduced.

Sanitise

This principle means to be tidy and avoid clutter. This helps make things easy to find, allows easy access of staff around the warehouse, and helps make a safe working environment. The warehouse manager's daily assessment of tidiness is a suitable measure of this principle, which is a subjective assessment.

There is the possibility that the assessment will be biased, especially if the warehouse manager who is undertaking the assessment is also having their performance evaluated on the tidiness of the warehouse. The characteristics of what constitutes a tidy warehouse, compared to an untidy one, will need to be defined. There is the possibility of inconsistent measurement if someone other the warehouse manager does the assessment, or the assessment is done at different times of the day.

Standardise

This principle involves finding the best way of undertaking a process or task, and applying it consistently. The suggestion of the number of accidents caused by goods which have not been stored or picked in the correct way would measure this. As NJN should aim to have no accidents, this should be a performance measure with a target level of zero.

Self-discipline

This principle relates to sustaining the other Ss by motivating employees. Motivation is subjective, and hard to measure. None of the performance measures the management consultant has suggested directly measure this principle. The consistency in which specific tasks or processes are performed could be a measure of how well they are being sustained.

14 Amal

Workbook reference

Performance indicators are introduced in Chapter 2, and Big Data is discussed in Chapter 5 of the Workbook.

Top tips

Part (a)

Note that there are effectively two parts to this requirement: (i) choosing and calculating appropriate performance indicators, and then (ii) commenting on the indicators you have calculated.

The context of the scenario could also be important here. Amal and Kayland Air both appear to be pursuing differentiation strategies, whereas Cheapo Air is a budget airline.

The requirement doesn't specify how many performance indicators you should analyse. The key point here is perhaps not the quantity of indicators you calculate, but making sure they are relevant.

We have chosen four in our answer below. However, this is not an exhaustive selection. If you have made other relevant calculations, and then commented on them, you would have got credit for this.

A sensible approach here is to select indicators which relate to Amal's key business issues (eg fuel costs), identify the key drivers behind them (eg fuel cost per seat kilometre) and then provide a short commentary showing how the indicator links to the companies' strategies and the issues mentioned in the scenario.

Part (b)

There are four areas for you to explain here, and eight marks available, so two marks per area. This means you are not expected to write in depth about any of the areas. However, make sure you explain how the areas could be used to help Amal's performance, rather than explaining what the benefits of Big Data Analysis are.

In effect, the key areas from the conference already identify the benefits of Big Data, so you need to think practically here, and assess how Amal could use them.

Examining team's comments for part (a)

The overall quality of the commentary which candidates provide in relation to numerical results they have calculated remains a concern. Simply putting the numbers which have been calculated into a sentence isn't an analysis of the figures. For example, saying 'Amal has a higher profit margin than either Kayland or Cheapo' doesn't add any value to a reader (who has already seen the calculations which show this). Consequently, such a statement will not score any marks.

However, good answers used the numerical work as an opportunity to show they have understood the scenario; for example, by commenting that Amal's higher profit was not surprising given that Amal is a 'premium airline'.

Marking guide

	Marks
(a) Calculations – up to 6 marks 1 mark for each meaningful indicator selected 2 marks for load factor or similar measure of capacity utilisation Commentary – 1 mark per relevant point, up to 7 marks Total – up to 12 marks	12
(b) For explaining how Big Data Analysis could improve performance in each of the four key areas identified – up to 2 marks per area Total – up to 8 marks	8

Professional skills

Analysis and Evaluation

- Use of information provided to perform a suitable/comprehensive evaluation of performance
- Appropriate use of the data to support discussion and draw appropriate conclusions
- Demonstration of reasoned and balanced judgement / assessment of performance
- Demonstration of ability to consider relevant factors applicable to Amal Co's situation
- Balanced appraisal of information

Marking guide	Marks
Commercial acumen	
• Effective use of examples and/or calculations from the scenario information and other practical considerations related to the context to illustrate points being made relating to Amal	
• Recognition of problems and opportunities	
Maximum	5
Total	25

(a) The following performance indicators could be used to analyse the three airlines:

	Amal	*Kayland*	*Cheapo*
Operating profit margin	630/5,430	54/7,350	127/2,170
	11.6%	0.7%	5.9%
Capacity utilisation (load factor)	79,619/100,654	82,554/105,974	40,973/46,934
	79.1%	77.9%	87.3%
Revenue/staff member ($'000)	5,430m/32,501	7,350m/56,065	2,170m/5,372
	167	131	404
Fuel cost/seat kilometre ($)	1,480m/100,654m	1,823m/105,974m	535m/46,934m
	0.015	0.017	0.011

Operating margin – Amal has the highest operating margin of the three airlines (11.6%), which suggests it is being run efficiently overall.

We might expect Amal to achieve a relatively high margin because it appears to be pursuing a **differentiation strategy**. However, Kayland, which appears to be pursuing a similar strategy, generates an operating profit margin of less than 1%.

Capacity utilisation – By showing, on average, how full each airline's aircraft are this indicator shows how well the airlines are using their asset base (ie their aircraft).

Amal and Kayland's performance is similar in this respect, but Cheapo's is significantly better. This is likely to be because Cheapo (a low cost airline) is pursuing a **cost leadership** strategy. Amal might consider reducing its prices to try to improve capacity utilisation, but it needs to do so in the context of its overall strategy. If it reduces prices too much, it may end up compromising the quality and service it offers to passengers, but these elements are crucial to its strategy as a differentiator.

Revenue per staff member – This is an important measure in the context of the recent disputes over working conditions and pay. Amal's staff appear to be performing better than Kayland's, which in turn might strengthen their claims for a pay rise.

The comparison between Amal and Cheapo's performance for this measure may be less meaningful. Cheapo **outsources** many of its activities, meaning its staff numbers will be significantly lower than Amal which carries out the corresponding activities **in house**.

Fuel costs – The board's interest in new fuel-efficient aircraft indicates that reducing fuel costs is an important concern for Amal.

Again, Cheapo appears to be controlling its fuel costs better than Amal or Kayland. This might be because it has more **fuel-efficient planes**, which would support the board's argument for Amal investing in new aircraft. However, Cheapo may have negotiated more favourable fuel contracts with its suppliers, or be using lower grade fuel.

> **Tutorial note.** It is important to use fuel cost per **seat** kilometre as the performance indicator here rather than fuel cost per **passenger** kilometre, because we are looking to monitor the fuel efficiency of the aircraft, rather than the airline's ability to fill their aircraft with passengers.

(b) Amal's business strategy as a premium airline, coupled with the difficult trading conditions, mean that it is increasingly important for the company to provide its customers with the best services and experiences possible, so that they choose to fly with Amal in preference to another carrier. Increasing the data it holds about customers, and potential customers, should help Amal's management make better decisions, and thereby should help the company achieve this.

Detecting key trends – Analysing conversations on social media could help Amal identify potential trends in customer demand; for example, if there are major events taking place in a particular place, or if certain resorts are increasing (or decreasing) in popularity as holiday destinations. Being able to forecast demand more accurately – and almost in 'real time' – could help Amal boost revenue, through applying **dynamic pricing**. For example, Amal could keep prices high on flights which are going to be popular, but could reduce prices on flights which look like they are going to have a lower capacity utilisation in order to try to boost demand for those flights.

Customer selection process – One of the key issues here is for airlines to understand the reason why potential customers have not completed their transaction – for example, this could be due to price, seat availability, difficulties in the booking process itself. In this respect, if Amal was able to capture data about the stage in the booking process which causes potential customers to abandon their booking, it could then look at ways to tackle the problem – for example, if there was a confusing user interface on the Amal website this could be amended to make booking easier. Equally, applying the 'velocity' aspect of Big Data, if a customer abandons a transaction, and Amal already has their contact details, the customer could immediately be sent an incentive to try to encourage them to complete the purchase.

In-flight sales – Amal currently offers a standard selection of in-flight products across all its flights. However, the amount of products Amal sells (and therefore the amount of in-flight revenue ancillary revenue Amal generates) is likely to depend on how well the products offered meet customer needs. By analysing the purchasing patterns of different passengers (or different types of passengers) on different routes, Amal could customise the range of products it offers on different flights, to focus on the products which are most likely to appeal to the passengers on a particular flight.

Customer satisfaction – In the same way that conversations on social media could help to identify trends in demand, they could also help to indicate how satisfied customers are (or aren't) with their flights and the service they receive from Amal. This type of **sentiment analysis** could be measured automatically using data analysis tools.

However, although knowing whether customers are satisfied or not is useful, perhaps the greater value will come from identifying any factors which are reducing satisfaction levels so that Amal can then address the causes of any problems and take steps to improve its performance in those areas.

15 Chicory

Workbook reference

Financial performance measures, including ROCE and EBITDA, are discussed in Chapter 6 of the Workbook. Benchmarking is covered in Chapter 3.

Top tips

Part (a). More marks are available in part (a) as a whole for the evaluation of the **measures**, than for evaluating the **performance** of the two organisations. The examining team have said that, at Strategic Professional level, candidates will not simply be asked to perform calculations, and this question provides a good illustration of that point. Although it is important you calculate the ROCE and EBITDA for both companies correctly, you then need to comment on the figures you have calculated ('Evaluate the relative financial performance...') before moving on to the advantages and disadvantages of the measures themselves.

Another point that the examining team make regularly is that theoretical knowledge alone is not sufficient to pass the APM exam. This is also pertinent here, because, to score well in this question, you mustn't just evaluate the usefulness of ROCE and EBITDA in general terms, but specifically in the context of the scenario. For example, in the first paragraph you are told: 'Chicory's objective is to maximise shareholder wealth' – but will using ROCE as a performance measure encourage that?

Part (b). The same point about making use of the scenario also applies to part (b). To score well here, you mustn't simply talk about the problems of benchmarking in general terms, but instead you should focus specifically on the problems of benchmarking Chicory's performance against Fennel's, using the data which Fennel has agreed to share.

The scenario should provide you with a number of clues you could use here. For example, Fennel is based in Veeland (whose economy is growing rapidly), while Chicory operates in Deeland (which is experiencing an economic slowdown) so how might this affect the comparability of the two companies' performance?

Also, don't concentrate purely on the written scenario, and forget about Appendix 1. For example – look at the dates for the data being proposed for the potential comparison. Fennel's data (31 December 20X5) is 18 months older than Chicory's (30 June 20X7). What implications does that have on its usefulness in the benchmarking exercise?

Marking guide			Marks
(a)	(i)	Calculation of Chicory's and Fennel's average capital employed – up to 2 marks	
		Calculation of both companies' ROCE – 1 mark	
		Comment on the results of the ROCE calculation – 1 mark	
		Evaluation of ROCE as a performance measure – up to 3 marks	
		Total for (a) (i) – up to 5 marks	
			5
	(ii)	Adjustments to operating profit to get EBITDA – up to 2 marks	
		Calculation of both companies' EBITDA – 1 mark	
		Comment on the results of the EBITDA calculation – 1 mark	
		Evaluation of EBITDA as a performance measure – up to 6 marks	
		Total – up to 10 marks	
			8

Marking guide	Marks
(b) Advising on relevant problems of the benchmarking exercise – up to 2 marks per point Total – up to 9 marks	
	7

Professional skills

Analysis and Evaluation

- Appropriate use of the data to support discussion and draw appropriate conclusions
- Demonstration of reasoned and balanced judgement
- Demonstration of ability to consider relevant factors applicable to Chicolry Co's situation

Scepticism

- Effective challenge and critical assessment of performance measures

Commercial acumen

- Effective use of examples and/or calculations from the scenario information and other practical considerations related to the context to illustrate points being made relating to performance measurement and benchmarking
- Demonstrating an awareness of organisational and external factors

Maximum	5
Total	25

(a) (i) **ROCE**

As can be seen in the Working, Chicory's ROCE is 13.6% and Fennel's ROCE is 14.9%. Fennel has apparently performed better than Chicory. One benefit of using ROCE as a performance measure in this benchmarking exercise is that it gives a percentage figure and can compare businesses of different sizes. ROCE does not, however, give the absolute level of return. In this case, Fennel has both a higher capital employed and a higher percentage return.

ROCE is easy to calculate and will be familiar to Chicory's management as it is currently one of Chicory's main financial performance indicators. The figures required to calculate ROCE are readily available from published data, which makes this a good financial performance measure for benchmarking.

ROCE shows a weak correlation with Chicory's objective to maximise shareholder wealth, which may limit ROCE's usefulness as a performance measure in this benchmarking exercise. ROCE may be distorted by accounting policies or where different businesses have different levels of intangible assets. This may lead to drawing incorrect conclusions from the exercise.

A big disadvantage of using ROCE in this benchmarking exercise is that it may encourage managers not to invest in new non-current assets, which contradicts Chicory's strategy of investing in charging points.

Working

ROCE calculations

Chicory:

Opening capital employed (Total assets – current liabilities)	\$78.0m	(138.0 – 60.0)
Closing capital employed	\$59.0m	(140.0 – 81.0)

Average capital employed	$68.5m	((78.0 + 59.0)/2)
ROCE (Operating profit / average capital employed)	13.6%	(9.3/68.5)

Fennel:

Average capital employed: (170 × 0.25) + (176 × 0.75)	$174.5	
ROCE	14.9%	(26.0/174.5)

(ii) **EBITDA**

Using Chicory's main financial performance indicators of ROCE, Fennel has performed better than Chicory. When depreciation of non-current assets and the write-off of goodwill in Chicory are added back to operating profit to calculate EBITDA, Chicory's performance, with an EBITDA of $52.0m, is slightly better than that of Fennel, which has an EBITDA of $51.0m.

EBITDA as a proxy for cash flow

EBITDA is easy to calculate from published data, and easy to understand. It is a measure of underlying performance, as it is a proxy for cash flow generated from operating profit. As Chicory is having cash flow difficulties following the unsuccessful acquisition, EBITDA would be a relevant measure for this benchmarking exercise. EBITDA does not, however, take into account the cash flow effect of working capital changes, for example, by Chicory negotiating longer payment terms with its suppliers.

Excludes items which are not relevant to underlying performance of the business

Tax and interest are distributions from profits, unrelated to the underlying performance of the business. Excluding them from measures of performance, therefore, gives a better understanding of the underlying performance of Chicory and Fennel. This is important for the benchmarking exercise since Fennel appears to suffer much lower rates of tax, probably due to the tax incentives given by the Veeland government. Loans underwritten by the Veeland government may be at artificially reduced rates of interest and should also be excluded when measuring performance.

Similarly, depreciation, amortisation and write-offs such as goodwill are not relevant to the current year's underlying performance and may relate to previous years. For example, adding back the write-off of goodwill in Chicory means the two businesses have identical EBITDAs, albeit that Fennel has much greater capital employed.

EBITDA affects comparability of the benchmarking data

Using EBITDA as a performance measure in the benchmarking exercise makes the data for the two businesses more comparable and removes one element of subjectivity, such as in determining useful economic lives of non-current assets. EBITDA does, however, ignore the replacement costs of these assets. This might limit the usefulness of comparisons between Chicory and Fennel if one were to lease non-current assets and the other to purchase them. The introduction of a new accounting standard on the treatment of leases may, however, remove this limitation.

Unlike Chicory's existing measure of ROCE, which is a percentage measure, EBITDA is an absolute measure and so makes it difficult to compare businesses of different sizes. As a profit-based measure, its usefulness is also limited by subjective assumptions made in the calculation of profit, or by inconsistent accounting policies. Development costs may be capitalised in Veeland, but not in Deeland, which may make a comparison against the benchmark difficult.

Working

EDITDA calculations

	Chicory	*Fennel*
EBITDA	$m	$m
Operating profit	9.3	26.0
Add back:		
Depreciation on non-current assets	18.0	25.0
Write off of goodwill	24.7	–
EBITDA	52.0	51.0

(b) **Benchmarking**

Benchmarking the performance of Chicory against a similar business implies that there is a best way to operate. Though Fennel may be similar to Chicory, there is no indication that it is best in class and benchmarking against it may be inappropriate.

For example, Fennel has taken advantages of tax incentives and loan guarantees to finance new investments. These do not exist in Deeland, so Chicory may be unable to fund investment in this way. It may have to consider leasing assets instead, or accept a slower rate of growth if it wishes to set up charging points in Deeland.

Benchmarking is essentially a catching up exercise. The financial data for Fennel is 18 months older than that for Chicory and may already be out of date. In 20X5, Fennel improved operational performance by investment in IT. The effect of this is not reflected in the financial data given. Benchmarking performance against historical data may not be relevant for current or future performance. The electric car market in Veeland has grown rapidly in the last two years. This growth is not reflected in the financial performance data given for Fennel, nor is the falling price of components for the charging points.

Although Fennel has agreed to share data, this data may be inaccurate or misleading. Though initially the benchmarking exercise is only against Fennel, it may be difficult to find other comparable businesses to benchmark against in the future. The data required for calculation of the three financial performance indicators used in the benchmarking exercise is likely to be readily available and audited, however, which means it is reliable.

A large part of Fennel's business relates to providing charging points for charging electric cars. Though this is a business model Chicory intends to follow in the future, it is very different to its existing business, and so benchmarking against Fennel may be misleading unless more detailed data relating to the two activities can be obtained.

Similarly, Fennel operates in a different country, where the economy is much stronger. Performance targets set following the benchmarking exercise may be unachievable for Chicory. Fennel's financial data has been converted into $ from its home currency. Movements in exchange rates may make the benchmarking data less comparable, especially if the economies in Deeland and Veeland are growing at different rates.

16 Landual Lamps

Workbook reference

Transfer pricing is covered in Chapter 7 of the Workbook.

Top tips

Part (a). As the requirement asks you to 'evaluate' the current system of transfer pricing, it might be useful to start by considering what the aims of transfer pricing are. Then, having identified the aims, you can then evaluate how well Landual's current transfer pricing system fits with those aims.

Does the current system promote goal congruence between the individual divisions and the company as a whole?

Does the current system enable the performance of the individual divisions to be measured fairly?

The distinction between the markets available for the two types of component is important: there is a readily available external market for electrical components, while there is no external market for housing components. Therefore, a market-based transfer price could be appropriate for the electrical components and a cost-based transfer price could be appropriate for the housing components.

But is it fair to include transport, marketing and bad debt cost in the transfer price for electrical components?

And is it fair that the price of housing components should be at cost only, with no mark-up? On the other hand, should the transfer price for housing components be based on actual production costs or budgeted production costs?

Part (b). The change being proposed is to include variable production costs only (rather than total production costs) in the transfer price for housing components. A key issue is what impact the changes have on the profitability of the two divisions. Does the revised position accurately reflect the value added to Landual as a company by the different divisions?

Part (c). The requirement here asks you to evaluate the impact of the changes on the profit in the divisions as well as on the company as a whole. So you need to look at the impact of the changes on four different elements: the new Housing Components Division; the new Electrical Components Division, the Assembly Division, and Landual overall.

Again, you need to calculate the divisional profits under the new structure, and then consider what benefits (or drawbacks) the changes might yield for the divisions, and for Landual overall.

The biggest change will see the Housing Components Division change from a profit centre to a cost centre. Although the 'profit' in the Housing Division will fall significantly because it no longer has any revenue, what might be the benefits of making this change? Remember, the housing components are only sold internally anyway.

Examining team's comments

This question was generally poorly answered with weak (often no) efforts at handling the quantification issues – recalculating the current transfer price; and calculating the impact of the two proposed changes on the various entities in the scenario. As a result, this meant candidates often had very little to say in evaluating or giving advice in the narrative parts of their answers.

For example, in part (b) if the (simple) quantification work was not done, candidates could not see that the proposed change will lead to lower profits in the division which provides the key competitive advantage of the company.

Marking guide

	Marks
(a) *Electrical components*	
Evaluation of the basic policy to use market-based transfer price – Up to 2 marks	
For comments on adjusting market price to exclude additional costs (of transport, marketing and bad debts) – 1 mark	
For calculating the impact on divisional profits of adjusting market price – 1 mark	
Housing components	
Evaluation of the basic policy to use cost-based transfer price – Up to 2 marks	
For comments including a mark-up on cost in the transfer price – Up to 2 marks	
For comments about the merit of using actual or budgeted costs as the basis of the transfer price – Up to 2 marks	
	8

Marking guide	Marks
(b) For calculating the new profit figures for each division – 1 mark For comments on the impact of the changes – 1 mark per valid point; Up to 4 marks	
	4
(c) For calculating new profit figures for each division (Housing, Electrical, Assembly) – 1 mark per entity – Up to 3 marks For evaluating the impact of the changes on the profit in the divisions – 1 mark per valid point – Up to 5 marks	
	8

Professional skills

Analysis and Evaluation

- Use of information provided to perform a suitable evaluation of the existing transfer pricing system
- Appropriate use of the data to support discussion and draw appropriate conclusions
- Demonstration of reasoned and balanced judgement
- Demonstration of ability to consider relevant factors applicable to Landual Lamps Co's situation

Scepticism

- Effective challenge and critical assessment
- Demonstration of effective challenge of information supplied

Commercial acumen

- Effective use of examples and/or calculations from the scenario information and other practical considerations related to the context to illustrate points being made
- Demonstrating an awareness of organisational and external factors
- Recognising key issues in a given scenario in terms of how to address problems, and possible obstacles that will need to be overcome in the process of doing this

Maximum	5
Total	25

(a) **Aim of transfer pricing** – The aim of transfer pricing is to ensure goal congruence between the divisions of an organisation and the organisation as a whole, by ensuring that the performance of the divisions is measured fairly and is not distorted by any internal transfers.

A good transfer pricing system will also maintain a level of managerial autonomy for the managers of the different divisions in an organisation.

Electrical components

Market-based transfer price – As there is already an external market for electrical components, it seems appropriate to use a market-based transfer price for electrical components. The Assembly Division can choose either to buy components from an external supplier or to source them internally from the Components Division, depending on the respective prices charged by the two sources.

Under the current system, the Components Division generates a contribution of \$383,000 to head office costs from the sale of electrical components: \$1,557,000 – \$804,000 – \$370,000. Given the generic nature of the components, we would not expect the contribution to profit to be very high, so this figure seems reasonable.

Adjustments to market price – However, the Assembly Division could legitimately argue that the transfer price charged by the Electrical Components Division should be lower than the open market price, because transferring the components internally doesn't incur transport or marketing costs in the way that an external sale would. Also, there is no risk of bad debt. Therefore, the $269,000 in respect of these costs should be deducted in order to get an adjusted market price.

If these adjustments are made, then the contribution to head office costs from electrical components within the Components Division falls to $114,000 ($383,000 – $269,000).

Housing components

Actual production costs – The transfer prices for housing components are based on actual production costs. Again, this seems appropriate because these components are designed specifically for Landual's products, so there is no external market for them.

However, because the price set for the housing components only covers the actual **production** costs, the proceeds from the sales of the housing components will not make any contribution towards the allocated head office costs.

As a result, since the housing components account for 84% of the division's total sales by revenue ($8,204/$9,761) it will be very difficult for the Components Division ever to earn a significant profit.

Since the housing components make a significant contribution to Landual's competitive advantage, it would seem fair if they are rewarded with greater divisional profit than they currently get. Therefore, rather than selling the components at cost, Landual could consider a transfer price which includes a mark-up on actual production costs. This would also redistribute the divisional profit between the Assembly and Components Divisions.

If a mark-up of 25% (for example) were applied to the total actual production costs of the housing components ($8,204,000) this would generate additional profit of $2,051,000 for the Components Division. If this mark-up were applied, the Components Division would then show a profit of $1,973,000, while the Assembly Division would only show a profit of $668,000.

Actual vs budget costs – Because the Components Division uses actual production costs rather than budgeted costs as the basis for its transfer price, there is no incentive for the Components Division to control or reduce its costs, because it knows it will recover any additional costs through the price charged to the Assembly Division. By contrast, if budgeted productions were used as the basis for the transfer price, the cost of any adverse variance would continue to be borne by the Components Division.

The current system, based on actual production costs, may be part of the reason behind the $575,000 adverse cost of sales variance in the Components Division for the last year.

(b) **Variable costs basis**

The proposal will reduce the profits of the Components Division (and correspondingly raise the profits of the Assembly Division) by $1,302,000.

This change further tilts the balance in the relative profitability of the two divisions towards the Assembly Division.

Given that the housing components are specifically designed for Landual's products, and therefore could be a source of significant competitive advantage, the proposed change doesn't seem particularly appropriate. The Components Division adds significant value to Landual's overall product, but the change seems to be emphasising the importance of the Assembly Division to the company.

If the results are balanced too heavily in favour of the Assembly Division, this will understate the importance of the work done by the Components Division, and could demotivate its staff. This would be a mistake given the intricate nature of the work.

Despite these concerns, the decision to use variable costs as a basis for transfer pricing (rather than total costs) is not necessarily a bad one. The clarity gained by using only variable costs may help Landual to set the optimal prices and profits for its products.

> **Tutorial note.** The following solution shows the full data for the two divisions under the revised basis. However, you did not need to show these figures in full to earn the marks available here (for the new revenue figure for the Components Division, and for the revised profits figures for both divisions). The bottom line is that the profit of the components division goes down by $1,302 (compared to the figure of (78) stated in the question) and the profit of the assembly rises by the same amount (from 2,719 to 4,321).

		Components	*Assembly*
Sales	Electrical	1,557	
	Housing	6,902	
	Sub-total	8,459	15,794
Cost of sales	Electrical	804	1,557
	Housing	6,902	6,902
	Sub-total	7,706	8,459
Fixed production costs	(No changes)	1,672	1,268
Allocated head office costs		461	2,046
Profit/(loss)		**(1,380)**	**4,021**

(c) **Housing Division**

Cost centre – Under the proposed changes, the Housing Division will be a cost centre only.

Given that the Housing Division only sells its (bespoke) products to the Assembly Division, and therefore the difficulty of determining a fair revenue figure for its work, it seems more appropriate to treat the Housing Division as a cost centre rather than a profit centre. Treating the division as a cost centre is better aligned with the ideas of responsibility accounting.

Moreover, because the focus of the division will now be on cost control, this should help avoid adverse cost of sales variances like the one incurred in the last year. The performance measures and reward packages in the division will also need to be redesigned to reinforce the focus on costs.

In addition, the change in status could enable a greater focus on the quality of the division's output, which will be important given the key role which the housing components play in Landual's overall manufacturing process.

In this respect, it is important that the change from being a profit centre to becoming a cost centre is not seen as downgrading the status of the division. If it is, such a perception will demotivate the divisional managers, and any fall in morale is also likely to filter through the staff.

Electrical Division

Under the proposed new divisional structure, the Electrical Division will make a profit of $335k (see Working at the end of the answer).

As the electrical components are generic and could easily be obtained externally, it is appropriate to continue treating the Electrical Division as a profit centre. Under this basis, Landual has the information it needs to decide whether to 'make or buy' the electrical components for its lamps.

The current figures, showing that the Electrical Division is making a contribution to head office costs, suggest that the Electrical Division should continue to supply components to the Assembly Division.

Assembly Division

The changes do not directly affect the Assembly Division. However, being able to see the Electrical Division's results more clearly will allow the managers of the Assembly Division to ensure that the Electrical Division remains competitive (compared to any external suppliers which could provide the components instead).

Working

Revised profits for each of the divisions

Allocated head office costs for the Components Division have been reallocated between the Housing and Electrical Components Divisions in proportion to their cost of sales.

		Housing	*Electrical*	*Assembly*	*Landual*
		$'000	$'000	$'000	$'000
Sales				15,794	15,794
	Electrical		1,557		
	Housing				
Cost of sales					
	Electrical		804	1,557	804
	Housing	6,902		8,204	6,902
Fixed production costs				1,268	1,268
	Electrical		370		370
	Housing	1,302			1,302
Allocated head office costs (apportioned in line with cost of sales)		413	48	2,046	2,507
Profit/(Loss)		(8,617)	335	2,719	2,641

17 Laudan Advertising Agency

Workbook reference

Objectives, critical success factors (CSFs) and key performance indicators (KPIs) – and the relationship between them – are discussed in Chapter 2 of the Workbook. Transfer pricing is discussed in Chapter 7.

Top tips

Part (a)

A key point in part a is to evaluate how the KPI helps (or doesn't help) to achieve each of the four objectives. The comments in Appendix 1 of the scenario relate to the KPI in question, so these comments should have provided you with some useful clues to help answer this part of the requirement.

Part (b). A sensible approach to a requirement like this – to assess the need for a transfer pricing policy – is to start by thinking what the main aims of the transfer pricing policy would be: for example, to enable performance evaluation of divisions; to maintain divisional autonomy; and to promote goal congruence.

Then think how well – or not – these aims are achieved under LAA's current arrangements (in the absence of a transfer pricing policy). The scenario provides a lot of information about how the current practices for transferring goods between the different divisions are causing problems, in terms of performance management, autonomy and goal congruence. These are the same areas which the transfer pricing policy would address. So, what does this suggest about the need for a transfer pricing policy at LAA?

Although ACCA's suggested solution (below) isn't specifically structured around the aims of a transfer pricing system, the examining team have stated that such an approach would have been acceptable for this question.

Part (c). In order to advise whether an organisation should use a particular approach to something, you need to consider what the potential advantages or disadvantages of that approach are. And, to score well in this requirement, that is what you need to do here.

The scenario tells us that LAA's current transfer pricing arrangements appear 'to be based on full cost' plus a substantial mark-up. So, in effect, you need to consider what the potential benefits, or problems, with using a market value transfer price would be, compared to the current 'cost plus' approach.

Marking guide	Marks
(a) Discussion of the KPI in relation to achieving the stated objectives – 1 mark per point	
	5
(b) For each relevant point about the need for a formal transfer policy – 1 mark each	
	8
(c) Benefits of a market value approach – up to 5 marks	
Problems with a market value approach – up to 5 marks	
Total for part (c): up to 7	
	7
Professional skills	
Analysis and Evaluation	
• Use of information provided to perform a suitable evaluation of the KPI	
• Demonstration of reasoned and balanced judgement ...	
• Demonstration of ability to consider relevant factors applicable to LLA Co's situation	
Scepticism	
• Effective challenge and critical assessment	
Commercial acumen	
• Effective use of examples from the scenario information and other practical considerations related to the context to illustrate points being made	
• Demonstrating an awareness of organisational and external factors	
Maximum	5
Total	25

(a) **KPI to buy 90% internally**

Setting a KPI should lead managers to try to achieve this target, as they are appraised (and presumably rewarded) according to their performance against the target.

Delight clients with quality of work – Having this target will only help achieve the objective of delighting clients if the quality of the design done internally exceeds that done by third-party external designers. Though LAA has set up the 'centre for design excellence', this does not automatically mean the quality of work is any better than external agencies.

Value for money – Encouraging managers to buy creative services internally does not necessarily help achieve the objective of giving value for money for clients. Managers at both B and C have indicated that the prices charged by the in-house design department are significantly higher than other agencies in the market. The use of the internal design department may not be best value for the client.

Specialist and local knowledge – Encouraging the use of internal services may not help achieve LAA's third objective to offer specialist and local knowledge to clients. The design department is based entirely in Geeland and may not meet the needs of clients in other countries. The manager of B has already commented that the department did not understand the requirements of consumers in Veeland. This is also inconsistent with the objectives to delight clients and to have them return to LAA.

Client retention – Similarly, managers in A have also commented that the internal department did not have specialist knowledge to meet the needs of a new client. Again, encouraging managers to use the internal department seems contrary to the objectives of providing clients with specialist knowledge in order to delight them and to have them as return customers.

(b) **Transfer pricing policy**

Autonomy of the subsidiaries

The purposes of a transfer pricing policy are to encourage subsidiaries' autonomy, facilitate performance evaluation and promote overall goal congruence with the aim of LAA to maximise shareholder wealth.

As the three subsidiaries are profit centres, they will tend to make decisions which maximise their own profit. This may be at the expense of the other subsidiaries. By charging a higher transfer price to B and C for design services, A will increase its own revenue and also the costs for B and C. This may also be at the expense of LAA as a whole, for example, as C's client was unhappy with the high charges levied by A.

A transfer pricing policy helps to prevent subsidiaries from acting in an entirely self-interested way where this may not be in the best interests of LAA as a whole. Though a transfer pricing policy should promote autonomy of the subsidiaries, LAA's head office should have the power to impose a transfer price to maintain goal congruence across the organisation. This is not currently happening, and the high transfer prices charged for design services are causing dissatisfaction.

Both B and C have commented that they have spent large amounts of time trying to negotiate transfer prices with A. This is a waste of managers' time. The ability of head office to impose a transfer price, or the existence of a clear transfer pricing policy, would allow managers more time to deal with other key aspects of the business, such as ensuring client satisfaction.

Performance measurement in the three subsidiaries

A transfer pricing policy will enable the performance of the individual subsidiaries to be fairly measured. If the policy is unfair, for example, the gross margin at subsidiary C was reduced by the seemingly excessive transfer prices charged by A, managers' motivation will be reduced, especially if this reduces the subsidiaries' managers' rewards.

Setting clear, transparent and understandable transfer prices

Managers at B have complained that the basis for setting the transfer price from A is unclear. A transfer pricing policy should ensure that the basis for setting the prices is transparent, straightforward and well understood by managers so that they do not see prices as being set unfairly and thus become demotivated.

The basis for the prices set between subsidiaries in different countries should also be clear about how exchange rate movements are reflected in the transfer price, so that managers' performance is not appraised on factors which are outside their control.

Also, the transfer pricing policy for transfers between different countries should ensure that the prices are likely to be acceptable to the local tax authorities. The tax authorities in Veeland, where B is located, are already investigating the transfer prices charged by A. This is presumably because the authorities suspect that the transfer price may be set at an artificially high level in order to reduce tax paid on profits earned in Veeland. Having a clear transfer pricing policy may help to demonstrate that B is operating within relevant taxation laws and is acting ethically in setting a fair transfer price. As the internal design department has no external customers, then it may be preferable to operate it as a separate cost centre and make all transfers at marginal cost.

(c) **Market value transfer prices**

Advantages of setting transfer prices on the basis of market value

Transfer prices on the basis of market value reflect the prices of purchasing creative design services on the open market. Both buying and selling subsidiaries will know what the market price is and be able to compare this to the price they are paying or charging internally.

Where subsidiaries have autonomy to negotiate their own transfer prices, in order to maximise the performance of the individual subsidiaries, the transfer price agreed is likely to reflect market price. The buyer will be unwilling to pay more than the price it can pay on the open market. The seller will be unwilling to charge less to sell internally than can be obtained on the open market. This encourages efficiency in A, which has to compete with external suppliers of creative design services.

Where a market value transfer price is used, it will usually be beneficial for buyer and seller, as well as for LAA as a whole, to transfer internally. This is because selling and administration costs overall for both parties are reduced, and the buyer should get better customer service and reliability of supply by buying internally.

The transfer price charged by A currently includes an allowance for marketing costs and bad debts. These are unlikely to be incurred where internal transfers are made. The cost savings may be shared by both parties and the transfer price reduced to a level below the market value. This lower transfer price is known as the adjusted market price.

If the transfer price charged by A is calculated on a different basis from market value, which appears to be the case as A's prices are higher than the market rates, the subsidiaries will waste time arguing over the transfer price. This current approach may improve the subsidiaries' own performance, but this is not in the best interests of LAA overall.

Disadvantages of using market price

The use of external market price will only be the optimal transfer price when a perfectly competitive external market exists. For example, though creative services can be purchased on the open market, those services may not be identical with those provided internally. Subsidiary A had to use a third-party design agency for its new client as it did not have the industry knowledge to do the work itself. In this case, there may not be an equivalent service available internally to those available externally, and vice versa. There may therefore be no realistic option to buy on the open market in this situation and the use of an external market price as a transfer price would be inappropriate.

The market price may be temporary, changing according to capacity of the service providers or changes in economic circumstances or, in the case of LAA, short-term variations in the exchange rate. In this case, the transfer price would need to be frequently changed if it were to continue to reflect market conditions. This would be time consuming and probably confusing to the subsidiaries' managers.

Where allowance is made in the transfer price for the reduced costs, for example, of marketing and bad debts, it may be difficult to agree an adjusted market price which is acceptable to both A and the subsidiary purchasing design services from A.

18 Jenson, Lewis and Webb

Workbook reference

The concepts of controllability and accountability are discussed in Chapter 7 of the Workbook. EVA™ is also discussed in Chapter 7.

Top tips

Part (a)

The context for this question is the issue of controllability, and the fact a manager's performance is not necessarily the same as a division's performance.

This is the point which the export division manager appears to be making when they suggest it is not appropriate to use the division's net profit margin to appraise here performance.

To score well in this question it is important that you relate your answer specifically to the scenario and the context, rather than talking about controllability and accountability in general terms.

For example, Appendix 1 shows that the division's net profit is shown after deducting apportioned head office costs – but is it appropriate to include them in an assessment of the divisional manager's performance?

Part (b)

The importance of looking, in part (a), at specific issues from the scenario is reinforced in part (b).

In effect, part (b) involves recalculating controllable profit – but the evaluation in part (a) should have helped to identify the items which need to be excluded from the original net profit figure in order to generate the controllable profit.

As so often in Advanced Performance Management questions, it is important to pick out all the clues from the scenario. For example:

- In the first paragraph, you are told the Export Division is a profit centre (whereas the Domestic Division is an investment centre). In terms of controllable profit, what is the significance of the Export Division being a profit centre rather than an investment centre?
- Similarly, in the second paragraph you are told that the $KL weakened by 15% against the £SL half way through the year. What is the significance of this?

Note, that although the majority of the marks in part (b) are for 'appropriate calculations', you also need to make a recommendation (based on your calculations) as to whether or not the manager should receive their bonus.

As always in Advanced Performance Management, make sure you consider the drawbacks of EVA™ specifically in the context of the scenario, rather than giving a generic discussion of its potential disadvantages.

For example, since the EVA™ calculation is influenced by WACC, is it appropriate for a profit centre (like the Export Division)? Or, since Appendix 1 suggests that the Domestic Division is significantly larger than the Export Division, how useful will EVA™ be in comparing the relative performance of the divisions (since it generates an absolute value, rather than a percentage)?

Examining team's comments

Part (a)

To score well in this part of the question, it was important to pick up on the issues mentioned in the scenario and examine their impact on the question. Those candidates who did this, scored well in this part.

Part (b), which required a calculation of the relevant profit to judge the manager's performance in order to assess their suitability for a bonus payment, was generally done well.

Marking guide	Marks
(a) Evaluation of manager's comments – 1 mark per relevant point	
Traceable net profit calculation – 2 marks	
	7
(b) Depreciation and allocated head office costs – 2 marks	
Currency gain – 2 marks	
Controllable revenue – 2 marks	
Controllable profit margin – 1 mark	
Conclusion/recommendation – 1 mark	
	8
(c) Drawbacks of EVA™ – 1 mark per relevant point	
	5

Professional skills

Analysis and Evaluation

- Use of information provided to perform a suitable evaluation
- Appropriate use of the data to support discussion and draw appropriate conclusions
- Demonstration of reasoned and balanced judgement
- Demonstration of ability to consider relevant factors

Scepticism

- Effective challenge and critical assessment
- Demonstration of effective challenge the opinions of the divisional managers
- Demonstration of effective challenge of information supplied

Commercial acumen

- Effective use of examples and/or calculations from the scenario information and other practical considerations related to the context to illustrate points being made
- Demonstrating an awareness of organisational and external factors

Maximum	5
Total	25

(a) **Assessing managerial vs divisional performance**

A key characteristic of divisional performance measurement is that divisional managers, and the divisions themselves, should only be appraised on performance that they control. For example, costs which are not controlled by divisional managers, such as JLW's apportioned head office costs, should be added back to profit when appraising manager's performance.

Similarly, as Export Division is a profit centre, divisional managers are not able to make capital investment decisions and so depreciation is out of their control and should be added back to profit for their appraisals. Domestic Division is an investment centre, so managers there can make investment decisions, and depreciation is a cost which they can control.

On 30 June 20X6, the $KL weakened by 15% against the £SL. This meant Export Division benefited from an increase in revenue which was not under the control of the divisional manager. This amount must be deducted from revenue when calculating the controllable net profit for Export Division.

The net profit arrived at after items which are not under managers' control are added back is known as the 'controllable profit'. This is what divisional managers should be appraised on. This is because it is unfair to appraise them on factors outside their control, and may mean they become demotivated or give up trying to improve performance, which is not in the interests of JLW as a whole.

Divisional performance should be evaluated on all the items which relate directly to the division which is its 'traceable profit'. Allocated head office costs do not directly reflect the activity of the division and should be excluded when calculating the traceable profit.

The traceable net profit for Export Division, after adjusting for allocated head office costs, was $KL905,000 (Working), and the traceable net profit margin was 11%.

A difficulty with calculating controllable and traceable profits in this way may be that it is difficult to determine which items are controllable or not. For example, though the new machine purchased for Export Division by head office did lead to improvements in productivity, the extent of this increase must be attributed to good management, or otherwise, by the divisional managers. This increase in productivity is therefore due partly to controllable factors, and partly to uncontrollable.

Working

Traceable net profit

	$KL'000
Reported net profit	545
Add back: Allocated head office costs	360
Traceable net profit	905
Traceable net profit margin (905/8,000)	11.3%

(b) **Export division manager's bonus**

The controllable net profit is arrived at after items which are not under the manager's control are added back. The net profit margin controllable by the manager of Export Division is 10%. Given that it is difficult to assess the effect of the increased productivity on controllable net profit, the manager should be awarded their bonus for the year. This is because the controllable net profit margin of 10% exceeds the target of 8%.

Workings

1 ***Controllable net profit margin for Export Division; year ended 31 December 20X6***

Controllable net profit	$KL'000
Reported net profit	545
Non-controllable items	
Add back:	
Depreciation	395
Allocated head office costs	360
Deduct:	
Currency gain	(522)
Controllable net profit	778
Controllable revenue	
Reported revenue	8,000
Deduct currency gain	(522)
Controllable revenue	7,478
Controllable net profit margin (778/7,478)	10.4%

2 ***Currency gain***

Six months revenue from 1 July 20X6 was increased by 15% due to currency gain.

Six months revenue before currency gain is 4,000/1.15 = 3,478.

Therefore, non-controllable currency gain is 4,000 – 3,478 = 522.

As the exact increase in productivity resulting for the new machinery on Export Division is unclear, it is difficult to accurately adjust the controllable net profit margin to reflect this. It would seem the divisional manager is benefitting from productivity improvements which are not entirely under their control. To reduce the controllable net profit margin to 8%, the threshold at which the manager is awarded their bonus, the net profit would have to fall by approximately $KL179,760 (778,000 – (7,478,000 × 8%)). This is equivalent to 3.7% of cost of sales (179,760k/4,800,000).

It is difficult to conclude, therefore, whether the 'significant' improvement in productivity would make the difference between the manager of Export Division receiving their bonus or not.

(c) Although EVA™ is consistent with JLW's objective to maximise shareholder wealth, it involves making many adjustments to operating profit and capital employed. These may be time consuming and be poorly understood by managers. The manager of Export Division has already commented that they find the bonus calculations difficult to understand. Failure of managers to understand the EVA™ calculations would make it difficult for them to work towards targets set for the division.

EVA™ is not suitable for comparing divisional performance as it is an absolute measure and does not make allowance for their relative sizes.

However, the calculation of EVA™ is backwards looking, and based on historical financial information, whereas shareholders need information about future performance on which to base their decisions.

The Export division is a profit centre and managers do not have control of investment decisions. Therefore, EVA™ is not a suitable measure for the evaluation of the performance on Export Division because there is no controllable capital employed.

Although the Domestic Division is able to control investment decisions, and does have controllable capital employed, to use the weighted average cost of capital (WACC) in the EVA™ calculation requires a number of assumptions and estimates to be made, for example, in calculating the cost of equity or market value of debt. The WACC is normally based on historic data, which may not reflect circumstances in the future, and may not be accurate.

19 Essland Police Forces

Workbook reference

The use of league tables in relation to measuring public sector performance is discussed in Chapter 8 of the Workbook.

Top tips

Part (a)

It is vital that you read the requirement very carefully before starting to answer this requirement.

In particular, note the following:

- You are asked to evaluate the **method** of calculating and measuring the force scores, not to evaluate the performance of the different forces based on their force scores.
- You need to evaluate how useful the league tables are in improving the performance of the police forces in the context of achieving the Department of the Interior's aims and goals.

The scenario reiterates this first point, with the reference to the CEO's comment: 'I'm not interested in the performance ... I'm interested in the method of assessment.'

Nonetheless, the statistics provided in Appendix 1 are very important to the question; for example, for indicating other measures which could potentially be included, eg number of police force employees per head of population.

In relation to this second point (about the usefulness of the tables) a key question is: how well do the variables included in the tables relate to the Department's overall aim (achieving value for money) rather than being linked to the Department's goals?

Part (b)

The CEO has raised concerns about how appropriate it will be to transfer league tables from the schools sector into the police forces. Are these concerns valid? A comparison of schooling and policing would be a sensible approach here.

Marking guide	Marks
(a) Evaluating the appropriateness of variables used in the context of achieving the overall aim of the Department of the Interior – 1 mark per relevant point – up to a maximum of 3 marks	
Evaluating the appropriateness of variables used in the context of achieving the detailed goals of the Department of the Interior – 1 mark per relevant point – up to a maximum of 5 marks	
For relevant comments on other indicators which could be included in the tables – up to a maximum of 2 marks	
Evaluating the allocation of the weightings across the different forces – 1 mark per relevant point – up to a maximum of 4 marks	
Up to 2 marks for other relevant points	
Total for part (a): up to 15	
	15
(b) Appropriateness of using league tables from schools in relation to the police forces – 1 mark per relevant point	
	5
Professional skills	
Analysis and Evaluation	
• Use of information provided to perform a suitable/comprehensive evaluation of the approach to performance appraisal	
• Appropriate use of the data to support discussion and draw appropriate conclusions	
• Demonstration of reasoned and balanced judgement	
• Demonstration of ability to consider relevant factors applicable to the situation	
Scepticism	
• Effective challenge and critical assessment of league tables	
• Demonstration of effective challenge of information supplied / identification of missing information	
Commercial acumen	
• Effective use of examples and/or calculations from the scenario information and other practical considerations related to the context to illustrate points being made	
• Demonstrating an awareness of organisational and external factors	
Maximum	5
Total	25

(a) **Choice of variables selected**

The variables used to measure the force score should be aligned to the aims and goals of the police forces. At the highest level, the two main aims of the police forces are: to provide a **value for money** service, and to ensure the **security** of the community.

Detailed goals – However, the detailed goals of the Department focus primarily on crime, justice and community support without providing any more detail about the economy, efficiency or effectiveness (value for money) of the policing service.

Choice of 'ranks' – In turn, the four 'ranks' used to calculate the force score appear to be derived from the detailed goals, rather than the overall aims.

Goal	'Rank' indicator used
Tackling the underlying causes of crime	Rank 1 – number of reported crimes
Bringing perpetrators to justice	Rank 2 – proportion of reported crimes solved
Providing protection and support for individuals and communities	Rank 3 – user satisfaction score (for service offered by police forces)
Responsiveness, accessibility and community engagement	Rank 4 – responsiveness (to calls) Rank 3 – user satisfaction will also reflect responsiveness, accessibility and engagement more generally

The indicators selected don't measure all aspects of the goals exactly, but they provide a reasonable coverage of them. For example, one way to reduce the number of reported crimes would be to tackle the underlying causes of crime so that fewer crimes are committed.

Nonetheless, the 'ranks' could still be improved. For example, the number of public meetings between the police and the local community could be used to measure the level of community engagement.

Value for money

More importantly, however, because the goals focus on tackling crime and promoting community safety, the ranks also focus on these aspects of performance rather than the degree of value for money achieved by the police services. For example, whereas the current Rank 2 is based on the solution rate for crimes, it might also be useful to measure the number of crimes solved per police force employee in order to assess the efficiency of the police service.

The data which the police forces already keep (Appendix 1 in the scenario) would be suitable for calculating some value for money performance measures. For example, using the data already available, the following additional 'rank' scores could be calculated:

	C	D	E	F
Number of police per 10,000 population	49.6	48.9	50.0	52.7
Cost of police force per head of population ($)	323.2	331.1	336.5	340.0
Number of crimes solved per police force employee	5.0	5.2	5.4	4.2

Weightings used

Another potential issue with the current system is that it assigns the same weighting to each of the four ranks. This approach has the benefit of simplicity, but it also presumes that each aspect of performance is equally important to the performance of the force. In practice, this may not be the case, but no explanation is given to justify the weightings used.

Importantly, however, the weightings used could affect the overall ranking of the forces in the league table. Currently, Force F is top ranked, while Force C is bottom ranked. However, if, for example, user satisfaction was given greater weighting than the other factors, this would be likely to mean that Force E became top ranked.

Equally, as we noted earlier, if value for money measures were included, the rankings would also change – particularly because Force F performs worst in relation to this area.

Therefore, the Department faces a trade-off between preserving the simplicity of the calculations and including additional factors and prescribing different weightings to different factors.

Additional point:

Impact of using ranks – The difference between the best and worst performing forces in relation to call handling is only 3 percentage points (94% vs 91%), whereas the equivalent difference for user satisfaction is 12 percentage points (80% vs 68%). However, both of these performance spreads generate a difference of 0.75 in the forces' scores. In this way, the ranking system currently being applied doesn't take into account the degree of variation in performance between the different forces for any of the measures.

(b) Although the introduction of school league tables may have been successfully applied in Essland's schools, there are some significant differences between schools and police forces which may make the use of league tables less appropriate for the police forces.

Users of the league tables – In particular, parents in Essland have a choice about which school their children attend, so they can use information about the relative performance of different schools to help them make that choice. However, residents cannot choose which police force is responsible for their safety and security – unless they relocate to a different area of the country. Therefore, whereas the school league tables can help users (parents) in their decision making, the police force league tables do not have an equivalent benefit for the residents of their regions.

Number of measures included – Additionally, the school league tables are entirely based on a single measure of performance (exam results) whereas the force score tries to include a wider range of factors. However, as we have already noted, this then raises questions about which factors should be included in the tables, and whether all the factors being considered are equally important.

Controllability and motivation – Perhaps even more importantly, the police forces do not have the power to affect the external environment, such as economic conditions. The number of reported crimes per 10,000 of population could reflect the social and economic conditions of a region. If the police forces feel their performance is being judged on factors they cannot control, introducing the league tables could serve to demotivate, rather than motivate, the forces.

20 Beeshire Local Authority

Workbook reference

The issues surrounding performance measurement in public sector organisations are discussed in Chapter 8 of the Workbook. The importance of non-financial performance indicators, and the difficulties around measuring qualitative aspects of performance are discussed in Chapter 9.

Top tips

Part (a). There are several different elements in the requirement, so it is important that you cover all of them to score the marks available in this part of the question.

In effect, the requirement can be broken down into three parts: (i) explain how value for money provision should be assessed; (ii) by suggesting (and justifying) suitable performance indicators; and then (iii) calculating performance in relation to those indicators.

Value for money is typically measured in terms of the three Es: economy, efficiency and effectiveness. So a useful approach to this requirement would be to explain the Es first, and look at each one in turn to suggest suitable performance indicators for it. The requirement to 'calculate justified performance indicators using the information in the scenario' should have been a reminder that the indicators you suggest need to be specifically relevant to the scenario, rather than being generic measures of economy, efficiency or effectiveness.

Part (b). A useful starting point for this requirement would be to think how qualitative factors of performance differ from quantitative ones. What are the key characteristics of qualitative data?

The key characteristic of qualitative data is that it is subjective (based on people's opinions). Once you identify this point, the difficulties of measuring it should become easier to identify.

However, note you aren't only asked to discuss the difficulties of measuring qualitative performance; you also need to suggest appropriate solutions to help BLA overcome the difficulties associated with measuring qualitative performance.

Marking guide	**Marks**
(a) General description of VFM (economy, efficiency, effectiveness) – up to 3 marks For discussing each heading (economy, efficiency, effectiveness) in relation to BLA – 1 mark per relevant point – up to 12 marks Total for part (a): up to 13	13
(b) For identifying difficulties of measuring qualitative factors of performance – 1 mark per valid difficulty identified For suggesting appropriate solutions for BLA – 1 mark per relevant point Total for part (b): up to 7	7
Professional skills	
Analysis and Evaluation	
• Use of information provided to perform a suitable/comprehensive evaluation of value for money	
• Appropriate use of the data to support discussion and draw appropriate conclusions	
• Demonstration of reasoned and balanced judgement	
• Demonstration of ability to consider relevant factors applicable to BLA's situation	
Scepticism	
• Effective challenge and critical assessment of qualitative information	
• Demonstration of effective challenge of information supplied	
Commercial acumen	
• Effective use of examples and/or calculations from the scenario information and other practical considerations related to the context to illustrate points being made	
• Demonstrating an awareness of organisational and external factors	
Maximum	5
Total	25

(a) **Value for money**

The extent to which BLA provides value for money services should be assessed in relation to:

Economy – the extent to which services of an acceptable quality are provided at the cheapest cost possible

Efficiency – the way BLA's services are organised, to ensure that the department maximises the benefits and outputs it obtains from its resources

Effectiveness – the extent to which the Waste Services Department's activities achieve its goals

Possible performance indicators at BLA

Economy

BLA's staff costs account for 44% of its total costs, and so the extent to which BLA controls its staff costs will have a significant impact on the economy of its services.

The average salary for BLA's waste collection staff is $31,429 compared to the national average of $29,825. The fact that BLA's average salary exceeds the national average suggests its services are not being provided as economically as they could be. However, this may reflect the fact that Beeshire is a wealthy area, so wage levels in general may be higher there than in other parts of the country. Equally, though, by paying above the national average for staff, BLA may be able to recruit more experienced or higher quality staff. As a result, this could improve its efficiency.

Another significant cost driver for BLA is likely to be its fleet of vehicles. Therefore, it could also measure economy in relation to the costs it pays for its vehicles, their fuel and their maintenance.

Efficiency

Benchmarking the performance of BLA's waste collections against the national figures indicates that BLA is relatively efficient:

	BLA	*Nationally*
Tonnes of waste collected per member of staff	629	583
Cost per tonne of waste collected ($)	114	123
Staff cost per tonne of waste collected ($)	50	51

This supports the point we made earlier: that although BLA's average salary is above the national average, BLA benefits from the greater efficiency of its staff.

Effectiveness

Effectiveness needs to be measured against a variety of aspects, linked to the need for waste collection:

Public health concerns – The fact that waste is only collected every 14 days (compared to the national average of 12 days) could suggest that BLA is less effective in maintaining public health. However, the level of public health concerns could also be measured by the number of complaints about vermin or other problems related to waste. If the level of complaints BLA receives is in line with national average (or below it) there would seem to be little reason to increase the frequency of the collections it carries out.

Clean and attractive streets – Finding a way to measure the cleanliness of BLA's streets could be difficult, because 'cleanliness' is inherently subjective, and therefore difficult to quantify. However, BLA could use the number of complaints it receives from residents or businesses as an indirect measure. If the number of complaints is relatively low, this would suggest that the cleanliness of the streets is being maintained at an acceptable level.

Increased recycling – The Government has set a target of 40% of all waste to be recycled, therefore BLA needs to measure the percentage of its total waste it recycles. It currently recycles 43% of all waste collected (950,000/2.2m). As such, BLA has already achieved the target level, and the proportion of waste it recycles is above the national average (41%).

Nonetheless, as the Government is planning to increase the levy charged on landfill, it will be important for BLA to ensure the proportion of waste that it recycles is as high as possible. As such, this remains an important indicator to monitor.

(b) **Difficulties of measuring qualitative performance**

Subjectivity – One of the main problems in measuring qualitative performance is that it is based on people's opinions and judgements and therefore is subjective. For example, people's assessment about what constitutes an acceptable level of cleanliness in BLA's streets may differ, and this in turn could affect the degree to which the area's streets are perceived to be 'clean'.

Equally, as Seeland is currently in a long recession, some people may prefer that waste be collected less frequently to allow the local government to save money, instead of, for example, increasing local taxes to pay for more frequent collections. In this case, people's priorities could dictate their willingness to complain about uncollected waste or the frequency of collections.

The fact that the underlying data is qualitative rather than quantitative can, in itself, create problems for measurement. For example, if the Waste Management Department receives a phone call from a resident complaining that some uncollected waste is 'disgusting', it will be difficult for the department to gauge whether this is a more serious or less serious problem than the uncollected waste described by another resident as 'foul'.

Currently, BLA records the number of complaints it receives, but there is no indication of the seriousness of these complaints – possibly due to the subjective nature of the data involved.

Scoring – One way of addressing the problem of subjectivity could be to try to make the data quantitative. For example, the Waste Management Department could introduce a scoring system to judge how satisfied residents are with the cleanliness of their streets. The scoring system could ask residents to rate cleanliness on a scale from 1 to 5, with '1' signifying 'Very satisfied' and '5' signifying 'Very dissatisfied'.

However, scoring systems are still subjective, because the level of cleanliness which one person grades as 'Very satisfactory' may only be deemed 'Satisfactory' by another person. In general, there is also a tendency to score towards the middle in this type of scoring system: people feel more comfortable selecting scores in the range '2' to '4', rather than using the extreme scores of '1' or '5'.

Trends – One way to reduce the subjectivity in non-financial performance measures is by looking at trends over time rather than one-off metrics – for example, monitoring trends in the average scores for cleanliness.

Although individual scores will still be subjective, looking at average scores over time can help to overcome this subjectivity and highlight changes in quality or satisfaction. For example, if the residents are surveyed about the cleanliness of BLA annually, and the average score declines from one year to the next, this should provide a good indication that the quality of the waste collection services is declining.

21 Teeland Universities

Chapter references

Not for profit organisations and the concept of 'value for money' are discussed in Chapter 8 of the Workbook.

Top tips

Part (a). Teeland's Government wants to assess the value for money provided by universities in the country, and a senior politician has asked for advice on how to do this. The reference to 'value for money' should have prompted you to think about the three Es – economy, efficiency and effectiveness – and these would have provided a useful framework for structuring your answer. (ACCA's marking guide also indicates that there were up to three marks available for a general description of the three Es approach in the context of assessing value for money in public sector organisations.)

Since the requirement refers specifically to the performance data in Appendix 1, a sensible way to approach this question would be to think what the data in the appendix can tell us about the universities' performance – in relation to economy, efficiency and effectiveness.

Remember that 'effectiveness' relates to the extent to which an organisation is achieving its objectives. The three objectives for universities in Teeland are clearly identified at the start of the scenario, so the universities' effectiveness should be judged in relation to these three points.

In this respect, as well as thinking about the relative performance of the four universities described in the scenario, it would be relevant to consider how useful the data in Appendix 1 is for assessing value for money. For example, one of the universities' objectives is 'to engage in high quality research' but would the data in Appendix 1 help the Government to assess the quality of the universities' research?

More generally, when thinking about value for money and the three Es, it is important to think about the linkages between the different Es. This point is relevant here as well. For example, if a university looks to reduce its costs (to improve economy) what impact might this have on the standard of education or the quality of its research (effectiveness)?

Part (b). It is important to note that the question refers to 'implementing the proposal to introduce league tables', and not simply 'league tables'. So it is valid to think about the practical implications of implementing the tables, not just the potential issues surrounding league tables more generally.

As is often the case, the scenario provides some useful clues here – in particular by highlighting the level of resources which will be needed to compile the league tables. (In Veeland, there is a special government department of 150 staff who administer a similar system of performance measurement.)

To score well in this question, you need to address both the benefits and the problems associated with the league tables, although on balance there are actually more problems than benefits (and the relative marks available in the marking guide reflect this).

The short descriptions in the scenario of each of the four universities should also have been useful for identifying some of the problems with the proposal – for example, by raising concerns about how comparable the universities actually are. However, the more general problems of league tables (for example, in terms of motivation or behaviour – what gets measured, gets done) would also be relevant here.

Note that the solution below is, deliberately, longer than an answer that a student would be expected to write under exam conditions, in order to show the range of valid points that could have been made in response to this question.

Examining team's comments

In **part (a)**, many candidates made good use of the three Es to structure their answers. Good answers also used the data in the scenario to illustrate the points being made.

Part (b) was answered fairly well in general, with candidates splitting their answers into two sections (benefits and problems) and illustrating their answers with specific issues relating to the universities in the scenario.

Marking guide	**Marks**
(a) General description of three Es approach (economy, efficiency, effectiveness) in public sector organisations – up to 2 marks Applications of the three Es to assess the performance of the three universities – 1 mark per relevant point – up to 11 marks Total for part (a): up to 11	11
(b) Potential benefits from the league tables (linked to improving the universities' performance) – 1 mark per relevant point – up to 5 marks Potential problems associated with the league tables – 1 mark per relevant point – up to 8 marks Total for part (b): up to 9	9

Professional skills

Analysis and Evaluation

- Use of information provided to perform a suitable/comprehensive evaluation of value for money
- Appropriate use of the data to support discussion and draw appropriate conclusions
- Demonstration of reasoned and balanced judgement
- Demonstration of ability to consider relevant factors

Scepticism

- Effective challenge and critical assessment
- Demonstration of effective challenge the opinions of the politician
- Demonstration of effective challenge of information supplied

Commercial acumen

- Effective use of examples and/or calculations from the scenario information and other practical considerations related to the context to illustrate points being made
- Demonstrating an awareness of organisational and external factors
- Recognising key issues in a given scenario in terms of how to address problems, and possible obstacles that will need to be overcome in the process of doing this

Maximum	5
Total	25

Tutorial note. The solution given below is very detailed, and is intended to give an idea of the range of relevant points which could have been made. However, candidates would not be expected to provide an answer of this length in the exam.

(a) Public sector organisations such as the Teeland universities receive all their funding from central government and do not have the generation of profit as an objective. Furthermore, their objectives such as 'improving the standard of education of the citizens of Teeland' cannot be measured in financial terms. The value for money of the universities can be assessed using the three Es framework of economy, efficiency and effectiveness.

ANSWERS

Economy

This involves obtaining the inputs to the service at the lowest possible cost, while still maintaining the quality of the inputs. In practice, this may be difficult to do, and a reduction in cost may lead to a reduction in quality.

From the performance data given, the average annual payroll cost per member of academic staff is highest in Northcity University at $62,286 ($109m/1,750). This is 51% higher than Eastcity University, which has the lowest cost at $41,237 of the four universities given. The high costs in Northcity University may reflect the fact that staff there may be more highly qualified or that highly skilled, trained staff are attracted to work there because of the high standards of teaching and academic research.

A higher payroll cost per member of academic staff may not necessarily mean a particular university is not giving good value for money. The relatively high salary costs in Southcity University of $62,083 may simply reflect the higher costs of living in the capital city and so comparison between the regions may be inappropriate.

As such, there may be a conflict between this performance measure and the ability of the universities to achieve their objectives, such as to improve educational standards in Teeland. The politician's proposal to reduce salary levels for new recruits may reduce the number of appropriately qualified and skilled staff who wish to work there. This may reduce the standard of teaching and academic research and, as a result, the universities' performance against their stated objectives.

This means that focusing solely on economy would not ensure the universities achieve value for money.

Efficiency

Efficiency measures the amount of outputs relative to the amount of inputs. The number of academic staff per student may be a suitable measure, but there may be differences between universities which would make it hard to compare results.

For example, there are 10.1 (17,600/1,750) students per member of academic staff in Northcity University, which is ranked number one in the Teeland Government's provisional league table. There are 17.9 in Westcity University which is ranked much lower at 21. It would seem, therefore, that increasing the number of students relative to the number of academic staff as per the politician's proposal may reduce the performance of the universities against their stated objectives and as such will not increase value for money.

The politician's comparison with the number of students per academic staff in neighbouring Veeland may not be appropriate. Whilst the politician's assertion that educational standards are higher in Veeland may be correct, the undertaking of high quality academic research may not be a key objective of the universities there, or the quality of research may be lower than in Teeland.

Effectiveness

Effectiveness measures whether the objectives of the organisation are being met. The stated objectives of the Teeland universities are to improve the overall standard of education of citizens in Teeland, to engage in high quality academic research and to produce well-qualified university graduates to meet the needs of the graduate jobs market in Teeland.

Objective to improve the overall standard of education in Teeland

Currently, there is no direct measure of the performance of the universities' stated objectives to increase the level of education of the citizens of Teeland. The number of graduates entering graduate jobs and the results of the TSOR survey may indirectly measure the effectiveness of the universities in achieving this aim. More direct measures such as the number of students completing their studies or obtaining good results in university exams may be more appropriate.

The effectiveness of the universities in improving the standard of education should really be related to the entry requirements of each university. Westcity University is the lowest ranking of the four universities in the provisional league table and has the lowest proportion of graduates entering graduate jobs at 50% (1,750/(11,200/3.2)). It also receives the lowest amount of research funding per student at around $1,250 ($14m/11,200), but it has the lowest entry requirements, which have been relaxed to encourage students from a more diverse range of backgrounds to study there. Therefore, the improvement in educational standards relative to students' attainment on entry may be higher than the position in the league table may suggest.

Objective to engage in high quality academic research

The stated aim of the universities to engage in high quality academic research is also not currently measured. The amount of research funding received from government and other organisations by each university may indirectly reflect the quality of the research there as providers of funds for research would probably look to fund high quality research.

This measure may, however, equally reflect that some types of research are more expensive than others. Southcity University, which is successful in science and technology subjects, receives $15,592 per student compared to $5,000 in Eastcity, which specialises in arts and humanities subjects. The funding received may be more indicative of the past quality of academic research rather than future quality, or may not even reflect the quality of the research and may be high due to wastage or inefficiency. The definition of 'quality' of research is unclear.

Objective to meet the needs of the graduate jobs market

The number of graduates from each university obtaining graduate jobs each year is an indirect measure of how well each university is achieving this objective. However, the number of graduate jobs filled may simply reflect the number of students at each university and demand for graduate jobs in the economy.

Many graduates, including the most talented of them, may take graduate jobs overseas, in which case the measure of graduate jobs filled may not be a clear measure of the objective to meet the needs of the graduate jobs market in Teeland. A more precise measure of graduates entering graduate jobs in Teeland may be more appropriate. Even this may be misleading, if graduates later return from overseas to enter graduate jobs in Teeland.

The definition of what is a 'graduate' job is subjective and likely to change over time, for example, as a result of changes in the economy. This again limits the usefulness of this measure in determining whether universities have met this objective.

The TSOR survey is a measure of effectiveness reflecting a basket of measures, one of which is students' own perceptions of their future job prospects. The measures in the TSOR survey are, however, highly subjective according to individuals' personal perceptions, for example, about students' job prospects and the quality of teaching at the university. Furthermore, the survey covers a wider range of factors such as their overall satisfaction with university life. As such, this may not reflect the stated aims of the universities in Teeland. The TSOR score for Westcity University is considerably higher than for all the other universities, despite it having the lowest overall ranking.

(b) **League tables encourage competition between universities**

The publishing of league tables of the performance of the universities in Teeland should stimulate competition for high ranking between them. This should encourage them to find better ways to improve the quality of the service, achieve their performance objectives, and deliver greater value for money.

Sharing of resources may be discouraged

However, this may discourage knowledge or even resource sharing between the universities if they see themselves in competition for the best students and limited research funding. This could particularly be a problem if the university leaders were given performance targets and rewards based on their university's position in the league table. They may be encouraged to undertake 'gaming' and focus solely on their position within the league table to the detriment of other aspects of performance. This may mean the objectives for the universities overall in Teeland may not be achieved.

University leaders may focus on a narrow range of objectives

Students' overall experience of university life may be influenced by access to social, pastoral and sporting facilities.

Management time and resources may be diverted away from these important areas by focusing on a narrow range of performance objectives such as improving educational standards and high-quality research in order to boost the position in the league table.

Use of league table to ensure accountability of the universities

If the performance league tables are made publicly available, for example, on the internet as they are in Veeland, this should ensure the performance of the universities is transparent. This will mean that they are held accountable by the public for the quality of service and value for money which they provide.

League tables give choices to students and staff

To be really effective, league tables should provide users of the performance data, such as the public, with the ability to make choices based on the data given. Prospective students and staff will be able to make choices about which university to study or work at according to their position in the league tables. In addition, providers of funding such as the Government will be able to identify where corrective action or additional funding may be required.

This could also be a disadvantage of using league tables, as the best students are likely to be attracted to the best universities, which are in turn likely to attract the most funding for academic research. This may cause a reduction in the overall performance of lower ranking universities, and therefore a failure of the universities as a whole to achieve the stated aim of improving educational standards in Teeland.

League tables may not reflect variation of standards at each university

There may also be considerable variation of the standards within one university, which a ranking in a league table will not address. For example, Southcity University offers courses in a variety of subjects and is particularly successful at science and technology subjects. This may mean that it achieves a high overall ranking in a league table, whereas its performance in other subjects may be weaker. For all of these reasons, the provision of league tables or performance data at a lower level, such as by subject area, may therefore be a better way to make the universities accountable to the public.

Regions may not be directly comparable

There may be inherent differences between universities which make comparison using league tables misleading or of limited value. For example, Eastcity University specialises in teaching arts and humanities. It may be inappropriate to compare it to universities offering a wide range of courses or specialising in science and technology subjects. Similarly, it may be misleading to compare universities of different sizes or in locations in different parts of Teeland. Universities which also attract students from outside Teeland, for example, those in capital or major cities, are likely to have more access to the most able students.

Due to its capital city location, Southcity University may incur additional costs of providing facilities and have to pay staff more to reflect the higher cost of living there. It may be more appropriate to produce league tables at a lower level, like within individual cities, to make the comparisons more meaningful and eliminate the effect of regional variations such as this.

There may be differences in the way different universities collect and report performance data. These problems can be reduced by the use of consistent and enforced policies for compiling performance data.

Resources required to produce league tables

Other problems relate to the targets chosen, external influences on results and cost of collating and measuring performance for the league table.

In Veeland, there is a sizeable government department dedicated to measuring performance. The cost of collecting performance data and compiling the league tables may therefore outweigh the benefits to be gained from doing so. It will use up resources which could be used, for example, in providing additional funding to the universities themselves.

Performance measures used to create league tables may be confusing and conflicting

By having a large number of targets such as in Veeland, this may cause confusion to managers, who may not know which to focus on. Similarly, it may be difficult to decide which performance measures are the most important.

Many performance measures chosen are likely to conflict. Reducing the salaries paid to academic staff may make it harder to recruit and retain experienced and well-qualified staff, which may lead to failing to meet the universities' key objectives.

Similarly, increasing the number of students per member of academic staff is unlikely to help achieve any of the universities' objectives as staff will have less time available for teaching and for engaging in high quality research.

League tables may demotivate staff and students

The Teeland politician's proposed target of a 5% annual increase in the number of students entering graduate jobs sounds very challenging and may be unrealistic. This will be especially so if accompanied by a reduction in the number of academic staff and a reduction of the salaries of new recruits. If the targets are felt to be unachievable by the university leaders, they may become demotivated, and give up on trying to achieve them altogether. This will especially be the case if this is an 'all or nothing' target. A more realistic target may at least ensure that some progress is made.

Students may also become demotivated if their university ranks poorly in league tables, even if the students themselves are satisfied with the standard of education they are receiving.

Similarly, some performance measures, such as the number of students entering graduate jobs, which may be highly dependent on the economic conditions in Teeland, are not entirely under the control of the university leaders. The economic conditions in Teeland will be a key factor in determining the number of graduate jobs available there. University leaders may become demotivated by this measure as well and stop trying to improve.

The relative importance of different performance measures is subjective

The weighting of the different performance measures used by the Teeland Government in arriving at the provisional ranking of the universities is subjective. It is difficult to determine which measures are the most important, and hence how each should be weighted. The opinions of different stakeholders on which are the most important measures will also vary. Academic staff and students may view different measures as important compared to the providers of finance (the Teeland Government) and organisations which recruit university graduates.

Determining the relative importance of different performance measures in order to publish a league table is therefore difficult. Furthermore, the measures chosen, and their relative weightings, could differ from those in other countries. This would make it difficult to benchmark performance against universities in other countries, such as Veeland.

22 Tosemary and Rhyme Hospital

Workbook reference

Issues surrounding performance measurement in not-for-profit organisations are discussed in Chapter 8 of the Workbook. Management styles are discussed in Chapter 11.

Top tips

Part (a)

A useful starting point for this requirement might be to think about the objectives of not-for-profit organisations, and how these differ from the objectives of commercial organisations. Then think how the nature of these objectives will influence the aspects of performance which are important to measure.

A key point to remember in relation to performance management in any organisation is that performance indicators should measure how well an organisation is performing against its objectives. The scenario clearly states TRH's objectives – eg to give prompt access to high quality medical treatment for patients. The key aspects of this objective (promptness; high quality) are non-financial; so what implications does this have for the type of performance indicator which are important for TRH to measure?

Part (b)

The second of TRH's objectives tells you the three elements of the value for money framework – economy, efficiency and effectiveness – and you should use these to structure your answer.

For each of the three Es you need to do two things: (i) select – and **justify** – an appropriate performance measure, using the data provided in Appendix 1; (ii) compare TRH's performance for that measure against the national average, in order to **evaluate** whether TRH is delivering value for money.

Note, however, that for the first element you aren't simply asked to identify a performance measure, but to justify it. To score well here you need to explain how the measure you have selected will help TRH assess the economy, efficiency or effectiveness of its performance as appropriate.

For the second element, you need to calculate the relevant performance indicators for TRH, and for the national average. However, remember the verb here is 'evaluate', and not just 'calculate'. So, for example, if TRH's performance for a given metric is worse than the national average, what does this suggest about how well TRH is delivering value for money?

Part (c)

The model underlying this requirement was Hopwood's management styles – budget-constrained; profit-conscious and non-accounting, and, the question you need to ask yourself is: what are the implications of a budget constrained style? The penultimate paragraph of the scenario could be very useful here. For example, if doctors at TRH have to work longer hours than their colleagues, often without being paid overtime, what could the consequences of this be – in terms of quality of medical treatment, or in terms of staff retention?

As we noted in relation to part (a), it is important that an organisation's performance management systems enable it to measure how well it is performing against its objectives. This point is also relevant here: if TRH's managers are focusing primarily on short-term financial performance, what implications could this have on TRH's ability to achieve its objectives?

Marking guide

		Marks
(a)	Importance of non-financial performance indicators – 1 mark per relevant point Maximum for part (a): up to 5 marks	
		5
(b)	Definition of value for money (3 Es) – 1 mark For each 'E' (economy, efficiency, effectiveness): Selecting, and justifying, an appropriate performance measure, and using this to evaluate whether TRH is delivering value for money – up to 4 marks each Maximum for part (b): up to 10 marks	
		10
(c)	Advising on the implications of a budget-constrained approach at TRH – 1 mark per relevant point	
		5

Professional skills

Analysis and Evaluation

- Use of information provided to perform a suitable/comprehensive evaluation of VFM
- Appropriate use of the data to support discussion and draw appropriate conclusions
- Demonstration of reasoned and balanced judgement
- Demonstration of ability to consider relevant factors applicable to TRH's situation

Scepticism

- Demonstration of effective challenge the opinions of the doctor

Marking guide	Marks
Commercial acumen	
• Effective use of examples and/or calculations from the scenario information and other practical considerations related to the context to illustrate points being made relating to TRH	
• Demonstrating an awareness of organisational and external factors	
Maximum	5
Total	25

(a) **Lack of profit-making objective**

Not-for-profit organisations do not, by definition, have profit as an overriding motive. Patients are not charged for receiving treatment, so TRH does not have a revenue stream. It may also be difficult to define a cost unit as this could be cost per patient arriving at hospital or cost per patient successfully treated.

Not-for-profit public sector organisations, such as TRH, have strict constraints on the amount of funding they receive, such as a fixed amount of funding received entirely from the government. They cannot obtain funding from elsewhere, so financial measures cannot be ignored completely. TRH must exist within its financial means, and the use of budgets to control costs is critical.

TRH provides an essential public service. Political, legal and social influences would prevent it from closing down a service just because it became more expensive or uneconomic to provide it. For all of these reasons, financial objectives are less relevant than for most commercial organisations, and its objectives are mainly non-financial in nature.

Not-for-profit organisations also undergo more public scrutiny and have multiple stakeholders, so non-financial indicators will be necessary to manage expectations. For example, patients are stakeholders who will have relatively little interest in how TRH exists within its financial constraints. They will have much more interest in non-financial performance, such as how quickly and successfully they are treated.

Multiple objectives

Not-for-profit organisations have multiple objectives, and it may be unclear which are the most important. Except for some aspects of giving value for money to the taxpayer, TRH's objectives are all non-financial.

The outputs or benefits of the services provided are non-financial in nature, for example, giving prompt and high-quality treatment to patients. Therefore non-financial performance indicators are required to measure performance.

(b) Value for money in public sector organisations can be measured using the 'three Es': economy, efficiency and effectiveness.

Economy

Economy means obtaining resources at the lowest cost. Doctors' salaries will be a significant expense for TRH, and salary per doctor is a suitable measure of economy. Doctors at TRH have an average salary of $150,000 ($3.75m/25), compared to the national average of $175,000 ($4.20m/24).

The relatively lower salaries of doctors may be due to differences in levels of experience or that they work unpaid overtime. It may also be one of the reasons why the staff satisfaction is so much lower at 9% compared to the national level of 89%.

Efficiency

Efficiency relates to obtaining the greatest possible outputs from the resources available. Treating patients is a key objective of TRH, and the number of doctors is an important resource. The number of patients treated per year by each doctor is a good measure of efficiency. In TRH, each doctor treats an average of 975 (24,375/25) patients per year, 17%

more (975 vs 833) than the national average 833 (20,000/24). This may be because they work longer hours than their colleagues in other hospitals.

Effectiveness

Effectiveness means how well TRH achieves its objectives. TRH has multiple objectives, one of which is to provide high quality medical treatment for patients. Where patients are re-admitted to TRH because their treatment had failed, this represents a failure to provide high-quality medical care, so the rate of re-admission of patients is a measure of effectiveness. The rate of re-admission at TRH is 7.5% (1,830/24,375), much higher than the national average of 1.5% (300/20,000). TRH seems to have performed relatively very poorly in this respect.

Summary

Overall, the results from the measurement of the 3Es are consistent with the doctor's comments that they are working without being paid overtime and treating more patients than their colleagues in other hospitals. TRH appears to deliver better economy and efficiency than the national average. This seems to be reducing performance, however, in respect of providing high-quality medical treatment for patients, where TRH is less effective than the national average.

Overall, the comments from the doctor are not valid because value for money is not just about cost control, it is also about achieving medical care objectives and this is not the case at TRH.

(c) **Implications of a budget-constrained approach at TRH**

A budget-constrained approach encourages financial discipline, which is vital given that TRH is operating within cash limits imposed by the government.

However, this management style encourages short-termism, by encouraging doctors to work long hours without being paid overtime, or not making funding available to recruit new doctors to alleviate the situation. An implication of this is that TRH may reduce its performance against its objectives, and this is already seen by the relatively high rates of re-admission as an indicator of a reduced quality of medical treatment. Job-related tension is a consequence of a budget-constrained management style, and the low staff satisfaction score could have resulted from this.

This management style also encourages manipulation of results, or the way they are measured, to show better performance. At busy times, more patients are referred to the nearby larger hospital. There is apparently no medical need for this, which is inconsistent with the objective to deliver high-quality treatment. It appears to be a way to distort waiting times to demonstrate improved performance in treating patients promptly. From patients' perspective, though, this will mean they are treated less promptly than if treated at TRH.

Being unable to recruit new doctors reduces TRH's flexibility in reducing waiting times at busy periods, as the steps already taken seem to have had minimal effect.

This style does not encourage innovation, probably because doctors have insufficient time for this. Though innovation may have long-term benefits, it seems to be taken as less important than the other objectives.

23 Pitlane

Workbook reference

Target costing and Kaizen costing are discussed in Chapter 10 of the Workbook.

Top tips

Part (a)

Although we often tell you that the majority of the marks in Advanced Performance Management relate to analysis and evaluation, calculations are still an important part of performance management – and therefore you should still expect there to be some calculations in the exam. All 6 of the marks for part (a) of this question relate to calculation.

The calculations themselves should not be difficult, but you need to work carefully through the scenario and the Appendices to gather relevant information; for example, a 15% net profit margin is required (fourth paragraph of the scenario); and there is a 10% uplift on the basic price (Appendix 1).

Note that you are asked to calculate the gap for each of the three years, so it would be sensible to lay out your answer in a three-column format, with one column for each year.

You should then be able to slot in the relevant figures, in a format something like this:

Price	×
Margin required	(×)
Target cost	×
Expected cost	(×)
Cost gap	**×**

Part (b)

The process of calculating the cost gap in part (a) should have reminded you how the process of target costing works:

- Set an acceptable price
- Determine the required margin
- Derive the cost

Thinking about these general principles could be a useful starting point for tackling this requirement. But note the requirement asks you to 'Advise on the extent to which target costing could help...' so, as well as the potential benefits of target costing, you also need to identify factors which could reduce the extent to which it could help and other techniques such as Kaizen costing (mentioned in the question) that may also be useful.

For example, identifying a target cost up front will allow management to Pitlane's managers to assess whether Booster can be produced for that price. If it can't, are there any ways to reduce cost?

However, the target cost ultimately depends on the price set. How does the uncertainty over price (for example, Pitlane's ability to charge 10% more than its competitors) affect the extent to which target costing could help Pitlane achieve the 15% net profit margin required by the shareholders?

The penultimate paragraph in the scenario also identifies that 'staff have never been encouraged to suggest any ways to improve the manufacturing process.' How would this situation be different under a Kaizen costing approach?

Examining team's comments

Part (a) required a basic calculation of the cost gap. Many candidates scored well on this part. However, a significant number chose to present their answers using absolute figures rather than 'per unit'. This is not only a failure to answer the question requirement, but it also illustrates a lack of understanding about the application of the method, where per unit calculations are most helpful.

Part (b). Candidates scored reasonably well on this part but often failed to score as many marks as they could because they did not analyse all the problems areas mentioned in the scenario. The scenario will often provide hints of areas to consider in an answer, and good candidates use these to efficiently compile high marks in the longer parts of questions.

Note. The Examining team's comment about using the hints in the scenarios is a very important piece of advice which applies to many, if not all, of the scenario questions in Advanced Performance Management.

Marking guide	Marks
Calculations:	
Estimated unit selling price – 1 mark	
Less: 15% net profit – 1 mark	
Target total cost per unit – 1 mark	
Less: Fixed cost per unit – 1 mark	
Target direct cost per unit – 1 mark	
Cost gap – 1 mark	
Total for part (a): up to 6	
General description of target costing – up to 2 marks	
Advice on target costing for Pitlane – 1 mark per relevant point	
Comments about additional revenue generated from features – up to 2 marks	
Advice on using Kaizen costing at Pitlane – 1 mark per relevant point (max 5)	
	20
Professional skills	
Analysis and Evaluation	
• Use of information provided to perform a suitable/comprehensive evaluation of target costing	
• Appropriate use of the data to support discussion and draw appropriate conclusions	
• Demonstration of reasoned and balanced judgement	
• Demonstration of ability to consider relevant factors applicable to Pitlane Co's situation	
Scepticism	
• Effective challenge and critical assessment	
Commercial acumen	
• Effective use of examples and/or calculations from the scenario information and other practical considerations related to the context to illustrate points being made	
• Demonstrating an awareness of organisational and external factors	
• Recognising key issues in a given scenario in terms of how to address problems, and possible obstacles that will need to be overcome in the process of doing this	
• Recommendations are practical and plausible, and commercially viable in the context of Pitlane Co's situation	
Maximum	5
Total	25

Calculate cost gap for each of the three years of the Booster's life

	20X8	*20X9*	*20Y0*
	$	$	$
Basic selling price	180.0	170.0	160.0
10% uplift for features/packaging	18.0	17.0	16.0
Estimated selling price	198.0	187.0	176.0
Less: 15% net profit	(29.7)	(28.1)	(26.4)
Target cost per unit	168.3	159.0	149.6

	20X8	20X9	20Y0
	$	$	$
Current expected cost			
Estimated total direct cost per unit	134.0	134.0	134.0
Estimated fixed cost per unit (see Working)	44.1	44.1	44.1
Estimated total cost per unit	178.1	178.1	178.1
Cost gap	**9.8**	**19.2**	**28.5**

Workings

1 ***Fixed cost per unit***

Fixed overhead cost per unit = Total fixed overheads/Number of units sold

= $10,000,000/227,000

= $44.05

Tutorial note. The solution for part (b) is a detailed solution showing the range of relevant points which could have been included, for tutorial purposes. Candidates were not expected to produce a solution as detailed as this.

Target costing

Pitlane currently operates a traditional cost plus pricing method, where customers pay a fixed mark up on Pitlane's standard cost. This has been appropriate because the components currently produced have been manufactured in the same way for some time and their cost structure is well understood. Actual costs of production are very close to the standard costs. There is little competition in the market for Pitlane's current products, as a long-term contract was recently renewed with its biggest customer.

In contrast, for the proposed Booster product, the market price is only estimated. To compete with similar products, the Booster will need to sell at a price reflecting that of competitors' products, taking into account the different benefits and quality which each product has.

Target costing begins with taking the price which the market will pay for the product for a given market share. From that, the required profit margin is deducted to arrive at a target cost. The difference between the estimated cost for the product and the target cost is the cost gap. Where the estimated costs exceed the target cost, steps are taken to reduce the cost gap. The product can then be sold at a price which the market will accept, and which generates an acceptable profit margin. Pitlane charges a 15% profit margin on its existing projects. The shareholders' financial objective indicates that they require the same profit margin to be earned on Booster.

Reducing the cost gap

A big advantage for Pitlane of using target costing is that it is often easier to reduce costs of a product at the design stage rather than after it has entered production.

As Boosters are not sold directly to consumers, the buyers of the product, who are professional installers, may not see value in the highest quality packaging. This could be a significant yet unnecessary cost, to be eliminated at the design stage. In deciding what costs to eliminate, Pitlane will have to take into account the effect of these on the quality and perception of the final product.

The features where the Booster can communicate with consumers' smartphones, and the use of highest quality packaging, are believed to enable Pitlane to charge 10% more than competitors' products. The $3.8m (see Working below) of estimated additional total revenue from the packaging and smartphone features may not justify the $2.8m upfront development costs for the smartphone feature alone, especially if the time value of money were to be taken into account.

Consumers may not value these two features or be prepared to pay more for them. Eliminating them would therefore have little effect on sales volumes and would enable Pitlane to charge a more competitive price, or obtain higher gross profit margins.

Due to damage of sub-components when assembling the prototype, the estimated assembly labour cost assumes highly skilled labour will be used. This is 30% more expensive than other labour. By providing additional training, lower paid labour could be used to produce the Booster, and hence reduce the cost gap.

Pitlane plans to purchase the four main sub-components in bulk from six different suppliers. Consolidating suppliers, or using suppliers in lower cost countries, could help reduce the cost gap by reducing purchase costs.

Moving to a just-in-time (JIT) production system, rather than buying supplies in bulk, would help reduce costs of holding inventory as suppliers would only deliver sub-components when needed. This may increase other costs such as by requiring investment in information technology. It would also take time to develop the close relationship required with suppliers.

Another source of waste is due to internal transport and handling, which forms over 5% of the total direct cost of the Booster. This will also increase production cycle times, and is an unnecessary process which does not add value. It could be eliminated by changing the layout of the factory, or reorganising production into teams and ensuring all production was done at a single factory, rather than in both of Pitlane's factories.

2 ***Additional revenue from smartphone feature and highest quality packaging***

20X8: 60,000 units × $198 = $11,880,000

20X9: 75,000 units × $187 = $14,025,000

20Y8: 92,000 units × $176 = $16,192,000

Total revenue (over 3 years) = $42,097,000

10% premium = $42,097,000 × 10/110 = $3,827,000

Problem 1: Determining the market price

Pitlane's marketing department has estimated the average market price of competitors' products and the likely market share over the three years of the scheme. The estimates are based on the success of a similar scheme in Veeland, and the assumptions used could be incorrect. Electricity prices may already be higher in Veeland than in Deeland, meaning consumers there would reduce their energy costs more by installing solar panels. Similarly, consumers in Veeland could save more on energy costs if there is more sunshine there than in Deeland, enabling solar panels to generate more energy. Both factors would, in this case, reduce the take up of subsidies by consumers in Deeland and the amount they would be willing to pay for solar panels.

The domestic solar energy market is new in Deeland, and Pitlane has no experience in estimating market share or price for this type of product. Pitlane's belief that consumers would be willing to pay a 10% premium for highest quality packaging, or for the Booster to communicate with consumers' mobile phones, may be incorrect.

Problem 2: Estimating the total costs of Booster

The total direct costs of Booster have been estimated at $134.00. The fixed overhead per unit relating to Booster for the three years of the scheme is $44.05, making total estimated costs per unit of $178.05. The cost estimates may be incorrect, especially as Booster is new, and different from Pitlane's existing products. As Booster includes costs which are fixed, estimating sales volumes is also crucial in determining costs per unit.

Pitlane has no recent experience of developing new products or of estimating costs and sales volumes for them. This makes it more likely that the cost estimates for the Booster will be incorrect. Estimating the total costs is needed for the next stage in the target costing process, to identify the cost gap.

Kaizen costing

Even though Booster's share of the market rises over the three years of the project, the market price falls, as does the size of the market. This means that in order to achieve the shareholders' financial targets, the direct costs of the Booster must fall over the three years. Continual incremental improvements using Kaizen costing, and measuring these improvements against targets from the previous period rather than the original estimated cost, could help to achieve this.

To benefit from Kaizen costing, Pitlane must undergo a culture change to encourage employees to suggest ideas, perhaps using quality circles, to reduce costs. That way, improvements could be made in the way sub-components are assembled during production, which would shorten the production cycle and lead to a reduced cost of scrapped items.

The Booster will be produced only for the three years during which the Deeland Government offers subsidies and tax incentives. Generally, Kaizen costing is used over longer periods, and it is likely the full benefits of this approach will not be achieved in such a short timescale. The target cost is the starting point for Kaizen costing. After production begins, each period's target is based on the previous period's reduced costs.

24 Posie

Workbook reference

Quality management and Six Sigma are discussed in Chapter 10 of the Workbook. Responsibility centres are covered in Chapter 7, while information systems and performance reports are discussed in Chapter 5.

Top tips

Part (a)

Arguably the most important words in the requirement are 'could be implemented'. This is because they indicate that the advice you need to give the board is about how the project could be implemented; not how Six Sigma could help Posie to reduce the level of returns from customers.

The specific reference in the requirement to the 'DMAIC' methodology should help you structure your answer. If you use each of the five elements of 'DMAIC' as headings to provide a framework for your answer, you can then assess the activities which Posie needs to undertake at each phase of the project.

Note, however, that the marking scheme indicates that there were more marks available for advice given in relation to the 'define' and 'measure' phases of DMAIC than for the other three. The CEO's concerns about the quality of Posie's data should have alerted you to the fact that 'measurement' of performance is currently an issue at Posie. This, in turn, is reflected in the marking scheme – where up to six marks are available for advising on the 'measure' phase of DMAIC.

Part (b)

The last paragraph of the scenario sets up the context for this requirement – identifying that the data generated by Posie's current IT systems isn't sufficient to identify which responsibility centres are the root cause of the problem of customer returns. This reference should highlight the need to produce performance information at a responsibility centre level.

However, the requirement is not only about responsibility centres; you should also think more generally about the qualities of good performance reports (eg level of detailed provided, timeliness) and whether the current returns data enables Posie's management team to manage returns effectively.

Examining team's comments

The standard of candidates' responses to part (a) was mixed, but responses to part (b) were, generally speaking, quite poor.

Part (a) asked how a Six Sigma project could be implemented using DMAIC methodology. The use of DMAIC methodology was central to this requirement but some candidates demonstrated little knowledge about how it worked. These candidates scored very few, if any, marks.

Candidates who explained the DMAIC methodology scored a few marks, but the majority of the marks in this question were earned by applying the methodology to the scenario. One of the main shortcomings in many answers was a failure to recognise properly how to relate the data given to each part of the methodology (ie define, measure, analyse, improve, control) and how this all connected to customer requirements and expectations.

Part (b) was answered poorly overall, as many candidates did not read the requirement properly and offered responses which considered the impact that identifying and improving the level of customer returns could have on the organisation's performance. Such responses scored few marks, because the question asked specifically about the impact on the organisation's information requirements.

The impact of Six Sigma projects and a DMAIC methodology on information requirements can be fundamental – in particular, in relation to the 'measure' and 'analyse' aspects of DMAIC.

More generally, candidates sitting APM need to be aware of the impact that new initiatives or developments could have on the information requirements in an organisation. For example, if a project is introduced, what information will be required to measure its performance? Can the organisation's systems provide the information required? How will the information be captured?

Marking guide

	Marks
(a) Use of DMAIC Define – 1 mark per point – up to 4 marks Measure – 1 mark per point – up to 6 marks Analyse; Improve; Control – 1 mark per point – up to 3 marks for each heading Total for part (a): up to 15	
	15
(b) Definition of responsibility centres – 1 mark Impact on information requirements of the need for greater detail about customer returns – 1 mark per relevant point; up to a maximum of 5	
	5

Professional skills

Analysis and Evaluation

- Use of information provided to perform a suitable/comprehensive evaluation of customer returns
- Appropriate use of the data to support discussion and draw appropriate conclusions
- Demonstration of reasoned and balanced judgement
- Demonstration of ability to consider relevant factors applicable to Posie Co's situation

Scepticism

- Effective challenge and critical assessment
- Demonstration of effective challenge the opinions of the CEO
- Demonstration of effective challenge of information supplied / identification of missing information

Commercial acumen

- Effective use of examples and/or calculations from the scenario information and other practical considerations related to the context to illustrate points being made
- Demonstrating an awareness of organisational and external factors

Marking guide	Marks
• Recognising key issues in a given scenario in terms of how to address problems, and possible obstacles that will need to be overcome in the process of doing this	
• Recommendations are practical and plausible, and commercially viable in the context of Posie Co's situation	
Maximum	5
Total	25

(a) The DMAIC process is a technique used to implement Six Sigma to improve existing processes. It is split into five phases as described below.

Define the problem

The CEO is concerned that the increase in returns from customers is increasing costs and threatens to affect the Posie brand.

Six Sigma focuses closely on the requirements of the customer, and it is important for Posie to be clear exactly what customers' requirements are, and specifically why products are returned.

The objective of the project needs to be clear – in this case to reduce the number of customer returns.

Customers will expect certain minimum requirements from the manufacturing and packaging process, for example, that they can assemble the furniture properly and all the necessary components for them to be able to do this are included in the box. Customers will also expect the goods to be delivered undamaged within a reasonable time, and at the time and date promised when the order was placed. Customers' perceptions of quality should correspond to the price paid, though different customers will have different expectations of this.

Beyond this basic requirement, there may be aspects of the manufacturing product which further enhance the customers' experience of the product, and presumably of the Posie brand. Customers may be particularly pleased with furniture which is delivered early or at a time especially convenient to them, or which is robust, durable and 'well made'. These perceptions are subjective, and may equally relate to design or the quality of raw materials as to the manufacturing process. By identifying where the products exceed customers' expectations, it may be possible to focus more on these aspects in the future. While products which significantly exceed customers' expectations will enhance the Posie brand, it may also indicate a quality of manufacture which is too high and allow Posie to reduce manufacturing costs in accordance with its cost leadership strategy whilst still having mainly satisfied customers.

Measure the existing process

The current returns figures do give some data to as to why products are returned, but their usefulness is limited as it is unclear which of the categories relate to defective manufacture, and which relate to activities of other divisions. The ambiguity of the data and category definitions will need addressing to enable the process to be measured effectively.

Returns in Category 1 could be because the goods were not manufactured or packed properly in the Manufacturing Division, but could also be due to poor design, or customers losing components or simply being unable to assemble furniture.

Damaged goods in Category 2 probably do not arise because of defective manufacturing either, though customers may wrongly categorise defective goods as damaged. For the other categories it is less clear. Though goods may become damaged by the distribution company, it seems that only a small number of returns relate directly to them.

Returns in Categories 3 and 4 could be due to defective manufacture or if the customer had simply changed their minds and no longer wanted the product. In Category 3, the identification of 'defective' items is too broad.

Returns in Category 5 which arrived late are clearly not due to manufacturing defects and, as this causes only 2% of returns, is relatively insignificant.

Currently 10% of Posie's sales are of products from other manufacturers. There is no indication from the data given how many of the returns relate to these products, nor of the total number of returns relative to the number of items sold.

Therefore, the existing data are insufficient to reliably measure existing performance and take no account of inputs such as raw materials. Only items which customers value should be measured. The CEO has suggested more detailed data are required, for example, on overall customer satisfaction with the manufacturing, but this is at 93% which already seems high and there is little point in incurring costs to measure what customers are already satisfied with. In the context of the Six Sigma project at Posie, there is little that can be done to improve this particular area and such items should not be measured.

Analyse the process

This stage is where the root causes of the problems are identified. Additional information may be needed, for example, to analyse customer returns by type of product, by country of sale or with a clearer definition of what is meant by 'defective'. By doing so, Posie may identify areas of the business where customer returns are particularly high and so be able to focus on these.

Improve the process

At this stage the proposals for improving the process are implemented and availability of resources and likely costs of making the improvements need to be carefully considered. Posie may need to consider which aspects of the production or packaging process could be improved, for example, by better maintenance or calibration of machinery. Additional training of staff may also be required.

Control

This is the ongoing monitoring that the reduction in customer returns due to defective manufacturing is being maintained. Reporting on the number of returns may be done by exception if they reach a particular level. In Posie, it seems likely that the data on customer returns used to manage this process will need to be redesigned to make it clearer in which responsibility centre the problems arise. The ongoing monitoring may indicate that some of the earlier stages in the DMAIC process need to be revisited.

(b) The CEO wants to identify which responsibility centres are the root causes of the problem of customer returns. A responsibility centre is a part of the business where a manager has specific authority and accountability for its performance and so Posie will need information relating to aspects of performance specific to the centre. For example, performance data relating to the reasons for customer returns need to be clearly segregated between responsibility centres. Currently, the information compiled on customer returns does not do this and some categories of return may result from manufacturing defects but some will be from problems outside the Manufacturing Division, or even outside Posie itself, for example, from poor quality raw materials purchased externally, or because of late deliveries or damaged goods caused by the distribution company.

Once information has been analysed and responsibility has been identified, then the managers of those areas will need the information drilled down into even further, as in order to improve they need to know which specific areas they can control. It would be unfair to make managers responsible for aspects of performance which they are unable to control, and the board member responsible for manufacturing quality has recently resigned because of this.

Posie needs to ensure it produces performance data to an appropriate level of detail so as not to overload the users with too much data. For board level reporting, the information in the current board reporting pack may be too detailed and it would be sufficient just to produce summary data on the overall level of returns relative to sales. Responsibility centres would need much more detailed information, perhaps even down to product or production line level.

However, Posie should also consider the costs and resources required to provide more detailed performance data. Given Posie's cost leadership strategy, the costs of data collection may outweigh the benefits of doing so.

Performance data should be provided at an appropriate frequency. For the Posie main board, monthly reporting may be sufficient to alert them to any problems. Responsibility centres will need much more frequent, even daily or weekly, details of the levels of customer returns so that they can react quickly to any problems identified. At the moment, the returns data are compiled every six months, possibly due to the difficulties in obtaining data from the IT systems in the overseas businesses. Even for a board level report, this seems much too infrequent.

25 Albacore

Workbook reference

Controllability and accountability are discussed in Chapters 3 and 7 of the Workbook. Performance management styles are discussed in Chapter 11.

Top tips

Part (a)

The scenario identifies that the budget in Albacore is imposed by the corporate centre and a number of costs are also controlled centrally. However, in terms of assessing a shop manager's performance, is it fair to assess them on factors they cannot control?

The current branch information measures the shop's performance, rather than the manager's performance. How would the branch information for the Tunny branch be different if it only included factors the manager could control?

Importantly, though, note that part (a) is not asking you to assess the performance of the branch manager; it is asking you to assess the suitability of the information as a means of appraising the shop manager's performance.

Part (b)

In effect, there are three component parts to this requirement: (i) analyse the performance management style; (ii) evaluate the current performance appraisal system; and (iii) suggest suitable improvements to the reward system for the shop managers. To score well here, you need to address all the different parts of the requirement.

Marking guide	Marks
(a) Calculation and discussion of operation and planning variances – 1 mark per point, up to a maximum of 4	
Discussion of other variances – 1 mark per point, up to 2	
For highlighting the importance of measuring controllable costs – 1 mark	
Revised performance report distinguishing controllable and non-controllable costs – 1 mark	
For highlighting the importance of controllable profit as a measure of the manager's performance – 1 mark	
Total: up to 8 for suitability of existing report	
	8
(b) Analysis of performance management styles – 1 mark per relevant point, max 6	
Evaluation of performance appraisal system – 1 mark per relevant point, max 6	
Total: up to 12	
	12

ANSWERS

Marking guide	Marks
Professional skills	
Analysis and Evaluation	
• Use of information provided to perform a suitable/comprehensive evaluation of the performance system	
• Appropriate use of the data to support discussion and draw appropriate conclusions	
• Demonstration of reasoned and balanced judgement	
• Demonstration of ability to consider relevant factors applicable to Albacore Co's situation	
Commercial acumen	
• Effective use of examples and/or calculations from the scenario information and other practical considerations related to the context to illustrate points being made	
• Demonstrating an awareness of organisational and external factors	
• Recognising key issues in a given scenario in terms of how to address problems, and possible obstacles that will need to be overcome in the process of doing this	
• Recommendations are practical and plausible, and commercially viable in the context of Albacore Co's situation	
Maximum	5
Total	25

(a) **Accountability** – The managers should only be held responsible for those aspects of performance they can control. However, the branch information does not appear to distinguish between the factors that the shop managers can control and those they can't, which suggests the information is unsuitable for assessing the managers' performance.

Budgets – If one measure of the manager's performance is comparing actual performance against budget, then it is important that the budgets are realistic and achievable.

The fall of 12% in sales across the industry as a whole suggests that the original shop budget (showing the same figures as the previous year) was unrealistic.

Although the shop shows an overall gross margin variance of $17,340 (adverse) based on the original budget, this can more usefully be split into **planning** and **operational** variances as follows:

Planning variance		$	
Original sales	(1)	266,000	
Revenue variance due to economic conditions (12%)	(2)	31,920	(A)
Gross profit variance (gross margin 60%)		**19,152**	(A)
Operational variance			
Actual sales		237,100	
Revised budgeted sales	(1)–(2)	234,080	
		3,020	(F)
Operational variance (gross margin 60%)		**1,812**	(F)

The operational variance more accurately reflects the shop manager's work in promoting sales, and here we can see that the manager's efforts have actually reduced the fall in gross profit by $1,812. The overall gross profit variance (of $17,340 adverse) comprises an adverse planning variance of $19,152 partially offset by a favourable operational variance of $1,812.

Discounting – One area where the managers have a degree of autonomy is in setting prices; for example, it is possible they could reduce the sales price of particular titles to boost sales of those titles. This is therefore an aspect of the manager's performance which could be measured, for example, by looking at the sales price and volume for individual product lines, and then looking at the impact of any promotions on gross profit.

The figures for the Tunny branch suggest that the manager has not made use of the discounting authority, though. The actual gross margin achieved for the year has remained constant with the budget (60%) but discounting would have led to a reduction in the margin percentage.

Controllable and non-controllable costs – A number of non-controllable costs are currently included in the manager's performance assessment. In particular, the shop manager will have very little scope to control **property costs**, as the shop heating, lighting and rental contracts will all be managed by the Central Purchasing Department. The shop managers may have some control over the amount of heat and light that are used in their shops, but the managers don't have any control over the unit prices paid for them.

Similarly, the managers cannot control their own wages. However, it is reasonable to classify the **part-time staff costs as controllable**. The managers manage the staffing for their shops, and so they could save on part-time staff costs by working longer hours themselves.

Consequently, a fairer way of assessing the shop managers' performance would be to distinguish costs into two groups: controllable (marketing; part-time staff) and non-controllable (managers' wages; property costs).

Controllable profit – Following on from this, a controllable profit could then be shown as well as the overall shop profit. The shop manager's performance should then be assessed on the controllable profit performance of their shop only.

If we apply this logic to Tunny branch, then instead of the shop manager facing an adverse variance of $12,840, they would have achieved a positive variance of $6,312, and would therefore have been entitled to a bonus, because they have actually been performing well in difficult economic circumstances.

(b) **Budget-constrained style**

The performance management style at Albacore seems to be **budget-constrained style**, in which the predominant focus is a short-term one, centred around achieving the budget set.

This style can be seen in the way the shop managers' performance is primarily evaluated on their ability to meet the budgets set, even though the general economic conditions mean that the budgets are no longer realistic or achievable.

Job-related tension – One of the characteristics of the budget-constrained style is that it leads to job-related tensions and poor relations between staff and the managers. This appears to be the case at Albacore, where the shop managers have complained about the way they are managed and their remuneration.

Performance manipulation – The budget-constrained style can often motivate staff to manipulate performance reports to try to make it look as if they have achieved their budget targets. However, given the centralised nature of control at Albacore, it seems unlikely that any such performance manipulation would be possible at shop level.

Alternative performance management styles

Profit-conscious style – In contrast to the short-termist nature of a budget-constrained style, under a profit-conscious style, a manager's performance is evaluated in relation to their ability to increase the general **effectiveness of their business unit** in relation to the organisation's **long-term purposes**.

It is possible that such a style could be suitable for Albacore, given the management team's aim of running the business in order to maximise profits. However, the long-term perspective may be at odds with the venture capitalist's likely requirements.

Non-accounting style – Budget information is relatively unimportant in performance evaluation, and other non-financial factors are deemed to be more important.

Performance appraisal system

Reflects budget-constrained style – The performance appraisal system at Albacore reflects the budget-constrained management style in the business.

Lack of discussion and negotiation – The shop managers appear to have little or no opportunity to influence their shops' budgets; they are simply presented to the managers at their annual appraisals.

Despite this, the bonus criteria appear to be rigidly enforced. If the Tunny branch manager's experience is representative of the other managers, it appears that the failure to achieve budget has led to no bonus being paid at all.

This is despite the shop still being profitable (making an operating profit of $43,160), and the manager's **controllable profits actually being higher than budget** (see part (a)).

This total lack of discussion and flexibility in the appraisal system, along with the apparent lack of appreciation of the managers' efforts in difficult economic conditions, is likely to **demotivate them**, and this appears to be the case, with the managers (justifiably) calling the current system unfair.

Improvements to the reward system

Focus on controllable aspects of performance – As we have noted in part (a), the reward system should distinguish between the **manager's performance** and the **shop's performance**.

If the managers feel that they are being judged on aspects of performance they can control, this should help to **motivate them**, and hopefully as a result also improve their performance.

However, given that Albacore's aim is to maximise profits, it is still important to monitor the shop's performance overall as well as the manager's profits. One possible solution might be to base part of the manager's bonus on their own performance (controllable profit) while another part of it could be determined by the shop's performance overall.

Stepped bonuses – Although the current bonus is 'up to 30% of basic salary', it is not clear how this is calculated. The current system seems to have an 'all or nothing' approach under which managers get a bonus if their shop achieves budget, and they don't if it does not.

One way this system could be improved is by introducing a graded system. For example, the amount of bonus the managers get will be determined by actual profit as a percentage of budget, with the bonus amount increasing above certain trigger levels. For example, above 90% of budget = 3% bonus; above 95% of budget = 6% bonus; above 100% = 9% etc.

Budgets agreed – Rather than the annual budget being determined centrally and then imposed on the shop managers, the managers should be involved in setting the budgets. The managers could be aware of factors that will affect the performance of their shops that central management are not aware of. Such a process may lead to more realistic budget targets being set for the shop, and in doing so increase the managers' motivation.

Nonetheless, it may still be necessary for the senior management team to adjust the budgets overall, to bring them in line with Albacore's overall financial objectives or any performance expectations the venture capitalist may have.

Non-financial factors – Finally, the reward system could recognise longer-term and non-financial factors in the manager's performance. For example, they could be rewarded for innovative marketing ideas and staff development (eg part-time staff from their branch who progress to become managers in other branches).

26 Cuthbert

Workbook reference

BPR is discussed in Chapter 4 of the Workbook. Reward systems are discussed in Chapter 11.

Top tips

Part (a). The scenario highlights that the cancellation of the army's order for jackets was 'the latest in a series of problems in production at Cuthbert' which has prompted the directors to look at using BPR 'to radically change the production process'.

The scenario also specifically identifies the three main elements of the proposed BPR project at Cuthbert:

(1) Reorganising production lines into teams

(2) Making machinists responsible for quality (changing job roles)

(3) Tracking batches with RFID tags (instead of the paper batch cards currently being used)

As such, it is vital to look at how each of these three specific elements could influence performance at Cuthbert, rather than simply considering the potential influence of BPR in general terms. A useful way to structure your answer would be to use each 'element' as a heading, and then assess how the changes arising from that element could affect operational processes at Cuthbert. For example, what are the potential implications of reorganising the production lines into teams?

Note. The 'operational' element is important here. Your answer needs to focus on how the BPR project could influence day to day activities and performance, not the wider impact it could have on Cuthbert's financial performance or its reputation.

Part (b) looks at Cuthbert's reward systems, but there are two distinct parts to the requirement, so make sure you address both of them in your answer:

(1) Evaluating the effectiveness of the current reward system

(2) Recommend – and justify – how the reward systems will need to change if the BPR project goes ahead

One of the key issues when evaluating any reward system is the extent to which it influences staff behaviour, and in turn how this affects their performance. This is an important consideration in evaluating Cuthbert's reward system. For example, the fact that the machinists are rewarded for the **number** of items they sew is likely to encourage the machinists to work quickly, but a focus on speed alone could have a negative impact on quality – and quality problems were a major factor in the army cancelling its order from Cuthbert.

Another important point to note from the scenario is that each machinist's weekly bonus is determined by the number of items that they, individually, sew each week. However, the proposed BPR process will lead to production lines being reorganised into teams. Moreover, machinists will now be responsible for quality (as well as quantity).

These points from the scenario should have helped you answer the second part of the requirement; for example, if machinists are now working in teams, bonuses based on team performance may be more appropriate than ones based on individual performance. Similarly, if machinists are responsible for quality, will bonuses based purely on the number of items produced be appropriate?

The requirement isn't only about the machinists, though, so it is important to consider the reward systems in relation to the different grades of staff identified in the scenario – machinists, supervisor, and factory manager.

Examining team's comments

Part (a) was generally well done, with those candidates who broke their answers down into a detailed discussion of the impact of each part of the BPR project scoring most highly.

Part (b) was also reasonably well done, with the candidates who addressed the specific issues in the scenario relating to each level of employees scoring most highly.

Answers to this question which used the detailed structure of the scenario (in relation to the BPR proposal and the existing employee hierarchy) generally made points that scored easily, since they directly addressed relevant issues for the business that was seeking advice. It is important to remember that, in APM, candidates need to apply their knowledge to the specific scenario, rather than just making generic points that could apply to any business.

Marking guide	Marks
(a) Up to 2 marks for an explanation of BPR	
For advising how each of the three elements of the BPR proposal could affect operational performance at Cuthbert – up to 3 marks for each of the three elements (up to 9 marks in total)	
For other practical advice about how BPR could affect operational performance at Cuthbert – 1 mark per relevant point, up to 4 marks	
	12
(b) Evaluation of Cuthbert's current reward system – 1 mark per relevant point; up to 5 marks	
Recommendations for changes to the reward system if the BPR project goes ahead – 1 mark per relevant point; up to 5 marks	
	8

Professional skills

Analysis and Evaluation

- Use of information provided to perform a suitable/comprehensive evaluation of the reward system
- Demonstration of reasoned and balanced judgement
- Demonstration of ability to consider relevant factors applicable to Cuthbert Co's situation

Scepticism

- Effective challenge and critical assessment of BPR and of changes to the reward system

Commercial acumen

- Effective use of examples and/or calculations from the scenario information and other practical considerations related to the context to illustrate points being made
- Demonstrating an awareness of organisational and external factors
- Recognising key issues in a given scenario in terms of how to address problems, and possible obstacles that will need to be overcome in the process of doing this
- Recommendations are practical and plausible, and commercially viable in the context of Cuthbert Co's situation

Maximum	5
Total	25

(a) **BPR** involves radical and fundamental changes in the way processes in organisations are designed. A focus on the needs of the customer, and customer satisfaction, are key to BPR. BPR aims to improve key performance measures such as reducing costs, improving quality, service delivery and customer satisfaction.

The proposal is to move away from the existing functional structure where staff are attached to only one stage of the production process, or even to one type of machine within each function, to team working. This is a radical change for Cuthbert and, as such, is an example of BPR.

Reorganising into teams

Currently, there is very little multi-skilling of production staff at Cuthbert. This was seen where there were insufficiently trained zip machinists available for the emergency order for the Ceeland army, even though there were enough machinists to sew buttons. This led to the emergency order failing to meet the customer's requirements as it was not delivered on time.

Furthermore, it seems that machinists also prefer to work on one particular type of machine. This is probably because they are currently rewarded according to the speed of production, rather than the quality of production, and can work faster when using just one machine.

A change to team working would imply job enlargement for machinists, who would need to be trained so that they were multi-skilled in different parts of the production process. They could then perform the roles of other members of their team, to ensure that there were no bottlenecks in production.

The cost of reorganisation and the costs of training the machinists should be outweighed by the resulting improved efficiency and flexibility of production. In this way, there is more focus on the outcome (goods of the correct quality produced on time) and less focus on the individual tasks within the process, which is a key principle of BPR.

Production teams are responsible for quality

Cuthbert's brand has a strong reputation, and the use of its products for protection in harsh environments and by the armed forces means that quality is a key element of customer satisfaction. Cuthbert must be able to manufacture goods which are free of defects, unlike the emergency order for the Ceeland army.

Reorganising the production into teams of machinists, sometimes known as production 'cells', would make machinists responsible for decisions about quality of a particular product type. This should lead to improvements in quality and therefore to meeting the needs of the customer.

Reducing the number of processes for checking is typical of a re-engineered process, and the quality checking currently performed by the supervisors would no longer be necessary. The production teams will be managing themselves in this respect, and the distinction between supervisors and machinists will be removed, which is again typical of organisations which have undergone BPR.

Encouraging machinists in each team to suggest improvements in the production process should bring about improvements in both quality and efficiency, and hence a reduction in costs. It is the machinists who are closest to the production process and may be able to see how it can be improved. Cuthbert could also consider a more formal system of incremental continuous improvements such as Kaizen costing.

Tracking with RFIDs

Typically, organisations with re-engineered processes end up having a flatter hierarchy. It seems that the supervisors' current roles will no longer be required if the proposal is adopted. Quality checks will no longer be undertaken by them, nor will recording of batches, which will become automated using RFID tags. This should save salary costs and improve lines of communication in the business.

The use of RFID tags would capture the information required to manage the production process at source, and there would be no distinction between the gathering of information and processing it. This is in contrast to the current system of inputting batch data into a spreadsheet, and is a feature in organisations which have undergone BPR.

Practical and cultural aspects of the proposal

New performance measures related to quality rather than just quantity produced will have to be developed and processes and systems developed in order to record and report these. New rewards systems will also have to be developed and introduced as a result of the changes proposed.

The proposal, by definition, represents a significant cultural change for Cuthbert, and may meet resistance by staff who may perceive it as a threat and a one-off cost-cutting measure rather than a fundamental long-term change in the business. It will also affect the organisational hierarchy, relationships between employees and the roles within Cuthbert. There will be significant costs with training staff and with the disruption the transition may cause.

(b) **The current reward system**

The machinists are currently paid a basic hourly wage plus an amount depending on how many items they sew. This will encourage them to work quickly, which will reduce product costs. However, as they are not directly rewarded for the quality of the work which they produce, they may not be motivated to produce high quality work. Furthermore, in order to work quickly, machinists prefer to work on only one type of machine. This reduces Cuthbert's overall flexibility to respond to customer needs, as illustrated by the failure to deliver the emergency order for the Ceeland army.

The production supervisors also receive a bonus according to how many items machinists in their team are able to sew. This too does not reward the production of high-quality work, and supervisors may also neglect quality in order to increase the speed of production. The machinists in their teams could also see it as unfair that the supervisors obtain a bonus based on what they see as their efforts.

The Production Manager does not receive a bonus for production or quality. It seems that they have currently no direct motivation to improve on either of these two aspects of the process.

At 5% of salary, the bonus related to Cuthbert's overall profits is relatively small and it is unclear whether it is a significant motivator to any of the employees. Furthermore, machinists in particular may perceive their own efforts as too remote from the company's overall profit for them to bother to achieve it. Even if they were to be motivated by this, it is unclear what proportion of the total costs are related to direct labour as Cuthbert incurs many other costs such as advertising to maintain the brand. If the costs of direct labour were relatively low, even a large improvement in production efficiency by the machinists may have little effect on overall profit.

Changes to reward systems under the new proposal

The existing reward systems would likely need to change if the move to team-based production were to be adopted.

It may still be appropriate to reward machinists with volume-related bonuses but, as they worked in teams, a team-based performance bonus would be more appropriate. In that way the rest of the team would ensure that any underperforming machinists would improve their performance.

Rewards based on other factors such as quality, innovation, on-time delivery and the ability to work as part of a team would also be appropriate and consistent with the machinists' enlarged job role. This would be a significant change for Cuthbert, where machinists are now being encouraged for the first time to bring about improvements in the production process. Rewards based on direct costs of production, or for the number of suggestions made by each machinist may be appropriate here.

New performance measures would need to be developed against which to align rewards to ensure that employees work towards the overall objectives of the organisation. New reporting systems will need to be put in place to feedback information regarding quality to each cell. This may incur additional costs in the development of existing or new information technology systems.

The commitment of senior management to these changes would be required, as well as communication and training of employees at all levels. This may again incur additional costs and divert management time away from existing activities.

27 Beach Foods

Workbook reference

Financial performance measures including EVA™, ROI and RI are discussed in Chapters 6 and 7 of the Workbook. Control and management styles are discussed in Chapter 11, and the BCG matrix in Chapter 1.

Top tips

Part (a). In this respect, it is important to note (from the second paragraph of the scenario) that Beach already uses EVA™, so we can assume that Beach's management accountants already know how to calculate it.

Part (b). The need to evaluate management's performance as well as the division's performance should have prompted you to think about issues of controllability. For example, if Baby's managers cannot control the R&D costs which are recharged to the department, is it fair to include them in an assessment of the manager's performance?

The reference to 'the assumptions made' also relates to the profit figure being used to assess performance – again, recognising the difference between divisional and managerial performance. Crucially, though, your 'assumptions' should relate to the level of profit to include, not the cost of capital figure to use. The cost of capital figures used must be that for the division (11%), not the one for Beach as a whole (7.5%).

Part (c). Note the requirement here is that you recommend suitable styles, rather than discussing or evaluating different styles. Also, note that you need to recommend a suitable way to control each division (cost/profit/ investment centre) as well as recommending a suitable management style (budget-constrained, profit-conscious and non-accounting). In both cases, the options to choose from were identified in the scenario – control styles in the third paragraph, and management styles in the fourth.

Importantly, the requirement asks for recommendations for **each** division, so you need to cover all three divisions – Baby, Chocolate and R&D – not just the two operating divisions.

Examining team's comments on part (c)

This part was poorly answered as many candidates clearly did not know the criteria for the choice of responsibility centre, even though the centre headings to choose from were given in the scenario. Such a lack of knowledge continues to surprise the examining team.

Lengthy descriptions of the three management styles were not helpful here either, as candidates were expected, instead, to demonstrate their understanding of the styles by applying it to the scenario.

Marking guide	Marks
(a) For relevant points assessing the use of EVATM as a divisional performance measure – 1 mark per point	
Total for part (a): up to 4	
	4
(b) Calculations:	
For applying the correct method to calculate RI – 1 mark	
For applying the correct method to calculate ROI – 1 mark	
For correct calculation of both RI and ROI based on different profit figures (controllable profit, profit after R&D, divisional profit) – 1 mark per profit figure used; up to a maximum of 4 marks	
Comments: 1 mark per relevant comment up to a maximum of 4 marks	
Total for part (b): up to 7	
	7

ANSWERS

Marking guide	Marks
(c) Up to 4 marks for valid recommendations for any one division All recommendations must be justified within the answer to gain credit High marks within the answer for any divisions can only be scored by discussing both the type of centre and the management style which would be appropriate Total for part (c): up to 9	
	9

Professional skills

Analysis and Evaluation

- Use of information provided to perform a suitable/comprehensive evaluation of appropriate management styles
- Appropriate use of the data to support discussion and draw appropriate conclusions
- Demonstration of reasoned and balanced judgement
- Demonstration of ability to consider relevant factors applicable to Beach Food's divisions' situation

Scepticism

- Effective challenge and critical assessment of EVA
- Demonstration of effective challenge the opinions of the managers

Commercial acumen

- Effective use of examples and/or calculations from the scenario information and other practical considerations related to the context to illustrate points being made
- Demonstrating an awareness of organisational and external factors
- Recommendations are practical and plausible, and commercially viable in the context of Beach Food Co's situation

Maximum	5
Total	25

(a) **EVA™ as a divisional performance measure**

Advantages

Maximising wealth – Beach's overall objective is to maximise the family's wealth through their shareholding – in effect, to maximise shareholder wealth.

One of the main benefits of EVA™ as a performance measure (rather than profit-based measures such as ROI) is that it is a value-based approach, and therefore it will be aligned to the overall objective of maximising shareholder wealth.

Goal congruence – Moreover, using EVA™ as a divisional measure will help to ensure that decisions taken at divisional level support the best interests of Beach as a whole, rather than just the individual division.

The **other advantages of EVA™** are:

(1) It gives an absolute measure of performance, and so shows the overall contribution the divisions make to the company.

(2) The basic test of performance is simple. If a division has a positive EVA™, then it is generating a return above that required by the providers of finance. (ROI requires a target level to be set, usually based on benchmarking to the industry sector.)

(3) The adjustments required when calculating net operating profit after tax mean that it is closer to cash flows than traditional accounting profits are, and also mean that EVA™ is less subject to choices in accounting policies.

(4) EVA™ encourages investment in the future (for example, in advertising and development) by adding back these costs to profit in the performance period and treating them like capital expenditure. This will reduce the temptation for dysfunctional, short-termist decision making, which could otherwise be a problem where the capital employed figure from the financial statements is used in ROI and RI. This is likely to be particularly appropriate at Beach where R&D is significant.

Disadvantages

The directors' complaint that EVA™ is complicated to understand appears reasonable, because of the number of adjustments which need to be made to the information from Beach's financial statements. By contrast, ROI and RI are derived from headline information in the financial statements which would be more familiar to the board. A related issue here would be the time and cost involved for Beach's management accountant in calculating the division's EVA™.

EVA™ (like RI) uses a charge for the capital employed in the division. EVA™ uses the weighted average cost of capital (WACC) for the company as a whole, which may not reflect the risks of the manufacturing divisions. Also, as an unlisted business, WACC may be difficult to estimate. By contrast, RI uses a notional cost of capital based on the risk of the divisions – although this will also be subject to an element of judgement and estimate.

Unlike ROI (which gives a percentage measure, rather than an absolute measure) EVA™ will not help to assess relative divisional managerial performance at Beach if the divisions are of different sizes.

(b) **ROI and RI**

A key consideration when calculating either ROI or RI for Baby is what profit figure to use for the calculations.

The data in Appendix 1 suggests three potential profit figures, which could be used for assessing the performance of Baby as a division, and its manager:

Controllable profit – The only costs included in controllable profit are those under the direct control of the divisional manager (ie the divisional operating costs of $121m).

R&D costs recharged – Although the divisional manager cannot influence the costs of the R&D Division, Baby's divisional revenue includes the profit which results from new products and ideas generated by the R&D Division. Therefore, in order to match costs with revenues more fairly, a proportion of the R&D Division's costs should be included in Baby's profit figure.

Divisional profit – The division's performance (as distinct from the manager's performance) should take account of all relevant costs, including Baby's share of the head office management fees. As such the divisional profit ($60m) would be an appropriate figure to use in this respect.

Performance analysis

Regardless of which profit figure is chosen, Baby seems to be performing relatively well. Baby's EVA™ is positive ($35m) and its RI is also positive.

In terms of ROI, the return based on divisional profit (14.2%) is lower than the ROI for similar entities (20%), but the return based on controllable profit, or profit after R&D, is higher than the benchmark figure. However, we do not know which profit figures were used in the benchmark figure, which means we cannot tell whether Baby's ROI figure is above or below the average achieved by similar entities.

	Controllable profit	*Profit after R&D*	*Divisional profit*
ROI			
Profit ($m)	99	88	60
Capital employed ($m)	424	424	424
ROI	**23.3%**	**20.8%**	**14.2%**

ANSWERS

	Controllable profit	Profit after R&D	Divisional profit
RI			
Profit ($m)	99	88	60
Cost of capital ($m)			
(424 × 11%)	46.6	46.6	46.6
RI **($m)**	**52.4**	**41.4**	**13.4**

(c) **Management styles for the divisions**

Baby Division

Responsibility centre – Baby's position as the star in Beach's portfolio, coupled with the fact it is developing and introducing new products, means that the division's focus should be on growth rather than cost control.

As such, it might seem appropriate for Baby to be treated as an investment centre, giving its managers autonomy to develop their business as they see fit.

However, it is not clear whether the divisional managers have the authority to make capital investment decisions or whether these are taken by head office. (Chocolate had to get approval from head office to upgrade its production line.)

If the authority for investment decisions remains with head office, then Baby should be treated as a **profit centre**, and managed according to its ability to generate profit.

Management style – A profit-conscious style focuses on longer-term performance and objectives (such as growth) whereas a budget-constrained style focuses on short-term performance and cost control.

Therefore, given the nature of Baby's market – and the market's rapid growth – the profit-conscious style would seem more appropriate for Baby.

However, elements of a non-accounting style (such as new product development) may also be appropriate.

Given the costs associated with new products and rapid growth (such as the publicity campaign Baby ran to support its new product launch), we recommend that a **non-accounting style** is applied initially.

However, once the market sector begins to mature, then given Baby's strong market share its focus should shift to optimising its profits – at which point, a profit-conscious management style should be adopted.

Chocolate Division

Responsibility centre – As the Chocolate Division is the cash cow in the portfolio, Beach needs it to generate the profits and cash necessary to support Baby's growth.

However, as a cash cow, and operating in a market with limited growth opportunities, Chocolate is unlikely to receive much investment. As such, it would seem appropriate to treat Chocolate as a profit centre.

Nonetheless, it appears that Chocolate does still makes some capital expenditure (for example, the upgrade to its main production line). As such, it could be appropriate to treat Chocolate as an **investment centre**, so that its managers have the autonomy to take these decisions, rather than having to wait for head office to approve them.

Management style – Because it is operating in a mature market with limited growth opportunities, cost control is likely to be crucial in maintaining Chocolate's profitability. As such, a **budget-constrained style** will be the most appropriate management style for Chocolate.

R&D Division

Responsibility centre – The R&D Division does not generate any revenue in its own right, and therefore should be treated as a cost centre.

Nonetheless, it is important that the contribution the division makes to the group (through the overall profit generated by the products it develops) is not overlooked. The complaints which Baby's managers make about the recharge suggests they are only thinking about the costs rather than the revenue which the new products have generated for them.

As such, whilst Beach should continue to treat the R&D Division as a cost centre for control purposes, it would also be useful to **monitor the profit generated by each new product** over its life cycle, to demonstrate the division's value to the group as a whole.

Management style – As the R&D Division is a cost centre, it might seem appropriate to apply a budget-constrained management style.

However, it is important that potentially profitable developments are not rejected simply to keep the division's costs within a fixed budget – and there is a danger this could be the case under a budget-constrained management style.

Therefore, elements of a non-accounting style might also be appropriate – with a focus on the number of new product ideas being generated, and the market reaction to new products being developed.

As such, it may be necessary to adopt a management style which combines some elements of the **budget-constrained style** with others from the **non-accounting style**.

28 Veyatie

Workbook reference

Non-financial indicators are introduced in Chapter 9 of the Workbook. The balanced scorecard is discussed in Chapter 12.

Top tips

Part (a). This will require a practical analysis, and better answers will use some of the data provided to specifically illustrate the problems in using and interpreting the customer satisfaction data.

1 mark was available for each relevant point, which is normally the case in APM, so about 4 relevant points will be required to secure a pass mark for this part of the question.

Part (b). The question scenario mentioned that the answer to this part of the question should include advice on how to refine performance measures. Therefore, a sensible approach would be:

(1) Discuss general problems with the scorecard possible points here could cover conflict between measures, information overload

(2) Illustrate specific problems with measures provided For example, no link to some CSFs (no. stores), types of training, imbalance in the number of measures selected

(3) Discuss on how to refine some of the measures (without recommending new ones) where appropriate eg types of training

(4) Difficulties in use: board scepticism, information systems

Again, 1 mark was available for each relevant point.

Examining team's comments

A common problem in part (b), which was surprisingly poorly answered, was that students chose to answer the question 'advise the board on whether the given set of indicators is suitable for a BSC at the company'; this was not the question that was being asked.

These answers frequently ignored the further guidance in the scenario that 'the board does not want you to give a detailed evaluation of the advantages and disadvantages of each performance measure or to suggest completely new measures.' Also, the answers did not focus on the actual requirement to address the 'problems of implementing and using the balanced scorecard (BSC) approach'.

Marking guide	Marks
(a) 1 mark per relevant point covering:	
• Subjectivity and customer perception	
• Mean and aggregated data	
• Incomplete data	
• Trends and seasonal factors	
	7
(b) 1 mark per point	
• Problems of selecting measures	
• Problems of measurement	
• The need for balance	

Marking guide	Marks
• Problems of conflicting measures	
• Need for board and management commitment	
• Collecting and interpreting data	
• Information system requirements	
• Use of illustrative examples from the measures in Appendix 2	
	13

Professional skills

Analysis and Evaluation

- Use of information provided to perform a suitable/comprehensive evaluation
- Appropriate use of the data to support discussion and draw appropriate conclusions
- Demonstration of reasoned and balanced judgement
- Demonstration of ability to consider relevant factors applicable to Veyatie Co's situation
- Identification of further analysis, which could be carried out to enable an appropriate recommendation to be made.

Scepticism

- Effective challenge and critical assessment
- Demonstration of effective challenge of information supplied / identification of missing information

Commercial acumen

- Effective use of examples and/or calculations from the scenario information and other practical considerations related to the context to illustrate points being made
- Demonstrating an awareness of organisational and external factors
- Recognising key issues in a given scenario in terms of how to address problems, and possible obstacles that will need to be overcome in the process of doing this

Maximum	5
Total	25

(a) **Subjectivity**

Customers' own assessments of satisfaction are subjective. Different customers could buy the same goods in the same store and at the same time, but still score their satisfaction differently. Different customers may have different expectations of their visit to the store and will attach different levels of importance to different aspects of their visit. Some may place a high importance on being able to move around the store and access goods easily, whereas to others this may be unimportant and would not affect their satisfaction.

Another reason why the data may be misleading is that, when rating their satisfaction, customers may tend to use the middle scores and be reluctant to use the highest and lowest scores. This appears to be the case in the data given where in most quarters customers do not give the scores of 1 or 5.

Aggregated and mean data

The collection of data of a single measure of customer satisfaction does not indicate what aspect of their visit to the store customers are satisfied, or dissatisfied, with. Customers may consider the price, design and quality of the goods, the comfort and layout of the store or the friendliness and product knowledge of the staff when scoring their satisfaction. Without knowing which aspects of their visit customers are satisfied with, it will be hard to know what to do to improve customer satisfaction.

Using the mean score may also make the data hard to interpret. For example, in Quarter 1 20X4, 50% of the customers are completely satisfied (a score of 5) and 50% of the customer are completely dissatisfied (a score of 1). This may be due to an error in collecting or compiling the data, but the mean score of 3 indicates that, overall, customers are satisfied, whereas 50% of them are completely dissatisfied. The calculation of the median or modal score may be preferable because this reduces the distortion to mean scores caused by very high or low scores.

Incomplete data

The data may not represent the views of a wide range of customers. The scores are collected when customers are buying goods at the till. This does not reflect the views of the customers who were so dissatisfied that they did not buy anything.

The prizes offered in the draw to encourage customers to leave the satisfaction score may appeal differently to male and female customers and to customers of different ages. For example, tickets to amusement parks may appeal more to younger customers than to older ones. Using this data as if it represents a wide range of customers' views may be misleading and lead to incorrect decisions being taken.

Identifying trends

Identifying trends is one way of overcoming some of the problems of interpreting the customer data, but it may be difficult to identify trends. In a fashion retailer such as Veyatie, there may be seasonal and short-term or cyclical trends, which make it hard to interpret what the long-term trend is.

In the limited data given, there appears to be a seasonal trend where customer satisfaction is worse in Quarter 4 than in any other quarter in each year. Overall there seems to be a downward trend, with every quarter being worse than the same quarter in the previous year.

(b) **Problems of implementing and using the balanced scorecard**

Selecting measures

Veyatie's strategic objectives are to maximise shareholder wealth by increasing the number of retail stores, making customers completely satisfied, ensuring its stores are attractive and offering the widest range of fashion clothing in the market. Measures must be selected which are congruent with Veyatie's critical success factors (CSFs) and strategic objectives. Though it is unclear what the CSFs are, at least one of the strategic objectives, to increase the number of stores, is not reflected at all in the measures selected. The lack of a suitable measure for this objective could be the reason why Veyatie is unlikely to open new stores in the near future.

Measures must not be selected just because they are easy to measure. The human resources department already records the total number of employee training days, so this measure could have been selected just because the data is readily available.

The number of days spent on the different types of training is unclear. Though clearly important, staff health and safety training does not directly help Veyatie achieve its strategic objectives. It may simply reflect Veyatie's legal obligations and so would not help gain competitive advantage. It would be better to measure the days spent training staff to understand the range of products available and how to display them attractively in the store, as this directly relates to Veyatie's strategic objectives.

One of the benefits of the balanced scorecard approach is that it presents a holistic view of a business, covering financial and non-financial and internal and external factors. The measures selected do cover all four perspectives of the balanced scorecard, but do not seem to be well balanced as there are more measures in the financial perspective than in each of the other perspectives. Also, most of the measures are internally focused.

The bias towards financial measures may reflect the fact that the board has so far seen little need for non-financial indicators. Financial measures, however, are backwards looking and measure the results of actions taken in the past. It is non-financial factors, such as customer satisfaction, which drive future performance and which will enable Veyatie to achieve its strategic objectives.

Conflicting measures

When selecting measures to use in the balanced scorecard, care must be taken to select measures which do not conflict with each other. Otherwise, without further guidance, managers will not know which measure to focus on, or may simply ignore one measure and focus on another.

Several of the measures selected by the consultant may potentially conflict with one another. For example, in order to achieve a low stock out percentage, Veyatie may have to hold higher levels of inventory which may worsen inventory turnover. This could apply at the overall company level or at individual stores.

The financial measure of operating profit margins conflicts with some of the measures in the other perspectives. The total number of employee training days has been selected to measure the learning and innovation perspective. The cost of this training, at least in the short term, will reduce operating profit margins. Similarly, having a high market share may imply that Veyatie will have to be competitive on price, which will also lower operating profit margins.

Board commitment

If the introduction of the balanced scorecard approach is to be successful, the commitment of the board is essential. Without this, other managers in the business are unlikely to work hard to implement and use the approach.

The board is already sceptical about the benefits of the balanced scorecard. There is the danger that it may simply be abandoned if it is found difficult to use, as was proposed for the collection of customer satisfaction data which was found to be difficult to interpret. The board's apparent disregard of non-financial performance measures is also clearly inconsistent with a successful introduction of the balanced scorecard approach.

Collecting and interpreting data

Interpreting the measures used in the balanced scorecard may be difficult, for example, for qualitative data such as customer satisfaction, which Veyatie has already had difficulties in interpreting. A lack of expertise in interpreting this data, may lead to wrong decisions being made.

The collection and interpretation of the data for the balanced scorecard will take time and resources. There may be staff resistance to the change, though this may be overcome by training in the benefits and use of the balanced scorecard.

Veyatie's information systems are basic for a business of its size and focus just on the use of financial information. They will need to be replaced or upgraded in order to collect and process non-financial and external data required for the balanced scorecard. The cost of implementing and using the balanced scorecard should be compared to the benefits of doing so.

29 Pharmaceutical Technologies

Workbook reference

The balanced scorecard is discussed in Chapter 12 of the Workbook.

Top tips

For part (a), you should be asking 'how well will the proposed measures help PT deliver its objectives and, in turn, its corporate strategy?' The scenario provided you with considerable detail about objectives and measures, and you should have used it to help answer this requirement.

Part (b)

Note there are two distinct parts to this requirement. The first is a pure test of knowledge: describing a method for analysing stakeholder influence. Mendelow's matrix seems the obvious choice here.

However, don't spend too long on this part of the requirement (**briefly** describe...), because the second part of the requirement is more substantial: analyse the influence of four different external stakeholders on the regulator. Note that the question refers to stakeholders who could influence the regulator (not PT). Although some of the stakeholder groups identified by the working group (eg doctors, patients) could also be stakeholders of the regulator, it is important that you analyse their influence in relation to the regulator.

However, as there are only eight marks available for part (b) in total you should only give a relatively brief analysis of each stakeholder's influence on the regulator – highlighting what power they have, and how interested they will be in exerting that power.

Part (c)

You need to establish how BDR differs from PT, because this will affect how the scorecard is applied in both organisations. In effect, the requirement is asking how the application of the scorecard would vary in a private sector organisation (PT) compared to a public sector one.

To score well here, you need to make a comparison between the two, rather than simply talking about the application of the scorecard at one or other of them.

Marking guide

	Marks
(a) 1 mark per relevant point – up to a maximum of 5 Relevant points include: Evaluation of whether the customer and learning and growth measures suggested cover the perspective intended Consideration of whether there are other suitable measures Discussion of linkages between the measures and the company objectives Discussion of the difficulty of collection of appropriate data, and ranking the measures Total: up to 5	5
(b) Description of suitable method of stakeholder analysis – 1 mark per point – up to a maximum of 2 Analysis of the power and interest of each stakeholder – 1 mark for power, and 1 mark for influence of each stakeholder – up to a maximum of 8 Total: up to 8	8
(c) 1 mark per relevant difference between the application of the scorecard at BDR and PT. Differences must be clearly linked to the scenario to score the marks available. Total: up to 7	7

Professional skills

Analysis and Evaluation

- Use of information provided to perform a suitable/comprehensive evaluation
- Demonstration of reasoned and balanced judgement
- Demonstration of ability to consider relevant factors applicable to PT Co's situation

Scepticism

- Effective challenge and critical assessment of measures
- Demonstration of effective challenge of information supplied / identification of missing information

Marking guide	Marks
Commercial acumen	
• Effective use of examples and/or calculations from the scenario information and other practical considerations related to the context to illustrate points being made	
• Demonstrating an awareness of organisational and external factors	
Maximum	5
Total	25

(a) **Customer perspective**

PT has two different types of customer: users (healthcare providers and patients) and the people who fund the drug use (insurance companies or government). The measure currently proposed seems to focus mainly on the end users. However, their concerns may not always be same as those who are paying for a course of treatment. For example, the healthcare providers and patients are likely to focus primarily on how effective the product is as a cure. However, the funding bodies will also be interested in the cost of the treatment in comparison to the cost of treatments from PT's competitors.

Therefore, PT should consider a measure looking at the cost of its drugs; for example, comparing the cost of its drugs against similar alternative drugs offered by rival manufacturers.

Learning and growth

The third of the objectives from the medium-term strategy highlights the importance of innovation in the drug approval process. The measures in the learning and growth perspective of the scorecard should therefore directly help PT to achieve this objective.

We are not told anything about the relative importance or ranking of any of the measures in the scorecard, but it is debatable whether the number of training days attended is the main measure of learning and growth. Reducing the time to market of new products, and increasing the percentage of drugs that gain final approval, are likely to be more directly strategically important.

Measurement issues

Management will also need to consider how practical it will be to collect data for some of the non-financial measures. Conversely, measures should not be chosen because only they are easy to measure. The number of training days undertaken by staff will be easy to measure by staff. However, there may be a danger that staff will simply end up going on training days simply to achieve a target number of days. Training will only be valuable to PT and its staff if it is relevant and appropriate for the people attending.

(b) **Stakeholder influence**

A stakeholder's influence over an organisation can be analysed in relation to the stakeholder's power and interest, using Mendelow's matrix.

Power identifies the extent to which a stakeholder (or group of stakeholders) has the power to influence a decision or situation. The level of **interest** reflects the likelihood that a stakeholder will exercise their power in relation to any given decision or situation.

This approach can be used to analyse the four key external stakeholders of BDR: the drug companies, the Government, healthcare providers, and patients.

Drug companies

Interest – likely to have a **high interest** in BDR, because it makes the final judgement about whether a product can be sold in the country. Without approval from BDR, the drug companies will not have any products to sell.

Power – **little power** to influence BDR. BDR's responsibility is to the public and to public health, rather than to the drug companies. Therefore, BDR needs to be (and be seen to be) independent from the drug companies.

Government

Power – **high power** because it appoints the board of trustees and also directly funds BDR.

Interest – will have a keen interest in public health overall, but their direct interest in BDR is likely to be **relatively low**. The Government has appointed the trustees to manage BDR on its behalf so it is unlikely to intervene in decision making at BDR (unless there is a specific financial or medical scandal which requires it to do so).

Doctors and healthcare providers

Interest – will have a **high level of interest** in the approval process, because they will want to be confident that any new drugs approved are safe for use. They will also have an interest in BDR's role in encouraging the development of beneficial new drugs. These new drugs could help them treat patients and diseases that they would not otherwise be able to treat as effectively.

Power – likely to have **low power** over the approval process because BDR is an independent regulator (although they may be able to exert some power by lobbying the Government).

Patients

Interest – will have a **high level of interest** in the drug approval process because they will want to be reassured that any drugs approved are safe. However, they will also have an interest in potential new cures being available on the market quickly.

Power – in the same way that healthcare providers only have low power, so patients also only have **low power** over any decisions made at BDR.

(c) **Differences in objectives** – BDR's objectives are less explicitly financial than PT's, not least because it does not have any shareholders. Therefore, the emphasis the balanced scorecard places on non-financial performance will be relevant for BDR.

Stakeholder structure – BDR is a public sector organisation, while PT is a commercial organisation, which means that the Government is a much more important stakeholder for BDR than for PT. It is likely that this will need to be reflected in BDR's scorecard, with there being a political dimension to measuring performance.

Complexity of the scorecards – BDR's scorecard is likely to be quite complex, because it needs to reflect the diverse nature of its stakeholders and their interests. For example, on the one hand, drug companies will be keen for new drugs to be approved as quickly as possible, while healthcare providers and patients will be most interested in the risk-benefit profile of any potential new drugs. Equally, the Government will want effective drugs and treatments to be available for patients, but in terms of paying healthcare providers the Government may not be willing to pay for drugs it considers to be too expensive.

In this respect, the **customer perspective** of BDR's scorecard is likely to be crucial because, in effect, the drug companies, healthcare providers and patients are all BDR's customers. In PT's scorecard the relative significance of the four perspectives is likely to be more equal. The financial perspective will be very important for satisfying shareholders, while the internal business processes and learning and growth perspectives will be crucial in developing and manufacturing the new drugs effectively. Process and innovation are likely to be less directly important in BDR because it doesn't develop 'products' of its own.

Selecting performance measures – However, the nature of BDR's work means that it will be quite hard to measure how well it is performing against its objectives. For example, determining whether a medicine has an 'acceptable balance of benefit and risk' will involve a degree of judgement and selectivity, and it is likely to be difficult to set a quantifiable performance measure to determine whether this objective is being achieved.

Potential conflicts – Of BDR's three objectives, the easiest to set quantifiable measures for is likely to be 'encouraging new beneficial product development' because a performance measure could be set around the number of new products developed. However, there is a danger that imposing quantifiable measures in this way may have unintended consequences. For example, it may lead to new drugs being introduced even if the new product is not a significant improvement on an existing drug.

30 Victoria-Yeeland Logistics

Workbook reference

The balanced scorecard (BSC) is discussed in Chapter 12 of the Workbook. Reward systems and reward management are discussed in Chapter 11.

Top tips

Part (a)

As the marking guide indicates, there are two marks available for each metric you recommend: one for calculating a suitable metric; and one for justifying why you have chosen it.

Therefore, as is so often the case in APM, the requirement is not simply about calculation. Justifying the metric you have chosen is equally as important as the calculation.

Note, also, that there is a second part to the requirement – a discussion about the problems of using customer complaints as a performance measure. For example, can Victoria be sure that all customer complaints are valid?

Part (b)

The requirement asks you to advise on 'the reward management issues outlined by the CFO'. The context for this requirement is provided by the last paragraph in the scenario, but crucially you need to recognise that there are two sets of issues here: one relating to the senior management bonus scheme, and one relating to the operational managers' bonus scheme.

As the marking guide indicates, you can only score up to five marks for advising on the issues with either scheme, so it is vital to analyse both schemes in order to score well on this requirement.

The fact that the shareholders have been complaining about the senior management's bonus should be a clue that agency theory is an issue here – is the scheme designed with shareholders' best interests in mind, or management's?

Similarly, in relation to the operational managers' scheme, the fact that the scenario identifies a change to the way that bonus targets are set should prompt you to question whether these changes are appropriate.

Examining team's comments

Many candidates used the building block model as a template for their answer but failed to go further than a generic response – around the need for standards to be fair, achievable and owned, and for rewards to be clear, motivational and controllable.

In order for answers based around the model to score well, candidates needed to show how each aspect could be applied to the specific scenarios at Victoria.

Candidates seemed unwilling to say that employees (either senior management or operational managers) may be unhappy but this need not be an issue for Victoria, as there will usually be a conflict of interest between employees and the company/shareholders.

Good answers identified and discussed how to address this issue fairly. However, simply stating that employees should set their own targets is not a practical solution, nor one which is commercially valuable to Victoria.

Marking guide	Marks
(a) Each suitable performance measurement recommended – up to 2 marks (for each of four perspectives; so up to 8 marks in total) (1 mark for calculating a suitable metric; 1 mark for justifying the choice of metric) For discussing the problems of using customer complaints as a performance measure – up to 4 marks Total for part (b): up to 11	11
(b) For relevant points relating to issues in the senior management reward system – 1 mark each, up to a maximum of 5 For relevant points relating to the operational managers' bonus scheme – 1 mark per relevant point, up to a maximum of 5 Total for part (c): up to 9	9

Professional skills

Analysis and Evaluation

- Use of information provided to perform a suitable evaluation of both reward schemes
- Demonstration of reasoned and balanced judgement
- Demonstration of ability to consider relevant factors applicable to Victoria's situation

Scepticism

- Effective challenge and critical assessment
- Demonstration of effective challenge the opinions of operational managers on the reward scheme

Commercial acumen

- Effective use of examples and/or calculations from the scenario information and other practical considerations related to the context to illustrate points being made
- Demonstrating an awareness of organisational and external factors
- Recognising key issues in a given scenario in terms of how to address problems, and possible obstacles that will need to be overcome in the process of doing this
- Recommendations are practical and plausible, and commercially viable in the context of Victoria's situation

Maximum	5
Total	25

(a) **Ability to meet customers' transport needs**

This success factor can be measured by the proportion of customer requests which Victoria is able to undertake.

$$\frac{\text{Total number of packages transported}}{\text{Total number of customer transport requests}}$$

$$\frac{548{,}000}{610{,}000} = 89.8\%$$

Ability to deliver packages quickly

This measure needs to take account of how far packages have to travel as well as how long it takes them to get to their destinations. Therefore, a suitable measure will be one which measures **time taken per kilometre** (rather than one which measures time taken per journey).

$$\frac{\text{Total package minutes}}{\text{Total package kilometres}}$$

$$\frac{131{,}520{,}000}{65{,}760{,}000} = 2.0$$

Ability to deliver packages on time

This measure needs to reflect the proportion of packages which are delivered within the time window given to the customer.

$$\frac{\text{Deliveries within agreed window}}{\text{Total number of packages transported}}$$

$$\frac{(548{,}000-21{,}920)}{548{,}000} = 96\%$$

Ability to deliver packages safely

This measure needs to reflect the number of packages delivered undamaged as a proportion of the total number of packages transported.

$$\frac{\text{Deliveries with no reported damage}}{\text{Total number of packages transported}}$$

$$\frac{(548{,}000-8{,}220)}{548{,}000} = 98.5\%$$

Problems of using customer complaints as a basis for performance measurement

Victoria delivers packages to a large number of different customers, and it could respond to problems with their delivery in different ways. This means it will be difficult for Victoria to get an accurate picture of the number of deliveries which were damaged or late.

Problems understated – Some customers may not bother to report that a package has been delivered late or was damaged. However, due to the inconvenience caused by the lateness or damage they will use one of Victoria's competitors to deliver their packages in future.

In such cases, the performance measure gives a misleading impression that Victoria is performing better than it is. And, given the importance of customer retention in Yeeland's competitive market, this could have very significant consequences on Victoria's revenue performance in the longer term.

If Victoria recorded its own delivery performance it could take direct action to try to retain customers who have suffered from late or damaged packages. For example, acknowledging the problem at the point of delivery, it could offer to discount the next order for a customer whose package is delivered late.

Problems overstated – In contrast to customers who do not report valid complaints, others may report unjustified complaints in the hope of obtaining a refund or a credit against future orders. Currently, the measures simply record the number of complaints received, even though some of these may not be valid.

In this respect, it would be better to measure the number of refunds or discounts given (as an indicator of the number of valid complaints) rather than simply recording the total number of complaints.

(b) **Senior managers' reward system**

Assuming that the members of the senior management team are all on the board, the potential problem here is that senior management could be deciding their own bonuses.

Agency issues – As such, there is a danger that the reward system will favour the managers' interests, rather than those of Victoria's shareholders. For example, if the targets used to determine managers' bonuses are easy to achieve, this will maximise the chances of managers receiving bonuses. This would justify the shareholders' complaints that the bonuses are not suitable – because they are not supporting Victoria's objective of maximising shareholder wealth.

The introduction of the BSC should help to align the senior management's objectives with those of the shareholders, particularly in relation to the financial perspective. However, the financial measures suggested for the BSC do not directly address shareholder wealth, because they are essentially still based around profitability rather than value-based management.

Controllability – The fact that the market is saturated, and dominated by two international companies, will constrain management's ability to grow revenue. Similarly, fuel prices – which management cannot control – will be a significant influence on profit margin. This again suggests these may not be the most appropriate measures to use when assessing management's performance.

Operational managers' reward system

Choice of measures – Although the senior managers assess the operational managers' performance, it is not clear what measures are used as the basis of this assessment. The measures of performance against which operational managers are assessed should be aligned to Victoria's overall objectives.

However, the measures should also relate to the aspects of performance that the operational managers can influence (and therefore will typically come from the 'customer' and 'business' perspectives in the scorecard).

Setting own bonus targets – However, the suggestion that the operational managers should be involved in setting their own bonus targets does not seem appropriate. In the same way that senior management shouldn't set their own performance targets, neither should operational managers.

Although it could be beneficial to explain the **target setting process** to the manager, this should not be confused with the idea of letting managers set their own targets. Targets should still be set by a higher level of management, and should be set at a level which is stretching but achievable.

The target set should then be explained to the managers so that they understand what they have to do in order to earn their bonus.

31 Harray Keyboards

Workbook reference

Non-financial indicators are introduced in Chapter 9 of the Workbook. The performance pyramid is discussed in Chapter 12.

Top tips

Part (a) required the completion of calculations for operational performance indictors (OPIs) and an evaluation of the OPIs.

A key issue here is that operational performance covers only 4 parts of the performance pyramid (cycle time, delivery, quality and waste). Failure to realise this meant that many candidates covered all 10 aspects to the PP instead of concentrating on these four. Candidates were less competent, however, at offering an evaluation of the indicator.

Part (b) required an evaluation of the non-financial indicators requested by the CEO (using the OPIs from part b). This was poorly answered because candidates failed to appreciate it was about the reliability of the data not its usefulness.

Examining team's comments

A common problem in **part (a)**, was that many candidates did not add anything additional by way of discussion or evaluation. The ACCA examiner's report noted that 'often candidates simply gave an indication as to what a measure might be – for example, % of late deliveries for the Delivery heading – without saying why that would be useful for Harray. A response which had indicated – "% of late deliveries would be an appropriate indicator to use for the Delivery heading, as a high proportion of late deliveries is likely to have an adverse effect on customer satisfaction. Whereas customers who receive their goods on time cannot always be assumed to be satisfied, it can be logically inferred that a high proportion of late deliveries would lead to unhappy customers" – would have demonstrated an evaluation of the suitability of the indicator.

In **part (b)** a good response would have taken each operational NFPI in turn and discuss how reliable it might be.

The ACCA examiner's report provided the following examples:

Quality:

This relies upon the quality inspector's count of the rejected keyboards. The quality inspector may not have counted accurately and/or, possibly, may have missed some keyboards which perhaps should have been rejected. The indicator in its current format is therefore unreliable and there should either be an automated way of ascertaining which keyboards should be rejected or someone else should work with the production manager to ensure that there is some verification of both the inspector's work and the number of rejected keyboards.

Delivery:

Harray is relying on information from Achall to detail the percentage of on time deliveries. As this information is supplied to Harray by Achall from Achall's systems, Harray seems to have little or no way of verifying that it is correct. We do not know what the service level agreement (SLA) between the two companies indicates but it can be safely assumed that Achall would not want to pass on to Harray information which indicates that it has broken the SLA and may be liable for a payment penalty. The information is not only unreliable, therefore, but Achall also would appear to have a motive to manipulate it should it be unfavourable for them."

Marking guide		Marks
Waste – up to 4 marks		
Quality – up to 6 marks		
Delivery – up to 4 marks		
Cycle time – up to 4 marks		
1 mark for correct calculation of each suitable indicator and 1 mark for each point in commentary		
1 mark per point	7	
		20

Professional Marks

Analysis and Evaluation

- Appropriate use of data to perform suitable calculations to complete the work started by the junior accountant
- Comprehensive evaluation is made of the four operational indicators

Scepticism

- Recognition that more than just working capital should be assessed under cycle time

ANSWERS

Marking guide	Marks
Commercial Acumen	
• Addresses in the three areas of focus requested in the advice on the reliability of the NFPIs	
Maximum	5
Total	25

There are four operational headings in the pyramid which shall be considered in turn.

Waste is about optimal use of resources and minimisation of non-value adding activity. There are 1·05 million keyboards produced but this only represents 86% utilisation of the capacity of the factory (2,695,680 minutes of production line time are available at 2·2 minutes per keyboard meaning that the factory can produce 1,225,309 at full capacity). Therefore, capital invested in the factory is underutilised, although an 80+% utilisation would be considered efficient for many manufacturing operations.

Quality can be measured through four cost types: inspection and prevention costs (which represent the costs of preventing faults in the production process and inspecting to avoid faulty goods leaving the factory) and internal and external failure costs (which are costs resulting from faulty goods being identified before and after delivery to the customer). There are no data given for 20X5 on the costs of inspection and prevention. However, the effectiveness of inspection can be measured in that only 0·4% of orders were returned while inspection stopped the delivery of 1·5% of faulty goods. There was a loss of $50,400 at standard cost from the scrapping of faulty keyboards although 60% of faulty boards identified were able to be repaired. The effectiveness of prevention can be measured in that there is a roughly 1·9% failure rate in total, which must reflect the good production practice at the factory. There are data on measures of the costs of internal failure from reworking goods ($18,900). But there are no data on the costs of external failures from 0·4% of customer returns which may incur further repair or warranty claim costs.

Delivery has been outsourced to Achall and Harray is reliant on Achall to provide the data on the quality of Achall's own service. This represents a risk which Harray can control by monitoring its own customer feedback to identify if Achall is under-reporting the late deliveries. Based on Achall's data, 92% of orders are delivered on time at an average time of 3·4 days.

Cycle time for working capital is being measured but this should be done for all the significant processes in Harray. The processes which have been identified so far are setting up production lines, running the production on an order and delivering the order. Measurement of production cycle times is likely to be particularly important in assessing the efficiency of such a cost-conscious business. There are data on delivery time (3·4 days on average) and on production time (2·2 minutes per production line). These should appear in the pyramid of indicators if they are deemed sufficiently important.

In order to understand the issues surrounding measurement of non-financial indicators, it is necessary first to consider the more commonly used financial ones. Financial indicators will be produced by Harray's financial systems. These systems will generate much of the cost information used, for example, in measuring the costs of quality. They are internally controlled and additionally monitored by the external auditors of the organisation. Such systems are by definition working with easily quantified data (invoice values). For these reasons, they are likely to be the most reliable data available.

However, for the measurement of headings such as cycle time, the data are often going to be nonfinancial. Cycle time requires measuring how long processes take, for example, the length of time it takes a production line to produce a keyboard. These data are within the control of Harray and the data will be obtained by production records and interviewing the key personnel. However, they will not be subject to the checking and controls over financial data and therefore, may be more prone to error.

Other non-financial data used may come from external sources. For example, at Harray, they are using the delivery data of Achall. This data must be treated carefully as there is an incentive for Achall to under-report late deliveries as there may be penalties for such non-performance in their contract with Harray (there is also the threat of losing the contract). Harray will want to ensure that Achall's data is reliable by checking it against its own customer complaint records. Also, the definition of non-financial data is more subjective, for example, what constitutes a late delivery (though this should be consistent with the service level agreed in the contract).

Tutorial note. There is a wide variety of possible answers to this question which will be given credit, provided they are consistent with part (a).

32 APX Accountancy

Workbook reference

The building block model is discussed in Chapter 11 of the Workbook.

Top tips

It is vital that you read the requirement for **part (a)** carefully and answer the question set. You are asked to evaluate APX's performance **management system**, not APX's performance.

Notice also the link between parts (a) and (b). In part (a) you need to evaluate the existing system, and then in **part (b)** you need to explain and suggest improvements. Therefore, you should not have suggested any improvements while you were answering part (b); but should have saved these for part (c) instead.

Part (c) – At one level, the marketing manager seems to be highlighting the importance of non-financial performance measures, which seems reasonable. However, they also seem to have overlooked the environmental factors which have contributed to the relative financial performance of the different service areas. Has the Business Advisory Division really performed best financially because it has the highest customer service score, or because the business advisory sector had a growth year across the industry as a whole?

Examining team's comments

It was sad to note how many candidates did not even know the names of the three building blocks. This demonstrated inadequate preparation for the examination.

Better candidates had read the full requirement to the question before beginning their answers, and so held back from offering improvements to the faults recognised in part (a) until their answers to part (b) of the question.

Professional skills

Analysis and Evaluation

- Use of information provided to perform a suitable/comprehensive evaluation of performance systems
- Demonstration of reasoned and balanced judgement
- Demonstration of ability to consider relevant factors applicable to APX's situation

Commercial acumen

- Effective use of examples and/or calculations from the scenario information and other practical considerations related to the context to illustrate points being made
- Demonstrating an awareness of organisational and external factors
- Recognising key issues in a given scenario in terms of how to address problems, and possible obstacles that will need to be overcome in the process of doing this
- Recommendations are practical and plausible, and commercially viable in the context of APX's situation

Maximum 5 marks

(a) Fitzgerald and Moon's building block model suggests that performance systems should be based on three concepts: dimensions, standards and rewards.

Dimensions – The model identifies six dimensions (competitive performance, financial performance, quality of service, flexibility and resource utilisation and innovation) and suggests that the performance measures companies choose should focus on these six areas.

The model also suggests that the dimensions can be divided into two sets: **results** (competitive performance and financial performance) and **determinants** (the other four). The logic here is that controlling and improving performance in respect of the determinants will then lead to improved results.

Standards – Here, the model highlights three key properties which performance measures (standards or targets) should possess: **ownership, achievability** and **fairness**.

Rewards – Finally, the model also highlights threee properties which reward schemes need to possess: **clarity, controllability** and **motivation**.

The current performance management system appears to be based primarily on financial performance, and so does not focus on a number of the determinants highlighted by the building block model.

Dimensions

Results – The current system does allow **financial** and **competitive performance** to be measured. The figures for **revenue growth** and **profit margin** can be used to measure APX's financial performance, while the data on accounting industry revenue can be used to calculate **market share**.

Determinants – However, the management information collected provides less opportunity to measure the determinants of performance. The customer service score could be used as an indicator of the quality of service offered, but there appears to be no information on which to measure flexibility and resource utilisation and innovation.

Standards

Measuring competitive performance – The industry figures will allow APX to monitor its market share, and its revenue growth relative to the industry as a whole, but they only look at revenue rather than profit. Therefore, it does not look as if APX can measure its profit margin against the industry as a whole.

Consequently, any standards for profitability will have to be **set internally**; for example APX could measure the profitability of each of its business streams. However, this could raise issues in relation to **achievability** and **fairness**. Given that Emland is currently in a recession, it is perhaps to be expected that the growth and margins in the audit businesses will be lower than those in the Business Advisory Division, so the fact that this is the case does not necessarily tell us anything about the relative performance of the divisions.

The scenario does not tell us anything about the target scores for customer service or how these are set, so we cannot comment on this aspect of the standards.

Reward system

Clarity – Non-partners receive a bonus based on their line managers' annual review, but the scenario does not indicate what aspects of their performance staff are judged on in this review. If they are not clear what their performance is being judged on, or if the judgement is perceived to be too subjective, this may serve to demotivate staff.

Controllability – APX's performance management system appears to focus predominantly on financial indicators, which may suggest that financial measures are used as the basis for the annual review. Again, though, this could be a cause for concern, because non-partners have relatively limited scope to influence revenue or profit margins.

Divisional or group-wide performance – There may be similar issues of controllability in relation to the partners' reward system. The partners currently receive a share of profit, but it is not clear if this profit share is based on APX's profit as a whole or the profit for their area of the business. If the partners feel their rewards are being based on measures they cannot control, this is likely to adversely affect their motivation. For example, if partners' rewards are based on group profits, then partners in the Audit Division may not maximise their own performance if they know that they will benefit (regardless of their own division's performance) from the favourable performance of the Business Advisory Services Division.

(b) **Cover all dimensions of performance** – One of the key improvements a building block system can make to performance management is ensuring that all the key dimensions of successful performance are measured.

At APX, this will mean considering the importance of flexibility, resource utilisation and innovation to the firm's success and then developing performance measures for these dimensions.

Flexibility – Flexibility is likely to be important for APX in terms of the scheduling of its work (to meet client deadlines) and, in this respect, flexibility is also likely to have an impact on customer satisfaction. Accordingly, APX could introduce a performance measure looking at the percentage of jobs delivered on time.

Resource utilisation – APX's key resource is its staff, so it would seem very important to measure staff utilisation rates. One way of doing this would be to measure the percentage of chargeable hours worked as a percentage of total working hours, and such a measure would provide APX with information about the productivity of its staff. Moreover, if this measure were recorded on a monthly basis it would highlight periods when the business is busy and when it is less busy. The partners could then try to win new clients who need work done in APX's less busy periods.

Innovation – Innovation could be useful for improving APX's internal systems and working practices, but its impact is likely to be greater in relation to the new services APX can develop for its clients. In this case, it may be useful to have a performance measure which looks at the percentage of revenue earned from new customer initiatives.

Standards and rewards

Although the introduction of additional measures which cover the non-financial dimensions of successful performance is perhaps the biggest improvement the building block approach could make to APX, there are also **issues with the way standards are currently set**.

To address this, APX needs to ensure that the measures chosen (and performance targets set) are **achievable** and **fair**. In turn, this should encourage the staff to try to achieve the performance targets.

Similarly, the current rewards system should also be reviewed to ensure that it serves to **motivate partners and staff**. For example, if this is not already the case, an element of the partners' profit share should be based on the profitability of the work from their divisions, rather than it all being based on APX's profitability overall.

Equally, it may also be beneficial to give the non-partners their own targets or objectives for the year, because then the line managers have some more clearly defined objectives to assess their staff against in the annual review process.

(c) **Top tip.** The measure being commented on is customer service, not customer satisfaction. You may have been tempted to discuss the potential trade-off between financial and non-financial performance measures – by suggesting that APX might be able to increase customer satisfaction by reducing its prices, and thereby also reducing its profit margins.

However, we have focused specifically on the customer service score, rather than customer satisfaction more generally, and so we have not included this more general argument in our suggested solution below.

Importance of customer service – Customer service is undoubtedly important for a service firm like APX, because if the service it offers its customers is poor it may look for other advisers.

It is not clear what factors contribute to the customer service scores which customers give, but the quality of the advice which APX gives its clients is likely to be an important factor in its ongoing success, so this aspect of customer service is important to measure.

Reasons for scores – However, the inherent nature of the services provided could also contribute to the customer service scores, and so, in this respect, the marketing manager's statement could be misleading.

APX's clients have to have an audit, and they may almost resent this if they perceive the audit brings them little value. So the fact that the audit gets the lowest customer service score may reflect this rather than the quality of APX's audit staff.

External environment – However, perhaps more importantly, the marketing manager seems to be attributing the Business Advisory Division's favourable performance to its customer service score alone, without considering the environmental factors which have also affected its performance. The current recession in Emland has led to an increase in demand for business advisory services across the industry as a whole. It seems likely that APX's performance reflects this more than its customer service scores.

Equally, the marketing manager's implication that the customer service score is a more important performance metric than financial measures is also misguided. Whilst it is important that APX considers non-financial aspects of performance, it should not do so at the expense of financial performance measures. Instead, APX's performance evaluation needs to consider both financial and non-financial performance measures.

33 Vunderg

Workbook reference

Activity based management (ABM) is covered in Chapter 12 of the Workbook.

Top tips

This was based on a windows manufacturer considering the implementation of ABM.

Part (a). This required advice on how ABM could improve strategic performance.

To score well this required a brief definition of ABM and then an extraction of relevant practical information from the scenario to support the introduction of ABM (high overheads, complexity of products and customers etc).

Part (b). This required an assessment of the limitations of ABM (eg of the impact of closure of a product line) and potential implementation issues (eg staff opposition).

To score well, this required an extraction of relevant practical information from the scenario to argue against the introduction of ABM (main product is standardised, ignores life cycle).

Examining team's comments

This was the most poorly answered question in this exam, with many candidates generally aware of activity-based costing, but much vaguer on ABM.

Part (a) of the question asked how ABM could help improve the strategic performance of the company. Some candidates took the productive path of discussing the general benefits of the method and then illustrating each of these for the relevant products. Many candidates though took the approach of treating each product type individually, which lead to answers that repeated the same general point several times (wasting time) and not discussing the impact of their advice on the business overall.

Part (b) of the question required candidates to assess the limitations of using ABM in context and the problems with its implementation. Candidates provided fair answers on the general problems of identifying cost drivers and issues in resourcing the implementation of ABM. However, their lack of knowledge of ABM lead to generally weak answers, lacking in detail relevant to the company.

There were a number of candidates who provided the benefits of ABM again in this part, so not answering the question.

Marking guide	**Marks**	
1 mark per relevant point		
Defining ABM	2	
Choosing which products to manufacture	3	
Review of costs, prices and designs	3	
Customer profitability analysis	3	
1 mark per relevant point		
Limitations of the ABM method	7	
Implementation	5	
		20

Professional skills

Analysis and Evaluation

- Use of information provided to perform a suitable/comprehensive evaluation of...
- Appropriate use of the data to support discussion and draw appropriate conclusions
- Demonstration of reasoned and balanced judgement
- Demonstration of ability to consider relevant factors applicable to Vunderg Co's situation

Marking guide	Marks
Scepticism	
• Effective challenge and critical assessment of ABM	
• Demonstration of effective challenge the opinions of the CEO	
Commercial acumen	
• Effective use of examples and/or calculations from the scenario information and other practical considerations related to the context to illustrate points being made ...	
• Demonstrating an awareness of organisational and external factors	
• Recognising key issues in a given scenario in terms of how to address problems, and possible obstacles that will need to be overcome in the process of doing this	
Maximum	5
Total	25

Activity based management

Activity based management (ABM) applies activity based costing (ABC) principles in order to satisfy customer needs using the least amount of resources. Activity based costing groups overheads into cost pools for an activity and identifies the cost driver for each activity. This gives a more accurate calculation of product costs.

ABM makes it possible to better control costs by controlling the activities which drive the costs. ABM would also help Vunderg to identify value added activities and non-value added activities. Activities which do not add value should be reduced, which would allow cost reduction without affecting the quality of service or product for Vunderg's customers.

Choosing which products to manufacture

ABM can help to improve Vunderg's performance in terms of deciding which products to manufacture. This is particularly important where a large proportion of a company's costs are overheads. This is the case in Vunderg, where overheads relating primarily to procurement, customer administration and product design are high. By understanding the cost of a product, and therefore its profitability, Vunderg can decide whether to discontinue an unprofitable product or whether to produce a new one. This will be relevant for the proposed large windows for commercial buildings. These are bespoke items and the cost will include a large amount of overheads, such as design.

Loss making products identified using ABM are often those which are highly customised and produced in low volumes, such as the conservatories. By using ABC principles, Vunderg could identify the high overhead costs of the sourcing of special materials and finishes for these by the procurement department. Using ABM, Vunderg could take action to reduce these costs, for example, by standardising the range of materials and finishes used so that the procurement department spends less time sourcing them. The conservatories earn 8% of Vunderg's total contribution in 20% of the factory space. This implies that conservatories account for a disproportionate level of factory overheads.

Review of costs, prices and designs

By understanding what drives the costs of a product, Vunderg can take actions to make an unprofitable product profitable – for example, in response to the initial quality problems when the glasshouses were first manufactured, but which now command premium prices. The use of ABM may have led to a faster resolution of these initial quality problems by identifying the causes, or drivers, of the product cost and taking action to manage these.

ABM will also help identify products which may need to be re-priced. For example, customers may be prepared to pay more for the use of special materials and finishes in the conservatories. Vunderg could charge customers more for the use of special materials and finishes to cover the high overhead cost associated with procuring them.

ABM may identify possible improvements to the design of a product by focusing on activities which add value for the customer and eliminating those which do not. Selling leaking conservatories does not add value to the customer and incurs rectification costs. The improvement in design to prevent the leaks occurring in the first place is an example of how ABM can be used to make the conservatories business more profitable.

Customer profitability analysis

Customer profitability analysis (CPA) involves apportioning overhead costs to different types of customers, or categories of customers, using ABM principles. This enables a better understanding of the profitability of selling to different customers and can help Vunderg to decide whether to stop selling to certain customers or take other actions to improve their profitability.

At Vunderg, CPA would be most useful for the glasshouses which are sold through 40 different retailers. Some of the costs of selling to these customers, such as trade discounts, should be relatively easy to identify. Other overhead costs, such as those driven by the number of customer orders processed, may only be identified using ABM principles and may differ considerably between customers as the size of orders they place varies greatly.

The profitability of selling to the 40 retailers will therefore also vary considerably. Vunderg could act to improve the profitability of the least profitable ones. This could include insisting on minimum order sizes to reduce the costs driven by the number of orders processed. They could also offer more product training or contribution towards advertising costs to increase sales volumes.

Limitations of using the ABM method identifying key activities and drivers

It may be difficult to separately identify all of the key activities and what drives them, which makes the application of ABC principles difficult. It may also be hard to assign responsibilities for individual cost pools which may cut across departmental boundaries.

Limited use

ABM is most useful where products are customised and contain high overhead costs such as design, procurement and customer administration. While the use of ABM may be worthwhile for the conservatories business, which is highly customised, and for the bespoke windows for commercial buildings, 84% (9,800/11,679) of Vunderg's contribution is from windows used in residential housing. These are highly standardised and are likely to include few overhead costs; for example, relating to design and after sales service. The manufacturing process after many years will already be efficient. The costs may already be well understood and controlled, in which case the implementation of ABM may not be worthwhile. Vunderg does, however, need a good understanding of the overhead costs, as the residential windows market is competitive.

As windows are highly standardised, Vunderg may be unable to pick and choose which items to produce. Design, specification and size will be dictated by the large construction companies who buy them and who will expect Vunderg to supply a complete range of windows. These companies would just buy from a competitor if Vunderg stopped producing the items they needed. As this market is very competitive, there may be little Vunderg could do to improve profitability, for example, by increasing prices, so the use of ABM to choose which products to sell could therefore be of little use. Similarly, as there are only a few large construction companies, the use of ABM may also not be worthwhile as Vunderg could not realistically stop trading with any one of them, nor could it raise prices because of the competitive market.

Incorrect decisions

Despite the difficulties in using ABC, for example, in identifying cost drivers, the use of cost drivers to charge overhead costs to conservatories should give a clearer indication of their profitability than under the current system. Vunderg can then take action to increase the profitability of these products, for example, by increasing the prices or reducing the costs.

The decision on whether these products should be discontinued should, however, take into account the effect on glasshouse sales as customers like to buy glasshouses which match the materials used in the conservatories. Discontinuing conservatories could reduce contribution from glasshouses by up to 17.1% (650/3,800), a total loss of contribution of approximately $166,000 (17.1% of $969,000), which is significant. As conservatories are at the start of their life cycle, expecting them to be profitable immediately could be unrealistic.

Just because a large proportion of factory space is dedicated to manufacturing conservatories, this does not mean that these costs will be saved in the short term if the products are discontinued. The depreciation or lease costs of the factory are fixed. Vunderg's main business is saturated and there is no prospect that the factory space could be better used in making other products. The factory may already not be fully utilised.

Problems of implementing ABM resource and cost impact

As Vunderg does not have an ABM system, considerable resources and management time will be needed to set this up. There may be resistance from staff, for example, because they do not want to change from the current costing system, which has been in use for a long time. Staff may not understand the benefits of ABM, or how it works. They would need training, which is expensive, and it may take a considerable time before ABM is working effectively.

As Vunderg has only basic information systems, it may need to invest in these in order to collect large volumes of data on costs. Vunderg will have to consider whether the benefits of implementing ABM are greater than the costs of doing so.

34 Bazeele

Workbook reference

Value-based management is discussed in Chapter 12 of the Workbook. Economic Value Added (EVA™) is discussed in Chapter 8.

Top tips

Part (a). A useful way to approach this requirement would be to begin by thinking what the key features of a VBM approach are. Having done this, you can then begin to assess how these differ from Bazeele's current approach, and therefore whether moving to a value-based management approach is appropriate to Bazeele.

Note that, in the scenario, the CEO has said 'The shareholders are unsure what VBM is' so it could be useful to begin your answer with a brief explanation of what VBM is.

However, the requirement doesn't actually ask you to describe the VBM approach, or how it might be implemented, but specifically whether the VBM approach is appropriate for Bazeele. So the main focus of your answer needs to be whether VBM would be appropriate in the context described in the scenario.

For example, the second paragraph of the scenario identifies Bazeele's current objective to maintain its level of ROCE, with business units having an objective to maintain net profit margins. In the fourth paragraph we're then told business unit managers have postponed staff training because it was expensive. But is this decision taken with a view to maintaining short-term profit, or generating value for shareholders in the longer-term? (And, if there are problems in Bazeele's current approach, could these be solved by moving to a value-based approach?)

Also, we're told that Bazeele currently has no information about customer satisfaction levels. But, if maintaining customer satisfaction is important in maintaining the company's success (and therefore its future value), is this something it will need to start measuring under a VBM approach?

More generally, might any changes to Bazeele's culture be required in order to adopt VBM successfully? In the scenario the CEO has said 'Personally, I dislike change, but would not object to the adoption of VBM if it was thought to be beneficial.' The fact that the CEO has made this comment, could be a clue that change **will** be required.

Part (b). Although the requirement asks you to advise whether Bazeele has generated economic value, this part of the question essentially requires you to calculate economic value added, using the information provided in Appendix 1. If EVA™ is positive this will mean Bazeele has generated value for its shareholders; if EVA™ is negative, this will suggest Bazeele has destroyed value.

Although you don't need to include this, it might be useful to write out the EVA™ formula at the beginning of your plan, to provide you with an overall structure for the calculation.

All of the points in Appendix provide you with figures, or adjustments, which are relevant to the EVA calculation, so you need to work methodically through them and assess how they fit into the calculations. For example, what adjustments need to be made to the stated net profit of $10m (Point 1) in order to determine the 'NOPAT' figure required. Similarly, what adjustments need to be made to the capital employed figure (Point 2) in order to calculate the figure for economic value of assets?

Examining team's comments

The discussion parts to this question were poorly answered and reflected a lack of understanding of the VBM approach. Many candidates provided lots of irrelevant information in an attempt to disguise their lack of knowledge.

Candidates' answers to part (b) were often good. However, a significant number of candidates made simple errors where they had correctly identified an adjustment to make to profit, or capital employed, but then added it when it should have been subtracted, or vice versa. This suggests candidates may have simply learned the adjustments, but then failed to do sufficient practice questions before the exam, so that they didn't know how to apply what they had learned.

Marking guide	Marks
(a) 1 mark per relevant point	
General explanation/evaluation of VBM – up to 2 marks	
Application to Bazeele – up to 4 marks	
Changes required on adoption of VBM – up to 4 marks	
Recommendation of whether VBM approach is appropriate for Bazeele – 1 mark	
Maximum for part (a)	
	10
(b) NOPAT adjustments:	
Depreciation – 1 mark	
Economic depreciation – 1 mark	
Interest – 1 mark	
Tax on interest – 1 mark	
Reduction in bad debt provision – 1 mark	
Advertising – 1 mark	
Capital adjustments:	
Difference in accumulated depreciation – 1 mark	
Add back: increase in bad debt provision	
Calculation of EVA™ – 1 mark	
Conclusion: whether value is created or destroyed – 1 mark	
Up to a maximum for part (c) of 10 marks	
	10

Professional skills

Analysis and Evaluation

- Use of information provided to perform a suitable/comprehensive evaluation of VBM
- Demonstration of reasoned and balanced judgement
- Demonstration of ability to consider relevant factors applicable to Bazeele Co's situation

Marking guide	Marks

Scepticism

- Demonstration of effective challenge of information supplied / identification of missing information

Commercial acumen

- Effective use of examples and/or calculations from the scenario information and other practical considerations related to the context to illustrate points being made
- Demonstrating an awareness of organisational and external factors
- Recognising key issues in a given scenario in terms of how to address problems, and possible obstacles that will need to be overcome in the process of doing this
- Recommendations are practical and plausible, and commercially viable in the context of Bazeele Co's situation

Maximum	5
Total	25

(a) In the context of VBM, value of a business is measured by discounting cash flows at the business's cost of capital. When investment returns exceed the cost of capital, value will be created for shareholders. When returns are lower than the cost of capital, value will be destroyed.

The VBM approach is to ensure that all activities and decisions in a business are undertaken so as to create value for shareholders. Currently, Bazeele's overall objective is to maintain ROCE at historic levels, but this does not necessarily create value for shareholders.

This is particularly so now that Bazeele has diversified into hiring large items of plant for use in major infrastructure projects. These projects last up to 10 years, so the time value of money is likely to be significant, as is the initial capital expenditure for the plant. Long-term hire agreements may give an acceptable ROCE, but may have a negative net present value, and hence destroy value for shareholders. The prediction of large increases in bank interest rates will increase Bazeele's cost of capital, and further reduce the net present value of long-term agreements.

Similarly, business unit and branch managers are given the objective of maintaining net profit margins. Thus, managers may currently avoid activities which reduce profits in the short term, but which have future long-term benefits and create value for shareholders, such as investment in staff training.

Changes required

To adopt a VBM approach, Bazeele would need to use a different set of performance indicators, as ROCE and net profit margin do not necessarily create value for shareholders.

Economic value added (EVA™) is a performance measure for shareholder value. Though more complex to calculate and more difficult to understand than the existing measures, EVA™ does encourage managers to make decisions, such as undertaking staff training, which have future long-term benefits. By encouraging managers to make investments which give a positive EVA™, value will be created for shareholders.

With VBM, managers would be given targets according to their areas of responsibility. For example, the board may have objectives to maximise value by making acquisitions which create value. Branch managers' objectives may be focused on non-financial value drivers such as customer satisfaction.

To identify value drivers, Bazeele will need good information which is accurate, reliable and timely, for example. It is unclear whether the current management information system is able to provide good information, but the CEO has said that information on customer satisfaction is not available. Certainly the costs of new information systems will need to be assessed.

Resources, such as financial investment, time and training, may be needed to improve Bazeele's management information. Managers may resist the change in culture which would be required to adopt VBM; not least the CEO would need to set the 'tone at top' for what would be a disruptive and major change to Bazeele. However, the benefits of adopting VBM seem to outweigh the costs of doing so.

With VBM, decisions are taken to create value for shareholders by considering value drivers, which are any factors which affect the value of the business. Value drivers may be non-financial, such as the customer satisfaction which may have been improved by the postponed staff training. VBM is therefore likely to encourage decision making that will encourage the creation of value for shareholders and as such a VBM approach is suitable for Bazeele.

(b) **Economic value**

As the economic value added (EVA™) is negative – ie ($13.1m) – Bazeele has destroyed value for shareholders.

Calculation of net operating profit after tax (NOPAT)

	$m	$m
Net profit after tax		10.0
Add: depreciation on non-current assets	6.0	
Deduct: economic depreciation	(14.0)	
		(8.0)
Add: interest (accounted for in the WACC)	15.0	
Less: tax on interest ($15.0m × 20%)	(3.0)	
		12.0
Deduct: reduction in bad debt provision		(4.8)
Add: advertising for long-term benefit		0.6
NOPAT		9.8

Calculation of economic value of assets

	$m
Capital employed at the start of the year	250.0
Deduct: difference in accumulated depreciation	(16.0)
Add back: increase in bad debt provision	4.8
Economic value of assets	238.8

Calculation of EVA™

	$m
NOPAT	9.8
Deduct: capital charge ($238.8 × 9.6%)	(22.9)
EVA™	(13.1)

35 Dibble

Workbook reference

ABC and ABM are discussed in Chapter 12 of the Workbook.

Top tips

The opening paragraph of the scenario tells us that 'Dibble has always absorbed production overheads to the cost of each product on the basis of machine hours'. In other words, Dibble currently uses a simple absorption method of cost allocation. In effect, the context for part (a) of this question is based around the differences between ABC and overhead allocation based on a simple absorption method.

Part (a). To score well here, it is vital that you appreciate the main characteristics of the Timber and Steel Divisions – and the differences between them. The Timber Division produces a limited range of standardised products. By contrast, the Steel Division produces a wide range of bespoke products. (And, as the fourth paragraph of the scenario tells us, the board of the Steel Division feels the pricing structure may be too simplistic, and it is not sure of the profitability of some groups of products.)

The key point to note here is that it seems likely that the Steel Division will benefit from a more detailed (and accurate) method of allocating overhead costs, and therefore ABC would seem to be appropriate for that division. However, the existing basis seems perfectly adequate for the Timber Division.

Note that, in the scenario, the CEO tells you they don't want detailed calculations. So you shouldn't waste time trying to use the figures from the management accounts to assess the impact of introducing ABC.

Note also – as a general point in APM exams – just because a model (or approach) is new, this doesn't necessarily make it better than the existing one. It needs to be appropriate to the context. ABC is more time consuming than absorption costing so, in this case, would the benefits it might generate for the Timber Division justify this extra effort?

Part (b) asks how ABM could be used to improve business performance in the company as a whole.

A useful approach to this requirement could be to think about the key principles of ABM – for example, satisfying customer needs while using the fewest resources possible; eliminating activities which do not add value for customers in order to focus on value-adding activities; improving the design of products – and then assess how Dibble's performance might be improved if it applied these principles.

For example, the scenario tells us that protective coatings are added to Steel products, by subcontractors, at the end of the production process. These are then returned to the Steel Division for dispatch to the customer. But does returning the products to Dibble add any value? Or could they be sent directly from the subcontractors to the customer?

Think also about how part (b) of the question fits with part (a). One aspect of ABM is the way organisations can use ABC information to help manage costs, and to focus on those activities which add value. The scenario has identified that the Steel Division has concerns around the pricing and profitability of its products; but introducing ABC could help to address these concerns. In turn, if Dibble has a better understanding of pricing and product profitability, could this help to improve its (financial) performance?

Examining team's comments

Part (a) required candidates to assess the appropriateness of ABC compared to the current costing systems in the Timber and Steel Divisions. This part was answered reasonably well, although the weaknesses in candidates' basic understanding of ABC often led to vague answers. In particular, it was surprising to find that candidates often seem unaware that ABC is specifically an overhead allocation system.

Part (b) asked candidates to advise on the benefits ABM would bring to Dibble. This part of the question was not well answered. Many candidates provided lists of benefits that were not specifically related to an activity-based approach, and again reflected candidates' lack of understanding of the general principles of such an approach – in particular, analysing activities' cost drivers, and cost pooling.

Marking guide	Marks
(a) Appropriateness of ABC– 1 mark per relevant point – up to a maximum of 5	
Problems with ABC – 1 mark per relevant point – up to a maximum of 5	
	8
(b) Improving performance using ABM – 1 mark per relevant point	
Differences must be clearly linked to the scenario to score the marks available.	
Total for part (b): up to 12	
	12

Professional skills

Analysis and Evaluation

- Use of information provided to perform a suitable/comprehensive evaluation of ABC
- Appropriate use of the data to support discussion and draw appropriate conclusions
- Demonstration of reasoned and balanced judgement
- Demonstration of ability to consider relevant factors applicable to Dibble Co's situation

Commercial acumen

- Effective use of examples and/or calculations from the scenario information and other practical considerations related to the context to illustrate points being made
- Demonstrating an awareness of organisational and external factors
- Recommendations are practical and plausible, and commercially viable in the context of Dibble Co's situation

Maximum	5
Total	25

(a) **Appropriateness of ABC**

ABC is especially useful where there is a wide range of complex products and where production overheads form a larger proportion of total production costs. In Steel Division, there is a large range of products, many of them bespoke or one-off designs. Production overheads form 28% (4,472/(20,605 – 4,533)) of total production costs, and the use of ABC will be appropriate in this division.

ABC enables a more accurate cost of production to be calculated, which is very useful in setting product prices. This could be especially useful in Steel Division which has a wide range of products subject to a number of manufacturing processes. It will help to ensure that each product is priced high enough in order to produce an acceptable margin, but not so high as to become uncompetitive. This is especially important as Steel Division's strategy is to produce bespoke products at prices comparable to competitors which produce simpler, more conventional products.

ABC enables managers to determine what activities drive the costs, and so focus on reducing those activities to control costs. Not all production overheads, for example, inspection costs of the coatings in Steel Division, are related to production volumes. It is equally possible to apply ABC techniques to overheads other than production overheads.

Problems with ABC

ABC is less useful in businesses such as Timber Division where there is a small range of relatively simple products and where production overheads only comprise around 1% of total production costs. Of the production overheads in Timber Division, storage is by far the biggest and is likely to be driven by production volumes.

It may be difficult to determine what the drivers of production costs are. Storage costs could also be related to the insolvency of a customer. It may be impossible to allocate all overheads to the specific activities which drive them and so management will have to apply judgement.

Calculation of ABC may be time consuming, complex and poorly understood by managers. As such, the time and expense of doing so may not be justified. This appears to be the case in Timber Division where there are only a few, relatively simple products and few production overheads. Whereas in Steel Division, where there is a wide range of more complex products and a high proportion of production overheads, ABC is more appropriate than the traditional absorption costing method currently used at Dibble.

(b) **ABM**

ABM is the use of ABC methods in order to improve organisational performance by meeting the needs of customers using the lowest possible amount of resources or costs. ABM can be applied at the operational level or to help develop strategy.

Product pricing

By accurately determining the cost of each product using ABC, Dibble would be able to ensure that prices are set so as to achieve an acceptable margin and also remain competitive with the prices currently charged in the rest of the market.

Steel Division charges customers a standard mark-up of 10% on top of the $650,000 subcontractor costs for the coating and painting of the steel. This means that customers are only being charged $65,000 whereas the costs of storage of goods awaiting subcontract work and of transporting the goods to the subcontractor total $695,000.

By identifying the cost pools relating to the subcontract work, Steel Division can determine that it is making a loss on the subcontract work as a whole. It could therefore adjust the price of painted and coated products to ensure that an acceptable contribution margin is achieved. This is an example of operational ABM. At the strategic level, this type of information could help Dibble decide which product types to develop or discontinue.

The same principle may also apply where ABC can be used to identify which types of customers are the most profitable. In that way, resources can be focused on retaining and managing these customer groups. Action can be taken by additional advertising or product development in order to focus on these particular markets. By analysing customer profitability, it may be possible to reduce costs or increase revenue to make certain customer groups or product lines more profitable, in both the short and long term.

By identifying lines of business with poor profitability, Dibble could discontinue selling to particular customers, or selling particular products, if appropriate action could not be taken to improve profitability.

Analysis of activities

By analysing the activities which drive the costs, Steel Division could determine which activities may not be required or could be done in a more efficient way. It may be possible to introduce improvements in the short term, for example, changes in the production process which may improve efficiency. In the longer term, strategic changes could be made to the way in which activities are undertaken, such as by outsourcing other activities in addition to the painting and coating which is currently outsourced.

Identifying the costs of transporting painted finished goods back from the subcontractors to Steel Division could lead them to evaluate ways to reduce this cost, for example, by despatching goods to customers directly from the subcontractors' premises. This is a non value added activity, ie one which consumes resources, such as time and cost to transport goods to and from the subcontractors, but which is of no additional value to the customer. In contrast, ABM may help identify value-adding activities, such as the coating and painting, which customers are prepared to pay for.

Of the five categories of production overheads, only machining time is a value-adding activity, sometimes categorised as a primary activity. Setting up the CAM machinery is a secondary activity, which does not itself add value, but is required in order to perform a value-adding activity (machining).

The other overheads, storage, transfer and inspection, are all non value adding activities which should be eliminated or reduced. By identifying the activities which drive these costs managers can attempt to do this.

However, given the nature of Dibble's products, it is likely that some inspection will still be required for safety or commercial reasons, as shown by the litigation case relating to the faulty product. The production manager's proposal to increase the costs of inspection is inappropriate as, having identified inspection as a non value adding activity, it would be better to focus attention on getting the product right first time.

Design improvements

Steel Division has a wide range of relatively complex or even bespoke products. ABM can help managers take decisions at the product design stage, where many of the product's costs are already committed. These can include using fewer or more standardised components, such as a more limited range of paints and coatings.

Where strategic decisions are being taken, for example, about new product lines or lines of business, such as with Steel Division's strategy to develop novel innovative products, ABM can help assess whether such developments are likely to be profitable at an early stage. This would help avoid development costs for products which could turn out to be unprofitable. This could also help allocate resources, such as capital investment, to the most profitable lines of business.

Performance measurement

For ABM to be successful, it will require the commitment of senior management and effective communication and training of employees at all levels in the organisation as to the benefits and methods of ABM. This will incur management time and cost, and divert attention from existing management activities.

New performance measurement systems will need to be developed. Employee rewards will need to be aligned to key performance measures, such as the reduction of non value adding processes like inspection. This will ensure that employees work towards the objectives of the organisation. Additional information gathering systems, or adaptations to existing information systems, will also be required, which will again incur additional cost and may disrupt existing activities.

36 Zones

Workbook reference

The Performance Pyramid (Lynch & Cross) is discussed in Chapter 12 of the Workbook. Six Sigma methodology is discussed in Chapter 10.

Top tips

Part (a)

The performance pyramid model is provided for you in Appendix 1, which should also help you identify relevant points in the scenario that you can use to illustrate how the model will be useful to Zones. Equally, however, the fact that the model is provided for you in Appendix 1 means that you should not spend time describing the model in generic terms; but rather focus specifically on how its features could benefit Zones.

Part (b)

The requirement refers specifically to 'operational performance' so it is important that you remember that the factors in the bottom row of the pyramid (quality; delivery; cycle time; waste) relate to 'operational' performance.

So, in effect, this requirement is asking you to evaluate how useful the three new measures identified in Appendix 2 (vehicle utilisation; fuel consumption; on-time stops) could be for measuring and managing these aspects of performance.

A useful way to structure your answer (and the approach taken in the solution below) would be to take each of the three new measures in turn and then assess how well it will enable Zones to measure and manage the aspects of performance. Note the verb here is 'evaluate' so you should try to include a balanced assessment, including aspects of the measure which make it suitable, as well as ones which make it unsuitable.

Instead of structuring your answer around the three measures, you could have structured your answer around the four operational factors identified in the pyramid. Again, though, to score well you need to 'evaluate' how well the measures will allow each aspect of performance to be managed.

Part (c)

Although your answer here needs to focus on the suitability of the two measures in Appendix 3, it would be useful to think about the characteristics of the Six Sigma methodology (and DMAIC) before assessing the suitability of the measures.

In particular, two of the key principles when deciding which aspects to measure (the 'M' in 'DMAIC') are: focus on what the customer thinks is important; and only measure things that can be improved.

In Appendix 2, we are told that customers make complaints if deliveries are not made on time, but a tiny fraction of these relate to deliveries which are not made within 30 minutes of the delivery time. If customers are happy for deliveries to be made within 30 minutes of the booked time, are on-time stops (within 10 minutes of the booked time) something which is important for customers?

Equally, is deliveries fail because the customer is unavailable, how does this affect Zones' ability to improve performance against this measure?

Marking guide — **Marks**

(a) 1 mark per point

Advising on relevant features of the performance pyramid that help Zones to achieve its corporate vision – up to 4 marks

Total for part (a): up to 4 — 4

(b) 1 mark per point

Evaluate the extent to which each measure can be used to measure and manage operational performance – up to 3 marks per measure

Total for part (b): up to 8 — 8

(c) 1 mark per point

Evaluating the suitability of the two measures – up to 4 marks each

Total for part (c): up to 8 — 8

Professional skills

Analysis and Evaluation

- Use of information provided to perform a suitable/comprehensive evaluation of performance measures
- Appropriate use of the data to support discussion and draw appropriate conclusions
- Demonstration of reasoned and balanced judgement
- Demonstration of ability to consider relevant factors applicable to Zones Co's situation

Marking guide	Marks
Commercial acumen	
• Effective use of examples and/or calculations from the scenario information and other practical considerations related to the context to illustrate points being made	
• Demonstrating an awareness of organisational and external factors	
Maximum	5
Total	25

(a) The performance pyramid makes extensive use of non-financial performance measures, such as on-time stops. Non-financial measures are leading indicators which can help to achieve long-term future financial performance. This would be useful to Zones, which has had excessive focus on financial objectives and inadequate systems to measure and manage performance of the underlying processes driving financial performance.

The elements of the pyramid are interrelated, and each level in the pyramid supports the one above it. For example, on-time stops will increase customer satisfaction, which will eventually lead to greater market share, one element of the corporate vision.

The pyramid ensures that all aspects, both internal and external, of performance are measured. The right-hand side of the pyramid covers internal efficiency, such as flexibility and productivity, while the left hand side covers external effectiveness, such as customer satisfaction. Using on-time stops again as an example, which relates to the quality (external effectiveness) element of the pyramid, will lead to improved performance up the left-hand side of the pyramid.

(b) Operational performance is represented by the four elements at the bottom level of the performance pyramid, which are quality, delivery, cycle time and waste. It is unclear what quality means in the context of the corporate vision, though the measure of on-time stops could be interpreted as a measure of quality, which is valued by customers. There is no direct measure of cycle time, for example, the time taken between collecting a parcel and delivering it. Also, there is no direct measure for delivery, which in this context would be the amount of time needed to arrange a collection or delivery.

Vehicle utilisation

This is a good way to measure waste. The greater the utilisation of vehicle capacity, the lower the waste, for example, of vehicle running costs. In the long run, higher vehicle utilisation would mean the number of vehicles operated could be reduced for the same level of activity. This would lead to increased productivity and financial performance, so helping to achieve the corporate vision.

Vehicle utilisation will vary, according to location, time of year and type of vehicle used, and is also measured inconsistently, according to the type of vehicle. Vehicle utilisation may be too broad a measure, making it difficult to manage performance. Areas of poor performance may mask other areas of good performance. Similarly, measuring utilisation as an average between that at the beginning and end of each day may not actually represent the average utilisation during the day.

Fuel consumption

Reducing fuel consumption would lead to a significant increase in financial performance at Zones. Measuring average fuel consumption per kilometre travelled does not, however, relate directly to activity, for example, to the number of parcels delivered.

Average fuel consumption will vary between type of vehicle and between rural and urban areas. A large vehicle may have high fuel consumption per kilometre travelled, but will also carry a large number of parcels. Average fuel consumption per kilometre is not a good measure of waste, or any other aspect of operational performance. To be useful in managing operational performance, this measure should be changed to average fuel consumed per parcel delivered. In this case, this would be a suitable measure for waste.

On-time stops

Customers are likely to value on-time stops very highly, and along with value for money, this will be one of the main reasons they will choose to use Zones. This is reflected in the corporate vision. The proportion of on-time stops is a measure of operational performance which relates to the quality element of the performance pyramid and is a key driver of customer satisfaction.

> **Tutorial note.** Answers structured on the basis of the four operational elements of the pyramid would also be acceptable.

(c) The DMAIC acronym stands for define, measure, analyse, improve and control. These are the five phases by which the Six Sigma methodology is implemented. To be suitable for use in the DMAIC method, measures defined must have certain characteristics.

Percentage of stops made within 10 minutes of the booked time

According to the Six Sigma method, only those measures which are valued by the customer should be measured. On-time stops will be valued by customers, and contribute to customer satisfaction.

Currently, however, of all complaints which Zones receives from customers relating to stops not made on time, less than around one per million of these relate to those made within 30 minutes of the booked time. This level of complaints is so low that this would already achieve the very low level of failures targeted by implementation of the Six Sigma methodology. (The goal of Six Sigma is to reduce failures to a rate of less than 3.4 in a million.)

It seems that customers will not value stops made within 10 minutes of the booked time, any more than they would value those within 30 minutes. Another principle of Six Sigma methodology is not to measure what customers are already satisfied with. They are already satisfied with stops made within 30 minutes of the booked time.

The percentage of stops made within 10 minutes of the booked time is not a suitable measure. The time and costs of making the measurements will exceed the benefits of doing so.

Failed deliveries

Failed deliveries will represent a considerable cost to Zones in terms of wasted fuel and driver time. It may also reduce flexibility by using up vehicle capacity which could be used to carry more parcels. Even though deliveries may fail due to traffic congestion, they will still reduce customer satisfaction.

The percentage of failed deliveries is currently 5%, well above the target rate for failures under the Six Sigma methodology (ie less than 3.4 in a million accuracy), and in this respect would be a suitable measure.

According to the Six Sigma method, only those measures which can be improved should be measured. Failed deliveries arising from customers being unavailable to take the delivery is completely out of Zones' control. Deliveries failing due to incorrectly addressed parcels could be reduced to some extent, for example, by the use of information technology to check the correct address, but most failures due to this are outside Zones' control. As failed deliveries cannot be significantly improved, this is not a suitable measure.

37 Roan

> **Workbook reference**
>
> The difficulties of managing performance in complex structures is covered in Chapter 13 of the Workbook.
>
> **Top tips**
>
> **Part (a).** This required use of the scenario to look critically at the potential problems. A key challenge here would be to make value-adding comments, rather than simply repeating the

information provided ie explaining the problem, linking points to each other, judging the potential significance of the issue.

Part (b). Many points could have been made, but the important skill being tested is the ability of the candidate to justify a practical performance measure in the context of a new joint venture.

Marking guide	Marks
(a) 1 mark per point	
Discussion of issues in relation to performance management – up to 8 marks	
Discussion of issues in relation to performance measurement – up to 8 marks	
	14
(b) For each stakeholder group:	
Justification of the measure – up to 2 marks	
	6
Professional marks	
Analysis and Evaluation:	
• Comprehensive evaluation of the problems of managing and measuring performance in the joint venture	
Commercial Acumen:	
• Demonstrate an understanding of the incompatibility of the objectives of the two organisations	
• Performance measures recommended for the three stakeholder groups are practical and plausible in the context of the organisation situation	
Maximum	5
Total	25

(a) **Managing performance**

Establishing common objectives

The initial problem with regard to managing performance in any joint venture is establishing its objectives and goals and the aims of each university for the joint venture of RSU are different.

Roan's main purpose for undertaking the joint venture is to find a new revenue stream. The word profit is not that Roan is seeking to make a financial return from this and that its focus will be on maximising that return rather than maximising revenue to the disregard of cost. In terms of performance management, therefore, the focus of Roan is likely to be on ensuring that these main goals are met and therefore areas of finance and resource utilisation and consumption are likely to form the core of the management system.

Saugh's main purpose for undertaking the joint venture is to enhance its status within its own country, and perhaps globally, as a renowned institution of learning. The focus for Saugh in terms of how performance of RSU is managed is likely to be on the reputation of Saugh, staff development and the destinations of its graduates.

Developing a joint venture in terms of its financial return and in terms of the contribution that it makes to society may be possible within a performance management framework but it is clear that these aims are contradictory. At a simple level, focusing on the financial aspects can lead to a lack of investment which may damage the quality of the joint venture's provision and, ultimately, the contribution that the graduates of RSU can make to society.

Lack of stable leadership

It is clear from the scenario that the rotational nature of the chairman of the management board (MB) will almost ensure that there is a lack of stable leadership. Unless the universities can agree on a common and mutually acceptable aim, the chairman is likely to be acting more in the interests of their own university than in the interests of the joint venture.

The inclusion of at least one government official from Deeland on the MB may also present problems from the perspective of Roan with regard to performance management. As the current balance of the MB membership is 50:50, the inclusion of representatives from Deeland would clearly tip the balance in favour of Saugh. This is likely to lead to a loss of control for Roan which would clearly have an effect on the manner in which the joint venture is managed in terms of its performance.

Measuring performance

Given the challenging funding environment in Teeland, reflected in the overall view of Roan with regards to what the aim of the joint venture should be, Roan will be focused on the financial return of RSU. This means that Roan would seek to measure traditional financial measures such as return on investment and operating surplus. Roan's focus is likely to be specifically on the fees charged, student numbers, costs incurred and on return on investment overall. The measures that Roan would like to see would therefore relate to fee growth, student numbers and cost reduction. It is not clear how quickly Roan is seeking to achieve a return on the investment but from the scenario it can be assumed, given the cuts to governmental funding, that it would prefer a return to be achieved in the short term as well as over the long term. Roan may therefore be keen to spend a significant amount on advertising, to boost student numbers in the short term, rather than wait for the reputation of RSU to grow by word of mouth.

Saugh appears to be free from any financial constraints, at least in the short term. Its funding is secure and this means that Saugh is unlikely to be interested in assessing the performance of RSU with any traditional financial metrics. As a result, this may place Saugh in direct conflict with Roan with regard to many decisions. For example, Saugh may feel that enhancing 18 classroom technology in RSU is necessary and should be undertaken immediately without understanding that this would represent a significant further investment for Roan.

Saugh will be more focused on the quality of the students that are admitted to RSU, their performance whilst at university and their occupation and perhaps salary level on leaving the university. There is likely to be conflict with Roan with regard to students that are admitted to RSU as Roan will be more focused on recruiting as many students as possible whereas Saugh will be more focused on the grades that these students have achieved either at school or in previous study.

Both universities will be interested in how the students perform at RSU. Roan's reputation would suffer significantly, for example, if it were to accept students who failed its programmes in large numbers. However, Roan will be less focused on the level of excellence achieved by students of RSU than Saugh. Again, this is likely to lead to conflict as Saugh will be motivated to undertake additional investment, be it in terms of staff time in the form of extra classes or through extra resources that are likely to help students achieve higher grades.

Roan is also likely to be interested in how graduates of RSU perform after graduation, but it is not as important to them as it is to Saugh. Saugh may therefore be keen to devote significant resource to developing strong links with local industry to ensure that RSU graduates are equipped with the correct skills. Saugh will also want to devote significant resource to monitoring and measuring how the graduates perform after graduation. Saugh may, for example, initiate surveys at various points following graduation at intervals of perhaps one, five and ten years. Given the focus of Roan, it is unlikely to want to devote much by way of resources to such measurement.

As a measure of commitment to the joint venture, Saugh will be motivated to measure how many of Roan's staff will teach at RSU. Saugh may try to impose specific measures here, such as percentage of Roan staff from Teeland teaching on each programme, as it is clear that the involvement of Roan is a critical success factor for Saugh in achieving its aims.

(b) **Government of Teeland**

The government of Teeland is only likely to be interested in the performance of RSU if there is a significant failing. The most obvious examples relate to a financial default through overspend or, potentially, a scandal involving staff of Roan in Deeland whilst working at RSU. It would be impossible to either plan for or meaningfully measure this latter scenario and hence the most likely aspect to be of interest to the government of Teeland is the liquidity of Roan.

A simple measure of this, even something as straightforward as the cash surplus of Roan, would confirm to the government of Teeland that Roan is unlikely to go into liquidation. This measure should be considered alongside the long term liquidity of Roan and the government would be interested in knowing if Roan had taken on any long term debt to fund the joint venture and, if so, its overall proportion in Roan's capital structure.

Teachers' trade union

The teachers' trade union would be interested in the number of programmes or courses that are being offered in RSU. The more programmes that are offered, the more likely it is that Roan staff will be required by their employer to teach in Deeland. Fewer courses would increase the possibility that local provision for teaching could be found. However, the more courses that are offered, the less likely it is that the necessary specialism could be found through local provision in a developing country.

Public pressure group

The public pressure group would be interested in how much time is being spent by staff of Roan, perhaps teaching staff in particular rather than those of a higher level of management, in Deeland. The pressure group would like to see this figure probably presented in absolute terms and measured month by month to allow for comparison and trend analysis. The higher this figure becomes the more active the pressure group is likely to become and the more the membership of the pressure group is likely to grow.

38 Forion Electronics

Workbook reference

ERPSs are discussed in Chapter 5 of the Workbook. Sources of data are also discussed in Chapter 5, while non-financial performance indicators are discussed in Chapter 9.

Top tips

Part (a). Even if you didn't know much about an ERPS, you should have been able to identify how deficiencies in the information sharing between departments could lead to the problems identified in the scenario.

Part (b). An important factor to consider here is the relationship between Forion and BAS. BAS is a supplier to Forion, and Forion has chosen BAS because of its reputation for quality and new product development. This suggests Forion considers these aspects of performance to be important (and Forion has previously identified it needs to have high-visibility, durable screens in order to be competitive – so visibility and durability could be considered as aspects of 'quality').

A useful way to answer the question would be to consider how well the performance measures chosen allow Forion to assess BAS's performance in the areas which it has identified as important.

In this respect, don't just think about the aspects of performance selected, but also think about the practicalities of measuring the performance. How easy will it be to measure whether or not BAS achieves the desired levels of performance?

Part (c). Note that the question requires you to make two separate comparisons: financial vs non-financial data; and internal vs external data. Also, it is important that you discuss the issues specifically in the context of the SLA between Forion and BAS. For example, will BAS be happy to use internal performance data prepared by Forion given that it (BAS) could be liable for a financial penalty if it fails to achieve the target performance levels?

Examining team's comments

(For part (c)) – Evaluating the reliability of data has been a common topic in past exams, yet candidates' answers to this question were unexpectedly poor. Many candidates seemed unaware of what constitutes internal and external sources, and – surprisingly – many considered audited, financial data to be amongst the least reliable sources. In addition, many candidates discussed the type of information that both parties to the alliance would need, without discussing its reliability (which is what the requirement actually asked for).

Marking guide **Marks**

(a) For specific discussion of the impact an ERPS could have on the problems at Forion: 1 mark per relevant point – up to 6 marks

Total for part (a): up to 6

6

(b) For relevant points about the usefulness of the three areas for measuring performance – 1 mark per point

Note. In order to score a clear pass, all three issues must be addressed.

Total for part (b): up to 8

8

(c) For relevant points about the relative reliability about the different types of data – 1 mark per point

Note. In order to score a clear pass, both issues (financial/non-financial; and internal/external must be addressed.

Total for part (c): up to 6

6

Professional skills

Analysis and Evaluation

- Use of information provided to perform a suitable/comprehensive evaluation of the agreement
- Demonstration of reasoned and balanced judgement
- Demonstration of ability to consider relevant factors applicable to Forion Co's situation

Scepticism

- Effective challenge and critical assessment of the performance areas

Commercial acumen

- Effective use of examples and/or calculations from the scenario information and other practical considerations related to the context to illustrate points being made
- Demonstrating an awareness of organisational and external factors
- Recommendations are practical and plausible, and commercially viable in the context of Forion Co's situation

Maximum 5

Total 25

(a) **The impact of an ERPS on performance management issues at Forion**

Information sharing – The board has suggested that a number of the performance management problems at Forion arise from poor communication and information sharing between departments; not least because each of the departments has its own information system rather than having an integrated system across the organisation as a whole.

As such, by providing an integrated system which assists the flow of information between departments, an ERPS could help to solve the three problems identified.

Amount of subcomponents ordered – This reflects a problem with the information being shared between the Purchasing Department (which orders the subcomponents) and the Manufacturing Department (which uses them). If the Purchasing Department has incorrect or out of date information, this will lead to it ordering the wrong amount of subcomponents, which in turn means that Forion's inventory handling and storing costs will be higher than they need to be.

However, if Forion had an ERPS, information from the Manufacturing Department would automatically be shared with the Purchasing Department, meaning the Purchasing Department should be able to identify the quantities of subcomponents to order more accurately.

Stock-outs or obsolescence – Both of these problems arise from the amount of goods being manufactured not reflecting the expected level of orders. Although the Marketing Department may produce good sales forecasts, if these forecasts are not shared with the Manufacturing Department, it will not know what quantities of different goods it needs to make. If it produces too few, this will lead to stock-outs (and a loss of potential revenue); while obsolescence results from producing too many units of a good which cannot then be sold. (The risk of obsolescence could be a particular concern for Forion as a manufacturer of electronic goods.)

If the Marketing Department's forecasts were captured in an ERPS, they would be available to the Manufacturing Department when it was setting its production plans.

Lack of delivery vehicles – The delivery schedule needs to incorporate sales information (customers' orders) and manufacturing information (when goods will be available).

If the Warehouse Department only becomes aware of a customer order after it has scheduled all its delivery vehicles this would help to explain why there seem to be insufficient vehicles to meet customer deadlines. Similarly, if there are delays in manufacturing which the Warehouse Department isn't aware of, this could mean that goods can't be included in their scheduled delivery, and will require an additional delivery and an extra vehicle to fulfil the customer order.

By linking the manufacturing schedule, customer orders, and the delivery schedule, Forion should be able to schedule its deliveries as efficiently as possible, to make best use of its delivery fleet.

Equally, though, by having greater visibility over orders and the manufacturing schedule, the Delivery Department should be able to identify in advance any times when it will not have sufficient vehicles of its own to fulfil all the orders required. Knowing this, it can then make arrangements for a third-party logistics company to deliver the order in time to meet the customer's deadline.

(b) **Usefulness of performance areas**

The three performance areas selected (quality of manufacturing; timeliness of delivery; technical upgrades) all seem appropriate. The 'quality' area derives from underlying logic behind the alliance – Forion's need for high-visibility, durable screens; timeliness of delivery will be important for the smooth operation of the production process; and the ability to make technical upgrades is likely to be critical in a rapidly changing market – such as the market for smartphones.

Quality of manufacturing – BAS's strong reputation suggests the number of faults should be low. Nonetheless, as screen manufacturing is a key part of the assembly process, and having high quality screens is likely to be a critical success factor for the phone overall, it will be important to measure performance in this area.

There could also be significant costs involved in remedying any faults with the screens. If the faults are identified during internal inspection, the time taken to fix them will delay delivery. If the faults are identified by customers, Forion will incur the cost of repairing – or replacing –

the faulty phone. Customers' dissatisfaction with faulty items may also mean they are less likely to buy a Forion smartphone again in the future.

Time of delivery – The screen is a key component of the phone so delays to shipments could cause significant disruption to the production process if Forion is trying to use a just-in-time (JIT) production process. Conversely, if Forion holds inventory 'just in case', then concerns about delayed shipments could lead to it holding higher levels of inventory than it might wish to.

If Forion wants to use a JIT production process, then implementing the ERPS and giving BAS access to the system could be very useful. For example, this would give BAS greater visibility around when screens are needed and in what quantity.

Technical upgrades – Whilst upgrades are likely to be important in keeping Forion's phone competitive, it will be difficult to measure BAS's performance against the metric as it is currently defined. For example, there is no timescale in which BAS needs to provide the upgrade, and deciding when the market demands an upgrade could be subjective.

If performance in this area cannot be measured effectively, BAS could pay less attention to it. Although, in theory, building financial penalties into the agreement is appropriate, Forion may not be able to apply them if it cannot measure whether or not BAS has achieved the target levels of performance.

Moreover, as Forion selected BAS as its strategic partner due to its strong reputation for quality of manufacturing and new product development, it is surprising that both of these acknowledged strengths are being measured, rather than any areas of potential weakness.

(c) **Reliability of financial vs non-financial data**

The requirement to produce annual accounts, and to have them audited, means that there should be robust controls in place around the production of financial data. Although non-financial data will be useful to management in controlling the business, it may not be subject to the same scrutiny and controls as financial data.

Similarly, financial data will be quantitative and objective, whereas non-financial data can sometimes be subjective; for example, an issue with a phone screen which some customers may report as a fault, other customers may not report.

Although the subjectivity of non-financial data can sometimes make it difficult to measure, this does not appear to be a problem in this context. The fault rates and the number of shipments overdue should be relatively easy to measure.

Internal vs external sources

Forion is likely to place greater reliance on its own data rather than external data (for example, as provided by BAS in relation to shipments supplied). As such, Forion is likely to use its own warehouse records to determine the number of shipments which are overdue, although this means that Forion will need to have sufficient controls in place to ensure that expected and actual delivery times are recorded accurately.

However, if both parties place greater reliance on their own data than the other party's data, this could be a source of problems for the alliance; for example, if the number of shipments BAS believes to be late differs from the number Forion believes to be late. This could be a particular issue here, given the financial penalties relating to performance.

In this case, it may be useful for both parties to have the right to inspect (audit) each other's data to confirm the reliability of that data.

39 Callisto Retail

Workbook reference

Performance management in complex business structures is discussed in Chapter 13 of the Workbook. Management reports and the problem of information overload are covered in Chapter 5.

Top tips

Part (a). Note that the requirement distinguishes between performance **measurement** and performance **management** issues. Accordingly, you need to consider both in your answer.

Note also that the requirement highlights that Callisto deals with two different types of external partner: individual workers (employees working remotely) and strategic partners (which are multinational companies). The issues Callisto faces in managing the performance of a multinational company are likely to be very different to those involved in managing an individual worker.

Part (b). The key problem with George's report appears to be information overload, so in the first part of your answer you need to consider how this will affect the usefulness of the report.

Examining team's comments

Although part (a) was presented as a single requirement, candidates were correct to split it into areas such as the general impact of such a complex structure on the business as a whole, and then the impact on employee management and strategic partner management. However, the key to scoring well was making points which were relevant for Callisto – related to the difficulties of measuring and managing home-working employees and strategic outsourcing partners.

Marking guide	Marks
(a) Up to 2 marks per relevant point relating to performance measurement Relevant points include (but are not limited to): Geographical distance; reliance on IT; difference between employees and strategic partners; technology solutions; use of service level agreements 1 mark per relevant point relating to performance management Employees – up to 4 marks Strategic partners – up to 6 marks	
	15
(b) Evaluation of proposed report and issues of potential information overload – 1 mark per relevant point – Up to 5	
	5

Professional skills

Analysis and Evaluation

- Use of information provided to perform a suitable/comprehensive evaluation of the issues
- Demonstration of reasoned and balanced judgement
- Demonstration of ability to consider relevant factors applicable to Callisto Co's situation
- Identification of further analysis, which could be carried out to enable an appropriate recommendation to be made

Commercial acumen

- Effective use of examples and/or calculations from the scenario information and other practical considerations related to the context to illustrate points being made
- Demonstrating an awareness of organisational and external factors
- Recognising key issues in a given scenario in terms of how to address problems, and possible obstacles that will need to be overcome in the process of doing this
- Recommendations are practical and plausible, and commercially viable in the context of Callisto Co's situation

Maximum	5
Total	25

(a) **Performance measurement issues**

Data collection – The main difficulties in performance measurement at Callisto are likely to arise from the fact that its employees do not work 'on site', and also a number of key business functions have been outsourced. As a result, before it can begin to measure its performance, Callisto first has to collect the necessary performance data for its remote workers and outsource partners.

IT systems – Callisto needs to rely on information technology for collecting and handling data from its partners and remote workers. As far as possible, this data should be collected and monitored automatically, for example making use of electronic data interchange.

Given the likely number of remote workers and partners that Callisto uses, it is likely that it will need a large database for storing this performance information.

However, in order for the database to be automatically updated (with inputs from remote staff and suppliers), Callisto will need the systems which staff and suppliers use to be compatible with its system.

While Callisto can control the systems its employees use, it seems unlikely that it will be able to exert much, if any, influence over the systems its strategic partners (which are multinational companies) use.

Measuring employees' performance – Callisto's employees log in to its own systems via the internet. In this way, although the employees are not physically in the premises, Callisto is still able to monitor aspects of their performance. For example, monitoring the number of hours employees are logged into the system gives an indication of the number of hours they have worked.

However, it is harder for Callisto to monitor the work the remote employees have actually done; for example, the number of videos they have edited, or the number of customer complaints they have resolved satisfactorily.

In this respect, it is important for Callisto to define its outputs clearly: for example, it should define the various steps which need to be completed for a video edit to be complete. If outputs are not defined in this way, there is scope for disputes between staff and managers about the amount of work they have done; for example, with staff claiming to have completed the editing on more videos than they actually have.

Strategic partners – Whereas Callisto's employees log on to its own systems, the strategic partners, such as RLR, will have their own systems. Therefore they will continue to use their systems rather than using Callisto's systems.

System reconciliations – As a result, there can be **discrepancies** between Callisto's systems and RLR's systems. Therefore, an added complication in the performance measurement process is that, before RLR's performance can be measured against the key SLAs, Callisto will first have to reconcile its inventory records with RLR's.

Lack of control – Without having any agreement over the figures, Callisto will not be able to enforce the SLAs. The disagreements with RLR illustrate this. For example, if an item is despatched late, it will be difficult for Callisto to prove that RLR has broken the SLA, if RLR argues that the item was not actually in stock when an order was placed, so that it couldn't be expected to despatch that item within three working days from when the order was placed.

The difficulty which Callisto faces is establishing whether RLR is responsible for the delay, or whether the product suppliers are responsible.

SLAs as controls – This lack of control over the SLAs is likely to be a significant problem for Callisto, because the SLAs represent its key control over the relationship with its strategic partners.

A potential solution would be for the partners to agree a standard reporting format for all data relating to the SLAs. This would then remove the need for the reconciliations Callisto currently has to carry out.

Performance management issues

Employee management – Because Callisto's employees work from home rather than at company premises, the brothers cannot monitor what the employees are doing in the same way as they could if everyone was working in the same place. For example, Jeff and George cannot monitor what hours their staff are working, or how productive they are being.

Equally, because Jeff and George have no direct contact with their staff, it is difficult for them to judge how motivated the staff are.

Reward schemes – Because the brothers cannot directly monitor or control how productive their employees are being, they need to ensure Callisto's reward scheme is designed such that it encourages productivity and motivation. One way to do this would be to link the reward scheme directly to achieving agreed outputs and targets for each employee.

Managing strategic partners

Reliance on partners – A key issue Callisto faces is that it is reliant on external partners (such as RLR Logistics) for the successful day to day operation of its business. The nature of Callisto's business structure means that some of the functions which have been outsourced are business critical.

For example, if RLR decides not to renew its contract (when it is due for renewal in two months' time) this could create major problems for Callisto. Equally, the reliability of partners such as RLR is vital, because Callisto's customer service reputation will be damaged if products are delivered late.

However, there is a danger that Callisto's reliance on strategic partners in this way strengthens the strategic partners' bargaining power in any negotiations with Callisto (because it is unlikely that Callisto will be able to replace a strategic partner immediately if it stopped working for Callisto).

Relationship management – However, the success of the relationship between Callisto and its strategic partners is likely to depend on establishing an atmosphere of trust between the parties. Currently, it appears the trust between the partners is limited; meaning, for example, that Callisto feels it has to reconcile performance data between RLR's figures and its own. However, such reconciliations do not ultimately add any value for Callisto, so they are a wasteful activity. Therefore, if Callisto was able to trust RLR's figures, this would be beneficial because the detailed reconciliations would no longer be required.

Pricing – Another issue which will have to be managed is how the agreements between Callisto and its strategic partners can be arranged so that they are motivating and profitable for both parties. George has already acknowledged that Callisto operates on small profit margins, so it needs to secure sales growth and high volumes of business in order to be profitable.

However, Callisto is dependent on partners such as RLR to deliver a good quality service to its customers. If the customers don't receive this, then Callisto's reputation is likely to suffer, which in turn will reduce its ability to achieve the sales growth it needs (either by retaining existing customers or acquiring new ones).

So, Callisto needs to negotiate contracts which motivate the strategic partners to deliver the high quality it needs, whilst at the same time not being prohibitively expensive for it. Therefore, Callisto needs to ensure that the contracts are motivating and profitable for both parties.

(b) **Content**

Information overload – Whilst having a daily report will mean that George has up to date and timely information, there is a danger that its frequency will actually lead to **information overload**. In practice, George may not have time to look through a detailed report each day. We do not know how many employees work for Callisto, but its turnover ($120m per annum) suggests there are likely to be quite a large number of employees. Therefore, George's report is likely to contain a large amount of data to look at each day.

There is also a danger that if George spends too much time looking at detailed, daily reports they may overlook more strategic issues in the business, or higher level trends in performance.

Control – It is not clear from the scenario whether the employees will be told that George is monitoring their productivity. However, if the employees know that George is monitoring their productivity on a daily basis, then this could prompt any who are not currently working as hard as they could to work harder. It seems likely that this is what George hopes will happen.

Usefulness of information – However, it is debatable how useful some of the measures George has chosen will be. For example, simply monitoring the number of complaints employees deal with doesn't reflect how long or complicated each complaint was. Equally, although an employee may have been logged on to the network this doesn't necessarily mean they have been working all the time they have been logged on.

The frequency of the reports could also be a problem in itself. If the reports looked at the average number of complaints employees dealt with in a month, this might be a fairer reflection of their activity than looking at a single day at a time.

Equally, it is not clear whether all the employees are expected to carry out all the tasks being monitored. For example, some may specialise in editing videos, while others concentrate on dealing with customer queries and complaints. However, this could mean that the report shows a large number of zeros in the columns for work the employees do not attend to.

50-mark (Section A) Questions

40 Freuchie Retail

Workbook references

Reporting is covered in Chapter 5 of the Workbook, operational gearing in Chapter 6 and 'what gets measured gets done' in Chapter 11.

Top tips

A major general weakness here was a tendency to present disorganised work, often based on single sentence paragraphs. This allows a point to be introduced but to score marks in APM you need to develop your points and brief bullet style points do not allow a candidate to develop their points to a level required to score marks.

The ACCA Examiner's comments also mentioned that 'candidate should also avoid writing responses, in part or in full (in some cases) on the excel spreadsheet'. The spreadsheet is provided for computational work only. All written responses should be provided in the word processing response area.

Part (a). A number of candidates evaluated the company's performance instead of evaluating the performance report; be careful not to make this common mistake.

Better answers will use sub-headings based on the company's mission and strategy.

Part (b). Note that inventory is not aligned to any part of Freuchie's mission and a specific operational area such as this has no place in a strategic performance report.

For the second part of the question (rewriting), at least have a go! Many candidates did not attempt to write their own version of the commentary at all. Up to four points were requested; ideally, these would be presented in order of importance.

Part (c). This part was not done well and emphasises the need to not neglect the technical content of the APM syllabus. Clearly if you do not know how to calculate operational gearing (there are a variety of acceptable approaches) then it is impossible to score any marks here.

Part (d). The main weakness was in applying illustrations from Freuchie's business; this requires more than the name of a company as part of a generic point. A good answer would develop the point clearly. An example of this from the ACCA Examiner's report is: 'gaming involves deliberately distorting performance to achieve goals [...] If Freuchie had performed very well in any given year and had achieved full bonus for all staff, it is possible that Freuchie's staff might consider holding back sales to ensure the next year starts very well for them.'

Marking guide	**Marks**
(a) 1 mark per point – must be based on scenario information	
Aim of performance report – 1 mark	
Breaking down mission – up to 3 marks	
Eg, identify priority of objectives, pick out strategies, comment on their connections	
Assessment of whether report meets mission – up to 10 marks	
Eg, clear statement of inadequacy for mission, addressing each of the elements of the mission, information for relevant decision-making by board	
Other points – up to 4 marks	
Eg, answering where growth is coming from (if not already discussed), lack of information on capital (for return on capital for shareholders) and liquidity (given poor profits), data overload, general presentation	
	16

ANSWERS

Marking guide	Marks
(b) 1 mark per point – must be based on scenario information Comments on existing commentary – up to 5 marks	
Eg, Achieving its mission; whether the three subsidiary strategies are measured, relevance and accuracy of points made	
Proposed new commentary	
1 mark for observing requirement to have a max of four points and placing them in a sensible priority order	
Up to 4 marks – considering each point individually	
	10
(c) Commentary on the general meaning of operational gearing – up to 2 marks	
Calculations:	
Revenue – variable costs	
Variable – excludes other operating costs	
Variable – excludes insurance, utilities and depreciation	
Handling staff costs correctly	
Operational gearing	
Commentary on results – up to 2 marks	
	7
(d) 1 mark per point	
	7

Professional skills marks

Communication:

- Report format and structure – use of headings/sub-headings and introduction
- Style, language and clarity – appropriate tone of report response, presentation of calculations, appropriate use of the CBE tools, easy to follow and understand
- Effectiveness of communication – content of the report is relevant and tailored to the question scenario
- Adherence to the CEO's specific requests eg to not provide more than four narrative points
- Analysis and evaluation
- Appropriate use of the data to support discussion and draw conclusions on operational gearing
- Balanced and reasoned appraisal of the reporting changes that are required given the specific situation in the scenario

Scepticism:

- Demonstration of the ability to question the validity of the current reporting approaches
- Recognition that the data provided does not allow some of the commentary to be completed in full

Commercial acumen:

- Practical and plausible points that recognise the scenario information and other practical considerations

Maximum	10
Total	50

To:	**The board of Freuchie Retail (Freuchie)**
From:	**An Accountant**
Date:	**September 20X5**
Subject:	**Performance reporting and management issues at Freuchie**

This report evaluates both the quantitative and narrative aspects of the current performance report used by the board for strategic review. Next, the meaning and calculation of operational gearing are discussed for Freuchie as are the implications of the results. Finally, the quote 'What gets measured, gets done' is discussed, along with certain other pieces of jargon with illustrations from the situation at Freuchie.

(a) **Current performance reporting: Quantitative**

The current report has a number of strengths and weaknesses. These will be discussed according to whether the report:

- Addresses the objectives of the business;
- Contains appropriate information for decision making; and
- Is well-presented.

The mission of Freuchie can be broken down into a main aim with supporting strategies. The primary aim is to deliver returns to shareholders above the average for the retail sector. This is to be achieved by providing a superior customer experience which, in turn, is done by:

- The appearance of the stores;
- The attractive range of clothes; and
- Selling with enthusiasm.

The report, as it stands, is designed from a traditional set of management accounts and is dominated by internally-generated, financial information. It is clearly not suitable to measure the achievement of the business' objectives.

(1) The primary aim is not fully measured. The return to shareholders is partly measured by dividend payments but there is no measure of share value to allow for total shareholder return to be visible. It is not compared as required to the retail sector average and this reflects a lack of external information in the report.

(2) The achievement of the supporting strategies is done through the customer experience although there is no measure of this in the report. Indirectly, revenue growth would provide an indicator. However, this indicator is currently unsatisfactory as it has not been adjusted for the increased number of stores, which increases sales without any change in the customer's experience of a store.

(3) The superior customer experience should be measured through the three ways in which this is to be achieved:

(i) Appearance of the stores is difficult to judge through financial indicators although, possibly, spending on fixtures and fittings and cleaning may give some indication. (These are not provided in the current report.) An assessment by an external expert comparing Freuchie with competitors may be required to give an indication, although this is likely to suffer from its subjective nature.

(ii) The range of clothes is not measured in the report. This should include the number of product lines which achieve certain gross margin or revenue targets (so measuring their attractiveness). Alternatively, fashion awards won might indicate the attractiveness although the proliferation of industry awards means that a comparison to competitors rather than the absolute figure would be needed.

(iii) Selling with enthusiasm is measured in the current report by revenue growth although, as already noted, this must be adjusted for the change in store numbers. The enthusiasm of the sales staff could be measured by the proportion who are paid a bonus for exceeding their target.

Other points in meeting best practice in reporting:

(1) At present, the report only reports on absolute sales and does not reflect the purchase of new stores. This distorts performance as it is unclear if the growth is organic or from these acquisitions. Revenue and operating profits per store or a categorisation of performance into existing and new stores would help to clarify this.

(2) There is no mention in the current report of the capital which is being used by the business. As a result, it is not possible to give any comment on the return which investors are getting per $ invested. The use of return on capital employed would address this.

(3) The current presentation of a detailed list of costs will tend to obscure important information and those headings which remain should relate to the main objectives. Therefore, it is recommended that all cost information not directly related to the achievement of objectives is removed from the report although there may be need from time to time to provide such information on an exception basis (such as if inventory losses became material in explaining performance).

(4) The report provides both budget and actual figures but does not show variances. This presentation is useful for a detailed control of costs. However, it may be too detailed for consideration of strategic performance which should focus on performance against external measures such as competitor performance.

(5) The report only shows the current year and previous year allowing a simple comparison. The board might want to consider if longer historic trends are of value, especially in a fashion business.

(6) In terms of presentation, the initial table of data is clear and in a form which would be easily recognisable to those used to reading accounts. However, much of this information is not necessary in forming a view about the achievement of the mission, being too detailed or not directly relevant, and so the report overloads the board with internal information but lacks the necessary information on the external environment.

    The section on other data in the report could be easily ignored as it appears to be a mere attachment to the main table of accounting data. It does get mentioned in the commentary (dividends). However, lacking structure or a necessary priority order, the importance of the points might be easily missed. For example, number of employees is placed first, while dividends paid is third in the list.

(b) **Current performance reporting: Narrative**

The current commentary in the report does not justify its conclusion on whether the business is achieving its mission. The actual measure of the primary objective is insufficient, as already noted. It shows the dividend but not total return to shareholders and does not show a return on their capital. The subsidiary strategies are only indirectly mentioned through revenue growth, which relates to enthusiasm of selling. There is no statement on shop appearance, the range of clothes or attractiveness of the clothes. The gross margin should probably be stated to three significant figures which would show a slight fall year-on-year from 40.8% to 40.6%. The final comment on inventory write-downs appears unnecessary as it is neither key to the mission nor material in its impact or year-on-year change.

Suggested improved commentary:

- Overall performance is satisfactory as the business has maintained its dividend and improved its profits although these remain marginal at 0.2% of revenue.
- Revenue is up by 10.5% on the previous period which reflects the purchase of new stores. Revenue per store is static at $15.2m reflecting an unchanged customer experience in the stores.
- The clothing range had X% of lines achieving their gross margin targets.
- The enthusiasm of the sales force was illustrated by X% receiving a bonus for exceeding their target.

> **Tutorial note.** There are many acceptable possibilities in the suggested commentary. For example, the first point here uses existing data but others might discuss percentage total shareholder return against the sector average.

(c) **Operational gearing and cost structures**

Operational gearing measures the business risk relating to how fluctuations in sales volume might lead to falling profits as fixed costs are not covered. The higher the ratio, the greater the risk. It can be defined as contribution/operating profit where contribution is revenue less variable costs. If the contribution is large but operating profit is low (as with Freuchie), then the fixed costs are only being marginally covered and a small loss of revenue could lead to losses (as happened in 20X4). It is difficult to measure precisely as most costs have both fixed and variable elements. The measure here has classified each cost into one or the other category based on their general expected behaviour.

Calculation:

	Budget	*Actual*	*Actual*
	20X5	*20X5*	*20X4*
	$m	$m	$m
Revenue	641.0	638.1	577.7
Cost of sales	380.5	378.9	342.1
Adjusted for:			
Other fixed costs noted	47.2	47.1	42.3
Variable element of staff costs	6.4	6.4	5.8
Contribution	301.3	299.9	272.1
Operational gearing (%) = contribution/PBIT	40.7	44.8	85.0

In these calculations, other fixed costs noted include rent and property costs, marketing, head office costs, insurance, utilities and depreciation; although all do change with the number of stores, they are not likely to change with changes in revenue per store. Staff costs seem to be mostly fixed but the variable bonus element has been calculated and adjusted for.

The results reflect the high fixed costs of Freuchie where, as can be seen by comparing this year and last year, a 10.5% change in revenue moved the business from overall loss to profit and more than doubled operating profit. Freuchie can be seen as a risky business with volatile results as a consequence.

Tutorial note. There are a number of possible acceptable definitions of operational gearing and these are given credit.

(d) **'What gets measured, gets done'**

The idea behind the quote, 'What gets measured, gets done', is that the staff will only react to the performance measures reported on. In other words, poor performance reporting can lead to inefficient management. If an area is not measured, then there is a danger that it is not efficiently managed and equally, if an area is measured, then there is the danger that it is over-managed. For example, the presence of inventory losses on the report might lead to a restriction in the clothing range in order to control this and so be to the detriment of the aim to have an attractive and wide range.

Tunnel vision is present within the quote as it refers to an undue attention on the aspects of performance which are measured and a consequent lack of resources being applied to unmeasured areas. The focus on revenue and dividend payment in the commentary may lead to a lack of attention to profit margins.

Sub-optimisation can be present within the quote as a criticism since if the areas measured are not optimally chosen, then if performance is only driven by the measured factors, the outcome will not be the best possible for the business. As commented above, there is a lack of measure of capital employed at Freuchie and this might be driving the growth by acquisition of stores without addressing the individual profitability per store.

Gaming does not necessarily follow from the quote as gaming is the deliberate distortion of performance in order to achieve the rewarded goals. This implies that what is being measured is not being done, merely being reported that it is done.

The quote may not be entirely applicable as management may still take action out of other motivations such as the results from training or personal motivation to demonstrate their own skills. However, the quote is intended to bring into focus the fact that many people will tend to focus effort on the explicit measures of their performance.

41 Iron Chicken

Workbook references

EVA™ – including the adjustments to accounting profit required to calculate it – are discussed in Chapter 7 of the Workbook. CSFs and KPIs are discussed in Chapter 2. Lean systems and enterprise resource planning systems (ERPSs) are discussed in Chapter 5. Just-in-time and Kaizen costing are discussed in Chapter 10.

Top tips

Part (a). The scenario tells you that the CEO wants your views about the use of EVA™ as the key performance metric at IC. However, they don't want a general discussion about the merits of EVA™. Instead, they want a specific response to their request about evaluating the accuracy of the calculation and the assumptions used in it.

The fact that the scenario mentions that there are doubts about the junior management accountant's ability to calculate EVA™ should have alerted you to the likelihood that some of the figures in the calculation are wrong. However, this doesn't mean that all of the figures are necessarily wrong.

As such, a sensible approach to this question would be to work through the calculation methodically (line by line) identifying whether each of the current figures is correct or not. Where a figure is incorrect, you then need to adjust the calculation accordingly. In addition – applying your knowledge of the adjustments to operating profit required when calculating net operating profit after tax (NOPAT) – you need to consider if there are any figures which have been (incorrectly) omitted completely.

Part (b). The wording of the CEO's underlying requirement – to explain 'a weakness' and to provide 'a justified alternative' – means that there are a number of possible answers to it. You may have recommended different alternatives to the ones suggested in the solution below, but provided they are relevant (ie they help to measure performance against the CSF) and you have justified your recommendation you would earn the marks available. Nonetheless, to score the marks it is vital that you recommend a KPI (ie something that could be measured), not an alternative CSF.

Importantly, you should not spend too long on this part of the question, as there are only six marks available for it. Given that there are three CSFs, this means there are only two marks for each CSF: one for explaining a weakness of the current KPI associated with it, and one for providing a justified alternative KPI. The instruction in the question to 'briefly explain' is important – you shouldn't waste time giving a detailed explanation, particularly as there is only one mark available per weakness.

Part (c). The short paragraph in the scenario above the two projects – with its reference to 'lean' manufacturing – provides the context for this requirement. In effect, the projects are ways of (hopefully) making IC's manufacturing 'leaner'.

As the projects are clearly identified separately, a useful way of tackling the requirement would be to address each project in turn.

Then for each project you need to do three things:

- Explain what the project is.
- Explain how the project will help to achieve IC's CSFs (again the reference to 'lean' in the introductory paragraph here could provide a useful pointer here, since eliminating waste (CSF number 2) is one of the key aims of 'lean').
- Explain what impact the project will have on the KPIs.

Note. Your focus here should be on the levels of performance as measured by the indicators; not on the choice of indicators.

Note that for the second of the three parts you need to explain 'how' the project will help, whereas in the third you have to explain 'what' the impact will be. The distinction is important, because in some cases – eg in relation to the number of products launched – the projects may not affect the KPI. Make sure you state this, though; saying that the project will not have an impact is a valid answer, and so would earn you a mark.

Part (d). This final paragraph of the scenario describes the new information system. In essence, the new system is an enterprise resource planning system (ERPS) so, in effect, the question is asking how an ERPS would help the three projects.

This part of the question is quite challenging, but, of the three projects, the benefits can perhaps most easily be seen in relation to JIT. For example, in a demand–pull system, with no inventory, sharing information between different departments is likely to be crucial in avoiding stock-outs.

More generally, note that the scenario says that IC's current systems can only handle quantitative data. So, also think about the nature of the information required by the projects. For example, in order to reduce the level of defects, IC will presumably need to know what is causing those defects. But can a system which only handles quantitative data provide that information?

Overall. Remember that you have been asked to write a report, so make sure the style and structure of your answer, as well as its tone, is appropriate for a report.

Examining team's comments

Part (a) asked candidates to 'evaluate the accuracy' of an EVA™ calculation that had been provided. Many candidates spent time discussing the advantages and disadvantages of using EVA™ (such as it being closely related to cash flow) but this was not asked for in the requirement. Although a brief explanation of a model/technique may add some value to an answer, it does not warrant a lengthy discussion – unless this has been specifically asked for.

This type of question – which requires an evaluation of whether or not something is accurate – also requires candidates to do more than simply state whether it is right or wrong. Candidates need to state what is inaccurate, explain what the correct treatment should be, and explain why this is the case.

Worryingly, some students incorrectly interpreted a debt:equity ratio of 100% as meaning that the company was financed entirely by debt, and there was no equity. This is a fundamental error, and one which the marking team was surprised to see at this level.

Part (b) was generally well answered, but answers to **part (c)** were mixed. Many candidates were limited by the fact that they appear to have little knowledge of Kaizen costing.

Part (d) required an assessment of the impact a new information system would have on the three improvement projects. Many candidates reiterated the features of the new system that were given in the scenario, but provided little in the way of 'an assessment' of the impact this would have on the projects.

For a question like this – requiring an assessment of the information system on the projects – a good answer will identify what the information requirements of each project are and whether or not the new system will meet those requirements. For example, the implementation of initiatives such as just-in-time manufacturing is heavily reliant on an appropriate information system allowing for co-ordination of deliveries and manufacturing schedules in order to meet customer demands.

Marking guide	Marks
(a) For calculation of corrected EVA™:	
1 mark for identifying correct treatment of each of the following and adjusting as necessary: • Non-cash expenses • Marketing expenses • Research and development • Tax paid • Capital employed – opening figure • WACC • Economic value added	
Maximum for calculation: 7 marks	
1 mark per relevant point evaluating the assumptions and advising on the corrections – up to 10 marks	
Total for part (a): up to 15 marks	
	15
(b) KPIs for CSFs – up to 2 marks for each CSF (1 mark for the weakness of the current KPI; 1 mark for the justified alternative)	
Total for part (b): up to 6 marks	
	6
(c) Quality improvement projects	
Definitions and descriptions of the projects – up to 2 marks	
Analysis of the impact of the projects on IC's CSFs and KPIs – up to 6 marks per project	
Maximum for part (c): up to 10 marks	
	10
(d) New unified database	
Definition and general points – up to 3 marks	
Interaction with each project – up to 3 marks each	
Other comments (eg quantitative vs qualitative information) – up to 3 marks	
Maximum for part (d): up to 9 marks	
	9

Professional skills

Communication

- General report format and structure (use of headings/sub-headings and an introduction)
- Style, language and clarity (appropriate layout and tone of report response, presentation of calculations, appropriate use of the CBE tools)
- Effectiveness of communication (answer is relevant, specific rather than general and focused to the requirement)

Analysis and evaluation

- Use of information provided to perform a suitable/comprehensive evaluation of EVA
- Appropriate use of the data to support discussion and draw appropriate conclusions
- Demonstration of reasoned and balanced judgement
- Demonstration of ability to consider relevant factors applicable to IC Co's situation

Marking guide	Marks
Scepticism	
• Effective challenge and critical assessment of EVA	
• Demonstration of effective challenge of information supplied / identification of missing information	
Commercial acumen	
• Effective use of examples and/or calculations from the scenario information and other practical considerations related to the context to illustrate points being made	
• Demonstrating an awareness of organisational and external factors	
• Recommendations are practical and plausible, and commercially viable in the context of IC Co's situation	
Maximum	10
Total	50

Report

To: **Board of Iron Chicken (IC)**

From: **Performance management expert**

Date: **[Today's date]**

Subject: **Performance management issues at IC**

Introduction

This report evaluates the accuracy and assumptions used in the calculation of EVA™. It then suggests new KPIs for the current CSFs at IC. Finally, it considers the impact of quality improvement projects on these CSFs and a proposed new information system.

(a) **EVA™**

Although some elements of it have been performed correctly, there are a number of errors in the existing calculation of EVA™. The correct treatments are described below, and then the corrected EVA™ is calculated.

Non-cash expenses are correctly added back to profit as such costs are treated as unacceptable accounting adjustments on a cash-based view.

Marketing activities for long-term benefit are also correctly added back as they generate future value for the business. The prior year marketing expenditure is also added into capital employed.

Research and development (R&D) expenditure should be added back to profit in the same way that the long-term marketing spending is. (**Note.** There was no R&D expenditure in the prior year.)

The **tax cost** in the calculation should be the amount paid, adjusted for lost tax on interest, not the adjusted amount of tax charged in the accounts.

The **WACC** is incorrectly calculated as it should be based on the post-tax cost of debt.

The **capital employed** figure should be based on the figure at the start of the year (opening capital employed), not the end of the year.

Economic value added		*Year ended 30 June 20X5*
		$m
Operating profit		551.4
Add back:	Non-cash expenses	15.1
	Marketing capitalised	23.1
	Research and development	10.0
Less:	Tax	130.0
	Lost tax relief on interest	24.5
NOPAT		**445.1**
Capital employed		
At 20X5 year start		2,282.0
Marketing spend capitalised from YE 30 June 20X4		23.1
Adjusted capital employed at 20X5 year start		**2,305.1**

WACC = (1/2 × 16%) + (1/2 × 6.8% × (1 – 30%)) = 10.38%

EVA™ = NOPAT – (WACC × Capital employed)
= 445.1 – (2,305.1 × 10.38%) = **$205.8m** (rounded to **$206m**)

The recalculated EVA™ has increased from 154 million to $206m which still indicates a positive position for the company as it adds to shareholder wealth.

In addition to the corrections above, the following assumptions in the calculation require comment:

(1) There is an implicit assumption that accounting depreciation (included in operating profit) is equivalent to economic depreciation (which should be used for EVA™ calculations). This is questionable generally, although there is no information to allow a more accurate calculation. Also, there is additional marketing spending which will probably have a limited economic life in building the brand. No estimation of this life and the resulting additional economic depreciation has been attempted in the above calculation.

(2) It has been assumed that no amortisation needs to be charged on the R&D costs since the product has not yet launched. This is in line with the accounting treatment of such items.

(b) **KPIs for the CSFs**

Greater staff productivity

The current measure of units produced per labour hour does not reflect the skill and effort which goes into producing different units. The products of IC range from complex to simple and so revenue per employee would better reflect the different skill levels involved in production.

Reduction of wastage

The weakness of the existing measure is that it only looks at one cost area of production (power consumption). Inventory (stock) obsolescence will measure the wastage due to technological change which is present in the complex products produced by IC.

Greater innovation of products

Measuring the number of new products launched doesn't reflect the extent to which IC's innovations can become a sustainable source of value for its shareholders. The number of patents filed will reflect greater innovation at IC, but patents also legally protect groups of products. This will represent a stronger measure of innovation than new products launched, since the patent gives legal exclusivity.

Tutorial note. There are many possible acceptable answers to this question. For example, alternatives you could have suggested are:

Greater staff productivity. Actual staff hours as a percentage of standard hours for actual production as this would measure staff efficiency in producing a wide range of products.

Reduction of wastage. Input/output analysis of material which looks at the percentage of material purchased which goes into the final product.

Greater innovation of products. Percentage of income earned from products which did not exist last year. This will measure the ability of IC to develop successful products. (The existing measure would record unsuccessful products as innovation.)

(c) **Lean manufacturing projects**

The three projects link together as improvements to the quality of the manufacturing process at IC. There are common elements to these projects in the elimination of waste and empowerment of employees which will occur in the long term. In the short term, there may be increased costs due to these disruptive changes.

Just-in-time (JIT) manufacturing

JIT seeks to produce on a pull basis to meet the customers' demands, rather than to produce products for inventory, which then acts as a buffer between production levels and demand. The main impact of JIT is the reduction of inventory which is held. The main enablers for such a system are a need for close links to customers and suppliers in order to predict demand and to quickly supply that demand.

In terms of IC's CSFs, this project will improve productivity as production lines must be made more flexible to meet changes in demand, although it should be noted that there could be a negative impact as constant changes in production lines will require more time to be spent setting up new production runs. It will also help to reduce wastage through losses in inventory as there will be less inventory. It also pushes some of the responsibility for improved quality of components (and reduced wastage) on to suppliers. However, it does not directly impact on product innovation.

The project will not necessarily immediately change any of the existing KPIs as it is about producing the right products at the right time, not necessarily producing more products for any given input, and it does not impact directly on new product launches.

Use Kaizen costing

Kaizen costing aims to reduce current costs of production through continuous improvement. Each period, goals for lower costs are set and then performance monitored against these using variances. At the end of the period, a new lower cost goal is set for the next period. The process also often uses target costing to set the initial planned cost of a product thus incorporating the idea of only producing what the customer values. The purpose is to build into the control of the production process the idea of continuous improvement.

This project has the explicit aim of reducing waste and improving productivity and so is directly linked to the first two CSFs. As a result, it will have an impact on the KPIs which are related to productivity and resource consumption. The project will also require the empowerment of staff to make improvement decisions within their quality circles (teams) and so it may give scope for more innovative thinking. However, this thinking is not aimed at producing new products but at improving the production process, so new product innovation may only be affected indirectly.

(d) **New information system**

The move to a single database for the organisation will integrate the subsystems from different functions (such as production and sales). It will require existing systems to be networked and compatible or else be replaced. It will affect overall decision making by improving the visibility of each function's operations to the others and to the strategic decision makers. This shift is often achieved by using an ERPS and a strategic enterprise management system.

The unified database will be critical in achieving the goal of JIT manufacturing as close links between production scheduling and demand forecasts will be required in order to match production runs with demand forecasts/orders. Also, the production schedules will need links to inventory levels in warehousing so that inventory is run down before new production is initiated. As closer communication with suppliers and customers will also be required, some change to existing information systems will be necessary in any case. It may be worthwhile to consider including electronic data interchange (EDI) in the specifications of the new system.

In using Kaizen costing, cross-functional communication will be important. The design team will need to communicate with the production team so that the design is more easily streamlined for production. The financial systems will need to be frequently updated for information from the quality circles as improvements are made. This will affect the Kaizen cost targets which need to be continually monitored and new targets set regularly. Quality circles often involve groups from across the business and so a common information system will facilitate communications amongst them.

The nature of the data used in the current system is quantitative but with the new projects there will be a need to communicate qualitative information, for example, relating to the nature of defects or the new production processes put in place. This will require a fundamental change to existing systems which again motivates the change to a new database.

42 FIAG

Marking guide	Marks
(a) (i) Misrepresentation by report	
1 mark per point including:	
Omitted industry averages	
Omitted certain year-on-year changes	
Misclassification of costs: exceptional costs and grant income	
Commentary misleading	
Additional credit given where points are correctly supported by calculation.	
	12
(ii) Measuring the achievement of the objectives of Fiag	
Breakdown objectives of Fiag – up to 2 marks	
Show hierarchy and break into measurable parts	
Measurement of objectives within the report – up to 10 marks	
Other points – up to 4 marks	
	14
(b) External business environment	
For each of Political, Economic, Socio-cultural, Technological:	
Discussion of the relevant issue in the PEST analysis – up to 2 marks	
Justification of suggested KPIs on the issue – up 2 marks	
Points must be related to Fiag's business.	
	14

Professional marks

Communication:

- Report format and structure – use of headings/sub-headings and introduction
- Style, language and clarity – appropriate tone of report response, presentation of calculations, appropriate use of the CBE tools, easy to follow and understand

Marking guide	Marks

- Adherence to the CEO's request to re-perform the PEST and to offer a justified performance indicator per PEST factor

Analysis and evaluation:

- Appropriate use of the data to provide relevant calculations to support discussion and draw a conclusion as to whether the report presents a manipulated picture
- Appropriate use of the data to support discussion and draw a conclusion as to whether the report supports monitoring of Fiag's objectives

Scepticism:

- Recognition that information relating to certain industry comparators can be difficult to obtain
- Recognition that failures in measuring the supporting strategies are because of only using financial systems

Commercial acumen:

- Recognition that the NED's criticism seems to be merited with supporting evidence
- Provision of suitable performance measures are practical and plausible in relation to the issues identified by the PEST analysis

Maximum	10
Total	50

Report

To: CEO of Fiag

From: A. Accountant

Date: September 20X5

Subject: Performance reporting and other management issues at Fiag

Introduction

This report evaluates the current performance report used by the board of Fiag, firstly against the accusations that it misrepresents performance and then, secondly that it fails to measure Fiag's performance against its objectives. Finally, justified recommendations of performance indicators arising from an analysis of the external business environment are offered.

(a) (i) **Manipulation of board report**

The non-executive director (NED)'s criticism of the current report seems to have good reason. The problems lie in omitting bad news by using classifications some of which appear to select only a positive view of performance and some that manipulate commonly used performance indicators.

Omitting the bad news

The report gives only one industry average (operating margin) but does not provide a revenue growth comparator. While cost and detailed profit information is often difficult to obtain, the revenue figures are clearly reported for most entities and so it should be straight-forward to see if Fiag's fall of 6% is representative of the market as a whole.

The report does not calculate many of the year-on-year changes. This may be because important headings such as gross profit show a deteriorating performance. It could be argued that many of these calculations are unnecessary (such as for the detailed cost headings). However, no such case can be made for not showing the percentage fall in operating profit.

The revenue performance fall may be worse than portrayed as the range without the electrical bicycle has seen revenue fall from $284m to $248m (13%). This category covers 91% of the current revenue earned by Fiag.

Misclassification of costs

Exceptional costs relate to the development of the new electrical bicycle which appears to be part of the main activities and a central part of the strategy of the business. These costs should be considered normal. Their placement after the operating profit line means that key performance indicators such as return on capital employed are not affected so over-stating performance.

Administrative expenses include government grant income which probably should be stated separately as it is material, short term and will not match to the full five years of costs associated with developing the electrical bicycle.

Commentary

The commentary appears misleading. It gives a positive impression of revenue growth by only selecting the growth in revenue from new models rather than noting the underperformance of the range as a whole. It quotes the improved profit before tax figure while ignoring the widely used operating profit figure, thereby bypassing the reason for the rise in profit before tax which is the fall in exceptional costs resulting from the completion of development of the new electrical bicycle model.

The description that a fall in operating margin is small ignores a number of facts. The fall is not 1.8% but 1.8 percentage points which is 27% on 20X4. Also, no reference is made to the industry comparator of 11% against which Fiag's 4.8% looks poor.

Thus, the commentary fails to address the falling revenue, gross profit and operating profit and so, is not representing the performance of Fiag accurately.

(ii) **Measuring the achievement of the objectives of Fiag**

The critical measure of whether the report is fit for its purpose is that it shows whether the business is achieving its objectives. Fiag's overall objective is 'to give the shareholders sustainable growth in returns' and it intends to do this by:

- Developing the best quality bicycles;
- Manufacturing the best quality bicycles; and
- Bringing the joy of cycling to a broad customer base in Beeland.

Overall, the report is in the format of a profit and loss statement, so it contains a number of common financial measures, but these are only loosely connected to the stated mission. The following problems are noted about how the report measures the achievement of the objectives:

(1) There is no direct measure of shareholder returns in the report, not even profit after tax which would allow an earnings calculation. There is no statement of the gains that shareholders would make in income (dividends paid) or capital terms. While it is not possible to give capital growth through share price rise as Fiag is unlisted, shareholder wealth changes could be measured through NPV or economic value added. Growth of the returns would require the change year-on-year of these indicators, and this is only partially recognised in the existing report where not all growths are provided.

(2) The sustainability of the returns are unclear from the report. These require the determinants of future performance to be measured. This should be done by examining the success of the supporting strategies.

(3) The first two supporting strategies of the overall objective relate to the qualities of Fiag's products. The report does not measure these individually. There is an indirect measure of customer attitude through the revenue growth figure but without competitor comparison or a market share it is not possible to draw a conclusion about any of the qualities of the products. These elements relating to the products are difficult to measure overall as they are likely to be dependent on each product line individually.

(4) The objectives also make clear the need to separately measure development and manufacture.

(i) There are no separate categories for all new products although there is a note on revenue from the Zoam. The number of development projects, their state of completion and then their market performance all require to be monitored.

(ii) There is little apart from the gross profit to indicate the efficiency of the manufacturing process.

(5) The failures in points 3 and 4 reflect the choice to use only data from the financial systems in the report. The measurement of these aspects requires Fiag to move beyond its traditional information systems.

(6) There is no measure of the customer base and so the broadening of the customer base cannot be commented upon. This final aspect would appear to be addressed by the Zoam which seems attractive to those who may previously have not been willing or able (elderly) to make the physical effort. This failure also reflects the lack of external competitor/market information in the report where the only external data given is the industry average operating margin.

Other aspects

From the perspective of a board report, it should provide information to allow the board to perform its tasks of planning for the future of Fiag and controlling its existing activities. For planning purposes, the lack of external information about customers and competitors makes some of the numbers difficult to interpret. For control purposes, there is previous year information given but not sufficient to establish a trend (which requires at least 3 years of information). Also, there is no indication of whether the business is meeting its budgets through the provision of variances.

In terms of presentation, the report is clear and in a traditional profit and loss format, would be easily understood by most readers. It uses terms that would be recognisable to those used to reading accounts. It is helpful that a narrative commentary is provided. However, problems with the quality of the narrative are noted above and often the commentary does not go beyond restating the figures in the table. It should provide the significant explanations for performance as measured by the key indicators which should be linked directly to the objectives of Fiag noted above.

(b) **External business environment at Fiag**

The political environment is characterised by government actions which appear aimed to increase the use of bicycles in Beeland. Tax allowances represent a financial incentive while the building of new cycle paths should make cycling safer and so increase participation. These factors are both beneficial to Fiag. Suitable indicators of the impact of these factors on Fiag would be the increased demand for their products (volumes purchased) and also the increased participation rates with total number of kilometres cycled or if this is not available then total market size for bicycles in Beeland. It is not unusual for retailers to ask if customers were buying under a government scheme and if Fiag did this it could measure how well it was exploiting this free sales promotion. The growth of these indicators should be compared with revenue growth at Fiag.

The broad economic environment is characterised by growth and the populace of Beeland has become wealthier. For Fiag, this should mean growing volumes and margins although the cost base (eg staff costs) will inflate too. Again, the size and growth of the overall market and Fiag relative performance against these will show if it is developing a competitive advantage. The introduction of tariffs will increase the costs and can be measured at Fiag by the negative impact on profit margins.

The socio-cultural factors include demographic trends and changes in customers' tastes. The increasing interest in health should again be a factor in driving the consumers' taste towards cycling and so, as above, indicators of the market size/growth and Fiag's relative performance are relevant. The ageing demographic factor should seem to increase the attractiveness of the electrical bicycle over other models and so the market/growth of this particular sector and Fiag's share along with the relative performance of electrical bicycles against the traditional models at Fiag should be monitored. Fiag seems at the forefront of this development and should be seeking to maintain that competitive advantage.

Technology impacts on Fiag in two ways. Firstly, the development of new models, such as the Zoam, where the lightweight aspect will further enhance the model's attractiveness especially to the elderly. In order to continue to monitor competitive advantage, the average weight of Fiag's models (especially the Zoam) should be compared to the average of its competitors. Secondly, new materials could improve further the contribution per unit as material costs are cut. The use of contribution or gross profit to measure this impact is plausible but may be indirect since this change may also influence the selling price. Therefore, a measure of direct material cost per unit would better capture the change.

43 Merkland Sportswear

Workbook references.

SWOT analysis is discussed in Chapter 1 of the Workbook. The performance hierarchy linking strategic objectives and performance metrics is discussed in Chapter 2. The value chain is covered in Chapter 4.

Top tips

Part (a)

There are two distinct parts to this requirement: assess the current metrics; and then make suggestions for improving them. As the marking guide illustrates, the marks available were distributed roughly equally between the two parts, so to score well you needed to give due weight to both parts of the requirement.

The first part of the CEO instruction is to 'assess' the existing dashboard metrics. A useful way to approach this requirement might be to ask yourself what the characteristics of effective performance metrics are, and then to consider how well MS's metrics demonstrate these characteristics. Importantly, performance metrics enable management to identify how well an organisation is performing against its critical success factors (CSFs), and how well it is achieving its strategy. In turn, this means that the aspects of performance which are being measured should be ones which are linked to key elements of an organisation's strategy.

Therefore, before you can assess MS's performance metrics, you also need to identify its strategy. The third paragraph in the question scenario – which identifies MS's aims and then its broad strategy for achieving them – is crucial here. In effect, your assessment of the metrics should be an assessment of whether or not they will enable MS's management to determine if the company is achieving its aims and strategy.

Having assessed the current metrics, you are then asked to make suggestions for improvements. However, crucially, are asked to do so within the constraints outlined by the CEO in the scenario – ie that the existing performance headings (financial, design and brand) are retained, and that there are no more than three financial metrics, and no more than two for each of 'design' and 'brand'. The post-exam review comments (see below) indicated many candidates in the real exam failed to adhere to these constraints.

Also, note that the CEO has specifically asked you to use the SWOT analysis as the basis for your suggestions. Therefore, a useful approach to this part of the requirement would be to ask if the current performance metrics will allow management to assess how the issues identified in the SWOT are affecting MS's performance. If factors in the SWOT are not being covered by the performance metrics, then these can provide the basis for your suggested improvements. However, remember, your suggestions must be within the constraints outlined by the CEO.

Examining team's comments for part (a)

Although part (a) was often answered reasonably well, there were still a number of weaknesses in candidates' answers. A 'significant minority' of candidates chose to assess MS's performance, rather than assessing the performance metrics.

Also, candidates need to remember that, when making suggestions, justifying the suggestion is crucial. Candidates will not score enough marks to pass the requirement by listing alternative performance metrics – to score the marks available candidates must explain why the metrics they are proposing would be beneficial to MS.

Most worryingly, however, the majority of candidates ignored the instructions from the CEO to limit the number of metrics suggested. Many answers contained long lists of new metrics, which was not what was asked for at all.

Part (b)

The CEO request is for you to assess the qualitative and quantitative impact of a change of outsourcing partners for footwear manufacture. The qualitative issues (around the ethical implications of using child labour) should have been relatively easy to identify from the scenario.

The information needed to calculate the quantitative impact is provided in Appendix 3, and the comment 'It would be helpful to know how many units we would need to sell in order to cover these increased costs' should have been a clear instruction that a breakeven calculation was required here.

As the marking guide indicates, four out of the eight marks available for this requirement related to the breakeven calculation. However, when this question was examined, the post-exam report suggested that a number of candidates appeared unable to perform the calculations, and the examining team reported that this was very worrying at Strategic Professional level (which is the level of the APM exam).

Part (c)

Here again there are two parts to the CEO's request: (i) evaluate the impact of the new factory on the figures in the dashboard (ie the results) and (ii) evaluate the impact of the new factory on the choice of metrics in the dashboard.

To identify the relevant issues here, it is crucial to think about the new factory in the context of MS's current business model. Currently, MS outsources all of its manufacturing. However, once the new factory is set up, MS will have its own manufacturing operation. This is particularly significant when thinking about the impact the factory will have on the metrics needed to assess performance.

The examining team's comments for this part of the question are also helpful here:

Examining team's comments.

Many candidates attempted to recalculate the dashboard metrics but ignored the fact that the new factory was bringing in-house an existing process and so the change in operating profit was the difference between the new factory's profit and that which was made from existing outsourced sales. However, even if no calculations were attempted a number of candidates earned enough marks to pass this requirement by simply going through the metrics and discussing how the new factory affected them and what changes should be made now that MS has a manufacturing operation – something which it did not have prior to this change.

Part (d)

Note that the CEO's instruction here does not ask you to describe the value chain, or to explain the implications of the value chain for performance management in general terms. Instead the CEO has asked specifically for an 'explanation of the implications of using the value chain for performance management at MS'. Linking your answer to the scenario was important to score well here.

A useful way of approaching this requirement could be to think how MS generates value through the different activities in its value chain, and then to consider what implications this has for the choice of performance measures or the way performance is measured at MS.

Report format

Finally, note that you were asked to write a report, and remember that there are 'professional marks' available for the quality of your report. In this respect, markers are looking for suitable report headings, a brief introduction, and a logical structure to your report – signposted by the use of headings. They are also looking for your report to be written in a clear, concise style.

Marking guide	Marks
(a) For identifying MS's aims and broad strategies – up to 2 marks	
For evaluating how well the metrics support each aim and strategy:	
Growth – 1 mark	
Shareholder wealth – up to 2 marks	
Innovation – up to 3 marks	
Marketing – up to 3 marks	
For other comments/suggestions linked to SWOT analysis:	
Comments about supply chain management – up to 2 marks	
Comments about social media and IT expertise – up to 3 marks	
Comments about brand ambassadors – up to 3 marks	
	16
(b) For calculations:	
Increased cost of sales – 1 mark	
Lost operating profit – 1 mark	
New contribution per unit – 1 mark	
Required sales – 1 mark	
Comments (on qualitative and quantitative issues) – up to 4 marks	
Total for part (b): up to 8 marks	
	8
(c) For calculations:	
Operating profit under third-party manufacturing – 1 mark	
Loss of operating profit – 1 mark	
New capital employed – 1 mark	
New ROCE – 1 mark	
No change to other metrics – 1 mark	
For comments (about the impact of the new factory on the values in the dashboard, and on the choice of measures in the dashboard) – up to 5 marks	
Total for part (d): up to 10 marks	
	10
(d) For relevant points about the implications of the value chain on performance management at MS – 1 mark per point	
Total for part (e): up to 6 marks	
	6

Professional skills

Communication

- General report format and structure (use of headings/sub-headings and an introduction)
- Style, language and clarity (appropriate layout and tone of report response, presentation of calculations, appropriate use of the CBE tools)

Marking guide	Marks

- Effectiveness of communication (answer is relevant, specific rather than general and focused to the requirement)
- Adherence to the details of the required report as specified

Analysis and evaluation

- Use of information provided to perform a suitable/comprehensive evaluation of existing dashboard
- Appropriate use of the data to support discussion and draw appropriate conclusions
- Demonstration of reasoned and balanced judgement
- Demonstration of ability to consider relevant factors applicable to MS Co's situation

Scepticism

- Effective challenge and critical assessment of ROCE assessment
- Demonstration of effective challenge of information supplied / identification of missing information

Commercial acumen

- Effective use of examples and/or calculations from the scenario information and other practical considerations related to the context to illustrate points being made
- Demonstrating an awareness of organisational and external factors
- Recommendations are practical and plausible, and commercially viable in the context of MS Co's situation

Maximum	10
Total	50

Report

To: Board of MS

From: Consultant

Date: [Today's date]

Subject: Performance management at Merkland Sportswear (MS)

Introduction

This report looks at a number of performance management issues at MS, particularly in relation to the range of performance measures included in the dashboard. We begin by evaluating the existing measures used, before looking at the way the company's response to the child labour scandal in the sportswear manufacturing industry could affect its performance and its performance measurement system.

We finish by looking at how value chain analysis could influence performance management at MS.

(a) **Evaluation of current metrics**

MS's overall commercial aims are to grow as a business and to maximise shareholder wealth.

As these aims are essentially financial, it seems appropriate for the dashboard to include three financial measures, but only up to one each for 'design' and 'brand'.

Financial performance measures

Growth – Comparing the revenue figures to prior years can give an indication of the growth being achieved by the business. Including percentage change figure (for 20X5 compared to 20X4) on the dashboard also highlights the amount of growth achieved year on year. Similarly, the operating figures show whether this growth is profitable for MS.

However, because the dashboard doesn't give any revenue figures for the sportswear market as a whole, we cannot gauge how fast it is growing relative to its competitors, and whether its market share is growing or not.

Shareholder wealth – Return on capital employed (ROCE) shows how profitably MS is using its assets and, as such, could provide some indication of how well MS is generating wealth for its shareholders. However, ROCE is ultimately not a good metric in this respect.

One of ROCE's weaknesses is that it could encourage strategic decisions designed to increase short-term profit, potentially at the expense of investment for the future. More fundamentally, though, ROCE is a profit-based measure, and shareholder wealth would be better assessed through a **value-based measure**, which provides some insight into MS's ability to generate future cash flows. In this respect, MS should consider using **economic value added** (EVA™) as a metric instead of ROCE.

Non-financial performance

MS's broad strategy also identifies the need to create innovative products and to have an effective marketing operation – the best in Ceeland.

The current dashboard headings ('Design' and 'Brand') reflect the importance of these elements of performance. However, there are still some potential problems with the metrics used in each heading.

Design awards won – The design awards acknowledge the look and technology in a finished product; they do not directly measure the level of innovation in MS. (For example, the number of new features added to our products, or the number of new products developed would provide a more direct measure for innovation.)

MS's strategy also identifies that its products should help reduce the risk of injury and enhance sporting performance by their customers. The current dashboard does not measure how effectively the products are doing this. However, it could be difficult to provide metrics which cover all of these areas, given the constraints on the number of performance indicators to be included in the dashboard. As such, MS will have to decide whether reducing the risk of injury or enhancing sporting performance is likely to be the more critical success factor for its products.

Brand awareness – The level of brand awareness is likely to be influenced by the effectiveness of MS's marketing operations. The fact that brand awareness is increasing might suggest that MS's marketing operations have been effective. However, without any comparison showing brand awareness for rival brands it is difficult to tell how effective they are, and therefore whether MS has 'the best marketing operation in Ceeland'.

In this respect, market share might be a more appropriate measure – not least because it also links back to MS's aim to grow as a business.

Moreover, just because people can identify MS's logo or name one of its products does not mean they have a positive impression of the company or any desire to buy its products. By contrast, market share statistics can provide a measure of how well MS is identifying and satisfying customer requirements, and how effectively its marketing activities are influencing their purchasing decisions.

Potential improvements

Although the SWOT analysis suggests that supply chain management is a CSF for MS, the CEO's insistence that no new headings be added to the dashboard means that performance in this area cannot be reported directly.

However, MS's ability to manage its supply chain effectively will, indirectly, affect its revenue and operating profit margins. As such, it may be preferable to replace the absolute operating profit figures in the dashboard with percentage margin figures.

The following improvements could also be made to the non-financial performance metrics:

Design – We have already suggested that the number of new features added to our products might be a better performance measure than design awards won. The SWOT analysis suggests that, rather than just looking at new features, we could monitor innovation in relation to the number of new products introduced.

Brand – We have already suggested that market share would be a better metric than brand awareness.

However, the SWOT analysis also suggests that social media is going to become an increasingly important aspect of marketing activities – although MS's weak IT expertise may limit its ability to take advantage of this.

Linked to the overall performance metric of market share, MS could also monitor the number of followers it has on social media (eg on Twitter, or the number of 'likes' it has on Facebook) as an indicator of how effectively it is using these marketing channels.

Brand ambassadors – Despite the growth of social media, brand ambassadors still play an important role in promoting MS's brand, and the SWOT analysis highlights this by acknowledging the loss of a key brand ambassador as a strategic weakness. As such, it could be useful to include a metric for 'Number of ambassadors' under the 'brand' heading on the dashboard. However, as we have already suggested metrics for market share and social media followers – and can only have two in total for 'brand' – the board will have to decide whether including a metric for the number of ambassadors is more important than either of these.

(b) **Impact of Response 1**

Qualitative impact

Although there is not currently any evidence that MS's suppliers are using illegal labour, the fact that MS does not appear to have any assurance over the labour practices used by its suppliers (and is having to review them now) means there is a risk that this could be the case.

This means that the review proposed under Response 1 should be carried out as soon as possible. If MS does find that the appropriate employment terms and conditions have been breached (and, in turn, MS's own ethical code has been breached) it should be transparent and own up to these failings. However, at the same time, MS should also explain the actions it has taken (through either Response 1 or 2) to redress the problems and to prevent them from recurring. Taking action in this way should help to restrict the level of negative stakeholder reaction to any findings.

In particular, MS will have to manage the reactions of customers and the regulator if it finds evidence of any unethical practices in its supply chain.

Customers – Such findings will damage MS's reputation for ethical sourcing, and there is a danger that customers could boycott MS's products, threatening revenue and profit growth.

Regulator – The regulator will review MS's sourcing policies (as it did with Nush), and is likely to punish MS in some way for using suppliers who have acted illegally.

Employees – Any such breach would mean that MS has failed to follow the requirements of its own ethics code (to source goods responsibly) and this could damage employees' trust in the company as a responsible employer.

Assurance procedures – More generally, the review required by Response 1 also suggests that MS could benefit from regular assurance processes over its supply chain – to ensure that its suppliers comply with relevant employment legislation on an ongoing basis. Although the constraints on the performance headings in MS's existing performance dashboard mean there isn't scope to monitor performance there, it could perhaps be monitored at departmental level within the Procurement Department.

Quantitative impact

Impact on shareholders – The increased manufacturing costs, coupled with increased compliance and marketing costs, mean that MS's operating profit will fall by $5.5m if the number of shoes MS sells remains the same. MS will need to increase sales by 106,000 pairs of shoes to make good this shortfall.

However, since the problem of child labour appears to be a common problem among suppliers to sports footwear companies, if MS is able to demonstrate that it has responded rapidly and decisively to any potential problems in its supply chain, this action could help to differentiate it from its competitors, and in doing so could help generate these extra sales.

Annual cost:

		$m
Increase in cost of shoes purchased	$2.1 × 2 million pairs	4.2
Supplier audits		0.5
Marketing cost		0.8
Total (per year)		**5.5**

Contribution per unit	$	
Price	75.0	
Direct cost ($21 + $2.1)	(23.1)	
	51.9	
Number of units required to cover lost operating profit:		**105,973**

(c) **Impact of the new factory on the dashboard**

Financial metrics (20X5)

	Existing factory	*New factory*	*Change (%)*
Revenue ($m)	273	273	–
Operating profit ($m) ($5m lower see Working 1)	71	66	–7.0%
ROCE (see Working 2)	41.7%	30.4%	–27.1%

The new factory will not affect the number of design awards won or brand awareness levels.

Impact on financial performance

Operating profit – The decline in operating profit indicates that manufacturing all of its footwear in-house will lead to an increase in MS's costs of approximately $5m per year.

Although the variable cost of manufacturing footwear in-house ($21–$23 per unit) is expected to be similar to that of buying footwear from an external supplier ($21 per unit), there will also be additional fixed costs associated with the new factory.

The increase in fixed costs will also lead to an increase in MS's **operational gearing**.

Non-current assets – As MS is primarily a product development and marketing operation – with no manufacturing operations of its own – it will have a relatively low level of fixed capital (buildings, equipment etc). As a result, it also has a relatively high ROCE.

However, establishing the factory will increase capital employed (as well as reducing operating profit), which explains the significant reduction in ROCE.

However, although establishing the factory (and taking full control of operations) may have a negative impact on ROCE in the short term, it could benefit MS in the longer term – for example, by helping it to avoid lost sales due to damaged reputation, or to avoid costs such as fines imposed by the regulator.

Impact on choice of metrics

Quality – If MS starts manufacturing footwear itself, then quality control will become an important aspect of performance management. Currently, product quality is not measured directly in the dashboard, but it would seem sensible to add an extra heading to reflect this new dimension – manufacturing – which has been added to MS's activities. (Alternatively, the 'design' heading could be expanded to allow additional metrics to be associated with it. But it would seem preferable to keep 'design' and 'manufacturing' as distinct activities.)

However, we must remember that MS has no experience of manufacturing. As such, it may be sensible to wait until the company has gained some operational knowledge of the factory operations before introducing a detailed metric for this area – for example, to avoid setting performance targets which are not realistic.

Gearing – The factory will cost $36m to build and equip, as well as increasing working capital by $11m. It is not clear how this additional capital will be funded, but if it involves debt then this will increase the company's financial gearing, and therefore the level of financial risk. There is not currently any measure of such risk on the dashboard, but again it may be necessary to add one.

Workings

1 ***Impact of new factory on Operating Profit***

Average selling price ($)	$75
Cost of shoes ($)	$21
Operating profit per shoe	$54
Operating profit on 2 million shoes bought/sold	$108m
Operating profit from the new factory (per board's estimate given in the question scenario)	$103m
Reduction in operating profit	$5m

2 ***Impact of new factory on ROCE***

Current capital employed (where operating profit (PBIT) is $71m and ROCE is 41.7%)	170.3
Additional capital employed: $36m + $11m	47
New capital employed	217.3
Revised ROCE: ($66m/$217.3m)	30.4%

(d) **Value chain**

A value chain provides an overview of the different activities within an organisation which combine to create value for customers. By identifying the activities which create value, the organisation can then focus on improving its performance in those areas – with the result that it also improves its performance overall.

Equally, however, the value chain can help an organisation to identify which aspects of performance are most important to measure – that is, those which relate to the key value-adding activities. In this respect, we might expect the metrics included in MS's dashboard to provide the board with information about how well the company is performing in these key activities. However, the current dashboard provides very little information about MS's performance in these activities.

Marketing and sales – To a degree, the dashboard heading for 'brand' could relate to the 'marketing and sales' activities in the value chain; but, as we have already suggested, simply monitoring brand awareness can only provide limited insight into the effectiveness of MS's marketing and sales activities.

Technology – In this respect, the linkage between technology (as a supporting activity) and marketing (as a primary activity) could also become increasingly important with the growth of social media as a marketing channel.

Logistics and operations – MS's current business model (with outsourced manufacturing and third-party retailers) means that a number of the primary activities (inbound/outbound logistics; operations; sales) are performed by third parties. Currently, MS does not appear to monitor the performance of its supply chain partners, but this is perhaps something it should consider doing, since these partners are responsible for generating a significant proportion of the value in MS's products.

Procurement – Although procurement is normally classified as a supporting activity on the value chain, MS's business model means that effective procurement (coupled with effective supply chain management, particularly with its upstream manufacturers) is likely to be crucial to the company's commercial success.

Moreover, the importance of outsourced manufacturers means that MS's performance management should not focus solely on its internal value chain, but also its value network (value system) more generally. (The Nush scandal provides an important reminder of this.)

Here again, the value chain also highlights the important supporting role that technology is likely to play – for example, in ensuring that the quantities of goods produced by different third-party suppliers responds effectively to the requirements of MS's third-party retailers (for example, to avoid either over- or under-production of different product lines).

Product design – Technology could also be important at MS in relation to creating innovative products; either through the way technology is used in the design process, or the way that technological developments make new materials available for use in MS's products.

'Design' has already been identified as one of the three performance headings in the dashboard, but technology development is likely to be a key supporting activity in relation to product design.

Although we have already suggested this point (in part (d) of this report) value chain analysis reiterates the idea that MS may need to include a wider range of metrics in its dashboard – to provide management with performance information about the range of activities which are critical in sustaining the company's commercial success.

44 Flack

Workbook reference

Performance reports are discussed in Chapter 5 of the Workbook, as are management information systems. Performance measures (including ROCE, RI) are discussed in Chapter 6.

Top tips

Part (a). A key point to note in this requirement is that you have been asked to evaluate the performance report, not Flack's underlying performance.

Also note that your evaluation needs to be in relation to the CEO's question of whether the performance report 'is fit for the purpose of achieving the company's mission'.

A key part of this requirement is identifying what information the performance report provides the board about the issues identified in the mission (eg earning customer loyalty; resource utilisation; serving shareholders' interests). A useful way to structure your answer could have been to use each of the issues identified in the mission as a sub-heading, and then consider what information – if any – the report provides the board in relation to that issue.

However, as well as evaluating the performance report in the context of Flack's mission, you also need to comment on whether the performance report is 'short-termist'. So, to score well in part (a), you also need to address this issue: do the aspects of performance being included in the performance report encourage a short-term focus?

Part (b). The context for this requirement is that the CEO wants an evaluation of how the two new measures (revenue per square metre; operating profit per square metre) could help Flack assess the objective of 'utilising all our resources'.

Make sure you look at the CEO's request in the scenario very carefully, because it contains a number of elements:

- Explain how the new measures relate to the objective
- What the ratios are (ie **calculate** the ratios themselves, using the figures from Appendix 1)
- Explain how the ratios could be used to manage business performance

To score well here, you need to address all three of the elements. However, note that there are only eight marks available in total for this part of the question, so you only need to cover each element quite briefly.

Part (c). The board currently uses divisional operating profit as the measure for assessing divisional performance, but is considering replacing this with residual income. You are asked to assess this proposed change.

It is important to recognise the context of this proposed change. Flack has been criticised for its stores looking 'run down' and store managers have been reluctant to invest in refurbishing existing stores, preferring instead to use capital to open new stores. A key issue here is whether the change in performance measures will change managers' behaviour in this respect.

A useful approach to answering requirements like this which require a comparison between current and proposed measures is to identify what the potential problems are with the existing measure and then consider whether the proposed new measure will help to address them.

Importantly, note that in the scenario, the CEO has told you that you are not required to calculate the current values. In other words, you need to focus on the measures themselves, not on the performance of the divisions.

Part (d). It could also be useful to think back to Flack's overall mission, one of whose key elements is 'earning customer loyalty' to give direction to the points being made.

Overall. Remember that you have been asked to write a report, so make sure the style and structure of your answer, as a whole, is appropriate for a report. For example, a report should have a short introduction explaining the key issues to be discussed in it, and should have headings for each section or part.

Examining team's comments

Part (a) was generally well done. Candidates performed well when they used the signposts given in the scenario to identify specific issues to look for in Flack's performance report.

Part (b) again required candidates to address specific requirements identified in the scenario. However, this part of the question was not answered well, with many candidates failing to identify how the new measures fit with the specific strategy point they were intended to address. In addition, candidates often didn't pick up the simple calculation marks on offer by failing to recognise that they were working in $'000.

Part (c) was answered reasonably well, with candidates structuring their comments into criticism of the existing performance measure and then analysis of how the proposed new measure would address the issues with the existing measure. Unfortunately, a number of candidates decided to focus their answer on a different, new performance indicator of their own choice, which cost them a number of marks.

Report format

As we have seen in previous sittings, those candidates who had practised writing professional answers prior to the exam performed admirably in the presentation area. The markers were looking for:

- Suitable report headings
- An introduction
- A logical structure (signposted by good use of sub-headings)
- A clear, concise style

Marking guide	Marks
(a) Performance report	
Breaking down the mission – up to 3 marks	
Two main aims and three CSFs/strategies – noting how these are logically connected	
Comments on how report addresses mission and strategies – up to 6 marks	
Missing information – up to 3 marks	
Lack of external info; margins by product category	
Report is 'short-termist' – up to 3 marks	
Comments on presentation – up to 3 marks	
Lack of narrative; data overload; rounding	
Maximum for part (a)	
	14
(b) New asset utilisation indicators	
Addressing the mission – up to 3 marks	
Calculations – 3 marks	
Use in managing business performance – up to 5 marks	
Maximum for part (b)	
	9
(c) Divisional performance	
Discussion of existing behaviour and measure – up to 5 marks	
Discussion of new measure – up to 5 marks	
Maximum for part (c)	
	9

Marking guide		Marks
(d) Data analysis		
How descriptive data analysis can help Flack	3	
How diagnostic data analysis can help Flack	3	
How predictive data analysis can help Flack	3	
		8

Professional skills

Communication

- General report format and structure (use of headings/sub-headings and an introduction)
- Style, language and clarity (appropriate layout and tone of report response, presentation of calculations, appropriate use of the CBE tools)
- Effectiveness of communication (answer is relevant, specific rather than general and focused to the requirement)

Analysis and evaluation

- Use of information provided to perform a suitable/comprehensive evaluation
- Appropriate use of the data to support discussion and draw appropriate conclusions
- Demonstration of reasoned and balanced judgement / assessment of performance measures
- Demonstration of ability to consider relevant factors applicable to Flack Co's situation

Scepticism

- Effective challenge and critical assessment
- Demonstration of effective challenge of information supplied / identification of missing information

Commercial acumen

- Effective use of examples and/or calculations from the scenario information and other practical considerations related to the context to illustrate points being made
- Demonstrating an awareness of organisational and external factors
- Recommendations are practical and plausible, and commercially viable in the context of Flack Co's situation

Maximum	10
Total	50

Report

To: Board of Flack

From: A. Accountant

Date: [Today's date]

Subject: Performance reporting and management issues at Flack

Introduction

This report evaluates the current performance report for Flack and the introduction of two new performance measures. Then, the effect of a proposed change in the divisional performance measure is assessed.

Finally, the report explains how improved data analysis can help to improve business performance at Flack.

(a) **Performance reporting at Flack**

The current report has a number of strengths and weaknesses. These will be discussed according to whether the report:

- Addresses the mission;
- Contains appropriate information for decision making;
- Shows signs of being short term; and
- Is well presented.

The current mission can be broken down into two parts:

- To be the first choice for customers; and
- To provide the right balance of quality, service and price.

There are three strategies for achieving this mission, reflecting stakeholder concerns:

- Earning customer loyalty;
- Utilising all resources; and
- Serving shareholders' interests.

Addressing the mission

Customer loyalty. The report does not address the first part of the mission (earning customer loyalty). This can only be measured using external data but the report is utilising only Flack's internal data. This part of the mission relates to the first strategy to gain customer loyalty. Customer loyalty could be gauged through repeat purchases or market share information but neither is supplied. This is clearly important to a retailer and may be more easily gathered once the data from the new information system are available for inclusion in this report.

The current report provides no measures of the balance of quality, service and price other than through the historic growth in revenue. It would only be through comparison with competitors or customer survey data that a picture of the mix of these qualities could be gained.

Utilising all resources. The second strategy of utilising resources requires that the key resources be identified. Clearly, the stores themselves (and thus the capital invested) are an important resource and the introduction of the revenue and profit per square metre and comparison with competitors will indicate the efficiency of their use. However, there are likely to be other important resources such as staff and no measure of their performance is offered. Staff costs are not shown in the trading account, although a more sophisticated measure such as revenue per employee is a commonly used metric and would address this.

Serving shareholders' interests. The report is much better on the third strategy of serving shareholder interests as it supplies two helpful measures: total shareholder return and return on capital employed. However, most shareholders will want comparison with benchmark returns within the retail sector and the market more widely, since these represent their alternatives.

Short-termism. The criticism of the company's management as being short term is reflected in the performance reporting. The only benchmarks in the report to compare actual performance against are the budget information and the previous year's figures. There are no longer-term forecasts or information on future capital investment. Also, there are few indicators which would be described as determinants of performance. These are often non-financial and focused on the external business environment (behaviour of customers and competitors).

As already noted, there is a significant gap in the information in the report as it contains no external information. Also, although revenue is broken down into broad product categories, no further information about growth within these categories nor the margins being earned is supplied. As a result, it could be questioned whether this breakdown is worthwhile.

Presentation. In terms of presentation, the data is clear and in a form which would be easily recognisable to those used to reading accounts. However, no narrative commentary is provided which would highlight the key features in the report such as major deviations from the budget or performance well outside industry norms. There should be a comment on each of the five areas within the mission and strategies as well as comments about specific, material issues arising in the period covered. The report could be made easier to read by reducing the volume of numbers present both by cutting out unnecessary measures (see earlier discussion of product categories) and also by rounding all figures to millions.

(b) **New asset utilisation indicators**

Revenue and operating profit per square metre reflect the utilisation of the key capital asset used in their generation (the store). Therefore, they are directly addressing a major part of the aim of utilising all resources; however, they do not address **all** resources which the business uses. There are likely to be significant staff costs and so similar measures of revenue and operating profit per employee could also be introduced in order to reflect these human resources.

	Metro	*Hyper*	*Flack*
Revenue per sq. metre ($)	13,702	13,165	13,251
Operating profit ($'000)	159,058	498,791	657,849
Operating profit per sq. metre ($)	987	592	656

These measures reflect the importance of the use of the store's space which is an area which the business does not give sufficient attention as is reflected in the problems with divisional performance measures. Focus on these measures will require addressing issues of volume of sales and the profitability of those sales. The two types of store at Flack will have different impacts on these measures. For example, the smaller Metro stores may be capable of earning higher margins as they are convenient to customers while selling lower volumes. The Hyper stores may concentrate on selling in volume to customers who come to buy in bulk. However, in terms of the overall performance of the business it is essential that Flack sells in high volumes as it is a low margin business but it must not sacrifice profitability, in effect buying customers' revenue by selling at or near a loss.

(c) **Divisional performance assessment**

The current measure of divisional operating profit reflects the trading in the period under consideration. Profit will link to the whole business's operating profit which is the correct level to reflect the efforts of the divisional managers. However, this measure only indirectly addresses the capital being used by the divisions (depreciation charged to operating profit). This is distorting the behaviour of the divisional managers.

The managers are not investing in refurbishing their stores which is causing the press (and presumably customers) to notice their run-down appearance. This may reduce the depreciation charge against operating profit. They are prioritising new store capital expenditure over the refurbishment since they are not being charged for the use of that capital (financing charges are deducted after operating profit is calculated). This may not be optimal since small spending on existing capital assets often yields higher returns than new spending (which may be subject to greater risks).

The proposal to change the divisional performance measure addresses the issue of not reflecting the capital used since residual income (RI) deducts an imputed interest charge. Divisions can then be set targets in terms of their RI. The difficulties in calculating RI lie in correctly setting the imputed interest rate and calculating the capital being employed by the division. However, since both divisions are types of stores they will have similar assets and so the same rules can be applied to each to fairly calculate the capital used.

An advantage of RI is that the imputed interest rate can be changed to reflect the different risks of the divisions. The two divisions here do not seem to have significant risk differences unless the geographical locations introduce these (city centres and city edges). However, it is worth noting that using RI can discourage investment. As net book values of assets fall over time, RI automatically increases and 'do not invest' could become an attractive option to the managers.

Overall, the proposed change addresses existing problems and would be considered a normal solution to measuring divisional performance in this industry.

(d) **The use of data analysis**

The loyalty card programme collects data from customers' purchases and stores it, and this is currently used for more effective marketing campaigns, targeting customers based on the types of product that they buy. However, the data could provide very valuable information that can be used to manage the business and potentially increase sales.

Data analysis can be categorised under the three headings mentioned by the CEO: descriptive, diagnostic and predictive.

Descriptive – this essentially involves providing summaries of the data in the system. For Flack, this might include information such as average spend per customer per week, and standard deviation of spend. Such analysis could be used for performance evaluation purposes, such as identifying whether customer spend is increasing or decreasing. It could also be used to understand customers better, if additional personal data is collected when customers sign up for the loyalty scheme, such as income levels, socio economic background, and gender, which could help Flack to know which segments of the market are its most important customers.

Diagnostic analysis aims to identify patterns in the data to understand why something happened. The data warehouse will allow data mining for relationships, for example, geographical preferences for products; links between price offers and volumes sold; products which are often bought together; and seasonality of product purchases. These relationships can then be used to address areas such as advertising, product range choices and price offers (eg if a particular price offer did not lead to increased sales of the product in the future). Customer churn (customers that move to competitors) could also be identified by diagnostic data analysis.

Predictive data analysis aims to use data to predict what may happen in the future. The types of analysis used, such as identifying patterns, and data mining, are the same as those used for diagnostic analysis. In order for Flack to be successful, it will need to be able to predict changes on consumer tastes. By examining trends in actual customer sales, Flack will be able to see which items are becoming more popular; and which, less. The company can plan their purchases accordingly. It may also be able to identify changes in customer's life stages, such as marriage or becoming parents, based on changes in their purchasing habits. This information can be used to promote specific products (eg baby foods) to those customers.

In summary, data analysis can help flack to increase sales by understanding their customers better, evaluating performance, evaluating promotions and predicting changes in what their customers want.

45 Monza Pharma

Workbook references

The balanced scorecard (BSC) is discussed in Chapter 12 of the Workbook. The importance of the link between performance measures and objectives is discussed in Chapter 2. Financial performance measures (including ROCE) are discussed in Chapter 6. Costs of quality, and TQM, are discussed in Chapter 10.

Top tips

Part (a). The BSC is one of the key performance measurement frameworks covered in the APM syllabus, so you should have a good understanding of it. However, the requirement here doesn't ask for you to describe the scorecard, or to explain how Monza could use the scorecard. Instead, the CEO asks specifically about the problems of using a scorecard at Monza. In other words, you need to think what the potential problems an organisation could face with using the scorecard, and then assess if these are likely to apply at Monza.

For example, one of the major problems with using the scorecard relate to choosing the measures to use – agreeing how many measures are required, and what the appropriate measures might be. Could this be a problem at Monza? The first paragraph of the scenario tells us that the board members frequently comment that 'it is good to have one easily understood measure for consideration' – but this would no longer be the case if the scorecard is introduced.

Part (b) requires you to evaluate two different sets of measures:

- The current performance measures (ROCE, average cost to develop a new drug, and revenue growth)
- The proposed measures presented by the consulting firm (ROCE, revenue growth, average cost to develop a new drug, training days provided)

As such, it is important that you address both sets of measures – but hopefully you noticed how similar the two sets of measures actually are in the scenario. So, are the measures the consultants have suggested really the most appropriate to use for the scorecard perspectives, or have the consultants simply rolled forward Monza's existing measures as far as possible?

One of the key issues when evaluating performance measures is the extent to which they enable managers to assess how an organisation is performing against its objectives. The opening paragraph of the scenario identifies that Monza's overall objective is to maximise its return to shareholders. Later on, the scenario also identifies that Monza aims to create shareholder value through innovation in drug development, efficiency in drug manufacturing, and success in selling its products. So the question is: how effectively do the performance measures enable Monza to assess how well it is achieving these aims?

Note that the CEO has asked you to 'evaluate' the choices of measures, so if there are some positive aspects to them you should include these in your answer as well as highlighting any problems or limitations with them.

Part (c). In order to 'evaluate the effect' of using the different measurements (as the CEO has asked you to do), you first need to calculate the returns using the different figures possible (as provided in Appendix 1).

At face value, Appendix 1 identifies four profit figures: gross profit, operating profit, profit before tax and profit after tax. However, the figures for the most recent accounting period also include restructuring costs of $482m. So, an additional consideration is the impact this could have on ROCE. Should the profit figures be adjusted to exclude these 'one-off' costs?

The marketing director's reference to 'using equity rather than all capital' should also have been a clue to calculate return on equity (ROE) as well as ROCE.

Remember, however, that the CEO has asked you to 'evaluate the effect' of using the different measures, not simply to calculate different measures. So you also need to consider what each of the measures shows. Think about the differences in the figures used to calculate the measures: for example, ROCE (operating profit/total capital employed) compared to ROE (profit after tax/equity capital).

Comparing the measures in this way is also necessary in order to 'recommend a suitable approach for Monza' – which is the final element of the CEO's request. In order to make a sensible recommendation, you first need to consider the usefulness of the different measures Monza could potentially use (and then recommend the one which is most useful).

As the marking guide indicates, only 4 (out of 11) marks in this requirement are available for calculating ROCE and ROE (with a further 1 mark for calculating gearing). Therefore, in order to pass the requirement, it is essential to make some relevant comments about the different metrics.

Here again, it is also important to think about Monza's underlying objective (to maximise its returns to shareholders). Which of the two measures (ROCE or ROE) is more suitable – and why?

Part (d). A useful starting point here would have been to categorise the information given in Appendix 2 into the different 'costs of quality' (prevention, appraisal, internal failure and external failure) and then to comment on the relative size of the costs in each category.

Even if you couldn't remember the individual 'costs of quality', you should still have been able to distinguish between 'costs' incurred in trying to prevent failure, as opposed to the costs incurred as a result of failure (or problems occurring).

The figures in Appendix 2 themselves should have given you a clue about the balance between prevention and failure, with the costs incurred on batches rejected and customer complaints being clearly the largest figures mentioned (thereby also suggesting that quality problems are having a significant adverse effect on the division's financial performance).

In this context, it should have been clear that the division's current approach to quality is substantially different to a TQM approach – where the focus is on preventing defects, and the ultimate goal is to achieve zero defects. Recognising this contrast should then help you answer the second part of the requirement: how implementing TQM would affect the division (and the way its staff think about quality).

Overall. Remember that you have been asked to write a report, so make sure the style and structure of your answer, as well as its tone, is appropriate for a report.

Examining team's comments

Part (a) asked for an assessment of the problems of using the balanced scorecard. In questions like this, candidates should focus on the theoretical areas where they believe the problems lie, and then to illustrate these by reference to the entity in the scenario. Unfortunately, what many candidates do is address the question by discussing another performance measurement system (which they believe may be more suitable). Making a suggestion as to an alternative may be worth merit, but it does not address the fundamental question asked. It is very important that candidates should know about the challenges arising from different management and control techniques, as well as the potential benefits from using them.

Part (b) asked for an evaluation of the current measurements and alternatives which had been suggested. Most candidates addressed the question asked, but they must appreciate the need to ensure that suggestions are justified and supported. For example, many suggested that 'more non-financial indicators are needed'. However, such comments are not worth merit unless they are supported by reference to points such as achievement of some of the company's specific objectives. When making comments like this, candidates should ask themselves: why is that relevant? Or, how/why would it benefit the company?

Part (c) was answered very poorly, as candidates did not demonstrate the technical knowledge that is expected at this level with regard to the composition of the measures of performance. At APM, candidates have to be able to interpret and discuss the results that measures are producing. Too many candidates described the measurements rather than evaluating their impact or usefulness. Candidates need to consider why some measures may be more appropriate than others. For example, which costs might one measure include that another doesn't? And why might this be significant in terms of performance measurement and management?

Marking guide	Marks
(a) Problems with using the BSC	
Up to 2 marks per relevant point, specifically related to using the scorecard at Monza	
Maximum for part (a): up to 8 marks	
	7
(b) Evaluating choice of current and proposed performance measures	
Evaluating current measures – 1 mark per relevant point, up to 6 marks	
Evaluating proposed measures – 1 mark per relevant point, up to 9 marks	
Maximum for part (b): up to 12 marks	
	12
(c) Variation in calculating return on investment	
For calculating appropriate ROCE figures (including ROCE adjusted for restructuring costs) – up to 3 marks	
ROE calculation – 1 mark	
Gearing – 1 mark	
Maximum for calculations – up to 5 marks	
For discussion of ROCE – 1 mark per point, up to 5 marks	
For discussion of ROE – 1 mark per point, up to 3 marks	
For justified recommendation of a suitable measure – 1 mark	
Maximum for part (c): up to 11 marks	
	11
(d) Quality costs and TQM in the Manufacturing Division	
Discussion of categories of quality cost – up to 2 marks	
Calculation/identification of quality costs – up to 3 marks	
Discussion of results – up to 3 marks	
Discussing how implementing TQM would affect the division – up to 5 marks	
Maximum for part (d): up to 10 marks	
	10

Professional skills

Communication

- General report format and structure (use of headings/sub-headings and an introduction)
- Style, language and clarity (appropriate layout and tone of report response, presentation of calculations, appropriate use of the CBE tools)
- Effectiveness of communication (answer is relevant, specific rather than general and focused to the requirement)

Analysis and evaluation

- Use of information provided to perform a suitable/comprehensive evaluation of quality costs
- Appropriate use of the data to support discussion and draw appropriate conclusions
- Demonstration of reasoned and balanced judgement

Marking guide	Marks
• Demonstration of ability to consider relevant factors applicable to Monza Co's situation	
Scepticism	
• Effective challenge and critical assessment	
• Demonstration of effective challenge of information supplied / identification of missing information	
Commercial acumen	
• Effective use of examples and/or calculations from the scenario information and other practical considerations related to the context to illustrate points being made	
• Demonstrating an awareness of organisational and external factors	
• Points made are practical and plausible, and commercially viable in the context of Monza Co's situation	
Maximum	10
Total	50

Report

To: The board of Monza

From: Performance management expert

Date: [Today's date]

Subject: Performance measurement and management issues at Monza

Introduction

This report addresses the problems of using the BSC within Monza. The current and proposed performance measures are evaluated and the main current measure is discussed in detail. Quality costs and the new quality programme at the Manufacturing Division are analysed.

(a) **Problems with using the BSC**

The BSC provides no aggregate or single summary measure of performance (in the way that cash flow is used in a value-based approach, or in the way that ROCE is currently used at Monza). Also, there is no simple, direct link between the BSC measures and shareholder value, the main objective of Monza.

The measures in the scorecard can conflict; for example, cost controls (financial perspective) can obstruct the investment needed in order to speed up manufacturing processes (internal business perspective). Overall, the measures should seek to align with the fundamental need to create shareholder value.

It can be difficult to select measures. In particular, there is the danger of losing sight of key information in a plethora of indicators. This may be an issue for Monza as it has only had three indicators in the past and this will now increase significantly – a potential of 12, if there is one for each level of management (strategic, tactical, operational) for each of the four perspectives of the BSC.

There must be management commitment to the change to the scorecard. In particular, there must not be a return to a focus on the financial measures which have been used in the past at Monza. Management should acquire the expertise for understanding non-financial measures through training.

There are potentially significant costs in collecting the additional information which will be needed for the new performance measures. Many of the measures will be non-financial and so new information systems will be required to collect and record the data.

(b) **Choice of current and proposed performance measures**

Current measures

The current measures are all historic, financial ones and so the BSC approach will bring a longer-term view by using non-financial measures which consider those factors which might drive future growth, for example, those in the learning and growth perspective.

The current measures do not directly link to shareholder value which appears to be the overall aim of the company. A measure such as economic value added would do this more effectively.

The three measures do give a broad view of financial performance, though. ROCE is a widely used measure which it should be possible to benchmark against competitors.

As far as the divisions are concerned, there is a measure of success in selling through revenue growth, though this may be due to not only the Sales Division but also the drugs brought to market by the Development Division.

Average cost to develop a new drug is a financial measure of the Development Division's performance but this does not measure its aim of innovation in development. Indeed, this measure may conflict with that aim, as cost control of development may hinder innovative thinking. It would appear more appropriate to have a cost control measure associated with manufacturing, as its goal is to be more efficient. The performance of the Manufacturing Division is only measured indirectly through its effect on the financial performance of the company as a whole.

Consultants' proposed measures

The suggested measures do not seem to deviate much from the existing measures, though there may be an advantage in this as the new system would use existing information systems and known measures in that case. However, this advantage is secondary to the need to find measures which will drive useful performance in the four perspectives.

The proposed measures from the consultants' interim report mostly fit within the standard four perspectives of the BSC, although revenue growth is more appropriate as a measure from the financial perspective. Customer perspective measures should focus on the strategies which will achieve success in the eyes of the customers rather than just measuring the results of those strategies. Examples of this would be measuring the efficacy of the drugs which are developed by Monza or the reputation of Monza's medicines among the medical community.

Taking the others in turn, ROCE does not seem to be directly linked to shareholder value as, for example, economic value added or net present value would be. ROCE considers the performance over the whole capital base while the shareholders will be more directly concerned with returns on their equity investment. As a profit-based measure, ROCE may also be failing to target cash generation which is ultimately driving dividend payments and value creation for shareholders.

As already indicated, cost control in business processes is important but other measures of success such as time to market for the development of new products and quality initiatives should also be considered.

The fourth perspective (learning) is particularly relevant to a high-technology firm such as Monza. There will be considerable competitive advantage in having a highly skilled workforce. However, the measure proposed is imprecise as it values all training days, whether for knowledge workers or unskilled labourers, as equally valuable. Measures of the number of innovations within each division may be appropriate as these will be qualitatively different (new compounds developed, manufacturing quality improvements and sales techniques/initiatives developed).

Overall, the initial proposed set of measures does appear limited and does not address the overall aim of Monza or the problem of the narrowness of the existing set of measures.

(c) **Variations in calculating return on capital**

	ROCE	Return on equity
Using:		
Operating profit (W1)	18%	
Operating profit before restructuring (W2)	23%	
Profit after tax (W3)		97%

Workings for calculations

Workings

Operating profit ($m):	1,811
Capital employed ($m):	1,161 + 8,739 = 9,900
ROCE:	1,811/9,900 = 18.3%

Operating profit ($m):	1,811
Add back restructuring ($m):	482
Operating profit before restructuring ($m):	2,293
Capital employed ($m):	9,900
ROCE:	2,293/9,900 = 23.2%

Profit after tax ($m):	1,126
Shareholders' equity ($m):	1,161
Return on equity:	1,126/1,161 = 97.0%

ROCE is normally calculated by dividing operating profit by capital employed (debt and equity). The calculations above illustrate the possibilities of using the different return (profit) and capital figures available.

The ROCE figure should not use gross profit, as this ignores the operating costs not directly attached to sales, and at Monza these will include significant overheads from the Drug Development and Manufacturing Divisions which are relevant to overall performance. The return figure should match with the capital used to generate that return. As ROCE is calculated based on the return on total capital, it should not include financing costs, and so profit before and after tax are not consistent with this view.

The one area that could be discussed is whether to include the one-off costs of restructuring in performance. It would probably be best to disclose both figures to the company's stakeholders and to identify how any competitor would perform such a calculation for benchmarking.

A suitable approach for Monza

ROE may be a more suitable measure given Monza's focus on shareholder (not debt provider) performance.

In this case, the relevant return figure is the profit after tax as this is the return available to shareholders after the debt providers have been paid. The figure here (97%) is very large. This is due partly to the fact that the capital figures used in these calculations are from the financial statements and are not market values. (Market values of equity and debt would give a more accurate measure of performance both for ROCE and ROE.)

Another reason why the ROE is large compared to ROCE is that Monza is highly geared (88%). ROE, therefore, demonstrates the benefit of the chosen capital structure of Monza.

Overall, therefore, ROE is a better measure than ROCE as it fits with the prioritisation of shareholders as opposed to all capital providers.

> **Tutorial note.** Although we have recommended ROE, using ROE could have the effect of encouraging the continued heavy use of debt finance. (If a company's gearing ratio becomes too high, this can be a problem, not a benefit.)
>
> By contrast, ROCE does not reward the excessive use of debt finance, so you could have added this point as a word of caution alongside the recommendation.

(d) **Quality costs and TQM in the Manufacturing Division**

Quality costs are usually broken into four categories:

- Prevention costs, which relate to avoiding producing defective items in the first place;
- Appraisal costs, which relate to ensuring that the products produced meet an acceptable standard;
- Costs of internal failure, which relate to products that fail appraisal and how these are handled; and
- Costs of external failure, which relate to products that fail the standard but are still shipped to customers.

At Monza, for the most recent period, the following quality costs have been identified:

Prevention costs: $8m (training)

Appraisal costs: $12m (product testing)

Costs of internal failure: $13m (batches rejected)

Costs of external failure: $27m = $5m (fines) + $22m (discounts for late delivery)

Total raw material costs might hide relevant quality costs if the company is buying higher quality material to prevent problems of quality; however, this cannot be quantified in this scenario.

It can be seen that there were $40m of failure costs (internal and external) in the period but only $8m was spent on prevention (training). A 10% improvement in the failures could generate $4m in cost savings. In the light of this, the budget for improvements to production which prevent such failures could be significantly expanded. The analysis of quality costs should help to emphasise the importance of prevention by showing its financial value and this could be an important argument in favour of a TQM approach.

Impact of TQM on Manufacturing Division

TQM focuses on the customer perspective and the need for each part of the organisation to avoid defects in the chain of production.

Prevention is the key to improvement and so management should focus on avoiding defects through training and improved process design rather than appraisal. All employees must accept personal responsibility for their work and act to remove defects from production. Quality certification programmes are often instituted in order to encourage the focus on 'zero defects'. Quality circles may be formed as small, autonomous groups aimed at devising solutions to quality problems.

46 Dargeboard Services

Workbook references

The performance hierarchy linking mission statements and performance indicators is discussed in Chapter 2 of the Workbook. Reward schemes are discussed in Chapter 11, as is the building block model.

Top tips

Part (a)

A mission statement identifies an organisation's key purpose. By doing so, it can help to identify – at a high level – the aspects of performance which are important for an organisation, and therefore those aspects according to which its performance needs to be measured.

This question looks at this link between mission and performance measures, and specifically – as identified in the fifth paragraph of the scenario – whether the current set of KPIs measure the achievement of DS's mission.

The fifth paragraph of the scenario also provides a clear instruction pointer for how to structure your answer: 'by showing how each [KPI] links to all or part of the mission'. In other words, you should use each KPI as a sub-heading, and then evaluate the extent to which it links to the mission, and therefore whether monitoring it will help DS's management assess if the company is achieving its mission.

Note the CEO has asked you to 'evaluate' the links, so you should try to consider both the strengths of the KPIs (where they are clearly linked to the mission) as well as their weaknesses (where they are not linked to the mission). One important question here could also be: are all the elements of the mission (given in the second paragraph of the scenario) covered by the current KPIs?

Importantly, though, note the instruction in the fifth paragraph of the scenario, that the CEO 'does not want suggestions of new indicators'. Therefore, if you identify limitation or problems with the current measures, you need to highlight these, but you shouldn't then suggest alternative measures which could replace them, because there would be no marks available for doing so.

Examining team's comments for part (a)

This part of the question required a common task (in a performance management exam) of identifying the mission from the scenario. Candidates were good at repeating the mission from the question, but few appeared to appreciate the structure of the mission, and how certain goals were subsidiary to an overall aim. However, most scored reasonably well, as they linked the indicators given to the parts of the mission.

Part (b)

As with part (b), your approach to part (b) should also be to work through each of the indicators in turn, assessing the assumptions and definitions used in calculating them.

The sixth paragraph of the scenario provides some important context for your assessment. There has been a suggestion that DS is producing biased results, designed to mislead the markets, and in turn to boost the share price and the value of senior management's shares. As such, a key part of your answer needs to be an assessment of whether the indicators are being manipulated to make DS's performance appear better than it is, in the way the press report is suggesting.

Note the number of marks available for this part of the question. There are 12 marks available, and there are 6 KPIs to assess. This should be a clue that, to score well in this part of the question, you can't just say there are problems with the assumptions or definitions; you need to go on and explain why this is the case, particularly, in relation to them making the results misleading.

Examining team's comments for part (b)

This part of the question required a detailed consideration of how performance measures are put together. However, candidates' responses tended to be very limited, with many candidates only scoring a single mark per indicator because they failed to develop their answers sufficiently. For example, it was often clear that a candidate had correctly identified that there was a problem with the calculation of a particular indicator, but very few candidates then attempted to quantity the impact of this problem.

Part (c)

A key issue when answering this part of the question is that you need to evaluate the dashboard in the specific context of DS, rather than evaluating performance reports in general terms.

For example, DS's mission says the company aims to provide 'world-class services' but does the information in the dashboard provide any indication about how well DS is performing against its competitors, or against best-in-class service providers?

Similarly, we know DS offers a range of different activities to its clients (cleaning, security, etc), but does the report provide any indication of how each of the different areas is performing?

Once again, note the CEO has asked you to 'evaluate', so you should try to give a balanced assessment of the dashboard – highlighting areas where it helps managers assess performance effectively, as well as its potential problems or limitations.

Part (d)

Although the requirement refers only to 'the building block model, you are not required to give an explanation of the whole model here. In the scenario, you are told the CEO specifically wants you to explain what is meant by results and determinants (in the model), and how the dimensions link to standards and targets. As these are the issues which the CEO has asked you to explain, these are the only issues which you should focus on in your answer.

Examining team's comments for part (d)

Responses to this question were generally poor, as many candidates ignored the detailed requirement of the CEO and provided a generic answer that irrelevantly described the whole model.

Part (e)

The sequence of requirements (d) and (e) and the context described in the final paragraph of the scenario should help provide you with some pointers for how to assess the two reward schemes.

The CEO is considering the Building Block model as a way of improving performance measurement at DS. So a good way of assessing the schemes could be to assess how well they display the characteristics of effective standards or rewards (as identified in the Building Block model).

For example, the Building Block model identifies that effective standards should be fair and achievable; and, in order for performance measure systems to operate successfully, rewards should be clear, motivating and controllable. How well do the two proposed schemes illustrate these characteristics?

The examining team's comments confirm that this was the expected approach here:

Examining team's comments for part (e)

This part of the question was generally well answered, with many candidates using the Building Block model concepts to good effect by illustrating how the two reward schemes demonstrated the ideal features from the model.

Report format

Finally, note that you were asked to write a report, and remember that there are four 'professional marks' available for the quality of your report. As is the case in all report questions, markers are looking for suitable report headings, a brief introduction, a logical structure to the report – signposted by the use of headings – and a clear, concise style.

Marking guide	Marks
(a) For breaking down the mission statement and identifying the key elements of DS's mission – Up to 2 marks For evaluating the links between the KPIs and the mission statement – 1 mark per relevant point Total for part (a): up to 8 marks	8
(b) Up to 3 marks for relevant comments on each indicator: • Operating profit margin • Secured revenue • Management retention • Order book • Organic revenue growth • ROCE Total for part (b): up to 12 marks	12
(c) 1 mark per relevant point about DS's performance dashboard Total for part (c): up to 8 marks	8
(d) For explanation of results and determinants – 1 mark per relevant point – Up to 2 marks For explanation of standards and targets, and key characteristics (ownership; achievable targets; fair): – 1 mark per relevant point – Up to 3 marks Total for part (d): up to 4 marks	4
(e) Up to 2 marks for general discussion of assessment or reward schemes For assessment of Scheme 1; 1 mark per relevant point – Up to 4 marks For assessment of Scheme 2; 1 mark per relevant point – Up to 4 marks Total for part (e): up to 8 marks	8

Professional skills

Communication

- General report format and structure (use of headings/sub-headings and an introduction)
- Style, language and clarity (appropriate layout and tone of report response, presentation of calculations, appropriate use of the CBE tools)
- Effectiveness of communication (answer is relevant, specific rather than general and focused to the requirement)

Analysis and evaluation

- Appropriate use of the data to support discussion and draw appropriate conclusions
- Demonstration of reasoned and balanced judgement
- Demonstration of ability to consider relevant factors applicable to Dargeboard Co's situation

Scepticism

- Effective challenge and critical assessment
- Demonstration of effective challenge of information supplied / identification of missing information

Marking guide | **Marks**

Commercial acumen

- Effective use of examples and/or calculations from the scenario information and other practical considerations related to the context to illustrate points being made
- Demonstrating an awareness of organisational and external factors
- Recommendations are practical and plausible, and commercially viable in the context of Dargeboard Co's situation

Maximum	10
Total	50

Report

To: Board of DS

From: Accountant

Date: [Today's date]

Subject: Strategic performance reporting and reward systems at DS

Introduction

This report assesses the coherence of the choice of key performance indicators (KPIs) with the mission of DS, followed by the assumptions used to calculate them. Other aspects of the presentation of the dashboard report are then evaluated. Finally, an overview of the operation of the building block model and an assessment of two proposed reward schemes are provided.

(a) **Linking the mission to the current KPIs**

The mission statement can be broken into several parts. The principal aim is maintainable, profitable growth, and this is supported by three further goals: developing the best talent; providing world-class services; and being efficient.

The KPIs are linked to elements of this statement as follows:

- **Operating profit margin** shows that the organisation is profitable and also as a margin, it indicates efficiency in cost control.
- **Secured revenue** indicates the amount of revenue which is contracted and so has greater likelihood of being earned. Contracts give an indication of maintainability here only in the short term, however.
- **Management retention** links to the need for best talent though it does not measure developing that talent.
- **Order book** shows the maintainability into the future of the business though it does not show the average length of the contracts.
- **Organic revenue growth** shows historic growth and may indicate what the management are capable of achieving in the future.
- **ROCE** demonstrates the efficiency of profit-generation from the capital base of DS.

None of the measures are external (looking at the competitive environment) and so it is not possible to indicate if DS has 'world-class services'.

(b) **Assumptions underlying the current KPI calculations**

Every KPI will involve some assumptions in its calculations. The aim of this section is to highlight how each indicator could be manipulated to show a better picture so that the business can avoid this in the future and the subsequent bad image portrayed in the investing community.

Operating profit margin is a standard performance measure and the only area which can be questioned is the categorisation of costs below this line; for example, the movement of

ANSWERS

operating costs into 'exceptional costs' below this line in order to artificially inflate this indicator. If the $55m reorganisation cost was included in overall operating profit, which was $91m (= 5.9% of $1,542m), then the business would show an operating margin of 2.3%. The catering business would show a loss of $39m.

Secured revenue represents long-term recurring revenue streams. A good picture will show a high percentage of secured revenue but will be below 100% so that management can indicate that budget targets are being exceeded. It is worrying that the budget is completed well after the year start as this may indicate such manipulation. If the original budgeted revenue figure is used then the secured revenue for 20X6 was 82%.

Management retention only includes retention of employees on full-time contracts which at 65% of all managers excludes a material number. Poor treatment (and thus retention) of part-time managers is therefore ignored. This may be a particular issue for managers with young children who often take advantage of such contracts.

Order book is a total 'value' figure, but is this the cash or present value figure? By choosing cash value of the contract, this will give a much larger figure than the discounted present value, especially where some revenues will not be received for ten years.

Organic revenue growth is calculated by using the total revenue figure as reported in the accounts. The main purpose of stating organic is that it is growth from within the organisation as it stands and so acquisitions should be ignored. Currently organic revenue growth is 7.2% (this is given), so the 20X6 revenue is $1,542m / 1.072 = $1,438m. Excluding the impact of the $48m from acquisitions (Note 7) means that organic revenue in 20X6 is $1,542m – $48m = $1,494m. This means that organic revenue growth would fall to ($1,494m / $1,438m) -1 = 0.039, ie from 7.2% overall to a less impressive 3.9%.

ROCE. Capital employed is being calculated using the statement of financial position figures which may exclude many intangible assets. As such it may overemphasise the tangible capital base which is not as important in a service business such as DS. The focus on this measure can lead to sub-optimal decisions.

(c) **Evaluation of the strategic performance dashboard**

The current information used by the board is both financial and non-financial allowing different elements of the mission to be measured. However, none of the measures are external, looking at the competitive environment, and so it is not possible to indicate if DS has 'world-class services'. Also, the measures do not focus on shareholder concerns, although the mission statement indicates that they are the principal stakeholders. Other measures beyond ROCE might have been expected given that priority, such as EPS or dividend per share. No breakdown of ROCE is provided for each business unit, this may be due to the lack of availability of capital employed figures for the units but it does seem an odd inconsistency since ROCE is the best KPI provided for shareholder use.

No revenue figures are given and as most figures are ratios it is not possible to gauge the absolute scale of the business. It is particularly surprising that an absolute profit measure is not included on the dashboard given the importance of profitable growth to shareholders.

Generally, there is a lack of external figures to allow benchmarking or the assessment of the competitive position of DS.

The breakdown of results into business sectors will help to judge the performance of the managers of those units but they may not be comparable; for example, comparing building services and security, it seems that building services is growing more rapidly but with weaker margins. Also, it may be that the employment market is different between each sector and so no comparison of management retention figures is sensible. Again, it may be helpful to provide either an external benchmark through industry averages or an internal one through a historic trend for these sector specific indicators.

The report does have good qualities as it is brief and clearly presented. The use of ratios makes for easy understanding.

(d) **The building block model**

The model takes the important step of distinguishing within the dimensions of performance between what is the desired outcome (results) and what are the drivers of those results (determinants). It then highlights the need to measure both of these within the performance reporting systems of an organisation.

The standards are the target level for the specific measures chosen for each dimension appropriate to an employee's performance. Employees must take ownership, so they need to be persuaded to accept the target and be motivated by the targets. Targets must be achievable and so challenge the employee without being viewed as impossible to achieve and therefore demotivating. For example, they must take account of external market conditions beyond the control of the employee, but this can be managed by benchmarking against an industry average. Targets must be fair; for example, different businesses within DS must be measured against their respective sector (catering, security, etc).

(e) **Assessment of the proposed reward schemes**

As the board is already considering using the Building Block model, it is appropriate to outline the main criteria in the model for reward schemes.

Rewards must be:

- Clear, that is, understood by the managers;
- Motivating, that is, of value to the employee; and
- Controllable, that is, related to their area of responsibility.

Scheme 1

The scheme has the benefit of continuing with the successful policy of offering an equity share in DS. It continues to utilise the knowledge of the line manager in performing the appraisal. It attempts to address a problem of the current scheme – that the breadth of the categories gives the line manager scope to continue to show favouritism to specific employees. The fact that the line manager's own bonus will be affected by how well they perform the appraisals should help to reduce the risk of favouritism, and improve the quality of the appraisal process. The fact that the new scheme also sets an expectation for the distribution of bonuses should bring greater transparency to the process. For example, if 50% of a manager's staff receive no bonus (rather than the expected 20%) this could indicate the manager is being too harsh in their assessment of their staff. Having an expectation of the distribution of bonus shares could also mean that forecasting staff costs will be simpler.

However, this scheme does not address the problem that the appraisal categories are vague and do not reflect the KPIs of DS. It also could create a problem, as line managers will give bonuses according to the stated expectation – for example, even where all staff are, in absolute terms, performing brilliantly, only 20% will get the maximum. Also, there is no mention of the scale of the scheme bonuses as there is for Scheme 2, where the maximum bonus available is stated as 50% of basic salary.

Scheme 2

Scheme 2 loses a key benefit of the current scheme in not rewarding in shares; however, cash is an acceptable alternative. Cash may well be a preferred option for the managers as it offers a certain value to them. This form of benefit also reduces the desire to manipulate share prices. It sets standards based on the KPIs and so should lead to greater focus by each employee on the goals of DS. Involvement of both strategic and line management in this process should lead to a better set of measures being used.

It is not clear, however, why five targets are being chosen. This seems an arbitrary figure and it may be more sensible to suggest a range from three to six (the number of strategic KPIs) to be decided by the managers in consultation. The size of the maximum reward seems likely to motivate but the equal weighting for each heading may not be effective. It requires that, say, operating profit margin has the same importance as management retention.

47 Thyme Engine Products

Workbook references

Performance reports are discussed in Chapter 5 of the Workbook, as is the role of the management accounting in providing information for integrated reporting. Target costing, total quality management (TQM) and costs of quality are all discussed in Chapter 10.

Top tips

Part (a). There is a technical article on ACCA's website (also mentioned in the Workbook) about 'Reports for Performance Management' which highlights four basis criteria which can be used to evaluate an organisation's performance reports:

- **Purpose** – What is the purpose of the report? Does the report provide information which is relevant to the organisation's performance against its mission or objectives?
- **Audience** – Who is the report produced for? Is it appropriate for its audience and their requirements?
- **Information** – What information is needed – financial and non-financial; quantitative and qualitative? Does the report provide the information which is needed to fulfil its purpose and satisfy its audience?
- **Layout** – Does the report make it clear for readers to identify the most important information?

Although you didn't have to use these criteria to answer the requirement, they could have given you a useful framework for answering this question. For example, does the report provide information which is relevant to its objectives and strategies (which are 'very similar' to Thyme's, as described in the first paragraph of the scenario)? Also, Thyme's board need information for 'planning and controlling', so does the report provide information which support both of those aspects of performance management?

Note, however, that the CEO doesn't simply ask you to evaluate the dashboard, but rather to evaluate why it was 'award winning'. Whereas an evaluation of the dashboard would require you to look at its advantages and disadvantages, your focus here should be primarily on its advantages (which have made it award winning).

Also, note that the CEO has mentioned that they think 'there may be some useful, specific comments to make about the contents of the dashboard given Thyme's recent problems.' The dashboard in Appendix 1 is for the award-winning company (not Thyme) so an issue to consider here is whether Thyme should include some additional measures on its dashboard in relation to the specific issues it has faced.

Part (b). The fourth paragraph of the scenario tells you that the CEO wants to know 'how integrated reporting might have an impact on the type of information prepared by the company's management accountants.'

As such, a sensible way to approach this question will be to think how the information required for integrated reporting differs from that used in traditional annual reporting – for example, in relation to the 'six capitals'. The management accountant's role will be to provide the information – but, as different information is required what impact might this have on the accountant? For example, will changes be required to the information systems to enable different aspects of performance to be measured?

Part (c). There are two elements to the CEO's request ('calculate...' and 'comment...') and it is important that you address both of them in your answer.

The requirement is worth 10 marks in total, but the marking guide shows it would be possible to score up to 6 marks for calculations. These should have been relatively easy marks.

However, once you've done the calculations don't just ignore them. Although the CEO hasn't specifically asked you to comment on the cost gap, it would be helpful to think what the implications of it are – in the context of the TQM approach at Thyme. For example, there is currently a cost gap, but this is a new product. As Thyme gains experience in producing it, might its costs per unit come down?

At the same time, think about the key features of the TQM approach – one of which is continuous improvement. How does this link to the idea of closing a cost gap?

Part (d). Although there is only a single question requirement – 'costs of quality' – there are four different elements to what the CEO has asked you to do in the scenario, so to score well here it is important that you address all of these:

- Categorise the quality costs
- Calculate the costs in each category
- Suggest cost areas to be examined
- Evaluate the relative importance of each cost category

The first element here is essentially a test of knowledge. What are the four categories of quality cost? (The final paragraph of the scenario identifies one of these for you – prevention costs – which should help jog your memory as to what the other three categories are.)

The second element should also be relatively straightforward: identifying which category the costs in Appendix 3 relate to, and then calculating the total for that category. Don't overlook the 'Notes' though: the cost of buying higher quality raw materials is also a quality cost, even though it is not included in the list of quality costs identified in the current year.

When answering the third element ('Suggest cost areas to be examined'), it is vital to remember exactly what you have been told in the scenario: '[the CEO] is happy that prevention costs are complete, but is worried some costs for the other three categories are missing, and needs suggestions of cost areas to be examined to identify these missing items.' Consequently, your suggestions should relate to appraisal, internal failure, and external failure; not prevention. One approach here could be to think about the costs which have already been identified in each category, and then think if there are any costs which might be associated with these, but which have not yet been identified. For example, although costs of re-inspection after repairs arising from final assembly testing are included, the costs of those repairs themselves don't appear to be.

When considering the final element of the requirement – the relative importance of each cost category – remember the context of the scenario. Thyme adopts a TQM approach, and one of the key aims of TQM is to get things right first time. Which of the costs of quality is likely to be most important in helping to get things right first time?

Overall. Remember that you have been asked to write a report, so make sure the style and structure of your answer, as well as its tone, is appropriate for a report.

Examining team's comments

Part (a). Similar questions to this have been examined in previous exam and, as such, candidates tended to score relatively well here. However, a significant number of candidates provided very superficial answers; for example, stating that 'there is not a lot of detail in the report'. This could be an advantage or a disadvantage, depending on the users of the report, so it is essential to explain why something is good or bad. Also, this particular question required candidates to focus on the elements of the report that were particularly good, so parts of answers that discussed negative aspects scored very few marks.

Part (b). This question explored the role of the management accountant in providing information for integrated reporting, so it was essential for candidates to relate their answers to integrated reporting. Many candidates did not seem familiar with this type of report, and so discussed – in general terms – changes to the role of the management accountant in recent years. The examining team would like to remind candidates that technical articles are made available on the ACCA website to assist candidates in their studies, and candidates should read these articles. Several of the topics examined in recent exam sittings, including integrated reporting, have been discussed in technical articles.

Part (c). The calculations in this section were performed well by most candidates. However, we would remind candidates to present calculations in a logical order to allow the marking team to award marks for method even if the final answer is incorrect. Good candidates also went on to discuss the results well.

Part (d). Many candidates performed well on the calculations although some were not able to categorise the costs correctly. Also, candidates should pay close attention to all the verbs within a requirement. This part of the question specifically asked for four things (categories, calculate, suggest and evaluate) and candidates' performance would be improved if their answers addressed each of these separately.

Marking guide	Marks
(a) 1 mark per relevant feature of the dashboard which helps to make it award-winning, with additional marks (1 mark per relevant point) for illustrating these features.	
Relevant features (and supporting illustrations) include, but are not limited to:	
Achievement of the strategies of the business	
Breaking down the strategy, and linking to measures in the dashboard	
Balanced view	
Financial and non-financial; different perspectives; results and determinants; internal and external views	
Planning and control	
Short and long-term views; forward focus for planning; trends/budgets for control	
Presentation	
Brevity; narrative points; link to other strategic issues; eg risks	
Specific issues at Thyme not measured in the sample template – up to 3 marks	
Total for part (a): up to 13 marks	
	13
(b) Description of Integrated Reporting – up to 2 marks	
Impact on management accountant – up to 5 marks	
Total for part (b): up to 6 marks	
	5
(c) Calculations: 1 mark for each of the following:	
Target cost: 2,125	
Production costs: 1,825	
Design and development: 100	
Sales and marketing: 500	
Target cost gap: 300 (12% of current cost)	
Current profit margin: $0.075m (or 3%)	
Discussion of cost savings – 1 mark	
Definition of target costing – 1 mark	
Definition of TQM – up to 1 mark	
Fit between target costing approach and TQM – up to 3 marks	
Maximum for part (c): up to 10 marks	
	10
(d) Definition of quality costs – up to 2 marks	
Calculations: 1 mark for cost in each category (either absolute value or % of revenue)	
Prevention: $139m, 1.21%	
Appraisal: $138m, 1.20%	

Marking guide	Marks
Costs of internal failure: $95m, 0.83%	
Costs of external failure: $279m, 2.43%	
Total: $651m, 5.66%	
Discussion of results – up to 2 marks	
Identification of other quality costs which appear to be omitted – up to 6 marks	
Relative importance of categories of quality costs – up to 4 marks	
Maximum for part (d): up to 12 marks	
	12

Professional skills

Communication

- General report format and structure (use of headings/sub-headings and an introduction)
- Style, language and clarity (appropriate layout and tone of report response, presentation of calculations, appropriate use of the CBE tools)
- Effectiveness of communication (answer is relevant, specific rather than general and focused to the requirement)
- Adherence to the details of the proposal in the scenario

Analysis and evaluation

- Use of information provided to perform a suitable/comprehensive evaluation of the costs of quality
- Appropriate use of the data to support discussion and draw appropriate conclusions
- Demonstration of reasoned and balanced judgement / assessment of the dashboard
- Demonstration of ability to consider relevant factors applicable to Thyme Co's situation

Scepticism

- Effective challenge and critical assessment
- Demonstration of effective challenge of information supplied / identification of missing information

Commercial acumen

- Effective use of examples and/or calculations from the scenario information and other practical considerations related to the context to illustrate points being made
- Demonstrating an awareness of organisational and external factors
- Recommendations are practical and plausible, and commercially viable in the context of Thyme Co's situation

Maximum	10
Total	50

Report

To: CEO of Thyme
From: Accountant
Date: [Today's date]
Subject: Reporting performance and quality issues at Thyme

Introduction

This report analyses the positive features of the award-winning dashboard identifying some areas which specifically apply to Thyme. Next, the role of the management accountant in providing information for integrated reporting is explained. Then, the target cost gap for the new engine is calculated and an evaluation is provided of the use of this target cost within the TQM approach. Finally, issues associated with the costs of quality at Thyme are addressed.

(a) **Positive features of the award-winning dashboard**

The following are features of the dashboard which will have impressed the assessors' minds when making the award. They are placed in a priority order of most important first, and then there are a few specific comments about the possible use of such a template at Thyme.

Achievement of the objectives and strategies of the business

The critical measure of whether the dashboard is fit for its purpose is whether it answers the question: has the business achieved its key objectives?

The dashboard measures all of the key objectives of the business growth of the firm:

- Shareholder wealth and returns through EVA™ and TSR; and
- Growth through revenue and market share growth.

It also measures the strategies used to achieve these results:

- World-class engineering to design engines through the class leading design specifications;
- High quality production through fault rates in manufacturing and delivery; and
- Customer service through those same fault rates and market share (an indirect indicator).

Balanced view

The report presents a balanced view of the business's performance. It deals with various perspectives (shareholders (TSR), customers (market share), internal business (fault rates) and innovation (design position)) which are used in the balanced scorecard approach. This is also achieved using both internal and external data (fault rates and average sector growth). It presents both the results and the determinants of those results by giving financial and non-financial indicators. For example, revenue growth will be driven by the customers' view of product and service, so design and manufacturing quality measures are important. Short- and longer-term measures are given such as profit margin and economic value added.

Planning and control

The dashboard should allow the board to perform both its vital functions in planning and controlling the business. The forecasts for next year (budgets) are given and also, as noted above, there are non-financial determinants of performance such as design and customer service which will drive the future short-term competitive position of the business.

The control activities of the board are served by providing historic trends and also current budget variances. The major headings are provided for under the financial headings with activity measured by revenue, profit by the margin and shareholder wealth by economic value added.

Presentation

The dashboard is kept brief as the board will have an opportunity prior to the board meeting to use it to identify issues requiring further analysis at the meeting. There is a short narrative commentary which deals with the major commercial points arising from the dashboard and also, gives further external market data as context for the figures (eg average sector growth). It is also worth noting that the narrative picks up on strategic issues of risk and opportunity which can be more difficult to capture in numerical form. Hence, the commentary appears appropriate to assist in an annual review of the business.

Specific issues at Thyme

There are certain issues particular to Thyme which may be added to the example dashboard, though if these are deemed short term, then they may not necessarily appear on this main dashboard view. The example dashboard does not show measures of cash flow performance (such as free cash flow generated) nor gearing ratio, although both of these measures would be important for future fund raising. There are no measures associated with governance and ethics which in the light of the bribery scandal may have a higher priority at Thyme. Ethical training costs may give a measure of this area.

(b) **Integrated reporting**

There is no standard format for integrated reporting. However, there are changes in focus of the company's reporting which will require the input of the management accountants of that business. Integrated reporting has a focus on opportunities and risk, how resources are allocated and performance both recent historic and expected in the future. There are six capitals involved in value creation including traditional tangible and financial assets but also including human, intellectual, environmental and social assets.

For the management accountant, these newer forms of capital will require information systems capable of capturing and processing such non-financial measures. The forward-looking nature of such reporting will require more information of a forecast nature (with the accompanying requirement to understand their estimating assumptions). The more strategic view which integrated reporting intends to give also requires reporting on factors which drive long-term performance.

A key part of the integrated report is linking performance to strategic goals and the ability to create value. This will require a less structured and more contingent approach to reporting. In other words, pro-forma reporting must be better tailored to the specific business's situation. However, it is considered a key requirement of such reporting that it is concise and so the management accountant must help to ensure that only the key information is reported.

It can be seen that the dashboard discussed in the above section of this report achieves many of these requirements.

(c) **New jet engine: target costing and TQM**

	$'000	
Target cost	2,125	(to give 15% profit margin on a price of $2,500k)
Production costs	1,825	
Design and development	100	
Sales and marketing	500	
Current cost	2,425	
Target cost gap	300	(12% of current cost)

The target cost for the new engine is $2.125m and the current estimated cost is $2.425m. Therefore, there is a need to cut costs by 12% to achieve the target profit margin. It is common for the initial costs to be higher than the target cost and for cost savings to be achieved as the product reaches maturity in its lifecycle. However, it should be noted that, even at this higher initial cost, the engine will be still making a small profit per unit (of $0.075m; giving a 3% margin).

Target costing involves setting a selling price based on what will be competitive in the market then deducting a target profit margin to obtain the target cost. An estimate is made of the cost of the engine based on the current design specification. The gap between this cost and the target cost is the target cost gap and opportunities to bridge this gap are sought by amending the product design or cutting costs in production.

Total quality management (TQM) is a management approach which seeks to have no defects in resource or relationship management. It aims to have a culture of continuous improvement in the organisation.

In this new engine project, the TQM philosophy will fit well with the need to cut a relatively small amount of costs (12%) in order to meet the target. The production team will experience a learning curve associated with such a new product, and will make small but frequent improvements as they do so, which should help the required cost savings to be achieved.

Given the size of the cost gap, it does not seem that a major redesign of the engine is required.

(d) **Quality costs**

There are four categories of quality costs:

- **Prevention costs** are costs to prevent the production of engines which fail to meet specifications;
- **Appraisal costs** are costs incurred in inspecting products to ensure that they meet specifications;
- **Costs of internal failure** are costs associated with making good products which are identified as sub-standard before delivery to the customer; and
- **Costs of external failure** are costs associated with making good products which are identified as sub-standard after delivery to the customer.

Working

Working: Costs of quality by category

	$m	
Prevention	139	(= training, 11 + higher quality materials, 92 + maintenance, 36)
Appraisal	138	(= performance testing: 110 + 28)
Costs of internal failure	95	(= re-inspection)
Costs of external failure	279	(= repairs and replacements, 223 + complaint handling, 56)
Total	651	

Tutorial note. The marking guide for this question indicates that if candidates showed the costs in each category as a % of total revenue, rather than $m figures, they also earned the marks available.

Comments on results

The total quality costs are 5.7% of revenue which seems surprisingly low for an organisation which recognises this as a key competitive advantage; notable is the large size of the external failure costs of 2.4%.

Possible other relevant costs

Overall, there are likely to be administrative costs associated with many of these categories and some attribution of overhead should be undertaken beyond the customer complaint handling mentioned.

Appraisal costs include performance testing of final assembly and performance testing of subcomponents from suppliers. There may also be costs associated with inspection of raw materials inward since these make a difference to quality (shown by the higher purchase costs).

Internal failure costs include costs of re-inspection after repairs after final assembly testing. There must also be costs associated with repairing faulty goods identified at final testing and possibly also scrapping failed products. It is possible that there is idle time costs due to work held up by internal identification of faulty products.

External failure costs include customer complaint handling and replacements under warranties. There is also the cost of damage done to Thyme's brand by such problems although many customers will accept that these are inevitable and provided they are infrequent and covered by warranty, they need not be important.

New products such as the new jet engine will likely generate additional failure costs while production methods are optimised.

Relative importance of categories

Given the high cost of external failure and the importance of reputation for Thyme, the most important category is prevention.

It would be appropriate for Thyme with a TQM approach to be spending heavily in this area. This will still need to be combined with warranty spending in order to protect the reputation of Thyme when problems do occur. As prevention succeeds, so the importance of the other categories will decline. It is worrying that external failure costs are more than twice internal failure costs, which suggests that final testing is not identifying a significant number of the faults in production.

48 Chiven

Workbook references

Performance reports are discussed in Chapter 5 of the Workbook, as are Data Analytics. The value chain is discussed in Chapter 4.

Top tips

Part (a). In the scenario you are told that the CEO wants your evaluation of the performance report split into two separate parts in your report; ie parts (a) and (b) of the question.

Your recommendations for the three new measures should be covered in part (b) of the requirement. Therefore, your focus in part (a) should have been:

- Evaluating the choice of existing measures used
- Evaluating the presentation in the report

In the Workbook, we referred to the technical article on ACCA's website about 'Reports for Performance Management' which highlights four basis criteria which can be used to evaluate an organisation's performance reports:

- **Purpose** – What is the purpose of the report? Does the report provide information which is relevant to the organisation's performance against its mission or objectives?
- **Audience** – Who is the report produced for? Is it appropriate for its audience and their requirements?
- **Information** – What information is needed – financial and non-financial; quantitative and qualitative? Does the report provide the information which is needed to fulfil its purpose and satisfy its audience?
- **Layout** – Does the report make it clear for readers to identify the most important information?

Although you didn't have to use these criteria to answer the requirement, they could have given you a useful framework for answering this question. For example, how well do the performance measures included in the report help the board assess Chiven's performance against its aims?

Similarly, in terms of the audience – is the information provided in the report suitable for board members (or is some of it too detailed, and more appropriate for operational managers?)

The points about 'layout' are also directly relevant to your evaluation of the way the report is presented: does the report make it clear for readers to identify the most important information? Remember that having large amounts of information in a report isn't always beneficial, because there is a danger of information overload. Could that be a potential issue here? Also, does the way the information is presented help the board members understand performance? For example, instead of presenting simply presenting revenue figures for 20X8 and 20X7 might it be more useful to indicate % growth between the two years?

Overall, note that there are 15 marks available for this part of the question though, so you need to cover a sufficient large number of relevant points to score well here.

Part (b). The CEO's request (in the second paragraph of the scenario) asked you to identify 'three new measures which you believe address key issues for the business' but are not currently on the report.

However, note that you also need to carry out appropriate calculations for the performance measures you recommend. So, to score all the marks here, you need to recommend (and justify) measures which not only address key issues, but can also be calculated using the indicators already provided in Appendix 1.

Although the CEO has identified increasing Chiven's online presence (ie increasing online sales) as one of their aims, there is no information available to calculate any performance measures you might recommend in relation to it. So, for example, if you recommended a measure relating to online sales, you would receive a mark for identifying a measure which relates one of the key issues the business is facing, but you would not be able to earn any marks for calculations.

Part (c). The paragraph in the scenario about 'Business integration and supply chain' identifies that the CEO believes that simplifying Chiven's supply chain could help improve the company's performance, but doing this will have implications for Chiven's performance measurement and information systems.

The CEO has asked you to advise on appropriate performance measures and systems when using the value chain approach to simply the supply chain. Importantly, the main focus of your answer needs to be on the supply chain, not the value chain. So, for example, you shouldn't spend time describing all the activities in the value chain. The only areas of the value chain which are relevant here, are ones which relate to the supply chain.

Also, note that the requirement asks you to advise on two different things: (i) performance measures which would be affected by the simplification, and (ii) information systems which would be involved. It is important you address both parts of this requirement. Equally, when advising on relevant performance measures, you should identify existing measures from Appendix 1 which are relevant to the supply chain, rather than introducing additional new measures of your own.

Overall. Remember that you have been asked to write a report, so make sure the style and structure of your answer, as well as its tone, is appropriate for a report.

Examining team's comments

Part (a). Responses to this part were disappointing, and candidates could have scored much better had they related their answers to the aims and critical success factors of the company in the scenario. Some candidates **did** indicate that the company had two aims, and evaluate whether the report addressed these aims. However, the company also had four subsidiary critical success factors, and very few candidates addressed whether the report measured these factors.

The ability to evaluate whether the measures in a report are appropriate for a company to help it achieve its critical success factors and overall aims is one of the main learning outcomes of the APM exam.

Some candidates also offered quite lengthy general descriptions about what a report should contain. While this might earn a mark for recognising the purpose of the report, to score well in this question candidates must discuss the contents of a report in the context of the company in the scenario. Candidates have to offer analysis and justification as to whether the specific report in the question has the content and presentation of a high quality report. If it does, then candidates need to be able to justify why the content and presentation are appropriate and of high quality. Alternatively, if it does not, then candidates need to be able to justify why the report, in its current format, is not helping the company achieve its aims and its critical success factors.

Part (b). This question was generally poorly answered. Candidates often ignored the CEO's instruction to use the data in Appendix 1 and recommended other measures based on a broader consideration of the business. Justified suggestions are rewarded where possible, but this approach made calculation impossible and so meant candidates inevitably lost marks.

Candidates must also recognise that it is the justification for measures which is tested in a question like this, not simply the calculation. Candidates need to demonstrate that they understand the company and its situation, and therefore how the measure they are recommending will improve on those already being used. Any improvement should be justified in terms of helping the company to better achieve its aims.

Part (c). Although the value chain was given as an Appendix, many candidates still spent time explaining the value chain, and offering definitions of each of the nine components. Such responses clearly did not address the question asked, and so earned few – if any – marks.

Few candidates appeared to appreciate that the focus of this question was on the supply chain and so the value chain was only relevant insofar as it might help simplify the supply chain. Therefore, candidates should have focused on the specific parts of the value chain that related to supply. However, most candidates failed to appreciate this and offered generic measures for different components of the value chain that did not relate to the scenario.

Part (d). Many candidates scored well on this question, particularly in relation to the benefits and disadvantages of analysis of social media discussions. Many students did not appear to know what sentiment analysis is, however.

Report. Candidates who had practised writing professional answers scored in the presentation area. Markers were looking for suitable report headings and sub-headings, an introduction, a logical structure, and a clear, concise style. Most candidates performed well in this area.

Marking guide

	Marks
(a) Identifying the company's aims, and key aspects of performance relating to them – 1 mark per relevant point, up to 4 marks Evaluating if the aims are measured – 1 mark per relevant point, up to 10 marks General comments about the presentation of the report and the measures included – 1 mark per relevant point, up to 10 marks Eg, repetition of measures, no grouping or structure, external information, focus on the strategic not operational, need for online measures as well as store-based measures. Total for part (a): up to 15 marks	15
(b) Justification of each performance measures – 1 mark each Calculations – up to 5 marks Other relevant points – up to 3 marks Total for part (b): up to 8 marks	8
(c) Defining the value chain – 1 mark Identifying the activity types relevant to the supply chain – up to 2 marks Advising on appropriate performance measures – up to 3 marks Advising on information systems – up to 3 marks Maximum for part (c): up to 7 marks	7
(d) Advantages of social media discussions - up to 2 marks each, if relevant to Chiven (max 4) Explanation of sentiment analysis - 1 mark Benefits of sentiment analysis - up to 2 marks each (max 4) Disadvantages of analysis of social media - up to 2 marks each (max 4)	10

Professional skills

Communication

- General report format and structure (use of headings/sub-headings and an introduction)
- Style, language and clarity (appropriate layout and tone of report response, presentation of calculations, appropriate use of the CBE tools)
- Effectiveness of communication (answer is relevant, specific rather than general and focused to the requirement)

Analysis and evaluation

- Appropriate use of the data to support discussion and draw appropriate conclusions
- Demonstration of reasoned and balanced judgement

Marking guide	Marks
• Demonstration of ability to consider relevant factors applicable to Chiven Co's situation	
Scepticism	
• Effective challenge and critical assessment of the impact of Big Data	
• Demonstration of effective challenge of information supplied / identification of missing information	
Commercial acumen	
• Effective use of examples and/or calculations from the scenario information and other practical considerations related to the context to illustrate points being made	
• Demonstrating an awareness of organisational and external factors	
• Recognising key issues in a given scenario in terms of how to address problems, and possible obstacles that will need to be overcome in the process of doing this	
• Recommendations are practical and plausible, and commercially viable in the context of Chiven Co's situation	
Maximum	10
Total	50

To: The Board of Chiven Stores (Chiven)

From: Accountant

Date: [Today's date]

Subject: Performance reporting and management issues

Introduction

This report evaluates the current performance report used for the annual board review and suggests three additional important performance indicators. The performance measurement aspects of the use of the value chain to help to streamline the supply chain is considered. Finally, the impact, risks and challenges of Big Data for Chiven are discussed.

(a) **Performance report for annual board review**

The basic role of the performance report is to allow the board to see if the mission is being achieved along with the subsidiary aims and strategically important initiatives set by the senior management.

Chiven's overall aim, or mission, breaks down into two parts:

- Becoming the largest clothing retailer in Beeland, which is measured by Chiven's market share, but without an indication of the market leader it is not possible to see if this is achieved; and
- Delivering exceptional value to its shareholders, which is measured through a number of measures (dividends, EPS, economic value added and ROCE). However, it is often the growth of these indicators year-on-year which would be more useful to assess performance rather than the absolute amounts. Additionally, market average information would be important for investors so they can compare their investment in Chiven with others in their portfolios.

The subsidiary aims and initiatives based on the CEO's comments are:

- Maximising opportunities from new technology
- Increasing web presence
- Making use of 'Big Data' in relation to Chiven's web sales
- Simplifying the supply chain

There are no measures of web sales or the impact of technology on the activities of Chiven which would allow measurement of the first three aims. The basic data does not appear to be collected as sales are reported in total and not for stores and for the website separately.

The final aim does appear to be measured by looking at the number of suppliers and also the number of product lines sold (number of suppliers × average number of product lines per supplier). Reduction of these numbers would indicate a more streamlined supply chain. This would also indirectly improve the probability of stock obsolescence and so reduce inventory write-downs.

General comments about the current report

The current report is likely to confuse the board as it presents too many indicators and so overloads the board with information. This could be improved by reducing the number of indicators. For example, it should be considered if there is a need for both economic value added and ROCE in the report as they perform similar functions.

The report does not appear to group or appropriately prioritise the indicators presented. Suggested headings for an improved report might be:

- Shareholder value performance
- Market leadership
- Impact of new technology
- Efficiency in the supply chain

For example, the main company aim relating to shareholder value should appear at the top of the report and include dividends, EPS, economic value added and/or ROCE. As already noted, the growth of these indicators year-on-year would be more useful rather than the absolute amounts.

There is a lack of external information (especially competitor information) such as the market leading market share.

There is a lack of forward-looking information which given the aim of innovation through new technology would be important. Expected growth of web sales in the market generally would allow measurement of Chiven's performance in this area.

There is a lack of a summary of property costs which could be especially useful for comparison with web operations.

There are a number of indicators which are about the detailed operation of the stores (such as average time between customer entry and employee greeting or average queueing time for customers). These are of a more operational nature and may be distracting and unnecessary in the board report, as it ought to focus on the strategic indicators.

However, the board may take the view that such customer-experience centred indicators are strategically important as they are commonly used in retail. In this case, there ought to be equivalent indicators for the web-based sales, for example, relating to number clicks or pages needed in order to make a web sale.

(b) **Three new performance measures**

There are three performance measures, which currently do not appear on the report, which would improve presentation of Chiven's results. As noted above, the current report contains many absolute figures and some ratios would simplify the work of interpreting these results.

Key issues in the current report and from the perspectives of running the physical stores are the number of employees and the floor space of the stores. Therefore, it is suggested that the revenue and operating profit per unit for each of these variables would be helpful and these are also common indicators used in the retail trade.

	Total	*Total*
	20X8	*20X7*
Revenue per employee ($)	64,988	66,142
Revenue per sq metre ($)	3,096.5	3,147.3

	Total 20X8	Total 20X7
Operating profit ($m)	434.3	430.0
Operating profit per sq metre ($)	510.9	519.3

Operating profit per employee has not been calculated as the general body of employees are more concerned with sales rather than cost control and hence profits.

Tutorial note. Workings are for new performance measures.

Working

		20X8	20X7
Revenue ($m)	From scenario	2,632	2,606
Employees	From scenario	40,500	39,400
Revenue per employee ($)		**64,988**	**66,142**
Floor space (square metres)	From scenario	850,00	828,000
Revenue per square metre ($)	Revenue/floor space	**3,096.5**	**3,147.3**
Operating profit margin (%)	From scenario	16.5	16.5
Operating profit ($m)	Revenue * margin	**434.3**	**430.0**
Operating profit per square metre	Operating profit/floor space	**510.9**	**519.3**

(c) **Streamlining the supply chain using the value chain**

The value chain divides the value activities of a business into different types and then examines the links between these in order to more efficiently build value within the business.

The supply chain simplification may involve reducing the number of suppliers and making the chain more efficient. The supply chain has an impact on three types of activity in the value chain: the main activity area is procurement (dealing with suppliers) but it could also include technology development (information systems) and inbound logistics. There may be other types of activity affected if these are outsourced.

The performance measures associated with this simplification are the number of suppliers and number of product lines supplied by each supplier (both areas are part of the existing reporting). They include the time taken to source new products and the revenue and profits obtained from these (new measures).

The information systems which would be involved would be those with contact to the suppliers obtaining product details and prices and also those liaising over delivery of these items. For example, these could be part of a just-in-time delivery system to reduce stock holding at Chiven.

(d) **Analysis of social media discussions and sentiment analysis**

Discussions on social media have the potential to provide a great insight into what people think about the products that Chiven sells. Discussions are likely to provide more information that simple questionnaires that businesses have traditionally used to obtain customer feedback. People might compare Chiven's products with those of competitors, for example, and might state why they prefer one to the other. This might help Chiven to understand why they have fallen from fourth largest retailer to fifth. Demographic and other information about the people having the discussions may also be available, so Chiven can gain insights into the preferences of different market segments, which may enable the business to identify which segments it should focus on.

Sentiment analysis is a tool that can analyse the mood reflected in text, voice and other forms of communication. It could be used alongside the analysis of discussion of Chiven on social media - do people appear to be happy or angry when they discuss Chiven. Voice analysis could be used to monitor the mood of customers that call Chiven's customer service departments. This could be used to ascertain whether customers are happy with the service they receive.

49 Fearties

Workbook references

KPIs are discussed in Chapter 2 of the Workbook. Issues relating to non-financial performance indicators are discussed in Chapter 9. ROCE is covered in Chapters 6 and 7.

Top tips

Part (a). Although this is a single requirement, the CEO has asked you to do a number of different things in the scenario, in the paragraph under the heading 'Existing KPIs and introduction of the balanced scorecard'. It is important you address all of these points to score well in this part of the question:

- The CEO wants an evaluation of whether the existing KPIs cover the financial perspective of the balanced scorecard.
- The CEO believes there is an error in the ROCE calculation in Appendix 1 which you should correct.
- The CEO also wants you to recommend, with reasons, two KPIs for each of the other three perspectives of the scorecard (ie six KPIs in total), relating to the key issues facing the business.

In relation to the first of these points, we are told in the second paragraph of the scenario that the Feartie family has tried to manage the business 'to increase profits without excessive risk-taking' and that they are 'dependent on the business through their pay and dividends.' Also, in the paragraph about 'Recent events' we are told that the owners now have a goals of 'increasing growth' by expanding into new countries. So, when evaluating the financial perspective, an important point to consider is how well the existing KPIs enable the board to assess how well the business is achieving these aims.

Although there is a specific instruction to correct an error in the ROCE calculation, you might also want to consider how useful ROCE actually is as a performance measure for a service business like Fearties. In terms of correcting the error itself, what should the ROCE figure in Appendix 1 be, given the financial information in Appendix 2?

In relation to recommending new KPIs, a key part of the instruction here is that the KPIs you recommend should relate 'to the key issues facing the business'. The 'Recent events' section of the scenario highlights these key issues (eg health and safety certification; difficulties in recruiting staff; legal claims). We also know that Fearties has a 'reputation for reliability' so could that be important – for example, in relation to the 'customer' perspective of the scorecard.

Importantly, you are asked to make 'reasoned recommendations' for your indicators. There are a number of possible indicators you could recommend, so the key to scoring well here is in justifying why the indicator you have recommended will help Fearties' board address the issues facing the business.

Part (b). The scenario tells you that Fearties' board has resisted the introduction of customer surveys due to concerns about their ability to measure performance using this method.

So, could the board's lack of familiarity with using non-financial performance indicators could be an issue in itself?

There isn't any information in the scenarios specifically about the customer surveys, so you need to draw on your own knowledge here, and one of the key things to remember here is that non-financial data (like customer satisfaction levels) can often be qualitative.

- What are the difficulties in **capturing** qualitative data? How can these be overcome?
- Also, what are the difficulties in **interpreting** customers' feedback in customer surveys? How might these be overcome?

Part (c). The paragraph headed 'Management style' in the scenario clarifies exactly what is required here:

- A brief definition of the three management styles (budget-constrained; profit-conscious; non-accounting)
- An assessment of the existing management style at Fearties
- A justified recommendation for an appropriate approach

A useful approach to this question would be to assess the current style, and then assess the potential advantages and disadvantages of each of the other two styles in turn, before recommending which style you think is most appropriate (based on the advantages and disadvantages you have identified for each of them).

The CEO's request doesn't specifically say the approach you recommend can't be the existing style. However, from the context of the request, it is reasonable to assume that the current approach is not the most appropriate, and therefore one of the other two might be more appropriate.

Overall. Remember that you have been asked to write a report to the board of Fearties. Is the style and structure of your answer, as well as its tone, appropriate for a board report?

Marking guide	Marks
(a) Current KPIs focus on financial aspects only; absolute figures less useful than relative figures; not covering the long-term perspective; not referencing external data – up to 3 marks Financial indicators: Revenue growth, operating margin, cash flows generated, dividend growth (long and short term) – up to 8 marks ROCE – 1 mark for calculation, 2 marks for discussion New indicators – up to 4 marks for each of the customer, internal and innovation perspectives. Marks are for justification and discussion of two new indicators NB: No marks for naming perspectives (done in the question). Total for part (a): up to 22 marks	22
(b) 1 mark per relevant point about problems with measuring and managing performance using non-financial performance indicators Total for part (b): up to 8 marks	8
(c) 1 mark for definition of each style – up to 3 marks 1 mark for identifying current style Up to 2 marks for assessing each style (budget-constrained, profit-conscious, non-accounting) in context of the scenario – up to 6 marks Up to 2 marks for recommending (and justifying) an appropriate style Total for part (c): up to 10 marks	10

ANSWERS

Marking guide	Marks

Professional marks

Communication:

- General report format and structure (use of headings, sub-headings and an introduction)
- Style, language and clarity (appropriate tone of report response, presentation of calculations, appropriate use of the tools, easy to follow and more than a negligible amount of content)
- Adherence to the CEO's specific request to provide only two indicators and only for the three balanced scorecard (BSC) elements

Analysis and evaluation:

- Appropriate use of data to perform suitable calculations for the financial perspective of the BSC
- Problems of NFPIs are clearly supported with examples from the use of customer surveys
- Demonstration of explanation of all three management styles at Fearties

Scepticism:

- Recognition of the need for both absolute and % growth figures in reporting
- Recognition that ROCE is not that useful for Fearties
- Recognition that although the KPIs reflect Fearties' focus on financial results, the KPIs do not reflect the new goal of growth

Commercial acumen:

- Recommendations of performance indicators for the BSC are practical and plausible in the context of the company situation
- Recommendation of the management style for Fearties is practical and plausible in the context of the company situation

Maximum	10
Total	50

Report

To: The board of Fearties Security (Fearties)

From: Accountant

Date: [Today's date]

Subject: Performance reporting and management issues

Introduction

This report evaluates the current choice of indicators within the financial perspective of the balanced scorecard and recommends new indicators to cover the additional perspectives of the scorecard. Additionally, it discusses the problems of measuring non-financial indicators. The current management style is evaluated, and a new approach is recommended to match the strategy of the business.

(a) **Key performance indicators**

Tutorial note. There are a number of possible KPIs which could be suggested for this scenario. Candidates will be given credit for the KPIs they recommend, based on the justification offered, even if the KPIs are different to the ones included in this suggested solution.

The balanced scorecard has four perspectives: financial, customer, internal business process and innovation and growth. Indicators are needed for each perspective. The indicators suggested here are for the use of the board at a strategic level and not detailed operational management.

Financial perspective

The overall business objective is to grow profit without taking excessive risks. This is focused on the financial aspects of the business and so it is consistent that the current key performance indicators (KPIs) are all financial, being taken or calculated from the accounting information supplied with them. However, they are open to criticism.

The figures provided are the absolute values where it may be more useful to provide the year-on-year change in order to show growth.

	20X5	*20X4*	*Growth*
	$m	$m	
Revenue	686	659	4.1%
Operating profit	36	34	5.9%
Cash flow from operating activities	64	64	0.0%
Dividends paid	14	13	7.7%

The operating profit figure is less helpful for control purposes than the operating margin which allows for the effect of increased sales activity. The figures above show operating profit improving but, in fact, this just reflects the increased sales, as the operating margin is constant at 5.2%.

The ability to generate cash from operations is one which should indicate if the company is at risk of failure and so it is a valuable measure of risk to the owners.

The dividend growth figure only shows growth for one year, but given the family's long-term involvement in the business, it might be more helpful to have a five-year average of growth, which can be calculated as 7.0%. This smooths out the fact that dividends are often only changed every few years once an increase appears sustainable.

Return on capital employed (ROCE)

The return on capital employed (ROCE) ratio is incorrectly calculated. The ratio calculated in the draft report is the return on equity (profit after tax/equity). This may be useful to a family-owned business where share values are critical, but it does not reflect the efficiency of the use of capital overall. The correct value for ROCE is 31.3% (operating profit/average capital employed = 36/(21 + 94)). However, this ratio is of limited value to Fearties, as it does not have a significant capital base. The business requires relatively little capital investment as its activities are mainly about the hiring out of its employees' time.

New KPIs

The existing KPIs do not adequately reflect the new plan to grow more rapidly by developing new markets. Figures for revenue growth and operating margin should be broken down as they are unlikely to be similar in the different markets.

Customer perspective

The customer's views are important for growth and so the scores of a customer survey may be used to indicate customer satisfaction. However, as discussed later, there are difficulties in measuring customer satisfaction and so customer retention (which could be measured through the percentage of revenue generated from existing customers) may be a better objective measure.

Reliability is listed as a key selling point, and some investigation may be required to identify on what aspects of the service the customers are basing this view. Possible measures could be the percentage of times that a security team of adequate size and experience are sent to each job, or the number of times when police have to be called to the customer's location (indicating a problem which the Fearties' team could not handle).

Internal business process

The operating margin indicator suggested in the financial perspective will supply useful information about the overall efficiency of internal processes.

Based on the issues facing the company, KPIs for this perspective should reflect employee recruitment and retention, so the average number of unfilled vacancies at the company over the year would be a relevant measure.

The success of the company's training process could be measured by the number and average size of the legal claims against its staff.

Innovation and learning

Training is a key issue for Fearties, so the percentage of staff who are qualified is an appropriate indicator. The time taken for this training and its costs may also be measures of the organisation's ability to learn and improve this process.

The operating margin changes over time which are generated in the new markets entered by Fearties would show the organisation's improvements in these new markets.

Obviously, revenue generated from new services offered would also measure innovation at Fearties. However, there appears to be little appetite for this at present as growth is to be driven from selling existing services in new markets.

(b) **Problems of using non-financial performance indicators**

The problems of using non-financial indicators can stem, at least in part, from management's lack of familiarity with them. This is a particular problem for Fearties given its history of using financial indicators. Such non-financial indicators can have issues in the different areas of recording/processing and then interpreting the information.

Customer satisfaction is a good example of an indicator with such difficulties.

Customer satisfaction is often surveyed and the results are expressed in language. It can be difficult to tell if a complaint which describes service as 'poor' is more or less serious than one which describes service as 'unacceptable'.

The most common way to try to overcome this problem is to turn the data into quantitative data. For example, surveys often use scoring systems to capture data on service. A scoring system will often ask the customer to rank their satisfaction at the service provided on a scale of 1 to 5 with '1' representing 'completely satisfied' and '5' representing 'totally dissatisfied'.

However, the problem remains that such scoring systems are still subjective, and it has often been found that there is a tendency to score toward the middle as people tend to feel uncomfortable using the extreme scores of 5 or 1. However, Fearties may suffer from an over-reaction response as the events it deals with are dramatic. For example, if there was a burglary at a factory it was meant to be guarding, then the loss is all blamed on Fearties' failure and a bad score given.

Also, there is the difficulty in interpreting qualitative data, such as customer satisfaction. It is essentially subjective since it is based on people's opinions. For example, in assessing quality of service, people have different expectations and priorities and so are unlikely to be consistent in their judgements. At Fearties, customer complaints will be driven by such opinions. Some customers may expect there will never be a security incident, but this is out of Fearties' control since it is criminal actions which will generate some of these cases.

One way to reduce the effect of subjectivity is to look at trends in performance since the biases in opinion will be present in each individual time period but the trend will show relative changes in satisfaction.

(c) **Management style**

The current style at Fearties would appear to be budget-constrained. The targets set are all financial and are short term in that they are only for the next financial year. This style of management leads to a focus on cost control and often staff are not rewarded if they take actions which will require investment or the foregoing of short-term profit, such as marketing to build a reputation for reliability as an outsourcing partner.

The profit-conscious style evaluates managers on their ability to build long-term profits for the business. This style would appear to suit Fearties' strategic goals, but it does not emphasise non-financial issues such as recruitment and retention. It would not fit with the increased importance of these non-financial factors under the balanced scorecard approach to management.

In the non-accounting style, budgetary information plays a less important part of staff's performance evaluation. It suits an emphasis on quality and on operational factors. It would fit with many of the new non-financial indicators being proposed from the balanced scorecard. However, it may not be strategically suitable for Fearties due to the importance to the family of the financial returns from the business.

Overall, a profit-conscious approach is recommended but one which uses both financial and non-financial indicators from the balanced scorecard to support the long-term financial goals of the company. The profit-conscious style will suit the financial needs of the family and its long-term goal of growth while a supporting non-accounting approach will suit some of the operational arms of the business, for example, dealing with legal compliance and employee issues.

50 Rezillos

Workbook references

Management reports are discussed in Chapter 5 of the Workbook, and issues around mistake and misconceptions in the use of numerical data for performance measurement are also discussed in Chapter 5. Benchmarking is discussed in Chapter 3.

Top tips

Part (a)

Sometimes in APM scenario, when the CEO asks you to do something, there are multiple elements to their request. However, in this case, the scenario (4th paragraph) simply tells you 'The CEO would like an evaluation of the performance reporting system used at the strategic board level.'

Nonetheless, the reference to 'strategic board level' is important when thinking about the criteria which can be used to evaluate an organisation's performance report:

Purpose – What is the purpose of the report? Does the report provide information which is relevant to the organisation's performance against its objectives (ie how effectively is it implementing its strategy?).

Audience – Who is the report produced for? Is it appropriate for its audience and their requirements? (ie Is the report suitable for board members?)

Another important criterion when evaluating reports is layout, and that is also relevant here: is the report well presented; is it easy for readers to find the key information?

However, the main focus of your evaluation here should relate to the 'purpose' of the report. The second paragraph of the scenario details Rezillos' objective: 'to deliver sustainable growth in value to the shareholders by working in partnership with customers to deliver innovative and value-for-money solutions utilising the skills of the highly-trained workforce.'

There are a number of different elements in this objective, so a useful approach to your answer would be to assess how well the report provides the board with information about the different aspects of this objective.

Part (b)

The CEO has asked you to 'assess the analysts' criticisms of the customer survey' so a useful approach to this question would be to question whether these criticisms are justified. Are there any potential problems or weaknesses in the survey? The scenario also tells us the analysts' criticisms centred on 'the method of calculation, sampling and the disclosures in the press release' so you should try to address all three of these elements: calculation; sampling; disclosures.

The information provided in Appendix 2 should have provided you with some useful clues here, for example:

- The press release says Rezillos has 'performed an extensive survey'. However, only 9 customers were surveyed out of a total of 180. How extensive, or even representative, is this? How were the customers selected?
- 6 of the 9 customers were from Beeland division; with only 1 from Teeland (the division with the biggest revenue). Again, how representative is this?

The key to scoring well in this question is to identify points in Appendix 2 which indicate potential weaknesses in the survey, and then to explain the implications of them.

Part (c) (i)

The final paragraph of the scenario tells you that the CEO has decided the three divisions should be benchmarked against each other – in other words, this is an internal benchmarking project.

Also, note you have been asked for an 'evaluation' of the usefulness of the proposed type of benchmarking, so you should try to consider a balanced assessment of its potential advantages and its drawbacks.

Part (c) (ii)

Here, the CEO's request in the final paragraph of the scenario identifies that you need to do three things:

- Complete the benchmarking exercise
- Comment on the metrics used in the benchmarking exercise
- Comment on the results of the benchmarking exercise

The first part of this request should be relatively straightforward: using the data provided to complete the missing figures for Veeland in Appendix 3.

(The 'Notes' in the Appendix tell you how to calculate incident rate, and utilisation of learning and development programme.)

Having calculated the missing figures you then need to comment on the performance metrics used in the exercise. A key issue here is whether the areas of performance being benchmarked are those which are most important to the organisation's success. So, how well do the metrics support the achievement of Rezillos' objective (as stated in the second paragraph of the scenario)?

For the final part of the requirement, you then to comment on the results of the benchmarking exercise itself: how does performance vary between the divisions? To score well here, it is important that you don't simply 'write out' figures from the benchmarking exercise – for example, don't simply say, Beeland has the highest number of face-to-face interactions with its key customers. Instead, try to think about potential reasons for the differences, and the implications of them. For example, what might the differences in face-to-face interactions with customers tell us about the division's marketing strategies, and what might be the implications of this?

More generally, are there ways the divisions could improve their performance by learning from others which are performing better than them for a given metric?

Overall

Remember that you have been asked to write a report, so make sure the style and structure of your answer, as well as its tone, is appropriate for a report.

Marking guide	Marks
(a) 1 mark per relevant point – points must be based on scenario information Breaking down overall objective and how Rezillos seeks to achieve this – up to 2 marks Assessment of whether report supports objectives – up to 10 marks Other points – up to 4 marks Point could include (but are not limited to): lack of targets; lack of information on capital and liquidity; general presentation (lack of narrative) Total for part (a): up to 12 marks	12
(b) Comments on average calculations – up to 3 marks Comments on calculation weightings – up to 2 marks Comments on sampling issues – up to 6 marks Summary comments about whether criticism is justified Total for part (b): up to 9 marks	9
(c) (i) Identify type of benchmarking proposed (internal) – 1 mark Evaluation of usefulness of internal benchmarking for Rezillos – up to 5 marks Total for part (c) (i): up to 5 marks	5
(ii) Calculations: Inventory days – 1 mark Order book growth – 1 mark % of revenue from new products introduced in the last three years – 1 mark Reduction in incident rate – 2 marks Utilisation of learning and development programme – 1 mark Comments on choice of metrics – up to 4 marks Comments on results – up to 10 marks Total for part (c) (ii): up to 14 marks	14

Professional marks

Communication:

- General report format and structure (use of headings, sub-headings and an introduction)
- Style, language and clarity (appropriate tone of report response, presentation of calculations, appropriate use of the tools, easy to follow and more than a negligible amount of content)
- Effectiveness of communication (answer is relevant, specific rather than general and focused to the requirement)
- Adherence to the CEO's request to evaluate the performance management system, not performance

Analysis and evaluation:

- Appropriate use of data to perform suitable calculations for the benchmarking exercise
- Demonstration of ability to consider the relevant factors regarding the performance report in light of Rezillo's situation

Marking guide	Marks
• Demonstration of reasoned judgement regarding the customer survey criticisms	
Scepticism:	
• Effective challenge and critical assessment of the performance report	
• Demonstration of effective challenge of information supplied / identification of missing information in the benchmarking exercise and the performance report	
Commercial acumen:	
• Effective use of examples and/or calculations from the scenario information and other practical considerations related to the context to illustrate points being made	
• Demonstrating an awareness of organisational and external factors	
Maximum	10
Total	50

Report

To: The Board of Rezillos Engineering (Rezillos)

From: Accountant

Date: [Today's date]

Subject: Performance reporting and benchmarking at Rezillos

This report begins by evaluating the current performance report used by the board for their strategic review of the business. Next, the report examines the methodology used in the customer ratings survey in response to criticisms of that survey. Finally, the method of benchmarking to be used for the divisions is evaluated, and the divisional benchmarking exercise is completed and initial conclusions drawn from it.

(a) **Performance report for annual board review**

The current report has a number of strengths and weaknesses. These will be discussed according to whether the report:

- Measures performance towards the company's overall aims; and
- Is well-presented.

The company's overall objective is to deliver sustainable growth in value to the shareholders, and it aims to achieve this by:

- Working in partnership with customers;
- Delivering solutions which are innovative and provide value for money; and
- Utilising the skills of the highly-trained workforce.

Shareholder value – Beginning with the overall objective of Rezillos, the report does not directly measure shareholder value and so does not report its growth despite this being a primary goal of the organisation. This could be done directly by measuring economic value added (EVA™) or total return to shareholders. Also, the report is wholly historical and contains no information about the future prospects necessary to judge whether the growth in shareholder value is sustainable. The current report uses period profits and return on capital employed as its main measures of performance. These can suffer from being short term unlike economic value added.

Non-financial measures – Overall, the report does not give information about the performance of the strategies which are in place to deliver the overall objective. These will require non-financial measures and so do not appear in the report which is dominated by standard accounting information.

Partnership with customers – There is no measure in the report of how the company works with customers. The company does collect data on interaction with customers at a divisional level, although measuring 'working in partnership' is a vague term which should be more accurately defined in order to be measured, possibly by measuring the number of joint product development projects undertaken.

Value for money – An indirect measure of the customer value-for-money is being offered through the gross profit which, when compared to the industry average, gives a partial measure of value but without data on the price/quality mix compared to competitors, it is difficult to be conclusive about this. Revenue growth is given but should be compared to industry growth in order to give an impression of the attractiveness of our offering to the customer.

Innovation – No measure of innovation is offered in the report either in terms of the number of new products or the revenue or profit generated from them. This appears to be an important fault as an engineering firm such as Rezillos will only be viable in the long term if it continues to innovate.

Workforce – There is no information on the training provided to Rezillos' workforce, or their skills, but given the emphasis on innovation and the sector in which Rezillos operates, these appear to be important factors.

There are measures appropriate for these strategies available within the divisions (see the benchmarking exercise later). These could provide easy solutions to many of these gaps.

Divisional performance – The report treats the divisions in the same way as the group, using profit and comparison to industry average margins and budgets as the main assessment tools. This may not be helpful as the divisions are in different markets and so may not be easily comparable. This problem could be solved by providing the targets set for each of the divisions for the major financial indicators.

Liquidity – It is unusual, given the preponderance of financial data in the report, that there is very little about the assets and liabilities of the company or its liquidity. This may be acceptable if the efficiency of capital use and the danger of insolvency are negligible but this appears unlikely as shareholder value is a key measure and the ROCE is quite low.

Presentation – In terms of presentation, the data are clear and in a form which would be easily recognisable to those used to reading accounts. However, it is common to provide a narrative commentary with such a report in order to highlight the key features in the report such as major deviations from target or performance well outside industry norms.

(b) **Performance report for annual board review**

In a recent analysts' meeting, Rezillos has been questioned about its disclosure that it has an average 7.0 customer rating. The average customer rating is correctly calculated as 7.0 from the sample data. However, there are a number of questions which could be raised over the method of calculation and sampling.

The first issue which might be raised is the definition of 'average' in this context. The method used for the calculation is the arithmetic mean but average can also be considered to be the mode (most common rating) or the median (the middle value of the sample, which here would be the 5th value). Both of these alternative methods of calculation would give the lower value of 6.0 for the rating.

The calculation method does not take into consideration the size of the account. The rating of the large accounts might be considered more important and so given some extra weighting in the calculation.

A larger area of concern would surround the sample selected for the calculation. There are a number of questions to be raised about this:

(1) A confidence interval and level should be supplied for the rating. If the sample is a small one or the confidence level required is high, then the confidence interval might be shown to be unacceptably large.

(2) The method of sampling is not disclosed. Ideally, it should be a random sample.

(3) There are various ways in which the sample might be biased:

(i) Only customers who are expected to give a favourable response may have been selected.

(ii) It could be that only the customers who chose to respond are included in which case the sample will often be populated with those at the extremes of opinion on Rezillos' service.

(iii) The majority of customers in the sample are from Beeland (six of nine) and only one from Teeland. This will not allow the rating to identify divisional performance, which, given each division has responsibility for customer support, may create a bias. In order to do this, random samples from each division should be taken separately.

(iv) There are only three customers sampled with an above average account size ($20.5m ($3,691m/180)). It is common in such surveys to ensure that all of the major accounts are sampled.

Overall, the criticism appears justified and in future, Rezillos should consider disclosing more detail of the method of sampling and the sample size in order to build trust with the investing community.

(c) (i) **Method of benchmarking**

Benchmarking involves comparing performance against another entity. The proposed benchmarking exercise is an **internal** one comparing divisions within the same organisation.

Evaluation of internal benchmarking

The major advantage of internal benchmarking is the ability to obtain detailed operational information and so to share best practice amongst the divisions. This will show the different divisions the advantage of being part of a larger company and assist in integrating them.

This method of benchmarking suffers the drawback that it will often involve non-financial data whose production is often less robust than the financial systems involving subjective judgements.

Also, it will not necessarily identify world-beating performance. Its internal focus may lead the company to ignore competitor performance. However, as a one-off exercise to harmonise and improve the divisions' performance, it seems to be suitable for Rezillos now.

(ii) **Divisional benchmarking exercise**

The benchmarking has been completed as follows:

	Beeland	*Teeland*	*Veeland*
Benchmarking metrics			
Growth of market	8.5%	3.2%	5.0%
Revenue growth	12.5%	3.2%	4.8%
Operating margin	10.6%	12.8%	15.0%
Inventory days	162	162	162
Order book growth	5.2%	5.3%	5.3%
Number of face-to-face interactions with top 10 customers	260	120	40
Percentage of revenue from new products introduced in the last three years	24.9%	29.0%	

	Beeland	*Teeland*	*Veeland*
Incident rate (20X8)	1.14	1.13	1.03
Incident rate (20X7)	1.18	1.13	1.18
Reduction in incident rate	3.4%	0.0%	12.7%
Utilisation of learning and development programme	1.20	1.26	0.98

Metrics used

The benchmarking metrics appropriately reflect many of the detailed strategies of the company:

- Order book growth reflects the sustainability of current levels of business;
- Number of face-to-face interactions with top ten customers reflects working in partnership with customers;
- Innovative solutions is measured by percentage of revenue from new products introduced in the last three years; and
- Caring for employees and nurturing their skills is measured by reduction in incident rate and utilisation of learning and development programme.

The major missing piece is the change in shareholder value or profit generated by each division.

Results of the benchmarking exercise

The initial three metrics identify the broad financial performance of each division:

- Beeland is operating in a high growth market and seems to be using lower prices (lower operating margin) and a sales drive (visiting top customers more regularly) in order to push growth above the market rate.
- Teeland operates in a more stable market, but one where the take-up of new products is higher.
- Veeland is growing more slowly than its market, possibly due to higher margins and a weak sales effort (with only a small number of visits to key customers).

So, the divisions apparently operate in markets with different characteristics, but there does appear to be scope to share practices between them in order to improve. Looking at the individual metrics in more detail:

- Inventory days is the same across the divisions, reflecting the new company-wide inventory management system. This indicates that some aspects of integration are working.
- Order book growth is an important measure of the growth and sustainability of profits in the business. All three divisions saw similar order book growth, although Beeland saw higher levels of revenue growth. Beeland visits its key customers much more frequently than the other two divisions (every two weeks on average), so the other divisions might learn from this in terms of increasing the number of interactions they have with their key customers in order to try to increase revenue growth.
- Teeland is seeing the highest proportion of sales of new products but this may reflect the fact that they operate in a more developed market. This could only be controlled by obtaining external data such as industry averages for each country.
- Veeland has shown a significant reduction in safety incidents and its training and operating procedures should be shared with the other divisions in order to see if similar improvement can be replicated there.
- Not surprisingly, the market with the largest proportion of revenue from new products (Teeland) is also the one which makes greatest use of training. The low training score in Veeland may reflect little sales training as the number of sales interactions shows the most dramatic difference of all the metrics.

51 Folt

Workbook references

CSFs and KPIs are covered in Chapter 2 of the Workbook, target costing and quality management are covered in Chapter 10.

Top tips

This was a relatively short question focusing on a range of classic APM issues including CSFs, KPIs and quality management – questions on these themes are common in the APM exam.

Part (a). This asked for a justification of a maximum of two KPIs to fit three CSFs that were provided in the scenario, and then an evaluation of the collection of KPIs that had been chosen. There were many possible answers to this, but all should be along the theme of creating a logical performance hierarchy of KPIs which tie back to the overall strategy.

Part (b). This asked for an analysis of the application of target costing, including a definition and an explanation of how it could be used. The main requirement was to use data provided to illustrate the target cost gap.

Part (c). This required an explanation of two of the the four categories of quality costs (2 marks) and then of who (of the company and an outsourced partner) had responsibility for each area. This required a close reading of the scenario to understand the split of responsibilities for quality management.

Part (d). This required an evaluation of the impact of an outsourced providers limited information systems on quality management. Even though the wording of the requirement was slightly confusing, the detailed instructions of what was required were contained within the relevant section of the scenario (this was also true for other requirements).

Examining team's comments

Part (a). This part of the question was out of 15 and candidates generally scored about half the marks available. Part of the problem candidates encountered here appeared to be in not fully comprehending, for the first CSF, that it was two particular groups of capital providers who had to be satisfied. Many responses suggested KPIs that were clearly not relevant to the scenario in this regard. It is also clear that many candidates felt that justifying the measure they had offered could be undertaken by providing a definition of that term. Clearly, such comments are not appropriate when a justification is being sought. Candidates also found it challenging to offer KPIs for CSFs that were essentially non-financial in nature, and many responses offered financial KPIs which were not justified in the context of the CSF they were discussing.

Almost all candidates ignored the second part of the requirement of the question.

Part (c). Though this question was generally well done, there was a significant minority of candidates who did not understand what quality costs were and discussed costs in general. This is a fundamental lack of basic knowledge and such responses did not address any part of the question asked.

Some candidates also struggled to divide responsibilities accurately and did not refer to the specifics of the scenario to explain their response.

Part (d). Candidates found this very challenging and most candidates did not pass this part of the question. Responses here were either brief or not relevant to the scenario. Many candidates responded to a slightly different question, which was much more focused towards the qualities that information should have. Such responses did score some marks but did not address the main focus of the question, which was around the sources of the information.

Candidates also often offered unjustified, commercially unaware suggestions such as the companies purchasing an Enterprise Resource Planning (ERP) system. Such systems are very expensive and the overall profit on the venture would not justify further expenditure of this nature.

Marking guide		Marks
(a) Recommended KPIs – up to 4 marks for each CSF, must be justified	12	
Staying within maximum of 2 KPIs per CSF	1	
Evaluation as a complete system for Folt	6	
		15
(b) Target costing		
Target cost	1	
Design	1	
Inspections	1	
Reworking	1	
Other costs	1	
Cost gap	1	
Definition of target cost	1	
Conclusion	1	
Impact on contract negotiations	4	
		10
(c) 1 mark per relevant point		
For each of the two quality cost areas: defining the cost areas with an illustration of how it applies to the scenario and giving a justified recommendation of its treatment under the contract		
		6
(d) 1 mark per relevant point		
Importance of quality information	2	
Need for systems at Xela	2	
Use Folt's systems	2	
Need for monitoring	3	
Impact on the contract (SLAs)	2	
Other sources of information	2	
		9

Professional skills

Communication

- General report format and structure (use of headings/sub-headings and an introduction)
- Style, language and clarity (appropriate layout and tone of report response, presentation of calculations, appropriate use of the CBE tools)
- Effectiveness of communication (answer is relevant, specific rather than general and focused to the requirement)
- Adherence to the details of the requirements in the scenario

Analysis and evaluation

- Use of information provided to perform a suitable/comprehensive evaluation of...
- Appropriate use of the data to both support discussion and also draw appropriate conclusions
- Demonstration of reasoned and balanced judgement
- Demonstration of the ability to consider relevant factors that are applicable to Folt Co's situation

Marking guide	Marks
Scepticism	
• Effective challenge and critical assessment	
Commercial acumen	
• Effective use of examples and/or calculations from the scenario information and other practical considerations related to the context to illustrate points being made	
• Demonstrating an awareness of organisational and external factors	
• Recognising key issues in a given scenario in terms of how to address problems, and possible obstacles that will need to be overcome in the process of doing this	
• Recommendations are practical and plausible, and commercially viable in the context of Folt Co's situation	
Maximum	10
Total	50

Report

To: The CEO of Folt Manufacturing (Folt)

From: An accountant

Date: [Today's date]

Subject: Performance measurement and outsourcing of manufacturing at Folt

This report recommends a set of key performance indicators (KPIs) for the identified critical success factors (CSFs) associated with the new strategy and evaluates these as a set of measures of the strategic performance of Folt. Further, in preparation for the negotiation of the outsourced manufacturing contract, advice is given on the use of target costing; the attribution of responsibility for areas of quality and the information required to monitor the quality of production.

(a) **Recommended KPIs for CSFs**

The chief executive officer (CEO) has identified three CSFs for the medium term. Performance towards these requires to be measured and so KPIs are recommended as follows:

Keep capital providers satisfied

There are two capital providers, the debt is all provided by the venture capitalist (VC) and the equity is provided by the management team and the VC combined with the management team taking the majority. A widely used and understood metric for performance would be return on capital employed (ROCE), which measures the returns to all capital providers as a group. It is defined as operating profit/capital employed. In order to properly understand performance, a target measure should be set for this, possibly by using an industry average as benchmark.

To break this down further would probably require return on equity and cost of debt measures and would, therefore, break the desire to keep the performance information brief. As there are only two capital providers and ROCE neatly summarises this, no other KPIs are suggested.

Build a world-class software development team

This is a difficult factor to measure with precision. Building a team could be measured by an increasing number of employees or number of projects undertaken. However, the important element in this CSF is the 'world-class' quality of the team. This could be measured by the input cost of the team, provided that they are recruited at competitive market rates, since higher wages would imply higher skills. Alternatively, it could be measured by the team's output in terms of commercial success (sales) or technical achievement (industry design awards).

Overall, therefore, being led by the output of the team, it is recommended that we use growth in number of projects undertaken and the number of industry design awards won as the KPIs for this CSF.

Ensure that quality of the imaging devices meets market standards

Again, this is a difficult factor to measure. Financial measures of quality are possible by looking at the effect on sales volume and profitability (both likely higher for higher quality). However, these are lagging indicators where quality effects can take some considerable time to trickle through to customer perceptions.

A more direct measure of the quality of current manufacturing would be through customer returns and product failure rates on factory testing. However, it can be difficult to obtain benchmarking information that will allow judgement of whether this is meeting market standards. Given that the company already does manufacture successfully, it should have historic data which, if products are selling at the required margins, would suggest that these data on failure rates and returns would be acceptable to the market. As the business is moving to outsourcing its manufacturing, it is the external failure rate data of the customer returns which will be more appropriate, as Folt will retain the key contact with the customer.

Overall, it is recommended that gross profit (a measure of both volume and profitability) of products and value of customer returns be used as KPIs. Both of these will need to be benchmarked to historic values in order to judge the maintenance of standards.

Performance measurement system

The KPIs suggested are:

- ROCE
- Growth in number of projects undertaken
- Growth in number of industry design awards won
- Gross profit
- Value of customer returns

The question of whether this is a suitable set of metrics to measure strategic performance really asks, does this measure the achievement of Folt's overall objective 'to provide an adequate return to its capital providers while growing the business into a world-class supplier in its areas of expertise'?

This objective can be broken down into:

- Providing an adequate return to its capital providers
- Growing the business
- Being a world-class supplier in its areas of expertise.

These KPIs do address the first part through ROCE and the second part partly through building the software team. However, the overall growth of the business is not measured financially through sales or profits and its target of being world-class is not measured through the number of markets which it has entered and is considered a leader. The final two KPIs have a more supporting role to play for the overall objective and these could be replaced by others measuring the concepts of growth and world-class supplier in order to provide a strategic view for the board of whether the company's mission is being achieved.

> **Tutorial note.** Credit is given for suitably justified metrics and then a consistent discussion of this in relation to the objectives of Folt.

(b) **Outsourced manufacturing: Target costing**

Working (per unit):

	$	$
Target price		175.0
Target profit		35.0
Target cost		140.0
Cost:		
Software	40.0	
Materials	37.0	
Machine costs	35.2	
Labour	12.5	
Packaging and delivery	8.0	
Design	8.0	
Inspections	0.8	
Reworking costs	0.5	
Total costs		142.0
Cost gap		2.0

Note. It is assumed that it is the total design costs which are relevant to pricing the product, although it would also be possible to consider the original design costs as sunk and so only include the redesign element.

The target cost is calculated as the estimate of a competitive product price less the desired profit margin.

The illustrative calculation above shows that the current estimated cost is $2 per unit too high and so the product or the manufacturing process will need to be redesigned to cut these costs in order to meet the desired margin.

The costs will be split under the contract between the two parties. Therefore, Folt could press Xela to make cuts in its costs to meet the cost gap as the gap is not large (2.3% of the total costs for manufacturing [ie excluding software, design and packaging and delivery]) and it is stated that Ceeland is a lower cost environment than Beeland for manufacturing. However, it may be dangerous to Folt's strategy if these cuts adversely affect product quality.

(c) **Responsibility for quality areas within outsourced manufacturing**

This discussion relates to the quality of the manufactured device and should exclude issues with the software, packaging and delivery, which remain Folt's responsibility. Taking each of the two areas of quality costs in turn, the cost area is defined and the appropriate treatment under the contract discussed:

- Prevention costs are incurred to prevent the production of products which do not conform to specification (eg design of the product and manufacturing process). The product design costs will obviously lie with Folt and the costs for design of the manufacturing process will lie with Xela, although it would be sensible for Xela to replicate Folt's current process and indeed this may be required in order to maintain quality. However, Xela may want autonomy on this in order to make further gains from streamlining processes. There will need to be liaison between Folt and Xela to ensure that process designs are acceptable to both parties.
- Appraisal costs are costs to ensure that the products output by the manufacturer conform to standards. These costs will mostly lie with Xela as it will be the manufacturer. However,

Folt will have to oversee this appraisal by checking on the quality data which Xela will supply under the contract.

- Obviously, all of these matters are subject to negotiation before the contract is finalised.

(d) **Impact of sources of quality information**

- The maintenance of quality standards is a critical success factor for Folt. The ability to ensure this is based on the SLAs in the manufacturing contract with Xela. The monitoring of these SLAs will be done through information systems and so the quality and reliability of the information is critical to Folt's success.
- The outsourcing contract must stipulate agreed quality metrics and also the targets for performance. These will have to be measured and reported by Xela to Folt. Xela does not at present have information systems capable of capturing the non-financial data which is likely to be required by the SLAs. It must therefore be a condition of the contract that suitable systems are put in place by Xela.
- In fact, a simple solution would be for Xela to duplicate the existing systems at Folt. This would avoid the need for Folt to authorise (under the contract) any new system as it would then have a familiar one. It will also mean that the format of the reports is familiar and this too will ease the handover of operations.
- However, this new system will be owned and operated by Xela, and so Folt will need to have access to it in order to verify that data is being input, processed and reported accurately. The detailed type of system audit work may be new to Folt. However, again by using the same system as currently exists, it should be possible to identify managers who monitor quality at Folt's existing manufacturing operation, to perform this task.
- In summary, it will be important that any metrics and targets for these which are used under the contract are unambiguous. It will also be important to stipulate in the contract that Folt be given access to verify that this information is being produced accurately. This will help to avoid the possibility of gaming the contract by Xela.
- Ultimately, customer complaints and returns will represent an external source of information on the quality of the products manufactured. However, it would be more effective to identify and address problems before they reach customers.

52 Arkaig

Workbook references

EVA™ – including the adjustments to accounting profit required to calculate it – are discussed in Chapter 7 of the Workbook. The performance hierarchy is covered in Chapter 2. The value chain is covered in Chapter 4 and performance reporting is discussed in Chapter 5.

Top tips

Part (a)

This is asking for a general assessment of the current reporting of performance as presented in Appendix 1, which presents a simple financial report for each sector (profit margin and ROCE) plus an overall statement of performance in the previous year and some industry averages.

This is a regularly examined area, and requires a firm understanding of the company's mission and whether the report supports this, in addition to general observations about the presentation, level of detail, and lack of commentary.

Positive remarks and negative remarks would both have been relevant but the lack of measures that directly and clearly support the company's strategy would have meant that the 'critical' points would dominate.

Part (b)

This is asking for an evaluation of the replacement of ROCE with EVA using data in Appendix 2 to provide illustrative calculations. 11 of the marks were for calculations; these were mainly straightforward, harder adjustments and easier adjustments were all worth the same marks (1 mark per adjustment) so even if some mistakes were made it was still possible to score well here. There were also 5 straightforward marks for discussing EVA compared to ROCE.

Part (c)

This is asking for a description of the nature of strategic, tactical and operational information required and how this is influenced by planning and control activity; using examples relevant to this company. Because strategic planning has been covered in part (a) more focus is needed on tactical (planning short-term resource allocation & control) which could include variances and NFIs, and on operational information which could include staff absenteeism and delivery performance. It is important to emphasise the need to link back to the company's mission in the discussion of the performance hierarchy.

Part (d)

The implications of a value chain analysis given in Appendix 3 which provides two observations using the value chain that require comment. These need to be assessed in a practical way (gaining 1 mark per point) and could sensibly highlight interlinkages to other parts of the value chain as that is the main purpose of value chain analysis.

Overall. Remember that you have been asked to write a report, so make sure the style and structure of your answer, as well as its tone, is appropriate for a report.

Examining team's comments

In part (a), good candidates focussed on the high priority question of whether the report answers the question of whether the company is achieving its objective(s). Weaker answers over-concentrate on minor issues of presentation and often, spend much time suggesting large amounts of additional information which would overload the users without sufficient justification. A decreasing but still notable minority of candidates continue to respond incorrectly to such a requirement with an evaluation of the performance of the company. This demonstrates failure to read the scenario where it was made clear that the CEO wanted the report evaluated and not the performance of the company.

In part (b), many answers solely discussed the benefits and problems of economic value added without the comparison to ROCE and this meant that fewer marks could be awarded. In part (c), which was generally well done, numerous candidates offered up a performance pyramid analysis of performance management at the company as an answer to this question. This did not directly address the question of the nature of the information for each level and tended only to score marks indirectly. Additionally, a notable minority could not correctly define the tactical and operational levels. Part (d). Here, candidates were able to discuss broadly the activities identified as critical but often; they did not clearly link to this to the company's circumstances.

Marking guide

	Marks
(a) 1 mark per point – must be based on scenario information	
Breaking down mission – up to 2 marks eg identify priority of objectives, pick out strategies	
Assessment of whether report meets mission – up to 11 marks	
eg Clear statement of inadequacy for mission, addressing elements of the mission, information for relevant decision making, illustrated by relevant examples	
Other points – up to 4 marks	
eg Lack of information in the commentary, data overload, general presentation	
	10

(b) Calculations:		
Amortisation	1	
Marketing capitalised	1	
Research and development capitalised	1	
Accounting depreciation (for replacing with economic depreciation)	1	
Tax paid	1	
Lost tax relief on interest	1	
Capital employed (for opening figure)	1	
Research and development asset	1	
Marketing spend capitalised and w/off		
WACC	1	
EVA™	1	
Comments on result	1	
Evaluation of EVA™ versus ROCE – up to 5 marks		
		15
(c) Each level of the hierarchy – up to 4 marks		
eg explanation of the nature of the information needed, impact of planning and controlling activity and illustrative examples		
		9
(d) Specific points relating to the areas of concern – 1 mark per relevant point		
Inbound and outbound logistics		
After-sales service		
Human resource management		
		6

Professional skills

Communication

- General report format and structure (use of headings/sub-headings and an introduction)
- Style, language and clarity (appropriate layout and tone of report response, presentation of calculations, appropriate use of the CBE tools)
- Effectiveness of communication (answer is relevant, specific rather than general and focused to the requirement)
- Adherence to the details of the requirement in the scenario (eg assessing the performance report, not the performance of the company)

Analysis and evaluation

- Use of information provided to perform a suitable/comprehensive evaluation of EVA
- Appropriate use of the data to support discussion and draw appropriate conclusions
- Demonstration of reasoned and balanced judgement
- Demonstration of ability to consider relevant factors applicable to Arkaig Co's situation especially in terms of the key features of the performance report

Scepticism

- Effective challenge and critical assessment of EVA

Commercial acumen

- Effective use of examples and/or calculations from the scenario information and other practical considerations related to the context to illustrate points being made
- Demonstrating an awareness of organisational and external factors
- Recommendations are practical and plausible, and commercially viable in the context of Arkaig Co's situation — 10

Total — 50

Report

To:	The CEO of Arkaig Manufacturing (Arkaig)
From:	An accountant
Date:	September 20X5
Subject:	Performance reporting and management issues at Arkaig

This report evaluates the current performance report used by the board for strategic review. Next, the use of economic value added (EVA™) at Arkaig is illustrated and its use compared to return on capital employed (ROCE). Then, the differences between performance measurement and management at the different levels of the management hierarchy are discussed with reference to Arkaig. Finally, the implications of a value chain analysis for performance management are assessed.

(a) **Strategic performance reporting**

The current report has a number of strengths and weaknesses. These will be discussed according to whether the report:

- Addresses the overall aims of the business;
- Contains appropriate information for decision-making; and
- Is well-presented.

The primary aim of Arkaig is to maximise shareholder wealth by providing suitable products for its customers. These products should have a number of qualities: be world-class; tailored; use technology innovatively; show improved machine downtime; and reduce energy consumption for customers.

This should be supported by an entrepreneurial culture among the employees.

Overall, the report contains a number of common financial measures but they are only loosely connected to the stated mission.

The following problems are noted about how the report measures the achievement of the mission:

(1) There is no direct measure of shareholder wealth in the report. The overall measure of performance for shareholders is provided through the absolute profit after tax and ROCE. It usefully benchmarks the net profit margin and ROCE with industry averages. However, these measures are only indirectly linked to value. The suggestion to use EVA™ is, therefore, appropriate for Arkaig.

(2) The supporting pillars of the mission are all qualities of the products produced by Arkaig. The report does not measure any of these individually. There is an indirect measure of customer attitude through the revenue growth figure but without competitor comparison or a market share, it is not possible to draw a conclusion about any of the qualities of the products. These elements relating to the products are difficult to measure overall as they are likely to be dependent on each product line individually. For each in turn:

(i) The 'world class' nature of the offering could be measured by market share or customer survey responses.

(ii) The tailored nature of the products could be measured by the cost of individual design for each installation or customer survey responses.

(iii) Technological innovation could be measured through comparison of features with the competition or alternatively, by number of industry awards won.

(iv) Machine downtime and energy consumption requires specific testing of each product line.

(3) There is no measure of the employee culture although there is a comment that it is being achieved but this lacks evidence.

The report shows the financial performance by sector as well as in total for the business and the provision of some industry averages is useful in benchmarking performance.

For planning purposes, the lack of external information about customers and competitors makes some of the numbers difficult to interpret. For example, there is no indication whether the fall in revenue is due to general economic conditions or specific faults with Arkaig.

For control purposes, there is previous year information given but not sufficient to establish a trend (which requires at least three years of information). There is no indication of whether the business is meeting its budgets through the provision of variances.

In terms of presentation, the report is clear and it avoids overloading the reader with data. It uses terms which would be easily recognisable to those used to reading accounts. It is helpful that a narrative commentary is provided. However, often the commentary does not go beyond restating the figures in the table. It should provide the significant explanations for each of the major changes commented upon. For example, by stating why the ROCE has exceeded the industry average.

The commentary is an appropriate place to handle the less quantitative aspects of performance such as innovation and employee culture but it does not offer anything substantive. For example, it would be helpful to state what mechanisms are in place to emphasise the entrepreneurial culture (such as percentage of employees who own shares and the total proportion of equity owned by staff).

(b) **Economic value added (EVA™)**

Working

	Year ended 30 June 20X5
	$m
Economic value added	
Operating profit	3,175
Add back:	
Amortisation	95
Marketing capitalised	90
Research and development capitalised	705
Depreciation	1,780
Less:	
Tax paid	694
Lost tax relief on interest	53
Economic depreciation	1,907
NOPAT	3,191

ANSWERS

	Year ended 30 June 20X5
	$m
Capital employed	
At 20X5 year start	19,404
Research and development asset	3,528
Marketing spend capitalised	900
Marketing written-off	(100)
Adjusted capital employed	23,732

WACC = (55% × 12%) + (45% × 3.8% × (1 – 25%))

= 7.88%

EVA™ = NOPAT – (WACC × capital employed)

= 1,321

The business has created $1.32 billion of value in the last year. The net operating profit after tax more than covers the cost of the capital used by the business.

The main benefit to EVA™ is its link to the overall corporate objective of maximising shareholder wealth. ROCE gives a much less direct link to shareholder wealth as it is less cash-like and more tied to the accounting assumptions around producing a profit figure.

The basic test of performance is simple since for EVA™ if it is positive, then the business is generating a return above that required by the providers of finance. ROCE requires a target level to be set usually based on benchmarking to the industry sector and the setting of this target return can be somewhat subjective.

EVA™ encourages investment for the future (for example, in advertising and development) by removing such costs from the performance period and treating them like capital expenditure. This will reduce the dysfunctional temptation for management to engage in some short-term decision-making, which can be a problem with the unadjusted capital employed figure from the financial statements which is used in ROCE. This is particularly relevant to Arkaig, where research and development is a significant activity.

EVA™ is consistent with net present value (NPV) as businesses with an increasing present value will increase EVA™. This will aid communication as NPV is a widely used appraisal measure for businesses.

Overall, however, the better link to shareholder wealth creation and the use of EVA™ in a value-based management framework may make this extra complexity worthwhile for a large entity such as Arkaig.

(c) **Performance hierarchy**

According to Anthony, there are three tiers to decision-making in an organisation and each one has different needs which impact on the performance information which is required.

The strategic level is the one associated with the higher levels of management (such as the board). Strategic performance is measured over longer periods (3–10 years) since this depends on the achievement of the strategies which will enable the achievement of the overall mission of the business. The information will be externally focused requiring information on competitors and markets against which the company's performance can be benchmarked. This information will be used mainly for planning rather than controlling. At this level of the hierarchy, forecasts will be prepared and broad targets will be set for the lower levels of management and their performance measured against these targets. Therefore, information will often be heavily aggregated and qualitative in nature (such as customer attitudes). The board report evaluated above is an illustration of this type of information.

At the tactical level, the middle layer of management will be concerned with shorter term and more detailed objectives (possibly over a quarter or year) than the strategic level. The information will be collected on the deployment of the company's resources and activities on a functional department or business unit level. This information will be used to see that the strategic objectives are being supported by the company's activities. It will contain information to aid some short-term planning but will focus more on assisting this layer of management to control the operations of the business. Much of the information at this level will be internally generated and will be combined with the targets supplied by the strategic level in order to make decisions. For example, generally, the achievement of budget targets or more specifically, the sales and marketing department might be required to report quarterly on changes in the order book in order that the strategic level can forecast future revenue levels.

The operational level focuses on the day-to-day activities of the business ensuring that specific tasks set by the tactical level are achieved. Therefore, information at this level is detailed and task-specific. It will be prepared on a regular basis (often daily or weekly). It will be aimed to assist management at this level in controlling the business in order to achieve its short-term plans (weekly sales or monthly profit targets). There will be little external information needed at this level as there is very little planning activity being carried out.

(d) A specific area of concern at Arkaig is inbound and outbound logistics where there is an old warehousing and distribution information system. For a business such as Arkaig which aims to use technology innovatively, this could lead to inefficiencies. A state-of-the-art system would be integrated with the production and sales systems and would allow better stock control with fewer errors in picking inventory and reduced obsolescence while improved distribution could lead to faster delivery to customers with reduced costs of transportation.

The concern regarding after-sales service may be due to an inconsistency in having an area which generates a significant amount of revenue but which relates in reality to the failure of reliability of the business' products. It would be important to identify that customers' attitude to product reliability is not affected and that they see this service as necessary (maybe by benchmarking failure rates/machine downtime against competitors).

Although the chain shows human resources as a secondary activity, it is recognised as important to achieving the entrepreneurial culture at Arkaig. This culture can be realised through the reward system where employees are rewarded by share ownership or a share option scheme. Its effect can be measured through improved profitability and increased innovation.

Mock Exams

ACCA

Advanced Performance Management (APM)

Mock Exam 1 (BPP)

Questions	
Time allowed	3 hours 15 minutes
Section A This ONE question is compulsory and MUST be attempted. Section B BOTH questions are compulsory and MUST be attempted.	

DO NOT OPEN THIS EXAM UNTIL YOU ARE READY TO START UNDER EXAMINATION CONDITIONS

Section A

This section of the exam contains one question.

This question is worth 50 marks and is compulsory.

This exam section is worth 50 marks in total.

1 Question 1

Write a report to the CEO of Kolmog to respond to their instructions for work on the following areas:

(a) The characteristics of service businesses **(4 marks)**

(b) The current strategic performance report and the choice of performance metrics used **(8 marks)**

(c) Evaluation of the outline balanced scorecard **(12 marks)**

(d) The difficulties in implementing and using the balanced scorecard **(7 marks)**

(e) Standards, and the managers' performance reward system **(9 marks)**

Professional marks will be awarded for the demonstration of skill in communication, analysis and evaluation, scepticism and commercial acumen in your answer. **(10 marks)**

(Total = 50 marks)

Exhibit 1: Company information and mission

Kolmog Hotels (Kolmog) is a large listed chain of branded hotels in Ostland. Its stated mission is: 'to become the No. 1 hotel chain in Ostland, building the strength of the Kolmog brand by consistently delighting customers, investing in employees, delivering innovative products/services and continuously improving performance'. The subsidiary aims of the company are to maximise shareholder value, create a culture of pride in the brand and strengthen the brand loyalty of all stakeholders.

The hotels in the Kolmog chain include a diverse range of buildings and locations serving different customer groups: large conference venues, city centre business hotels and country house hotels for holidays. For reporting purposes, the company has divided itself into the four geographical regions of Ostland, as can be seen in a recent example of the strategic performance report for the company used by the board for its annual review (see Appendix 1). At the operational level, each hotel manager is given an individual budget for their hotel, prepared in the Finance Department, and is judged by performance against budgeted profit.

Exhibit 2: Strategic changes

Kolmog is planning a strategic change to its current business model. The board has decided to sell many of the hotels in the chain and then rent them back. This is consistent with many other hotel companies which are focusing on the management of their hotels rather than managing a large property portfolio of hotels.

In order to assist this strategic change, the chief executive officer (CEO) is considering introducing the balanced scorecard across Kolmog. They have tasked you, as a management accountant in the head office, to assist them with this work.

The CEO is worried that the BSC might be perceived within the organisation as a management accounting technique that has been derived from the manufacturing sector. In order to assess its use at Kolmog, they have asked you to explain the characteristics that differentiate service businesses from manufacturing ones, using Kolmog to illustrate your points.

Also, before introducing any new performance measurement systems, the CEO wants to assess the current information which is produced for the board (Appendix 1). To assist with this, they have asked you to evaluate the current strategic performance report, and the choice of metrics used.

Exhibit 3: Balanced scorecard

Senior executives at the head office of Kolmog have drawn up a preliminary list of perspectives and metrics as an outline of the balanced scorecard:

Table 1: Performance metrics for the balanced scorecard

Key strategic perspective	Metric
Strategic financial performance	Financial performance benchmarked to Kolmog's main competitors (share price and return on capital employed)
Customer satisfaction	Customer satisfaction survey scores
Hotel performance against budget	Variance analysis for each hotel
Employee satisfaction	Staff turnover

The CEO has asked you to help him review the preliminary work done on the development of the scorecard in order to ensure that it is consistent with the goal of meeting the strategic objectives of the company by tying operational and strategic performance measurement into a coherent framework. To this end, the CEO has asked you to evaluate the outline Scorecard (Appendix 1), suggesting suitable improvements where appropriate.

The CEO also wants your thoughts about any practical issues arising from introducing the scorecard. Therefore, they asked you to include a section in your report which describes the difficulties in implementing and using the balanced scorecard at Kolmog.

Exhibit 4: Reward systems

The history of rewards at Kolmog has not been good, with only 1% of staff receiving their maximum possible bonus in previous years, and 75% of staff receiving no bonus. This has led to many complaints that targets set for the reward system are too challenging.

Under a new performance reward system, employee targets are to be derived from the balanced scorecard strategic measures depending on the employee's area of responsibility. The new system is for hotel managers to be given challenging targets based on their hotel's performance against budgeted profit, industry-wide staff turnover and the company's average customer satisfaction scores. The hotel managers will then get up to 30% of their basic salary as a bonus, based on their regional manager's assessment of their performance against these targets.

The CEO wants to use Fitzgerald and Moon's building block model to assess the new system. They are happy with the dimensions of performance but wants your comments on the standards and rewards being applied here. They asked you to evaluate the standards and rewards for the hotel managers' performance reward system, using the building block model as the basis for your evaluation.

Exhibit 5: Appendix 1

	East region	*West region*	*North region*	*South region*	*Total*	*Total 20X2*	*As % of revenue for 20X3*
	$m	$m	$m	$m	$m	$m	
Revenue	235	244	313	193	985	926	
Cost of sales	28	30	37	21	116	110	11.78%
Gross profit	207	214	276	172	869	816	
Staff costs	61	65	78	54	258	245	26.19%

	East region	West region	North region	South region	Total	Total 20X2	As % of revenue for 20X3
	$m	$m	$m	$m	$m	$m	
Other operating costs							
Hotels	68	70	97	54	289	270	29.34%
Head office	—	—	—	—	158	150	16.04%
Operating profit	78	79	101	64	164	151	16.60%
Financing costs					78	73	7.92%
Profit before tax					86	78	8.73%

	20X3	20X2	Growth year on year
Capital employed	$1,132m	$1,065m	6.29%
EPS	$1.36	$1.27	7.09%
Share price	$12.34	$11.76	4.93%
ROCE	14.49%	14.18%	

Section B

This section of the exam contains two questions.

Each question is worth 25 marks and is compulsory.

This exam section is worth 50 marks in total.

2 Question 2

Respond to the FD's request for work on the following areas:

(a) Evaluating the suitability of incremental budgeting **(9 marks)**

(b) Recalculating the budget and assessing the use of rolling budgeting **(8 marks)**

(c) Recommending a suitable budgeting method for the Marketing Division (M) **(3 marks)**

Professional marks will be awarded for the demonstration of skill in analysis and evaluation, scepticism and commercial acumen in your answer. **(5 marks)**

(Total = 25 marks)

Exhibit 1: Company background

The Drinks Group (DG) has been created over the last three years by merging three medium-sized family businesses. These businesses are all involved in making fruit drinks. Fizzy (F) makes and bottles healthy, fruit-based sparkling drinks. Still (S) makes and bottles fruit-flavoured non-sparkling drinks and Healthy (H) buys fruit and squeezes it to make basic fruit juices. The three companies have been divisionalised within the group structure. A fourth division called Marketing (M) exists to market the products of the other divisions to various large retail chains. Marketing has only recently been set up in order to help the business expand. All of the operations and sales of DG occur in Nordland, which is an economically well-developed country with a strong market for healthy non-alcoholic drinks.

The group has recruited a new finance director (FD), who was asked by the board to perform a review of the efficiency and effectiveness of the Finance Department as their first task on taking office. The FD has just presented their report to the board regarding some problems at DG.

Extract from FD's report to the board:

> The main area for improvement, which was discussed at the last board meeting, is the need to improve profit margins throughout the business. There is no strong evidence that new products or markets are required but that the most promising area for improvement lies in better internal control practices.

Exhibit 2: Control

As DG was formed from an integration of the original businesses (F, S, H), there was little immediate effort put into optimising the control systems of these businesses. They have each evolved over time in their own way. Currently, the main method of central control that can be used to drive profit margin improvement is the budget system in each business. The budgeting method used is to take the previous year's figures and simply increment them by estimates of growth in the market that will occur over the next year. These growth estimates are obtained through a discussion between the financial managers at group level and the relevant divisional managers. The management at each division are then given these budgets by head office and their personal targets are set around achieving the relevant budget numbers.

Exhibit 3: Divisions

H and S Divisions are in stable markets where the levels of demand and competition mean that sales growth is unlikely, unless by acquisition of another brand. The main engine for prospective profit growth in these divisions is through margin improvements. The managers at these divisions have been successful in previous years and generally keep to the agreed budgets. As a result, they are usually not comfortable with changing existing practices.

F is faster growing and seen as the star of the Group. However, the Group has been receiving complaints from customers about late deliveries and poor quality control of the F products. The F managers have explained that they are working hard within the budget and capital constraints imposed by the board and have expressed a desire to be less controlled.

The Marketing Division has only recently been set up and the intention is to run each marketing campaign as an individual project which would be charged to the division whose products are benefiting from the campaign. The managers of the manufacturing divisions are very doubtful of the value of M, as each believes that they have an existing strong reputation with their customers that does not require much additional spending on marketing. However, the board decided at the last meeting that there was scope to create and use a marketing budget effectively at DG, if its costs were carefully controlled. Similar to the other divisions, the Marketing Division budgets are set by taking the previous year's actual spend and adding a percentage increase. For M, the increase corresponds to the previous year's growth in group turnover.'

The FD has asked for a brief, justified, recommendation of a suitable budgeting method which could be used at the Marketing Division (M).

Exhibit 4: Budgeting methods

At present, the FD is harassed by the introduction of a new information system within the Finance Department which is straining the resources of the department. However, they need to respond to the issues raised above at the board meeting and so is considering using different budgeting methods at DG. They have asked you, the management accountant at the Group, to do some preliminary work to help them decide whether and how to change the budget methods. The first task that they believe would be useful is to consider the use of rolling budgets. They think that fast-growing F may prove the easiest division in which to introduce new ideas.

F's incremental budget for the current year is given below. You can assume that cost of sales and distribution costs are variable and administrative costs are fixed.

	Q1	*Q2*	*Q3*	*Q4*	*Total*
	$'000	$'000	$'000	$'000	$'000
Revenue	17,520	17,958	18,407	18,867	72,752
Cost of sales	9,636	9,877	10,124	10,377	40,014
Gross profit	7,884	8,081	8,283	8,490	32,738
Distribution costs	1,577	1,616	1,657	1,698	6,548
Administration costs	4,214	4,214	4,214	4,214	16,856
Operating profit	2,093	2,251	2,412	2,578	9,334

The actual figures for Quarter 1 (which has just completed) are:

	$'000
Revenue	17,932
Cost of sales	9,863
Gross profit	8,069
Distribution costs	1,614
Administration costs	4,214
Operating profit	2,241

On the basis of the Q1 results, sales volume growth of 3% per quarter is now expected.

The FD has requested an evaluation the suitability of incremental budgeting at each division.

The FD has also requested that you recalculate the budget for Fizzy Division (F) using rolling budgeting and assess the use of rolling budgeting at F.

3 Question 3

Respond to the board and the FD's request for work on the following areas:

(a) Evaluating the performance of SS using EVA™ **(13 marks)**

(b) Assessing if SS meets its regulatory ROCE target and commenting on the impact on performance management **(7 marks)**

Professional marks will be awarded for the demonstration of skill in analysis and evaluation, and commercial acumen in your answer. **(5 marks)**

(Total = 25 marks)

Exhibit 1: Company background

Stillwater Services (SS) is a listed water utility company providing water and sewage services to the public and businesses of a region of Teeland. The company was formed when the government-owned Public Water Company of Teeland was broken up into regional utility companies (one of which was SS) and sold into private ownership over four years ago.

Exhibit 2: Industry regulator

As a vital utility for the economy of Teeland, water services are a government-regulated industry. The regulator is principally concerned that SS does not abuse its monopoly position in the regional market to unjustifiably increase prices. The majority of services (80%) are controlled by the regulator who sets an acceptable return on capital employed (ROCE) level and ensures that the pricing of SS within these areas does not breach this level. The remaining services, such as a bottled water operation and a contract repairs service, are unregulated and SS can charge a market rate for these. The regulator calculates its ROCE figure based on its own valuation of the capital assets being used in regulated services and the operating profit from those regulated services.

The target pre-tax ROCE set by the regulator is 6%. If SS were to breach this figure, then the regulator could fine the company. In the past, other such companies have seen fines amounting to millions of dollars.

The board is concerned about this and has asked for an assessment of whether SS meets its regulatory ROCE target and a brief comment on the impact of such a constraint on performance management at SS.

Exhibit 3: Economic value added (EVA™)

The board of SS is trying to drive the performance for the benefit of the shareholders. This is a new experience for many at SS, having been in the public sector until four years ago. In order to try to better communicate the objective of maximising shareholder wealth, the board has decided to introduce economic value added (EVA™) as the key performance indicator.

The finance director has asked you to calculate EVA™ for the company, and to use it to assess SS's performance, based on the following financial information for the year ending 30 September 20X2:

Exhibit 4: Stillwater Services

	Regulated	*Non-regulated*	*20X2 total*
	$m	$m	$m
Revenue	276.0	69.0	345.0
Operating costs	230.0	47.0	277.0
Operating profit	46.0	22.0	68.0
Finance charges			23.0
Profit before tax			45.0
Tax at 25%			9.5
Profit after tax			35.5

	20X2	*20X1*
Capital employed:	$m	$m
Measured from published accounts	657.0	637.0
Measured by regulator (for regulated services only)	779.0	761.0

Notes.

1 Total operating costs include:

	20X2	*20X1*
	$m	$m
Depreciation	59	57
Provision for doubtful debts	2	0.5
Research and development	12	–
Other non-cash items	7	6

2 Economic depreciation is assessed to be $83m in 20X2.

Economic depreciation includes any appropriate amortisation adjustments.

In previous years, it can be assumed that economic and accounting depreciation were the same.

3 Tax is the cash paid in the current year ($9m) and an adjustment of $0.5m for deferred tax provisions. There was no deferred tax balance prior to 20X2.

4 The provision for doubtful debts was $4.5m on the 20X2 statement of financial position.

5 Research and development is not capitalised in the accounts.

6 It relates to a new project that will be developed over five years and is expected to be of long-term benefit to the company. 20X2 is the first year of this project.

7 Cost of capital of SS

Equity	16%
Debt (pre-tax)	5%

8 Gearing of SS

40% equity, 60% debt

Answers

DO NOT TURN THIS PAGE UNTIL YOU HAVE COMPLETED THE MOCK EXAM

Exam success skills

In any APM exam, it will be important to apply good general exam technique by using the six exam success skills identified at the start of the Revision Kit, in the section covering 'essential skills'. These skills are: 1. Case scenario: Managing information; 2. Correct interpretation of requirements; 3. Answer planning: Priorities, structure and logic; 4. Efficient numerical analysis; 5. Effective writing and presentation; and 6. Good time management.

Some examples of how to apply these skills in this exam are provided in the table below.

Skill	Examples
Managing information	It is crucially important to assimilate the information in the question scenario. In longer questions, such as the 50-mark question, it is difficult to assimilate information by simply starting at the beginning and read to the end because there is so much information to take in. Instead, it is sensible to take an **active approach** to reading each question. Read enough of the question to get an idea of the basic scenario and then read the initial requirements so that you understand the first things that you are expected to do with this information. *For example, in question 1 the lengthy scenario makes a lot more sense if, before reading all of it, you are aware that the first requirements relate to performance reporting for a service business.*
Correct Interpretation of requirements	Be careful to interpret the verbs used in the question requirements carefully. *For example, Q1 part (b) requires you to evaluate the company's current performance report. It is vital that you evaluate the report itself, rather than the company's performance which is shown in the report (a common mistake in the exam).* Also be careful to identify where a question requirement contains more than one instruction. *For example, in Q1 part (e), the question is actually multi-faceted because it is based on a comment from the CEO in the final paragraph of the question. Many candidates will ignore the full extent of the question because the CEO's requirements were* ***embedded in the main scenario*** *of the question, as opposed to being in the requirement per se.*
Answer planning	Planning is always important in APM questions, because most of the marks are available for discussion and if your discussion points are not relevant to the scenario then they will not receive any credit. As a general rule, you should spend at least 20% of your time, reading the scenario and planning your answer.
Efficient numerical analysis	It is essential that the marker can follow your workings and your logic. If you make a mistake early in your calculations that affects your later calculations then the marker will only penalise the error you have made, and not its follow-on impact on other calculations. This means that it is not normally a good use of your time to correct such errors during the exam.

Skill	Examples
Effective writing and presentation	In APM this is a very important skill. You are often expected to be able to employ **critical analysis**, and this will sometimes mean that you will reject innovative and modern ideas in favour of less exotic tried and tested performance management tools. It is also very important to **relate your points to the scenario** and to the requirement wherever possible. *For example in Q1 part (b) a key issue is to consider how well the measures are linked to the company's mission – to become the No. 1 hotel chain.* Relating to the scenario will often require you to apply your theoretical knowledge to the scenario, and here you need to avoid simply repeating a rote-learned technical point. However, you **will** be tested on your understanding of the theoretical content of APM and **you will not be able to apply your theoretical knowledge to the scenario if you do not possess a strong understanding of the theories in the first place**. *For example, in Q1 part (e) it is not possible to apply the building block model to the scenario unless you have a strong understanding of this concept in the first place.* Finally, in Q1, to score the **marks** that are available you should use suitable report headings, an introduction, a logical structure, signposted by the good use of subheadings in the answer, and a clear, concise style.
Good time management	The exam is 3 hours 15 minutes long, which translates to 1.95 minutes per mark. There are 20 professional marks in the exam and therefore 80 technical marks. If you build in an allowance of 20% of your time for assimilating the scenario and planning, this still leaves you with 1.95 minutes per technical mark available. At the beginning of a question, work out the amount of time you should be spending on: • Planning: for a 25-mark question this will be 1.95 × 25 marks × 20% = 10 mins. For a 50-mark question this should be about 20 minutes. • Writing your answer to each requirement: Take the mark allocation and multiply by 1.95 minutes per technical mark.

Diagnostic

Did you apply these skills when reading, planning, and writing up your answer? Identify the exam success skills where you think you need to improve and capture your thoughts here of what you want to achieve when attempting questions in future.

Section A

This section of the exam contains one question.

This question is worth 50 marks and is compulsory.

This exam section is worth 50 marks in total.

1 Question 1

Workbook reference

The characteristics of service industries are highlighted in Chapter 4 of the Workbook. The Balanced Scorecard is discussed in Chapter 12, while Fitzgerald and Moon's building block model is discussed in Chapter 11.

Top tips

Part (a). Although you have been asked to 'explain' the characteristics, there are only five marks available for this part of the question. So you should keep your explanations relatively brief. There are five key characteristics which differentiate service businesses from manufacturing ones, meaning that there is only one mark available per characteristic. However, don't forget that you need to illustrate how the characteristics relate to Kolmog Hotels. Don't just talk about the characteristics of service businesses in generic terms.

Part (b). The CEO has asked you to evaluate Kolmog's current strategic performance report, and the word 'report' is crucial here. It is vital that you evaluate the **report** and the choice of metrics used in the report, rather than evaluating Kolmog's strategic **performance**.

A key issue to evaluate here is how well the performance report allows Kolmog to assess its performance against its mission. For example, does the report (or the metrics selected in it) help assess Kolmog's performance in relation to it becoming 'the No. 1 hotel chain in Ostland'?

Also think about the 'segmentation' of the report. For example, how useful is it to know how each of the four regions has performed, as opposed to how each type of hotel has performed?

Part (c). One of the key problems with Kolmog's current performance report (which, hopefully, you identified during your evaluation in part (b)) is that the report only includes financial metrics, rather than a range of metrics which can be used to measure performance in relation to the different elements of Kolmog's mission.

By contrast, the different perspectives included in the proposed BSC look at key aspects of non-financial performance as well as financial performance. This should be beneficial for Kolmog.

However, while the idea of introducing a BSC may be a good one, note that the CEO has asked you to 'suggest suitable improvements' to the scorecard where appropriate. So, are there any ways which the proposed metrics could be improved so that the aspects of performance being measured support the mission and objectives more effectively?

Part (d). Your evaluation in part (c) should have highlighted that some of the measures originally proposed for the outline scorecard could be improved. In turn, this should have highlighted one of the main difficulties of implementing the scorecard: choosing what measures to actually include in it.

As Kolmog has not used the scorecard before, selecting appropriate measures and then educating the managers in how to interpret the reported results are likely to be significant challenges in relation to implementing the scorecard.

Part (e). The scenario highlights that 75% of Kolmog's staff have received no bonuses in previous years, and there have been many complaints that the targets are too challenging.

This suggests that the staff don't regard the bonus targets as achievable, and consequently the staff are not motivated to try to achieve them.

Achievability is one of the three key 'standards' identified in the building block model (along with ownership and fairness). Similarly, motivation is one of the three key aspects of 'rewards' identified in the model (along with clarity and controllability).

The key issue in this part of the question is whether the new performance reward system fits with these standards and rewards any better than the old system appeared to. For example, will hotel managers feel they 'own' their performance targets if the budgets are imposed by head office?

Overall. Once again, remember that you have been asked to write a report, so make sure the style and structure of your answer, as a whole, is appropriate for a report. For example, a report should have a short introduction explaining the key issues to be discussed in it.

Examining team's comments

It was pleasing to note in part (b) that, compared to previous sittings, there were fewer examples of candidates evaluating the performance of the company and many more evaluating the performance **report**, which was what was required by the question.

Most candidates handled part (c) relatively well, but they could have scored more efficiently if they attended to the mission of the company, and how the scorecard would help the company achieve its mission.

However, part (d) was answered very poorly, with many candidates choosing to discuss improvements required rather than the **difficulties** faced in implementing and using the BSC at Kolmog. It is vital to answer the question set!

In part (e), most candidates demonstrated good understanding of the use of 'stretch' targets and the reward system implications at Kolmog. However, there was weaker understanding of the 'standards' element from Fitzgerald and Moon's building block model.

Marking guide	Marks
(a) Service industry characteristics – 1 mark per characteristic (intangibility; inseparability; variability (or heterogeneity); perishability) Characteristics must be illustrated in relation to the hotel industry to score the full mark available for each characteristic. Total for part (a): up to 4 marks	4
(b) For comments on how well the current report enables Kolmog to measure performance against its objectives – 1 mark per point; up to 5 marks For comments on the choice of measures used in the report – 1 mark per point; up to 5 marks	8
(c) For comments on the outline BSC proposed for Kolmog; evaluating current metrics and suggesting suitable improvements to the scorecard – 1 mark per point, up to 4 marks for each scorecard perspective Other relevant comments about the scorecard – 1 mark per point Comments must be linked directly to the scorecard proposed for Kolmog, rather than being a generic description of the scorecard. Total for part (c): up to 12 marks	12
(d) For difficulties in implementing and using the scorecard at Kolmog – 1 mark per point Again, to score the full marks available difficulties should be linked directly to implementing the scorecard at Kolmog. Total for part (d): up to 7 marks	7

Marking guide	Marks
(e) Standards – for explaining the criteria of ownership, achievability and fairness; 1 mark per standard; up to 3 marks Rewards – for explaining the criteria of clarity, motivation and controllability; 1 mark per reward; up to 3 marks For comments on the new reward system which has been proposed at Kolmog – 1 mark per point; up to 5 marks Total for part (e): up to 9 marks	
	9

Professional skills

Communication

- General report format and structure (use of headings/sub-headings and an introduction)
- Style, language and clarity (appropriate layout and tone of report response, presentation of calculations, appropriate use of the CBE tools)
- Effectiveness of communication (answer is relevant, specific rather than general and focused to the requirement)

Analysis and Evaluation

- Use of information provided to perform a suitable/comprehensive evaluation
- Appropriate use of the data to support discussion and draw appropriate conclusions
- Demonstration of reasoned and balanced judgement
- Demonstration of ability to consider relevant factors applicable to Kolmog Co's situation
- Identification of further analysis, which could be carried out to enable an appropriate recommendation to be made.

Scepticism

- Effective challenge and critical assessment

Commercial acumen

- Effective use of examples and/or calculations from the scenario information and other practical considerations related to the context to illustrate points being made
- Demonstrating an awareness of organisational and external factors
- Recognising key issues in a given scenario in terms of how to address problems, and possible obstacles that will need to be overcome in the process of doing this
- Recommendations are practical and plausible, and commercially viable in the context of Kolmog Co's situation

Maximum	10
Total	50

Report

To: CEO Kolmog Hotels

From: Accountant

Date: June 20X3

Subject: **Performance measurement and targets at Kolmog Hotels**

Introduction

This report explains the key characteristics which differentiate service businesses from manufacturing ones, and then evaluates the performance reports and measures which are being used to monitor Kolmog's performance. The report then evaluates the balanced

ANSWERS

scorecard (BSC) which has been proposed for use at Kolmog, and describes the difficulties which could be associated with using the scorecard.

Finally, the report explains the purpose of setting challenging targets, and uses Fitzgerald and Moon's building block model to evaluate the standards and rewards which are applied to the managers' performance reward system at Kolmog.

(a) **Characteristics of service businesses**

There are five key characteristics of services that distinguish services from manufacturing.

(1) **Intangibility** – In contrast to manufactured goods which are tangible, physical products, services do not have any substantial material or physical aspects. When a customer books a room in one of Kolmog's hotels, they are not buying a physical product; rather they are buying their overnight accommodation in the hotel. The fact that Kolmog isn't producing a physical product also helps to explain why its cost of sales (at around 12% of revenue) is much lower than the equivalent figure would be for a manufacturing business.

(2) **Inseparability (or simultaneity)** – Whereas manufactured goods need to be produced before they can be consumed, services are created at the same time as they are consumed. For example, a guest's experience of one of Kolmog's hotels is formed during their stay in the hotel.

(3) **Variability (or heterogeneity)** – One of the key issues which service businesses face is ensuring consistency in the standard of their service. For example, it could be difficult for Kolmog to control the level of service provided to customers by the different hotels in the group, not least because the behaviour of individual staff working in a hotel on any given day will have a significant impact on the level of service which customers receive.

(4) **Perishability** – Services are innately perishable. If a room is unoccupied (unused) for a day, then the revenue which could have been earned from the room for that day can never be recovered. This explains why room occupancy rates are often used as key performance measures by hotel companies.

(b) **Current strategic performance report**

Financial information only – The strategic performance report should help the board monitor how well Kolmog is performing in the light of its stated mission.

However, despite the mission highlighting non-financial aspects of performance, the performance report currently includes only financial information. As a result, the report does not provide any indicators of how well Kolmog is performing in relation to the non-financial elements of the mission, such as **customer satisfaction, employee development** or **product innovation**.

Shareholder value – The report covers the subsidiary aim of maximising shareholder value by providing figures for earnings per share (EPS), share price performance and return on capital employed (ROCE), although total shareholder return and economic value added might be better measures than ROCE in this respect.

Importantly, however, maximising shareholder value is only a subsidiary aim, rather than a primary aim of the mission.

Key performance indicators – Hotels often have high levels of operational gearing because many of their costs (such as staff costs and property costs) are fixed. Consequently, their profit levels are likely to be sensitive to relatively small changes in revenue. As a result, hotel chains often view measures such as occupancy rates and revenue per available room as key performance indicators. Kolmog's performance report could be improved by including some key performance indicators like this – particularly indicators which are linked to revenue performance.

Market position – Perhaps the most important aspect of Kolmog's mission is the desire to 'become the No. 1 hotel chain in Ostland'. However, the report does not provide any indication as to how well the chain is performing in this respect, for example by measuring Kolmog's market share.

The absence of any external data is significant in this respect. Not only does it prevent the board from measuring overall market share, it also means it cannot benchmark Kolmog's performance in key performance areas against competitor hotels. For example, although the ratios of staff costs and hotel operating costs are useful, it would also be useful to know how these figures compare to the equivalent ratios for competitor hotels.

Segmental analysis – Although it is useful for the board to have information about how different segments of the chain are performing, breaking down the results into **geographical areas** may not be the most valuable basis of segmentation. For example, if the **mix of hotel types** varies significantly between each region, then simply comparing the performance of the four geographical regions may not be very instructive. In this respect, it may be more useful for the operating results to be broken down by hotel type (for example, conference venues, city centre business hotels, and country house hotels).

Budget figures – Although the individual hotel managers are judged by their hotel's performance against budget, the strategic performance report doesn't show any budget figures. This appears to be a significant weakness in the report. Including budget figures and variances in the report would enable the board to identify any significant deviations in actual performance compared to budget, and take corrective action where necessary.

(c) **The balanced scorecard**

In general terms, the balanced scorecard (BSC) is intended to help a company translate its mission into objectives and measures such that the measures are coherent with, and support, the overall mission. A company can also use the measures in its scorecard to inform its employees about the key drivers of success.

The BSC also highlights the importance of measuring both non-financial performance and financial performance. This could be particularly valuable to Kolmog, given the importance of the non-financial elements in its mission.

Although it may be easier for Kolmog to measure aspects of financial performance than non-financial performance, the long-term success of the hotel chain is likely to depend on how it performs in key non-financial areas. Nevertheless, it remains important to measure financial performance, and the financial perspective of the scorecard highlights this.

Financial perspective

The financial perspective in the outline BSC focuses on measures of strategic financial performance: **share price** and **ROCE**. This fits with the overall objective of maximising shareholder value, although it would be useful to measure **dividend per share** as well as share price in order to reflect **total shareholder return**.

Operational gearing – Although ROCE is often used as a measure of overall performance, the change in Kolmog's business model may make it less suitable as a measure for the company. Once Kolmog has sold and rented back many of its hotels, the business will have a much lower capital base. However, its fixed costs (notably rental costs) will be much higher. Therefore, it may be more appropriate to include a measure such as **operational gearing** in the scorecard.

Revenue growth – It would also seem appropriate to include **revenue growth** as a measure, given Kolmog's stated intention to 'become the No. 1 hotel chain in Ostland'.

Customer perspective

Customer satisfaction survey scores – This measure seems to be appropriate because it is aligned to the mission and the aim of 'consistently delighting customers'.

Brand loyalty – However, measuring customer satisfaction alone does not provide any indication as to whether loyalty to Kolmog's brand is strengthening. In this respect, it would also be useful to measure the number (or proportion) of customers who are repeat customers, as opposed to customers who are staying in a Kolmog hotel for the first time.

Alternatively, it could be useful to measure the value of the revenues (or the proportion of the revenues) which are generated by returning customers, as distinct from customers who are staying in a Kolmog hotel for the first time.

It is not clear from the scenario whether Kolmog has any kind of loyalty card programme. If it does, then a measure based around the number (or value) of bookings from loyalty card customers could also be a useful measure in relation to brand loyalty.

Internal business perspective

Variance analysis – In the outline scorecard, variance analysis (comparing actual performance to budget) for each hotel has been proposed as a measure to support the internal business perspective.

Occupancy rates – In this respect, it will be important for the budgets to include non-financial performance indicators as well as financial ones. As we have already noted, room occupancy rates are a key factor in shaping a hotel's performance, and so should be monitored here alongside financial variances.

However, as we noted in relation to segmental analysis, it is also important to recognise that different business processes or elements of performance may be important in different types of hotel hotels. For example, city centre business hotels may be able to maintain reasonably consistent occupancy rates throughout the year, whereas occupancy rates in the country house hotels are likely to exhibit greater seasonality. Likewise, operating margins in the country house hotels may vary more during the year, because they will still be incurring fixed costs even in months when occupancy rates are low.

Therefore, it may be necessary to adapt the key scorecard measures being used for different types of hotel.

Internal benchmarking – Nonetheless, the performance of individual Kolmog hotels can be compared against others of the same type. Internal benchmarking in this way should enable Kolmog to identify which hotels are performing best, and in turn whether there are any 'best practices' which can be shared between those hotels and others which are not performing so well.

In this way, knowledge sharing between different hotels may help Kolmog to 'continuously improve performance', which is one of the aims of its mission.

Innovation and learning perspective

The innovation and learning perspective of the scorecard should underpin this drive to continuously improve performance. Equally, the measures chosen in relation to the perspective should be ones which encourage the delivery 'of innovative products/services', which again is an aspect of Kolmog's mission.

New products/services – There are not currently any measures proposed which relate to innovation or new products. A measure which could be appropriate here is a measure of the proportion of revenue which is generated from new products or services; for example, any new packages which might be offered by the country house hotels. However, as the hotel industry in general is now a fairly mature industry the scope to deliver innovative products and services may be relatively limited.

Employee satisfaction – As a service business, Kolmog's employees play a particularly important role in delivering customer satisfaction. If the staff in a hotel are happy and motivated this is likely to lead to guests in that hotel enjoying their stay more than if staff were grumpy and unhelpful. The performance metric of staff turnover could give an indication of how satisfied staff are with their jobs. In general, the higher staff turnover rates are, the less satisfied staff are likely to be with their jobs.

Alternatively, instead of using staff turnover as a surrogate for employee satisfaction, Kolmog could perhaps also introduce staff surveys in which staff satisfaction scores could be measured more directly.

No. 1 hotel chain in Ostland – Whichever measures Kolmog finally chooses for its scorecard, it is important to remember the underlying emphasis of the stated mission is 'to become the No. 1 hotel chain in Ostland'. Therefore, wherever possible, Kolmog should seek to benchmark its performance in all of the scorecard areas against its competitors, in order to identify whether or not it is actually achieving this 'No. 1' status.

(d) **Implementing and using the BSC**

The BSC has not been used at Kolmog before, and therefore, as with any new framework, the company could face difficulties as it is introduced for the first time.

Selecting measures – In the previous section of this report we have suggested some alternative measures to the preliminary ones proposed by senior managers at head office. This highlights the first potential difficulty in using the scorecard: selecting which measures to include.

When deciding which measures are the most appropriate to include in Kolmog's scorecard, it is important to include measures which are related to key business processes and activities which add value to the company, not simply those that are easy to measure.

It is also important to remember the scorecard's role in translating strategic measures down to the operational level. So, for example, while there might be an overall measure focusing on customer satisfaction levels, at the operational level this may need to be broken down further into customer satisfaction on the service they received at reception, or the cleanliness and comfort of their room.

The innovation and learning perspective can often be the most difficult to measure directly. However, Kolmog appears to have worked round this problem by selecting measures relating to employee satisfaction.

Equally, it is important not to include too many measures. There is a danger that if the scorecard contains too many measures the impact of them will be reduced as a result of information overload.

Conflicting measures – Some measures in the scorecard may naturally conflict. For example, Kolmog may look to improve customer satisfaction scores by recruiting extra staff in some of its hotels. However, the costs of these staff could adversely affect financial performance in those hotels (at least in the short term).

The board may find it difficult to decide what combination of measures is likely to encourage the best results for Kolmog, but when making such decisions it will be important to look at how well each possible measure helps the company achieve its overall mission.

Interpretation – Even if Kolmog selects an appropriate set of measures for its scorecard they will ultimately only prove valuable to the company if managers can interpret the results of the measures adequately, and use them to initiate appropriate actions to improve performance. If managers have difficulty analysing the figures, or interpreting what the figures are demonstrating, then it will be difficult for the managers to know what actions need to be taken in the light of the results being indicated by the scorecard.

Again, this also reinforces the importance of not including too many measures, in order to avoid information overload.

Management commitment – The scorecard is only likely to be effective if senior managers are committed to using it. If they revert to focusing solely on the financial measures they are used to, then the value of introducing additional (non-financial) measures will be reduced.

In this respect, the proposal to derive employees' targets for the performance reward system to the BSC seems sensible, because it encourages managers and staff to focus on all four perspectives of the scorecard.

(e) **Standards**

In their 'building block' model, Fitzgerald and Moon highlight that in order for performance measures to be effective, employees must view the measures as being **fair** and **achievable**, and the employees must take **ownership** of them.

Achievability – The fact that 75% of the staff have not received a bonus in previous years suggests that Kolmog's reward scheme has historically not been an effective tool for motivating employees. If the staff feel the bonus targets are unachievable, they will only put in the minimum amount of effort they need to keep their jobs, rather than making any extra effort in the hope of receiving some extra reward as a result.

If the new targets are to be more effective in this respect, it is important that they are perceived to be more realistic to achieve.

Ownership – If the performance targets are based on budgets set by the Finance Department, this may also contribute to the sense of staff not accepting the targets and trying to achieve them. In particular, hotel managers' performance should only be judged against factors they can **control**. For example, if there is a downturn in market conditions, there is likely to be a downturn in revenue which managers cannot control.

Fairness – As we noted earlier in relation to segmental analysis, there are likely to be differences in the performance of different types of hotel. The concept of fairness suggests that targets should be adjusted for different types of hotel. For example, targets for city centre hotels should be comparable to each other, but may not be comparable to country house hotels.

Rewards

Rewards are the motivators which encourage employees to work towards the standards set. In order for rewards to be effective, they need to be clear, motivating and controllable.

Clarity – The employees need to be clear about the goals they are working towards.

Motivating – Employees need to be motivated to work towards the targets and in pursuit of the organisation's strategic objectives.

Controllability – Staff should not be held responsible for aspects of performance over which they have no control.

Issues with the proposed system

Ownership – The new system will propose that managers' targets are based on their hotel's performance against budgeted profit. However, if the budgets continue to be set by the head office Finance Department with no input from the managers, then there is likely to be a lack of ownership of the targets. Therefore, hotel managers should be involved in the budget-setting process.

Fairness – Comparing staff turnover against an industry-wide standard may not be fair if managers cannot control staff wages. If wages are set centrally, and are not attractive compared to the wages offered by other hotel chains, staff turnover is likely to be high, and there will be little that managers can do to prevent this. A fairer measure would be to compare the staff turnover for individual hotels against other hotels of the same type within Kolmog.

Aligned to mission – Customer satisfaction is a controllable factor for hotel managers and therefore customer satisfaction scores should be an important element of performance assessment. However, given Kolmog's stated mission 'to become the No. 1 hotel chain' it would be better to compare customer satisfaction scores against the scores achieved by Kolmog's competitors. The current proposal (to measure managers against the internal average) will not directly help Kolmog improve its performance against its competitors.

Clarity – The hotel managers' bonuses will be determined by their regional manager's assessment of their performance against the targets. In order for the reward system to be effective, the regional managers will need to explain the structure of the new scheme (for example, if there are different levels of bonus below the full 30%), and also the factors which will influence their assessment of the hotel managers' performance.

Ultimately, the success of the new scheme will depend on the extent to which it motivates staff and managers to help Kolmog achieve its mission. To do this, the targets will need to be stretching, but also to be perceived as achievable. In this respect, Kolmog should monitor the number of staff receiving bonuses to assess whether more staff are qualifying for some kind of bonus than under the old scheme.

Section B

This section of the exam contains two questions.

Each question is worth 25 marks and is compulsory.

This exam section is worth 50 marks in total.

2 Question 2

Marking guide	Marks	
(a) Evaluation of the advantages and disadvantages of incremental budgeting in general – 1 mark per relevant point	5	
Recommendations about the suitability of incremental budgeting in S and H Division – 1 mark per relevant point	3	
Discussion about the suitability of incremental budgeting for F – 1 mark per relevant point	3	
Discussion about the suitability of incremental budgeting for M – 1 mark per relevant point	3	
		9
(b) Explanation of the rolling budget process – 1 mark per relevant point, maximum 2	2	
Calculations (up to 6 marks in total for calculations):		
Actual figures in Q1	1	
Revenue; Cost of sales; Distribution costs; Administration costs; Operating profit – 1 mark for correct figures for each line in the budget	4	
Budgeted figures for Q1 in the next year	1	
Comments on the use of rolling budgets at F – 1 mark per relevant point	3	
		8
(c) Recommendation of an appropriate method (1 mark), plus 1 mark per valid point justifying the choice of method	3	
		3

Professional skills

Analysis and Evaluation

- Use of information provided to perform a suitable/comprehensive evaluation
- Appropriate use of the data to both support discussion and also draw appropriate conclusions
- Demonstration of reasoned and balanced judgement
- Demonstration of ability to consider relevant factors applicable to DG Co's situation

Scepticism

- Effective challenge and critical assessment

Commercial acumen

- Effective use of examples and/or calculations from the scenario information and other practical considerations related to the context to illustrate points being made
- Demonstrating an awareness of organisational and external factors
- Recommendations are practical and plausible, and commercially viable in the context of DG Co's situation

Maximum	5
Total	25

(a) **Incremental budgeting**

Advantages

Not too time consuming – DG currently uses incremental budgets. One of the main advantages of incremental budgets is that they are relatively quick and easy to prepare. This is a general advantage at DG given the time constraints which the Finance Department is currently experiencing in relation to the information systems implementation.

Stable environment – Incremental budgets are also appropriate for stable environments, where current or historic figures can provide a reliable basis for projecting future figures, and where only small changes are required to those figures.

Disadvantages

Accepts inefficiencies – A major problem with incremental budgets is that, by their nature, they reinforce existing practices. The fact that the FD has identified that the most promising area for performance improvement lies in better internal control practices suggests that there are inefficiencies in DG's current processes, which are likely to be reflected in its current figures. However, by basing future years' budgets on the current figures, these inefficiencies will be perpetuated rather than challenged. Consequently, for example, DG may miss opportunities to make cost savings.

Can encourage spending – Similarly, managers may feel they have to spend the full amount of their current year's budget in order to preserve the same level of budget next year, even though the expenditure may not actually be required at the moment. Once again, such an approach could lead to DG's costs being unnecessarily high.

H and S Divisions

Stable markets – Both H and S Divisions are in stable markets. The fact that sales growth is unlikely suggests that incremental budgeting could be appropriate for them.

Moreover, such an approach would fit with the managers' preference for maintaining existing practices rather than changing them.

Margin improvements – Because H and S have limited opportunities to increase revenues, in order to increase their profitability they will need to improve their margins. However, incremental budgeting will not be suitable to help them do this.

In order to improve their margins, the divisions will need to challenge and reduce their costs. However, by basing future budgets on current figures, an incremental approach will not provide the stimulus for continuous improvement which is required.

F division

Rapid growth – F's rate of growth means an incremental approach is unlikely to be suitable for it. Its rapid growth means that budgets based on current results will quickly become out of date.

The customer complaints and the managers' complaints could both be symptoms of the constraints which incremental budgets have placed on the business. For example, the complaints about late deliveries and poor quality could result from F trying to satisfy rapidly increasing demand whilst also facing budget constraints – which mean it either doesn't have sufficient capacity to keep pace with demand or it has to use poorer quality materials in order to reduce material costs.

The managers' complaints pick up on this point further. If the cost budgets have been set in line with current levels of demand, they are unlikely to be sufficient to cope with the higher levels of demand.

M Division

Justifying costs – The managers of the manufacturing divisions are sceptical of the need for a marketing department and using an incremental budget will not do anything to change their opinion of this.

The current budgetary approach at M (simply adding a percentage to the current year's expenditure) doesn't require M to justify its spending. Until it does this, however, it seems unlikely that M will be able to change the other division's perceptions of it.

Perhaps more importantly, though, simply adding a percentage to the current year's spend could lead to unjustified expenditure. For example, if the Marketing Division commits some expenditure this year on the basis that it is currently within budget (rather than because the expenditure is necessary and will add value for DG) next year's budget will be uplifted from the higher figure. Under such circumstances, the budget will continuously be higher than it needs to be. Again, this would justify the other managers' scepticism about the amount of value that M adds to the company.

(b) Under a rolling budget, another accounting period is added to the budget when the most recent one finishes. The budget is then recalculated using the actual data from the most recent period as a basis.

Because F Division's budget is based on a quarterly basis, the rolling budget will include actual figures for Quarter 1 of the current year, and then forecasts for Quarters 2–4 of the current year, along with Quarter 1 of the following year.

Based on the assumption that cost of sales and distribution costs increase in line with sales, and that administration costs remain fixed as in the original budget, F's rolling budget would be as follows:

	Q1	*Q2*	*Q3*	*Q4*	***Total***	*Q1*
	Actual	*Forecast*	*Forecast*	*Forecast*	***Forecast***	*Forecast*
	$'000	$'000	$'000	$'000	**$'000**	$'000
Revenue	17,932	18,470	19,024	19,595	**75,021**	20,183
Cost of sales	(9,863)	(10,159)	(10,464)	(10,778)	**(41,264)**	(11,101)
Gross profit	8,069	8,311	8,560	8,817	**33,757**	9,082
Distribution costs	(1,614)	(1,662)	(1,712)	(1,764)	**(6,752)**	(1,817)
Administration costs	(4,214)	(4,214)	(4,214)	(4,214)	**(16,856)**	(4,214)
Operating profit	2,241	2,435	2,634	2,840	**10,149**	3,051

As we noted in part (a), F is growing rapidly, and the rolling budget gives F's managers the scope to increase their variable costs to reflect that growth, rather than being constrained by the original budget.

As a result, F should be better able to sustain its growth, and the level of complaints about late deliveries and poor quality (which could otherwise jeopardise its growth) should be reduced.

Moreover, the rolling budget should provide managers with more realistic targets against which to compare actual performance. In this way, the rolling budget provides a more effective control mechanism than an annual budget, which could potentially be disregarded as being out of date.

It is likely that additional resources in the Finance Department will be required to prepare rolling budgets, because updated budgets will need to be prepared each quarter rather than on an annual basis as they currently are. However, the benefits which F's managers would derive from having rolling budgets should outweigh the additional costs incurred to prepare them.

(c) **Justifying expenditure** – The scepticism from the managers of the manufacturing divisions about the need for a marketing department (M), in conjunction with the board's requirement that M's costs should be carefully controlled, suggests that an incremental budget may not provide a robust enough framework for M.

Zero-based budgeting – By contrast, a zero-based budgeting approach may be appropriate, and this is the approach recommended for M.

As each marketing campaign is run as an individual project, it seems more appropriate for M to budget for the campaigns on a project-by-project basis. A zero-based budget approach would provide a suitable framework for doing this, with the cost of each campaign having to be justified at the start before the campaign is approved.

Under a zero-based budget, M would need to justify every cost which is required for a specific marketing campaign. If a cost element cannot be justified, then no resources will be allocated to it in the budget.

Tighter control – Such an approach should also appease the managers of the manufacturing divisions because it will mean that marketing expenditure is being much more tightly controlled.

3 Question 3

Workbook reference

EVA™ is discussed in Chapter 7 of the Workbook. Stakeholder management and the potential impact of stakeholders on performance are discussed in Chapter 4.

Top tips

Part (a). Up to ten of the marks available in part (a) are for calculations. There should be some relatively easy marks here (for example, for identifying the adjustments to operating profit), even if you don't get all of the figures correct.

A few months before the exam which included this question, a technical article was published on ACCA's website – 'Economic value added versus profit-based measures of performance'. This article explained the adjustments to operation profit which are required in EVA™, as well as the logic behind them. Candidates who had read (and understood) this article should have been well placed to tackle this question. This highlights the importance of reading relevant technical articles on ACCA's website as part of your preparation for your exams.

One particular point to note in relation to the EVA™ calculation itself: Remember that your calculations for the capital employed figure need to be based on the published accounts figure at the start of 20X2, not at the end of it.

However, also note that the question requirement isn't simply to calculate EVA™; you should also have used the EVA™ figure you have calculated to evaluate SS's performance. In other words, how well is it creating value for its shareholders?

Part (b). As in part (a), this part of the question combines calculations with a discussion related to the figures you have calculated. Crucially, though, you must make sure your ROCE calculations relate solely to the regulated parts of SS's business.

Also, it is vitally important that you recognised that the ROCE target of 6% is the upper limit that SS can achieve on its regulated business, not a minimum target it is trying to achieve.

This is very important because the presence of this target means that SS has very little scope to increase its profits from regulated business. So, in terms of performance management for SS as a whole, what implications does this have for the role of unregulated business in increasing the company's profits?

Examining team's comments

The calculation of EVA™ was discussed in a technical article on ACCA's website, and had clearly been well prepared for by many candidates who scored most of the calculation marks available in part (a). The calculations of net operating profit after tax (NOPAT) could be done by starting from PAT, or from Operating Profit, and both approaches gained credit. The weakest area of the calculations was the adjustments to capital employed.

Most candidates realised the need to comment on the figures they had calculated and gave a summary sentence. However, many candidates did not offer any broader comment on the key assumptions in the EVA™ method, or the limitations of the method. This could be seen as a failure to appreciate the need to 'evaluate' performance using EVA™, rather than simply to 'calculate' performance.

Part (b) was generally poorly answered, with many candidates not appearing to realise that the ROCE target was an upper limit on the company. Few candidates spotted that the constraints on the regulated side of the business would mean that the unregulated side would be the engine of growth for SS, while the regulated side could act as a cash cow.

Marking guide	Marks	
(a) Adjustments to operating profit:		
Non-cash items	0.5	
Accounting depreciation	1	
Doubtful debts	1	
Research and development	1	
Interest	0.5	
Tax (cash amount paid; tax on interest)	2	
Capital employed figure:		
Capital employed (per accounts) at start of year	0.5	
Provision for doubtful debts	1	
Other non-cash items	1	
WACC	1	
EVA™	1	
Note. Maximum 10 marks available for calculations	10	
Comments about SS's performance, consistent with EVA™ calculation – 1 mark per relevant point	3	
		13
(b) *Calculations:*		
ROCE (on regulated business only)	1	
Maximum regulated operating profit allowed	1	
Operating margins (regulated vs non-regulated business)	1	
Other relevant calculations	1	
Commentary:		
On calculations – 1 mark per relevant point	2	
On performance management of regulated areas of SS – 1 mark per relevant point	2	
On performance management of unregulated areas of SS – 1 mark per relevant point	2	
		7

Professional skills

Analysis and Evaluation

- Use of information provided to perform a suitable/comprehensive evaluation
- Appropriate use of the data to support discussion and draw appropriate conclusions
- Demonstration of reasoned and balanced judgement
- Demonstration of ability to consider relevant factors applicable to Stillwater Co's situation

Commercial acumen

- Effective use of examples and/or calculations from the scenario information and other practical considerations related to the context to illustrate points being made
- Demonstrating an awareness of organisational and external factors

Marking guide	Marks
• Recommendations are practical and plausible, and commercially viable in the context of Stillwater Co's situation	
Maximum	5
Total	25

(a) Performance of SS using EVA™:

	$m	$m	*Comments*
Operating profit		68.00	
Add back:			
Depreciation	59.00		
Doubtful debts	2.00		
Research and development	12.00		
Other non-cash items	7.00		
		80.00	
Less:			
Economic depreciation		–83.00	
Tax		–9.00	Cash only
Tax adjustment on finance charges		–5.75	$23m × 25%
		—	
NOPAT		**50.25**	

		$m	*Notes*
			Based on figure b/f at start of 20X2
Capital employed		637.00	
Add back:			
Provision for doubtful debts	2.50		(See Working)
Other non-cash items	6.00		Non-cash items in 20X1
		8.50	
		645.50	

		$m	Notes
WACC:			
Equity: 40% × 16%	6.4%		
	2.3%		
	8.7%		
EVA™:			
NOPAT – (Capital employed × WACC)			
50.25 – (645.5 × 0.087)		**–5.91**	

No adjustment for depreciation required at the start of 20X2.

Working	$m
Provision for doubtful debts at end of 20X2	4.5
Movement in year	–2.0
Provision at start of year	2.5

Negative EVA™ – SS's negative EVA™ figure for 20X2 suggests that, instead of creating wealth for its shareholders, it is actually destroying value. More specifically, the value which SS is generating (NOPAT) is not sufficient to cover the economic cost of the capital it has employed to generate that value.

Such a position is not sustainable in the long run, and will lead to dissatisfaction amongst SS's shareholders. SS could look to address this issue either by increasing its net operating profit or by reducing its cost of capital; or through a combination of both.

NOPAT – SS's current NOPAT of $50.25m leaves it with a negative EVA™ of $5.91m. At the current cost of capital, SS would need to increase its NOPAT to $56.16m to break even on EVA™.

Cost of capital – Alternatively, SS would break even on EVA™, with its current level of NOPAT, if its WACC was 7.8% ($645.5m × 7.8% = $50.3m). In this respect, SS's current cost of equity (16%) appears high, particularly given the highly regulated nature of the industry. Moreover, given that 80% of SS's sales (for water and sewage services) are for services which are necessities for everyday life, there is relatively little risk that demand will fall. Again, this suggests that SS's cost of equity should be lower than it currently is.

Asset base – SS could also look to reduce its asset base by selling under-utilised assets. If it could reduce the amount of capital employed without any significant reduction in its NOPAT, this could help its EVA™ break even or become positive.

(b) Target ROCE: 6%

Operating profit from regulated business: $46.0m

Average capital employed: (779.0m + 761.0m)/2 = $770.0m

ROCE: 5.97%

Alternative calculation:

The examining team's answer uses capital employed at the end of 20X2, rather than average capital employed during the year.

Under this basis ROCE is: 46.0m/779.0m = 5.90%.

Return within prescribed limit – The return which SS generates from its regulated business (5.97%) is within the limit set by the regulator (6.0%).

However, because SS's current return is so close to the limit there is very little scope for it to increase the profitability of the regulated aspect of the business. The maximum operating profit that SS could generate in its regulated business is $46.2m ($770m × 6%).

Non-regulated activities – The constraints on the regulated business increase the importance of the non-regulated activities as a potential source of profit growth for the business.

Additionally, the operating profit margins which SS earns from non-regulated business are significantly higher than those from regulated business.

Regulated services: \$46m/\$276m = 16.7%

Non-regulated services: \$22m/\$69m = 31.9%

Consequently, SS should be looking to expand its non-regulated business, as a source of profitable growth.

In effect, SS's regulated business could be seen as a 'cash cow'. SS should look to invest cash generated by its regulated business to help support the expansion of its non-regulated business (either through organic growth or through acquisition).

Cost control – The regulator's primary concern appears to be that SS doesn't increase its prices unjustifiably. If SS has little scope to increase prices, then in order to maintain its profits it needs to ensure that its costs do not increase significantly either.

Therefore, controlling costs will be a key element of performance management within the regulated part of the business. On the one hand this highlights the importance of variance analysis (comparing actual costs to budget), but on the other hand it also suggests the importance of identifying potential cost savings (for example, through efficiency improvements).

Lack of investment – The target level of 6% is lower than SS's WACC (of 8.47%; see part (a)). If SS uses WACC as a discount rate for decision making, then it would be reluctant to invest in the regulated part of the business at all.

The infrastructure in the regulated side of the business is likely to suffer as a result. This could have an adverse effect on other aspects of SS's performance. For example, if SS has increasing problems with burst water mains due to lack of investment in its infrastructure, this could lead to an increase in repair costs, and also a decline in customer service if customers' water supplies are disrupted.

Growth – By contrast, the focus of performance measures for the non-regulated services should be on revenue and profit growth. For example, SS should look to set targets for revenue growth or market share growth. However, it is equally important for SS to set targets for profit margins, to ensure that it doesn't sacrifice profitability in search of revenue growth.

ACCA

Advanced Performance Management (APM)

Mock Exam 2 (ACCA Specimen from Sept 2022)

Questions	
Time allowed	3 hours 15 minutes
Section A This ONE question is compulsory and MUST be attempted. Section B BOTH questions are compulsory and MUST be attempted.	

DO NOT OPEN THIS EXAM UNTIL YOU ARE READY TO START UNDER EXAMINATION CONDITIONS

Section A

This section of the exam contains one question.

This question is worth 50 marks and is compulsory.

This exam section is worth 50 marks in total.

1 Question 1

The following **exhibits**, available on the left-hand side of the screen, provide information relevant to the question:

(1) Organisation information – the background, new mission statement and four key areas of action for the organisation: Deeland Police (DP)

(2) CSFs and KPIs – details of work required by the chief executive officer (CEO) on the critical success factors (CSFs) and key performance indicators (KPIs) for DP

(3) Value for money – information on a request for an evaluation of the value for money (VFM) of the service provided by DP

(4) League tables – details of an evaluation required on the use of police force performance league tables

(5) Appendix 1 – data currently used when considering the performance of DP

This information should be used to answer the question **requirements** within your chosen **response options(s)**.

Required

It is now September 20X5.

Write a report to the CEO of the Department of Internal Affairs to respond to their instructions for work on the following areas:

(a) The critical success factors and key performance indicators for Deeland Police; **(16 marks)**

(b) An evaluation of the value for money service provided; and **(14 marks)**

(c) The use of league tables in measuring the performance of Deeland Police. **(10 marks)**

Professional marks will be awarded for the demonstration of skill in communication, analysis and evaluation, scepticism and commercial acumen in your answer. **(10 marks)**

(Total = 50 marks)

Exhibit 1: Organisation information

You are a performance management consultant brought in by the chief executive officer (CEO) of the Department for Internal Affairs (DIA) for the country of Deeland. The department handles, among other areas, the policing of Deeland. The CEO is a government employee reporting to the Minister for Internal Affairs. The Minister for Internal Affairs is an elected politician appointed by the leader of the Deeland government.

The government of Deeland has recently changed and the new Minister for Internal Affairs has instructed the CEO of the DIA to improve the performance of the Deeland Police (DP) by implementing the Minister's new mission statement for DP: 'to protect the community and prevent crime while providing a value for money service.' As part of this implementation, the CEO has identified the following four key areas for action:

(1) Protecting and supporting those at risk of harm

(2) Ensuring criminals are caught and brought before the courts

(3) Achieving long-term sustainable solutions to the causes of crime

(4) Addressing new forms of crime arising in the virtual world

The new Minister wants general improvement in the first three of these areas, as their political campaign was based around criticism of the previous government's perceived failure on these points. It is widely agreed that in the second area, the major concern is the catching of criminals since, historically, there is a high probability that once caught they are brought before the courts. The third area is being addressed through increased involvement with local communities in order to identify and address the causes of crime. The fourth area of crime in the virtual world (the use of computers to facilitate crime) was hardly addressed under the previous government and the Minister wants to see the creation of a task force which will develop skills in detection and prosecution of virtual crime.

Exhibit 2: CSFs and KPIs

In a recent meeting with the CEO, the Minister indicated that the four key areas were too vague and in order to better focus actions, the Minister's adviser has suggested the following critical success factors (CSFs):

(1) Greater protection and more support for those at risk of harm

(2) Be better at catching criminals

(3) Reducing the causes of crime by increased involvement with local communities

(4) Create a task force to develop skills in detection and prosecution of virtual crime

Initially, the CEO did not see why the four key areas originally given could not be used as CSFs. They want you to provide justifications in the light of the Minister's concerns for the changes which the adviser has made to each of these. Then, using the above CSFs, they want you to provide justified recommendations of up to two key performance indicators (KPIs) per CSF in order to measure performance.

In order to help you with the KPIs, the CEO has provided you with a table of data (Appendix 1) which has been used in the past when considering DP's performance. However, you are allowed to suggest new data which would help in measuring performance. The CEO has made it clear that at this stage, no calculations are required.

Exhibit 3: Value for money

Since DP is funded wholly through Deeland's general taxation, the CEO wants to be able to report on whether DP is providing a value for money (VFM) service as required by the new mission statement. They have heard of the 3Es (economy, efficiency and effectiveness) but needs an explanation of these three headings and how this links to the work on CSFs and KPIs already requested. Then, they require an evaluation, using the data given in Appendix 1, of whether DP provides such a service. They understand that the evaluation may be limited, as Appendix 1 may not give a data set to perform a full VFM exercise.

Exhibit 4: League tables

The Minister is interested in benchmarking as this was often done during their days in business. As a result, they joined an international initiative for creating a league table of fire service data by sharing information with other nearby countries. The CEO believes that the Minister will want to introduce this idea for DP and so wants an evaluation (including recommendation) of the use of an international police force performance league table and its link to targets for DP. The CEO is especially concerned about the police officers' reaction to this new idea as they have a powerful union, which has widespread public support. Therefore, they also need you to explain how the use of league tables and targets might affect police officers' behaviour.

Exhibit 5: Appendix 1

Deeland Police data for each year ending 30 June

	20X5	*20X4*	*20X3*
Population ('000s)	11,880	11,761	11,644
Number of police officers	37,930	38,005	38,400
Number of administrative staff	12,320	12,197	12,075
Number of crimes reported in the year	541,735	530,900	520,282
Number of violent crimes reported in the year	108,347	106,180	104,056
Number of crimes solved in the year	297,954	300,934	303,943
Number of complaints	7,624	7,512	7,483
Response to an incident within the allocated time limit	84%	86%	87%
Cost of police force for the year ($m)	2,248	2,226	2,203
Staff costs (all staff including police officers) ($m)	2,026	2,103	2,141

Section B

This section of the exam contains two questions.

Each question is worth 25 marks and is compulsory.

This exam section is worth 50 marks in total.

2 Question 2

The following **exhibits**, available on the left-hand side of the screen, provide information relevant to the question:

(1) Company information – the industry sector and challenges faced by a key customer of the company: Coruisk

(2) Purchasing and production – information related to the current purchasing policy and current production methods used by Coruisk

(3) JIT and costs of quality – information related to a request by Ericht to move to a just-in-time (JIT) purchasing system and a costs of quality exercise requested by Coruisk's CEO

(4) Appendix 1 – Coruisk's cost of quality report

This information should be used to answer the question **requirements** within your chosen **response options(s).**

Required

It is now September 20X5.

Respond to the CEO's request for work on the following areas:

(a) The introduction of a just-in-time (JIT) system; and **(13 marks)**

(b) Cost of quality changes. **(7 marks)**

Professional marks will be awarded for the demonstration of skill in analysis and evaluation, scepticism and commercial acumen in your answer. **(5 marks)**

(Total = 25 marks)

Exhibit 1: Company information

Coruisk is a clothing manufacturer in Teeland which produces a range of dresses which it sells to Ericht. The range of dresses are the only products which Coruisk produces and Ericht is its only customer.

Ericht is a well-known retailer in Teeland. Ericht has recently been affected by changes in consumer purchasing preferences to buying clothes online and, as a result, is keen to reduce its inventory holding as a way of reducing its costs. Ericht is also finding that it has an excess of goods which it has to discount as consumer tastes appear to change more quickly than in the past.

The chief executive officer (CEO) of Coruisk has given you some tasks.

Exhibit 2: Purchasing and production

Current purchasing policy

Coruisk currently obtains its raw material from four suppliers. Each of these suppliers operates differently in terms of the processes and procedures which they adopt in trading with Coruisk. Coruisk has been agreeable to this, as the quality of the raw material supplied has generally been acceptable.

More recently, however, Coruisk has found reason to question the accuracy and quality of the raw material delivered from one supplier. Additionally, another supplier now only despatches material to Coruisk in full-load quantities as it wishes to optimise the use of its delivery vehicles.

Current production methods

The performance metric at Coruisk for production efficiency is the number of dresses produced per period. Coruisk's method of production is to produce individual dresses in long production runs which has helped in maximising output. Staff working in the production department have their bonus based on this metric.

Coruisk has a practice of testing goods at the final stage of production and before they leave the factory. Goods which have not been produced to the required standard have traditionally been rejected at the end of the production process. Coruisk's production control manager has indicated to you that the current production methods have been successful, as the company only has 5% of its goods returned from Ericht due to poor quality.

Exhibit 3: JIT and costs of quality

Just-in-time (JIT)

Ericht would like to move to a just-in-time (JIT) system of purchasing its goods from Coruisk and as a result Coruisk is contemplating major changes to its working practices.

Coruisk's CEO has asked you, as a management consultant, to assess the changes which Coruisk will have to make in the areas of purchasing and production in order to supply goods to Ericht on a JIT basis.

Costs of quality

Coruisk's CEO has also made available to you a cost of quality report which they believe address all relevant costs of quality. This report is in Appendix 1.

They would like you to discuss the potential quality cost changes in light of the proposed move to JIT. They indicated that some of these costs have never been measured before and have been given financial values to help you in your discussion. They also told you that Coruisk's current revenue is $4.5 million.

Exhibit 4: Appendix 1

Cost of quality report

	$'000	*$'000*	*% of revenue ($4.5m)*
Costs of conformance:			
Prevention costs:			
Preventative maintenance	8		
Total		8	0.18%
Appraisal costs:			
Quality control supervisor	35		
Quality audit	2		
Total		37	0.82%
Costs of non-conformance:			
Internal failure costs:			
Rework cost	72		
Machine downtime	38		
Scrap	58		
Total		168	3.73%
External failure costs:			
Cost of complaints from Ericht	135		

	$'000	$'000	% of revenue ($4.5m)
Foregone contribution from lost sales*	85		
Product recalls and cost of goods returned	180		
Total		400	8.89%
Overall total		613	13.62%

* the foregone contribution from lost sales is an estimate of potential sales lost to Ericht due to problems related to production and delivery experienced by Coruisk.

3 Question 3

The following **exhibits**, available on the left-hand side of the screen, provide information relevant to the question:

(1) Company information – the background, current performance measures and changes in the market of the company: Totaig

(2) Value based management (VBM) – advice from a consultant about the use of VBM at Totaig and a request for work by the directors on this area

(3) Measuring value – details of work required on the introduction of EVA™ as a performance indicator to measure value

(4) Appendix 1 – the consultant's presentation slide showing the four steps involved in the implementation of VBM

(5) Appendix 2 – financial information supplied in order to establish if Totaig has generated value

This information should be used to answer the question **requirements** within your chosen **response options(s)**.

Required

It is now September 20X5.

Respond to the directors' request for work on the following areas:

(a) The implementation of Step 2 of VBM; and **(15 marks)**

(b) Measurement of value. **(5 marks)**

Professional marks will be awarded for the demonstration of skill in analysis and evaluation and commercial acumen in your answer. **(5 marks)**

(Total = 25 marks)

Exhibit 1: Company information

Totaig manufactures high quality and innovative small electrical appliances such as hairdryers and vacuum cleaners. All of the board of directors, who are the strategic decision makers, have always worked in the business and are members of the Totaig family. Most of the operational managers joined as factory workers when the business started and have taken on more responsibilities as the business has grown.

Totaig has basic and outdated IT systems for a business of its complexity and has always used traditional financial performance measures such as return on investment (ROI) and operating profit margin.

Totaig has historically had few competitors and the directors have focused on improving financial results from one year to the next, with little long-term planning. A number of overseas competitors have, however, recently entered Totaig's market. It is estimated that, within one year, these competitors will be able to produce at a similar unit cost to Totaig and that within three to five years, the quality of the competitors' products will be comparable to the current quality of

Totaig's products. Totaig may have to invest heavily in product development and make acquisitions in the future in order to compete effectively.

Exhibit 2: Value based management (VBM)

A consultant has recently told the directors that implementing value-based management (VBM) may help Totaig to respond to the increase in competition over the next one to five years. The consultant has defined VBM as 'the alignment of the business strategy, management processes and culture on maximising shareholder wealth by focusing on key drivers of value'. The directors have accepted this as a reasonable definition of VBM and most of them now agree that VBM would be useful, though others are not yet convinced.

The directors have, however, asked you for further advice on one aspect of the implementation of VBM at Totaig. At their recent presentation, the consultant presented a slide (Appendix 1) showing the four steps in implementing VBM. The directors want your advice on how to implement Step 2, which is defining performance targets and your advice should be focused on the following four areas:

(1) Selection of appropriate measures and targets

(2) Timescales to which the targets should relate

(3) Management levels (strategic and operational) in the business to which the targets should relate

(4) Difficulties in measuring and managing performance using VBM

Exhibit 3: Measuring value

The directors are unsure of a suitable financial performance indicator for them to use to measure whether Totaig is creating value. As an illustration, they have asked you to evaluate, by calculating economic value added (EVA™), whether Totaig has generated value for the year to 30 June 20X5. You should use the financial information given in Appendix 2.

Exhibit 4: Appendix 1

Four steps in implementing VBM:

Step 1: Produce a strategy for maximising value

Step 2: Define performance targets

Step 3: Create a plan to achieve the targets

Step 4: Set up measurement and reward systems

Exhibit 5: Appendix 2

Income statement for the year to 30 June 20X5

	$'000
Operating profit	10,000
Interest expense	(1,500)
Profit before tax	**8,500**
Tax at 22%	(1,870)
Profit after tax	**6,630**

Notes.

1 During the year $450,000 of advertising cost that will generate sales in future periods was expensed to the income statement.

2 The allowance for doubtful debts at the end of the period was $300,000, a reduction of $200,000 from the beginning of the period.

3 The capital employed at the beginning of the period was $88,944,000.

4 Totaig's after-tax weighted average cost of capital (WACC) is currently 9%. The company is financed by a mixture of equity and fixed and floating rate loans.

Answers

DO NOT TURN THIS PAGE UNTIL YOU HAVE COMPLETED THE MOCK EXAM

Exam success skills

In any APM exam it will be important to apply good general exam technique by using the six exam success skills identified at the start of the Revision Kit, in the section covering 'essential skills'. These skills are: 1. Case scenario: Managing information; 2. Correct interpretation of requirements; 3. Answer planning: Priorities, structure and logic; 4. Efficient numerical analysis; 5. Effective writing and presentation; and 6. Good time management.

Some examples of how to apply these skills in this exam are provided in the table below.

Skill	Examples
Managing information	It is crucially important to assimilate the information in the question scenario. In longer questions, such as the 50-mark question, it is difficult to assimilate information by simply starting at the beginning and read to the end because there is so much information to take in. Instead, it is sensible to take an **active approach** to reading each question. Read enough of the question to get an idea of the basic scenario and then read the initial requirements so that you understand the first things that you are expected to do with this information. *For example, in Q1 the lengthy scenario makes a lot more sense if, before reading all of it, you are aware that the first requirements relate to KPIs and CSFs.*
Correct Interpretation of requirements	Be careful to interpret the verbs used in the question requirements carefully. Also be careful to identify where a question requirement contains more than one instruction. *For example, in Q3 part (a) the question required an analysis based around 4 areas as specified within the scenario.*
Answer planning	Planning is always important in APM questions, because most of the marks are available for discussion and if your discussion points are not relevant to the scenario then they will not receive any credit. As a general rule, you should spend at least 20% of your time, reading the scenario and planning your answer.
Efficient numerical analysis	It is essential that the marker can follow your workings and your logic. If you make a mistake early in your calculations that affects your later calculations then the marker will only penalise the error you have made, and not its follow-on impact on other calculations. This means that it is not normally a good use of your time to correct such errors during the exam.
Effective writing and presentation	In APM this is a very important skill. You are often expected to be able to employ **critical analysis**, and this will sometimes mean that you will reject innovative and modern ideas in favour of less exotic tried and tested performance management tools. It is also very important to **relate your points to the scenario** and to the requirement wherever possible. This means that you will need to apply your theoretical knowledge to the scenario, not simply repeat a technical point as something that you have memorised. However, you will be tested on your understanding of the theoretical content of APM and **you will not be able to apply your**

Skill	Examples
	theoretical knowledge to the scenario if you do not possess a strong understanding of the theories in the first place. *For example, in Q2 it is not possible to discuss JIT and cost of quality unless you have a strong understanding of this concept in the first place.* **Relating your points to the scenario** does not mean simply repeating the details from the question, but using this information to help to explain the point you are making. Finally, in Q1, to score the **marks** that are available you should use suitable report headings, an introduction, a logical structure, signposted by the good use of subheadings in the answer, and a clear, concise style.
Good time management	The exam is 3 hours 15 minutes long, which translates to 1.95 minutes per mark. There are 20 professional marks in the exam and therefore 80 technical marks. If you build in an allowance of 20% of your time for assimilating the scenario and planning, this still leaves you with 1.95 minutes per technical mark.). At the beginning of a question, work out the amount of time you should be spending on: • Planning: for a 25-mark question this will be 1.95 × 25 marks × 20% = 10 minutes. For a 50-mark question this should be about 20 mins. • Writing your answer to each requirement: Take the mark allocation and multiply by 1.95 minutes per technical mark.

Diagnostic

Did you apply these skills when reading, planning, and writing up your answer? Identify the exam success skills where you think you need to improve and capture your thoughts here of what you want to achieve when attempting questions in future.

Section A

This section of the exam contains one question.

This question is worth 50 marks and is compulsory.

This exam section is worth 50 marks in total.

1 Question 1

Workbook references

CSFs and KPIs are covered in Chapter 2 of the Workbook, value for money and league tables are covered in Chapter 8 and non-financial performance indicators in Chapter 9.

Top tips

A report was requested on the following areas.

This focused on performance management issues for a police force.

This was a slightly unusual 50-mark scenario question in that it was based around a not-for-profit scenario. However, the topics tested within this question have all been tested before and should not have come as a surprise. The question was also relatively short, which would have meant that it was not too time-consuming to analyse.

Part (a)

This mainly required an assessment of how four CSFs could be measured by up to two KPIs per CSF. Data was provided in Appendix 1 to assist with this discussion although no calculations were required here. This is a regularly examined area.

Part (b)

This mainly asked for an explanation and evaluation of VFM using data provided in Appendix 1 (calculations were required here).

This required an ability apply VFM numerically, again this is regularly examined.

Part (c)

This required a general evaluation of league tables, but this needed to be applied to this scenario to achieve a strong pass mark (especially in terms of the potential behavioural impact).

Marking guide

	Marks
(a) **CSFs and KPIs**	
4 marks for the four CSFs	
Up to 4 marks for discussion of KPIs for each area	
	16
(b) **VFM**	
3 marks for defining each of the 3Es	
Up to 3 marks for comments on the link to the CSFs/KPIs	
Up to 3 marks each for discussing each heading at DP	
	14
(c) **League tables**	
Up to 7 marks for the general evaluation of league tables	
Up to 7 marks for the link of tables to targets and police officer reaction	
	10

Professional marks

Communication:

- Report format and structure – use of headings/sub-headings and introduction
- Style, language and clarity – appropriate tone of report response, presentation of calculations, appropriate use of the CBE tools, easy to follow and understand
- Effectiveness of communication – content of the report is relevant and tailored to the question scenario
- Adherence to the CEO's specific request to not provide more than two KPIs

Analysis and Evaluation:

- Appropriate use of the data to support discussion and draw conclusions on performance in relation to VFM, including recognition of further analysis which could be carried out to enable a full evaluation of VFM to take place
- Balanced appraisal to make a recommendation on the introduction of league tables, demonstrating reasoned judgement when considering key organisational matters and impacts

Scepticism:

- Demonstration of the ability to probe into why the CSFs were refined
- Recognition that the data provided does not allow some of the CSFs/KPIs to be adequately measured

Marking guide | **Marks**

Commercial acumen:

- Effective use of examples drawn from the scenario information and other practical considerations related to the context to illustrate points being made throughout the report

Maximum	10
Total	50

To: The CEO, Department of Internal Affairs (DIA)

From: An Accountant

Date: 1 September 20X5

Subject: Performance measurement and management at Deeland Police (DP)

This report recommends and justifies critical success factors (CSFs) and key performance indicators (KPIs) for DP based on the four critical areas of performance. DP is then evaluated on the value for money (VFM) provision of its service. Finally, the use of a league table of police performance and the setting of targets for DP is assessed, with comment on the employee reaction to such a management approach.

(a) **Critical success factors (CSFs) and key performance indicators (KPIs)**

The CSFs must follow from the four areas which are addressing the overall mission. The four key areas to consider are:

(1) Protecting and supporting those at risk of harm

(2) Ensuring criminals are caught and brought before the courts

(3) Achieving long-term sustainable solutions to the causes of crime

(4) Addressing new forms of crime arising in the virtual world

The first three areas are on-going in the activities of DP and the Minister wants improvement in each. The adviser's suggested CSFs all appear to be reasonable improvements to manage the Minister's concerns about the vagueness of the key areas as follows:

(1) Greater protection and more support for those at harm (a straight-forward improvement to the existing position in this area)

(2) Be better at catching criminals (bringing them before the courts does not appear to be critical as it seems to automatically follow)

(3) Reducing the causes of crime by increased involvement with local communities (improvement using the mechanism suggested)

The fourth area is relatively new, so it will be more in the nature of a separate project to:

(4) Create a task force to develop skills in detection and prosecution of virtual crime (as desired by the Minister)

The KPIs for the four CSF areas

Area 1

The CSF breaks into two parts – protecting and supporting. There should be a KPI measuring the change in each of these areas:

- Percentage change year on year of the number of victims of violent crimes, once they are identified as at risk (a register of 'at risk' people would need to be created)
- Percentage change of staff hours spent with each victim on average in support activities

Neither of these KPIs can currently be measured as the data is not collected. The first point could be indirectly addressed by measuring the number of victims of violent crimes, which should see a fall if those at risk are better protected.

Area 2

This CSF is looking at what is often referred to as the clear-up rate, which is the percentage of crimes where the criminal is caught. The data given allows this to be measured through:

- The percentage change in the percentage of crimes solved (although care must be taken that 'solved' is not the same as 'criminal caught' as there may be cases where the police know the criminal, but they escape capture)

The second part of bringing the criminal before the courts once caught does not appear to be a critical area needing measurement since this appears to be a low-risk possibility. The critical area might be better stated as 'Ensuring crimes are solved and criminals are brought before the courts' since the second part would then be an appropriate area to measure.

Area 3

From the data in Appendix 1, the KPI could be:

- The percentage change in the total number of crimes in Deeland in the year

The effect of reducing the causes of crime would be to create a long-term trend downwards in this measure. It may be better to use a three-year moving average of the change as a result. However, there may be many factors which cause such changes including the number of police officers and so the underlying causes of crime may not be accurately measured. The suggested KPI does not capture whether the changes are sustainable in the long term, which will be difficult to do.

Area 4

The KPIs for the fourth area require examination of the number and qualifications of those working on the task force on virtual crime. The data in Appendix 1 is not sufficient to measure this.

KPIs could include:

- Percentage of roles in the task force filled (this requires that there is a plan for the organisation of a suitable task force, which may be complicated as this is a new area where knowledge of how many staff and what qualifications they should have may not be present)
- Percentage of virtual crimes reported which are solved (shows the effectiveness of the task force)

(b) **Value for money (VFM)**

The standard criteria for analysis of the value for money of a service are:

- Economy – the optimisation of the resources which the organisation has; ensuring the appropriate quality of input resources are obtained at the lowest cost;
- Efficiency – the optimisation of the process by which inputs are turned into outputs; and
- Effectiveness – how the outputs of the organisation meet its goals.

The 3Es above link to the CSFs and KPIs in the area of effectiveness. The KPIs measure the achievement of the goals of DP and all relate to outcomes rather than processes or inputs in this case.

In order to judge VFM, comparison can be made internally to the historic performance of DP, but it should also be benchmarked against external organisations. The need for external data is also reflected in the desire to benchmark in league tables although no data is given for this here and so the VFM can only be judged against previous years' data.

Considering the situation at DP specifically

Economy could be measured by looking at the cost of buying inputs; the principal input is staff (90.1% of total costs) and so the cost per employee ($40,318) is relevant. This represents a 3.8% reduction on the previous year although it should be noted that the mix of staff is changing with more administrative staff replacing police officers who may be more expensive as they are more qualified. It would be useful to obtain the data on the average police officer salary as they make up 75.5% of the total staff and they are critical to the achievement of outcomes.

As noted above, in order to judge whether this is good or bad, the Department should also compare this to external figures such as the national average wage and, also, the average salary of staff in other police forces in similar countries.

Efficiency can be measured in a number of different ways.

	20X5	20X4	20X3
Solved crimes per police officer	7.855	7.918	7.915
Solved crimes per employee (police officers and admin staff)	5.929	5.994	6.022
Police officers per 1,000 population	3.19	3.23	3.30

The trend in the number of police officers is downward which would suggest improvement. However, the more important outcome is not the resources poured in but the crime results and these show that by decreasing the number of police officers, the number of crimes which each is solving is falling (down 0.8% from 20X3). Performance in this area is therefore poor.

Effectiveness must be measured against DP's goals in its four areas:

(1) Protection and support of those at risk – the percentage of violent crime remains flat over the three years of data at 20% of the total number of crimes reported. This suggests that protection remains broadly unchanged. As noted above, there is no measure of support provided.

(2) Solving crimes – the clear-up rate has fallen from 56.7% to 55.0%. This probably reflects the change in staff mix as police officer numbers have fallen.

(3) Causes of crime – the trend is clearly upwards with an increase of 2% each year over the last two years which may again reflect the falling numbers of police officers in DP.

(4) Virtual crime – as noted above, it is not possible to measure the achievement of the creation of the task force from the data provided.

(c) **League tables**

The use of league tables effectively benchmarks performance and can have a positive effect on behaviour. The sharing of data on performance can indicate areas of best practice and so offers the possibility of improving performance by copying that best practice. Additionally, the use of league tables gives, by the rank in the table, a clear, immediate answer to questions of relative performance.

However, the use of league tables only measures relative performance. The best force in the table could still be producing an unacceptable performance in absolute terms. The different forces in different countries will face different external environments. Each force will have to react to the economic situation in that country and may allocate resources differently according to the priorities of the government of that country. So, it will be difficult to get a single measure, such as the rank in the league table, to balance these competing factors.

This leads on to another area which will prove difficult, which is how to rank the different forces. Usually, there is a scoring system giving points across different areas for each force's performance. The selection of the areas and the weighting given to them within the rank score will affect the position of the different forces. In an example of 'what gets measured, gets done', it may be that the DP management will change their priorities from those given by the DIA to those measured in the rank score and so undermine the alignment of their behaviour with the given mission of DP. Therefore, to be of value to the Minister, the calculation of the rank must encompass the key variables which will drive DP's desired performance.

Therefore, there is a link between league tables and employee behaviour which comes from the setting of targets based on the league table rank.

The impact on the employees includes whether they feel a sense of accountability for the score. If the police officers do not feel that they can affect the rank, then they may ignore it or actively undermine it in public through their union's public statements. This will present the government with difficulty as the police are considered the experts in this area of public policy and their criticism will carry weight with the electorate.

Specifically, the police officers may be demotivated by the league tables if they feel:

(1) That the league table rank does not reflect the valuable work which they do (for example, in creating the new virtual crime task force); or

(2) That the rank is driven by factors outside of their control. (For example, the budget for the force may be cut, as appears to be happening with DP, or there may be a link between the number of crimes reported and the economic conditions in Deeland which they do not have power to affect).

Appendix 1: (spreadsheet extract)

Deeland Police data for each year ending 30 June

	20X5	20X4	20X3
Population ('000s)	11,880	11,761	11,644
Number of police officers	37,930	38,005	38,400
Number of administrative staff	12,320	12,197	12,075
Number of crimes reported in the year	541,735	530,900	520,282
Number of violent crimes reported in the year	108,347	106,180	104,056
Number of crimes solved in the year	297,954	300,934	303,943
Number of complaints	7,624	7,512	7,483
Response to an incident within the allocated time limit	84%	86%	87%
Cost of police force for the year ($m)	2,248	2,226	2,203
Staff costs (all staff including police officers) ($m)	2,026	2,103	2,141
Workings			
Economy			
Staff costs/total cost (%)	90.1	94.5	97.2
Cost per employee ($)	40318	41891	42417
Efficiency			
Solved crimes per police officer	7.855	7.918	7.915
Solved crimes per employee	5.929	5.994	6.022
Police officers per 1000 of population	3.19	3.23	3.30
Economy			
Clear up rate (% of crimes reported that are solved)	55.0	56.7	58.4
Violent crime (% of crimes reported classified as violent)	20.0	20.0	20.0
Increase in crime reported year on year (%)	2.0	2.0	

Section B

This section of the exam contains two questions.

Each question is worth 25 marks and is compulsory.

This exam section is worth 50 marks in total.

2 Question 2

Workbook reference

Quality management and JIT are discussed in Chapter 10 of the Workbook.

Top tips

Candidates that structured their answers with a brief description of JIT followed by **more lengthy, detailed advice about how this system impacted on the existing purchasing and production systems** would score well. In APM you should always try to apply your knowledge to the scenario, and excellent scores were achieved by candidates **who used the details of the current systems:**

- Poor-quality raw materials purchased
- An untailored approach to deliveries by the company's suppliers
- The existing quality review process
- The remuneration scheme

Examining team's comments

In part (b) 'a significant minority of candidates could not identify the difference between the easily distinguished, broad categories of conformance and non-conformance costs'. It was also noted that, in part (b), markers had latitude to allow for different but justified allocations of quality costs.

Marking guide	Marks
(a) Definition of JIT – up to 1 mark Purchasing and production – 1 mark per point up to 13 marks	
	13
(b) Quality cost changes – 1 mark per point	
	7

Professional marks

Analysis and Evaluation:

- Balanced and reasoned assessment of the changes which will be required to both purchasing and production as a result of introducing JIT
- Appropriate use of the data to support discussion on quality cost changes and draw relevant conclusions

Scepticism:

- Demonstration of effective challenge of the assumptions of both the production manager and CEO

Commercial acumen:

- Effective use of examples drawn from the scenario information and other practical considerations related to the context to illustrate points being made

Maximum	5
Total	25

(a) Just-in-time (JIT) is defined as a system which has the objective of producing or procuring products as they are required and not for inventory purposes. Coruisk is being asked to produce to JIT principles, the basis of which is where production is driven by demand for the finished product. Each part of the production process is therefore determined only by what is required for the next stage of production.

Purchasing

Coruisk has too many suppliers at present. Adhering to JIT production principles involves reducing suppliers to a minimum and establishing strong relationships with them, based on flexibility and understanding of each other's needs. Coruisk's four main suppliers are too many to develop this type of close relationship with, especially since these suppliers operate to different working practices. The effect of this, from a JIT production perspective, would be that Coruisk would require to undertake discussions with each supplier about the fundamental changes which would be required for the supply of goods in a JIT production environment. Coruisk would not have the time to do this with all four suppliers nor would the supply of goods from four companies be desirable. Coruisk should choose two of the companies it feels it has the strongest relationship with and initiate discussions with them around its needs when producing to JIT principles.

When producing to JIT principles, suppliers will effectively be an extension of Coruisk's own business. As such, Coruisk must be aware of and must understand how changes in suppliers' operations will affect Coruisk's own operations. It is clear that Coruisk does not currently have this level of relationship. The supplier who is seeking to optimise the cost of its delivery vehicles, for example, is undertaking practices which are very much opposed to the type of practices which Coruisk will need when it is producing to JIT principles. JIT only produces goods when needed by the next stage in the process (the 'kanban' principle) and Coruisk would need its supplier to understand this and be willing to supply it with goods accordingly. This would clearly be impossible for a supplying company which is insistent on supplying full-load quantities only.

Coruisk must also ensure that the raw material it receives is defect free, unlike the goods which are received currently from one supplier. Having the wrong quantity of material or material which is sub-standard, is unacceptable if Coruisk is producing to JIT principles as such problems will mean an inevitable delay in supplying goods to Ericht. Coruisk will therefore need to spend time in defining and agreeing requirements with suppliers to clarify requirements in terms of both quality and quantity and may need to also develop improvement teams with their suppliers to ensure that the raw material it receives is reliable.

Coruisk will most likely need to undertake official supplier assessments as part of this as such assessments and on-going reviews are a vital part of ensuring the quality of the raw material in a JIT production system.

Production

The manner in which Coruisk produces its goods will need to change significantly. Efficiency can no longer be measured by volume of output. Ericht will seek supply of goods as and when required in order to avoid obsolete inventory and Coruisk must adapt to this. The concept of producing as much as possible is one which Coruisk may struggle to abolish. It is clearly embedded in the culture of the organisation with its importance confirmed by the awarding of a bonus based on the quantity of goods produced. Presumably this bonus has been awarded without taking account of any goods which have been rejected and it is possible that the current system is encouraging production to be undertaken quickly with rejected goods seen as an acceptable part of the production process.

Producing to JIT principles would demand a fundamental rethink at Coruisk in terms of the way production runs are determined. Of most significance, initially, is that such runs would be shorter as all parts of the production process should match the rate at which Ericht is demanding the final product. For example, Coruisk can no longer focus on producing large runs of one dress. Necessary changes here may involve the development of machine cells. Such cells are composed of groups of team members to facilitate operations by eliminating setup and unneeded costs between operations. Cells might be designed for a specific process or part of a product. In Coruisk's case, this may mean workers being grouped together by the dress they are producing at that time rather than as part of a long production run.

Enhancing worker flexibility and developing their skill set in several areas of the operation, may be the best way to react to this new environment where demand is much more unpredictable. This may also involve changing the layout of the factory to try to ensure production is as flexible as possible.

Coruisk cannot supply faulty goods to Ericht and the previous belief that a 5% rejection rate was acceptable practice must be replaced by an understanding of the zero defects philosophy. This will require more fundamental change as quality of the finished good will need to be assured throughout the production process and not simply inspected at the end. This will most likely involve an initial discussion with Ericht as to the quality level it is seeking and, potentially, a redesign of the current processes and systems to which Coruisk is operating. For example, prevention and appraisal costs would be expected to increase as Coruisk would have to establish both goods inwards testing procedures and testing procedures for work in progress. There would also be a need for Coruisk to develop a culture where workers are flexible in terms of their capabilities and trained much more in identifying defective products (and ensuring they do not progress further on the production line) than in ensuring the maximum quantity of output is produced.

(b) The results of the cost of quality report are representative of a company which undertakes quality control as opposed to quality assurance in that the majority of the costs relate to failure, either of an internal or external nature. Additionally, since the costs have been amassed for the first time for this task, it is possible that they are inaccurate and probably understated as some costs are likely to have been omitted.

Costs of conformance

Coruisk will need to invest more in quality audits and, possibly, in testing equipment to ensure that the product is being produced to the right standard as it progresses through the production process. Whereas there may still be a requirement for final inspection, it should not be someone's full-time occupation and the supervisor may be more meaningfully deployed elsewhere for at least part of their role. These practices should reduce both the internal and external failure costs, particularly those of scrap and rework, which both appear very high currently. Machine downtime is perhaps due to the very little amount currently spent on preventative maintenance and the cost of internal failure should also fall with enhanced maintenance.

Costs of non-conformance

The significant external failure cost is of most concern. To operate to the JIT principles which Ericht is seeking, Coruisk has to ensure that these costs are as close to zero as possible. It is concerning, for example, that 3% ($135,000) of the revenue figure is taken up by dealing with complaints from Ericht. Some of this may be due to misunderstandings between the companies which could be rectified by the closer working relationship that JIT production principles demand. Nevertheless, it is clear that Coruisk must ensure that it addresses these costs as it is completely reliant upon Ericht for its business.

The amount of money attributed to product recalls and cost of goods returned (4% of the revenue figure) is concerning as this suggests that defective products have not been detected in Coruisk's current quality control system. This may be due to the bonus system currently in place and the desire to produce quantity, quickly, and not quality. A change to the production process should address this but it could be met with hostility if the workers' bonus is under threat and Coruisk may need to introduce an alternative bonus scheme based on a quality-related metric which specifies, for example, the percentage of defects detected.

The forgone contribution from lost sales is also concerning as it indicates that Ericht has alternative supplier(s). It is possible, given the cost detailed of dealing with complaints from Ericht, that this figure is considerably higher than Coruisk is estimating.

The balance of the costs must change so that the majority of Coruisk's costs are prevention and appraisal (costs of conformance) and not costs of internal/external failure (costs of non-conformance). Coruisk must ensure that it is producing to the standard which Ericht requests at the first time of asking and therefore Coruisk must ensure that it provides more training for staff, more preventative machine maintenance, more supplier appraisal and vetting as mentioned previously and moves to encourage a culture of zero defects with no faulty goods moving forward in the production process.

3 Question 3

Workbook reference

EVA is covered in Chapter 7 and value based management is covered in Chapter 13.

Top tips

In part (a), the question presented a four-part structure for this advice, which included: selection of measures and targets, timescales, appropriate management levels and difficulties in managing performance using VBM. A good answer required practical comments on these areas, not in generic terms but in a way that was applied to the scenario; 1 mark was available per point.

In part (b), don't forget to earn the mark available for commenting on your numbers.

Marking guide	Marks
(a) 1 mark per point (under the four headings):	
• Selection of measures and targets	
• Timescales	
• Management levels	
• Difficulties	
	15
(b) Calculation of NOPAT:	
Advertising cost – 1 mark	
Decrease in allowance – 1 mark	
Interest – 1 mark	
Calculation of adjusted capital employed – 1 mark	
Calculation of EVA™ – 1 mark	
Conclusion – 1 mark	
	5
Professional marks	
Analysis and Evaluation:	
• Demonstration of reasoned and balanced judgement to support arguments and communicate advice on the introduction of VBM	
• Use of the information provided to perform an evaluation on EVA™	
Commercial acumen:	
• Effective use of examples drawn from the scenario information and other practical considerations related to the context to illustrate points being made on the implementation of Step 2 of VBM	
Maximum	5
Total	25

(a) **Selection of appropriate measures and targets**

Value drivers create long-term value. Totaig is facing competition from overseas businesses, which will soon be able to produce at a similar unit cost to Totaig and produce items of comparable quality. The unit cost of production and product quality would be value drivers for Totaig and targets should be set for these two measures.

Targets should be both financial and non-financial. This will ensure that there is not too much emphasis on financial targets, which tend to be backwards looking, rather than relating to the present value of future cash flows, which is the focus of value-based management (VBM).

The existing targets of return on investment (ROI) and operating margin are backwards looking. They will also discourage managers to make investments, for example, in product development, which might be detrimental to Totaig's long-term performance. This is because investments in new products will reduce both of these measures in the short term.

Having targets related to product quality would ensure that the business does not focus too much on cutting the unit cost of production, for example, by using cheaper, lower quality materials. It appears that to create long-term value, Totaig must be competitive on both unit cost of production and product quality.

Timescales to which the targets should relate

Totaig must set short-term and long-term targets, which should be linked together, for key value drivers. Competitors will be able to produce at a similar unit cost to Totaig within a year. A suitable short-term target would therefore be to reduce unit production costs within that timescale. As VBM is concerned with long-term value, Totaig should set longer term targets relating to quality in anticipation of the new competitors' ability to improve on this aspect within three to five years.

The possible need to invest heavily in product development and make acquisitions will probably require longer term targets to be set.

Levels in the business to which the targets should relate

Value can be created at all levels in the company and targets should be set according to the different layers of management. Targets relating to unit cost of production and product quality are under the control of operational managers and these would be suitable for this level of management.

Targets relating to possible future acquisitions are under the control of the directors, who are the strategic decision makers.

Difficulties in measuring and managing performance using VBM

Totaig will require good information to implement VBM. It may be difficult to identify value drivers and reporting systems need to be able to provide the information which is required. Currently, IT systems are basic and outdated for a business of its complexity. This may mean that it is difficult to identify value drivers for the setting of targets. The implementation of VBM may require significant investment in IT systems to measure performance against targets and take up management time. The costs of implementing VBM may exceed the benefits.

The operational managers are unlikely to have any experience of VBM since most of them joined Totaig, which itself has never used VBM, when the business first started. They will require training on VBM if they are to understand the targets set. For example, new value-based performance measures, such as EVA™, will be needed, which will be unfamiliar to directors and managers in the business.

Using VBM to manage performance at Totaig will require a culture change amongst all employees, who will need to work towards creating shareholder value. The directors will need to demonstrate commitment to the use of VBM in order to motivate operational managers to accept the change. Currently, some directors at Totaig seem not to be convinced of the usefulness of the approach.

It may be difficult to measure economic depreciation, for example, or to determine whether and for when the anticipated heavy investment in product development will create value. These difficulties will affect the reliability of performance measures for value, such as EVA™, in managing performance.

(b) **Calculation of EVA™**

	$'000
Profit after tax	*6,630*
Advertising costs expenses	450
Decrease in allowance for doubtful debts	(200)
Interest net of tax (1,500 × 78%)	1,170
NOPAT	8,050
Opening capital employed	88,944
Opening allowance for doubtful debt	500
Adjusted opening capital employed	89,444
NOPAT	8,050
After-tax WACC × adjusted capital employed (9% × 89,444)	(8,050)
EVA™	0

As EVA™ is zero, Totaig has neither created nor destroyed value.

ACCA

Advanced Performance Management (APM)

Mock Exam 3 (Based on ACCA Mar/June 2021 exam)

Questions	
Time allowed	3 hours 15 minutes
This exam is divided into two sections. SECTION A This ONE question is compulsory and MUST be attempted. SECTION B BOTH questions are compulsory and MUST be attempted.	

DO NOT OPEN THIS EXAM UNTIL YOU ARE READY TO START UNDER EXAMINATION CONDITIONS

Section A

This section of the exam contains one question.

This question is worth 50 marks and is compulsory.

This exam section is worth 50 marks in total.

1 Question 1 (Mar/Jun 2022)

The following **exhibits** provide information relevant to the question:

(1) Company information – the background, organisation structure and current position of the company: Calavie Manufacturing (Calavie)

(2) Divisional performance measurement – details of the overall, strategic performance indicators for assessing the performance of Calavie's divisions and the work required by the CEO on this area

(3) BCG analysis – instructions from the CEO regarding how she wants a BCG (Boston Consulting Group) analysis prepared by a consultant to be applied to Calavie's divisions

(4) Management information – explanation of the current information systems used by the divisions and the advice requested by the CEO for the board on a good approach to management information

(5) Appendix 1 – financial performance data for the divisions for year ended 30 June 20X5

(6) Appendix 2 – the consultant's BCG analysis

This information should be used to answer the question requirements within your chosen response option(s).

Required

It is now 1 September 20X5.

Write a report to the board of Calavie to respond to the CEO's instructions for work on the following areas:

(a) Divisional performance measurement **(14 marks)**

(b) The BCG analysis **(15 marks)**

(c) Management information at Calavie **(11 marks)**

Professional marks will be awarded for the demonstration of skill in communication, analysis and evaluation, scepticism and commercial acumen in your answer. **(10 marks)**

(Total = 50 marks)

Exhibit 1: Company information

Calavie Manufacturing (Calavie) is a listed, multinational manufacturer of household refrigerators. It is made up of three divisions: Doilet, Essan and Fada.

- Doilet makes basic refrigerators which are sold across all of its geographical markets.
- Essan makes high-quality, premium-priced refrigerators for sale in the wealthier markets in which it operates.
- Fada makes a variety of hardware and software systems which link refrigerators and other household goods to a home management system which, for example, in the case of the refrigerators, will automatically scan the contents of the refrigerator and reorder food from web-based suppliers as required.

The business has concentrated on growth over the last five years but its weak share price performance has led to complaints from its investors, who feel that their wealth is not being maximised. The board believes that they need to take an overview of the whole business, beginning with its performance measurement methods. They have engaged a consultant to perform a Boston Consulting Group (BCG) analysis of the position of the three divisions and from this, they want to look in more detail at the performance measurement and management issues within each division.

Exhibit 2: Divisional performance measurement

Calavie uses return on investment (ROI) as a strategic performance indicator to assess the three divisions. There has been debate at the board level as to whether this is an appropriate divisional performance indicator. The bonuses of the management of each division are assessed against this indicator. As the year's performance report is being prepared, the chief executive officer (CEO) has suggested that you evaluate the performance of the three divisions using both ROI and a suggested replacement, residual income (RI). As part of this work, she wants you to include an analysis of the different ways these measures could be calculated, taking into consideration the effect of head office costs and the effect of the research and development and brand marketing costs. She needs the calculations you provide to be clear and justified. She also wants you to evaluate the appropriateness of ROI and RI for divisional performance measurement. At this stage, she does not want any other indicators to be considered. She has supplied you with data in Appendix 1 to do this.

Exhibit 3: BCG analysis

The consultant's BCG analysis is given in Appendix 2. The CEO wants you to assess how this can be used to assist in performance management generally and then, using your knowledge of performance measurement to apply it to each division in turn, recommending, with justification, up to two suitable, financial key performance indicators (KPIs) for each division.

Exhibit 4: Management information

The existing information systems at Calavie have been developed within each division and the divisions separately supply reports to head office for use by the company's executive.

Each division operates on a functional basis with its own manufacturing, sales and marketing and administration departments. As a result, the board feels that they lack a clear understanding of what is driving the performance of each division. The CEO wants to redesign existing information systems to bring the divisions and the board into a closer connection. However, as this project has not yet begun, she feels that the board needs a broad understanding of a good approach to management accounting information. Therefore, first, she wants an explanation of the general aims of management accounting information at the different levels of the organisation and then second, the board needs your advice on how applying the qualities of good information can improve the communication from Calavie's divisions to the company's executive.

Exhibit 5: Appendix 1: Divisional performance

Spreadsheet

Edit Format

100% 11

	A	B	C	D
1	**Calavie Manufacturing**			
2	**Divisional performance (y/e 30.6.20X5)**			
3		**Doilet**	**Essan**	**Fada**
4		**$m**	**$m**	**$m**
5	Revenue	484	223	32

6	Variable costs	248	81	10
7	Divisional overheads	94	41	5
8	Research and development	0	1	8
9	Brand-building marketing	5	12	0
10	Apportioned head office costs	36	14	2
11	Total operating costs	383	149	25
12				
13	Operating profit	**101**	**74**	**7**
14	Restructuring costs	0	11	0
15	Profit before tax	**101**	**63**	**7**
16				
17	Capital employed	615	261	31

Notes.

1 The notional cost of capital used is 11% per annum.

2 The current cost of debt is 6%.

3 Essan moved its main office to a prestigious building incurring restructuring.

4 The average return on investment for the industry is believed to be 15%.

5 The research and development and brand-building marketing costs are made by the divisions for the long-term benefit of Calavie.

Exhibit 6: Appendix 2: BCG analysis

Key features of the divisions:

Doilet makes basic refrigerators for use across all of its geographical markets. The management aims to be a cost leader in its markets which are not growing significantly.

Essan makes high-quality, premium-priced refrigerators for sale in the wealthier markets in which it operates. The divisional management has successfully created a market-leading brand which is seeing high growth in both sales and profits as its markets are becoming wealthier still. However, the competition and requirement to spend heavily on brand-building makes this a riskier business sector.

Fada was set up to create a system to link refrigerators to a home management system. This project was initially successful and as a result, it was realised that there were other opportunities to link household items into the internet. Fada has pursued a number of such development projects to launch a number of new products. However, there have been technical difficulties and varying levels of sales of these new products. As a result, Fada is only one of many similar sized companies within this market segment and it has seen weak financial results, while requiring considerable investment to support its development.

BCG categorisation:

Doilet can be reasonably treated as a cash cow as it is one of the two largest businesses by market share in a low growth market.

Essan is the star of Calavie as it is the market leader in a rapidly growing market.

Fada is a problem child as it is in a high-growth market but does not have a large market share.

Section B

This section of the exam contains two questions.

Each question is worth 25 marks and is compulsory.

This exam section is worth 50 marks in total.

2 Question 2

The following exhibits provide information relevant to the question:

(1) Company information – the background, industry and operating conditions of the company: Vaa

(2) Transfer pricing – details relating to the problems of setting transfer prices between the R and S divisions

(3) International acquisition – information about the possible acquisition of a subsidiary in Teeland and the factors to be considered when determining international transfer prices

This information should be used to answer the question requirements within the response option provided.

Required

(a) Advise Vaa on the criteria for designing a formal transfer pricing policy for its two divisions in Essland. **(7 marks)**

(b) Explain the disadvantages for Vaa of using market-based transfer prices. **(6 marks)**

(c) Advise Vaa on the factors it should consider when setting international transfer prices in relation to the potential acquisition in Teeland. **(7 marks)**

Professional marks will be awarded for the demonstration of skill in analysis and evaluation, scepticism and commercial acumen in your answer. **(5 marks)**

(Total = 25 marks)

Exhibit 1: Company information

Vaa is a manufacturer of electronic consumer goods. It is made up of two divisions, R division and S division, and a head office which provides the overall management of Vaa. Both the divisions and head office are based in Essland, where they manufacture all goods and where there is currently an economic recession. The corporation tax rate in Essland is 25%.

A large proportion of the electronic goods manufactured by R division use a key component which R division transfers in from S division. There are several companies throughout the world who manufacture a component which fulfils the same function as the component produced by S division. The component produced by S division, however, has much lower energy consumption than those of its competitors.

Both R and S divisions are profit centres. Both have the autonomy to be able to negotiate the price at which the key component is transferred between the two divisions and to be able to choose whether to purchase or sell the key component externally.

Exhibit 2: Transfer pricing

Despite R and S divisions having similar revenue and capital employed, R division has only broken even in recent years, whereas S division has made substantial profits. R division managers have complained that this is due to the high transfer price for the key components which are transferred from S division.

Head office is concerned about the amount of time divisional managers spend arguing about a suitable transfer price, when their efforts would be better focused on other important areas of the business, such as finding ways to utilise spare capacity.

There is also concern from the head office that the divisions negotiate in a self-interested way, so that head office often has to intervene and impose a transfer price which maximises the performance of Vaa as a whole. Head office is considering setting up a formal transfer pricing policy.

R division managers have proposed that the components be transferred at the market price in future, because they believe that R division should have a share of the cost savings which S division would make compared to if S division sold externally, such as administration costs and bad debts.

Head office understands the potential benefits of this approach but not the disadvantages.

Exhibit 3: International acquisition

Vaa is considering acquiring a subsidiary in the country of Teeland, which would be known as T division and would also be managed as a profit centre. Teeland is one of the largest producers of electronic consumer goods in the world and uses a different currency to Essland. The Teeland government is concerned about the level of competition to local manufacturers from imported goods and is considering introducing a range of protectionist measures, for example, the introduction of import tariffs, to deal with this. The corporation tax rate in Teeland is 16%.

Vaa plans to use the key component manufactured by S division in T division's products and has asked for advice on the factors which it should consider when setting international transfer prices, assuming the acquisition goes ahead.

3 Question 3

The following exhibits provide information relevant to the question:

(1) Company information – the background, mission statement and structure of the company: Breac

(2) Manufacturing agreement – details of a manufacturing agreement struck between Breac and another company: Gowan

(3) Value-based management – information about the possible introduction of value-based management (VBM) at Breac

(4) Appendix 1 – an example of Breac's strategic performance report

This information should be used to answer the question requirements within the response option provided.

Required

It is now 1 September 20X5.

(a) Assess the problems which may be faced by Breac when developing a service level agreement (SLA) with Gowan. **(8 marks)**

(b) Evaluate how the introduction of VBM would affect the current measures in the strategic performance report prepared by the SBUs and recommend, with justification, as to whether VBM should be introduced at Breac. **(12 marks)**

Professional marks will be awarded for the demonstration of skill in analysis and evaluation, scepticism and commercial acumen in your answer **(5 marks)**

(Total = 25 marks)

Exhibit 1: Company information

Breac is a sports clothing goods company which operates globally. It purchases sports clothing goods which have already been partly manufactured, completes the manufacture of the goods and then sells these goods through its global retail outlets. Breac's mission is to be the best sports clothing goods company in the world. Breac has 25,000 employees and a turnover of $8 billion approximately. Each country of operation is classed as an individual strategic business unit (SBU).

Exhibit 2: Manufacturing agreement

Breac has agreed with Gowan, a large global manufacturing company, that Gowan will manufacture the major part of all sports clothing goods for Breac. Breac will then complete the manufacture of these clothing goods. This completion work includes Breac adding its own brand name, specialist climate cool material and synthetic waterproof fabrics. Breac will then despatch the clothing goods to its retail outlets.

Breac's manufacturing departments have highlighted that the clothing goods received from Gowan are often neither up to the required standard nor delivered on time. Problems have also been identified in both the retail outlets and by the end-user which have been attributed to the poor quality of material supplied by Gowan. Specific quality problems have included stitching disintegrating, poor quality of material and clothing goods being incorrectly sized.

Breac and Gowan each have their own individual information systems. Breac's is an advanced computerised system whereas Gowan's is more basic and parts of it are manual. The two companies' systems are unable to communicate with each other.

Breac's staff at various levels in the organisation have suggested that a formal service level agreement (SLA) with Gowan is required if the agreement is to continue.

Exhibit 3: Value-based management

Breac's chief executive officer (CEO) was recently at a presentation on value-based management (VBM) where the main presenter indicated that it was a management methodology best suited to a large-scale manufacturing company such as Breac. VBM was further explained as a methodology which takes the idea of creating value through the return of future cash flows and embeds this in an organisation's culture. It should align all a company's processes with the key drivers of value.

An example of Breac's strategic performance report is provided in Appendix 1. This strategic performance report is produced by each SBU for the Management Board of Breac on a monthly basis. The format and structure of this strategic performance report has not changed in three years.

The CEO now wishes to investigate the possibility of using VBM in all of Breac's SBUs and he has asked you, as an external consultant in this area, for your views on this. He has indicated to you that he specifically requires you to consider the effect of the introduction of VBM on the measures in the example strategic performance report.

Exhibit 4: Appendix 1

EXAMPLE OF BREAC'S PERFORMANCE REPORT

Financial

Sales revenue

Gross profit margin

Operating profit margin

Manufacturing

Percentage of goods returned (from either end user of the retail outlet)

Percentage of goods produced and delivered on-time to the retails outlets

Number of stock-outs per month per retail outlet (Note 1)

Marketing

Marketing spend

Marketing contribution to revenue (Note 2)

Notes.

1 A stock-out is when the retail outlet does not have inventory of a particular product.

2 The % of overall SBU revenue that can be tracked back to the marketing team's efforts.

Answers

DO NOT TURN THIS PAGE UNTIL YOU HAVE COMPLETED THE MOCK EXAM

Exam success skills

In any APM exam it will be important to apply good general exam technique by using the six exam success skills identified at the start of the Revision Kit, in the section covering 'essential skills'. These skills are: 1. Case scenario: Managing information; 2. Correct interpretation of requirements; 3. Answer planning: Priorities, structure and logic; 4. Efficient numerical analysis; 5. Effective writing and presentation; and 6. Good time management.

Some examples of how to apply these skills in this exam are provided in the table below.

Skill	Examples
Managing information	It is crucially important to assimilate the information in the question scenario. In longer questions, such as the 50-mark question, it is difficult to assimilate information by simply starting at the beginning and read to the end because there is so much information to take in. Instead, it is sensible to take an **active approach** to reading each question. Read enough of the question to get an idea of the basic scenario and then read the initial requirements so that you understand the first things that you are expected to do with this information. *For example, in Q1 the lengthy scenario makes a lot more sense if, before reading all of it, you are aware that the first requirements relate to analysis of the divisional performance.*
Correct Interpretation of requirements	**Answer planning** Be careful to interpret the verbs used in the question requirements carefully. In APM exams the requirements are embedded within the scenario, so identify these and then ensure you are clear about what you are required to do. Also be careful to identify where a question requirement contains more than one instruction. *For example, in Q1 part (a) the question required an evaluation of the performance of the two divisions using ROI and RI, an analysis of how these could be calculated in different ways, based on the how head office costs were treated, and an evaluation of which of the two methods would be most appropriate for Calavie.*
Answer planning	Planning is always important in APM questions, because most of the marks are available for discussion and if your discussion points are not relevant to the scenario then they will not receive any credit. As a general rule, you should spend at least 20% of your time, reading the scenario and planning your answer.
Efficient numerical analysis	It is essential that the marker can follow your workings and your logic. If you make a mistake early in your calculations that affects your later calculations then the marker will only penalise the error you have made, and not its follow-on impact on other calculations. This means that it is not normally a good use of your time to correct such errors during the exam.
Effective writing and presentation	In APM this is a very important skill. You are often expected to be able to employ **critical analysis**, and this will sometimes mean that you will reject innovative and modern ideas in favour of less exotic tried and tested performance management tools.

Skill	Examples
	It is also very important to **relate your points to the scenario** and to the requirement wherever possible. This means that you will need to apply your theoretical knowledge to the scenario, not simply repeat a technical point as something that you have memorised. However, you will be tested on your understanding of the theoretical content of APM and **you will not be able to apply your theoretical knowledge to the scenario if you do not possess a strong understanding of the theories in the first place.** *For example, in Q1 a strong understanding of divisional performance measures, ROI and residual income is required.* **Relating your points to the scenario** does not mean simply repeating the details from the question, but using this information to help to explain the point you are making. Finally, in Q1, to score the 10 **professional marks** that are available you should use suitable report headings, an introduction, a logical structure, signposted by the good use of subheadings in the answer, and a clear, concise style.
Good time management	The exam is 3 hours 15 minutes long, which translates to 1.95 minutes per mark. There are 20 professional marks in the exam and therefore 80 technical marks. If you build in an allowance of 20% of your time for assimilating the scenario and planning, this still leaves you with 1.95 minutes per technical mark available.. At the beginning of a question, work out the amount of time you should be spending on: • Planning: for a 25-mark question this will be 1.95 × 25 marks × 20% = 10 minutes. For a 50-mark question this should be about 20 mins. • Writing your answer to each requirement: Take the mark allocation and multiply by 1.95 minutes per technical mark.

Diagnostic

Did you apply these skills when reading, planning, and writing up your answer? Identify the exam success skills where you think you need to improve and capture your thoughts here of what you want to achieve when attempting questions in future.

Section A

This section of the exam contains one question.

This question is worth 50 marks and is compulsory.

This exam section is worth 50 marks in total.

1 Question 1

Workbook references

Divisional performance evaluation is discussed in Chapter 7 of the Workbook. The Boston Consulting Group matrix is covered in Chapter 1. Management information is covered in Chapter 5.

Top tips

Part (a) required candidates to do three things, so it was important that you did attempt all three of these. This would have been quite time pressured, so time allocation was important. In the third part of the requirement, to evaluate the use of RI, it is important to try to bring in information from the scenario to avoid writing a textbook style answer. The calculations could have been done in the spreadsheet section of the computer-based exam interface, which would have saved time on the calculations.

Part (b) It was important to be clear about exactly what was required for this part of the question so note the embedded requirements carefully. (1) assess how the analysis in appendix 2 can be used in performance management. (2) Recommend with justification two suitable financial KPIs for each division (based on appendix 2).

Part (c) In questions about information systems, a good approach is to ignore the word 'system' and focus on the information needed. Again, try to avoid giving answers that are too theoretical and bring in issues specific to Calavie and the three divisions.

Examining team's comments

Part (a). Most candidates successfully attempted both ROI and RI for all three divisions [...] however a significant number of candidates only calculated ROI and RI once for each division. Given the exhibit stated that the CEO wanted an analysis of the different ways that these could be calculated it would have been a sensible approach to demonstrate the different ways, eg excluding the costs that were not controllably by the division.

Some candidates did not attempt the final part of this question at all [...] this was a relatively straightforward. Candidates should remember that the focus of APM is application and as such, although some markers were awarded for explaining the advantages and disadvantages [...] candidate needed to consider these in relation to the three divisions.

Part (b). There is little benefit here describing the BCG. Phrases such as 'how it could be useful' should encourage candidates to discuss the benefits to the company of using the model. The second part of part b) – Candidates should be prepared to discuss why are recommended KPI is suitable for a division [...] it is the explanation that demonstrates a solid understanding here as opposed to the long list of measures with no discussion that were produced by some candidates.

Marking guide	Marks
(a) Divisional performance measurement	
Calculations – 1 mark for each set (need all three divisions correct for mark)	
Discussion of results (up to 8 marks) – 1 mark per point must be based on the scenario	
Healthy ROI, over average and cost of capital	
Positive RI, also healthy	

Simple measures

Controllability

Long-term effect

Comparing ROI and RI (up to 5 marks) – 1 mark per point

ROI is simple

RI can use differing cost of capital per division

ROI is relative

Neither aligned to shareholder wealth

Note: No marks for the definition.

14

(b) The BCG analysis

General discussion of BCG use in performance management – up to 6 marks

Allows company to view prospects of division and where to invest

Simple method

Not created for performance measurement

Not all products in all divisions match the classification of the division overall

Does not consider links between divisions

Application to the divisions – up to 6 marks for each division:

Up to 2 marks for broad approach for the division: strategy and measurement

These marks are for broadly describing appropriate strategies, etc for each division, given their relative location in the BCG matrix

2 marks for stating the KPIs (1 mark per KPI) – must be financial KPIs

2 marks for the justification of the KPIs (1 mark per KPI) – judgement on other KPIs not stated in model answer, but MUST be financial KPIs

There are no marks for generically discussing life cycle of products/division unless it is in relation to how this would affect its movement from one quadrant of the grid to another.

15

(c) Management information at Calavie

Explain briefly the aims of management accounting information – up to 5 marks each

General aims of management acting information

Performance management occurs are different levels of the organisation

Qualities of good information with example – 2 marks per quality point (1 mark for explanation and one for example/implication) up to 8 marks

Maximum 4 marks for generic points, i.e. to score the remaining marks, must be related to the scenario

No marks for stating/listing ACCURATE, etc

Tutorial note: A candidate does not need to use the ACCURATE acronym in order to score marks here.

11

Professional marks

Communication:

- Report format and structure – use of headings/sub-headings and introduction
- Style, language and clarity – appropriate tone of report response, presentation of calculations, appropriate use of the CBE tools, easy to follow and understand

- MaximumEffectiveness of communication – content of the report is relevant and tailored to the question scenario

Analysis and Evaluation:

- Appropriate calculations of ROI and RI in part (i) and the use of these to inform the discussion
- Balanced appraisal to make a recommendation, demonstrating reasoned judgement when considering key organisational matters and impacts

Scepticism:

- Discussing the appropriateness of the BCG matrix for performance management

Commercial acumen:

- Using judgement and knowledge of Calavie's situation in making recommendations relating to appropriate divisional performance measurement
- Showing understanding of the different management styles appropriate for the different product types per the BCG analysis
- Making appropriate recommendations with regard to management information systems for Calavie 10

Total 50

To: The board of Calavie Manufacturing (Calavie)

From: An Accountant

Date: September 20X5

Subject: Divisional performance and its measurement

This report evaluates each division's performance using return on investment (ROI) and residual income (RI). It considers detailed aspects of the calculation and a comparison of these two divisional performance indicators. Second, the use of the Boston Consulting Group (BCG) analysis is discussed in general and then, specifically for the divisions of Calavie, where key financial performance indicators are recommended. Finally, the general aims of management accounting information are described and the qualities which good information should have are illustrated for Calavie.

(a) **Overall divisional performance measurement**

Working

	Doilet	Essan	Fada
Simple measures:			
Non-controllable ROI (operating profit/capital employed)	16%	28%	23%
Non-controllable RI (operating profit – notional charge) ($m)	33.4	45.3	3.6
Adjusted measures:			
Controllable ROI (HO costs added back to operating profit)	22%	34%	29%
Controllable RI (HO costs added back to operating profit)	69.4	59.3	5.6
Long-term spending as an asset (R&D and brand marketing added back to operating profit and to capital employed)			
Non-controllable ROI	17%	32%	38%
Non-controllable RI	37.8	56.9	10.7

On the simple measures, all divisions are performing well. They make a healthy ROI beating both the cost of capital and the industry average. Also, all divisions make a positive residual income which again implies healthy returns.

The simple measures of performance do not take account of the controllability of the profits of the divisions nor the long-term effect of some of the spending of the divisions.

Controllability – The appropriate measure of the divisional management's performance should only include those elements which are controllable by them and so should exclude allocated head office costs. This is especially important as management's remuneration depends on this measure and it would be counter-productive if the divisional management felt this was being measured unfairly.

Long-term effect of spending – Essan is building its brand for the long term through marketing and Fada is building its portfolio of products through research and development. It should be considered whether it is appropriate to include this spending as a period cost or whether it should be capitalised and then written off over a longer period from the balance sheet. The capitalisation and amortisation of these costs may encourage divisional management to persist with these plans for the long-term benefit of Calavie. The calculation here is very crude as no estimate of opening balance of historic spending is possible nor one of the amortisation charge to the profit figure.

It is noteworthy that the use of operating profit in all of these calculations avoids the problem of including one-off costs (eg, the restructuring costs) which would occur if profit before tax were used.

These adjustments to the divisional performance measures do not change substantively the conclusion of good performance by both divisions. However, they may provide unexpected results such as the notably large ROI of Fada if the effect of R&D spending is capitalised.

Comparing ROI and RI

ROI is a simple, commonly used measure of divisional performance. However, it can encourage divisions to delay investment in new assets since this measure improves as assets are depreciated with age.

RI offers the possibility of applying different costs of capital to divisions with different risk profiles which is appropriate for Calavie, especially at the higher risk Fada.

Unlike ROI, RI would not help to judge relative divisional performance at Calavie as the divisions are not of similar size and so an absolute measure is not comparable.

It is worth noting that neither of the indicators is directly aligned with the aim of increasing shareholder wealth and so do not ensure a detailed match between divisional and corporate goals. Both ROI and RI have the disadvantage of being based on profit measures of performance rather than cash. Measures such as net present value and economic value added use cash flows, which are less subject to the interpretation of accounting rules, and are more directly aligned with shareholder interests.

(b) **BCG analysis and performance measurement within the divisions**

The BCG analysis can be beneficial as it allows the company to view the prospects of its different divisions. A different style of management should be applied to each division based on this analysis. Those businesses which are in faster growing sectors will require more capital to be invested and may not generate cash as efficiently from profits (eg Fada). However, those businesses in slower growing mature markets should have a focus on cost control and cash generation. Business units identified as cash cows and, particularly, dogs should not be dismissed since if they are properly managed, they can provide a rich source of cash as they are run down.

The performance management systems and metrics used by the divisions should therefore be adjusted to reflect this analysis. The metrics for high growth prospects, Essan and Fada, will be based on profit and ROI while those in lower growth, such as Doilet, will be focused on margins and cash generation.

However, the BCG matrix is a very simple method of analysis. For example, using relative market share measured against the largest competitor, where a value of 1·0 is used as the cut off between large and small, means there is only one star or cow per market. It is notable that the consultant has treated Doilet as a cash cow although it might not strictly be judged as such.

BCG was designed as a tool for product portfolio analysis rather than performance measurement. As a performance system, it seems to downgrade traditional measures of performance such as profit and shareholder wealth and therefore may not be well aligned with all of the key stakeholders' objectives. Therefore, although it may have been an appropriate view in the past as Calavie focused on growth, this may no longer be the case.

Additionally, it may be that different products within each business unit may not fit the unit's classification. For example, Fada seems to have a variety of products performing at different levels. The model also fails to consider the links between the business units, for example, where the brand and products developed at Essan might have a valuable effect on the perception (by association) of Doilet's products.

Doilet

As a cash cow, Doilet should focus on cash generation to fuel the growth of the other divisions where there is the need for brand-building and research and development. It should also focus on cost control in order to meet its aim to be a cost leader. Therefore, cash flow ROI or more simply net operating cash flow for the period may be better overall measures. Also, in order to address the aim of being a cost leader, either gross or operating profit margin compared to the industry average could be suitable. The decision between these measures will depend on the importance placed on the non-production overheads compared with its competitors.

Essan

As the star, the appropriate measure for Essan is profit based. Therefore, ROI or RI should be used depending on the board's decision about which is to be the measure of divisional performance. It would appear that growth has been important in the past to Calavie and as the principal generator of growth for the company, this should continue to be monitored by growth of profit before tax. This would also show the strength of Essan's brand which appears important from its marketing spending.

Fada

Fada depends significantly on research and development in order to develop a portfolio of new products. It should be judged on revenue growth as a method of measuring the success of these new products. In the early stages of product development, profit-based measures may not be suitable. A second measure may be the research and development spending since this will need to be maintained in the face of failures as the division seeks to find successful products for its portfolio.

(c) Word Processor:

Management information

The general aims of management accounting information are to support measuring performance, controlling the business, planning and making decisions.

Performance measurement will occur at different levels within the organisation (company, divisional and departmental level). It also links to the assessment of the performance of individuals, for example, the rewards paid to divisional managers are based on divisional performance. This performance measurement then allows the business to be controlled by measuring performance against targets or budgets. The information also feeds forward in time to assist in the preparation of plans and forecasts. Finally, managers must make decisions at strategic, tactical and operational levels of the business. These will often require management accounting information such as profit margins or (at the operational level) average time taken to produce a component.

The qualities of good information are that it should be:

Accurate – That is fair and free from bias. There is a danger that, motivated by the desire for the reward payment, divisional management provides an overly positive view of their performance.

Complete – All information must be reported. For example, project failures at Fada must be reported so that lessons can be learned for further new product development.

Cost-beneficial – The information should be more valuable than the cost to produce it. This would be especially true at Doilet since the business is mature and may not merit heavy investment as it is a well-understood division.

User-targeted – It is important that the divisions do not swamp the executive with detailed operational information so that they are unable to obtain an overview of the business.

Relevant – Different board members will have different skills and areas of interest and they should be supplied with more detailed information appropriate to those responsibilities, while all of the board should receive the same overview information.

Authoritative – The source of the information should be suitably qualified. This may require board information to be reviewed and signed off by senior divisional management if it is produced at a lower level within the division.

Timely – Information must reach the executive in time so that they can make strategic plans in time.

Ease to use – The information should be formatted for easy understanding. Financial information should be presented in a standardised format to make for easy comparison between divisions. The use of a single, agreed measure of divisional performance will aid this.

Tutorial note. A candidate does not need to use the ACCURATE acronym in order to score marks here.

Section B

This section of the exam contains two questions.

Each question is worth 25 marks and is compulsory.

This exam section is worth 50 marks in total.

2 Question 2

Workbook reference

Transfer pricing is discussed in Chapter 7 of the Workbook

Top tips

All three parts of this question should have been straightforward if you know transfer pricing theory. Do remember to apply your knowledge to Vaa rather than just recite the theory – eg in part (a) you should mention information such as the fact that the current system does not seem to provide a fair measure of the performance of division R. In part (b) the question asked for disadvantages only, so don't discuss advantages.

Examining team's comments

This question was generally answered quite badly [...] in general candidates seemed at times unclear on the principles underlying transfer pricing and the operation of it.

The essence of APM is application [...] candidates would definitely benefit from asking questions such as "how does this apply to this company in its current situation?" rather than, as seems to be the case currently "what can I remember about transfer pricing and in which part of the question should I put this information?"

Marking guide	Marks
(a) 1 mark per point:	
Criteria for setting a transfer pricing policy – up to 9 marks	
Include up to 2 marks for brief discussion of the benefits of a policy	
No credit for discussing specific bases for setting transfer price	
	7
(b) 1 mark per point:	
Disadvantages of market value price – up to 8 marks	
	6
(c) 1 mark per point– up to 6 marks, e.g. tax, measures to protect local manufacturers, exchange rates, other points:	
Consideration of legal or ethical constraints – 1 mark	
	7

Professional marks

Analysis and Evaluation:

- Appreciating the existing situation at Vaa and demonstrating understanding of how transfer pricing methods currently in use are impacting this

Scepticism:

- Being able to challenge the proposed use of a market-based transfer pricing system in a balanced and courteous manner

Marking guide	Marks
Commercial acumen:	
• Providing discussion that appreciates the situation at Vaa	
Maximum	5
Total	25

(a) Word Processor:

Criteria for the design of a transfer pricing policy

Divisional autonomy

A transfer pricing policy should allow divisional autonomy for managers to negotiate transfer prices. This ensures management is motivated to act in the best interest of their divisions. Both R and S divisions already have the autonomy to negotiate the price at which the key component is transferred between them and to choose from whom to purchase and to sell to in the external market.

Both divisions must want to transfer internally if this is to take place. There is no point, for example, in R trying to purchase the key component from S, if S does not want to sell to it.

Goal congruence

As profit centres, R and S divisions will seek to act in their own interests, which may not be in the interests of the other division, or of Vaa as a whole. This does seem to be the case, as Vaa head office often has to intervene in the negotiations between the divisions in order to impose a transfer price which maximises the performance of Vaa as a whole. For this reason, the transfer pricing policy needs to allow head office to retain some control over the transfer price to ensure that the divisions are pursuing goals which are congruent to those of the organisation as a whole.

Divisional performance evaluation

As profit centres, R and S divisions' performance will be measured according to divisional profits and managers will prioritise the profits of their own division. The transfer pricing policy should ensure that divisional managers see the transfer price as fair because the transfer prices will affect the profits of the divisions and hence the evaluation of their own performance.

Recently, R has only broken even, whereas S has made substantial profits. It has been suggested that this is due to high transfer prices charged by S. Though the basis on which the transfer price is negotiated is unknown, this suggests that S division may have the stronger negotiating position, perhaps because the component produced by S division has much lower energy consumption than those of its competitors. The current system may not be fair and therefore may not allow a meaningful evaluation of divisional performance.

The transfer price should allow each division to earn a fair return for the work it has done, otherwise managers will not be motivated to improve performance. For the same reason, the basis of determining the price should be clearly understood by divisional managers. The transfer pricing policy should allow transfer prices to be easily calculated and recorded to minimise the amount of time and resource spent doing this.

Profit maximisation of Vaa

There are concerns about the amount of time divisional managers spend arguing about a suitable transfer price. A transfer price policy should be designed so that less time is spent doing this and so that managers can focus on improving performance in other areas, such as finding ways to utilise spare capacity.

The transfer price should be set to maximise Vaa's overall profits rather than the profits of the divisions themselves. The policy should set a transfer price which reflects the true cost to the organisation.

(b) **Disadvantages of market-based transfer prices**

Setting a market-based transfer price may be difficult because the market price may be only temporary. There is currently an economic recession in Essland, which may temporarily lower the demand for, and hence the price of, electronic consumer goods. These products will also be subject to rapid changes in technology. This may lead to falling market prices for components as they are superseded by newer versions.

There may be no equivalent product on which to set a market value price. There are other companies which manufacture a component which fulfils the same function as that produced by S division, so it appears that it would be possible to set a market value for this.

The key component produced by S division, however, has lower energy consumption than competitors' products, and so in some sense may be unique. It is unclear how significant this energy saving is relative to that of the finished product, but the fact that it is in some degree unique, suggests that the price charged by S may be higher than the market price. The use of average market price of other components may be inappropriate, as this would put S at a disadvantage. This may be unfair and could reduce motivation in S division.

Market price may discourage divisions from utilising spare capacity in the selling division, for example, because the buying division can purchase more cheaply from the open market. There is said to be spare capacity in Vaa, but it is unclear in what division(s) or whether this has anything to do with the component's transfer price.

If a market-based transfer price is used, this may increase the amount of any spare capacity in S as the price charged by S is likely to exceed the market price. This would encourage R to purchase from the external market. A market-based transfer price may not therefore maximise Vaa's overall profit and so would be a disadvantage in using it.

In reality, any market-based transfer price is likely to be an adjusted market price. This is due to that fact that internal transfers do not incur as many costs to the selling division, such as administration and bad debt costs, as external transfers do. Establishing the extent of these costs may be complicated and time consuming and may need to change over time. In the end, the adjusted market price would also have to be negotiated between the divisions. S division may need to share cost information with R division, so that the negotiation can be done on a fair basis, which it may be unwilling to do so. Given the difficulties the two divisions have in negotiating a transfer price, it seems likely head office would also have to intervene to impose an adjusted market price, which detracts from the benefits of using this basis.

(c) **Factors to consider when setting international transfer prices**

Tax

The corporation tax rate in Teeland is lower than that in Essland. This gives Vaa the opportunity and incentive to minimise its overall tax liabilities by charging a low transfer price for the key component. This would increase profits in T division, where the tax rate is 16% and decrease profits in Essland where the tax rate is 25%.

Vaa should consider whether trying to minimise its tax liabilities in this way would be legal or ethical. Whatever transfer price is charged, the tax authorities in Essland and Teeland may tax Vaa as if the components transferred from S division to T division had been transferred between unrelated parties at an arm's length price.

Import tariffs and anti-dumping legislation

Teeland is one of the largest producers of electronic consumer goods in the world. There may be many competitors there supplying the key component. In order to be competitive, Vaa may have to reduce the costs to T division by charging a lower transfer price.

However, the Teeland government is considering introducing a range of protectionist measures to protect local manufacturers from competition from imported electronic consumer goods. Import tariffs imposed on the value of imported components would increase Vaa's costs. Vaa could consider charging a low transfer price to reduce this cost of the import tariff, again subject to legal and ethical considerations. The Teeland government may require all transfers to be at arm's length value to try to protect local manufacturers by restricting companies from importing goods to Teeland.

If Vaa were to charge a lower transfer price to T division, the Teeland government may perceive this as unfair competition with local manufacturers and be more likely to use protectionist measures such as anti-dumping legislation.

Exchange rates

The transfer price of the components would vary over time according to the movements in exchange rate between the currencies in Essland and Teeland, which could make planning and budgeting more difficult. Exchange rate movements could also change the price of the component in the external market, which could affect each division's decision to buy from or sell to the external market.

The transfer price would have to be adjusted to reflect exchange rate movements. Otherwise, divisional managers could become de-motivated if their performance was evaluated based on factors outside of their control. This would make calculating and recording the transfer price more complex and may make it harder for managers to understand.

3 Question 3

Workbook reference

Performance management in complex business organisations is discussed in Chapter 13. Value based management is covered in Chapter 12.

Top Tips

Part (a) requires you to use application, and you trust your own ideas about the problems faced by Breac in developing the service level agreement with Gowan. There were plenty of clues given in Exhibit 2 about issues that would need to be dealt with in the SLA. Any sensible suggestions will gain marks.

Part (b) does require knowledge of VBM. A good approach is to think about what type of measures are used in VBM and compare those with the current performance measures, to help you think about changes that must be made. Don't forget to recommend whether VBM should be introduced at Breac.

Examining team's comments

Part (a). Most candidates correctly identified from the scenario, some of the main issues that were causing difficulty between the two companies. Candidates were less able to fully develop these points however, or make them relevant to the specifics of an SLA.

Part (b). This part of the question was very badly done, primarily because it was clear that many candidates did not know what VBM was.

Of those who did have an understanding of VBM [...] these candidates did not seem to fully appreciate what the question was asking which, at its core, was quite straightforward: if the company adopted VBM, would it continue to measure the areas that is currently does? If so, why and if not, why not?

Marking guide		Marks
(a) 1 mark per relevant point		
		8
(b) Financial measures	4	
Manufacturing measures	4	
Marketing measures	4	
Justified recommendation	2	
		12

Professional marks

Analysis and Evaluation:

- Evaluating the current performance measures at Breac and considering whether or not these would be appropriate under VBM

Commercial acumen:

- Demonstrating awareness of the problems that will face Breac when developing a service level agreement with Gowan

Professional scepticism

- Being able to objectively consider whether the introduction of VBM at Breac would be appropriate

Maximum	5
Total	25

(a) **Responsibility for damaged and/or faulty goods**

One of the problems which the management board (MB) of Breac will need to address in the service level agreement (SLA) is the point at which Gowan ceases to be responsible for the faulty goods. Breac must ensure that Gowan is responsible for the defect, most likely with a financial penalty, whenever the defect is detected. This point may depend on the nature of the actual problem detected. For example, as Breac is undertaking additional manufacturing work on the clothing, it may be relatively easy for the manufacturing departments at Breac to detect if the quality of the material is sub-standard or if the stitching has disintegrated at this stage.

However, issues of poor quality and stitching disintegrating may manifest themselves later when the goods have been purchased by the end-user. Additionally, Breac would be unwilling to undertake the time-consuming process of checking that every good which it receives is correctly sized and would probably only check a sample of the clothing for this error. It is possible, therefore, that this problem may also be detected by the end-user.

Unless Gowan can guarantee that the clothing goods it supplies are defect free, that the stitching will not disintegrate and that all correct size labels are on the respective items of clothing, Breac has to be able to hold Gowan to account whenever these problems are detected. Breac would be very keen to impose different levels of financial penalty on Gowan depending upon when the fault was detected. Faulty goods detected by the end-user, for example, are likely to bring significant reputational damage to Breac and Breac would be keen to impose a stronger financial penalty on Gowan for faults detected at this stage.

This is an area where Gowan is likely to resist. Gowan would be keen to ensure that its liability is limited to initial inspection on arrival of the material at Breac's manufacturing plant and that any quality-related problems detected thereafter are the responsibility of Breac.

Currently, for example, it is not clear that all the quality-related problems Breac is experiencing have been caused by Gowan. These problems may well have been caused by the additional work Breac has undertaken or, perhaps, Breac may have damaged the goods which Gowan has supplied somewhere in Breac's manufacturing process.

Delivery time

Another problem may arise regarding any agreed delivery time. Both Breac and Gowan are global companies and therefore delivery to individual countries may depend upon global trading regulations and, most likely, shipping conditions. Given this situation, it should be clear in the SLA exactly what Gowan is responsible for and which conditions are considered to be out of Gowan's control. For example, Breac may wish to place the entire responsibility for delivery onto Gowan and suggest that if there is a problem with shipping that Gowan must find another way to deliver the material, which would most likely be by air. Gowan would be keen to resist this given the cost implication.

Information systems

It is very clear that the information systems of both these companies cannot communicate with each other. This may prove to be problematic with regard to the actual operation of the SLA. It is important that Breac is aware of Gowan's production schedules, for example, to ascertain when it is likely to receive batches of goods from Gowan. It would also be very helpful for Breac to have access to Gowan's own internal quality control data as Breac may have concerns over the quality of material being sent to it if Gowan's internal failure rate is high.

Specific targets will also be set between the two companies around such areas as quality assurance and delivery times. It would be beneficial to the operation of the SLA if these targets could be agreed upon and shared on a common platform. Without a shared system, there is the potential for disagreement between the companies based on different interpretations of this data. For example, it would be helpful to Breac if Gowan's quality control data were displayed on such a platform. This would, potentially, remove any suspicion that Breac may have about the accuracy of that data.

(b) **Financial measures**

Value based management's (VBM) main ethos is that the value of a company is measured by its discounted cash flows. Companies therefore enhance their value when they invest in projects which return a positive net present value. It is clear that Breac is not using the cost of capital in its financial measurements at all, with the main measures being profit-based in the form of operating and gross profit margin. The revenue figure is less helpful from a VBM perspective as it offers no indication of any costs which have been incurred to achieve the revenue.

A common form of financial measure for companies which adopt a VBM approach is economic value added (EVA). The EVA calculation involves both the capital employed and the cost of capital in its computation. For Breac to accept this new calculation, a culture change would be required. The fact that the current performance report has been in place for at least three years would suggest that the behaviour which the current measures encourage is embedded within the company. There is therefore likely to be both a widespread lack of understanding in the company of the new measure of EVA and a reluctance to change. Nevertheless, it is recommended that Breac adopt this measure if it adopts a VBM approach.

Manufacturing measures

The manufacturing departments throughout Breac are likely to be under more pressure to ensure that what they produce is right first time and that it is delivered on time. If not, it is very likely that the manufacturing departments would be blamed by the retail outlets for any shortfall in their targets. It is likely, therefore, that the measures of percentage of goods returned and percentage of goods delivered on time would remain and that the emphasis on them would be increased with any change to a VBM approach. Such emphasis may also result in the further development of Breac's quality assurance processes to ensure that the material which is delivered to Breac is to the required standard and on time. As a result, further specific quality assurance measures may be introduced and Breac could consider introducing quality costing to allow it to analyse, understand and correct problems in this area.

The measurement of stock-outs per month is likely to continue in a VBM environment. Managers of each strategic business unit (SBU) will be responsible for the capital at their disposal and will be required to make a return on it. The inventory which the managers hold is a significant part of that capital and it will be important for managers to ensure that they have sufficient amounts of inventory to satisfy demand. If they do not have the inventory, manufacturing and/or delivery departments are likely to be blamed if the SBUs do not achieve the required return on capital.

Marketing measures

The measure of marketing spend alone is unlikely to be useful in a VBM environment. Spend alone offers no indication as to whether that expense has returned value. Perhaps if the spend was measured alongside any change in brand value, then it could be said that there was a connection between marketing spend and brand value. However, this would be impossible to measure at the level of each individual SBU as the brand value would relate to the entire company and not any individual retail outlet. Breac should therefore not continue with this measure in a VBM environment.

The measure of marketing contribution to revenue, however, does ensure accountability and would be appropriate in a VBM environment. This measure seeks to attribute revenue directly to specific advertising spend and, as such, makes an attempt to relate spend in a specific area to an increase in revenue from that spend. However, there are significant problems with this measure. First, advertising spend is being linked with revenue and not value. A more accurate measure would be to link advertising spend with enhanced EVA rather than revenue. Second, it is also difficult to establish a clear link between advertising spend and either revenue or EVA as these factors may have increased due to other aspects, such as growth in the market, rather than because of the individual marketing spend of the SBU.

Recommendation

There is a strong argument for introducing VBM into Breac. This argument is based on a recognition that Breac is a large-scale manufacturing company and therefore has significant capital at its disposal. It is not currently assessing whether that capital is being utilised effectively as the required return on it is not being measured. However, the culture change involved in introducing VBM into the entire company at once may be too difficult to undertake in a practical sense and it might be helpful to introduce VBM into one SBU initially. This would allow Breac to learn from any mistakes which may be made before embedding it within the entire organisation.

ACCA

Advanced Performance Management (APM)

Mock Exam 4 (Sept 2022)

Questions	
Time allowed	3 hours 15 minutes
Section A This ONE question is compulsory and MUST be attempted. Section B BOTH questions are compulsory and MUST be attempted.	

DO NOT OPEN THIS EXAM UNTIL YOU ARE READY TO START UNDER EXAMINATION CONDITIONS

Section A

This section of the exam contains one question.

This question is worth 50 marks and is compulsory.

This exam section is worth 50 marks in total.

1 Question 1

The following exhibits, available on the left-hand side of the screen, provide information relevant to the question:

(1) Company information – the background, overall aim, competitive environment and new strategic approach of the company: Belivat Manufacturing (Belivat)

(2) Product development budgeting – details of work required by the CEO on a proposal to change the budgeting method to zero-based budgeting (ZBB) for new product development

(3) Kaizen costing – instructions from the CEO on the possibility of introducing Kaizen costing at Belivat

(4) Interaction of ZBB and Kaizen – details of board discussion on the new budgeting and costing systems proposed and the subsequent request for work from the CEO

(5) Inventory management – information related to current inventory management practices at Belivat and the CEO's request for advice on a potential project to improve matters in this area

(6) Appendix 1 – an extract from the project specification report for improving inventory management

This information should be used to answer the question requirements within your chosen response option(s).

Required

It is now 1 September 20X5.

Write a report to the CEO of Belivat to respond to her instructions for work on the following areas:

(a) Product development budgeting **(12 marks)**

(b) Kaizen costing **(9 marks)**

(c) The interaction of ZBB and Kaizen **(6 marks)**

(d) The inventory management project **(13 marks)**

Professional marks will be awarded for the demonstration of communication, analysis and evaluation, scepticism and commercial acumen in your answer. **(10 marks)**

(Total = 50 marks)

Exhibit 1: Company information

Belivat Manufacturing (Belivat) is a world leader in the manufacture of temperature sensors used in many industrial processes. It aims to deliver growing returns to its shareholders in the long-term.

It operates in an increasingly competitive environment where profit margins are under pressure. In order to address these forces, the board of Belivat has decided that they need to change their strategic approach. They intend to increase revenue and drive down costs by becoming more innovative in the two keys aspects of the business: the development of new products; and the production process.

Currently, the business uses standard costing and incremental budgets in order to control costs. The same methods of production and accounting have been used for many years at Belivat.

The board recognises the need for a cultural change to fit the new strategic approach. The board also believes that they have an excellent workforce which is under-utilised. It has been decided that this can be capitalised upon by two changes (one to product development and the other to the general production process). Product development should be addressed by a more project-based approach, where products are developed by teams of workers. In addition, the organisation of production of all products will also now be handled by teams whose aim is to reduce costs as far as possible while maintaining competitive levels of quality.

The board has begun discussing these changes and the chief executive officer (CEO) has asked you, as a performance management expert, for your assistance on a number of proposals relating to changes to costing and budgeting at Belivat. There is also a plan to improve the operation of the warehouse by introducing new technology in inventory management.

Exhibit 2: Product development budgeting

It is proposed that a new budgeting method be used for new product development and it has been suggested that zero-based budgeting (ZBB) may be a more useful approach.

The CEO wants a critical comparison of ZBB with the existing method of budgeting. This should include a description of the ZBB approach and how it fits with Belivat's plans and aims.

Exhibit 3: Kaizen costing

The board has been investigating new methods of production and cost control in order to achieve the cost reductions needed to remain competitive. The board has been considering various Japanese production control techniques and has shown particular interest in the possibility of introducing Kaizen costing to replace the existing standard costing system.

As none of the board are experts, the CEO has requested an explanation of the process of Kaizen costing, the implications of the change in costing method for production management and a recommendation as to whether this change is appropriate for Belivat.

Exhibit 4: Interaction of ZBB and Kaizen

In the discussion of the budgeting and costing changes at a recent board meeting, one director suggested that ZBB should become the method of budgeting for the whole business (beyond just product development). Another director expressed concern that Kaizen costing did not fit with ZBB, neither on practical nor cultural terms. The board meeting then dissolved into a confused discussion of the new costing and budgeting methods.

The CEO would like you to provide the board with an evaluation of whether Kaizen costing would fit with ZBB in controlling production costs at Belivat.

Exhibit 5: Inventory management

Belivat has large warehouses containing a large inventory of many different types of sensors so that they can offer quick solutions to customer orders. However, as the business has grown, the scale of the warehouse operation has outgrown its ability to efficiently pick products for orders and identify obsolete items. The CEO believes that by tagging all items with radio-frequency identification devices (RFIDs) picking would be made more efficient, inventory control would be simpler and obsolescence reduced. She is aware that this has cost implications beyond merely buying and placing tags on each item in inventory and she wants your advice on the costs and benefits of introducing such a new system. As part of this advice, she has asked that you quantify your conclusions where possible using the illustrative data for one warehouse in Appendix 1.

Exhibit 6: Appendix 1

Title: Introduction of RFIDs at the warehouse

Aim: The aim of this project is to reduce costs and improve efficiency in the warehouse.

The system will apply to finished orders only and not components purchased.

The following are further details provided in relation to the project:

Spreadsheet

Edit Format

	A	B	C	D
1	**Costs:**			**$**
2	1	Average wage in the warehouse per annum		25,000
3	2	Average cost of each tag		0.75
4	3	New software needed to collate data from the tags		60,000
5	4	RFID sensors for the warehouse		50,000
6	5	On-going annual service cost for the new system		15,000
7	6	Updating current inventory management software to make it compatible with the collated RFID data		35,000
8	7	Other hardware required for the warehouse		25,000

Other inventory and warehouse information:

It is expected that 120,000 finished sensors will come into the warehouse in the year.

It is expected that the same number of items will be picked in the year as there is no inventory building planned in the period.

It is expected that the new system will last for eight years.

Currently, there is an average loss each year due to obsolete inventory write -downs of $120,000. It is expected that obsolescence will fall by 65% with the new system.

It is expected that picking efficiency will improve, saving 35% of staff time. There are currently seven staff involved in picking orders.

Section B

This section of the exam contains two questions.

Each question is worth 25 marks and is compulsory.

This exam section is worth 50 marks in total.

2 Question 2

The following exhibits, available on the left-hand side of the screen, provide information relevant to the question:

(1) Company information – the background, overall objective and plans of the company: Eck

(2) Measuring divisional manager performance – details of the possible introduction of EBITDA (earnings before interest, tax, depreciation and amortisation) and EVA^{tm} (economic value added) at Eck

(3) Proposed reward scheme – a new reward scheme for divisional managers

(4) Appendix 1 – performance data for Blue division

This information should be used to answer the question requirements within your chosen response option(s).

Required

It is now 1 September 20X5.

Respond to the board of Eck's request for work on the following areas:

(a) Measuring divisional manager performance

Note. There are eight marks available for the first piece of work on this area and there are five marks available for the second piece of work on this area. **(13 marks)**

(b) Proposed reward scheme **(7 marks)**

Professional marks will be awarded for the demonstration of skill in analysis and evaluation, scepticism and commercial acumen in your answer. **(5 marks)**

(Total = 25 marks)

Exhibit 1: Company information

Eck is a privately owned, capital-intensive manufacturing business. It has several similarly sized divisions which operate as profit centres. These divisions operate in different regions of Eck's home country, where the average tax rate is 40% and where the average rate of interest for commercial lending is 6%. Eck is financed by equal amounts of equity and debt.

Eck's overall objective is to maximise shareholder wealth. The company's board of directors, who are also the shareholders, make all investment and financing decisions.

The board is considering expanding Eck's product range, which will require the company to purchase a large amount of new plant and machinery. The shareholders are unable to provide any more capital and are unwilling to issue any form of equity finance. Eck is already close to breaching borrowing conditions and limits set by its lenders and is unable to raise any more debt finance.

Eck has recently revised the estimated useful economic life of existing large items of manufacturing plant, which is permitted under local accounting regulations.

Exhibit 2: Measuring divisional managers' performance

The board has recently been told that if the plans to expand its product range are to be successful, Eck needs better systems for measuring the performance of divisional managers and rewarding them. None of the divisional managers have any financial qualifications or experience. The board is, therefore, considering two possible measures of divisional manager performance: EBITDA (earnings before interest, tax, depreciation and amortisation) and EVA^{TM} (economic value added) and would like you, as a performance management expert, to undertake two pieces of work:

- The board is unfamiliar with EBITDA and want an assessment of its usefulness to measure a divisional manager's performance. The board does not require any calculations of EBITDA.
- The board has already been advised on the benefits and drawbacks of using EVA™ as a suitable performance measure, but has not yet seen how EVA™ is calculated for a particular division. As an example of this, the board would like to know whether the Blue division has created value using the information given in Appendix 1.

Exhibit 3: Proposed reward scheme

Based on the review of the two possible performance measures, the board has proposed a new reward scheme for divisional managers. Each manager will receive a reward equivalent to 45% of their annual salary if their division achieves a target EVA™ for the coming year.

Divisional managers have participated in the setting of the scheme. Market conditions in which each division operates will be considered when setting the target EVA™, which for Blue division is $25m. Eck has effective internal procedures to ensure the reliability of performance data and to prevent managers from focusing too much on a particular target while ignoring other important factors.

The board would like advice on whether this proposed new reward scheme will help improve the performance of the Blue division.

Exhibit 4: Appendix 1

Performance data for Blue division:

Spreadsheet

	A	B
1	Net profit after tax ($m)	50
2	Opening net assets ($m)	496
3		
4	Cost of equity	15%
5	Cost of debt (pre-tax)	12%
6		
	Tax rate	40%

Notes.

Net profit after tax for the year is after charging:

(1) Interest of $20 million

(2) Development expenditure of $5m was incurred during the year.

The development expenditure is to be amortised over five years.

3 Question 3

The following exhibits, available on the left-hand side of the screen, provide information relevant to the question:

(1) Company information – the background and existing performance management system of the company: Scye

(2) Value-based management – information about the introduction of value-based management (VBM) at Scye

(3) New project appraisal – details of a new graphic visualisation system being developed

(4) Appendix 1 – information gathered on the new graphic visualisation system

This information should be used to answer the question requirements within your chosen response option(s).

Required

It is now 1 September 20X5.

Respond to the CEO of Scye's request for work on the following areas:

(a) Value-based management (VBM) **(12 marks)**

(b) New project appraisal. **(8 marks)**

Professional marks will be awarded for the demonstration of skill in analysis and evaluation, scepticism and commercial acumen in your answer. **(5 marks)**

(Total = 25 marks)

Exhibit 1: Company information

Scye is a listed company of architects who imagine concepts for new buildings and then prepare detailed plans for their production. The business' performance has fluctuated over years and recently seen a reduction in profits.

The shareholders have demanded greater focus on their long-term returns rather than the quarterly dividend and a new chief executive officer (CEO) has been put in office, along with several new directors, in order to achieve this aim.

The new CEO has identified that the system of performance measurement and management is at fault in the business losing focus. It is based on a dashboard containing a wide mix of more than 15 financial performance indicators drawn from the financial reporting records from across the activities of the organisation. The report then benchmarks these indicators against competitors. Regular reports on these indicators are used at board meetings to guide the management of the business.

Exhibit 2: Value-based management

The CEO was at a recent meeting of business leaders where he heard that a move to value-based management (VBM) might help achieve the shareholders' goal. However, he was warned then that the use of economic value-added (EVA™) as a primary measure would not be ideal for VBM. Also, one of the new, non-executive directors at Scye commented that he had found EVA™ to be complex to understand and so Scye's board has agreed to avoid its use.

The CEO requires you to provide an understanding of the basic principles of VBM and then evaluate VBM compared to the existing performance dashboard, which is based around traditional profit-based measures of performance. He wants your evaluation to include both how VBM would affect the different management levels (strategic, tactical and operational) in Scye and how its implementation would affect the organisation.

Exhibit 3: New project appraisal

The next work the CEO requires is an example calculation of shareholder value (using the net present value (NPV) method) and he has given you information in Appendix 1 in order to allow you to do this for a new project at Scye. The project is the purchase and use of a new graphic visualisation system which will give a virtual tour of any new building design.

A non-executive director had also mentioned modified internal rate of return (MIRR) as another indicator that he had seen used to assess projects and so the CEO also wants a calculation of this for this same project and a final recommendation.

Exhibit 4: Appendix 1

Information gathered on the new graphic visualisation system:

(1) The system is expected to earn an additional $6.4m each year after operating costs.

(2) Operating costs include $8m of depreciation per year.

(3) Additional costs beyond those in operating costs for marketing and training staff are estimated at $0.7m in year 1.

(4) Tax will be charged at 20% paid in the year profits occur and all costs including depreciation are deemed allowable.

(5) There will be an initial spend of $25m to purchase the system, which will be totally replaced as new systems become available.

(6) The project will last for three years.

(7) It is reasonable for this exercise to assume that all revenue and costs will be paid or received in the year incurred.

(8) Working capital of 10% of the revenue after operating costs will be put in place at the start of year 1 and then working capital will be recovered at the end of the project.

(9) Scye's discount rate for such projects is 10% based on its cost of capital.

(10) Formula for MIRR = $(PV_R/PV_I)^{1/n} \times (1 + r_e) - 1$

Answers

DO NOT TURN THIS PAGE UNTIL YOU HAVE COMPLETED THE MOCK EXAM

Exam success skills

In any APM exam, it will be important to apply good general exam technique by using the six exam success skills identified at the start of the Revision Kit, in the section covering 'essential skills'. These skills are: 1. Case scenario: Managing information; 2. Correct interpretation of requirements; 3. Answer planning: Priorities, structure and logic; 4. Efficient numerical analysis; 5. Effective writing and presentation; and 6. Good time management.

Some examples of how to apply these skills in this exam are provided in the table below.

Skill	Examples
Managing information	It is crucially important to assimilate the information in the question scenario. In longer questions, such as the 50-mark question, it is difficult to assimilate information by simply starting at the beginning and reading to the end because there is so much information to take in. Instead, it is sensible to take an **active approach** to reading each question. Read enough of the question to get an idea of the basic scenario and then read the initial requirements so that you understand the first things that you are expected to do with this information. *For example, in Q1, start by reading the first sentence under Exhibit 1, so you know what Belivat does. After this, read the initial requirements so you know what topics you will be required to discuss, and the relative importance of each one. After this read the exhibits, using the highlighter tool to highlight key information.*
Correct Interpretation of requirements	**Answer planning** Be careful to interpret the verbs used in the question requirements carefully. In APM exams the requirements are embedded within the scenario, so identify these and then ensure you are clear about what you are required to do. Also be careful to identify where a question requirement contains more than one instruction. *For example, in Q1 part (ii) the requirement, which is embedded in Exhibit 3, required: (1) An explanation of Kaizen costing, (2) an explanation of the implications of the change in costing method for production management, and (3) a recommendation as to whether this is appropriate for Belivat.*
Answer planning	Planning is always important in APM questions, because most of the marks are available for discussion and if your discussion points are not relevant to the scenario then they will not receive any credit. As a general rule, you should spend at least 20% of your time, reading the scenario and planning your answer.
Efficient numerical analysis	It is essential that the marker can follow your workings and your logic. If you make a mistake early in your calculations that affects your later calculations then the marker will only penalise the error you have made, and not its follow-on impact on other calculations. This means that it is not normally a good use of your time to correct such errors during the exam.

Skill	Examples
Effective writing and presentation	In APM this is a very important skill. You are often expected to be able to employ **critical analysis**, and this will sometimes mean that you will reject innovative and modern ideas in favour of less exotic tried and tested performance management tools. It is also very important to **relate your points to the scenario** and to the requirement wherever possible. This means that you will need to apply your theoretical knowledge to the scenario, not simply repeat a technical point as something that you have memorised. However, you will be tested on your understanding of the theoretical content of APM and **you will not be able to apply your theoretical knowledge to the scenario if you do not possess a strong understanding of the theories in the first place**. *For example, in Q1 a strong understanding of Zero Based Budgeting, and when it is appropriate would have been necessary to be able to attempt parts (i) and (iii).* **Relating your points to the scenario** does not mean simply repeating the details from the question, but using this information to help to explain the point you are making. Finally, in Q1, to score the 10 **professional marks** that are available you should use suitable report headings, an introduction, a logical structure, signposted by the good use of subheadings in the answer, and a clear, concise style.
Good time management	The exam is 3 hours 15 minutes long, which translates to 1.95 minutes per mark. There are 20 professional marks in the exam and therefore 80 technical marks. If you build in an allowance of 20% of your time for assimilating the scenario and planning, this still leaves you with 1.95 minutes per technical mark available. At the beginning of a question, work out the amount of time you should be spending on: • Planning: for a 25-mark question this will be 1.95 × 25 marks × 20% = 10 minutes. For a 50-mark question this should be about 20 mins. • Writing your answer to each requirement: Take the mark allocation and multiply by 1.95 minutes per technical mark.

Diagnostic

Did you apply these skills when reading, planning, and writing up your answer? Identify the exam success skills where you think you need to improve and capture your thoughts here of what you want to achieve when attempting questions in future.

Section A

This section of the exam contains one question.

This question is worth 50 marks and is compulsory.

This exam section is worth 50 marks in total.

1 Question 1

Workbook references

Budgeting is covered in Chapter 3 of the Workbook. Kaizen costing is covered in Chapter 11. RFID tags are covered in Chapter 5.

Top tips

The requirement for part (c) was difficult. Many candidates seeing this at the start of their question attempt might have panicked – but it was only worth 6 of the 40 marks, so give it your best shot, and ensure that you aim to write good answers to the other three parts of the question to make up for this.

As always with APM questions, you must apply your knowledge of the technical areas to Belivat's circumstances, rather than just recite your theoretical knowledge.

Examining team's comments

Performance on this question was, overall disappointing [...] other candidates did not identify the fundamental difference in part (d) between the one-off costs and those occurring year. Performance in the professional skills marks was also slightly disappointing as candidates often did not fully address the requirements of the question, although the format, style and structure of the responses was generally an area where candidates scored well.

Responses should always justify the use of models in relation to the scenario, ie why is something important in this particular situation, as opposed to simply discussing features of a model or just its advantages and disadvantages.

Marking guide	Marks
(a) Description of ZBB – up to 4 marks	
Critical comparison of ZBB and incremental budgeting – up to 10 marks	
Costs and complexities of the systems	
Evaluation of fit of ZBB with Belivat's plans:	
cost control, innovation, culture, top-down v bottom–up	
Recommendation – 1 mark	
	12
(b) Explanation of Kaizen costing – up to 4 marks	
Implications for production management – up to 6 marks	
Change from standard costing	
Fit with aims and culture of Belivat	
Recommendation – 1 mark	
	9
(c) Differences of approach – up to 6 marks	
ZBB controlling manufacturing process	
ZBB compared to Kaizen	
Cultural issues	

ANSWERS

Marking guide		**Marks**
Practical issues		
Conclusion – 1 mark		
		6
(d) Cost benefit analysis	8	
Calculations		
Hardware		
Tags	1	
Sensors	1	
Other hardware	1	
Software total cost (1 each)	2	
On-going servicing cost	1	
Benefits of new system (cost savings):		
Warehouse -picking	1	
Obsolete inventory	1	
Conclusion		
Other costs/benefits – up to 6 marks		
		13

Communication:

- Report format and structure – use of headings/sub-headings and introduction
- Style, language, and clarity (tone of report response, presentation of calculations, appropriate use of the tools, easy to follow and more than a negligible amount of content)

Analysis and evaluation:

- Critical comparison of zero-based budgeting to incremental budgeting is provided
- Cost/benefit analysis of the new inventory system is performed on a one-year basis
- Recommendations/conclusions have been supplied for all work requested by the CEO

Scepticism:

- Demonstration of ability to challenge the use of ZBB and Kaizen together
- Recognition that not all costs have been considered for the new inventory management system

Commercial acumen:

- Demonstration of practical understanding of the impact of Kaizen costing on production for Belivat
- Suggestions of additional costs and the benefits of the new inventory systems are relevant and plausible for Belivat

Maximum	10
Total	50

To: The CEO of Belivat Manufacturing (Belivat)

From: A Accountant

Date: September 20X5

Subject: Budgeting, costing, and inventory management at Belivat

This report evaluates the use of zero-based budgeting (ZBB) to control new product development and assesses the implications of changing to a Kaizen costing system for control of production. Then, an evaluation is conducted into whether ZBB can be extended to production and will fit with a Kaizen costing approach. Finally, advice is provided on the introduction of a radio-frequency identification device (RFID) system in the warehouse.

(a) **Product development budgeting**

The first step in ZBB is defining the decision package which involves producing descriptions of all the activities to be funded by this budget. The packages may be incremental where a base level of work is justified with incremental levels of effort to perform additional tasks or they can be mutually exclusive packages where different methods of the organisation's goals are put forward. Cost benefit analysis is then conducted to establish which packages demonstrate value for money.

Each decision package is then evaluated and ranked. Finally, the budget allocates resources to those packages deemed acceptable within the overall budget limits.

The major difference between zero-based budgeting (ZBB) and the current system (incremental) is the starting point. Incremental budgeting assumes that last year's figures can be used as a basis for estimation of this year's costs with adjustments for inflation and changing activity levels. ZBB encourages a more questioning attitude where the budget setter requires justification for each activity carried out.

The existing system is much simpler than ZBB and so cheaper and less time consuming. ZBB will also require retraining of staff in its use which adds further costs. However, incremental budgeting tends to ossify existing practices and so does not fit with the aim of cost reduction. ZBB introduces a much more questioning attitude and so is more likely to lead to innovation in practices, which result in cost reduction.

The ZBB's innovative approach will also fit with the overall cultural desire to be more innovative in product development at Belivat. Each new product is likely to require innovative thinking, which matches the starting point of ZBB. ZBB is more commonly used in situations of discretionary spending such as new product development. Incremental budgeting fits a more conservative approach to new ideas which will not sit so easily with the changing technological environment which Belivat operates within. Practically, as there is no previous budget for each new product, incremental budgeting will have no obvious starting point.

Belivat is introducing a project-based approach where teams work on new product development. ZBB is a good fit to these concepts as it is more objective focused. Each decision package could then be prepared by the relevant team leader. Incremental budgeting is an over-arching approach which would tend to be imposed from the top-down in an organisation and so would not fit so well with a team-based approach where the autonomy of the team to come up with new solutions is respected. ZBB is a more bottom-up approach to budgeting being driven by operationally based teams.

Therefore, ZBB is a better cultural match than incremental budgeting for the aims, methods, and control of new product development at Belivat.

(b) **Kaizen costing**

Within a lean manufacturing system, the first year's costs would often arise from a functional analysis of the product design producing a target cost. Kaizen costing is a control system which takes these first year's costs of production of a new product and sets targets which reduce these costs in the next period. In each subsequent period, new tighter targets are set based on the previous period's actual results and so there is motivation to continuously improve. The process of continuous improvement is achieved by elimination of waste and the improvement of the quality of manufacturing activities.

Continuous improvement is an incremental process where the employees work in teams and make changes to day-to-day activities. This process is incremental and not radical. It fits with the plan to move to team-based production where quality circles are set up in order to drive these small improvements to activities.

The existing system of standard costing is used to control rather than reduce costs. It tends to assume that manufacturing processes are not changing. Standards are set often for a year and controlled by variances between standard and actual costs. Culturally, employees are seen as the cause of problems and a blame culture can result.

Kaizen costing sets cost reduction targets (often on a monthly basis) and then continuous improvement to production processes are sought by the production teams in order to meet each new set of cost targets. Culturally, employees are empowered and seen as the source of solutions to the need for improvement.

Kaizen costing seems to fit with the target of reducing cost and being more innovative in production processes. This addresses the competitive pressures on profit margins being felt by Belivat. It also matches the culture of team-working and an innovative organisation where new ideas are encouraged from all layers of business. Therefore, Kaizen costing is recommended as a better approach for Belivat.

(c) **Interaction of ZBB and Kaizen**

ZBB sets budgets based on decision packages which start from scratch. These budgets are then used to control operational projects. This fits the process of developing new products and being innovative. However, it encourages revolutionary rather than evolutionary change. In general, this does not seem as appropriate for an existing, well-respected manufacturing operation such as Belivat. It would represent a dramatic change in culture from the existing incremental budget control method.

Kaizen costing has some similarities to incremental budgeting in that each period sees changes based on the previous control targets. However, Kaizen is different in that it demands reductions on these targets rather than the inflationary increases often seen in more well-worn incremental budgeting cultures.

Starting from scratch with each period's budget does not fit with Kaizen costing which deliberately builds its targets on the previous period's costs with agreed reductions applied. Although both approaches build their control of costs from the bottom-up and have the similarity of demanding improvement, ZBB demands a more dramatic rethinking of budgets and so there will be a cultural mismatch.

Therefore, due to these cultural and practical differences, it is not recommended that ZBB and Kaizen costing operate together in managing production.

(d) Inventory management project

Cost/benefit analysis:

Annual costs of new system:

Hardware		
Tags	90,000	= 120,000 × 0.75
Sensors	6,250	= 50,000/8
Other hardware	3,125	= 25,000/8
Software total cost	11,875	= (60,000 + 35,000)/8
On-going servicing cost	15,000	
	126,250	

Benefits of new system (cost savings):

Staff costs	$	
Warehouse – picking	61,250	= 7 x 25,000 × 35%
Obsolete inventory	78,000	= 120,000 × 65%
	139,250	

Net benefit (per annum): 13,000

The introduction of RFID devices at the warehouse will yield a net benefit of $13,000 per annum and so the project is financially acceptable.

However, there are other costs and benefits which are not included in this analysis and should be estimated before a final decision is made.

Additional costs:

- Redundancy/retraining of the staff whose workload has been reduced
- Training costs for staff on the new system

Additional benefits:

- Reduced need for inventory counts as RFIDs can provide real-time inventory information
- Better decision making based on more accurate and real-time inventory information. This would allow earlier identification of popular product lines and adjustment to the production schedule to match actual rather than planned demand.
- The system could be extended to cover goods inward at the additional cost of fitting tags on goods delivered. Again, this would improve picking efficiency and reduce obsolescence. However, this may not be worthwhile for low value components which are held in bulk.

> **Tutorial note.** An analysis using other methods such as payback or accounting rate of return is acceptable.

Section B

This section of the exam contains two questions.

Each question is worth 25 marks and is compulsory.

This exam section is worth 50 marks in total.

2 Question 2

Workbook reference

EBITDA is covered in Chapter 6 of the Workbook. EVA™ is discussed in Chapter 7. Reward systems are covered in Chapter 11.

Top tips

Ensure you read the requirements carefully – you are NOT required to calculated EBITDA for example, and you are NOT required to discuss the advantages and disadvantages of EVA™.

In the calculation of WACC, remember that the cost of debt has to be adjusted from the pre-tax rate, given in the question as 12% to the post tax cost of debt.

When interest is added back to profits to calculate NOPAT, the interest net of tax is added back – that is interest × (1-tax rate).

Examining team's comments

Many candidates struggled with EBITDA and some candidates did not progress beyond offering definitions of the words that made up the different letters of the EBITDA acronym.

Others struggled with the specifics of the proposed reward system and offered generic comments on rewards and bonuses that did not address the specific areas of Eck's scheme. Most candidates passed the EVA™ calculation but very few scored full marks.

Marking guide	Marks
(a) Usefulness of EBITDA for measuring divisional manager performance – up to 10 marks	
Calculation marks	
Add back after-tax interest to net profit	
Add back development costs, less one year of amortisation	
Use of opening net assets figure	
Calculate WACC	
Calculate EVA™	
	13
(b) Impact of the bonus scheme on performance – 1 mark per point, up to 7 marks	
	7

Analysis and evaluation:

- Assessment of EBITDA addresses a range of points in relation to its usefulness for measuring divisional manager performance
- Appropriate use of the data (calculation and conclusion) on EVA™

Scepticism:

- Recognition that EBITDA has some limitations as a performance measure for divisional managers

Marking guide	Marks
Commercial acumen:	
• Conclusion/recommendation on the proposed reward scheme is practical and commercially sound for Blue division	
Maximum	5
Total	25

(a) **Measuring divisional manager performance**

Assessment of earnings before interest, tax, depreciation and amortisation (EBITDA)

Proxy to cash flow

EBITDA is calculated by adding back interest, tax, depreciation and amortisation to net profit. As such, it is often regarded as a proxy to cash flow.

The board is considering expanding the company's product range. Because of this, it would appear appropriate to measure performance using divisional EBITDA. This would align managers' objectives with the need to maximise cash flow during this period, when Eck's financial resources will be stretched.

This is important because the shareholders are unable to provide finance for the expansion and unwilling to allow new equity to be issued. Eck is unable to take on further borrowings and seems reliant on cash generated from trading operations to fund the expansion.

Cash flow is clearly an important issue for Eck. As EBITDA can be said to be a proxy for cash generated from trading operations, it can therefore be considered a relevant measure for Eck. EBITDA does not, however, take into account the cost of purchasing plant and machinery and investment in working capital required for the expansion. Other measures relating to cash flow may also, therefore, be needed.

EBITDA is easy to calculate and objective

EBITDA is generally considered to be easy to calculate using figures from the statement of profit or loss. However, it is unclear whether this will be easily understood by divisional managers, who do not have financial qualifications or experience, and who are familiar with having their performance measured using divisional net profit. Managers can only improve performance against a measure if they fully understand it. In this respect, EBITDA is better than economic value added (EVA™), the other measure being considered, which is difficult to calculate and to understand. It may be that divisional managers need some training or support in order to fully understand the calculation of EBITDA.

EBITDA excludes subjective assessments, such as the useful economic lives of assets and the amortisation period for development costs. The recent revision of the estimated useful economic lives of existing assets illustrates the difficulties in making these estimates. In this respect, EBITDA allows managers' performance to be measured more objectively than at present.

Clear view of operating performance

EBITDA does not include finance costs and tax, which are distributions of profit to lenders and to the government respectively. As such, EBITDA gives a clear assessment of operating performance.

EBITDA also removes these uncontrollable factors, as well as depreciation, from the measurement of managers' performance. This is likely to increase their motivation to improve performance. The effect of these factors will be significant because Eck operates in a high tax economy and pays interest at twice the market rate.

A disadvantage EBITDA as a divisional performance measure, however, is that it ignores the value of capital employed and changes in working capital used to generate the EBITDA and also ignores the cost of capital.

EVA™

Calculation of EVA™

Calculation of NOPAT

	$m
Controllable net profit	50.0
Add back:	
Interest net of tax at 40% ($20m × 0.6)	12.0
Development costs	5.0
Less:	
Amortisation of development costs ($5m/5)	(1.0)
NOPAT	66.0

Assets

	$m
Opening net assets	496.0
Economic value of net assets	496.0

WACC

	$m	
Equity:	50% × 15%	0.075
Debt:	50% × (12% × 0.6)	0.036
Total		0.111 or 11.1%

	$m
NOPAT	66.0
Capital charge (496 × 11.1%)	(55.1)
EVA™	10.9

Blue division has created value for its shareholders of $10.9m during the year.

(b) To improve performance, the proposed reward system should encourage divisional managers to work towards any standards set. Rewards should be clear, motivational and controllable.

Clear

The target EVA™ figure of $25m is clear, but the calculation of EVA™ involves adjustments to accounting profit. Therefore, it may be unclear which expenditure is value-building for the future and so which costs should be added back. For these reasons, managers, who are not financially qualified, may not understand the adjustments. Managers may not understand what they need to do in order to improve performance of Blue division and so will not be motivated to do so.

Motivational

Managers receive the whole of their reward based on whether they achieve the target EVA™. Managers who fail to meet the target by a small margin are likely to become de-motivated from trying to achieve future targets. If it becomes clear that managers will not achieve the target, they may give up on trying to improve performance altogether. Managers have no incentive or motivation to further improve performance once they have achieved the target.

The reward scheme seems reasonable, in that market conditions are considered when setting individual targets. The $25m target seems much higher than the $10·9m calculated for the most recent year. It may therefore be unachievable, which will reduce managers' motivation to improve performance.

The value of the reward, equivalent to 45% of managers' annual salary, is very high. This will give a strong motivation to improve performance, to achieve the reward. It may also result in managers taking excessive risks in order to do so, which may be inconsistent with Eck's risk appetite.

Controllable

As the divisions are profit centres, the net profit after tax is controllable by divisional managers. There may, however, be costs which are relevant to divisional performance, but which cannot be controlled by divisional managers, such as head office costs.

Some other parts of the EVA™ calculation are outside of the control of divisional managers. For example, the board takes all investment and financing decisions, which influence the value of net assets and the cost of capital. These determine the calculation of the capital charge, an element of the overall EVA™ calculation. It would be unfair and de-motivating to measure managers' performance against these factors. It would also be pointless, because they cannot improve performance in these areas.

Conclusion

The high value of the proposed reward will motivate divisional managers to improve the performance of Blue division. However, their lack of financial qualifications and experience mean that they may not understand the EVA™ calculation used to determine whether they receive the bonus. Some significant parts of the calculation are also outside of their control. On balance, it seems that the reward scheme using a target EVA™ is not a good way to improve the performance of Blue division.

3 Question 3

Workbook reference

Value based management is discussed in Chapter 12 of the Workbook. Net present value (NPV) and modified internal rate of return (MIRR) are covered in Chapter 6.

Top Tips

In part (a), there are four things you need to do in the embedded requirements: (1) Explain the basic principles of VBM; (2) Evaluate VBM compared to the existing performance dashboard, (3) Evaluate how VBM would affect the different management levels (4) Evaluate how its implementation would affect the organisation. Your answer should attempt all four parts in order to gain all the marks available.

Examining team's guidance

A significant minority of candidates did not know what VBM was, with some confusing it with the three 'Es' of economy, efficiency and effectiveness and others believing it was total quality management. The majority of candidates did understand VBM but failed to apply it to Scye's scenario in a meaningful manner. Many candidates failed to undertake the NPV calculation accurately with some being unaware of the importance of the timing of cash flows and most candidates being unaware of the decision rule for MIRR.

Marking guide		Marks
(a) General discussion of the principles and value mind-set – up to 3 marks		
Evaluation of VBM compared to existing dashboard – up to 6 marks		
Implementation considerations – up to 6 marks		
		12
(b) NPV:		
Additional costs	1	
Tax at 20%	1	
Add back depreciation	1	
Investment	1	
Working capital	1	
Discount factor	1	
Net present value	1	
MIRR		
PVI and PVR	1	
MIRR	1	
		8
Analysis and evaluation:		
• Evaluation of VBM considers all levels of the organisation		
• Justified conclusions based on the respective decision rules are provided		
Scepticism:		
• Recognition of the challenges of introducing VBM at Scye		
Commercial acumen:		
• Implementation issues raised are practical and relevant for Scye's context		
Maximum		5
Total		25

(a) **Principles of value-based management (VBM)**

VBM focuses on the idea that the value of a company is measured by its discounted cash flows. Although economic value added is often used as a proxy for discounted cash flows, it is only aligned in the very long term. It requires a large number of adjustments to the existing financially reported figures which makes it complicated to understand in detail as claimed by the director.

The VBM approach aims to align the activities at the strategic, tactical and operational levels of management and focuses all activities on creating value for the shareholder. VBM sets goals based on a more long-term view (through cash flow forecasts) and what drives the discounted cash flows (the value drivers). The identification of value drivers is complex and often uses scenario analysis to see the interaction between various factors and which ones should be given priority.

VBM compared to existing performance dashboard

A traditional profit-based approach will record the past performance of Scye. VBM will look at future value creation by the business. This is evidenced in the historic basis of past performance indicators as opposed to the use of forecasts in value calculations. This reflects the shareholders' desire for future long-term returns.

VBM aims to focus the business on the shareholders' objective of greater value creation in the long term. The fundamental change in using VBM is a move away from traditional profit measures to discounted cash flow (value). The traditional profit measures may not lead to long-term value for shareholders. Management may be encouraged to suppress projects with long-term value in order to improve the short-term performance of the company and meet its next dividend payment. VBM will drive a greater emphasis on the growth and sustainability of returns from management decisions. The VBM approach will consider a mix of short and long-term factors and financial and non-financial indicators.

VBM aims to align all levels of management towards the same goal of maximising shareholder value. Senior managers have a single clear overall objective (maximising value) and rules for deciding on conflicts with other objectives (eg environmental sustainability). The approach gives a logical analysis of the factors which drive the value of the business and all lower-level performance indicators are tied to the production of value. Thus, it simplifies and focuses management thinking in decision-making. It is, however, complex and the links between value and its drivers at the tactical and, particularly, the operational levels can be difficult to see. This may lead to a disconnection between managers and shareholders which is often addressed by using suitable compensation packages for the managers.

An example would be the head of a large building project for Scye would have a specific financial goal of the net present value (NPV) of a project. A sales department head within that project might have a goal of reaching a level of customer service. A procurement department head might have a goal of negotiating a specific cost per unit of materials to be used in the building project. These goals relate to the value drivers which link upwards into the calculation of NPV for the project.

Implementation of VBM

VBM requires good information and, in particular, the identification and measurement of value drivers. A common criticism of VBM is that it creates large, complex valuation spreadsheets which often obscure their dependence on fundamental assumptions. For example, in the project appraisal below, the answer will be heavily dependent on the predicted revenues.

The focus on value drivers and their logical connections to value may require a restructuring of the organisational hierarchy away from traditional departmental/functional roles. This change combined with the change in performance measures can cause disruption. The introduction of VBM will require strong leadership from the top of the organisation in order to be successful.

A major pitfall of VBM is its tendency to produce complex forecasts leading to discounted cash flow valuations of business units. Management can become over-focused on the process of making assumptions leading to a valuation to the exclusion of addressing the actual problems of the business.

(b) Project appraisal

NPV	Year 0	Year 1	Year 2	Year 3
	$m	$m	$m	$m
Revenue after operating costs		6.40	6.40	6.40
Additional costs		(0.70)		
Operating profit before tax		5.70	6.40	6.40
Tax at 20%		(1.14)	(1.28)	(1.28)
Add back depreciation		8.00	8.00	8.00
Investment	(25.00)			
Working capital	(0.64)	(0.64)		
Free cash flows	(25.64)	12.56	13.12	13.76
Discount factor	1	0.909	0.826	0.751
PV	(25.64)	11.42	10.84	10.33

Net present value = \$6.95m

MIRR

PVR (\$m)	32.59
PVI (\$m)	25.64
r	10%
n	3 years
MIRR	19.2%

The NPV is positive and the MIRR is above the cost of capital and so both methods indicate that the project is financially acceptable. It adds value to the shareholders.

Tell us what you think

Got comments or feedback on this book? Let us know.
Use your QR code reader:

Or, visit:
https://bppgroup.fra1.qualtrics.com/jfe/form/SV_9TrxTtw8jSvO7Pv

Need to get in touch with customer service?

www.bpp.com/request-support

Spotted an error?

www.bpp.com/learningmedia/Errata